Quantity Food Purchasing

Fifth Edition

Quantity Food Purchasing

Lendal H. Kotschevar
Professor Emeritus
Florida International University

Richard Donnelly

Merrill,
an imprint of Prentice Hall
Upper Saddle River, New Jersey   Columbus, Ohio

Library of Congress Cataloging-in-Publication Data

Kotschevar, Lendal Henry
    Quantity food purchasing / Lendal H. Kotschevar, Richard Donnelly.
—5th ed.
      p.   cm.
    Includes bibliographical references and index.
    ISBN 0–13–095881–6
    1. Food service purchasing.   I. Donnelly, Richard.   II. Title.
TX911.3.P8K68   1999
647.95'068'7—dc21   98–18805
                                                        CIP

Cover art: Stock Works
Editor: Kevin M. Davis
Production Editor: Linda Hillis Bayma
Design Coordinator: Karrie M. Converse
Cover Designer: Brian Deep
Production Coordination: Carlisle Publishers Services
Production Manager: Laura Messerly
Illustrations: Carlisle Communications, Ltd.
Director of Marketing: Kevin Flanagan
Marketing Manager: Suzanne Stanton
Advertising/Marketing Coordinator: Krista Groshong

This book was set in Garamond Light by Carlisle Communications, Ltd. and was printed and bound by Courier/Westford, Inc. The cover was printed by Phoenix Color Corp.

Photo credits: Photos on pages 4, 5, 7, 13, 80, 126, 129, 130, 132, 133, 141, 142, 146, 148, 153, 426, 448, 469, and 629–646 supplied by Lendal H. Kotschevar.

Printed in the United States of America

10 9 8 7 6

ISBN 0-13-095881-6

PRENTICE-HALL INTERNATIONAL (UK) LIMITED, *LONDON*
PRENTICE-HALL OF AUSTRALIA PTY. LIMITED, *SYDNEY*
PRENTICE-HALL CANADA INC., *TORONTO*
PRENTICE-HALL HISPANOAMERICANA, S.A., *MEXICO*
PRENTICE-HALL OF INDIA PRIVATE LIMITED, *NEW DELHI*
PRENTICE-HALL OF JAPAN, INC., *TOKYO*
PEARSON EDUCATION ASIA PTE. LTD., *SINGAPORE*
EDITORA PRENTICE-HALL DO BRASIL, LTDA., *RIO DE JANEIRO*

Preface

Since *Quantity Food Purchasing* was first published nearly 40 years ago, the task of purchasing for a food service has changed. In the 1950s and 1960s almost all food was prepared from scratch on the premises. Quality of product was often specified by grade. Today many of the items purchased are of the convenience or added-value type for which there are no grades: quality must be specified by brand. We must observe many more laws and regulations that affect purchasing. Sanitation and safety regulations require added attention. Paperwork and record keeping have increased both in amount and complexity. The market has also changed. In the past, buyers could expect the market to be guided by seasonal supply. Now with rapid air transport, imported foreign foods destroy this pattern. The variety of foods offered on the market has also increased. Often patrons demand exotic and unusual foods, forcing buyers to expand their market range. Sanitation, adequate nutrition, and safety of food are growing patron concerns, forcing governmental regulations that buyers must observe. The facsimile, computer, and Internet are changing the way purchasing is conducted. Competition and improved technology have forced food services to operate more efficiently. The gap between income and expense has narrowed to the point that a food service can no longer enjoy the luxury of a large inventory or an elaborate menu. In almost every area, management has been forced to make changes to operate the business successfully. Buyers have not escaped this drive for greater efficiency. Even nonprofit operations find they must observe the bottom line. Changes such as these are the way of life today.

The buyer who has not adjusted to these changes will find it difficult to compete in today's market. To the buyer who keeps abreast of the market and knows how to function in it, meeting such change has not been a problem. Such a buyer studies new developments, evaluating their implications. It is said that luck is "being prepared when opportunity strikes." The buyer who recognizes new trends and comprehends their meaning is "lucky." There are few problems when change is taken in stride.

This fifth edition recognizes such change. It covers a number of the new laws and governmental changes that have influenced purchasing. The changing varieties of food offered are recognized as food categories and are discussed. A chapter is devoted to the many advantages of the computer. Considerable discussion is devoted to how the market functions and how buyers can more efficiently function in the market. The amounts required to serve a specific number of portions are often given. The quality required for a certain production need is also frequently noted. The kind of specification needed to get the right product is also defined. In every way possible, methods are explored that make the purchasing task simpler and better.

ACKNOWLEDGMENTS

Our thanks to the following individuals who reviewed our manuscript: Judy Kay Flohr, University of Massachusetts, Amherst; Rob Heiman, Kent State University; Cathy H.C. Hsu, Iowa State University; Carol A. Perlmutter, Montclair State University; and Virginia Soliah, University of Southwestern Louisiana.

Brief Contents

Contents

CHAPTER 5   Getting the Goods   **115**

CHAPTER 6   The Computer in Purchasing   161

CHAPTER 7   Meat   187

CHAPTER 13   Groceries   461

CHAPTER 14   Alcoholic Beverages   499

CHAPTER 1

Introduction to Purchasing

1596 The Interrupted Dinner. Original etching from "The Illustrato of Petrarca" first edition 1595. From the Louis Szwathmary collection, Culinary Archives and Museum, Johnson and Wales University, used by permission of Dr. Szwathmary and Johnson and Wales University.

Chapter Objectives

1. To define purchasing as it applies to food services.
2. To indicate who makes decisions in purchasing.
3. To inform readers on what a buyer must possess to have adequate purchasing competency.
4. To indicate briefly the material to be covered in this text.

WHAT IS PURCHASING?

Purchasing is a series of activities resulting in the selection and acquisition of desired commodities or services. An exchange of values must occur between a buyer and seller, usually money being given by the buyer for goods or services. Sometimes

1

this function is called **buying,** or procurement, or shopping; whatever the name, the function is the same—goods or services are obtained for something of value.

In food services, much of the purchasing activity is in the selection and acquisition of food, and this text emphasizes that aspect. However, there is some discussion of the purchase of items other than food. A food service also uses important commodities or food-related services, and those charged with the responsibility of obtaining them should know how to select and buy these items.

Effective purchasing is part of a complete organizational and financial strategy that includes controlling the purchase system so all financial and other objectives are met. Every dollar saved through effective purchasing directly increases the profit line.

Purchasing is a dynamic function, one that is always changing. What may be true one day may not be so the next. The control of supply is not in the hands of the buyer, or sometimes not in the hands of anyone in the market. A drought, a freeze, or a storm may cause a sudden drop in supply, or some factor may influence supply so as to cause a market glut and an oversupply. Kinds and varieties of items on the market may suddenly change. Demand for a product may suddenly shoot up or tumble. It is a fickle market and buyers need to be constantly alert to keep up with its changes. Learning and relearning must be constant. Continued vigilance must be maintained if the purchasing is to be done correctly.

The market in which buyers must function is highly complex, and buyers require a lot of knowledge and skill to move in it. Foods move from production to processing and then to ultimate users. Buyers need to know how the market functions and how goods or services flow through it to reach ultimate users, and they also need to know how foods change as they move through this market. These changes may be important in obtaining the right product. In addition, buyers must be able to equate price to quality and to quantity.

A **buyer** buying for his or her own use is known as an **ultimate buyer,** but if a buyer purchases goods for manufacture or resale to be used by someone else, the buyer is known as an **industrial buyer.** It is much simpler to purchase for one's own use than to purchase for someone else's. We usually know what we want, but to interpret what others may want is a much more difficult task.

Buyers have many aids to help them. Over the years, we have compiled information on how much to buy to serve a specific number of portions. This text provides a great deal of information on quantities needed. Quite a lot of this information is also available from the federal government. Today, much of our food has grades, and buyers can specify quality wanted by using these. The science of purchasing has grown and we know a lot more about how the market functions and how we can function in it. We also have a well-defined set of laws. A reliable system for gathering and disseminating market information is in place so buyers have a better sense of what is happening or might happen in the market. We have developed better transportation methods and better storage, and continue to develop methods that improve products and lower product cost to the consumer. Packaging has made dramatic strides in improving shelf life, while preserving quality and nutritional values. Tight specifications exist that allow buyers to better search the market and get the right product for the production need. Sellers are also better informed when such specifications are used. The development of systems like the **Institutional Meat Purchase Specifications (IMPS)** and the **Universal Product Code (UPC)** has made it possible to more clearly identify items on the market. The use of computers has simplified many clerical and other purchase tasks. It is now possible for buyers and sellers to do much of the negotiation task in purchasing and even conclude a sale via the computer. Better communication systems are functioning which make it easier for buyers and sellers to get together. E-mail and facsimile machines have also helped to speed the exchange of information. The **Internet** and communication highway allow a vast amount of valuable purchase, market, and product information to be available at the click of a switch. This trend in constant improvement and simplification will continue to make purchasing increasingly simple.

Much purchase information is available to buyers. The various food divisions of the U.S. Department of Agriculture, the National Marine Products Division in the U.S. Department of Commerce, the U.S. Department of Health and Welfare, the U.S. Food and Drug Administration, and other federal agencies supply tremendous amounts of free information. Similarly, professional associations like the National Restaurant Association (NRA), Club Managers of America Association, and the American Hospital Association can be of great assistance. Professional organizations like the National Livestock and Meat Board, American Dietetic Association, and Cereal Institute devote much time and money in getting product information to buyers. Buyers also must not forget that one of the best sources of information is the buyer's own purveyors. Some operate test kitchens and otherwise provide helpful information on product selection and use. Salespeople who call in by phone or visit the facility can be tremendously helpful. They can advise buyers of a shortage of product. Thus, if the canned tomato pack is short for the year, the salesman can so advise the buyer and be helpful in building an inventory so that when tomato products become scarce later, the buyer is protected without having to pay the high prices that a scarce product can demand. Also, many newspaper, journal, trade magazine, TV, and radio reports can alert a buyer to a particular market situation and lead to a better market decision. For instance, the food buyer for a large university read in spring one year that there was a big freeze in the Idaho, Oregon, and Washington potato growing districts. He immediately purchased heavy supplies of canned, frozen, and dehydrated potato products and stored them, so when the price of fresh potatoes in the winter more than doubled, he advised the university's food service system that fresh potatoes would only be available for baked potatoes. He advised that the processed potato products be used for other potato needs and that rice, noodles, and other farinaceous products be used instead of potatoes. This buyer saved the university food service system thousands of dollars by being alert to changes in the market.

In spite of all the progress, however, the purchasing task remains highly involved and buyers will need to constantly study and learn to keep up with developments.

DECISION MAKERS IN PURCHASING

Five individuals or groups of individuals make decisions regarding what is purchased. The first and very dominant in influence is the patron, the second is production (kitchen staff and related units), third is service (dining room and related units), fourth is the buyer, and the final and very important element is management.

Patrons

The **patron** may be a guest, an inmate, or a patient having food needs that must be met, and, if these needs are not met, the foodservice operation has no reason to exist. What patrons select from a menu will dictate specific purchases that must satisfy their needs (see Figure 1–1). Patrons of fast food establishments need different items than patients in hospitals. Making purchase decisions based only on the needs of the enterprise may invite failure. The needs of the individual selecting and consuming the food are paramount.

Production (The Kitchen Staff and Related Units)

Purchase decisions made without considering needs of production can be risky. The ability of cooks and others to properly produce foods may impose limitations; limitations of equipment or other facilities may do so as well. **Production** staffs, no matter how competent, can only produce so much in a given time, and this must be recognized. For example, a staff given the task of preparing food for the regular dining room of a hotel, as well as preparing an elaborate banquet, may fail in both because too much was asked of it, and a decision may have to be made to use ready-prepared foods for the banquet or to hire extra staff to solve the problem. Buying the proper items to solve problems like this can be a big aid in lessening the load on the production department.

Figure 1–1
Patrons ordering from the menu determine what is purchased.

The kitchen production staff usually uses what the buyer buys. Thus, the item purchased should suit the production need (see Figure 1–2). Much satisfaction can come from food that not only tastes good but looks good too.

A cook cannot make a "silk purse out of a sow's ear"; therefore, buyers need to keep in close touch with production and service to see that the right products are obtained to suit the production need. An apple that bakes up into a hard, shriveled product or breaks up in cooking is not suitable for making good baked apples. The buyer should select an apple that cooks up into a mellow, soft product that holds its shape, such as Roman Beauty apples rather than Yellow Transparents.

Production can also provide information on amounts to purchase. While management or others on the staff may indicate the number of servings required, production often must determine how much to purchase to fill this order. Buyers should also possess some expertise in calculating quantities required, and management should supervise such determinations to see that overbuying is not occurring.

Figure 1-2
The production department is an important part of deciding what is purchased, since it usually knows best how to make a product patrons will find acceptable.

Service

Buyers must keep in mind that items must not only taste good and be of proper size but should also look good. Satisfaction in eating is influenced greatly by the appearance of what is to be consumed. Production cannot always make servings attractive. A lobster without a claw will not please the lobster connoisseur. An overly tender cake that breaks on cutting looks messy when served. Or, an item may not hold well in the steam table and be a very unattractive product on the plate. Products must fit the equipment available for service. Servers depend on pleased patrons for good tips and want food that looks good to help keep patrons happy. The service staff can also influence decisions on what is purchased. They serve the food and beverages and see the reaction of patrons to what is served. Buyers should set up a system in which the service staff can pass this patron reaction on to them. Through this system, buyers can learn what pleases patrons. For example, Total® packets may be purchased instead of Sweet n' Low® because servers report that a majority of people served indicate such a preference. Presentation, rather than product selection, can be a factor. Servers might tell the buyer that two pork chops take up too much space on the plate, resulting in an unattractive appearance. Buyers respond by providing one thicker chop. The service staff, as the sole user of many items, can also help ensure that the right products are purchased in adequate quantities. Feedback from the service staff is of great importance in making for a successful purchasing program.

The Buyer

The buyer must obtain reliable and proper information on the availability of foods on the market, prices, and other factors. It is often the responsibility of buyers to see that proper levels of goods are maintained. Buyers will have to make decisions as to market cost and whether an item can be purchased in view of the menu price. Buyers should know much about what it takes to produce satisfactory foods, so they can purchase the appropriate items. The information compiled by the buying staff is used by management in making financial and other decisions. Patrons are interested in eating safe, healthy food and the buyer must properly interpret these patron needs. Items must be purchased from clean and sanitary facilities that seek to provide safe food that is adequate in nutrient values.

It is usually the buyer who places the order and negotiates the sale. Purchase decisions are not made alone, but only after considering the needs of patrons, management, production, and service. In a way, the purchase task is one delegated by these four entities to the buyer. Too often buyers forget this and act as if they are the only authority empowered to make purchase decisions. Buyers are not cooks and do not possess as much knowledge as cooks of what is needed to make satisfactory products. They should be experts in organizing orders to be placed, searching the market, and negotiating: It is here that the job of purchasing lies (see Figure 1–3).

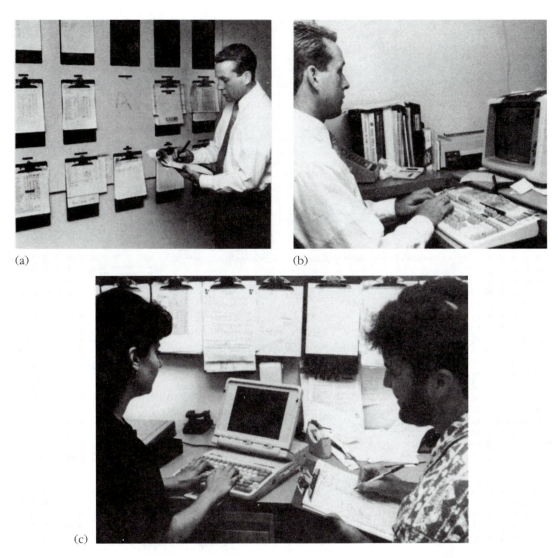

Figure 1-3
(a) The buyer checks requisitions to ascertain purchase needs; (b) placing orders by computer interfaced with the computer of the supplier; or (c) giving orders to a salesperson who puts the order into a laptop computer.

Management

Management[1] has the overall responsibility of establishing, supervising, guiding, and controlling the entire purchase function. To fulfill this responsibility, management

---

[1]Management in this text includes all management personnel to whom purchasing department employees report.

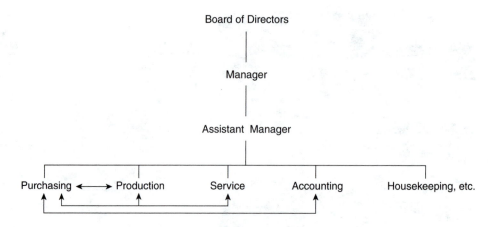

Figure 1-4
Organizational diagram for a foodservice operation.

should set up standards of quality, cost, portion size, and other basic factors that decide what is served and how it is served, and all policies and procedures affecting purchasing such as accounting procedures, internal controls, accountability procedures, and ethical standards.

Management should not make purchasing decisions on its own, but should do so after considering patron needs and after consulting with departments affected by the decisions. It can delegate some of the functions that must occur to obtain needed items, such as searching the market, or perhaps when and where to place orders, inventorying, issuing, and so forth. However, if delegated, functions should be closely supervised by management. Purchasing is too important an area not to do so.

Figure 1–4 shows an organizational diagram where the purchasing department is separate from other operating departments as might be seen in a large organization.

PURCHASING IN THE OPERATION

In large operations, the purchasing department may be a separate department; in a smaller one, it might be part of another department, or even just one unit in the entire system. Whatever the case, the part the purchasing function plays in the operation will be much the same.

Although a purchasing department will have its own goals, these should in no way supersede those of the enterprise, but should be consistent and supportive of the goals of the enterprise. To do a satisfactory job, a strong relationship needs to be maintained by the purchasing department with all areas of an operation. Figure 1–5

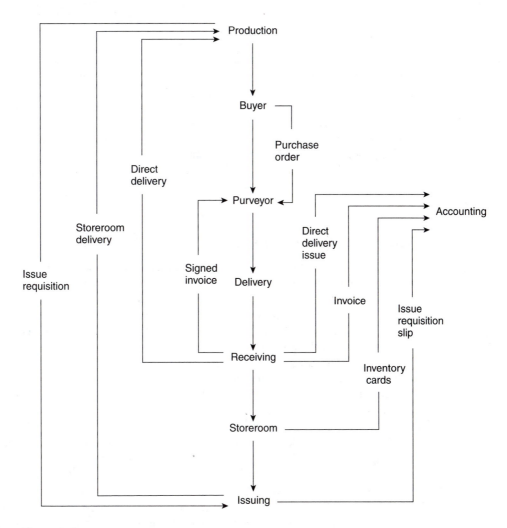

Figure 1-5

This graph shows how a production need arises in production and is forwarded to the buyer who sets up an order and forwards it on a purchase order to a purveyor, who in turn delivers it. The order is received by the facility where a part of it goes directly to production while another part goes to the storeroom where it later is issued and goes to production. All of these steps take considerable paperwork. Production sends a requisition to the buyer who might send the purveyor a purchase order. The purveyor in turn sends with the delivery an invoice, a copy of which is retained by delivery to give to the purveyor showing acknowledgment of delivery, while another copy of invoice goes to the receiving department, which forwards it to accounting. Some type of direct delivery slip must be signed by production when it receives the direct delivery part of the order and this goes to accounting so it can charge this part of the order as a cost. Inventory cards are prepared for the part sent to the storeroom and these form the inventory record. After the goods are issued to production, a signed issue slip is sent to accounting so it can remove the item from its inventory records and charge off the issue as a cost. It is a very involved process and this path will be followed in subsequent chapters so students will learn the process more completely.

shows how a purchasing department interfaces with other parts of an operation. Good coordination, cooperation, and communication must be maintained in this organization.

The food and beverage department, housekeeping, and others that use purchases, along with the accounting department, are especially important areas with which purchasing must keep in touch. Buyers and users of what is purchased must always be in close touch with each other. Accounting needs financial information and is an important factor in helping provide good accountability of purchasing, inventory, and issues.

The Foodservice Buyer's Profile

As noted, the primary responsibility of a buyer is to organize the purchase system in the operation, decide with others on the right needs and amounts to purchase, search the market for the best quality goods available at the best price, and buy at the right time. Buyers need to be reliable, dependable, intelligent, and observe proper ethics in purchasing. The buyer is responsible for a considerable amount of the firm's money and resources and must see that the funds are expended to the best advantage. Buyers need to be persistent in seeing that they receive the best value for the money paid. Skill in **negotiation** is required, and a knowledge of how prices on the market are derived is often very helpful in deciding when a price is too high and when it is not.

The buying function is given very little thought and time in many operations. It becomes merely a process of call and order an item, get it, and then use it. Little analysis or investigation occurs to see if better products could be purchased for the same cost or if money could be saved.

Buying is too important to an operation to be treated casually. It needs time and attention. It decides the quality of the product served and a satisfactory financial performance. Buyers should know the market and what is happening on it. In large organizations where there is a separate purchasing department, buyers spend a lot of time just studying the market and getting information that can be helpful in purchasing. Market reports are read and analyzed every day. Buyers and sellers communicate frequently on market conditions and what is happening or likely to happen. The more buyers know, the better the job they can do.

Buyers should inform management and production plus any other interested individual or group about important market changes and make recommendations as to how to act. Sometimes the amount of money involved is considerable, and buyers need to keep in touch with management regarding how to properly expend funds. A careless buyer can easily handicap an operation or even cause it to fail.

Figure 1–6a is a **job description** for a buyer and Figure 1–6b is an advertisement for a **purchasing agent.**

Coordinates activities involved with procuring goods and services such as foods and supplies needed for the preparation of menu items, paper supplies, detergents, dishware, flatware, and other items needed by a food service. Reviews requisitions; may write specifications for the items purchased. Confers with vendors to obtain product or service information, such as price, availability, and delivery schedule. Selects products for purchase by testing, observing, or examining items. Estimates values according to knowledge of market price. Searches market for availability of items and to determine their best quality and price. Maintains a close touch with the market and its operation and changes. Determines method of procurement such as direct purchase or bid. Prepares purchase orders or bid requests. Reviews bid proposals and negotiates contracts within budgetary limitations and scope of authority. Maintains manual or computerized procurement and other records relating to the purchase function such as receiving, costs, inventories, issuing, and product quality or performance. Discusses defective or unacceptable goods or services with inspection or quality control personnel, users, vendors, and others to determine the source of trouble and take corrective action. May approve invoices for payment. May expedite delivery of goods to users.

(a)

Purchasing Representative
Minimum requirements: associate degree plus 2 years of purchasing experience; understanding of the competitive bid process; understanding of financial and economic principles (lifetime costing, cost analysis); strong communication skills; ability to analyze problems and implement solutions; ability to travel as required. Preferred requirements: food and beverage industry experience a plus; bachelor's degree. Submit resume and salary requirements to:

(b)

Figure 1–6
(a) An example of a job specification for a buyer adapted from the U.S. Labor Department's Dictionary of Occupational Titles, 1991, 162.157-038, purchasing agent (buyer). (b) The qualities needed by one food service are set forth in this advertisement.

THE THREE SPHERES IN PURCHASING

Buyers for food services will find they must function in three spheres: (1) the **patron sphere,** (2) the **inner sphere** or the enterprise, and (3) the **outer sphere,** or the market. Buyers must function adequately in all three to satisfactorily perform the purchase function. Figure 1–7 shows how the three spheres in turn form the purchasing sphere.

The Patron Sphere

The patron is the focal point of purchasing, since this is who must be satisfied with what is purchased. This is true of profit and nonprofit operations. As pointed out, the industrial buyer has a much harder task of purchasing than the ultimate buyer, because the former must decide what someone else will like, while the latter buys to satisfy himself or herself. It is therefore necessary, in setting up any purchase program, to find out what patrons want and then design the purchasing program to suit their expectations.

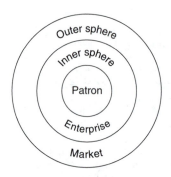

Figure 1-7

The three spheres of purchasing interface to complete the purchasing function.

Patrons differ. Some may want a quick lunch in a cafeteria, while others may decide to go into a drive-in for a quick hamburger and milk shake. For another neither would do; he or she might want a full meal in a white-linen establishment. Young people generally want different foods and more of it than elderly people. A buyer must know the market from which an establishment draws its patrons. Without knowing this, the proper foods will not be purchased.

In determining patron wants, all preferences must be considered and consolidated into the purchase program. Thus, the way foods and beverages are to be served needs consideration. Also, things like ethnic or religious factors must be recognized. In a restaurant located in a kosher area, it is wise to observe some kosher practices, even though the operation may not be a strictly kosher restaurant. A food service located in a Polish area in Chicago would probably be more successful if it served the types of foods typically eaten by that ethnic group.

The Inner Sphere

Most of a buyer's time is spent in the inner sphere, where purchase needs are determined, orders are placed and goods are received, stored, issued, and used (see Figure 1–8). A proper organizational structure is needed to support the entire process. The buyer must have adequate time to do the job. A good communication system is needed so information flows to and from management, accounting, and production through buyers to sellers. Management must set policies and procedures for controlling and directing this flow of work. Forms have to be devised and specifications set up to define the products needed. Lists of approved purveyors and what each supplies need to be formulated.

The physical facilities at which the purchasing is done in some operations can be simple—just a desk and a phone with a computer and a file in a quiet, nonbusy corner. In a large operation, the purchase department may be a separate department with an office equipped with furniture, equipment, computers, and facsimile machines. Much record keeping is required and proper forms and files must be provided.

Buyers need to know where to go in the market to find items. They must also possess the skill and knowledge to negotiate successfully. Many factors come into

Figure 1-8
Obtaining specialty items sometimes takes a lot of a buyer's time.

play, such as quality and price decisions, amounts to purchase, delivery arrangements, and more.

Management usually sets up the item **specifications** (short statements indicating exactly the quality and kind of item wanted), purchase orders, receiving reports, inventory forms, and other paperwork needed to do a proper job in purchasing. Sometimes, however, this is the responsibility of the purchasing department with the close supervision or cooperation of management.

Often the buyer places an order with a purveyor who then proceeds to deliver it, presenting on delivery a delivery slip that acknowledges delivery when signed by an *authorized* person of the receiving facility. Most orders will be placed and received in this manner, but sometimes the order is placed more formally by sending the purveyor a purchase order or other affirmation of a desire to buy goods or services. The purveyor then acknowledges the order making the deal legal, which binds both parties in a contract. The purchase department is usually responsible for the receiving, storing, and issuing of items purchased. If not, then these functions must be closely watched by purchasing even though the responsibility for them may rest with others.

Once a purchase program is set up, it should be reviewed frequently to see if it is functioning properly or can be improved. As noted earlier, purchasing is a dynamic function and never stays the same over a period of time.

The Outer Sphere

The third sphere of purchasing is outside the enterprise and is generally called the market, or outer, sphere. Some call it a jungle because it is a complex and difficult area to know and move in. Buyers need to know this area, at least the part of it in which they participate—the manner in which the market is organized and functions requiring completion to get the right product at the right price. Grades or other quality factors must be known, in addition to many specific market terms and practices.

Marketing agents who do the buying for an operation exist because they perform a service that sellers are willing to pay for. Often operations have found they are worth the money charged. These agents not only know the market better and do a better job, but they are able to reduce costs over what an operation might have to pay to do its own purchasing.

Market supply and prices are influenced by many factors, and buyers need to know what these are and how they can affect their buying. The ability to forecast market actions can greatly enhance the purchasing task.

No buyer can know everything about the market. Even the most expert buyer must constantly strive to learn more. The market is also very dynamic, and buyers need to discard old, unnecessary information regularly and learn the new.

The Need for Good Communication Flow Among Spheres

One of the challenges buyers face is establishing an adequate communication system among the other spheres and also within the buyer's own internal sphere. Some find that having periodic meetings with these other entities works well. Others establish a system of paper flow in which desired information is forwarded between various operating units. Maintaining contact with the outer sphere has become easier with the advent of the computer, facsimile, e-mail, and Internet, but personal contact with salespeople and others in the market must still be maintained. It is most important that the system established provide an adequate flow of information both into and out of the purchasing department.

Today many buyers work in a central office and purchase for separate operating units of the company. This complicates the communication system. The purchasing department now must not only maintain contact with the central office's management and various departments, but also must maintain contact with individual unit managers, production, accounting, and so forth. The delivery function is now lost, it being the responsibility of individual units. What usually happens is that in order to maintain adequate contact with operating units a much more elaborate system of paper flow is set up among the units and the central purchasing office, making it almost another sphere in which the buyer must function. The computer and other modern technologies have again simplified such paper flow systems and increased their speed.

AN OVERVIEW OF CHAPTERS

Chapter 2 is a discussion dealing with the patron sphere; Chapter 3 is an overview of the market (outer sphere) in which a buyer functions. Chapter 4 continues the explanation of the purchasing function, tracing the steps in detail that are taken in the purchase function. This chapter and others then cover activities that take place in the inner sphere, covering the criteria used to select suppliers and the placing, receiving, and issuing of orders. In other chapters that follow, how to develop specifications is discussed, followed by how the computer is used today in purchasing.

The next section covers in detail the factors that are important in the purchase of fresh fruits and vegetables, processed fruits and vegetables, dairy, groceries, poultry and eggs, marine products, meats, and alcoholic and nonfood items frequently purchased by food services.

SUMMARY

Purchasing is an activity in which goods or services are exchanged for something of value. The market in which a foodservice buyer deals is highly dynamic and must be watched carefully. It is also extremely complex and a buyer needs a great deal of knowledge about foods and how the market operates to do a successful job. The buyer must not only be competent in this market area but must also be able to coordinate the purchasing department's activities and goals with those of other departments. Buyers will find they can get much assistance from government agencies, purveyors, and their salespeople, from laws that regulate the market, and from the market itself.

What is purchased will be decided by five entities: patrons, production, service, the buyer, and management. The decisions of all are important, but patron needs and management's direction are paramount. Patrons decide what is purchased by selecting menu items; the production department dictates purchase needs by its production needs, and service does the same because of its needs. The buyer's decisions are shaped by the needs of the other four plus having to deal in the market and modify the purchasing program to be able to obtain the required items. Management is responsible for the successful functioning of the operation and so must see that all views are considered along with its own.

A foodservice buyer functions in three spheres. The first is that of the patron, and adequate functioning in this area is achieved by purchasing what gives patrons satisfaction.

The sphere in which the buyer functions is the inner sphere, which is the operation itself. Here the buyer must properly interpret the needs of production and service while following management's dictates. Good coordination between the facility's different departments affected by buying must be achieved. Proper records must be maintained and a close liaison with the accounting department kept to see that adequate financial control is achieved. Items must be given good security and be properly cared for so as to preserve their quality.

The outer sphere is the market itself. Here the buyer must deal with purveyors, negotiate purchases, make financial arrangements, and so forth. One of the biggest needs in this outer sphere area is the competency to negotiate.

REVIEW QUESTIONS

1. Discuss in class how the three spheres interrelate and influence the purchase function. For instance, consider the following but add your own ideas also: What might exist in the internal, or second, sphere that would make it impossible to follow completely the desires of patrons? In discussing this, consider cost, facility limitations, personnel limitations, and so forth. What might exist in the third, or outer, sphere that would make it impossible to follow the desires of patrons?

    How could factors in the internal sphere dictate how a buyer might function in the external market? For instance, consider how cost restrictions on how much one can buy might make it impossible to purchase in larger lots and thus save money. Or consider how turkeys below a certain size have to be purchased because the ovens of the facility are not high enough to hold the larger turkeys, thus raising costs. (Might there not be a solution in this by having the seller cut the larger turkeys in half lengthwise and thus make it possible to roast the halves laying down? In your class discussion see if you can come up with answers to problems like this.)

2. What steps would you take to find out what patrons want?

3. Discuss the knowledge, traits, and other characteristics that a good buyer should possess. How about honesty? Ability to get along with others? Attention to detail? Mathematical and computer ability? Knowledge of the market?

4. Set up a very short menu for a luncheon and then have one class member, representing the chef, explain to another class member, representing the buyer, the production need when purchasing the various items. If it's a lamb chop, what kind—loin, rib, or shoulder?—size or weight, type of cut, and so forth. If it's a stuffed tomato, what size, what ripeness, and what else is desired? The buyer might have to explain to the chef that a desired item was not then available on the market, or that the cost of the item was too high and something else might have to be offered instead. Develop a good scenario using your imagination to portray how such a meeting might occur.

KEY WORDS AND CONCEPTS

buyer	outer sphere
buying	patron
industrial buyer	patron sphere
inner sphere	production
Institutional Meat Purchase Specifications (IMPS)	purchasing
	purchasing agent
Internet	service
job description	specifications
management	ultimate buyer
negotiation	Universal Product Code (UPC)

CHAPTER 2

The Patron Sphere

Pleasures of the Mean Rich Man and the Misery of Poor Lazarus. Poor Lazarus who died in the dust of poverty, whose soul was received in the bosom of Abraham. From the Louis Szwathmary collection, Culinary Archives and Museum, Johnson and Wales University, used by permission of Dr. Szwathmary and Johnson and Wales University.

Chapter Objectives

1. To indicate what patrons generally want when they eat out.
2. To show how buyers can assist in an operation's goal of satisfying patrons.
3. To discuss concerns that patrons have about the healthful and nutritional qualities of the foods they consume away from home and also their concern about the sanitation and safety of this food.

4. To view some of the concepts patrons have about pesticides and additives in food.

5. To detail concerns patrons have about the nutritional value of items served and how food services can respond.

6. To discuss nutritional labeling on menus.

INTRODUCTION

Although food buyers may think they are remote from the patron sphere, they are not. Patrons are one of the most important driving forces in almost everything the purchasing department does. The purchasing department buys for patrons—not management, not the chef or cook, but patrons. Knowing what patrons want can help a buyer do a better job of pleasing them while still staying within budgetary limits.

KNOW YOUR MARKET

There are many kinds of food services because there are many kinds of patrons. No one food service could ever serve all patrons. This is because patrons have so many different wants that no one operation could meet all of them. Food services differ because they try to serve a specific kind of patron who has specific wants. McDonald's serves hamburgers and Kentucky Fried Chicken serves fried chicken because their patrons want them and they are designed to serve this trade. A seafood and fish house specializes in serving those foods, but a few meats and poultry may appear on its menu because some patrons want them.

The patrons an operation is designed to serve are often referred to as the operation's **target market**—operations aim their sales programs at this market. The more precisely an operation can define this market and understand its wants, the better the chance for that operation's success. The phrase "know your market" is heard so often that it becomes trite, but it is one of the truest axioms in the business world. A food service *must* know its market and then serve a product this market *wants*. Not to do so gives a person about the same odds for successful operation as going outside at night in pitch blackness, randomly shooting up in the air, and hoping to see a turkey drop. Today some food services use a computer to set up **patron profiles** and then summarize these to define their target market.

Once a market is defined, a menu designed to meet its needs can be planned, and this second step is equal in importance to proper definition of a market, because unless a food service gives a targeted market what it wants, it is not going to patronize the place. A men's college dormitory must serve different foods in larger portions than a women's dormitory food service. A family restaurant is not going to try to serve foods that satisfy the big expense account patron. Elderly people want smaller portions because of lower appetites and often foods that are easy to chew because their teeth are not as strong as those of younger patrons.

After the menu is planned, a series of steps must occur so the proper items are served. How well each entity of an operation does its specific tasks in moving this process through to a conclusion will determine how well the operation satisfies its market. The person who does the buying is one of these entities, working as a team player with management, menu planners, the kitchen (production), and service to satisfy this market.

WHAT DO PATRONS WANT?

How do you determine what a market wants? The simplest way to find out is to ask it. Management and others often have a chance to ask patrons how they liked their food and if they would like it prepared differently or would like other items. An operation's service staff can also be a rich source of information since the staff is most often in contact with patrons. Some operations place a small placard on the table asking for guests' comments. Hiring a firm that specializes in obtaining the information can be done, but is usually too expensive for small operations. Large chains frequently produce an item and then try it out on a limited test market. If the test is successful, the product is marketed by the entire chain.

Are complaints a good source of information about how you can better please patrons? Very much so. A person complaining has found something that does not please. By patient, sympathetic, honest listening, you can learn what this is—how you missed satisfying a want. Handling angry patrons is not easy but, if done properly, can do much to placate and keep patrons while teaching you how to better meet patrons' desires.

Outside sources can often give good information. Paying attention to what the competition is doing can keep you informed about what your operation might also do to better please, since the competition is serving the same market. Trade magazines, journals, and other media often report eating trends or successful promotions by others that your patrons might like. Vendors may be a good source of new menu items that patrons might like.

The **National Restaurant Association (NRA)** and other groups periodically make surveys of what patrons want when they eat out. High on the list are good food and good service. Close to these and sometimes ahead of them in desirability are clean and sanitary food that is safe to eat and free of pesticides, chemicals, and unnatural substances. Another important factor is food adequate in nutrient values, discussed later in this chapter. Other factors that frequently come up in surveys are value and convenience. These last two are not discussed in this chapter because they more properly receive emphasis in the chapters that follow.

Good Food

Although price often seems to be one of the main factors influencing the selection of items, quality should bear equal weight. Buyers need to know what item they want and what quality is needed to produce the item desired and how to secure it at the right price. As we shall learn in a later chapter, purchasing the *right* quality needs a lot of attention and thought. Small differences can make a big difference in quality and the better a buyer knows exactly what is needed, the better he or she can select the quality needed to make items patrons like.

Good food, however, is not guaranteed just because items of the right quality have been secured. After selection of quality items, they must receive proper handling so they do not lose their quality. The receipt of several crates of delicious, fully ripe strawberries may satisfy a quality need, but not after they are left to stand in the hot sun for several hours before sending them to storage.

The receiving, storage, and issue functions are usually a buyer's responsibility and, if done poorly, food will deteriorate and patrons will not get good food. Inventory management is also usually a buyer's responsibility, and stocks on hand should be adequate to meet needs but not such that there is a loss of quality because of overstocking or because the buyer fails to notify production or others of the need to move items into production before quality is lost.

Good Service

Can what is purchased be an influence on whether patrons are satisfied with the service? Certainly. Buyers often see that foods are obtained in a form that enables the production department to make an attractive product, thus improving a patron's impression of what is served. One large tomato slice that covers a slice of bread completely gives a much better appearing bacon and tomato sandwich than several smaller tomato slices; it is also much easier for the patron to handle because smaller slices tend to slip out. The buyer for such sandwiches should know that size "maximum large" tomatoes should be specified.

Obtaining items at their proper ripeness can also assist in seeing that foods have plate and taste appeal. Well-glazed red, ripe strawberries covering a fresh strawberry pie will arouse the interest of most patrons, but offer one covered with strawberries that still show plenty of green and white and the takers will be few. It is up to the buyer to see that items are right for production so menu items have high sight appeal when served.

Items when served should look like a picture in a frame, the plate edge being the frame and the food being the picture. Food should not cover the frame. Food hanging over a dish edge is unattractive and also may become contaminated if it touches other things. A buyer should know the serving sizes of dishes used and fit portions to these.

Service speed is important in facilities where patrons are in a hurry. A downtown restaurant will usually do the most business at lunch, when patrons are in a hurry. Their lunchtime is limited and they are often anxious to get something else done besides eat, such as running errands, before they have to return to work. Service can be speeded up if items are obtained that reduce service handling as much as possible. Thus, a vendor might offer the same brand of chicken pot pie in individual serving dishes rather than in half steam table pans. The cost per portion for the individual pie is only several cents more than one from the pan. The buyer informs management of the availability of the two and the cost difference, pointing out that the speed of serving individual pies over dishup from the pan plus the attractiveness of the serving should warrant the extra cost. Management agrees. Whereas just one item like this might not help much to improve overall service speed, a buyer might find enough suitable items that can be served individually so that overall service speed is considerably improved. Besides resulting in better satisfied patrons, an improved turnover rate occurs so more patrons can be served, giving a better bottom line. Patrons in a hurry who get food they like and get out quickly tend to return.

Safe, Clean, and Sanitary Food

Patrons can become ill as a result of eating out; in fact, it happens often enough to be an industry problem. Cases such as 30 people coming down with *hepatitis A* after eating a restaurant's contaminated salad or 912 people getting sick from *Salmonella* poisoning after eating at a Mexican fast-food establishment get wide publicity and often cause people to feel the situation is worse than it is.

Our government estimates that in this country between 6.5 and 33 million cases of **foodborne illnesses** occur each year along with about 10,000 related deaths. The health cost is estimated to be around $10 billion.[1] Although many of these illnesses and deaths are caused by food consumed at home, a significant number are traced to food services. In recent years we have also had some dramatic events occur in the area of food sanitation and these have augmented an already public concern. Some of these events include the following:

- An influenza virus infecting chickens in Hong Kong caused a number of deaths and illnesses to people eating these chickens. It also resulted in the slaughter of vast numbers of Hong Kong chickens, thorough sanitizing of the raising areas, and cessation of such raising for about a month. This incident received international attention.

- In the state of Washington four children died and hundreds of other individuals became ill after eating a food service's hamburgers contaminated with **Escherichia coli.** Another child playing with the one that had eaten the hamburgers caught the bacteria and died. (The contaminated hamburgers were undercooked.)

- In Japan at least 11 people died and as many as 10,000 people, including more than 6,000 children, became ill after eating food contaminated with the deadly *E. coli 0157—coliform* bacteria, which came from the fecal waste of animals. *E. coli* can be spread to nonanimal products by cross-contamination or by contacting manure and other fecal matter in fertilizers. These Japanese were from one area and became ill not only from food eaten in food services but also from food consumed in the home.

- A wide number of illnesses were reported after people drank one processor's unpasteurized fruit juices contaminated with *E. coli.*

- Evidence is increasing that poultry and eggs are not the only cause of *Salmonella* bacterial poisoning but that pork and even beef and lamb are also to a

---

[1]David Parkes, "Creating Awareness," *Restaurant Hospitality,* September 1996, p. 46.

degree greater risks than suspected. Poultry is also a frequent source of illnesses caused by *Listeria monocytogenes* and *Campylobacter jejuni* bacteria.

- Beef from cattle infected with **bovine spongiform encephalopathy** (BSE, or mad cow disease) bacteria can cause encephalitis or brain fever in those eating such infected meat. (Although this is thought to be true only of beef produced in Great Britain, the danger of this disease coming to the United States is sufficient as to cause us to take steps to contain it.)

- Recently several other *E. coli* group poisonings resulted in much publicity. One was caused by contaminated alfalfa sprouts, another from ground turkey, and the third from hamburger, the latter resulting in the recall of more than 1.3 million pounds of the product. Thus, the fact that nonmeat items such as alfalfa sprouts and the fruit juice mentioned earlier were involved and that the Hazard Analysis Critical Control Point (see below) had not completely solved the meat problem brought home the need for safer uncooked food preparation methods by producers and the need for consumers to cook meats above 160°F, especially ground meats.

Because of public concern over these and other incidents involving meat or poultry items, President Clinton announced in July 1996 that the government's 90-year-old meat inspection program would be amended to include new ways to test for and control bacterial contamination in meats and poultry. In addition to the present visual and odor inspection—called the "hunt and poke" method—actual testing for bacterial contamination would occur, and limits of the amounts of specific bacteria that could be allowed in such foods would be established.

This 1996 regulation, which extended the federal government's meat and poultry inspection program, is called the **Hazard Analysis Critical Control Point** (HACCP) and required that **Sanitation Standard Operating Procedures** (SSOPs) be established at all critical points in the processing of meats or poultry to prevent contamination. The new program was to take effect in steps, so buyers might not see complete evidence of it until the year 2000. In addition, later in 1996 President Clinton announced the allocation of sizable funds to improve the safety of marine products.

Also, as part of the program, a number of federal agencies began investigations on how to reduce contamination in our food supply and also how to improve awareness of its existence when it did occur. In 1997, as a part of this stepped-up program, the **Food Safety and Inspection Service** (FSIS) announced the approval of irradiation to destroy harmful bacteria in poultry before it is marketed. This approval was later extended to meats. Thus, buyers may soon see the international symbol for **irradiation** (see Figure 2–1) and read the words "Treated with Irradiation" or "Treated by Irradiation" on poultry and meat packages they receive. Other investigations are ongoing, such as the development of sensitive wraps on meats that would turn from blue to red if a product were contaminated with *E. coli*.

A repetition of the *E. coli* incidents, the BES presence in British cattle, and continued problems with *Salmonella* and other bacteria or viruses are something the meat and poultry industries do not want. Consumption of their products can be severely damaged by these adverse events. These industries now label all packages

Figure 2-1
The international logo used to indicate that a product has been irradiated.

containing their products with a warning to use proper care in their handling and cooking (see Figure 2–2).

The new regulation did not meet with universal approval. Some critics claimed it was too little, too late. Specific criticisms centered around three factors: (1) It did not increase the number of inspectors, (2) it did nothing to improve inspection procedures, and (3) the regulation was too lax in some of its sanitation standards. A recent **General Accounting Office** (GAO) report on food plant inspections made between 1989 and 1994 was used to support their claims[2] as follows:

1.   Inspections in this five-year period declined by around 50% despite the fact that federal spending for them increased by 10%—the reason given was that, although there was an increase in the number of plants, the number of inspectors remained the same. In this five-year period, the **Food and Drug Administration** (FDA), charged with inspecting dairy, seafood, and most kinds of food processing plants, inspected a plant on an average of every eight years instead of every three, which was the case when the GAO started its study in 1989—4,789 inspections were made in 1994 versus 6,368 in 1989, a decline of 25%. The FSIS, charged with the inspection of meat and poultry plants, increased the number of chickens requiring inspection by 7.4 billion in the five-year period—a 28% increase; the number of hogs by 90 million—an increase of 10%; with similar increases in beef and turkeys. Only lamb remained about the same. The number of inspectors in the FSIS did not increase.

2.   Inspectors are forced to go through inspections too fast to do a thorough job. Some inspectors have to inspect more than a dozen plants a day. Under the HACCP, inspectors will not physically inspect the plant but will inspect instead its sanitation maintenance records.

3.   Standards for *Salmonella* bacteria in poultry have been set at what poultry might have when it is processed in a well-operated, sanitary plant, a standard that is too high. This means that 25% of the chickens and 49% of the turkeys marketed will be permitted to show such contamination, a standard that is dangerous and too high.

The answer of the HACCP proponents to these criticisms is "Give HACCP a chance. We easily can take steps to correct omissions later."

---

[2]Donald F. Puzo, "The Federal Government Is Spending More on Food Safety but Doing Less Than in 1989," *Los Angeles Times,* June 13, 1996.

MEAT/DEPT

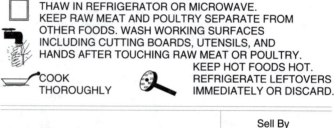

SAFE HANDLING INSTRUCTIONS

THIS PRODUCT WAS PREPARED FROM INSPECTED AND
PASSED MEAT AND OR POULTRY. SOME FOOD PRODUCTS
MAY CONTAIN BACTERIA THAT COULD CAUSE ILLNESS IF THE
PRODUCT IS MISHANDLED OR COOKED IMPROPERLY. FOR
YOUR PROTECTION FOLLOW THESE SAFE HANDLING
INSTRUCTIONS.

KEEP REFRIGERATED OR FROZEN.
THAW IN REFRIGERATOR OR MICROWAVE.
KEEP RAW MEAT AND POULTRY SEPARATE FROM
OTHER FOODS. WASH WORKING SURFACES
INCLUDING CUTTING BOARDS, UTENSILS, AND
HANDS AFTER TOUCHING RAW MEAT OR POULTRY.
COOK
THOROUGHLY
KEEP HOT FOODS HOT.
REFRIGERATE LEFTOVERS
IMMEDIATELY OR DISCARD.

	Sell By Feb 12, 97

Net Wt/Ct	Unit Price	Total Price
0.94 lb	$1.49/lb	$1.40

Figure 2-2
*This type of label with safe handling instructions now appears on
all retail packaged meat.*

Foodservice Industry Concerns and Progress

The foodservice industry is very much concerned with sanitation and food safety.
The NRA and a number of professional associations strongly support programs designed to produce the highest standards in these areas. The health departments of
many states or localities conduct frequent and rigorous inspections to see that proper
standards are met. A number today require food services to have at least one certified graduate of the **Educational Foundation of the NRA's** sanitation course on
duty during all hours of operation.

Over the years progress has been made. Sanitary conditions in food services
have improved. In the early 1900s when the industry was a fledgling one, rats and
mice were a constant problem; few products were available to combat vermin—
cockroaches roamed at will. Things like chlorine and other sanitizers were unknown;
dishes were washed in a sink—"pearl diving" was the job classification name because dishwashers had to reach down so deep into sinks filled with sudsy water to

get the dishes. There were no sanitation inspections. Boxes used ice to cool food (refrigeration wasn't available), so foods kept for only short periods of time. Hot substances could not be put into the ice box since that would raise the temperature and everything would spoil. Toilets were often outhouses with no running water for the cleansing of hands, and floors were wood, not hard quarry tile from which soil was easily removed. Who knows how many cases of foodborne illnesses or deaths from these conditions occurred? They were probably never reported! Pasteurized foods were unknown; canned ones were just beginning to appear. While electric street cars droned in the larger cities, electric lights were just beginning to light our streets. Some parts of the United States were still frontier. It was the day of the nickel beer and a free lunch! Perhaps romantic to look back at, but lacking in many of the standards we commonly accept today.

Over the years we have seen a gradual improvement in our National Health Code. The Sanitation Foundation of the University of Michigan has gone a long way to see that we have better equipment with which to maintain good sanitary conditions. We have also established tighter regulations on the production, processing, and marketing of foods. Packaging standards have been established that give far better protection to our foods. Limits on the bacterial content of our foods have been reduced. And, although we still have a long way to go, we at least know that we are making progress.

Pesticides and Food Additives

Patrons want food that is not contaminated with pesticides, chemicals, and other added substances. A number of regulations exist today that limit the amounts of them that can be added or used with foods. Some are entirely prohibited, such as DDT. However, many feel the regulations should be more strict, whereas still others feel they should be relaxed. Recently in Congress we have seen moves toward relaxation.

Pesticides are substances used largely during the growing process to destroy pests or insects or to further growth. Producers of items treated with pesticides claim that because better and more products are produced the public benefits. They also cite the fact that federal tests have established safe levels for these substances in foods and the public should be reassured by this that such food is safe to consume. Some buyers search out items called *natural* or *organic foods* that have not been treated with pesticides or grown in chemically fertilized soil so patrons will be satisfied. However, the supply of these is limited and sometimes nonexistent. The price is usually considerably higher so patrons must be willing to pay the added price if such items are purchased.

Food additives are substances added to foods largely during their processing either to preserve, retain color, stabilize, emulsify, or do other desirable things to them. The federal government publishes a list of the substances that may be added to foods. It is known as the **GRAS (generally regarded as safe) list.** Some are substances commonly added to foods, such as sugar (sucrose) and table salt (sodium chloride). (A GRAS list of substances that can be added to poultry products appears in the chapter on poultry.) GRAS list items have been tested by the federal government and limits set on the amounts that specific foods can contain. Some criticize these limits as too liberal, while others claim they are too limiting. Some buyers must secure foods free of such additives to satisfy patrons, often paying much more for them and passing the added cost onto the patrons who are willing to pay. Other buyers find they must purchase foods containing additives if they are to have them at all.

Pesticides and food additives are not the only substances in foods that are of concern to patrons. It has become a common practice for many growers of animals to give hormones and other substances to animals to ward off diseases and to promote growth. Whether they are harmful is again subject to argument. The problem is too complicated and outside the range of purchasing to spend time on it here, but buyers should know of their existence and the feelings of patrons about their use.

Carriers of Food Contamination

Foods can be contaminated with harmful or undesirable substances in a food service by animals, pests, and insects, by individuals, or by allowing equipment, work surfaces, or other places that foods come in contact with to remain in an unclean condition and develop harmful or undesirable substances on them. Carriers of such substances are called **vectors.**

Contamination more often comes from personnel rather than the facility. Employees handling foods should have clean bodies and wear clean clothing and be healthy and free from any condition that might cause contamination. Hands and nails should be cleaned and washed frequently. Cuts, sores, and other body abrasions are places where *Staphylococcus* bacteria develop and then get into food, developing a toxin that makes one ill. A person can have a cold and sneeze, spreading staph infection on food.

It is best to change clothing when entering a food service. Barring that, many operations require a garment be worn over the regular clothing. Many local health boards require foodservice personnel to wear head gear to prevent hair or soil from the head from getting into food. When such a regulation does not exist, the facility may make it a requirement.

Meats and poultry can carry bacteria that can contaminate other food. That is why the warning labels on their packages say to wash surfaces they touch well and to wash the hands after handling them (see Figure 2–2). They should be thawed under refrigeration or in a microwave and used soon after, but until used, they must receive adequate refrigeration. Carryover items should be kept refrigerated. The use of date tags on meat and poultry to record receiving dates is recommended.

The receiving, storage, and issuing units must not only be clean and sanitary but vectors such as mice and rats and insects such as ants, weevils, flies, and cockroaches should be eliminated completely. Shelving, floors, and other units with which items come in contact should be clean and sanitized. Items should not be stored directly on the floor nor close to wall surfaces. Trash should not be permitted to remain on the premises. Items are sometimes taken from larger units and transferred to smaller packaging for issue. The area where this is done should be such that contamination is not possible. The smaller containers should be clean and sanitary. Prior to removal, garbage and trash should be stored so that contamination of other substances is not possible.

Proper Handling

Items in receiving, storage, and issue should be handled with care so as to prevent breakage, bruising, or other damage. Even metal cans can be dented to the point that the seal breaks.

Accidents can and do occur. A jar of salted nuts may break and small pieces of glass fall into an open bin of flour. The nuts that fell into the flour may perhaps be picked out as well as some of the larger pieces of glass but not the small, tiny glass pieces. This actually happened in one operation and the manager was informed. He instructed the storeroom clerk to carefully remove the top layer of flour to a depth of about four inches. This was done, but it was a serious mistake. About a week later this manager was notified that a patron eating a piece of cornbread had crunched on something hard, cutting her mouth. On removing the item, she found she had bitten into a piece of glass. Examination of some flour in the kitchen bake shop showed a few additional pieces of glass! The patron threatened to sue. The incident was quietly settled out of court, but it cost $7,000 to do so. Management learned a lesson. The whole bin of flour should have been discarded. There is a big difference between $7,000 and $32.89, the cost of the flour. What if management had said "Sift it and get the glass out?" No. Some very fine pieces of glass could get through the sifter. "Best not take a chance" is the safest rule.

Separation of Storage Spaces

If detergents, chemicals, or other nonfood items are stored with foods, there is danger that they can be mistaken for a food items or somehow become mixed with food items. This can be a real danger and can lead to food loss or possibly poisonings. A separate storage space should be provided for such items, even a small cabinet, and it is best to have it locked at times when items are not being removed or stored there.

Here's an example of what happened in one foodservice operation when such a rule was violated. One day some additional cornmeal was needed to make a tamale pie, and the cook in charge sent a helper to the storeroom to get a bit more cornmeal to complete the preparation. The helper hurried to the storeroom and dipped out a can of what was thought to be cornmeal. (The storeroom was what we call an *open storeroom,* where items were removed as needed without any record being made.) The cook added some of what the helper brought and suddenly saw the mixture develop a heavy froth. Tasting it, she found the mistake. She had added a phosphate detergent instead of cornmeal. The two looked identical. Worse things can happen than this and do, but this is sufficient to indicate the need for such separation.

NUTRITION AND PLANNING

Planning Menus and Purchasing for Health

The first requisite to purchasing **healthful foods** is to know what they are and to put them on the menu. This means more vegetable and fruit dishes, whole-grain foods, foods that contain less fat and fewer calories, and perhaps less of some kinds of meat items. Fewer fried foods and foods wrapped in rich crusts or breading should be offered. Cooking foods by methods that keep off added calories, such as poaching, boiling, broiling, or roasting, is also recommended. The kitchen should undersalt foods, allowing patrons to add more if they wish. Ways need to be found to take old high-calorie favorites and trim off some of their calories, yet keep the taste as good as ever. Many people have been successful in doing so. The success of Chef Tower in introducing highly gourmet items that are healthful has led to the creation of what is called the "New Cuisine." It has many imitators today because operators have found that serving foods that are good and at the same time healthful wins customers.

Foods adequate in nutrition are a result more of proper menu planning and preparation than purchasing. Buyers can, however, assist in seeing that nutritious foods are served, but to a lesser degree than these other two areas. Fresh fruits and vegetables are most nutritious at the peak of their season; they are usually lowest in cost at that time as well. Buyers should see that the freshest possible items are delivered and give them proper care afterward. They should also specify that meat be as free of fat as is feasible for the production need. (Some meats, fish, and poultry need a certain amount of fat to process them as patrons want them. You need only try to broil an extremely lean piece of veal to see why this is true. A yield grade No. 1, quality-grade [Select] rib of beef will fill quite well the requirement for a very low-fat meat, but an operation trying to serve it as a prime rib roast might not like the patron reaction to tough meat).

A food service wishing assistance in planning menus or in other ways meeting the nutritional needs of patrons can secure considerable help from associations such as the American Dietetic Association, the American Heart Association, and the American Diabetic Association. The federal government has many agencies that also can be of assistance. The American Heart Association (AHA) has a program that it offers to food services along with menus, recipes, etc. A food service in this program that produces foods approved by the AHA is entitled to place a symbol of a heart after each food selection, indicating that it is one recommended by the AHA.

A buyer can assist in the nutrition program in the following ways:

- Purchase the freshest foods possible and move them to production as soon as possible. Freezing may preserve a food but not all the nutrients; while nutrient loss may be slowed slightly, there still is a loss.

- Store and handle fresh foods in a manner so as to preserve nutrients. Dehydration can even destroy as stable a vitamin as vitamin A. Spoilage causes a loss of all nutrients as well as the product.

- See that storage areas are held at the proper temperature and humidity.

- Do not pack fresh fruits and vegetables in storage areas too tightly; they are living organisms and need air and moisture to live.

- Keep storage areas and areas where foods are handled clean and sanitary so that chances for spoilage and contamination are reduced.

- Normally, paring and other prepreparation of items occur under the jurisdiction of the production department, but if this processing is the responsibility of purchasing, safeguards should be taken to see that foods are soaked as little as possible, items pared as thinly as possible, etc. If a meat cutting unit is operated, trim meats well of fat.

- Order foods containing dietary supplements and thus increase the nutritional value of the foods obtained. This must be done carefully, however. There are some authorities that say we are adding too many supplements to our foods and are actually endangering good nutrition rather than ensuring it. Eating a varied diet following the amounts recommended in the **dietary pyramid** (see Figure 2–3) is still favored. (See also the food storage recommendations in Appendix B.)

What Do Patrons Want in Nutrition?

Surveys of what people want when they eat away from home show that not all are concerned with diet. A significant number still want a meat and potatoes type of diet and are not especially concerned with nutrient values. They don't want to eat foods

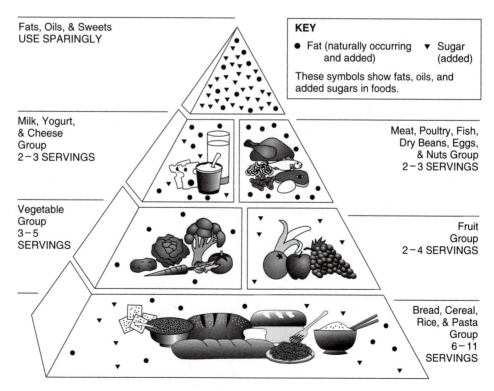

Figure 2-3
The guide to a complete diet. (Courtesy USDA.)

detrimental to their health, but are not going to go out of their way to eat foods especially high in nutrients. First of all, they want foods they have learned to like. After that, if nutrition comes, well, that's fine. To some, foods offered as "good for you" are rabbit foods. Foodservice operators quickly learn that trying to be a missionary by changing patrons' views on how they should eat is not a profitable way to operate a business. It is said that "It is harder to change people's eating habits than it is to change their religion." Patrons having a free choice of *what* and *where* they want to eat will soon weed out places that do not serve the foods they want and will patronize those that do.

Thus, offer healthful foods to those who want them but remember that some patrons don't particularly want them. This may be true of some who follow a dietary regime at home but, when they go out to eat, say "I'm not following my diet tonight. I'm going to eat what I want." When those planning the menu hear that people are eating less beef and red meat, they should think twice before cutting back on their red meat offerings. That steak or prime rib will look awfully good to someone who has not had red meat at home for some time.

How much responsibility should a food service have in seeing that its patrons have an adequate diet? The answer is that it varies according to the mission of the operation. A hospital must see that its patients eat as healthful a diet as possible and even instruct them on how to select one. An institution where all the food a person gets comes from the institution should offer adequate nutrition and encourage it, but should not go so far as to force it. When an operation offers only partial meals such as a drive-in, offering a completely adequate diet might not be possible, but the operation should see that the nutrients that should be in the food offered are there so patrons will at least get that much. A facility offering complete meals has the obligation to see that the selection of an adequate diet is possible and that the nutrients foods should have are there.

Many commercial operations can render a service to patrons by informing them about which foods on the menu are most healthful and why. By means of posters, placards, and other informational material, they can also encourage good nutrition but should in no way force such information on patrons.

The main concerns patrons have about healthful foods is that the foods be lower in fat, lower in salt (sodium), lower in calories, and lower in cholesterol. To this they add foods free of additives, pesticides, and chemicals—natural foods—that contain no harmful substances. A large number are suspicious of new foods and new technology. We could be using more irradiated foods, but many have the notion that foods treated this way to retain quality and appearance are harmful.

We need a public better educated about what good nutrition is and which foods will provide it. The public also needs to understand the part that nutrition plays in promoting health. This understanding is growing, and food services are finding more and more interest in good nutrition and patrons who know what good nutrition is and how to select it, but there is still much misinformation about nutrition among the public about exactly what are healthful foods. Quack diets abound. You can pick up any number of popular magazines from the newsstand and read in almost every one about one sensational diet or another that knocks off pounds in a few weeks.

The trouble is that people believe and follow these diets and often expect a food service to honor them. A lot of strange, quirky ideas about healthful foods are brought to foodservice operations by patrons and made a part of their request in the foods ordered. For the most part, these requests are harmless, cost nothing to satisfy, and please the customer.

Food services need to be better informed about what good nutrition is and how to offer it. Too many times an item will be offered as having healthful qualities, when actually it lacks them and might even be considered a food to avoid. Thus, a menu that offers a skinless chicken breast that is breaded and deep-fried is missing the boat. While removing the skin removed many of the fat calories, more were probably added by the breading, which soaked up considerable fat. In a study of more than 60 foodservice menus that offered low-calorie items, only 21 really did.

Unless your serving staff is informed about the nutritional qualities of menu items, they cannot talk intelligently about these qualities to patrons. Because patrons have become better informed, it is necessary for those working in the industry to become so also. Establishing a program to see that employees are better informed about nutrition is recommended.

The situation is not all negative, however. A significant part of the foodservice industry is aware of the public's growing demand for improved nutrition and is moving to supply it. Operations are changing menus, ways of purchasing, food preparation, and service to meet this demand. Fast-food establishments now offer salad bars and put tomatoes and lettuce and other healthful foods in hamburgers. Many offer menus having foods of high nutrient value. Such foods are identified by being placed in a special section of the menu or are identified by a small heart or other symbol.

For the most part, no particular food is bad, but too much of almost any food can be. Around 55% or more of our calories should come from carbohydrate foods such as rice, flour, pasta, sugars, and so forth, placing the most emphasis on whole-grain products.

As we learn more and more about the healthful qualities of foods, we may see an extension in the use of foods containing dietary supplements, not to provide adequate nutrition, but to provide curative powers such as is found in medicine. Thus, a doctor may prescribe a specific frozen dinner to help cure or prevent some illness. The fact that soy proteins might play a role in reducing the risk of cancer and heart disease is tempting some food companies to develop foods containing soy. Others show an interest in developing foods that carry antioxidants such as vitamin C or E or beta-carotene to prevent cancer, cardiovascular disease, or cataracts.

Nutrition Labeling on Menus

The FDA in 1996 decided that after May 2, 1997, menus of food services making health or nutrient claims must follow the same rules that food manufacturers follow in **nutrition labeling.** If a menu states that the amount of calories, cholesterol, mineral content, and so forth of a food item is such and such, the menu is making a nutrient claim, and if the menu says the food is "heart healthy" or uses a heart or apple symbol near it, a claim of health is being made. The operation making a claim must use a *reasonable basis* in making such claims. Thus, if an operation claimed that a glass of orange juice contributed 200 mg of ascorbic acid to your diet and it had taken the information from a reliable list of nutrient values, the rule would be followed. Other sources that can be used are cookbooks, databases, analysis software, and textbooks. The best source and one that will bring about the least argument is a nutrient value published in a government document.

Usually, nutrient claims on items are based on a reference amount of 100 grams. A "low-fat" meal must contain 3 grams or less of fat per 100 grams of the meal. Thus, if the amount were 400 g, the fat must be 12 g or under. If under the salad and vegetable offerings, you make the statement that "eating five fruits or vegetables a day can help provide a healthful diet," you are not making a health claim. If a claim is made about a specific item, one should then be careful to see whether it is a health or nutrient claim. Making claims such as "high in vegetables," "baked, not fried," "made with less oil," and so forth, need not be substantiated. An operation must make information substantiating nutrient or health claims on menus available to patrons. This can be in the form of posters, fliers, charts, brochures, or word-of-mouth reporting.

If a menu states that something meets the FDA-published **Dietary Guidelines for Americans,** it must; thus it must yield 30% or fewer calories from fat, 10% or fewer calories from saturated fat, moderate or less amounts of cholesterol, sugar and sodium, and provide fruits, vegetables and/or grains.

The May 1997 regulation further indicated that the use of terms such as "lean," "low fiber," or "lighter fare" must meet the FDA's definition of that term. Thus, a cup of soup claimed as "low sodium" must have less than 140 mg of sodium per 245 g (about an 8-oz portion). If "low fat," the soup must not contain more than 3 g of fat. Serving a "bowl" of soup means the portion size is 2 cups and to meet the requirement for "low," the amounts of fat or sodium can be doubled over that of a cup. If one serves oatmeal muffins with a breakfast, the menu can claim the presence of "oatmeal bran, a high-fiber food" but not that the whole meal is "high in fiber." Definitions indicate just what can be claimed and often what might not be claimed. Thus, the term "lighter fare" means the item may be served as a "smaller portion," "be served with sauce or dressing on the side," or be "made with half the usual amount of oil." The reference amount or size of a portion used to establish the criteria for using terms such as "low," "reduced," "free," etc., is given in the regulation.

SUMMARY

Important factors in providing patron satisfaction are examined and the part that buyers play in assisting a facility to achieve these goals is discussed. The first step in setting about to please customers is to know who they are and what they want. This is called the facility's *target market*. After the market is determined, a menu to satisfy these patron needs is often planned and at that point the buyer's role begins.

Operations ascertain what their market wants by asking, observing, hiring others to find out, studying complaints, or finding out what others in similar markets are doing. New ideas about foods that might please can come from publications, vendors, or others. Surveys by trade associations have indicated that patrons want good food, and good service, as well as clean, safe, healthful, and nutritious food.

The buyer assists in seeing that patrons get good food by searching out items of the exact quality needed by production and service and then, in subsequent handling procedures, the buyer sees that this quality is maintained until issued. Good service can come from a buyer's efforts to provide proper portion sizing and to purchase food that has good eye appeal and that speeds service.

The public has concerns about the safety of and sanitary qualities of items offered by food services. The number of foodborne illnesses and deaths is startlingly high in this country. We have also recently experienced some dramatic incidents in food services regarding illnesses and deaths from meats and poultry contaminated with *E. coli, Salmonella, Listeria monocytogenes, Campylobacter,* and others. As a result, the regulations governing the inspection of meats and poultry for wholesomeness were amended in 1996 and instead of only vision, touch, and smell being used, actual testing for bacteria on these products will occur to see if the findings are within allowable limits. The new program is called the HACCP (Hazard Analysis Critical Control Point) with SSOPs (Sanitary Safety Operating Procedures) established to make inspections at critical points in the processing chain. Additional funds were granted for improving sanitation in marketing fish and seafood.

The need to reduce chances for food contamination by carriers and to prevent improper handling or mistakes in identifying foods is discussed.

Patrons have begun to voice considerable concern about the healthfulness and nutritional qualities of the foods served to them. Although a fairly significant number are not overly concerned with nutrition and health—they want good food that satisfies them first of all—the number of those that express concerns is growing. The need to get more healthful food to the public can be furthered by more knowledge on the part of the public and the foodservice industry about nutrition and what constitutes healthful food. Steps are being taken by the foodservice industry to meet this growing expression of need for improved nutrition.

Recently the FDA instituted regulations governing the nutritional labeling of foods on menus. These follow much the same regulations required of food manufacturers.

REVIEW QUESTIONS

1. A small food service is located near a large high school. Define its target market and this market's wants. Do the same for a retirement home for wealthy people who have small apartments. Do the same for a neighborhood family restaurant.

2. Set up a small placard to set on dining tables. Design it to obtain information about who your patrons are and what they want.

3. A patron tells you, the manager, "I know what I want when I come to a place to eat. Above all, I want good food." This is an opportunity for you to find out what a patron wants, but the word *good* can mean a lot of different things to different people. How would you try to direct the conversation you next carry on with this person to ascertain just what is meant by *good?*

4. Pair the correct letter designator for a word or phrase on the right with its mate on the left:

    ___Vector

    ___*E. coli*

    ___HACCP

    ___*Salmonella*

    ___*Staphylococcus*

    ___Natural

    ___Pesticide

    ___Salt

    a. Kills ants

    b. A bacteria common on poultry and eggs, now also known to be found on meats

    c. Grown in organic fertilized soil

    d. A carrier of contamination

    e. New regulation for meat and poultry inspection

    f. Bacteria that develops in sores and body abrasions

    g. Food additive

    h. Bacteria often found in fecal matter

5. Why have new food services that emphasize nutrition and healthful foods largely failed whereas those offering such foods along with others have not?

6. Your manager asks you to prepare a checklist for your employees to use when maintaining your storage spaces so everything is adequately covered. Prepare one you might submit to him.

7. A large number of students do not eat meat. How does such a diet agree with that pictured in the dietary pyramid? Have you ever heard that combining legumes (beans, peas, lentils, etc.) with cereals was nearly the equivalent of meat in the diet? What about soybean curd? Is that nearly equal in nutrient values to meat?

8. A menu has certain foods followed by a tiny heart. What does this mean?

9. Obtain a menu that makes certain health claims about some of the foods listed. How would you change this menu to conform to the new regulations? What else would you do to meet the requirements?

KEY WORDS AND CONCEPTS

bovine spongiform encephalopathy (BSE)

Dietary Guidelines for Americans

dietary pyramid

Educational Foundation of the NRA

Escherichia coli (*E. coli*)

food additives

Food and Drug Administration (FDA)

Food Safety and Inspection Service (FSIS)

foodborne illness

General Accounting Office (GAO)

GRAS (generally regarded as safe) list

Hazard Analysis Critical Control Point (HACCP)

healthful foods

irradiation

National Restaurant Association (NRA)

nutrition labeling

patron profiles

pesticides

Standard Sanitary Operating Procedures (SSOPs)

target market

vectors (carriers)

CHAPTER 3

The Markets

The Graphic New York, March 5, 1870. Columbia Fish Market–The First Sale. From the Louis Szwathmary collection, Culinary Archives and Museum, Johnson and Wales University, used by permission of Dr. Szwathmary and Johnson and Wales University.

Chapter Objectives

1. To indicate what markets and marketing are, along with types of markets and some of the functions performed in them.

2. To discuss marketing agents and how they function.

3. To explain how goods move through the distribution system of our markets and understand the costs involved in such movement.

4. To show how the market is regulated with special emphasis on the food market.

5. To discuss some legal factors that control marketing actions between buyer and seller.

6. To cover some of the ethical considerations buyers and sellers should follow.

INTRODUCTION

Bartering is a simple and good example of marketing. It gets goods to users, transferring ownership. Although this works in simple societies, today with our complex social structure, we need a much more sophisticated marketing system.

For this text, a formal definition of a **market** is "where the activities of transferring foods from producers to consumers take place with an exchange of ownership." The physical location of a market is not as important as the action that occurs there. A market can be a telephone, a receiving dock, an office, or a street corner. Markets carry the impression of a place or facility where transactions take place. Today, that definition can be extended to be a room full of computers and telephones, exchanging products verbally or in computer language. Essentially, transfer of ownership should occur at this place.

Marketing involves creating a commodity or giving it time, form, place, or utility. Any activity concerned with the growing or production of a commodity, its harvest, processing, manufacture, storage, transportation, or distribution is a marketing function. Traditionally, the marketplace was the open-air area where sellers and buyers met to select goods, make bargains, and complete transactions. This transaction would be in the form of exchanging goods or bartering goods as a form of payment, or using the legal tender. Today the market encompasses all contact points. As this term is used in the economy today, it is not confined to one specific place and time as it was years ago. Markets were only set up at certain seasons of the year. Now, markets are not as visible, since most of the buying is done via telephone, facsimile, or computer, and the markets are highly competitive and complex. As a result of this, the purchasing manager must be aware of the different markets and their form of functioning.

TYPES OF MARKETS

Markets differ according to their function. **Primary markets** are those that set basic prices, quality standards, and other overall factors that promote the movement of goods and their sale. What happens in these markets affects the entire market. Liverpool, England, is the world's primary market for grain; it sets world prices and grading standards. Chicago is the U.S. primary market for grain, but it is strongly influenced by what happens in Liverpool, the world's primary grain market. Chicago is the primary market for meat in the United States, and what happens there influences national trading of meat. Events in the primary coffee market in New York control coffee prices all over the country. Buyers watch primary markets to see what is happening, hoping to get advance information on what their local market is going to do (see Figure 3–1).

Secondary markets are often the physical functional units of the market system. They accept or produce products and distribute them to local markets. Actions in secondary markets often influence primary markets. Omaha, Kansas City, and Los

Former Marketing Path of Cattle					
Texas Cattle Grower	Chicago Stockyards	Iowa Feeder	St. Louis Butcher	Houston Wholesaler	Houston Restaurant

Present Marketing Path of Cattle			
Texas Cattle Grower	St. Louis Feeder and Butcher	Houston Wholesaler	Houston Restaurant

Figure 3–1

Formerly cattle buyers bought up cattle and shipped them by train to Chicago, where they were unloaded at the stockyards and Iowa feeders purchased them, loaded them back onto train cars, and shipped them to Iowa where they were fed for a month or so. Then they sold them to a butchering firm, loaded them onto train cars, and shipped them to this firm, where they were slaughtered and shipped as carcasses or side beef to a wholesaler, who cut the meat up into wholesale or portion cuts and sold it to a user. Today, the path is shortened. Buyers no longer ship to Chicago but directly by truck to a combined feeder and butcher, who feeds only a short time compared to the former feeding time. (New grading standards, improved breeding, and other factors make this shorter feeding time possible.) The carcasses are boned out and wholesale cuts are boxed and shipped, saving shipping costs on unused bone and fat and shipping space. In some cases, the wholesaler is bypassed by the restaurant, which can buy boxed meat directly from the feeder-butcher. By shortening the path in this manner, considerable time and money are saved.

Angeles, all secondary meat markets, can send signals back to Chicago that influence that primary market. Secondary markets have become more influential in recent years and, to some extent, have taken over some of the primary market functions. Secondary markets now receive direct shipment of cattle from sellers (see Figure 3–1). Direct shipment of fresh fruits and vegetables to user points has also reduced Chicago's importance as a primary market for those products.

Local markets receive goods from secondary markets and act as distributors to consumers. They have less influence in setting prices and establishing standards and market procedures than primary or secondary markets. In some cases large buyers bypass local markets and purchase in the secondary or even primary ones. This is most often done to ensure a better price, but it can be done for other reasons.

Regional markets are the point to which products are shipped by marketing agents and offered through wholesalers to interested parties. **International markets** are where merchandise is offered globally.

MARKET FUNCTIONS

Generally, the functions of a market include the following:

- Exchange of commodities
- Supply of information pertaining to all aspects of commodities

- Physical supply of commodities
- General business rules and laws pertaining to the commodities.

1.   Exchange functions are buying, selling, merchandising, price setting, and other functions needed to transfer ownership. This may involve a search for goods, search for buyers, and evaluations and comparison of offerings. Specification negotiation, inspection, and receiving follow. Exchange functions cease with transfer of ownership. This often occurs in food services when goods are received at the operation and the buyer signs for them.

2.   Up-to-date information is necessary to function well in the market. A pool of water depends on a constant exchange of fresh water to stay vital and fresh. Without a constant inflow and outflow, the pool becomes stagnant. Our purchase information should be like a pool—its freshness depends on a constant inflow of new knowledge and the outflow of old, outdated information. Buyers need to keep up on market changes, conditions, new technology, new products, and a host of other things to better direct purchasing.

A vast amount of information is available to keep buyers up to date. Newspapers carry news every day on what is happening to commodities. Headline news is sometimes important—a big freeze, floods, hurricane, or drought can quickly cause a scarcity and change prices radically. Trade magazines and journals also give helpful information on new products, market trends, and happenings (see Figure 3–2). Advertisements can be revealing. Political events, such as a change in import quotas, or a trade treaty, may be meaningful. The end of a strike or a pay raise to workers can be significant.

E-mail has made it possible for sellers and buyers to exchange information much more rapidly. In a matter of a few minutes, a seller can forward to a potential buyer market information and prices on items wanted and the buyer can return a purchase order. The Internet has also opened up new areas of market information. Throughout much of the world, large library collections are now available in one's place of business. Vendors can be located, product information obtained, market quotes studied, and other vital purchase information obtained. The National Restaurant Association (NRA) and the American Hotel-Motel Association (AHMA) have home pages on the World Wide Web that connect the marketplace with vendors and markets.

Vendors are often a rich source of information because they are close to the market and often know the latest happenings. It is wise to remain in contact with them and to discuss market conditions and probable developments.

The federal government and state agencies are a rich source of information. One need only write the U.S. Government Printing Office to get its list of publications, most of which can be ordered at a nominal price. The U.S. Department of Agriculture (USDA) offices in various cities publish daily market reports indicating market conditions, prices, amounts available, and other data, all free of charge. Consumer indexes, plentiful and low-cost goods lists, harvest forecasts, and other facts are frequently published by federal or state agencies (see Figure 3–3).

Inflated coffee prices perk retail 'brewhaha'

Cost could increase 5 to 10 cents per cup

By Richard L. Papiernik

An escalation in world coffee prices has begun hitting restaurants, roasters, retailers and suppliers, according to experts who say the pressure is forcing the price of the brewed beverage up 5-cents-to-10-cents a cup.

"We've already been advised that as of March, we'll have to be paying 70 cents to 80 cents more a pound," said Richard Kubach, president of the Melrose Diner, one of the most popular eateries in Philadelphia.

(a)

The news brought the price of coffee soaring upward in the latter part of February. An already volatile rollercoaster ride on the New York Coffee, Sugar and Cocoa Exchange had taken prices from $1.20 to more than $1.70 and then back down again before hitting a two-year high of nearly $1.83 a pound in a five-week period after the Brazilian crop report.

(b)

Figure 3-2

Two short excerpts from an article appearing in Restaurant News, March 3, 1997. (a) This excerpt indicates the foodservice industry's reaction to "Escalating World Prices" of raw coffee beans. (b) This excerpt indicates that bad weather conditions in Brazil caused the price of coffee to soar on the New York coffee, sugar and cocoa exchange. An astute buyer reading this would immediately contact his or her coffee sources to see if a contract for a year's supply of coffee might not be made at a stable price for the year.

Market information is also available from organizations via computer. Daily, weekly, monthly, and annual forecasts are projected and compared to the actual market activity to see the accuracy of the forecasting. However, there is a fee for these services, which will link your computer to a host computer that stockpiles this information. Together they constitute a valuable package of information on expectations about the market (see Figure 3–4). The Internet can also give daily information on market activities.

Attending conventions, seminars, and meetings is one of the best ways to keep up on new merchandise. One can see products and talk to purveyors. Memberships in associations such as the NRA, AMHA, and others can also be helpful. These organizations have libraries and resource people who are rich sources of information.

Anyone purchasing a significant quantity of meat should subscribe to Urner Barry Publications' Yellow Sheet. It keeps buyers up to date on what is happening in the meat market. (See Chapter 7 for an explanation and an example of the information given in this publication.) Urner Barry Publications also publishes up-to-date news on fish, seafood, poultry, and produce. Other trade publications are also available. Information published by markets and the government can also be informative.

Labeling is an information function. The amount of information given can vary. The National Canners Association promotes **descriptive labeling,** using single words or phrases of known definition to indicate quality, rather than trying to give foods a quality rank. It recommends that other voluntary information be given.

```
- - - GRAPEFRUIT:     STEADY
FL 4/5 Bushel ctn Indian River Red 23-27s 9.00-10.00 few higher 32-40s
9.00-9.50 occ higher White 23-40s 8.50-9.50 occ higher
- - - LEMONS:     HIGHER
AZ/CA ctns 95s-115s 18.00-20.00 occ higher 140-165s 18.00-21.00 occ
higher 200s 22.00-23.00 fair quality 140s 15.00-16.00 occ higher 165s
14.00-15.00 occ higher 200s 13.00-14.00 occ higher
- - - LIMES:     STEADY
Persian Seedless 38 lb ctn MX 150-175s 17.00-18.00 occ higher 200s
16.00-17.00 occ higher FL one label 106s 36.00-37.00 160-205s 41.00-
46.00 occ lower Bulk approx 50 lb ctn fair quality various sizes FL
18.00-19.00 occ lower VZ 20.00
- - - ORANGES:     STEADY
4/5 Bushel ctn Navels CA 56-88s 14.00-16.00 fair quality 72-113s 10.50-
12.00 occ higher FL Valencia 56-72s 10.00-11.00 occ higher fair quality
8.00-9.00 occ higher
- - - TANGERINES:     STEADY
FL 4/5 Bushel ctn Murcot 80s-100s 18.00-19.00 occ lower Bulk approx. 40
lb ctn fair quality 14.00-15.00 occ higher
- - - GRAPES, TABLE:     ABOUT STEADY
CL 18 lb lug Flame Seedless 15.00-16.00 occ lower & higher Thompson
Seedless 15.00-16.00 occ higher & lower Black Seedless 12.00-13.00 occ
higher
- - - KIWIFRUIT:     STEADY
CA/IT 1 layer flats tray pack Hayward 36-39s 8.50-9.00 occ higher
- - - MANGOES:     LOWER
One layer ctn VZ Haden 8s One lot 14.00 9-14s 8.00-9.50 occ higher fair
quality 8-10s 6.00-7.00 occ higher
- - - NECTARINES     STEADY
CL 2-layer Traypack Flame Kist 40s 13.00-14.00 occ lower 50s 12.00-13.00
occ higher
- - - PAPAYA:     ABOUT STEADY
1 layer ctn DR/JM 7-8s 10.00-11.50 occ lower HI 8-9s 14.00-15.00 occ
higher 10-12s 15.00-17.00 occ higher FL Bulk approx. 50 lb 15.00-16.00
- - - PEARS:     ABOUT STEADY
Ctn wrapped D'Anjous WA US No. 1 70-90s 24.00-26.50 occ higher 100-120s
21.00-23.00 occ higher US Fancy 60-90s 20.00-22.00 occ lower 100-120s
17.50-18.50 occ higher 135s 16.00-17.00 occ higher WA Bosc Fancy 21.00-
```

Figure 3-3
*Market information available from
the USDA is transferred in a daily
market report by a private company.*
(Courtesy of Pronet/Vance
Publishing Corp.)

Nutrient labeling is now required on most packaged foods. Specific nutrient values must be given per stated size serving, and these amounts interpreted as to the percent yield they contribute to a person's recommended daily intake of that nutrient. Thus, Figure 3–5 indicates that if someone on a low-salt diet wanted to know how much sodium a serving (1/2 cup or 130 g) this particular hominy would give, the label shows the person would get 550 mg or 23% of a normal person's recommended daily intake of sodium, providing the person consumed a 2000 calorie a day diet. If a nutrient claim is made on a label such as "contributes to good bone formation," the claim must be substantiated. Some people want more information provided, such as drained weight (net yield), additives, and specific ingredient contents rather than a general statement. For instance, they want each spice specified rather than allowing the word *spice* to be used to indicate the whole range of spices.

Labels must list the ingredients in food mixtures from greatest amount to least. There are a few exceptions. Thus, catsup labels can omit this information because the government says that everyone knows so well the ingredients catsup contains, the information is not needed. Recent government regulations require that a label must be

```
MARKET AND INDUSTRY NEWS HIGHLIGHTS
   03/24/92   3:00 PM CST

Calif. Broccoli Quotes Inching Up . . . High Onion Prices Likely To Continue . . .

* Calif. dists. BROCCOLI market soaring as deal enters supply gap . . . Desert
    areas finishing season . . . Rain, seasonal lull in other areas pushing
    prices toward ceiling . . . Quotes, bnch. 14s: $11-12 . . .

*Higher quotes likely to continue for ONIONS nationwide . . . Idaho/E. Ore.,
    Wash. jumbos at $18-20 . . . Few prior commitments continue . . . Some orders
    taken f.o.b. inspection final basis . . . Good quality still available . . .
    Demand far outweighs availability . . .

*Strong movement should continue this week as active demand exceeds light
    TOMATO volume . . . Sources previously expected more balance next week
    between supply and demand, but now uncertainty arises since volume may
    not increase enough in Fla.'s Homestead, Immokalee and Naples, and
    crossings from Mexico remain scarce . . . Quotes in Fla. jumped from $25
    to $30 on x-lg., with Mexico prices few, at $30 across board . . .

*Active movement should continue in Fla., Mexico with ZUCCHINI, EGGPLANT
    volume limited . . . Demand good, should support quotes through week's
    end . . . Zucchini fancys at $14 in Fla.; $16, Mexico through Nogales,
    Ariz . . . Eggplant, 1 1/9-bu. crtn.: Fla, $30; Mexico, $20 . . .

*Soft BANANA undertone could be seen this week on E. Coast market . . . In-
    creased volume expected . . . Shipments nationwide will total about 3.6
    million 40-lb. crtns . . . Prices $10-11 for palletized fruit; $10.50-
    11.50 for fruit in containers . . . Fair demand should turn more active at
    lower prices . . .

*Steady prices should continue on Fla. GREEN BEANS, with demand fair for
    moderate volume . . . Quality good . . . Machine-picked quotes mostly at $8,
    few at $10 per bu . . . .
```

Figure 3–4

Market forecasting is available via modem. Your computer is connected to a host computer that provides access to market trends and future projections. (Courtesy of Pronet/Vance Publishing Corp.)

attached to meat, fish, and poultry packages indicating proper handling and preparation practices. Alcoholic beverages must carry a health warning on their labels.

3. Physical supply functions often revolve around storage and transportation. Improved shipping methods and refrigeration have broadened market offerings and improved the quality of holding. Improved packaging, handling, and storage facilities have also reduced loss and improved quality.

Without storage the orderly flow of goods would be disrupted, and losses would be high. Bonded storage is provided for security and financing. Bonded storage, cold storage, and some other storage facilities operate under government supervision.

Improved storage for perishable foods is now available. It not only controls humidity but introduces inert gases, special lighting, and other factors that give foods a longer shelf life. Tremendous amounts of fruits, vegetables, meats, and other foods are held in large low-temperature storage facilities today. Excellent cold storage facilities for eggs, butter, meats, fruits, and vegetables hold food at temperatures from 30° to 45°F.

As of December 1997, the Food Safety and Inspection Service required that poultry labeled "fresh" must refer to birds that had never been held below 26°F. Poultry held below zero must be called "frozen" and the terms "hard chilled" and "previously hard chilled" would no longer be used to indicate the market condition of poultry.

Cold storage means holding food under refrigeration for up to 30 days. Eggs, butter, meats, fresh fruits, and some kinds of vegetables are held in cold storage. How long foods can be held may be limited by local or state authority. Foods removed from cold storage usually cannot be returned to storage. Freezer storage foods are held for much longer periods, but quality is sometimes lost in a very short time, so the period of storage may only be three months. The maximum time is usually a year. Often buyers are tempted to purchase frozen turkeys at bargain prices in August or September; a small purchase is recommended, however, because they are usually last year's stock and turkey fat goes rancid easily.

4. Financial procedures usually dominate general business functions in the market. They facilitate buying and selling and reduce costs. The cost of carrying inventories, risk, and other cost factors should be understood by buyers. Purveyors who sell goods on the first of the month expecting payment on the tenth of the following month are carrying interest for up to 40 days. Delivery costs can be high—buyers who want frequent delivery are running up purveyor's costs, which they pass on. Vendors do not give advantageous prices unless they profit from them.

Figure 3-5
This part of the label gives the nutrition labeling required plus most of the other information required on labels for this particular hominy. (Courtesy of Bush Brothers and Company.)

THE MARKET DISTRIBUTION SYSTEM

To produce the food and supplies needed by consumers, a massive marketing structure is necessary, starting with producers such as growers and ranchers and with business activities such as lumbering, mining, transportation, manufacturing, storage, grading, and packaging. In making their way through this system, many items go through a number of changes of form.

This process of moving through the marketing system does not work alone. A number of facilitators must work to see that the process works and goods move to end up in the hands of users. These facilitators are called **middlemen.** The number of middlemen handling any item may be many or few depending on the marketing pathway the item must travel through and how much must be done to the item before it reaches the food service. Each product or group of similar products has its own particular pathway and the middlemen required to facilitate it. Figure 3–6 shows a simplified version of some typical distribution paths for items going from the original producer to the user. These are not the only pathways that such products take; they are merely examples.

Canned Peas

Contract→Grower→Processor→Commission Agent→Broker→Wholesaler→Food Service

A grower contracts to grow peas with a frozen food processor. The peas are grown and delivered to the processor and frozen. A commission person representing the processor contacts a broker indicating the availability of the peas of a certain quality at a certain price. The broker contacts a wholesaler and arranges for a large shipment to the wholesaler. The wholesaler breaks the lot up into smaller ones, selling them to various food services.

Butter

Dairy Farm→Creamery→Wholesaler→Food Service

A dairy farm produces milk and a creamery truck picks it up, taking it to the creamery where the cream is removed and churned into butter, which is sold to a wholesaler who sells it to a food service.

Beef

Ranch→Cattle Buyer→Feeder-Butcher→Processor→Broker→Wholesaler→Food Services

A rancher grows cattle and sells them to a cattle buyer who ships them by truck to a feeder-butcher. The butcher sells some to a food processor who makes the beef into a frozen stew. This processor contacts a broker who sells the frozen stew to a wholesaler who in turn sells it to a food service.

Turkeys

Hatchery→Poultry Raiser→Processor→Hotel Head Office→Food Services

A hatchery in April hatches out some turkeys that it sells to a poultry raiser. The poultry raiser cares for them all summer and then ships them in November to a poultry processor who butchers them and processes them into frozen birds. The purchasing agent of a hotel chain arranges with this processor for the shipment of a number of lots of these birds to its various hotels, which store them and use them as needed.

Figure 3-6

Various paths food items may take in moving through the market distribution system.

MIDDLEMEN (MARKETING INTERMEDIARIES)

As noted, a middleman or intermediary, called variously *commission man, broker, jobber, manufacturer's representative, manufacturer's agent, wholesaler,* or *retailer,* sees that the goods in their proper form and condition move through the market system from producer to user. The cost of rendering the various services required to do this differs, depending on the service rendered. Thus, if fresh corn is purchased from a grower and turned into canned corn, labeled and stored, and later sold to a jobber who in turn distributes a part to a wholesaler who contacts a restaurant selling three cases of the lot, many services have been performed such as financing, storing, changing form, and transporting that must be paid for. However, if a grower sells fresh corn to a restaurant, much less marketing is done and hence the marketing cost is less.

The cost of the service a middleman makes, called a **markup,** is added to the original cost of the product. This markup usually includes not only original cost and costs of the middleman but a profit. Thus, the final price a food service pays will depend on the original price plus these markups. Figure 3–7b shows that the basic February price of live cattle was around $0.63 to $0.64 a pound, whereas Figure 3–7a shows that, after butchering, choice 1–3 550–700 pound beef carcasses were quoted at $0.9178, a markup of around $0.28. On this same date the price of choice grade No. 109 oven-ready prime ribs was quoted on other markets at $3.25/lb. Thus, the original cost of $0.64 a pound beef on the hoof ended up at $3.25 at the food service. Such an increase comes not without reason as pointed out in the following section on Values Added in Marketing.

Commission men and **brokers** do not take possession of the goods they move. They find someone who wants something moved to another marketing area and then facilitate the process, acting sort of like salesmen for the owner of the goods. They may add 1% to 5% for such a service. Brokers usually do a bit more to promote the movement of goods through the market and therefore charge a slightly higher fee. **Jobbers** are much like brokers except they often own the items they transfer through the market distribution system; they may even take possession but usually do not. Their charge may go as high as 25%, depending on the service rendered.

Manufacturer's representatives and **manufacturer's agents** bring buyers and sellers together. They often own and take possession of the things they distribute, warehousing and delivering them. However, they can act as intermediaries only by merely bringing together a seller and buyer. The charge for full service is usually 25% or slightly more. The buyer usually pays for the goods in one of two ways: (1) The representative or agent adds a markup to the seller's charge, and bills the buyer this amount. The buyer pays the agent or representative who in turn pays the seller his or her charge. (2) The seller bills the buyer directly and then remits some of this charge to the agent or representative in payment for the service rendered. The second billing method usually occurs when the agent or representative facilitates the sale between seller and buyer, but does not own, take possession of, or deliver or finance the goods.

CASH PRICES

Wednesday, February 12, 1997

(Closing Market Quotations)

GRAINS AND FEEDS

	Wed	Tues	Year Ago
Barley, top-quality Mpls., bu	uz	z	3.85
Bran, wheat middlings, KC ton	u89-92	90-92	112.50
Corn, No. 2 yel. Cent. Ill. bu	bpu2.65½	2.65½	3.75
Corn Gluten Feed, Midwest, ton	96-108	96-108	118.50
Cottonseed Meal, Clksdle, Miss. ton	180.00	185.00	203.75
Hominy Feed, Cent. Ill. ton	75.00	75.00	116.00
Meat-Bonemeal, 50% pro. Ill. ton.	260.00	255-60	225.00
Oats, No. 2 milling, Mpls., bu	uz	z	2.40½
Sorghum, (Milo) No. 2 Gulf cwt	u4.91	488-89	7.34½
Soybean Meal, Cent. Ill., rail, ton 44%	u253-55	248-50	219.50
Soybean Meal, Cent. Ill., rail, ton 48%	u259-65	254-60	230.50
Soybeans, No. 1 yel Cent.-Ill. bu	bpu7.56½	7.43	7.22½
Wheat, Spring 14%-pro Mpls. bu	u439¼-49¼	436¼-48¼	5.97¾
Wheat, No. 2 sft red, St.Lou. bu	bpu3.46	3.50½	4.92
Wheat, hard KC, bu	4.52¼	4.59	5.69¼
Wheat, No. 1 sft wht, del Port Ore	u4.12	4.11	5.75

FOODS

	Wed	Tues	Year Ago
Beef, Carcass, Equlv.Index Value, choice 1-3,550-700lbs.	u91.78	92.05	93.20
Beef, Carcass, Equlv.Index Value, select 1-3,550-700lbs.	u88.14	88.46	89.30
Broilers, Dressed "A" lb.	ux.5918	.5941	.5332
Broilers, 12-Cty Comp Wtd Av	u.5962	.5962	.5581
Butter, AA, Chgo., lb.	u1.01½	1.01½	.72
Cocoa, Ivory Coast, $metric ton	1,419	1,429	1,521
Coffee, Brazilian, NY lb.	n1.86½	1.78½	1.28¼
Coffee, Colombian, NY lb.	n1.93½	1.85½	1.37¼
Eggs, Lge white, Chgo doz.	u.76-81	.79-84	.77½
Flour, hard winter KC cwt	11.10	11.20	13.55
Hams, 17-20 lbs, Mid-US lb fob	u.73	.73	z
Hogs, Iowa-S.Minn. avg. cwt	u52.30	52.25	47.00
Hogs, Omaha avg cwt	u53.00	51.50	47.50
Pork Bellies, 12-14 lbs Mid-US lb	u.65-66	.66	.58½
Pork Loins, 14-18 lbs. Mid-US lb	u102-13	107-16	1.18
Steers, Tex.-Okla. ch avg cwt	u63.00	63.00	63.00
Steers, Feeder, Okl Cty, av cwt	u76.88	76.88	60.50
Sugar, cane, raw, world, lb. fob	10.88	10.90	12.97

(a)

Figure 3-7

An example (a) of prices quoted on the February 12, 1997 market for some commodities and (b) future prices quoted on the same day for some livestock and meat.

FUTURE PRICES

Wednesday, February 12, 1997
(Closing Market Quotations)

LIVESTOCK AND MEAT

CATTLE-FEEDER (CME) 50,000 lbs.; cents per lb.

Mar	67.35	67.95	67.35	67.57 +	.22	70.45	56.15	6,267
Apr	68.10	68.47	68.10	68.35 +	.35	70.65	57.75	3,298
May	69.20	69.60	69.20	69.47 +	.42	71.70	59.80	4,867
Aug	72.42	73.05	72.42	72.80 +	.37	75.42	64.05	4,195
Sept	72.85	73.60	72.85	73.22 +	.47	75.75	65.60	1,489
Oct	73.50	74.05	73.50	73.82 +	.42	76.50	66.10	1,834
Nov	74.65	75.25	74.65	75.05 +	.42	77.50	67.95	541

Est vol 2,462; vol Mn 4,198; open int 22,535, −970.

CATTLE-LIVE (CME) 40,000 lbs.; cents per lb.

Feb	63.47	64.25	63.47	64.00 +	.57	66.25	60.15	7,487
Apr	65.52	65.97	65.45	65.65 +	.37	67.90	62.65	43,145
June	63.45	63.97	63.45	63.65 +	.22	66.75	61.00	17,056
Aug	63.40	63.77	63.40	63.42 +	.10	66.75	62.00	17,741
Oct	66.60	66.85	66.55	66.67 +	.10	68.10	64.55	11,046
Dec	68.60	68.80	68.60	68.65 +	.12	70.35	65.25	4,393
Fb98	69.90	70.10	69.90	70.00 +	.17	71.65	67.15	2,114

Est vol 15,901; vol Mn 20,657; open int 102,982, −2,993.

HOGS (CME) 40,000 lbs.; cents per lb.
New contract prices begin with Feb97

Feb	74.30	74.65	74.12	74.35 +	.02	80.30	63.15	4,180
Apr	73.05	73.95	73.05	73.85 +	.55	77.20	61.15	15,624
June	78.10	78.95	78.05	78.90 +	.47	81.40	67.60	8,356
July	76.30	77.00	76.12	76.77 +	.27	79.05	67.40	1,895
Aug	73.50	73.80	73.22	73.70 +	.05	75.40	66.00	2,145
Oct	66.90	67.10	66.67	67.00 −	.02	68.50	60.60	1,384
Dec	64.70	65.15	64.70	64.95 −	.10	70.40	60.10	797
Fb98	64.10	64.45	64.10	64.30 −	.10	68.05	61.75	252
Apr	61.00	61.10	60.85	60.85 −	.20	63.40	57.00	145

Est vol 8,016; vol Mn 7,356; open int 34,801, +1,198.

PORK BELLIES (CME) 40,000 lbs.; cents per lb.

Feb	75.95	76.50	75.52	76.22 +	.07	89.75	60.82	1,402
Mar	75.00	75.90	74.90	75.75 +	.55	89.35	60.60	2,447
May	76.00	76.60	75.70	76.10 −	.05	87.80	60.50	3,241
July	75.80	76.15	75.30	75.95 −	.25	88.00	63.00	647
Aug	73.70	73.70	73.02	73.02 −	.25	83.47	65.45	502

Est vol 2,195; vol Mn 3,370; open int 8,239, −217.

(b)

Figure 3-7 *continued*
An example (a) of prices quoted on the February 12, 1997 market for some commodities and (b) future prices quoted on the same day for some livestock and meat.

Wholesalers take possession of the goods they sell and warehouse and deliver them. Wholesalers give credit, maintain a sales force, and do other things that cost money. The markup is usually around 25%. In recent years, more and more wholesalers have tried to become one-stop sellers—selling groceries, dairy products, eggs, poultry, marine products, fresh fruits and vegetables, cleaning supplies, paper goods, everything a facility might want—instead of offering just one item. Volume of sales is increased and delivery, salespeople, and other costs are reduced, resulting in a profit to both the buyer and seller. Buyers find this system desirable not only because prices may be slightly lower, but because one call instead of many, one delivery instead of many, one billing instead of many, and so forth, makes for simplification of the purchase function.

A surprising number of small operations purchase through **retailers.** This is because retailers, being much bigger volume buyers than the agents that normally sell food services, purchase at very favorable prices. Furthermore, the food service assumes the cost of sending someone to the store, who picks out the items, pays for them, and carries and delivers them to the food service, making it possible for the retailer to save on costs these other agents have to bear. Even though the usual retailer markup is 35%, their prices are still highly competitive. (Today many discount supermarkets are taking less than 35%, expecting to make up their costs with added volume.)

VALUES ADDED IN MARKETING

As goods move through a marketing distribution system, a value is often added to them, justifying their added as-purchased (AP) cost. Thus, when they are moved to a location closer to a buyer, value is added because they are easier and quicker to obtain. Grading adds a value. Changing form, such as processing fresh peas into a frozen product, adds a value.

The following summarizes some of the ways value is added in marketing:

- **Place value.** Getting goods to the right place adds value such as delivering them to a facility.

- **Time value.** Holding them in stock to have them there when needed is an example of time value.

- **Form value.** Cutting a strip loin into individual steaks puts them into a more usable form. Splitting a case of four gallons of soy sauce and delivering one gallon only to a buyer is adding form value. Cleaning and shredding lettuce and delivering it changes its form.

- **Information value.** While taking an order, a salesperson indicates how using a product can increase its portion yield thus lowering the basic cost of the item per portion. Such information is of value to the operation. A buyer may pay for a daily market broadcast obtaining information of worth in purchasing.

- **Source value.** A buyer is searching for a scarce item on the market; he is told where it can be obtained. Such information is of value.

- Those in the market often do special things of value, such as extending credit, sending a buyer a complete list of goods available along with price, doing some special packaging, taking special care in transporting, or storing goods because a buyer does not have room for them. All of these things are of value to a buyer and make the service rendered worth more.

As items travel through a distribution system, various costs are incurred, such as storage, grading, transportation, and packaging, so the AP price grows. In some cases far more of these marketing costs are incurred than the cost of the base product. No marketing agent wants to render his or her service for nothing and so the marketing cost usually contains the marketing agent's profit in addition to expenses. You can see that if an item passes through many hands, its price can increase considerably.

Buyers must realize that adding a cost for a service rendered is logical and legitimate. We discuss later the values these agents add to products as they pass through their hands. Some authorities feel, however, that these agents add too much to the cost. The small share that basic producers (farmers, growers, ranchers, etc.) of our food supply get out of the total spent for food by consumers has prompted criticism from many. Figure 3–8 shows that while the price index of all farm products rose between 1990 and 1995 from approximately 120% to 122%, the retail food price index rose in the same period from about 128% to 148%, an increase ten times that of the farm products. This chart also shows that farm prices have risen very little since 1990. Another study by the Food Institute showed that the 1994 farm value of the American food dollar was only 21%.

Later in this chapter we discuss value analysis. This is one way in which a buyer can examine market costs and decide whether to pay them, or somehow avoid them, or have the buyer's facility do the service. Simple things such as deciding on whether to use fresh or frozen string beans, or getting a lower price by volume buying, or purchasing ready-to-serve cakes are quickly decided. Purchasing a truck, however, or assigning someone to do the purchasing and pickup of dairy items, vegetables,

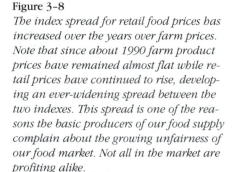

Figure 3–8

The index spread for retail food prices has increased over the years over farm prices. Note that since about 1990 farm product prices have remained almost flat while retail prices have continued to rise, developing an ever-widening spread between the two indexes. This spread is one of the reasons the basic producers of our food supply complain about the growing unfairness of our food market. Not all in the market are profiting alike.

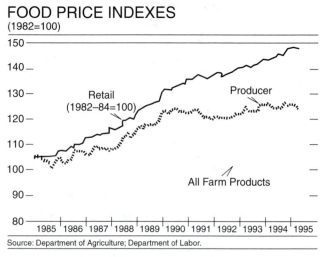

FOOD PRICE INDEXES
(1982=100)

Source: Department of Agriculture; Department of Labor.

meats, poultry, fish, and so forth, saving perhaps 25% or more on the middleman, involves a considerable commitment of funds and action. Few buyers on their own would be authorized to make such a decision; management would have to be involved. The buyer, however, should gather the data so management can make an informed decision.

Other factors may also be important. If the operation is in Glacier National Park, which is several hundred miles away from sources of supply, such a daily run, say, to Great Falls, Montana, might be feasible and worthwhile. Normally today, foodservice industry management concentrates its effort on building the business and pleasing customers and has less to do with food production. The trend is for the foodservice industry to become more of a service-retailing industry than a production-service industry. The attitude in the 1990s is to let others do jobs they can do better and more efficiently. Thus, if the operation were in an area where one had a choice of many suppliers close by, management might not even think twice about making such an arrangement as sending out a truck to pick up items.

MARKET SETTING OF AS-PURCHASED PRICE

As noted, middlemen move goods through the marketing system, adding value but also adding to the AP cost because of their market service. As indicated, the number of agents handling the goods and the nature of the services have much to do with the final product cost. Also, these marketing costs are compounded, so the final cost a buyer pays may be considerably more than just what each individual market agent sets. Thus, if a grower gets $0.15/lb for oranges, and various middlemen add 1%, 5%, 10%, 5%, 25%, and 35%, the cost to the buyer is $0.31, more than double what the grower received.

Certain fundamental economic factors establish AP price: (1) basic cost of producing the goods, (2) marketing costs, (3) supply offered on the market, and (4) market demand.[1] Normally factors 1 and 2 are fairly steady, allowing supply and demand to set the final AP price, but at times conditions may exist that throw this normal price setting process into a tailspin.

Although normally a buyer can expect there to be a steady, consistent relationship between these four price-setting factors, at times such a relationship will go awry and a price much different from what one might have expected will be quoted. In 1996 ranchers sold cattle below their production cost because herds were built up to a point of producing a beef oversupply, causing a market glut. The price of beef on the hoof to ranchers dropped to slightly above 50¢ a pound, the lowest it had been in years. An example of price-setting factor 2 going awry might be when a fruit dealer has far too much cantaloupe and decides to obey

---

[1]The authors assume the reader remembers that boring Economics I course he or she took.

the inexorable laws of marketing of "move it or lose it" and "sell it or smell it," selling his goods below cost.

Competition can also disturb these basic cost-setting factors. A community may have a limited number of suppliers who have a good command of their market and pricing. Things for these suppliers go smoothly. Then, a big national one-stop supplier moves in and creates a completely different competitive situation. Prices drop.

When there is over-production, the supply factor may take control and dictate prices regardless of the other factors. This happened to some extent in the over-production of cattle just cited. When a monopoly exists and the supply is under a few or even one supplier's control, the supply factor also can dominate, obviating the effect of the other three factors.

In some cases, governmental action influences the AP price. For instance, in the state of Montana a liquor board establishes prices for alcoholic beverages. When we import and pay the government a duty, we influence price. We also pay a much higher price for sugar and rice than the world does because our country protects our growers with a tariff. Government subsidies and purchase programs can also influence prices. Each year the government has the option to step in and stabilize the beef, turkey, chicken, wheat, butter, or other market items by purchasing and storing huge quantities. These foods are then given to our school lunch program, hospitals and charity organizations, foreign subsidy programs, and so forth.

Trade associations and boards representing special food products, such as the Wheat Institute and American Association of Meat Purveyors, can influence prices by promoting their products and seeing that favorable conditions exist for them.

The day-to-day price of many commodities is influenced by the future markets on which they are traded. In such a market, the expected price on a certain date of a commodity is predicted. Thus, Figure 3–7 indicates that live cattle prices will be about $0.05 a pound higher in December than at the present time. Such a forecast of a higher or lower future price can influence the present price. Thus, if the future price of hamburger-type beef were to be estimated as being exceptionally high, hamburger processors might enter the market and buy up a lot of such beef, process it into hamburgers, and hold it frozen until they could cash in on this higher price. This sudden demand for beef would tend to raise the present price of hamburger-type beef.

Better refrigeration and transportation, improved communication, and other technological advances have led to improvements in our methods of marketing goods, resulting in lower prices. At the present time, material advances in packaging are extending the shelf life and appearance of many products, lowering food losses. Had the fruit dealer we used as an example earlier stocked cantaloupe that had been irradiated, which considerably increases shelf life, he may not have been forced to put the fruit on the market at a loss.

We must also realize that what happens in foreign lands can influence our prices considerably. In 1997 grain prices rose in this country because Russia and some other countries had poor crops. However, while our grain producers profited, others in this country who used this grain did not, because farmers feeding animals such as poultry and hogs and those using grains for manufactured items such as cereals had to pay more. As a result, food services found that their prices also increased. A further drop in the already low beef prices occurred because the cost of grain made it too costly to feed cattle and so they were shipped to market, further adding to the oversupply. Fortunately, this oversupply was partially corrected by added beef shipments to Great Britain and Europe (no one was buying English beef because of bovine encephalitis) and increased exports to Japan.

Waste, spoilage, poor use in production, and other mismanagement factors within the facility can also cause an increase in the ultimate price although the facility might not realize it. Buyers with poor buying techniques can also cause suppliers to increase prices to cover their costs. Causing too many deliveries because enough of a particular item was not ordered, asking for too many split cases, or demanding too many other services can result in making a supplier ask a higher price than otherwise might be asked.

Then there are always the vagaries of our market. A heavy freeze, a drought, a sudden change of growers to another variety of onion or peas or strawberries, an eating trend, or some discovery by science of the medicinal benefits of a certain food can change market conditions such that a sudden, dramatic change in price occurs. The alert buyer is constantly watching for signals of such a change. Being alert to these signals can help much to get buyers over the rough spots.

The knowledgeable buyer who sets up a tight, well-organized buying program can obtain optimum prices. Suppliers know that their quoted price and quality are going to be carefully scrutinized and otherwise weighed. If they are to get the business, their prices have to be tight. There can be no "gravy." A suitable price can often be obtained after good negotiation and buyers need to become adept in this important part of the buying function. The purpose is not to *beat* the market—leave that to the speculators. The goal is to know the market as well as one can, play it with understanding, and do a job that satisfies the needs of your operation.

COST ANALYSIS

A large part of any buyer's job is analyzing prices to see if they equate properly to quality. As indicated, quality need not just mean quality of product but can include things like supplier's service, convenience in use, and so forth. Price analysis can be simple or quite complex. Deciding on the fairness of price between two identical products offered by two purveyors is often simple, but figuring out if it is better to purchase whole lamb carcasses or just legs of lamb can be quite complex. Weighing values often deals with the concepts of value perception and value analysis.

Value perception is a subjective evaluation of what a person believes an item's value is after weighing a number of conceptual quality factors the item is believed to possess. It deals with a *perceived* value, which may differ from its actual value. It usually has no numerical value but is the total worth of a commodity's desirable attributes as the buyer sees them at that particular moment and set of circumstances. Perceived value can vary. Thus, when Shakespeare has King Richard the Third cry out after being dismounted in battle, "A horse! A horse! My kingdom for a horse!" his perceived value of a horse at that moment was far above what his perceived value of a horse would be when seeing one on another occasion feeding in a peaceful pasture. In that moment of battle stress, his perceived value rose to great heights. He was willing to offer his whole kingdom for one!

To a buyer, goods may have a different perceived value at one time than at another. Factors other than price can influence the perceived value. Thus, demand can be a strong factor, considerably influencing the cost a buyer is willing to pay for an item. A buyer's perceived value of fresh raspberries when they are a *must* item for some menu dessert is different from the perceived value when no such demand exists. At another time the operation's demand for fresh raspberries might be such that regardless of price, this buyer would not want them.

Value analysis differs from value perception in that it is often a concrete numerical value based on an item's monetary worth. The formula V (value) $= Q/P$, where Q equals quality and P equals price, is used in a value analysis. If Q remains the same, but P changes, V will change—if P drops, V increases, but if P increases, V drops. Now, if P remains the same and Q drops, V drops but if P remains the same and Q increases, V increases. The following example illustrates this:

Frozen peas have a grade score (Q) of 88 and price (P) per case of $38.70, V is 2.33 (88/37.80 = 2.33). If P drops to $35 but Q remains the same, V is 2.51 (88/35 = 2.51), but if P rises to $40 with Q remaining the same, V is 2.20 (88/40 = 2.20). Now with P remaining at $38.70 but Q rising to 92, V becomes 2.38 (92/38.70 = 2.38), but if Q drops to 84 with P the same, V is 2.22 (84/38.70 = 2.22).

Assigning Quality Scores

In the preceding illustration the quality of the peas could be illustrated with a grade score. What if an item does not have such a numerical score such as in the case of, say, cherry pies? Some buyers make a mental evaluation of the quality of products and then try to come up with a value. However, all items can be scored on a scale of 1 to 100. While the process still may be highly subjective, it at least results in a concrete number. Thus, suppose based on color of the pie filling, flakiness of the crust, and amount of cherries to filling, a buyer compares the cherry pies of two bakeries and comes up with the following (Pie A, given a quality score of 90, is quoted at $4 each and Pie B, scored for quality at 88, at $3.88):

Pie A: 90/$4 = 22.5   Pie B: 88/$3.88 = 23.2

Pie B is the better buy, but is the quality difference enough in Pie A to warrant paying the higher price? Value analysis says "no" but the buyer, management, or someone else must decide.

Buyers often feel that factors other than quality enter into a logical reason for the purchase of one specific item over another. Factors such as supplier services (better delivery, better credit, etc.), convenience in using the product, or packaging might be counted as part of the quality and equated to price. Normally a buyer makes a mental evaluation of these other factors and decides on which supplier will get the order, but it is possible in such a case to use a scale of, say, 1 to 100 to give a numerical score for each factor to be evaluated and then come up with a score. The following example serves as an illustration:

A buyer for an airline food service gets the same-price, same-quality quote from Supplier A and Supplier B for 50,000 individual orders of cream cheese to use with a bagel and cheese breakfast offering. The price each supplier quotes is $80/per case of 500 1-oz aluminum foil individual packs. The quality of both is Grade AA. Since quality and price are identical, the buyer might feel the selection of either supplier is warranted. However, Supplier A offers to warehouse a large part of the amount purchased and deliver in lots as needed while Supplier B does not. But Supplier B has a foil pack with a special tag insert that makes it much easier for the guest to open the pack and squeeze out the contents. The buyer decides to evaluate Q (quality) for each as 100. Price is $80. Supplier A gets a 90 for service while Supplier B gets 75. However, the buyer has been on flights to observe guests' response to menu offerings and has noted how some struggle with a sealed foil pack and end up making a mess of the whole thing. He weighs Supplier A's pack as 70, but gives Supplier B's a 95.

Thus, the numerical evaluation would be:

$$\text{Supplier A: } \frac{100 + 90 + 70}{\$80} = 3.250$$

$$\text{Supplier B: } \frac{100 + 75 + 95}{\$80} = 3.375$$

The numerical value is in favor of Supplier B. Actually, in value analysis many buyers feel that since the evaluations for quality, supplier service, and convenience are subjective evaluations, why bother with numbers? Make a subjective evaluation of the whole thing without going to all this trouble.

Eliminating Factors and Value Analysis

Another reason for using value analysis is to examine commodities to see if factors in them can be eliminated or reduced without reducing their ability to satisfy their need. Again, the goal is to see which of the market offerings is the best buy. Let's compare three kinds of carrots all considered equal in quality when served to patrons: A, fresh carrots; B, already pared and sized fresh carrots; or C, canned

Table 3–1
Example of a value analysis

Type Carrots	As Purchased Price	Labor Cost	Cooking Cost	Total Cost
A	25 lb × $ .12/lb = $3.00	$5.06	$0.55	$8.61
B	21 lb × $ .40/lb = $8.40		$0.55	$8.95
C	4 No. 10 cans @ $3.07 each = $12.28		$0.28*	$12.56

*Cost of opening cans and reheating.

carrots. The fresh carrots require labor to pare and size. Already pared and sized fresh carrots do not need such labor, but both require cooking to be ready for service. Canned carrots are already pared, sized, and cooked, and need only reheating. Is it better to buy fresh, unpared and unsized carrots, or sized and pared ones, or canned ones? A buyer makes a calculation based on the quantity required to give 100 3-oz. portions of each (see Table 3–1). Clearly, canned carrots are not to be considered, and the buyer has to make a decision on whether to purchase A or B. Because of the small difference in portion cost, B might be the better purchase because of their convenience in eliminating preparation time.

As-Purchased, Edible Portion, and As-Served Considerations in Value Analysis

Often buyers must compare the value of goods based on their **as-purchased** (AP) price, **edible portion** (EP), or **as-served** (AS) requirement. Thus, the menu calls for hash brown potatoes. Fresh potatoes are quoted at so much a 100-lb sack, and peeled at so much a pound. Frozen potatoes ready to be made into hash browns are available at so much a 30-lb carton. Which is the best buy? Factors such as labor, storage and other space needs, equipment cost, operating cost of equipment, and heating cost are required to bring the fresh and peeled potatoes to the same state as the frozen ones, which are ready to use. Often some costs are difficult to determine and estimates of them must be made. In such a case, the comparison can end up sort of "iffy."

To make a good, worthwhile comparison, a lot of knowledge is required of the buyer. Knowing food production thoroughly can be a big help. Knowing where to find information so a valid calculation can be made is also worthwhile. The following is an example of one of the most complex types of comparisons, calculating the final AS cost of a meat item. (The figures needed to make this calculation were derived from price quotations at the time this text was written. Some figures used come from the buying and operation experience of the authors.)

The menu calls for pot roast of beef for which the chef wants shoulder clods of beef. He estimates he will need about 25 pounds to meet the menu forecast of servings needed. The buyer has a choice of purchasing (A) whole IMPS 126 boneless armbone chuck (about 50 lb each) at $1.58/lb, cutting out the clod and using the remaining beef for other purposes; (B) boned and tied clods IMPS 114B at $2.95/lb; or (C) frozen cooked, sliced clod at $3.40/lb.

The boneless armbone chucks average about 46 lb each and to get two clods, two chucks are needed (about 92 lb). There is a 5% fat and trim loss in preparing these chucks into cookable meat, a loss considered as having a salvage value of $5.25. After trimming and deducting trim value from chuck cost, clods and remaining meat are considered equal in price. Clods are about 28% of a trimmed A126 chuck. The butchering cost of cutting out the clod and tying it for roasting is estimated as being $0.25/lb or $6.25 for the 25 pounds. Cost of cook time including slicing time and cooking cost for both A and B are $3.10. There is a $5.25 cost for making two gallons of gravy for the precooked product C. Items A and B will produce their own base for making the gravy and each will require 20 oz. of flour ($0.22 worth) to make the two gallons of gravy needed. The estimated cooking shrink on A and B is 32%. Which is the most favorable buy between the AP (chuck), EP (roast-ready clod), or AS (roasted and sliced clod)? The buyer's calculation follows:

A 92 lb No. 126 chuck × $ 1.38/lb = $ 126.96 total cost of chucks

$126.96 − $5.25 (salvage value) = $121.71 cost of cookable meat

$0.28 (clod portion of chuck) × $121.71 = $34.08 + $ 6.25 (butchering cost) = $40.33

$40.33 + $3.10 (cook's time and cooking cost) + $0.22 gravy cost = $43.65 total cost

B 25 lb clod @ $ 1.95 = $48.75 + $ 3.10 + $0.22 = $52.07 total cost

C 17 lb sliced cooked pot roast × $ 3.40 = $ 57.80 + $5.25 (gravy cost) = $63.05 total cost˙

Seventeen pounds of cooked sliced meat at 4 oz. per portion (4/lb) will give 68 portions and so the portion costs are

A $43.65/68 = $0.64

B $52.07/68 = $0.77

C $63.05/68 = $0.93

MARKET REGULATION

Many laws and regulations control the market, and buyers need to know these laws plus the prevalent trade practices in the market. Control is necessary for systematic performance in the market and assurance that proceedings are fair to all operations that participate in the market.

Federal Laws

A large number of federal regulations control general business practices including marketing. In 1887 the **Interstate Commerce Act** was passed. It governed shipping of goods between states. Recent court interpretations of this act have extended its provisions to control even commerce within states. Thus, any firm doing more than $200,000 in business a year is treated as one engaged in interstate commerce whether it actually does or not. Meat producers are especially affected by this regulation.

Early in the twentieth century the **Sherman Anti-Trust Act** was passed. It was intended to prevent businesses from restraining trade and creating monopolies. Large corporations were threatening to destroy smaller ones and control the market. In subsequent years, this law was amended with even greater restrictions. The **Wheeler–Lea Act,** the **Robinson–Patman Act,** the **Clayton Act,** the **Tydings–Miller Act,** the **Celler–Kefauver Act,** and the **McGuire Act** all advanced the original Sherman antitrust concept and further controlled competition and businesses' practices in obtaining sales. For example, it is illegal in the liquor industry to offer credit for more than 20 days. No price reduction or discounts can be offered to encourage sales unless a similar inducement is offered to all consumers on equal terms. If one consumer will take less in service or in some other value, the price reduction is authorized. Price tie-ins, special rebates, or other hidden means of inducing trading are illegal. All business dealings must be open and aboveboard. The ramifications of these laws are too extensive to be covered here by more than a short summary, but they should be known by all buyers.

In 1914 the **Federal Trade Commission** (FTC) was created for the purpose of promoting fair business and trade practices, prohibiting false or misleading advertising, reducing competition that restricts trade, and preventing unprofessional actions in the market. False or misleading advertising was particularly emphasized.

Food and Drug Act

The **Food, Drug, Cosmetic and Device Act** of 1938 (revised 1967) was originally passed in 1906. It had far-reaching effects, forcing sellers to offer clean, safe, and sanitary products. The old adage of "let the buyer beware" was undercut and some safeguards were offered to protect consumers. Under this act, inspectors can enter any establishment at reasonable hours to inspect for sanitary and maintenance standards and to see if food is "prepared, processed, and packaged in a sanitary manner." No product of a "diseased animal, contaminated, filthy, putrid, decomposed, or otherwise unfit food" can be used. Damage or inferiority cannot be concealed; no substandard food can be added to increase bulk or weight or create an illusion of greater value than the food has. No valuable part of the food can be omitted, and one food cannot be sold under the name of another.

Many examples of how far-reaching this law is could be given, but two will illustrate the point. It is illegal to put on a menu "Roquefort Dressing" when the cheese used is bleu cheese. No label on a package can show a picture of a product that does not truthfully and realistically show the actual product in the package.

The law provides that the labels of packaged food do the following:

1. Bear the common name or names of the food.[2]
2. Contain the name and address of the manufacturer, packager, or distributor.

---

[2]Later, the importance of what is called the *common name* is discussed.

3. List the net contents by count, fluid, or avoirdupois measure.

4. Be sufficiently prominent to be easily comprehended.

5. Contain no foreign words to circumvent label requirements.

6. Bear the specific name and not generic term of ingredients if the product is not a common food, except that group words such as *spice, flavoring,* and *coloring* can be used instead of the exact spice, flavoring, or coloring.

7. Bear the names of ingredients, in order from greatest to least in proportion, if the food is not a common one; thus, it would be illegal to list ingredients for corned beef as beef, potatoes, and onions if there are more potatoes than there is beef.

8. Bear the exact definition of dietary properties if claims are made for them.[3]

9. Bear the term *artificial* if artificial coloring or flavoring is used or the term *chemical preservative* if a chemical preservative is used.

Later amendments regulated the use of food additives, colorings, preservatives, and other harmful substances. The government no longer tests products to see if they are harmful; the manufacturer is required to submit substantial proof that products are not harmful. This is a burden to some small producers. Under authority of this act and others, the government publishes the list of authorized substances **generally regarded as safe** (**GRAS** list) in foods.

The **Delaney Amendment** is another addition that has far-reaching effects. It requires removal from the market of any food suspected of being carcinogenic. Saccharin's removal is an example, although Congress later passed a law allowing its use. Other food additives on the **Food and Drug Administration's** (FDA's) GRAS list are under scrutiny, such as sodium nitrate and monosodium glutamate, and may be removed. PCB is definitely off.

The GRAS list has come under attack from food manufacturers. They say the FDA has overreacted in some cases. Cyclamate, banned because it was shown to cause cancer in rats, has never been proven to cause cancer in human beings; one would have to drink at least 138 12-oz. bottles of a soft drink containing cyclamate each day to take in an amount equivalent to what the test animals were fed. As a result of such criticism, the FDA has become more flexible in its administration of the GRAS list. However, it is responsible for protecting the nation's health by forbidding harmful substances in food and is backed in this not only by Congress but by a public that is concerned about the safety of its food supply.

Under the **Pure Food and Drug Act** and other regulations, the FDA has established what are called **Standards of Identity** for foods. This is a list that very exactingly and precisely defines how a food must qualify for its name. Canned pears, for example, must be of the variety *pyrus commis;* if the label says *halves,* they must meet the defined standards for a pear half. The word *egg* on a noodle package means the noodles contain at least 5½% eggs on a dry basis. *Ice cream* is defined as a product not less than 10% milk fat if a light flavor, weighing 4.2 lb/gal, and with other

---

[3]See later how nutritional labeling further increased this requirement.

stated characteristics. This use of Standards of Identity has led to the stabilization of names in the trade and helped sellers and buyers know exactly what products are. Product names used in specifications now have legal meaning. The act is administered by the FDA.

Because the Food and Drug Act did not go far enough in preventing deceptive packaging, the **Hart Act** was passed in 1966. It achieved its purpose in the first objective, which sought to eliminate misleading descriptions and illustrations, but has not been as successful in standardizing packaging. We still see a wide assortment of package sizes. What is needed is a standardization somewhat like the American Canners Association has achieved for canned goods.

Meat Act

The **Meat Inspection Act,** passed in 1906 with a major revision in 1967, provides for the inspection of meats and meat products wherever they are processed. A circle stamp, indicating the product is fit for human consumption, bears the words **"Inspected & Passed, USDA,"** with an official plant number that identifies where the meat was processed. Occasionally one sees initials underneath the circle; these identify the individual who made the inspection. Any product containing 2% or more of meat must bear such a stamp if shipped interstate. Basically, the law provides inspection to do the following:

1. Detect and destroy diseased and unfit products.
2. Require clean and sanitary preparation and handling.
3. Require display of the federal circle stamp.
4. Prevent the use of harmful substances.
5. Prevent false and deceptive labeling.

The Meat Act is administered by the Animal Plant Health Inspection Service (APHIS); the USDA Veterinary Service and Plant Protection and Quarantine Agencies also have responsibilities. If a state has stricter provisions than the federal law, it can follow them.

In 1957 the act was extended to cover poultry, and in 1968 the Wholesome Poultry Products Act extended further the government's powers to regulate the production of poultry. In 1996 the method for inspecting meats and poultry was changed to better detect contamination. The regulation enforcing this change is known as the Hazards Analysis Critical Control Point (HACCP) and is discussed more fully in Chapter 2.

Fish Regulation

The **National Marine Fisheries Service** and the **National Oceanographic and Atmosphere Administration** in 1970 in the **U.S. Department of Commerce** took over responsibility for fish and fish product market supervision. They provide for some inspection and grading and also act to control certain marketing practices on the primary and secondary fish markets. A fish processor can have continuous inspection of products for a fee. This is a voluntary program, and labels can state "packaged under federal inspection." Also the Commerce Department provides a quality grading service for a fee. The Food and Drug Act and the FDA hold responsibility for inspection of sanitation, storage, wholesomeness, and labeling of marine products. There is a feeling among many that the administration of fishery products is too broken up among federal agencies and that the total responsibility should be concentrated under one agency.

Sanitation Regulation

The **U.S. Public Health Service** inspects seafood beds to ensure they are sanitary and contain no disease-carrying products. It gives a certificate number to each shipping package and requires that all records be kept on where the product came from for six weeks, so that any incident of diphtheria, hepatitis, or other disease relayed by the product can be traced back. Because shipping packages are often broken down into smaller lots or processed, buyers may not receive the certificate number. This can be obtained from purveyors.

Serious outbreaks of botulinum poisoning in processed foods and other problems prompted the passage of the **Good Management Practices Act** in 1970. It combines sanitary safeguards and other safety and regulatory features in processing plants.

Grading Standards

The **Agricultural Marketing Act** of 1953 (revised in 1957) was far-reaching in its effects, especially in establishing quality grades for food groups and providing for the inspection and grading of fresh and processed foods. The USDA was given the authority to set up inspection and control divisions. Cereal, dairy, fresh fruit and vegetables, poultry, eggs, and meats were handled in separate divisions, which control the marketing of these products. Each division sets quality standards for its products. These standards were often adapted from grading practices on the market, but this has gradually changed to standards developed by the federal government. One example of grade changes is occurring in the grading of processed fruits and vegetables.

Standards are published first as "tentative" and then after testing are made "official" standards. In 1956 some of the provisions of the Agricultural Marketing Act were applied to fish and shellfish so that processed fishery products could be graded.

Grading is usually not mandatory but is performed only at the request of some individual or agency. A **certificate of inspection** is made out after grading is done. (Buyers can get a copy on request; see Figure 3–9.) Graded products may not show the grade, but shipping packages often show the certificate number so that buyers can ascertain the basis of the grade.

Inspectors often assign grades on the basis of scores for different quality factors. These factors differ for different product groups. Processed foods are often scored by color, absence of defects, character, color of liquor, and other factors. Meat may be scored on the amount of marbling in the meat, the quality of the meat, and so forth. Butter is scored on the basis of color, texture, salt content, and other qualities. **Grade scores** and not grade may be of interest to a buyer. Thus, one frozen pea lot may grade 80 whereas another may grade 89 although both are Grade B. If there is no price difference, the second is perhaps the better buy. Also, buyers may be interested in factor scores that make up the total score. If color is not important in an

F. P. I. 20

ORIGINAL

UNITED STATES DEPARTMENT OF AGRICULTURE

VIRGINIA DEPARTMENT OF AGRICULTURE AND IMMIGRATION

INSPECTION CERTIFICATE № 4377

This certificate is issued in compliance with the regulations of the Secretary of Agriculture governing the inspection of various products pursuant to the Act making appropriations for the United States Department of Agriculture, the Acts of Virginia Assembly, and is admissible as prima facie evidence in all courts of the United States and of Virginia. This certificate does not excuse failure to comply with any of the regulatory laws enforced by the United States Department of Agriculture, or by the Virginia Department of Agriculture and Immigration.

Inspection point Winchester, Va. *Billing point* Winchester, Va. *Date* Oct. 4, 19

Applicant Winchester Packing Co. *Address* Winchester, Va.

Shipper Same *Address* Same

I, the undersigned, on the date above specified made personal inspection of samples of the lot of products herein described, and do hereby certify that the quality and/or condition, at the said time and on said date, pertaining to such products, as shown by said samples, were as stated below:

Car initial and number FGEX 5 1 8 1 3 *Kind of car* Refrigerator

Inspection begun 1:30 P. M. Oct. 4, 19 (Hour, date) *Inspection completed* 6:15 P. M. Oct. 4, 19 (Hour, date)

Car equipment and condition at completion of inspection:

Products: York Imperial APPLES - in tub type bushel baskets labeled "W Brand, Winchester Packing Co., Winchester, Va." and stamped "U. S. No. 1, $2\frac{1}{4}$ inches up, York." Loader's count 516 baskets.

Loading: Through load, end to end offset, 3x3 rows, 4 layers.

Pack: Tight. Ring faced. Paper pads under lids. Good amount of oiled paper distributed uniformly through baskets.

Size: Generally $2\frac{1}{4}$ to 3, mostly $2\frac{1}{4}$ to $2\frac{1}{2}$ inches in diameter.

Quality and condition: Mostly well formed, some fairly well formed, clean, 15% to full red, mostly 25% to 50% good red color. Grade defects within tolerance. Generally hard. No decay.

Grade: As marked, U. S. No. 1, $2\frac{1}{4}$ inches up.

Fee \$5.16

Expenses

Total 5.16

L. F. Laney

Inspector.

PLEASE REFER TO THIS CERTIFICATE BY NUMBER

Figure 3-9

A certificate of inspection completed after the goods have been graded. (Courtesy of USDA.)

apple that is to be peeled, a buyer may not worry too much when this factor is graded down.

Marketing agents prefer to purchase by grade but sell to consumers by their own brand, though this varies. Eggs, dairy products, and many meats and poultry are sold to consumers as graded products; few processed or fresh fruits and vegetables are, although there are exceptions. Some states require inspection and grading. Florida requires it for citrus products but does not require the label to show the grade; the package, however, bears a blank grade shield showing it has gone through grading.

In recent years there has been a trend to break away from federal grades and use brand or other quality determinants to indicate quality. This is especially true for processed canned items. Much more ungraded boxed meat, called "no roll" because the government roller stamp indicating grade is missing, is on the market. Most fresh fruits and vegetables no longer bear labels showing grade. However, butter, eggs, and some other products continue to be graded.

The cost of grading is borne by the agency or person who requests it. The cost is significant, and so the amount graded must be large enough to warrant the cost; small buyers often find this cost prohibitive and so cannot make use of the service.

Quality grades are often too broad for use by foodservice buyers. Because narrower range is needed, buyers include the grade in their specifications but narrow the quality factors to get a suitable product within that grade. A buyer, for example, may specify frozen broccoli to come as "floret style 1 to 2 inches long, be Grade A with a quality grade score of 95 or more, scoring not less than 18 points out of a possible 18 for color." Just specifying Grade A might not be specific enough. It may be desirable to indicate a specific score or value for a factor such as color, clarity of juice, freedom from defects, and so forth.

Although the use of a quality grade is voluntary, standards of sanitation, identity, and fill are not. Seizure and destruction of offending goods is possible if the food is unwholesome, misbranded, or does not meet standards of identity, quality claimed, or fill. Prosecution may occur, and offenders may be forced out of business, fined, or sent to jail, or receive a combination of these penalties.

Federal inspectors can be hired to work continuously in a plant, inspecting for quality and grading goods. This is called **continuous inspection.** If an inspector inspects only a lot or several lots and is not present all the time, the inspection is called **intermittent.** Meat packers, poultry processors, egg and dairy units, and some fruit and vegetable processors operate under continuous inspection.

Buyers can send samples of products to federal inspectors for grading, but the grade applies *only* to the sample and not to the lot from which it came. For a grade certificate to apply to a lot, federal inspectors must randomly select and inspect a representative sample from the lot. Federal shields shown in Figure 3–10 indicate a federal grade.

Acceptance Buying

Large buyers often set up their own specifications[4] and send copies both to purveyors and to a federal inspection service. They then require purveyors to submit products for examination by the inspection service to ensure that the products meet the buyer's specifications. If they do meet the specification, the package, invoice, and

---

[4]A specification is a statement of all the factors a product must possess for purchase. Buyers use these as a reference in setting up needs, but sometimes they send specifications to vendors so there is a clear understanding of what is desired.

Figure 3-10
An example of federal grade shields used for merchandise.
(Courtesy of USDA.)

other papers are stamped with an "acceptance" stamp (see Figure 3–11). Tapes and other seals on the package are also stamped so that, if the package is opened after inspection, this can be detected. The procedure is called **acceptance buying.** The buyer often pays the cost of inspection.

Standards of Fill, Weights, and Measures

The standards of fill vary for different products and different packaging. False bottoms and slack or deceptive fill are prohibited. Products failing to meet the standards of fill are labeled "Below Standard of Fill." To ensure that a container has been filled properly, buyers often state the container size and then add the minimum weight of product in the container. Thus, a buyer would require a 4/5 bushel of California oranges to have a minimum weight of 38 lbs but a 4/5 bushel of Florida oranges to have a minimum weight of 42.5 lbs.

The **Bureau of Standards** in the Department of Commerce administers our laws regulating weights and measures. For the most part, it is an advisory body rather than a regulatory one and most states and local jurisdictions pattern their weights and measure laws on the bureau's code.

Three federal laws apply: (1) The barrel must be 7056 cu. in. or 105 qt; it will hold two 98-lb sacks of flour. The cranberry barrel was fixed at 5826 cu. in., enough to hold 100 lb of cranberries. (2) Climax baskets can be 2, 4, or 12 qt and standard berry and till boxes are 1/2 pt, 1 pt, 1 qt, and multiples of a quart dry measure. No other sizes are permitted. (3) The capacity of hampers and stave baskets can be 1/8, 1/4, 1/2, 5/8, 3/4, 1, 1 1/4, 1 1/2, and 2 bushels. Splint baskets are limited to capacities of 4, 8, 12, 16, 24, and 32 dry qt. Recently the bureau approved new bottle sizes

Figure 3-11
A federal acceptance seal indicating the product has met the buyers quality standards. (Courtesy of USDA.)

for the alcohol industry as well as allowing some malt and other beverages to be dispensed in small cans, other than the common 12-oz and 16-oz ones used in the past.

Special Exception Laws

To assist in the control and marketing of some foodstuffs, special laws have been passed exempting certain food groups from antitrust or other laws. The **Perishable Agricultural Commodities Act** is one. It regulates fresh fruit and vegetable trade practices by licensing dealers and establishing certain procedures. Inspection of fruits, vegetables, or other items may be required. The USDA administers the act.

The **Agricultural Adjustment Act** (1933) and Agricultural Marketing Act (1937) waive certain antitrust and marketing restrictions of the Sherman Anti-Trust Act for agricultural products. Thus, producers can band together to form large cooperatives or large marketing units. Buyers and sellers of agricultural products are also exempt from the law in dealing with such organizations. Thus, it is possible for states to have a milk board that controls the amount of dairy products produced, their transportation, and even their price. Dairies and others dealing in such a restricted and controlled market can do so without fear of violating the Sherman Anti-Trust Act.

Alcoholic Beverages

Alcoholic beverages must meet Standards of Identity requirements and other requirements of some of the other laws mentioned here. Control of alcoholic beverages comes under the **Alcohol, Tobacco and Firearms Division** of the **U.S. Treasury Department.** Some of the details of the regulations enforced are discussed in chapter 14 on alcoholic beverages. Another law that has come to the fore in recent years is the **Dram Shop Law,** which is in force in many states. This makes those engaged in the sale or dispensing of alcoholic beverages partly responsible for the actions of those they serve. Heavy fines and court awards for damages have been levied against operators, forcing producers of alcoholic beverages and the industry to change some of their marketing procedures to help solve the problem. Some localities today require that those serving alcoholic beverages to the public take and pass a special course dealing with responsibility today in serving alcohol to the public.

Franchising

When franchising was in its early days, the franchisor could write contracts requiring franchisees to purchase much of their requirements from them. The courts decided this was a restraint of trade, and the provision is now illegal. Franchisees can now purchase where they desire but can be required to meet franchise standards and specifications. Recent court decisions, however, have stated that franchisers *can* require franchisees to purchase through them if they do not profit from it.

Storage

The **U.S. Warehouse Act** provides for the warehouse certification of agriculture and processed food products moving in interstate commerce. Thus, time and type of storage can be verified. Bonded, cold, and other types of storage are covered by the act.

Nutrition Labeling

The requirements for the labeling of contents on a package were changed in 1990 with the passage of the **Nutrition Labeling and Educational Act** (NLEA), which went into effect in May 1993. Regulation was extended to cover raw fruit, vegetables, meat, fish, and poultry, but left it to the discretion of the company marketing the item whether to add such nutrition information to the package label. (Buyers will note that some supermarkets publish a list of the nutrients in their fresh fruits and vegetables in a separate sign so buyers can see what the nutrients are in the products purchased.) Few quantity merchants have done anything about extending the law to cover these other products.

The NLEA requires changes in advertising. Instead of the Federal Trade Commission having jurisdiction over food advertising, the Food and Drug Administration will have jurisdiction and will regulate claims about health benefits. The act requires the FTC to use the same definitions, regulations, and standards established by the FDA, making the two agencies consistent in their standards. The bill gives the FDA the authority to embargo any product that an inspector feels violates the regulations.

The NLEA requires that the stated size portion given on the label be the basis of the percent of one's daily intake. Figure 3–5 shows a label meeting these requirements. Buyers interested in the nutritional value of products can learn much from the information given on such labels, but some advocates of good nutrition feel that even more information is desirable.

Summary of Market Regulations

There are a number of other laws and regulations in which the market can be supervised and controlled, but the preceding material covers most of the important ones. Taxes can be an important marketing influence. This is particularly true of alcoholic beverages. Imports also influence prices and thus supply. Another influence in causing governmental action is legislation affecting the economy, bringing about growth or retardation. Policies of the USDA, Treasury, Federal Reserve, and others away from markets can cause significant changes in government actions that influence the market.

Legal Considerations

Buying procedures are affected by court decisions. These are forceful guidelines for market action, and buyers who do not know them can get themselves and their firms into difficult and expensive controversies that could end up in the courts. Many buyer–seller dealings can be legally binding; buyers need to know when they have made a legal commitment or entered into an arrangement that requires specific action. The following subsections summarize some of the most important factors covering legalities in purchasing, but more information is needed when specific actions are required. Usually, a course in business law covers many of these in greater detail. If one is an active buyer, legal advice should be sought if there is any doubt. (Also see Appendix A, The Law of Purchasing.)

Law of Agency

Buyers, salespersons, and others represent their firms in doing business. To what extent can they make legal commitments for their firms? A salesperson can take an order and agree on a price, delivery date, and other factors but still have no agreement because he or she does not have the company's permission to make a bond. The purchase order must be taken to the firm and be signed by a company official or someone authorized to do so. Buyers often cannot make such arrangements unless authorized to do so. The extent to which agents can act for their firms should be known. Some are limited in their authorization to make contracts or are allowed to purchase only up to a certain amount, after which someone higher up has to validate a greater commitment. Others acting for the agent assume the agent's limitations. (See Case Study No. 1 at the end of this chapter.)

Law of Warranty

A warranty is a guarantee that an item will perform in a specified way. Guarantees can be implied or expressed. Goods are sold with the understanding that they are suitable for purchase; if a seller knows the goods will not suit the intended purpose, the seller is guilty of a breach of warranty. Vendors should understand how the goods or services are to be used. "Trade puffing" or a salesperson's statement of a product's worth cannot be interpreted as a warranty guarantee. A warranty exists if a responsible person in the salesperson's firm confirms the claims, or indicates the firm is bound by the statements, or if there is fraud. Items sold "as is" are under no warranty.

Law of Contracts

Food services often enter into contracts for services or goods. A contract requires an offer, an acceptance, and a consideration. For instance, if a food service advertises for bids, receives and accepts one, and the seller posts bond, a contract is made. When a purchase order includes a promise to ship by a specified time, this implies order acceptance. No contract exists when a seller acknowledges receipt of a purchase order, unless the seller promises shipment. If only part of an order is shipped, the seller is contracted to send all of it.

Any change in *any way* of the original terms without agreement of both parties voids a contract. If a counteroffer is made and accepted, a contract exists. Written or even verbal matters relating to an original order can be considered a part of a contract providing they satisfy the basic requirements of a contract agreement. If only one party is bound, there is no contract; both must be. Usually, the buyer agrees to pay a certain sum, and the seller agrees to sell and deliver goods or services under specific terms and conditions.

Nonperformance on a contract is a breach of contract subject to penalty. A contract containing indefinite provisions can be canceled by either party upon due notice; ambiguity about conditions or other factors may make a contract nonbinding. When one or more considerations are decided by only one party, the contract is not binding because of the lack of mutual agreement. Approximate amounts can be legally binding if exact ones are not known; often a range is acceptable. Sometimes a variation by amount or percentage over or under suffices. Some prices may be assumed to be understood, and the purveyor must notify the buyer only if a price change occurs. If a price or quantity is subject to confirmation, acceptance of even a partial order by the buyer can be considered acceptance of quantity and price. Escalator clauses are used in contracts to allow for variable prices or conditions if certain specified conditions, events, or factors change.

Contracts usually hold for a specified time, but provision for cancellation is often made by agreement of both parties before this time, if desired. Cancellation clauses are sometimes effective when certain conditions arise. Provisions should be established to protect either party from loss from cancellation. Cancellations can be made on the basis of default by either party. If the ramifications of a cancellation provision are not clearly understood, legal advice should be obtained.

Failing to meet a delivery date, delivering the wrong quantity or quality, or other variation from the agreed terms constitutes default. If no protest is made, however, no violation is considered to exist; if continued violations are permitted, it is impossible for a buyer to later claim default. Written agreement can be given to accept a violation only one time, without agreeing to further violations. Violations that occur as a result of "acts of God" such as fires, earthquakes, or floods do not constitute default. The failing party should issue a formal notice that the contract is no longer valid because of a failure to perform. An injured party to a contract can sue for damages. Buyers can complete the seller's obligation in the market and charge the seller for whatever costs are incurred over and above what would have occurred. If a buyer cancels, the seller can recover for any harm done. Mutual agreements to cancel should be in writing. A mutual agreement to change a condition of a contract cancels the contract unless the entire contract's other provisions are affirmed by both parties.

Contracts should clearly define delivery or other times; if the agreed time is violated, default exists. Inclusion of the clause "time is of essence" gives a buyer the right to refuse orders or services that do not arrive at specified times. Contracts are void if made in violation of a law or regulation. Thus, a contract that violates wage and hours laws is no contract; validity is also lost if the contract is based on fraud. Conditional contracts give buyers or sellers certain repossession or other rights if terms are not met.

Law of Title to Goods

Buying or selling involves a transfer of ownership or title. Time and place are important considerations. Title can pass at any point, but it often passes at the time goods are delivered to the enterprise and delivery is acknowledged by signing the invoice. The seller loses control at this point and the buyer assumes it. One does not have to see the goods for title to pass. If goods are refused, the seller is obliged to pick up the goods or they may be returned at the seller's cost. Damages can be assessed against the seller if they can be proven. The buyer must have a legitimate reason for refusal; otherwise the seller has the right of recourse.

Goods delivered **free-on-board (FOB)** become the responsibility of the buyer at that time. Insurance, transportation charges, and other costs are the expense of the buyer. If a carrier in any way damages a shipment, the seller is not responsible unless the damage occurs FOB point of origin. After delivery FOB to the carrier, a seller cannot reclaim the goods if the buyer is found to be bankrupt or otherwise unable to perform. When a seller who retains merchandise a buyer pays for, such as storing liquor, goes bankrupt, the seller is liable to the buyer only as a creditor; the buyer cannot claim the goods. If a seller invalidates any contract terms, the buyer does not have to assume title upon an FOB delivery to a carrier. To be able to transfer title FOB, the seller must take due precaution to see that goods are properly packed for shipment, are of the declared value for insurance and carrier liability purposes, and follow the buyer's shipping instructions. If these things are not done, the buyer does not have to assume title. The seller shipping goods by independent carrier under FOB at the *buyer's designated place* (called FOB designation) does not transfer title until such delivery and assumes full responsibility until this time. If the carrier fails in any way, the seller and not the buyer must seek recourse. Tax liability and other considerations vary depending on where title transfer occurs. If title passes in Ohio, that state's laws apply and not those of Indiana, from where the goods were shipped. **CIF** means cash, insurance, and freight paid at destination by the buyer. Title passes at time of payment.

SUMMARY

The market in which a foodservice buyer functions is a highly complex structure divided into international, regional, primary, secondary, and local markets. Middlemen or market intermediaries act to move items through this market. They are composed largely of commission men, jobbers, brokers, manufacturer's agents, manufacturer's representatives, wholesalers, and retailers.

As goods move through the market, markup costs are incurred that add to their basic cost. In some cases these marketing costs can be quite high, dwarfing the original cost of the product. However, these marketing agents create added values in the goods they handle. These values are called place value, form value, information value, and source value, but other services may also be rendered.

The basic AP (as-purchased) price of goods on the market is set by (1) original cost, (2) marketing costs, (3) demand, or (4) supply. The government, trade associations, future market quotations, technological improvements, world events, loss, and unpredictable events can influence this basic price. An important part of a buyer's job is analyzing prices to see if a lower price with adequate quality can be obtained.

Value analysis is a method used by buyers to analyze prices. The formula V (value) $= Q$ (quality)$/P$ (price) is used. Quality refers to quality of product, convenience of use, value of supplier services, and so forth. Value perception differs from value analysis in that actual or real value may have little to do with the value that a buyer assigns to goods at a specific time and occasion.

The market is controlled by a number of laws, most important to a food buyer are the Food, Drug, Cosmetic and Device Act, the Meat Inspection Act, several agricultural acts, and regulations by U.S. governmental agencies. Laws also act to control buying and selling; these are mainly law of agency, law of warranty, law of contracts, and law of title to goods.

REVIEW QUESTIONS

1. A number of trade associations like the National Restaurant Association, American Hotel-Motel Association, and Club Managers Association offer their members information of value in buying. They also have state units that can assist buyers with information needs. Contact one and see what information of this type they offer.

2. In addition to the coverage mentioned in this chapter, what else do you think should be covered by laws and regulations of the foodservice market? For instance, should we have a law requiring food services to hire a dietitian to write menus and supervise food purchasing, production, and service to see that nutritious foods are served?

3. What are the differences between primary, secondary, and local markets? What is the trend in this area?

4. Identify the distinguishing feature of these marketing intermediaries: commission man, jobber, broker, manufacturer's agent, manufacturer's representative, wholesaler, and retailer.

5. What do the laws of agency, warranty, contract, and title to goods cover? Just summarize, giving only the high points.

6. Suppose a severe drought occurred during the summer in Western states starting with Texas and New Mexico and reaching up to Montana. What would you expect to see happen to the cattle market? If both California and Florida had severe frosts during the winter, what would you expect to see happen to the fresh fruit and vegetable market? Violent storms during the winter months in the New England market disrupt fishing. What would you expect to happen to the fish market? Good rains in the Midwest bring a promise of one of the best corn crops in years. What would you expect to see happen on the poultry, hog, and cereal markets?

7. Name one of the four market functions and indicate what this function is.

8. What is the NLEA? What are the responsibilities of the FDA and FTC in administering this act?

9. What does the term *fresh* mean when applied to poultry?

10. Gather at least five items from some news media, government publication, magazine, or newspaper, on happenings on the market that would be of interest to a buyer for a hospitality operation.

11. A salesperson offers a buyer the same brand of vanilla in single strength at $10.50/gal or double strength at $19.00/gal. One uses half the amount of double strength to get the same flavor yield as when one uses single strength. Set up a $V = Q/P$ formula for both so an evaluation can be made as to the best buy.

Answer: Single strength: $Q/10.50/gal$, double strength: $Q1/2$ $(19.00/gal)$ = $9.50/gal.

12. Which is the best buy?: Frozen string beans at $1.35/lb or fresh ones at $0.75/lb? Trim waste on the fresh beans is 12% and it takes a worker 1 hour and 12 minutes at $6/hr to prepare them. The amount needed to serve 100 3-oz. portions is required. There is no cooking loss for either and cost of cooking each is considered equal.

Answer: 100 portions × 3 oz. or 18.75 lb of cooked beans is needed (300/16 = 18.75) Cost of labor is $0.10/minute, and 1 hr 12 minutes is 72 minutes so the cost of labor is $7.20

Frozen beans: $1.35/lb × 18.75 lb = $25.31

Fresh beans: 18.75 lb = 21.3 lb fresh beans are needed to yield 18.75 lb (100% − 12%) of trimmed, cooked beans (21.3 × $0.75) + $7.20 = $23.32

KEY WORDS AND CONCEPTS

acceptance buying

Agricultural Adjustment Act

Agricultural Marketing Act

Alcohol, Tobacco and Firearms Division

as-purchased price

as-served

broker

Bureau of Standards

Certificate of inspection

CIF

Clayton Act

Celler–Kefauver Act

cold storage

commission man

common name

continuous inspection

Delaney Amendment

descriptive labeling

Dram Shop Law

edible portion

Federal Trade Commission (FTC)

Food and Drug Administration (FDA)

Food, Drug, Cosmetic and Device Act

form value

Franchising Law of Agency

Free-on-Board (FOB)

Generally regarded as safe (GRAS)

Good Management Practices Act

Grade Score

grading standards

Hazard Analysis Critical Control Point (HACCP)

Hart Act

information value

"Inspected and Passed, USDA"

intermittent inspection

international market

Interstate Commerce Act

jobber

Law of agency

Law of contracts

Law of title to goods

Law of warranty

local market

manufacturer's representative or market agent

market

market distribution system

market regulation

markup

McGuire Act

Meat Inspection Act

middlemen (marketing intermediaries)

National Marine Fisheries Service

National Oceanographic and Atmosphere Administration

nutrient labeling

Nutrition Labeling and Educational Act

Perishable Agricultural Commodities Act

place value

primary market

Pure Food and Drug Act

regional market

retailer

Robinson–Patman Act

secondary market

Sherman Anti-Trust Act

source value

Standard of Identity

standards of fill, weights, and measures

time value

Tydings–Miller Act

U.S. Department of Commerce

U.S. Public Health Service

U.S. Treasury Department

U.S. Warehouse Act

value analysis

value perception

Wheeler–Lea Act

wholesaler

CASE STUDY NO. 1

A chef has sent the buyer a requisition for 10 No. 109 ribs of beef averaging 20 to 22 pounds each. The buyer calls a meat supplier and receives a price of $1.89/lb. He makes a quick calculation. The total price will be around $415. He places the order. The supplier thanks him and then asks, "Did you know that we are offering a special price of $1.56 a pound for orders over $1,000?" The buyer says, "Sorry, I'm only authorized to place orders up to $500. I will have to get permission from my boss to order that much. I'll also see if the chef wants that much." "OK, but this sale is only on through tomorrow." The buyer calls the chef, who when he hears the price is interested and says he would have no problem selling prime ribs the next week and could use about another 200 pounds. The buyer then calls the head office of his chain to see if permission will be granted for the larger purchase. He is told that the official who can give permission is in the hospital and cannot be contacted, but the person answering the phone assures the buyer that he sees no problem. But the buyer is not sure and calls the supplier telling him he does not want to take the responsibility and would have to purchase only the 10 ribs. The supplier replies, "How about my sending the order in three billings, each bill slightly under $500 so you'll not be exceeding your authority?" The buyer thinks a moment and agrees. The ribs are received with the buyer signing the three orders that totaled 28 ribs weighing 588 pounds, for a total of $1499.40, each bill totaling $499.80.

However, the official at the head office, on finding out about the purchase, objected, saying the buyer had exceeded his authority. He said he understood that the buyer was acting on what he thought was the best interest of the company, but he was objecting because of the devious way the buyer went about exceeding his authority. The buyer was seriously reprimanded.

What do you think? Did the buyer really exceed his authority? Was collusion going on between the supplier and the buyer? What do you think of the ethics of the supplier in suggesting such a way to make the purchase? Did the buyer have a right to exceed his authority because the head office told him it was all right? Did this person really have the right to grant permission? Was the head office official right in reprimanding the buyer, not because the purchase was harmful to the company, but because it set a precedent in which the buyer could exceed the $500 order restriction? Was this really nothing more than a tempest in a teapot and the official should have said, "Well in this case it's all right, but never do it again?" You decide!

CASE STUDY NO. 2

A company has sold a food service a very high proof brandy substance to use in flambéing foods at the patron's table. It is shipped with a nozzle that permits the server to effectively shoot the brandy into the pan to be flamed. Two couples are celebrating a first-year wedding anniversary, and one of the young women, a beautiful girl, orders Bananas Flambé. The server is proceeding to prepare the order when suddenly the flames from the pan leap up and follow the brandy through the nozzle down into the brandy bottle. There is an explosion and the bottle contents shoot out of the bottle in flames and strike the young woman. She is immediately in flames. Fortunately, the server had the presence of mind to grab the draperies on the windows near the table and smother the flames, but not until the girl was horribly burned about the face, neck, and arms. When she healed, she was terribly disfigured. She became a recluse, refusing to see people, and even asked her husband for a divorce, which he reluctantly gave. She refused to accept a child that was born to her five months after the accident; her husband's parents took the baby to raise. Her life was ruined. She sued but because the assets of the food service, were very limited, the manufacturer of the brandy was included in the suit, the plaintiff claiming that the seller of the brandy product, by selling the product for use in flaming, had an implied warranty that it was safe to use, and that the bottle lacked a proper warning about the use of the product.

Do you think including the seller of the product in the lawsuit was justified? Wasn't the food service alone responsible because it misused the product and allowed the flames to get too close to the nozzle? Shouldn't the server have pointed the bottle in a direction where no harm would have resulted if such an ignition occurred? Under the law of warranty in your text you read that "Goods are sold with the understanding that they are suitable for purchase" and "vendors should know how the goods or services are to be used." Do you think a court would interpret this as making the seller responsible because of a failure to adequately warn the user about the dangers of using such a product? (*Note:* This was an actual case. The instructor's manual has the court decision. Your instructor may wish to tell you what the court decided after your decision.)

CASE STUDY NO. 3

A food service advertises for bids on a number of processed food items. The food service selects one of the bids and notifies the purveyor of its acceptance. No bond is submitted. However, a bid with bond is submitted after the closing date of the bids. It is a much favorable bid and the company calls the other bidder and cancels the order. The unsuccessful bidder sues claiming there was a contract, that an offer was made and accepted, and that the bid of the other purveyor could not be accepted because it had not been submitted within the time frame stated in the advertisement for bids? In either case, was there a contract?

CASE STUDY NO. 4

A purveyor signs a contract to deliver goods in several lots. It fails to deliver the last lot on the due date and the buyer cancels the contract. Can the buyer do so?

CASE STUDY NO. 5

A company purchases a large amount of liquor from a company but cannot take complete delivery of it. The seller agrees to store the remaining product in its warehouse and deliver on order of the buyer. On the first delivery, the buyer pays for the goods, takes the partial delivery, and signs the invoice for the entire lot. Then the unforeseen happens. A tornado strikes the warehouse destroying the buyer's stored liquor. The seller claims no responsibility saying that the tornado was an act of God over which the seller had no control and therefore had shown no negligence and that it was only doing the buyer a favor by storing the goods. The buyer claimed that, even though payment had been made, delivery had not been made and that therefore the liquor was the property of the seller and the seller should bear the loss. Whose loss is it? Did title really pass? Read the material on law of title to goods carefully and decide. There was also another problem. The buyer was in North Dakota but the seller was located in Minnesota. Where did title to the goods delivered to the buyer pass? Where did title to the stored goods pass, if it passed? Which state's laws apply in this case?

CHAPTER 4

Supplier Selection, Specifications, and Steps in Purchasing

May 30, 1831 Market Prices, Island St. Helena. (Napoleon was exiled here from 1815 until his death in 1820.)
From the Louis Szwathmary collection, Culinary Archives and Museum, Johnson and Wales University, used by permission of Dr. Szwathmary and Johnson and Wales University.

Chapter Objectives

1. To discuss factors important in the selection of suppliers.
2. To cover some ethical factors important in buyer–seller relations.
3. To describe what specifications are, what they should do and the advantages of using them.
4. To cover the steps that normally must be taken to adequately purchase for a foodservice operation.

INTRODUCTION

Before a buyer purchases items, certain information must be available. A list of suppliers must be on hand and this list must be complete so that all items normally required by a foodservice operation will be offered by a supplier or, preferably, by a choice of suppliers. In addition, the buyer should know *exactly* what is required. To this end an operation usually compiles a written list giving the details of what items must possess to meet the production need. This list of details for each item is known as a *specification*.

The buying task should be organized to suit the needs of the operation. Forms need to be set up to handle the various steps in purchasing. When these things are done, the buyer is ready to put together orders and buy.

SUPPLIER SELECTION

The suppliers selected by a facility are most important to that facility's success. The price offered, quality of product, and satisfaction with deliveries and other services of a supplier are critical. Supplier selection, therefore, must be done with great care. Selection is largely a management function but it can be delegated if management stays close to the decision-making process. It is also important, once a selection has been made, that management maintain surveillance to see that adequate supplier performance is achieved.

Kinds of Suppliers

There are four distinct kinds of **suppliers,** or **purveyors,** from which a selection can be made: (1) full-line, (2) local specialty wholesaler, (3) national jobber, and (4) supermarkets and discount houses.

Full-line Suppliers

In the last several decades full-line (diversified or one-stop) suppliers have become one of the leading suppliers to foodservice operations. They carry large inventories of different foods and supplies, attempting to furnish a facility with almost anything it needs from chemicals, to paper supplies, to frozen, processed, or fresh vegetables and fruits, meats, fish, and poultry, to equipment.

The reason for their popularity is convenience. Before these suppliers came into being, a food service dealt with a number of suppliers—one study showed 19 on the average. Using a full-line supplier makes it possible to eliminate almost all others and concentrate your buying power. It eliminates buying time, paperwork, receiving time, and so on. The simplicity of placing just one order instead of a large number of orders is especially attractive to the usually busy buyer who also must act in a number of other capacities. They often will deal in broken lots.

Local Specialty Wholesalers

Specialty wholesalers often carry a limited product line, such as only groceries and canned goods, or just meats, or fish, or produce. In this way, they are able to specialize in product variety and quality. They can deal with small or large orders. A specialty food service such as a fish and seafood house would deal with such a supplier for its needs in fish and seafood.

National Jobber

Large purchasers, such as the military, multiple-unit operations, school districts, cruise lines, and cooperative buying units, purchase from national jobbers who often sell a restricted product line. Some may be locally based and deliver a limited product line such as Kraft and Company with its cheese, salad dressing, and related item products. This latter type might sell in small or even broken lots, but the others only deal with whole lots, sometimes in carloads.

Discount Warehouses or Supermarkets

Some food services sporadically purchase only limited quantities. This might be a small family operation, or an operation such as a caterer that may have quite busy and slow periods. Other operations have so little volume that other suppliers will not bother with the account. The quantities purchased are often quite small. Discount warehouses or supermarkets require cash, with the buyer picking up the merchandise and taking it to the facility for use. It is inconvenient, but often the only way supplies can be obtained. A significant amount of purchasing is done with these operations.

Selection Criteria

The selection of suppliers should usually be based on (1) price, (2) quality of services rendered, and (3) quality of product. It is possible at times for one of these factors to completely dominate the decision, but often the best policy is to have a balanced approach. Sometimes these three criteria may have to be ignored and play no part in the selection, such as reciprocity selection and others, discussed later.

Price

One of the big mistakes inexperienced buyers make is that they overemphasize price in buying and end up neither saving money nor achieving other satisfactory results from their purchasing efforts. Price *is* an extremely important factor in the selection of purveyors, but should not be emphasized such that it overshadows the other two factors—quality of services rendered and quality of product. It is often said that "when one buys by price, the seller writes the menu."

As discussed in Chapter 3, a markup is applied to items as they pass through the hands of various marketing agents. Therefore, the elimination of agents should result in lower prices. Large volume buyers are often able to do this. Small buyers may not have this opportunity. However, by knowing the various markups agents take, one can at times find those who are willing to shade this a bit to get the business.

Sometimes buyers purchase services or quality not needed. Examples of purchasing unneeded quality have been given. Unneeded services can run the gamut from unneeded packaging to unneeded processing. What the good buyer must learn to do is to have true value perception and be able to do a value analysis as discussed in Chapter 3.

Quality of Services Rendered

A supplier can offer many services other than just providing a product, and often these services are such that they add value to a product. Another supplier may have the identical product at a slightly lower price, but because of the **quality of service** rendered by the higher priced supplier, it is advisable to purchase from the latter.

One of the most important of these supplier services is reliability of time of delivery and kind. Hospitality operations often work on a tight schedule between supply and service of items to patrons, and suppliers whose delivery times are unreliable are a risk that not only can be frustrating but cost money in patron satisfaction or lost sales. Some operations like to get their items early in the morning so they can be processed during the day. Other times are not convenient. Kind of delivery can also be important. Some suppliers deliver goods in more convenient ways to handle and check than others. Some may have better refrigerated trucks, so items arrive in better condition. Pallet loading may make it possible to check the goods and then move them promptly into storage with less handling (see Figure 4–1).

Figure 4-1
An example of a pallet properly loaded with goods for delivery.

Sometimes just the friendliness and cooperation of the driver can differentiate one delivery over another.

Buyers need to look at many other factors in the category of services rendered, such as time lag between order and delivery, billing, policy on returns, credit, ability to supply what is needed, and even having a sales representative with a nice personality who can be helpful in suggesting ways to improve menu items. Also, if they show buyers how to use new items, or even show how to prepare products, they add value to their service.

Some salespeople use laptop computers so orders can be quickly transferred to the home base for delivery. Suppliers can also have regularly scheduled tastings and also provide advice from experts on the utilization of products. All of these things add value to the products sold.

Buyers should be alert to suppliers who offer attractive services at the start but then slack off and actually provide poor quality service.

Credit.   Credit is a service supplied by the vendor in that it allows a facility to order merchandise and then use it without paying for it until later. It is often a risky business for the vendor because many hospitality ventures are undercapitalized, most of the equipment may be leased, and the operator has little or no resources to back up the enterprise. Thus, if the buyer cannot pay, the vendor has little to fall back on.

An operator should work to earn a good credit rating. A good rating can have many advantages, such as obtaining favorable credit terms and gaining the goodwill and trust of suppliers who will then vie for the business. Obtaining good credit can be helpful because it can have a significant effect on a company's operating capital. It is not uncommon for a food service to have trouble at times paying bills. If good credit is established, vendors are more likely to be flexible and work with the buyer during difficult times. Establishing good relations with credit managers and others in the supplier's business can help to establish good bonds. It is often wise to invite vendors to see the facility so they understand better the nature of the business and how it operates.

Payment plans made with suppliers should be respected. Food services usually expect immediate payment from their patrons—not a promise to pay later. In the same way, vendors expect buyers to meet payments when due, not at some future date. A vendor who sells a facility goods on the first of the month and gets payment on the 10th of the next month has financially supported the facility for 40 days. Paying later than the agreed 40 days is an imposition placed on the vendor. Buyers should remember that extending credit costs money, and should make every effort to meet their share of the bargain so as to reduce costs to the supplier.

Some suppliers offer discounts for purchases paid ahead of due dates. Some suppliers add a penalty payment if purchases are not paid for on time.

Credit arrangements can be time consuming; buyers should submit credit information as much as two weeks ahead. The more accurately, concisely, and quickly this is done, the more favorable will be the rapport between supplier and buyer. Establishing good credit with one or more purveyors often makes it much easier to get good credit with others. Often, for an account with a supplier to be activated, the following components must be completed by the food facility:

- A **credit application** must be completed with authorized signatures (see Figure 4–2).

- The buyer's bank account number and an authorization for the bank to provide financial data on a confidential basis is often needed.

- Records of past credit granted may be requested for review.

- A Personal Guarantee must be completed.[1]

- The authenticity of corporate officers must be validated by some governmental agency that can do so. Public corporations must submit annual financial statements to be analyzed.

- Other documents or information from financial institutions, commercial credit bureaus, and trade references may be needed.

A number of different types of credit are usually available. These often involve an agreement in which no credit is granted, to credit lasting 30 days or more. After the due date, there is usually a grace period giving a few days more for payment. If the goods are not paid for at the end of the grace period, the account is usually put **on hold.** When this happens, no more goods will be shipped until payment is made.

Cash on delivery (C.O.D.) is an arrangement in which merchandise cannot be left at the food service unless payment is received. While suppliers must use it to be sure of receiving payment, it has its disadvantages. Drivers are often held up because someone must be found who can pay. Also, after payment the driver is responsible for the safety of the money until it is turned over to the seller. It also involves more accounting work. It is easier to post one check per month than post one for each delivery.

Seven-day credit is an arrangement in which credit is extended for 7 days plus a 3-day grace period, making a bill due in 10 days. A *7-day recourse* arrangement is the same, except there is no 3-day grace period.

Biweekly credit arrangements require that all purchases are due and payable 14 days from date of invoice, and on hold after 17 days.

Twenty-one-day credit means all purchases are due and payable 21 days from date of invoice and on hold after 24 days. **Twenty-eight-day credit** is similar, with payment on hold starting 31 days after invoice date. Monthly arrangements mean that all purchases are due and payable on the tenth of the month following the purchases and go on hold on the 20th. In some cases, buyers may be able to get even more favorable credit terms.

Quality of Product

Quality of product purchased is closely correlated to quality of finished product. Don't expect a baker to make fine breads with pastry flour, nor tender pie crusts with bread flour. In one laboratory demonstration, two C grade tomatoes were opened

---

[1]This is primarily a goodwill document indicating the owners or managers of the property will stand behind it with their personal signatures. It is looked on as showing a sense of honor and good faith even to the point of being personally responsible. It can be a helpful document to the vendor in case the facility goes into Chapter 11 bankruptcy.

CREDIT APPLICATION

Account No. _____ Sales Rep. # _____ Terms Requested _____

TAX CERTIFICATE NUMBER _____

S
H Corporate Name _____
I
P (dba) Trade Name _____

T Address _____
O
City, State, Zip _____ Phone # _____

B
I Corporate Name _____
L
L (dba) Trade Name _____

T Address _____
O
City, State, Zip _____ Phone # _____

BUSINESS FACTS

Proprietorship [ ]   Corporation [ ]   Partnership [ ]

Length of time at present location _____
years

Person to contact _____
Name   Title

Does customer have existing accounts under another name? _____
(Name)   (Acct.#)

Monthly Gross Sales Volume $_____

Does Operator Own Premises?

Yes [ ]   No [ ]

Name, Address and Phone No. of Mortgagor

Is your Company responsible for purchases? _____
Or is foodservice consigned to another? _____
Name of Foodservice Consignes: _____
If Leasing, Name, and Address of Lessor

_____
_____
_____

_____
_____
_____

Complete the following information for all corporate officers, partners, or an individual proprietor.

Name and Title _____

Home Address _____

City, State, Zip _____

Home Phone No. _____

Social Security Number _____

Name and Title _____

Home Address _____

City, State, Zip _____

Home Phone No. _____

Social Security Number _____

Name and Title _____

Home Address _____

City, State, Zip _____

Home Phone No. _____

Social Security Number _____

Name and Title _____

Home Address _____

City, State, Zip _____

Home Phone No. _____

Social Security Number _____

BANKING

Bank Name _____

Adress _____

City, State, Zip _____

Account Number _____

Figure 4–2
Sample of a credit application.

for class inspection. One had good color and flavor but was broken up; however, the product would make an excellent sauce, soup, or other dish where broken tomatoes were needed. The other tomatoes were dark in color and poor in flavor and also broken; while they were lower in price, any cook would be challenged to make a satisfactory product from them.

As stated later in the discussion on specifications, the products purchased should be suited to the production need. Also, the highest quality sometimes does not make the most suitable product; a lesser quality is much better. The right item must be used to make the right product.

At times it may be much wiser to pay a higher price and purchase a higher quality than to purchase a lower priced item. This may be because a higher quality product makes a higher quality item. Another reason may be that the eventual yield as served is higher, so it makes sense to pay the higher price. One may get a very low price quoted on sea bass, but when the head, scales, skin, entrails, and other wastes are taken into consideration, the yield may cost more than the higher priced fillet sea bass (see Figure 4–3).

In this text, the loss in trimming or other preparation prior to obtaining the edible portion or as-served portion is often given. Buyers should watch these estimates to arrive at final product yields. While they are averages, they form a base for making much more reliable estimates on yields than plain guessing. The purpose of making yield tests has been discussed previously.

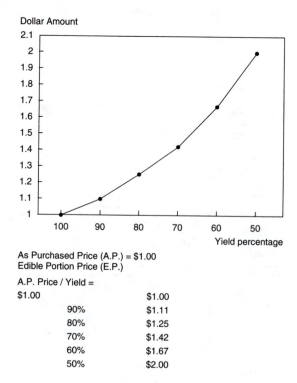

Dollar Amount

As Purchased Price (A.P.) = $1.00
Edible Portion Price (E.P.)

A.P. Price / Yield =

$1.00		$1.00
	90%	$1.11
	80%	$1.25
	70%	$1.42
	60%	$1.67
	50%	$2.00

Figure 4-3

Notice the increase in price as product yield decreases.

Objective Methods of Supplier Evaluation

The most used method of evaluating a supplier is to compare quality of service, quality of product, price, and perhaps some other factors. This is called the *categorical approach*.

Another method used by some is the cost–ratio method. This is a much more detailed value analysis procedure in which not only purchase cost, but other operating costs associated with use of the item are added together to get a price. Values such as supplier services, convenience, and others are grouped together and a ratio calculated. Another method is the *linear-averaging* or *weighted-point* method, which places a numerical value on price, quality, supplier services, and other factors. The value given reflects the relative importance of the factor. It gives a high degree of cost effectiveness. Both the cost–ratio and the linear-averaging methods are beyond the scope of this text.

Other Selection Factors

There are factors other than those mentioned that can influence supplier selection. These factors are often so compelling that they totally dominate and the buyer has little choice.

The most obvious is when a facility is located where there is a limited number of suppliers—perhaps only one. Of course, the buyer has no choice. It's that or nothing.

Another restriction can occur if a facility gets all of its supplies from a central commissary. In that case the buyer is put into the position of merely being an order giver naming quantities and little else. Someone else is making most of the purchase decisions.

Another factor that is not unusual is **reciprocity,** in which the facility is obligated to purchase from one supplier. This can occur when a facility is so obligated to a supplier that no other choice is feasible. For instance, a hospital receives each year a sizable grant from a local meat dealer who has an adequate product, service, and price. To change suppliers could mean the loss of the grant plus only a small gain.

While one may feel that supplier services, quality of product, and price are major factors in supplier selection, certain other factors can sometimes influence a selection decision. Visits should be made to the premises of suppliers to see how well they are set up to serve needs. Make note of sanitation. A supplier may have good service, quality, and price, but because of poor sanitation, a buyer under no circumstances would want items from that facility. How well is the place organized? In what condition are their trucks? Do they have refrigerated trucks for the delivery of perishable, chilled, or frozen items? Does the facility and management overall impress one as being an ongoing operation? Such factors may be important and assume a major place in making a final decision.

In some cases a supplier's financial position may be something a buyer is interested in. If the seller stores an item for a buyer and then goes bankrupt, the buyer becomes a creditor. A bond arrangement or insurance is one option for ensuring protection. In cases of bid awards, bonds are frequently posted.

A study by the Center for Advanced Purchasing Studies had buyers rank the importance of selection factors for sellers from 1 (highest) to 5 (lowest). Ranking from 1.17 to 1.60 were "accuracy in filling orders," "consistent quality level," "on-time delivery," "willingness to work together to resolve problems," "willingness to respond in a pinch," and "reasonable unit cost." From 2.00 to 2.28 were "reasonable lead times," "frequency of delivery," "technical competence," "lowest unit cost," and "reasonable payment policy." Ranking from 3.23 to 3.85 were "ability to single source (one-stop)," "training in product use," "willingness to break a case," and "provision of recipe ideas."

Buyer Sources

Buyers often identify themselves to a potential seller by calling in person on the facility or through some other communication media. One can also meet them and talk with them at trade conventions, shows, and other gatherings. Buyers frequently belong to a buying group in their field and sellers often attend these meetings. Trade magazines and other publications carry many seller advertisements. Often lists of sellers with a short description of some product they have for sale are grouped together and a buyer need only check a list to receive information on the product. One of the best ways to find a good supplier is to ask others about the suppliers they use. Another is to use the Yellow Pages.

Ethics in Purchasing

The problem of ethics in business is not restricted to the hospitality area. It has become so widespread in business and many professions today that schools of business and other professional disciplines are including courses on ethics in their curriculum offerings. In the past many professors never mentioned patterns of conduct to the students. Today many do so. When a buyer and vendor agree to a dishonest practice, it is called **collusion.**

High ethical standards are a requirement for satisfactory performance of the purchasing task. Most buyers are honest and adhere to a high standard of ethics, but unfortunately some are not. Most suppliers are basically honest, but because some few resort to questionable or illegitimate practices in their dealings, they, along with the dishonest buyers, make for ethical problems in the entire market. Unfortunately, we often hear only about the flagrant ethical violations. The wide number of honest suppliers and buyers who daily go about their business while practicing high ethical standards are forgotten.

Vendors use many ways to influence buyers—from a cup of coffee to a trip abroad. While plausibly legitimate, this can lead to overpurchasing. For example, a vendor offered luggage for quantity purchases of a gelatin dessert; investigation of the storeroom of one hospital that was purchasing from that vendor showed its storeroom had more than a 10-year supply of gelatin desserts. In this particular case, the nun doing the buying thought it was the perfect way to get some nice luggage for a number of the hospital's nuns. Usually, however, the matter is not one of innocence but one of downright collusion between seller and buyer.

Buyers are constantly tempted and they must know how to resist. Buyers who do not observe high ethics move frequently. They get a new job, but sooner or later they are discovered, are quietly discharged, and move on to another facility. Operations are often reluctant to persecute. It would be far better if they would, so the violators would become known and could no longer get positions. Operations should also refuse to recommend such violators for other positions. Buyers should, when a supplier acts in any illegitimate way, notify management and discontinue use of this supplier. This hastily corrects many of these problems.

Professional groups usually endorse a standard of ethics for its members to follow. This is true of the medical profession, law, clergy, and others. The National Restaurant Association has established a code of ethics for buyers in the foodservice profession. It is advisable that every operation set up its own code of ethics and prominently display it so all employees know its contents. A sample code of ethics appears later in this section (see Figure 4–4).

In addition to setting a code of ethics, a firm should send to vendors a statement of the policies and procedures that it will follow in purchasing. Such information is helpful in indicating to vendors the proper way to conduct affairs with that company. These policies and procedures should make it clear that all avenues for participation in the firm's purchasing program are open and that purchase awards will be made only on the basis of equality of product, service, and other factors important to the satisfactory function of the purchase program for that firm. They should also emphasize that gifts or other gratuities that would influence buying practices are not acceptable.

The buyer for a food service should realize that he or she has power, the power to give to purveyors the privilege of selling to the firm so that purveyor can make a profit and stay in business. This is a forceful wedge with which the buyer can force concessions and gain favors. However, buyers should understand that they hold a position of trust and should not use such power to benefit themselves but should use it wisely and fairly to the benefit of the company they represent. By observing proper conduct in conducting the affairs of purchasing, a buyer not only gains vendor approbation but also gains a favorable impression of what the firm they represent stands for and how it conducts its business.

Many inducements will be offered to buyers in order to get the business the firm has to offer. Some accounts can run into millions of dollars and so a vendor has a high stake in getting the business. They can afford to give high rewards to those that give them a big share of this business.

Here are some ways in which buyers reward vendors in payment for their favors:

- Giving them most of the firm's business for a group of purchases
- Agreeing to pay a higher price than what they could get from competitors for identical items
- Certifying delivery of a false amount
- Returning items but getting the credit paid to them
- Certifying invoices for which no delivery was made

- Be courteous at all times.
- Establish regular hours for salespersons to call and adhere to the schedule. See out-of-town salespersons at once, if convenient; prearranged appointments should have priority. See everyone but devote only the time needed to do business.
- Be fair. All purchase situations involve give and take. Keep a sense of humor.
- Think problems out. Use a rational approach; evaluate all factors; remember that buyers are largely industrial and not ultimate buyers.
- In dealing with competing vendors, do not play one against the other. Do not disclose confidential information and do not pass out information.
- Use your company's money and other assets as you would your own.
- Do not discuss business affairs out of the office.
- Set a high standard of conduct, and others will benefit from it.
- Never compromise your freedom of action as a buyer by accepting favors from vendors.

Figure 4-4
Sample Code of Ethics

- Accepting a lower quality than billed
- Selling things such as grease and garbage and pocketing the money.

The failure of vendors to comply with product specifications can be often detected at the receiving dock. Rigid inspection of all items should occur because at this point the goods often change ownership and the buyer is responsible once the invoice is signed accepting the goods. A common way of cheating is to deliver an item of a smaller size than ordered. A case of large eggs should weigh net 45 lb. A scale check at the receiving dock reveals a case of eggs being delivered weighs 49.5 pounds. Cardboard fillers and the case itself average 9 lb, so the net weight of the eggs is not 45 lb but 40.5 lb, the average weight of medium, not large, eggs. A gallon of ice cream should average 4.5 lb if it is not whipped to a foam over 100% of original liquid volume. By placing ice cream containers on a scale and getting the total weight and deducting the weight of packing, you can quickly ascertain if the vendor is selling a legitimate product. (Specifications requiring that ice cream be whipped to not more than an 80% volume give a better ice cream, so it is best that the ice cream weigh 5 lb 10 oz rather than 4.5 lb.) Putting a case of whiskey on the scales can quickly indicate if a bottle is missing. Buyers should use the scales consistently to check vendor performance.

As noted, purchasing is a responsibility of management but it is often delegated. However, this delegation does not relieve management from frequent checking to see that the purchase program is proceeding as it should. Management should go out on the receiving dock and receive items, noting the procedures used. It should also check records and even contact vendors to verify charges. Carefully check all practices in ordering, inventorying, and other actions that are a part of the program.

Detecting deviations is not easy and management needs to be constantly alert to possible discrepancies.

Buyers are often faced with the problem of whether they should allow their interest to supersede that of their company's. When it comes to things that deal solely with the function of purchasing and other company matters, the interests of the company are first. The matter of conflict of interest in company affairs largely concerns buyers becoming obligated to vendors because of favors rendered by vendors to the buyer. The buyer then acts not to promote the interest of the company but that of the vendor and himself or herself. This, as we have noted in the preceding discussion, is illegitimate and buyers should see that they do not fall into such a trap.

Figure 4–4 is a list of ethical principles the buyer of a food service should follow that was compiled by a student as a class assignment. They bear publishing.

The last principle is most important. Buyers are often invited to have a cup of coffee or even a meal with a vendor. This is legitimate if the vendor is doing so as an act of friendship and if the buyer is not giving up the right to make decisions free of any obligation for the courtesy. Often it is much easier to conduct a difficult problem of negotiation in an atmosphere other than the rigid atmosphere of an office. Buyers should see that they do not in any way lose their freedom to choose.

SPECIFICATIONS

A **specification** is a statement of all the characteristics a product must have to fill a purchase need. If such a need changes, then some part of the specification must be changed. Specifications serve as an anchor about which the purchasing function revolves. They are the heart of purchasing. Few goods or services should be purchased without a specification. If a buyer orders "10 Grade A, RTC broilers, 3.5 lb each," that is considered a specification; the kind of item and its class, amount, and size have been specified. Specifications should be stated in market language, and be as short as possible while covering all essential factors. They may be written or verbal.

Written specifications are used in the more formal types of buying such as bid buying or acceptance buying, but they may also be given to the suppliers with whom one deals orally so they have a written record of the products ordered. If a supplier has your specifications on hand, they need not be given a new set every time an order is placed. If any change must be made for a particular order, this can be done verbally. However, it is best to make any changes in writing if time allows and it is convenient.

Often day-to-day informal telephone orders are specified verbally, the buyer indicating the factors an item being ordered must possess. They may also be used in giving orders in person to a salesperson or when making a phone inquiry as to a product's availability, price, and so forth. However, even though verbal, some written notes will usually be used to make sure all the factors needed in an item are given. These notes can also serve as a record of the transactions. These verbal specifications will usually be very brief and serve merely as summary notes. Such notes should be retained to verify deliveries.

It is common for large companies to set up specifications for most of their product needs. Smaller companies may not do so as often. Without specifications, however, a buyer must depend on memory, something that is not infallible. If one's specifications are computerized, recall is simplified.

Kinds of Specifications

There are three kinds of specifications: (1) internal, (2) external, and (3) general.

Internal Specifications

Internal specifications are also called *menu specifications;* they are used solely within an operation, and are derived from menu offerings. They should be supported by information as to what an item should be for use, portion size, how items should be cooked, how they should appear on the plate, and how they should otherwise be handled. Cost calculations and price calculations may be included.

Internal specifications should give employees all the information needed to indicate what is required to provide a satisfactory product. These specifications can aid management control. Personnel should glean from them how management expects to please guests. Some internal product specifications are presented in Figure 4–5.

External Specifications

External specifications are often derived from internal product specifications but differ in that they list the factors needed in a product so vendors can quote on the right product and the facility can get what it needs. This text deals largely with external product specifications, and from now on the term *specification* is used to

---

MENU (INTERNAL) SPECIFICATION

Menu Items: T-bone steak, frozen, 1 in. tail, 3/4 in. thick, No. 261. Order as IMPS 1173A, 1 in. tail, 14 oz each +– 1/2 oz, top choice. Minium stock level 80 steaks, maxium 160.

Broil to order: garnish with 1/8 oz watercress, vegetable du jour, potato choice on 10 in. platter; steak marker (rare, medium, well done) inserted. Rare, very red; medium, traces of pink throughout; well done, no pink at all. Thaw 24 hours prior to service in walk-in; hold no thawed steak over 2 days.

Figure 4-5
An example of an internal product specification for operational control.

mean the external product specification. If a reference is made to an internal or general specification, the full term will be used.

General Specifications

General specifications define business factors and conditions that apply to the overall purchasing program, such as times of delivery, delivery procedures, credit and bill payment, submission of price quotations, etc. They often head up a list of specifications for items (see Figure 4–6). However, they may be written and presented separately along with a number of individual specifications. At other times,

---

INVITATION, BID, AND AWARD

Issued by	Address	Date _____
Manager	1122 Supply Street	
Ever-ready Restaurant	Happy Haven, Maryland	

Sealed bids in duplicate will be received at the above office until _____ _____, 19 ____ for the items and in the quantities indicted for delivery on the dates indicated. Quantities indicated are approximate and may be reduced on instruction of the buyer.

All items to be officially identified by the U.S. Department of Agriculture for class and quality. Costs of such service to be borne by vendor.

Items	Supplies	Quantity	Unit	Unit Price	Amount
1.	Chicken, fresh chilled fryer, 2-1/2 - 3 lb, ready-to-cook-U.S. Grade A	500	lb		
	To be delivered_ _ _ _ _ _ _ _ _				
2.	Chicken, fresh chilled fowl 3-1/2 - 4lb, ready-to-cook, U.S. Grade B	100	lb		
	To be delivered_ _ _ _ _ _ _ _ _				
3.	Turkey, frozen, Young Tom 20-22 lb, ready-to-cook, U.S. Grade A	100	lb		
	To be delivered_ _ _ _ _ _ _ _ _				
4.	Ducks, frozen roaster duckling, 5-5-1/2 lb, ready-to-cook, U.S. Grade A	50	lb		
	To be delivered_ _ _ _ _ _ _ _ _				

Vendor _____

Figure 4-6
A sample of general specifications is listed at the top section of this invitation to bid.

arrangements such as those included in general specifications may be submitted orally with the understanding that they apply whenever orders are placed.

Advantages of Specifications

Experience has shown that when specifications are used these results are reaped:

1. Costs are lowered.
2. Purchasing is better organized.
3. Product quality is improved.
4. Fewer misunderstandings occur between buyer and seller; sellers understand better what is acceptable and this lowers returns.
5. They serve as a written record of what is wanted.
6. They aid in negotiation and in obtaining competitive pricing and service.
7. They save time in many ways, such as in checking substitutes.
8. They aid employees in making judgment calls on problems in shipments.
9. They allow for better verification that what has been ordered has been delivered.
10. They limit stock-outs (running out of items).
11. They give better management control.
12. They give better satisfaction.

Who Writes Specifications?

Management is responsible for seeing that specifications are written and often writes them. All employees, however, from executive staff to hourly paid employees, should be involved. Feedback from everyone is needed and can be meaningful, since employees are on the "firing line" and see the results of purchasing.

Specifications used by others can be helpful in setting up specifications, but generally these should be used as models rather than used as is, because the needs of different facilities are seldom exactly the same. Assistance in writing specifications may be obtained from manufacturers, processors, salespersons, or trade associations. State and federal agencies often have specifications that can be used as models. They are often done by authorities who know the product in depth and can serve as reminders of factors that might be omitted.

It is management's responsibility to see that the proper product, of the proper quality and cost, is specified. The production department should be brought in to advise on kind of products needed, their quality, and other factors required to produce satisfactory results. Buyers may often write the final specification and have it approved by management and production. Sellers can advise in the writing of specifications as to what is available, quality, and cost. Sometimes they may make helpful suggestions to improve a specification.

Experimental specifications may be written and improved on later. It is necessary to constantly review specifications to see that they meet market conditions or take advantage of more favorable prices, products, or other factors.

Sometimes specifications may be written by a consultant or other outside person or agency. If so, such an outsider should be thoroughly familiar with the needs of the operation.

The Specification Form

Specifications can be set up in many forms, but no matter how they are written, all must include much the same information. Six items usually must be named in a specification:

1. Item's name
2. Quantity desired
3. Quality desired, brand, or other details needed to get the right quality, etc.
4. The form in which the item will come
5. The unit on which the price will be based
6. Miscellaneous factors that must be in the specification to ensure that the right product is obtained (see Figure 4–7).

Specification Sheet Listing Area of Purchase:

1. Trade or Common Name: _____

2. Amount to be purchased for 100: _____

3. Quality factor (grade/brand/description): _____
   _____
   _____

4. Packaging (weight/unit of purchase): _____
   _____
   _____

5. Unit on which prices are quoted: _____

6. Specific factors needed to obtain exact item: _____
   _____
   _____
   _____

Miscellaneous Remarks and Information: _____
_____
_____
_____
_____
_____
_____
_____
_____

Figure 4-7
A form that could be used for specification formulation.

Name

Shakespeare once asked, "What's in a name? A rose by any other name would smell as sweet." In buying, using the right name means a lot. It often determines exactly what an item is and differentiates it from others. Often using the right name results in getting the right product and avoids confusion. Sometimes product names vary from region to region, and buyers should learn what the right name is in the region. Thus, a "hip" steak in the west would mean a sirloin steak elsewhere. "Dover sole" in Seattle might mean the true Dover sole from England or a local product that closely resembles it in quality.

Although we have gone a long way toward establishing names that precisely identify a product, we still have a way to go, and buyers need to use names carefully to indicate exactly what is wanted. Be sure the name used exactly indicates the product. Perhaps at times some description may be necessary to set up the proper definition.

Government Names.   The government has established what are called Standards of Identity in which products carrying specific names are precisely defined, and these have been accepted by courts as legal descriptions of the product. As an example, the Standards of Identity state that singlefold vanilla flavoring must contain 13.35 oz of vanilla beans and 1 oz of vanillin per gallon. Or, when the word "cheese" is used in a specification, the product must on a moist basis be 51% or more of milk fat plus other things or it cannot be called cheese.

The government **Institutional Meat Purchase Specifications (IMPS)** precisely define meat cuts, giving each an identification number. This number means a lot along with the proper cut name. Thus, a No. 109 beef rib means an oven-ready rib roast with 7 ribs, cut and tied in a specific way. A buyer can put in a specification this name and number of a cut and know that the product should conform to the *legal* description of the IMPS.

There are other ways in which governmental names for products help identification for specification use.

Trade Names.   The market also uses many names that precisely define what a product must be. Thus, the terms "No. 10" or "No. 2" can means cans of specific size and nothing else. The words "60% patent flour" mean a flour made of only the first 60% of the flour siftings taken in milling. A No. 5 pea is a pea of a specific size. The term "close trimmed" means lettuce or cabbage with no more than four wrapper leaves. Using such terms gives more accuracy in naming what is wanted and also simplifies the writing of specifications. There are thousands of these and buyers need to know them if they are to do an adequate job in purchasing.

The **UPC (Universal Product Code)** system is a method of using 12 numbers to indicate a product and the producer of the product. Vertical lines of different thickness, and depth of print, plus a special arrangement of these lines indicate these numbers and make it possible for machines to read the number automatically and thus tell exactly what the product is. The UPC is proving to be useful in eliminating confusion over what food names mean. It is also proving to be helpful in identifying products on inventory, and so forth. (see Figure 4–8).

Figure 4-8
The vertical lines on this label are what the laser scanner reads. (Courtesy of ComSource™ Independent Foodservice Companies, Inc.)

Quantity Wanted

A specification needs a statement to indicate how much is wanted. Usually this is a numerical amount plus the kind of package or unit the item will be delivered in. Thus, a specification may read "6 cases No. 10's." Such a description makes it unnecessary to add in the specification both listings 4 (the form in which the product will come) and 5 (the unit on which the price will be based) since the term "cases of No. 10's" covers both. The product must arrive in 6 individual cases of 6 No. 10 cans in each case. However, if additional information is needed in either of a specification, it should be added at the proper place, such as "The six cases should be tightly wrapped together by 1″ steel bands" or, in 4, "Price should be based on price per dozen cans." However, if the quantity desired in a specification is stated as 125 lb, then it may be necessary to include additional information in items 4 and 5 to precisely inform sellers what is expected as to form of delivery and unit of price. Thus, the form might be 25-lb boxes, so 5 boxes will be delivered to make the 125 lb, and the unit on which the price may in this case be based will be per 25-lb box and not per lb.

Ways to calculate quantities needed are discussed later in this chapter.

Quality

The quality of product needed is based on what is needed to give a satisfactory product. Buyers who specify only the best are often wasting money and may not be getting an item that will in certain cases produce the best product. Why purchase choice grade sirloins and then grind them up for hamburger? A lower grade meat would make a more flavorful hamburger. Why purchase grade A chickens to make a chicken soup stock, when backs will do as well and cost much less? Items of adequate quality are needed to make quality menu items, but not always the highest grade and most costly.

Brand or Grade?   Brands can ensure quality. They are set to give a certain quality and buyers can usually assume that by specifying brand, they will get the quality desired. A brand may be purchased because patrons recognize its standard of quality—A-1 sauce, for instance. Buyers should understand that brands need meet only the brand owner's standard and do not conform to standard classifications such as federal grades.

The grading of many foods is the job required of a number of agencies proscribed by the federal government, largely under the Agriculture Marketing Act, enacted to ensure that a consistent standard of quality would be maintained in many products. They are meant to help both buyers and sellers in negotiating sales and in giving stability to the market.

Different standards must be used to determine the quality or grade of different foods. Thus, meat usually is graded on the basis of quality of flesh, marbling, age, and other factors, and butter on flavor, color, salt, texture, and so forth.

Many foods today are not graded, and this sometimes challenges buyers in naming the quality of product desired. Often, buyers will resort to brands. When there is no brand or grade, an item's quality description can be involved and complex for buyers.

Federal grades may be certified and given a **certificate of grade.** Each certificate carries its own number, and packages in this certified amount, invoices, and other papers relating to shipment can be stamped with this number to indicate that the goods have been certified as to grade. It is often possible for buyers to request certification and get a copy.

Just because a food carries a federal or other grade does not mean the food is of that grade upon delivery. The grade may change after grading, although the label on the food says it is of a different grade. Eggs may stand in the hot sun and drop a grade as a result. A frozen or fresh product may do the same. This is why buyers put in their general specifications, "The grade of the item named in the specification should be that upon delivery." Using acceptance buying, explained in Chapter 3, is one way of seeing that graded products are the grade named, but even then a delay in delivery can mean a change of grade in some foods.

The Form in Which the Product Will Come

Purveyors often need to know in what form the product is to be delivered. If canned grade B half peaches in light syrup are ordered, the purveyor wants to know what size can is ordered, and what the count of peach halves is per can. It is often necessary to specify the size of the product wanted. Thus, a buyer wants 12-lb salmon, plus or minus a half pound, because such a fish slices best into salmon steaks, or may specify 8-oz. tenderloin steaks (± 0.5 oz). A 64-count (actually now 32 per carton) grapefruit is a good size unit to cut into half-grapefruit portions.

When the unit of delivery is a case, it is sometimes highly desirable to specify the minimum weight per case. Thus, fresh spinach delivered in bushel hampers should be specified as containing not less than 18 lb of spinach each. A hamper of spinach in which the spinach is lightly tossed to make it appear full may only be 14 lb; this short weight just adds to the cost of the product if paid for by the hamper.

Packaging customs and product sizes vary considerably in different markets. A carton of Texas citrus fruit is 7/10 bushel, but a carton of Florida or California–Arizona citrus fruit is 4/5 bushel. A California lug is of a different size than other lugs. What may be called a large size on one market is called medium or even small on another. Buyers need to know what the standards for sizing and packaging are in their own markets so as to properly interpret needs and figure out costs.

The Unit on Which the Price Will Be Based

Purveyors will want to know on what unit price will be based: case, sack, barrel, pound, hamper, and so forth. If this is made clear in the specification, the danger of misunderstandings is reduced.

Buyers want to know what the price is based on to figure out costs. Thus, a facility may want to run a special on strawberry shortcakes during the peak of the strawberry season, but might want to know what the price might be before setting up its publicity. Or, a buyer might want to know what the price of a No. 180 boneless short cut strip loin is to see if the printed menu price of the steak is adequate to cover the cost.

Price decisions are easier when items are purchased in portion sizes. Thus, getting a price on 10-oz T-bone steaks (IMPS No. 1174A) makes it easy for a buyer to figure out what a menu price should be or whether the price quoted is suitable for the price on the printed menu.

Miscellaneous

Most specifications need particular information specific to the item being ordered, and this category of miscellaneous items can be used to add such details. The miscellaneous information may ensure that the right product is secured.

The information carried in this section may be quite varied. The following items might be considered miscellaneous:

Geographical area of production: Oregon Bluelake string beans, Florida limes, Hawaiian pineapple, Colombian coffee, Sea Island cotton, or Louisiana rice might have desirable quality attributes.

Feed: Corn-fed or grass-fed steers, Smithfield or Iowa hams, milk-fed chickens, and Snake River trout have special flavors because of the feed.

Variety: Gravenstein apples are excellent for applesauce but too soft for baking. Telephone peas freeze well but do not can well. Marshall strawberries freeze better than other varieties.

Type: Long-cut or short-cut string beans, skinned or unskinned hams, fresh-chilled or frozen poultry, and so forth.

Style: Sticks, slices, or tidbits of pineapple; cream-style or whole-kernel corn may be desired to suit a production need.

Weave: Terry, huckaback, cut pile, or serge weaves make a lot of difference in a fabric.

Count or portion size: Olives per gallon, a 4-oz veal cutlet not over or under 1/4 oz, 83 count oranges per case, or a 5-oz baking potato.

Syrup density: Water, light, medium, heavy, or extra-heavy syrup pack.

Packing medium: Syrup, sugar, juice, or water; dry or wet pack for shrimp or corn; brine or dry pack for cured meats, and so forth.

Concentration or specific gravity: Used mostly for tomato products.

Percent mixture: Percent fat in ground meat, pork, or cereal in sausage; various fruits in fruit cocktail; blend in Bourbon; type fibers in a fiber or yarn.

Weight tolerance or fill: Struck full or rounded full on bushel baskets; fill equal to facing in cherries, tomatoes, and peaches; drained weight for canned products; pounds per case of eggs; maximum and minimum weight for meat cuts; count in container, and so on.

Age: Terms such as yearling steers, tree-ripened apricots, and young turkeys.

Cut: Side, quarter, or primal cut, portioned or oven-ready for meats; bias for fabric; sliced, diced, julienne, or short cut for canned items.

Cutting style: Chicago cut for cattle, Boston cut pork shoulder.

Type processing: Kiln cure for dishes; annealing for hardening glasses; rendered for lard, dry salt cure in meat.

Condition upon receipt: Hard frozen, fresh, or interior temperature 40°F.

Pure or imitation: Pure jam or jelly, imitation vanilla.

Type flavor or other: Sweetened or unsweetened, salt-free.

Sex: Cow, steer, capon.

Performance: Btus/gal, moisture absorption power for a linen towel.

Trim: Close clipped, well trimmed; 1/2 in. fat on large cuts of meats and 1/4 in. on smaller ones.

Yield: Orange juice yield of 4/5-bushel carton not less than 2 1/4 gal; minimum yield AP to EP; minimum wear (washings per sheet).

Form: Whole, cut, sliced, molded.

Aging or ripeness: Cheese age; wine vintage; pinks for tomatoes; hard ripe (bananas); aged 14 days in Cryovac (for beef).

THE STEPS IN PURCHASING

Purchasing is a process requiring that certain actions be performed to accomplish it satisfactorily. While every purchase may not require the same actions, they will usually follow a common pattern. Some may be simple at one time and complex at another. It depends on the product, the market, and other conditions at the time the purchase is made. These steps in purchasing are as follows:

1. Ascertaining a need
2. Ascertaining quantity

3. Ascertaining quality
4. Searching the market
5. Ordering and negotiating the purchase
6. Receiving
7. Storing
8. Issuing
9. Evaluating how well the steps were performed

In this chapter only the first four steps are discussed; the others are examined in future chapters.

Ascertaining a Need

As noted, needs are decided primarily by patrons. Menus should reflect patrons' wants, and from this many needs will arise. Production of these menu items gives rise to other needs such as equipment, dishwashing compound, and paper goods.

Management and production will also decide needs. Management may influence needs by selecting menu items, specifying cost and desire for profit, and other considerations. Production decides needs because it is charged with the responsibility of producing the menu items. Production must not be bypassed in deciding a need, especially quality of product. A buyer must have a very good reason for overruling production. In such override situations, both management and production should be informed and told the reason. Service can influence a need because of some service requirement. A buyer must weigh these influences and decide what on the market will best satisfy it. Figure 4–9 shows this relationship between entities and the steps in purchasing.

A rule in purchasing is "Buy for the production need." Specific items are needed to produce desired results in food production. Just *any* flour won't work for many things. A good quality bread flour is needed to make good rolls and bread. An all-purpose or pastry flour lacks this ability. Trying, however, to make a good pie dough using bread flour is challenging. A soft wheat pastry flour is needed. To give good deep-frying results, one type of shortening is needed, another type is needed for cakes and cookies, and yet another for common cooking purposes.

The highest quality product is often not produced from the highest priced item; in fact, poor quality may result just because it was. Fowl (old discarded laying hens) make a more flavorful chicken pie than more expensive tender broilers. Why purchase whole pecan meats when the bakeshop takes them and chops them up for pecan rolls? Fancy canned tomatoes are firm and whole; adding them to a sauce or soup makes it necessary for the cook to use extra labor in breaking them up so they suit the need. Purchasing a lower cost, lower grade of broken tomatoes better does the job; also, they are riper and have a better tomato flavor.

A buyer should be constantly exploring the market to see if better or lower priced products are available to meet needs. New products are constantly arriving on the market and old ones are being changed that may make it possible to get a

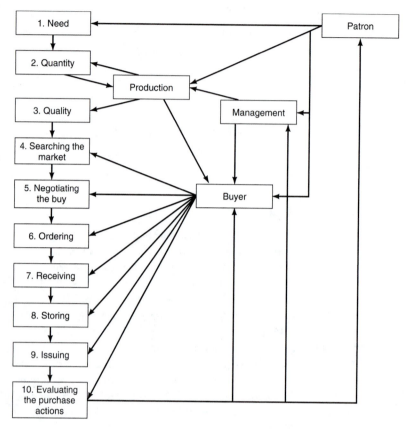

Figure 4-9
Chart of purchasing steps.

better product for the production need at a lower cost. The production department should be willing to try out new products to test their suitability.

Requisitioning

A common way for departments in an operation to let buyers know their needs is to use what is called a **requisition,** which is a list of items one wants (see Figure 4–10). These are sent to the purchasing department or storerooms to be filled. Blank copies of requisitions should be kept under control by those authorized to use them. They should be numbered so a record can be kept of them.

Requisitions are usually made out in duplicate, one copy being retained with the other sent to the storeroom or purchasing department. In some operations, three and even more copies must be made out, depending on whether accounting, receiving, or other departments require a copy. The ordering person signs the requisition, and often some supervisor countersigns it before it is sent to be filled. It is the responsibility

REQUISITION

No.

Date: _____

Location: _____

Order by: _____ Date: _____

Issued by: _____ Date: _____

☐ Kitchen

☐ Wine

☐ Store Room

ITEM	UNIT	ORDER	ISSUED	PRICE	EXTENSION

Authorized Signatures

TOTAL ☐

Figure 4-10
Example of a requisition form.

of the countersigner to see that the proper item is ordered, that it is needed, and that it is received and used properly. Some employees like to have "plenty" on hand and often tend to overorder, a practice called *sandbagging* in kitchen vernacular.

If an item ordered from the storeroom is not in stock, the storeroom must in turn notify the buyer of the need. Requisitions sent directly to the buyer for ordering may be called purchase requisitions and a different form may be used. Figure 4–11 depicts the information a purchase requisition might have.

Ascertaining Quantity

Calculating the quantity to purchase to produce a specific number of portions can be a challenge that is often more easily solved by looking into a crystal ball than trying to make a calculated estimate. Time and again the most knowledgeable and able person will be wrong. However, resorting to ordering "plenty just to be sure" can lead to added cost and oversupply. Even though faulty, it is best to use the information available and try to come up with a quantity as close to the production need as possible.

Foods lose weight in storage, by spoilage, preparation, cooking, carving, or serving. Knowing what these losses are is essential when calculating the correct quantity needed. Yields on meats are especially difficult. If cubed steaks are to be cut from rounds and hind quarters are purchased, the round averages only a certain percent of the hind quarter, and after trimming and cutting, only a small portion of the quarter is used. The yield of the resulting steaks is hard to calculate, and buyers often estimate for lack of better information.

No.		Date		Department	
Item	Quantity		Price	Total	Other information

Total _____

Orderer _____

Approved _____

Filled or ordered by _____

Figure 4-11
Example of a purchase requisition.

The quantity to purchase can be calculated in a number of ways; some are simple while others are quite complex. A method that is good for some facilities might not be helpful for others. No facility uses just one of the many ways in which quantity needs are calculated; usually a number are combined.

Minimum/Maximum Order or ROP and Par Level

Many facilities use the minimum/maximum or reorder point, and par level method to calculate quantities to order. This method is helpful in indicating when and how much to order. It is a simple system and lends itself to the purchase of almost any item.

Minimum level is the least number of items that should be in stock at any one time. The **maximum level** or **par stock** is the highest number of items that should be in storage at any time. Figure 4–12 shows how one facility listed items and then wrote in par stock levels. The amount of goods on hand is inventoried and this amount is put down under "INV." The amount to order is the par minus the inventory amount. In the case of puff paste, the amount on inventory is two cases, par is three cases, so one is ordered; for croissant dough, a half case is on hand so the order is for four cases. In each case, the stock is brought up to a par or maximum level.

The minimum stock level is often called the **reorder point (ROP).** This minimum level must be set so enough stock is on hand to last between the time of order and the time of delivery, plus an added safety factor. This is done by establishing par levels or maximum stock levels, giving due consideration to usage rate and lead time from time of ordering to delivery. Usage time may be calculated in units per day, per week, per month, or any group of days.

As an example of how this might work, suppose an operation uses fried potatoes at an average rate of four cases per day. It takes three days after an order is

COMPANY		CONTRACT WORKSHEET BY LINE			RUN 02/18/92 AT 16:35:48 PAGE: 2						
CONTRACT #			EFF DATE: 3/01/92	END DATE: 3/31/92							

ITEM	DESCRIPTION PACK/SIZE BRAND	PAR	INV/ORD	INV/ORD	INV/ORD	INV/ORD	INV/ORD	INV/ORD	INV/ORD	INV/ORD	INV/ORD
202838-9	DOUGH PUFF PASTRYHEETS 10x15(20/12 OZ PENNANT	3cs	2 1								
206175-2	CROISSANT DOUGH BUTTER 20/12 OZ RICH	4cs	1/2 4								
206387-3	ENGLISH MUFFINS (H) 120/2.25 OZ THOMAS	3cs	1 2								
216039-8	BLUEBERRIES IQF CULTIVATED 6/12 CT PACKER	1cs	1 0								
216123-0	STRAWBERRIES SLICED CALIF 4+1 1/30 # SIMPLOT	30#	31 0								
262913-7	TORTILLAS FLOUR 12" H.S. 6/6 1/2 # CHIQUITA	3cs	2 1cs								
262930-1	TORTILLAS FLOUR 6" H.S. 1/24 DOZ CHIQUITA	4cs	2 2cs								
270662-0	POTATOES CURLY Q 1/4 CUT 4/6 # TATERBOY	50#	20# 2cs								

Figure 4-12

Example of ROP and par level to order goods. ("INV" is the amount on inventory and "ORD" is the amount to order.)

placed to get the order, or when the order is placed the operation will use 12 cases before the new delivery is made. Management also decides it wants two additional days or 8 cases as a safety factor. Thus, 20 (12 + 8) cases is the minimum stock !evel or ROP. Management also sets a maximum or par stock limit of 40 cases. The number of cases that must be purchased at ROP is 20. The calculation is as follows:

Maximum or par stock level	40
Delivery time 3 days times 4 cases per day	= 12
8 cases safety factor	+8
Minimum stock level or ROP	−20
Amount to order (maximum stock level or par)	20

A computer can signal ROP and do the necessary calculations, indicating how much to order. All one need do is feed the proper information into the computer. If a perpetual inventory is maintained in the computer, the amount on hand can be quickly ascertained and compared against the ROP.

Storeroom clerks often check stock levels to see when the ROP is reached. If an inventory card is maintained in front of the stock, a count is not needed because the card records stock coming in and stock removed so the amount on hand is always tallied (see Figure 4–13).

Tables or Percentage Yields

Often buyers refer to tables to ascertain how much to order. Many of these have been compiled for various foods and are the results of years of experience and testing. In this text you will frequently find such a table giving the amount to purchase for 100 portions. Or, in many chapters, a **yield percentage**—either EP (edible portion) or AS (as-served)—will be given. Thus, a buyer is given the information that during the

ITEM					STORAGE AREA			NUMBER
Date	Amount				Unit	Price	Comments	Initials
	Received	Issued	Returned	Balance				

Figure 4-13
Example of an inventory card.

week 350 10-oz top sirloin steaks will be needed, and the facility buys No. 183 trimmed and boneless sirloins averaging 14 lb, of which 54% cuts into top sirloin steaks. The calculation is 350 × 10 oz = 3,500 oz of steaks are needed or = 219 lb, so 219/0.54 = 406 lb. Since each sirloin equals 14 lb, 406 lb/14 lb = 29 No. 183 sirloins are needed.

In this example only the actual amounts needed are being ordered. It was shown earlier how such amounts less amounts on hand plus a safety factor and an allowance for delivery time can change these figures.

Yield Tests

Facilities often run **yield tests** to see how much is obtained of an item from its aspurchased (AP) state to either its EP or AS state. Thus, on a number of such tests a certain size of a variety of Florida orange yields in juice AS on the average 33% of its AP weight. (Later we show, using this information, how the calculation is made to obtain a certain number of orders of juice.) Figure 4–14 shows a meat-cutting test. Of the original 102 lb of No. 103 ribs purchased, 57 lb of oven-ready No. 109 ribs are obtained, and 44 lb of other items; hence, there is a 1-lb shrinkage. Information such as this can be helpful to buyers in predicting quantities needed. Normally, we say that a pound of No. 109 rib must be purchased per portion, so if the buyer had to purchase enough for 100 orders, this order would have to be 100 lb, which means, if the ribs average 21 lb each, 5 ribs.

Standardized Recipes

A standardized recipe gives a known quantity of known quality items and thus is a good base on which to establish amounts needed. If a file of recipes is put into the computer and the computer is programmed properly, the computer can calculate the

Test Amount 3 Full (No. 103) ribs	@ $1.80/lb	$183.60
Yield:		
Roast-ready rib (No. 109)	57 lb @ $2.75/lb	$156.75
Short ribs (No. 123)	15 lb @ 1.85/lb	97.75
Cube steak (No. 1100)	1 lb @ 1.95/lb	1.95
Trim meat	11 lb @ 1.40/lb	$ 15.40
Bone	9 lb @ 0.10/lb	0.90
Fat	8 lb @ 0.05/lb	0.40
Total value if purchase in this state		$203.15
Total cost		
Butchering labor 42 min @ $8/hr	$ 5.60	
Unbutchered meat cost	183.60	
Total cost		$189.20
Saving in purchasing full ribs		$ 13.95

Figure 4-14

Meat-cutting test that will determine the yield of oven-ready ribs (#109) from full ribs (#103).

amount needed for a varying number of orders. It can even translate quantities given in the recipe AS or EP into AP, so the buyer knows how much to purchase.

If the computer is told which recipes are used and given a forecast of how many portions of each recipe are needed, it can come up very quickly with a consolidated list of ingredients required. It can also separate ingredients that should be in stock in the kitchen, those available from stores, and those that have to be ordered. Chapter 6 discusses how a computer can compile such information.

Portion Size Quantities

Many calculations of amounts to purchase are quite simple to make. Ordering by the portion is very easy. If 10-oz portion steaks are served, all the buyer has to do is to order the number of 10-oz steaks needed. Or, if a facility serves two 2-oz franks per order and 80 orders are needed, 160 franks are needed times 2 oz or 320 oz or 20 lb. If 60 8-oz portions of canned soup are required, and the soup is purchased in cases of 12 46-oz cans (net), the need is 60 portions × 8 oz = 480 oz/46 oz or 10.4 cans, so the buyer will purchase 1 case of 12 No. 46 oz cans.

Often, the portions obtained from certain size purchase units are so standard that buying needs can be quickly calculated. Thus, buyers know that canned vegetables packed in liquid are about 2/3 of the total can contents, so a No. 10 can containing 106 oz net of, say, canned string beans will yield 106 oz × 0.67 = 71 oz, and since a portion of vegetables equals about 3 oz, a No. 10 can yields from 20 to 25 portions depending on its drained yield. Fruits that come by can counts make yield calculations simple. If a case of 6 No. 10 can half pears is ordered, and a count of 30 to 40 is specified, a buyer knows that approximately 210 pear halves will be received (6 cans × 35 = 210)—each 30 to 40 count can averages 35 pear halves.

AP, EP, and AS Calculations

As previously noted, buyers must often translate quantities needed from the (1) as-served (AS) state to an (2) edible portion (EP) or (3) as-purchased (AP) state or vice versa. There is little difficulty if you are working with actual amounts. Thus, if one pares 100 lb of potatoes and has a 25-lb loss, the EP yield is 75 lb (100 − 25 = 75). The calculation is more difficult if you must use percent of change, but is also merely a matter of arithmetic if you follow the rules.

If you use percents, you must know the total portions needed, the portion size, and the percent of change in yield between the two states being compared. Follow these steps:

1. Find the total amount served by multiplying number of portions by portion size.

2. Divide the result by yield percent.

3. Reduce the result into purchase or requisition from stock units.

Thus, 6-oz cube steak EP is desired to fry for a luncheon of 120 covers. Boneless round with shank and rump off (IMPS 165) is used; the rounds average 50 lb. The steak yield from them is 89%. The calculation is:

1. 120 portions × 6-oz portion = 720 oz AS

2. 720 oz/0.89 (yield) = 809 oz required AP

3. 809 oz/16 oz/lb = 50.56; the buyer would buy a round over 50 lb

Note that to make the calculation you must know the yield percentage. If instead, the percent loss is known, then to get the yield percentage, you must deduct this percent loss from 100% to arrive at the yield percent. Thus, if 100 3-oz portions of cooked asparagus are desired and the preparation loss from AP to AS is 49%, then 100% − 49% = 51% and the calculation is:

1. 100 portions × 3 oz = 300 oz

2. 300 oz/0.51 (yield) = 588 oz needed AP

3. 588 oz/16 oz = 36.76 lb needed AP

The two examples just given converted amount needed to serve (AS) to amount to purchase (AP). The calculation is the same if one wants to go from EP to AP or AS to EP.

As an illustration of EP to AP, consider this example. Forty luncheon-size crab salads are needed. Each salad requires 3 oz of chopped lettuce. The preparation waste is 25%. How many pounds of lettuce must be requisitioned? First, the yield percent is 100% − 25% = 75%. Then, 40 portions × 3 oz = 120 oz and 120/0.75 = 160 oz or 10 lb (160/16 = 10). As an illustration of AS to EP: 100 3-oz portions of shrimp cocktail must be prepared and EP frozen, raw, peeled, and deveined shrimp will be boiled for this with a preparation loss of 50%. The yield percent is 100% − 50% = 50%. Then, 100 portions × 3 oz = 300 oz of cooked shrimp needed and 300 oz/0.50 = 600 oz EP, which divided by 16 oz gives 37.5 lb. Since the shrimp come in six 5-lb frozen packages per case, the buyer will have to purchase two cases unless the seller will break a case.

What if there is an increase instead of a loss in yield? Is the calculation method different? No. Thus, if a dormitory system is to serve 8,500 students baked beans for lunch, the portion is 8 oz, and there is a 225% yield in soaking and cooking the dried beans, how many pounds of dried beans must the warehouse plan to issue? The calculation is 8,500 × 8 oz = 68,000 oz, and 68,000/2.25 = 30,222 oz of dried beans needed, which divided by 16 equals 1,889 lb. The buyer needs 19 100-lb bags of dried navy beans in stock.

What if there's an increase in yield and then a loss? Does this make a difference in the calculation method? Again, no. Calculate the percent yield and go on as usual. Thus, a menu forecasts a need for 50 4-oz breaded fried scallops for luncheon. There is a 25% increase in breading and then a 40% shrink in deep frying— thus a gain and a loss. Calculate the final percent yield first and then go on. Thus, 100% + 25% = 125% and 125% − 40% = 85% final yield. The calculation is 50 portions × 4 oz = 200 oz needed to serve, and 200 oz/0.85 = 235 oz needed of raw EP scallops, which divided by 16 oz indicates about 15 lb are needed (235/16 = 14.7).

Economic Order Quantity

The **economic order quantity (EOQ)** is a composite calculation considering order cost, usage, item cost, and storage cost. It is used to calculate either the most economical dollar amount or the most economical number of units to order. It is suitable for use for items that are stored for some time; fresh or perishable items should be ordered by different means. It is also best used for calculating large quantities; it may not be useful for small units which usually order in small amounts. Because of this, the concept of EOQ is presented in appendix C.

Ascertaining Quality

Normally we think of quality on a scale of highest to lowest, meaning the best to poorest in attributes (standards) we think something should possess for its intended use. This is how we use the term here. As noted in previous discussions, the market's highest quality may not be the best for the intended use. Prime grade beef is of highest quality according to standards established for beef, but it is not of highest quality for making hamburger. Standard or even Commercial grades, federal 4th and 5th grades, are much better for this purpose. Although they lack tenderness (which grinding corrects), they are leaner and have more flavor. Therefore, Standard or Commercial grade beef is the highest quality one should use for making hamburger.

The quality of food and beverage item purchased is often set by production, but management must approve of and often dictates the quality. Quality can often be specified by using a brand or grade term. If not, then the quality must be described in longer terms. Often purveyors are selected on the basis of the quality of product they supply equated to price and service rendered. Many purveyors learn what quality a facility uses and do not have to be told what to furnish, unless the use is to be different from the usual one. A purveyor that delivers a varying quality often loses business. It is important that the quality of product purchased be consistent. Purveyors may at times offer bargains, a product of desirable quality at a favorable price. Buyers should be careful about the purchase of these bargains. Perhaps such a product has to be used in a short time to retain quality, but such a constraint may work for the buyer's intended purposes.

Quality can change in items. Grade A eggs may be delivered, but because they are left to stand on a warm receiving dock they can rapidly lose quality to become a lower grade. Fruits and vegetables can do the same, as well as other perishable items like meats, poultry, or fish. A buyer is usually responsible for seeing that the quality delivered is the same as that ordered and then for seeing that the quality is maintained until issued for use.

Quality identification at delivery is not difficult to determine if it is set by brand or grade. However, the quality of a brand and grade can change. The federal grade given a product is set at the time of grading. There is no assurance that the product delivered is that grade. A frozen vegetable may have thawed and deteriorated, yet on the market, that product goes under the grade given it at the time of grading. Brands can also change. Therefore, accepting even branded or graded items without inspection is not recommended.

The individual inspecting the item should be capable of identifying quality. Thus, allowing a pot and pan washer to accept a delivery of meat is risky; such an individual may know nothing of meat grades and will not be able to tell whether or not the right grade has been delivered. One of the best ways to ensure quality is to select purveyors that will deliver the quality of item specified. The inspection problem is considerably simplified when this is done.

Searching the Market

Normally searching the market is not a problem for the buyer, because purveyors who sell to the operation can usually furnish what is required. Thus, the selection of purveyors who carry a wide enough range of items to normally satisfy a facility's needs is often an answer to this problem.

In addition to this, buyers who *know* the market simplify market search. They know who carries what and how to get in touch with them. A buyer who usually purchases from a local market may at times have to go to a secondary or primary market to get special items and knowing one's way around in these can be very helpful. It might even be necessary at times to go to an international market to get needed items. A buyer wanting fresh, not frozen, Dover sole may have to contact a dealer in England and arrange to have this special fish flown in.

Dr. Lillian Gilbreth, the famous industrial engineer, once said in a lecture, "The best way to simplify a task is to let someone else do it for you." This can be true of market search. If something special is needed and the purveyor called cannot furnish it, let this purveyor search the market and get it. If a patron of a facility insists on having mangos as a first course for a dinner she is giving in March when relatively few foreign mangos may be on the market, let the fruit and vegetable purveyor do the searching and get them. This purveyor usually knows the market better than the buyer and probably has contacts that can supply the item.

Using the Yellow Pages is often an answer to a market search problem. Also, reading journals, advertisements, visiting trade shows, and belonging to associated trade groups are more ways in which buyers learn where items can be obtained.

Often market search problems become complicated because of time. The item may be needed within a short time period. Sometimes this is because someone in production or elsewhere neglected to notify the buyer of the need. This delay in requisitioning creates a problem for the buyer. Setting up times by which requisitions items *must* reach the buyer can help solve this.

SUMMARY

Before any purchasing can be done, those who are to supply the item must be selected. Buyers will find they have a wide selection or narrow one depending on their location and other market circumstances. Normally, jobbers or wholesalers are those from whom the smaller operations purchase, but larger operations often purchase from those that are national in scope. Suppliers may vary from those selling one type of goods to those selling many. The trend is to purchase from the latter since this simplifies purchasing. Larger operations will purchase on a more single supplier item base.

Selection of suppliers is often based on (1) price, (2) quality of product, and (3) quality of services rendered by the supplier, but other factors may enter into the decision such as credit arrangements.

Buyers should follow high ethical standards in the performance of their duties. While most suppliers are honest, some are not and will seek illegitimate ways to obtain business. A firm should set up its own policies and procedures in this area and publish them prominently so employees are aware of them. Vendors also need to be aware of policies so they will not expect the firm's employees to violate them.

Before a purchase can be made a buyer must also be able to specify to the supplier exactly what is wanted. Three kinds of specifications are used: (1) internal, used largely for service and internal operation procedures; (2) purchase specifications; and (3) general specifications, which apply to most purchases and include general requirements, such as delivery times, payment restrictions, and so forth.

One can name the quality of product desired by grade, brand, or description. Best quality for a particular use may not be the highest, but should be suitable for the need. Quality standards of an operation will be set by the particular need. It is wasteful to purchase the highest quality and then use it for a purpose in which a lesser quality would have done as well or may even do a better job.

Normally there are few problems in finding items in the market. Purveyors from whom one usually purchases are able to supply what is needed, but occasionally one must go outside of this source to get needed items. The buyer that is highly knowledgeable in the overall market can often easily find needed products. Assistance may be given by purveyors. Yellow pages, trade journals, trade shows, and other means are helpful in making a market search.

Management usually writes specifications but may delegate the job to others, possibly agents outside the operation.

A specification for a product should contain (1) the item's name, (2) quantity wanted, (3) quality wanted (brand, grade, etc.), (4) form in which the product must come, (5) unit on which price will be based, and (6) any miscellaneous factors needed to define precisely what is needed.

Buyers in purchasing will often follow the usual steps: (1) ascertain need, (2) ascertain quantity, (3) ascertain quality, (4) search the market, (5) order and negotiate the purchase, (6) receive, (7) store, (8) issue, and then (9) review the entire purchase process to see where improvements may be made. Only the first four factors were discussed in this chapter. The other factors are discussed in future chapters.

The name of products can be defined by market terms or practices, government standards, or by a buyer's requirements. The amount needed may be decided by various means. Among these are ROP, use of tables or quantity yields, standardized recipes, portion size quantities, EOQ, yield tests, and calculations from AP or AS to quantity needed. Quality definition is best obtained by grade, brand, or buyer definition. The definition of quality in products is changing and buyers need to be more and more alert to the need to specify factors that determine it.

REVIEW QUESTIONS

1. What factors are important in the selection of purveyors? Would you want to include other factors not mentioned in the text? If so, in what rank would you place them?

2. Cite the advantages and disadvantages of one-stop buying.

3. What six factors should a specification cover?

4. Why would one want to purchase by grade rather than brand?

5. What is meant by ROP? Par stock? Inventory card?

6. The specifications for a state require that meat items be federally graded and conform to IMPS standards. What is meant by IMPS?

7. Why would a company want to have a good credit rating?

8. What are the three kinds of specifications and what does each cover?

9. In setting up an order who should decide quality of product, the chef or the buyer? Would there be any case in which one would overrule the other?

10. What three factors are usually most important in choosing a supplier?

11. What is a full-line supplier? A local specialty wholesaler? A national jobber? A discount warehouse or supermarket?

12. What is the Universal Product Code (UPC)?

13. What are the main ethical problems that buyers encounter?

14. You are a manager and are suspicious of certain things going on in the purchasing department between the buyer and certain vendors. Cite things you might be suspicious of occurring and what you would do to try to detect them.

15. The menu forecasts a need for 40 4-oz portions of roast turkey. The cooked yield of turkey from the AP ready-to-cook (RTC) state is 50%. What size turkey must the buyer order?

Answer: 20 lb

16. A banquet of 500 is to be served prime ribs of beef. IMPS No. 103 ribs will be purchased, which yield 56% in IMPS No. 109 ribs that are RTC. A generous portion is desired and the chef plans a pound of No. 109 per portion. How many pounds of No. 103 ribs must the buyer purchase?

Answer: 910 lb

17. If you were a buyer, how would you rank sellers according to price offered, quality of product offered, other services such as prompt and frequent delivery, good credit, good billing, and accounting?

KEY WORDS AND CONCEPTS

cash on delivery (C.O.D.)	par stock
certificate of grade	purchase requisition
collusion	purveyor
credit (7-day, biweekly, 21-day, or 28-day)	quality of service
	reciprocity
credit application	reorder point (ROP)
economic order quantity (EOQ)	requisition
government name	specification (internal, external, and general)
Institutional Meat Purchase Specifications (IMPS)	
	supplier
maximum level	trade name
minimum level	Universal Product Code (UPC)
on hold	yield percentage
par level	yield test

CASE STUDY NO. 1

You have come to know a salesman quite well and see him at his booth at a trade show. You greet him and he says, "While I have them here, let me show you some of our new products." They are of interest to you and you spend some time looking at the items and having the salesman cite their virtues. You finally decide you have finished and thank him and get ready to leave. Before you can, he says, "Oh, by the way, I have two tickets to tonight's banquet but can't go because I have to leave for Chicago right after we close down our booth tonight. I'd like you to have them, because otherwise they'll just go to waste." Should you accept his offer? If you do, are you committing yourself to return the favor? Or is it just a matter of goodwill on his part?

CASE STUDY NO. 2

A buyer is about to make a year's contract with a fruit and vegetable purveyor to purchase all produce on a cost-plus basis. The contract will specify that total purchases be made with the contracting purveyor, unless this purveyor releases the order so the facility can purchase elsewhere. Two purveyors are under consideration and a decision must be made as to which one will be selected. Previous buying experience has given some idea of what to expect from each. Both are considered de-

Table 4-1
Supplier Comparison

Pluses	Minuses
BUYER A	
Often lower price than B; often gets specials	Quality often lower than B
Delivers on time	Drivers are difficult to deal with
	Trucks not refrigerated; lack good sanitation
	Packaging often not good
Gives good credit terms; not pushy in collecting	
Manager easy and nice to deal with; very friendly	
Billing often late; makes more errors than B	
Has wide variety; seldom is out of stock on items; can quickly get needed items	
BUYER B	
Price often higher than A; specials are seldom	Quality often higher than A
Erratic on delivery times	Courteous, cooperative drivers
	Clean refrigerated trucks
	Good sanitary packaging
Strict on payment times; refuses delivery if late on payment	
Very business-like in dealings; friendly but formally so	
Prompt on billing; few errors	
Carries only standard stock; has more stock outages than A; often not too cooperative in getting items not carried	

sirable suppliers. The buyer jots down the pluses and minuses of each purveyor (see Table 4–1). Weigh the pluses and minuses of each and then decide on which supplier you would choose.

How important is price if it's on a cost-plus basis? Does A's lower prices indicate a lower price base or a lower markup? Is the lower price an indication of why the quality is slightly lower? Would factors like these have to be checked? How important is it that A carries a larger variety of stock and has fewer outages? What about better, cleaner trucks and better, more sanitary packaging? With which supplier would you rather deal? Is there any one factor that outweighs all others and makes the decision of granting the contract undisputed?

CHAPTER 5

Getting the Goods

Of the German land. From the Louis Szwathmary collection, Culinary Archives and Museum, Johnson and Wales University, used by permission of Dr. Szwathmary and Johnson and Wales University.

Chapter Objectives

1. To cover the purchasing step of ordering.
2. To indicate the part receiving, storage, and issuing should play in the purchase function.
3. To discuss the forms most often used when ordering, receiving, storing, and issuing.

INTRODUCTION

Prior to ordering, most of the work in purchasing is planning and desk work, but after those preliminary steps are done, a series of greater physical activities occurs. These activities are ordering, receiving, storing, and issuing. At times, these activities are quite simple; at other times, they are quite complex. It is possible to bypass the storing and issuing steps when **directs** are received, which is where items are ordered, received, and then sent directly to production for use. In this case, the storage function is eliminated and the issuing function occurs immediately after receipt.

An important part of a buyer's job is to study market costs and see if somehow they can be avoided or reduced. The following list provides just a few of many ideas about how a buyer might be able to accomplish this when fulfilling the ordering step:

- Pay cash on delivery and avoid seller's charges for credit.
- Purchase in a different market form and make the desired form change in the operation.
- Avoid unnecessary packaging such as purchasing strip steaks in layered 20-lb boxes instead of individually wrapped.
- Change the quality. Why purchase nicely dried seedless dates when they are to be chopped up for baking? Jumble, mass-packed will do just as well.

ORDERING

Much ordering is still done over the phone (house buying) and with salespersons calling (off-the-street-buying), but the trend is moving away from these methods to the use of the computer or the fax. Sellers of some items are also offering them on the Internet. Bid buying is often used by large and institutional buyers, especially for nonperishable items. As previously noted, purchasing at a discount warehouse or supermarket is also done.

Order procedures differ among foodservice operations. Usually an order is a straight phone statement encompassing a need–price–quote–acceptance arrangement—a quick and simple method. Other arrangements include cost-plus, blank check or complete open, negotiated purchase, or futures. A method of ordering called *call sheet buying* is nothing but a variation of phone or house buying. Cooperative buying or having an outside buyer is another arrangement that is sometimes used.

Kinds of Ordering

Off-the-Street-Buying

Salespersons representing wholesalers or jobbers may contact customers to make a sale. This may be a routine weekly call or a random call to see if a new customer might be obtained. Such a call allows a buyer to place orders, gain market information, or otherwise act to perform the buying function. The salesperson often carries a laptop computer, which can be connected to a modem so the order can be placed directly in the seller's computer. The computer can acknowledge the order, relay credit arrangements, indicate outages or the need to back order, and provide any other information relating to the order on a real-time basis.

House Buying
When the buyer picks up the phone and calls in an order, a **house buying** purchase is made. It is possible to discuss with the salesperson taking the order various factors needing clarification so the right items are secured.

Call Sheets
A **call sheet** is a list of items required divided by categories. The amount and quality wanted, plus other needed information to make the right purchase, may also be on the sheet. The buyer takes this sheet and contacts various purveyors in a specific category. After all vendors have been called and prices and other information recorded, the buyer studies the sheet and decides from whom the purchase will be made. In Figure 5–1, a circle around this purveyor's price indicates that this is the purchase to be made and then a clerk can place the orders. Call sheets are also called **quotation sheets** or **quotation lists.**

Cost Plus
Cost plus buying is a good way to purchase. The buyer and seller negotiate for the purchase of items based on a price plus an agreed markup. Thus, a facility might arrange with a fresh fruit and vegetable or meat purveyor to purchase all of these requirements from the seller; in return the seller's price will be based on the seller's cost plus the agreed markup. Sellers must agree to have all their records open to buyers, so at any time a buyer wishes to check on a price, the buyer can do so.

Blank Check or Complete Open
Blank check or **complete open buying** is an arrangement in which the purveyor is told "get it at the best possible price" and charge for the item based on cost plus the seller's markup—usually the markup is not fixed. This gives the seller a free hand in searching the market and then charging what must be received for the service and goods. As the name implies, selected sellers are authorized a sort of blank check privilege.

Negotiated Purchase
An arrangement called **negotiated purchase** is somewhat like bid buying, but on a restricted basis that takes a much shorter time to complete. The negotiations are usually verbal, but may be written. As the degree of formality in the negotiation process increases, more of the conditions and discussions are put in writing, such as including product specifications. This type of negotiation saves time and avoids confusion in getting the right item or items. The method is used in these cases:

- The amount is small and not worthwhile to get a large number of sellers' prices.
- The number of sellers must be limited.
- Time is restricted and fast action must be taken.

Meats	Unit	Suppliers	
		Smith Co.	Higgins Bros.
Pork loins 10/12#	6	$1.69	$1.72
Bacon hotel slice	50#	1.88	1.83
Boiled ham 8#	6	2.10	2.05
Corned beef brisket	50#	1.55	1.67
Calves liver	10	2.05	2.05
Hamburger	50#	.89	.90
Square chuck	150#	1.33	1.32
Round "good"	150#	2.05	2.03
Lamb 50-55#	3	1.68	1.68

Fish	Unit	Suppliers	
		City Market	Seafood, Inc.
Jack salmon dressed	50#	$3.20	$3.25
Filet sole	50#	1.85	1.80
Butterfly whiting	30#	1.90	1.92
Filet ocean pike	30#	2.10	2.15
Halibut—1 fish	35#	2.75	2.70
Shrimp—headless 26/30	20#	4.85	4.90

Perishables	Unit	Suppliers	
		Green Co.	Acme Co.
New cabbage, 100# Bg.	3	$.15	$.16
Carrots, bunches	10	.12	.12
Cauliflower, 45/50# Ct.	3	6.00	6.05
Celery, Pascal, 72/92# Ct.	3	6.50	6.60
Lettuce, Iceberg, 24's Ct.	2	5.20	5.10
Mushrooms, 4 qt. basket	3	4.60	4.50
Onions, Bermuda, 50# Bg.	3	6.00	6.10
Lemons, 360's	2	.96	.92

Figure 5–1
Call sheets are also called quotation sheets or lists.

- The product or products are highly perishable and must be moved fast through the marketing channel.

- It is not practical to allow for more competitive bidding.

Three or more sellers' quotations are desirable but not always practical. In discussions with each, good notes are taken; the buyer studies these and chooses a seller. The notes are kept as a record to prove that not just one seller was involved. Negotiated purchasing is sometimes called the **informal purchase** method.

Bid Buying

Bid buying starts with a published written notice that specific goods are desired. The specifications for these goods, the amount, and general conditions are usually also presented. All the detail needed should be given so sellers know what is wanted and the conditions of the sale. Sellers are to reply in writing, giving prices and any other information on conditions of the sale. Usually two samples of each product bid on must also be given. Bidders are to furnish bond as a guarantee they will perform. The bids are opened all at one time, usually in public. One of the two samples is now opened and inspected and the buyer selects the items desired. The other sample is kept for opening when the goods are delivered.

A deterrent to bid purchasing is that suppliers may not wish to commit themselves to long price agreements because of market instability. This is especially true of highly perishable items like fresh fruits and vegetables or meats. This can be avoided by basing the bid on a market cost plus markup.

The advantages of bid purchasing are

1. Lower prices
2. Consistent quality assurance
3. Reduced paperwork
4. Reduced labor costs.

Futures Purchasing

Contracting to purchase certain commodities at a specified price at a future date, called **futures purchasing,** is often used by large companies. The market for goods purchasable by such a method is found on the Chicago Board of Trade, and is used for future purchases such as poultry, pork, beef, butter, coffee, sugar, and wheat.

The delivery of the commodity is seldom made, however, because futures purchasing is used only to guarantee a price during a specified period. Thus, suppose a chain plans to run a promotion on prime ribs of beef during August, and wants to start promotion by getting posters and other advertising materials together in June, along with an advertising program. It needs a price guarantee of choice grade No. 109 beef ribs and makes a futures delivery contract to buy during August 100,000 lb of these ribs at a price of $2.25. This is called *hedging,* since the company now knows it has ribs guaranteed by the seller accepting this order for this price and amount.

Now, suppose the market rises to $2.50 by June. By August, the seller doesn't deliver the ribs; instead, the seller pays the company $0.25 a lb or $25,000. The company now goes out in the market and buys the ribs paying $2.25 a lb of its own money and using the seller's $25,000 to pay the extra. Or, suppose the price drops to $2.00. The buyer now pays the seller $0.25 a lb or $25,000 and goes out on the market and buys the ribs for $2 a lb. While it was not to its advantage to pay this $25,000 to the seller, it nevertheless is not paying any more than it figured it would have to pay in setting up its costs, so it is not hurt.

This is an oversimplified explanation—there are costs involved in making a futures contract in commissions to agents and so forth. What we have tried to do is show the logic of the system, omitting certain details. Figure 3–7b shows futures quoted on livestock and meat.

Cooperative Purchasing

A group of food services may pool their purchase needs, buying them together to get the advantage of larger orders. Deliveries are usually made to the individual companies, but the cooperative effort may go as far as getting just one delivery at a warehouse operated by the cooperative and then the cooperative delivers. Sometimes the buying arrangement is such that each firm can name its own brand or grade.

In many cases a cooperative purchasing arrangement results in lower prices with little inconvenience to buyers. Some cooperatives work on the basis of cost plus a markup to cooperative members needed to operate the cooperative.

Purchase Agents

Purchase agents may also be retained to do the purchasing for a food service. This may eliminate the need for an in-house purchasing system, reduce paperwork, and improve the purchasing function. A purchasing agent may receive percentage fee or a set fee. Their use is increasing.

Standing Orders

Many items are used on such a consistent basis that a standard stock of the item is carried. As it is used, the supplier automatically replenishes the supply, bringing it up to an agreed-on par level. Often this replenishment takes place daily or every several days. The salesperson (usually the driver also) stops with a load of the items used, checks the amount on hand in the facility, and then adds to the stock to reach the desired quantity. A sales slip is prepared usually in duplicate; one is signed indicating receipt of the goods. The salesperson takes this slip back so a bill can later be sent. It is important when using such an arrangement that the salesperson place the new stock in back of the old, following the FIFO (first in, first out) principle. It is also important to see that the amount charged on the sales slip is actually received. Breads, dairy products, coffee, and similar daily high-use items are handled by this method. Only certain individuals in the operation should be allowed to sign for such deliveries. Purchasing by **standing order** is simple, takes little or no time, and satisfies the need.

Computer Ordering

More and more facilities and suppliers are purchasing by computer. The buyer's computer talks to the supplier's computer and names items wanted and asks for price, quality, and other information. The supplier's computer gives the desired information and the buyer can by computer signal whether an order is placed or not.

Computers can also supply a tremendous amount of market, supplier, and product information to buyers through the Internet. Databases containing desirable market information also are available to buyers.

Facsimile Ordering

Another in-house method of ordering that is quite common is to order via facsimile. It is possible to fax a supplier inquiring as to the price, quality, and so forth of items and then fax a return order. The supplier can reply by fax with an acceptance if necessary.

Order Costs

The more frequent the ordering, the higher the costs. Labor and supplies are involved. Each order compiled and placed takes time. Receiving time and storage time are increased, as is accounting time. Suppliers often add a delivery charge for each delivery. Some authorities estimate that each order placed by a facility costs from $5 to $65; others make no dollar estimate, but place the cost as 1% of inventory.

Large Versus Small Orders

Buyers have to decide at times if it is wise to purchase larger amounts to get better prices. The following are advantages of small orders:

- Lowers storage costs, including risk, interest on inventory, storage space cost, and some paperwork such as keeping inventory. One facility calculated its storage cost per dollar of inventory as 1% risk, 10% interest, 2% space, and 1% paperwork, for a total of 14%.

- Allows fresher product to be purchased with reduction of risk of spoilage.

- Increases chances for taking advantage of price drops.

- Lessens demands on financing.

- Does not take up valuable storage space.

- Allows for a wider choice of purveyors over a period of time.

- Reduces pilferage because missing items are more noticeable with less stock.

All of these advantages for small orders are also disadvantages for larger orders. The advantages of large orders include these:

- Reduces goods' price because of lower supplier delivery costs and quantity discounts.

- Reduces risk of stockouts and ensures an adequate quantity on hand.

- Reduces labor and material costs, as mentioned before.

- Gives the buyer more time for other purchasing.

- Allows one to set selling prices knowing that costs are somewhat stabilized.

For the most part, the advantages of larger orders are also disadvantages for the smaller ones.

Negotiation in Ordering

After a buyer finds a supplier from whom he wishes to buy, the buyer then negotiates for purchase. Negotiation is a part of all buyers' lives. They negotiate with the chef, with accounting, and with others in their own enterprise and they are in almost constant negotiation with suppliers in the market. Thus, one's ability to negotiate is a critical part of one's capability as a buyer.

Just what is negotiation? For our purposes, it is two or more individuals exploring areas of disagreement or areas needing clarification so they can come to terms or agreement on them. If there are no differences, there may be no need for negotiation. Negotiation builds a bridge between parties so they have a way of reaching a common goal. It removes roadblocks that might stand in the way of agreement.

A buyer can make negotiation a painful and difficult process or make it pleasurable and a game to be played. Negotiation can be a test of wits and skill in which the players face a challenge. The objective is always to reach an amicable agreement in which the interests of all parties are taken into account before the purchase is made.

The Simple Negotiation

Many negotiations are almost spontaneous and simple. A hundred or more may be made in a day. Many occur in phone calls where a buyer indicates to a seller the purchase needs. A quantity of a product of specific quality, size, and so forth is desired. The supplier quotes a price. If satisfactory, the buyer accepts and goes on to the next item. While quick and simple, such negotiations are only so when the buyer knows exactly what is wanted and the price that can be paid for it. If a buyer is not well organized, what should be a simple negotiation can quickly become a difficult one. A well-prepared, skilled, and knowledgeable buyer can quickly negotiate a problem without complication.

Be flexible yet firm. Be prepared to listen and to evaluate. Often you can gain valuable information on how to proceed as a result of something the other party said. Negotiations often require that compromises be made. A concession should be made only if another concession of equal value is obtained or if the negotiation is advanced significantly on its way. A request for concession should be met with a counteroffer. Be sure that it is understood that all concessions made are tentative and to be honored only if the negotiations end satisfactorily. It is easy to become emotionally involved in a negotiation to the point that you lose position. A buyer can become angry or frustrated to the point that perspective and judgment are lost. Keep calm and evaluate everything from a position of remoteness. A collaborative negotiation rather than a competitive one is usually most productive.

Purchasing experience often teaches buyers to be organized and to have the necessary skill and knowledge to negotiate well. Building a good rapport with vendors also can do much to speed and simplify negotiations. If a vendor has sold to a particular operation over a long period, the vendor learns the buyer's needs and also knows how to deal with the buyer and the organization. If a buyer says that the operation needs about 50 pounds of pot roast, that's all such a vendor needs to know. The roast to be supplied will be a low choice grade, IMPS No. 114B (Chuck, Shoulder Clod, Rolled and Tied), Range C (18–21 lb). These requirements are known to the vendor because this is the firm's usual order when it has pot roast on the menu.

The Complex, Involved Negotiation

Not all negotiations will be the simple day-to-day kind. Some can be quite formal and complex and can involve negotiations resulting in some kind of contract or bid acceptance, or a change in conditions from some previous contract, or a failure of buyer or seller to perform as agreed on. The negotiation may even require lawyers because of questions of law that might be involved.

Negotiating with more than one or several individuals can complicate the process and make the negotiation even more difficult. The various individuals involved may have different viewpoints and interests. Thus, several members of the school board, school officials, the school district's foodservice management, the accounting department, and others assemble with vendors to negotiate bids for food and supplies for the coming year. On the board is a mother with several children in the schools who is bent on seeing that the most nutritious foods are purchased. She has some odd ideas on what is and what is not nutritious. Another board member is one who wants to lower costs by all means. Another board member wants to throw as much business as possible to one bidder. The school officials want the least trouble possible and try to throw oil on troubled waters. The foodservice management team wants quality and suitability of product. The accounting people want a reduction in paperwork and lower costs. A definite rivalry exists among the vendors for acceptance of their bids. When these interests enter into a negotiation, a buyer is hard pressed to come up with the same results that might have been achieved had the buyer negotiated alone with the vendors. Coming out with anything close to it is a test of a buyer's skill in negotiation.

Another type of complex negotiation is one in which a large quantity is purchased or where purchasing is to cover a long period of time. A number of discussions may be required to come to an agreement. A good market search may be required to find those that can supply the need. The arrangement will usually end up in a complex contract involving lawyers. Suppose a large national foodservice chain wants to set up a contract with a national jobber for purchase of its frying oil. The quantity involved is huge and the product specification is complex and highly technical. The chain's buyer is highly specialized in oils and probably knows frying oil as well as those who sell it. Various separate discussions may be held among a number of jobbers, and much correspondence and many phone calls will occur before negotiations are completed and a contract signed.

To conduct such negotiations successfully, a lot of preparation and organization is needed. We could liken it to the preparation a lawyer might make before going into court on a difficult case. It has to be well documented and set up to achieve a goal. Even with the best of preparation, a complex negotiation may be a real challenge. The most experienced buyer should take time to be well prepared with facts, figures, knowledge of the law, and so forth. Some, but certainly not all, of the things that might have to go into preparation for a negotiation are as follows:

- An *exact* knowledge on the part of the buyer as to his limits in authority to commit his firm

- A knowledge also of how much authority the other party has to commit his firm

- An *exact* knowledge of what is wanted, such as quality, size, and quantity

- Time and date needed along with delivery requirements
- What concessions can be made on price, amount required to get a specific price, and so forth.

The Purchase Order

After negotiation and an understanding of terms, a **purchase order** (PO) is issued to the supplier that lists items to be ordered and often a delivery date. All of the information needed by the supplier to determine exactly which items and the amount to deliver is usually included along with the agreed-on price. Figure 5–2 is an ex-

GOLDMAN & CO.	No. 118743
P.O. BOX 890	(This number must appear on all invoices,
LOS ALTOS, CA 92122	packing slips, cases, bills of lading, etc.)

PURCHASE ORDER

VENDOR	SHIP TO

Date_____   Account No_____

Item	Unit	Unit Price	Total

Terms_____

Signed_____ Title_____ Date_____

Signed_____ Title_____ Date_____

Supplier Signing_____ Title_____ Date_____

Figure 5-2

A simplified example of a purchase order.

ample of a purchase order. The number of copies made of the order may vary. In some operations there may be only one, which is retained by the buyer. In others, copies may be sent to production, accounting, receiving, and storage to inform them that such an order has been placed so they can be prepared to handle it.

POs should be numbered so they can be identified. They should be carefully stored and only certain individuals should be allowed to fill them out. Often the order must be countersigned by some official of the company. If it is, it becomes a legal document that an official of the supplying firm can acknowledge, making it a legal contract between the two parties.

A purchase requisition from some department in the firm is often the basis for the order placement. At other times, verbal, computer, or other information compilation serves as the basis. It is desirable to make a written memo of verbal requests that serve as the basis for a PO.

RECEIVING

Receiving is basically the process of checking purchases to see that they include items that were ordered and whether other ordered factors are proper. It is a management function, but is often delegated. Management, however, should closely supervise this task because of its importance to quality and financial control. Buyers should be aware that a fewer number of deliveries reduces labor and some other costs.

Good receiving ensures that care taken in purchasing prior to receiving is not for naught; specifications and purchase orders are checked to see that the kind of item, amount, quality, packaging and form, price, and other factors are as ordered. Discrepancies such as shortages, omissions, product damage or deterioration are noted, and affected people in the organization and outside informed. The discrepancy is noted on the invoice or bill of lading or is written up on a discrepancy memo. Good receiving leads to better accountability and control of items received. Keep receiving as simple as possible, while at the same time keeping up required receiving standards.

The transfer of ownership of goods occurs at delivery. Up to that time the seller owns the delivery and has responsibility for it. After the goods are received and accepted, ownership transfers to the buyer, who then assumes responsibility for it.

Receiving Organization and Facilities

The receiving division usually is under the purchasing department, but, in some organizations, it may be put under the accounting department, because some feel it affords better accountability and merchandise control. However, since it is looked on largely as a part of the purchasing function, the division is more often under purchasing. In fact, the receiving office may just be an extension of the purchasing department. Since purchasing originates specifications and purchase orders, and arranges the delivery, it is usually easier to compile receiving reports and other records in the receiving department than in accounting. Also, if problems arise, accounting must contact purchasing to get information and perhaps help in solving the problem. Thus, giving receiving to purchasing may make for a simpler and actually more efficient system.

It is wise when ordering to plan for deliveries to arrive during hours the receiving department is in operation. While the delivery time arranged may not be honored, it usually makes for better organization and control if delivery times are planned. It is wise to stagger deliveries so the receiving office has a steady flow of work rather than a rise and fall.

It is desirable, especially in larger operations, to have a delivery dock built to handle big trucks backing up to them, with proper height and good depth (see Figure 5–3). Space must be planned for the storage and holding of receiving equipment.

Figure 5-3
Docks should be designed to allow plenty of space for goods awaiting storage and for unloading and other work.

Oftentimes waste storage is located here; this should not interfere with receiving, but should be located off to the side. Proper equipment should be on hand such as scales, thermometers, rulers, dollies, platforms, conveyor belts, a laser gun for scanning UPC labels (see Figure 5–4), lift trucks, and trolleys for carcasses or other large pieces of meat, if received that way.

Three kinds of scales may be desirable. One large scale, preferably counter-sunk to floor level, should be available to weigh heavy items. This scale should be equipped with an automatic time and date stamp, as well as a stamp for the weight. A platform scale, for weighing in smaller items, is also good to have. A smaller scale, often a balance scale, is available for weighing small amounts. In a small operation, a platform scale and a balance scale may be all that are needed. Scales should be located at the point of delivery and not some place inconvenient that would discourage their use (see Figure 5–5).

Personnel

The receiving clerk is the main employee in receiving and in some operations may be the only one, and may even work part time. In small operations, the receiver may be the cook, chef, or other individual. It is important that, if possible, in both small and large operations this person be someone other than the storage clerk, and not be associated in any way with the storage function. It has been found that combining receiving and storage is not wise because it gives a greater opportunity for collusion and dishonesty. An operation is at fault if it allows such a situation, since it is deliberately inviting problems. Receiving personnel should not be permitted even to move items to storage. In large operations, a number of people may be assigned to

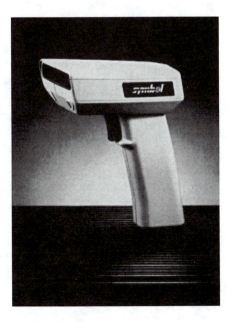

Figure 5-4
A laser gun used to scan UPC information.
(Courtesy of Symbol Technologies, Inc.)

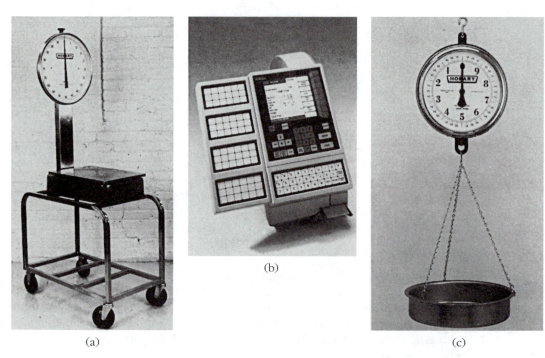

(a)   (b)   (c)

Figure 5-5
(a) A typical scale mounted so it is mobile, allowing it to be moved to where it is needed. (b) a new comput-erized scale that can be used to record weights on a platform scale or other scales to which it is attached. (c) a handy scale that can be used to make quick but fairly accurate weight checks. (Courtesy of Hobart Corporation.)

receiving, working under the receiving clerk, who then becomes more of a supervisor than a worker.

Receivers should be intelligent, alert, knowing, sagacious, and capable of doing the job of checking quantity and quality, do the necessary mathematical calculations, and properly compile reports (see Figure 5–6.) Receivers should know their operation and its needs. Some operations find it is wise to train receivers for the job. If a receiver is not capable of making certain judgments, such as judging the quality of meat delivered, some other competent person, even the manager, should be called to do it.

Receivers should be trained to handle deliveries fast and expeditiously, maintaining good control at every step (see Figure 5–7). Drivers are under pressure from their superiors to move fast and make as many deliveries as possible. At the start of a shift, the receiver should note the deliveries to be received and plan for them, even to the point of setting up some sort of schedule with times that each delivery will be handled; of course, such a report must be looked on as only tentative, since delivery times may not agree with the plan and throw everything off. However, it is better to have a plan than none at all (see Figure 5–8).

Figure 5-6
The receiving clerk checks a delivery as it moves out of the delivery truck. Note that there is enough work room, allowing also for storage, and that the dock level is about that of the truck, allowing easy removal of heavy items.

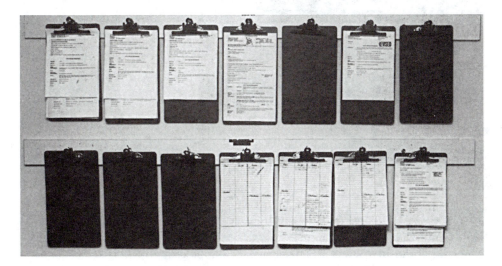

Figure 5-7
Files are hung on a wall at the receiving dock, indicating incoming deliveries expected in a specific period. Each file contains all the information needed to receive one delivery. The system is organized, efficient, and leads to fewer errors and faster turnaround time, thereby causing less confusion.

Figure 5-8
(a) A count check is made on the package to see if the size ordered has been delivered, (b) the package is opened, and (c) the count is verified.

Invoices

An **invoice** is a paper that lists shipping information. It has its own number, and gives the name of the company, quantity, quality, price, total price per type item shipped, and total for the invoice. Other information may be on the invoice. The invoice verifies the order.

If an invoice does not come with the order, a dummy invoice is made up by receiving. If this is done, the driver should sign or initial it, indicating it is a copy of

Date ——————— Company and Invoice No. ————————————

Received by ———————————— Driver ————————————————

Approved by ————————————— Rejected ————————————————

Date ————————————————————————————————

Weight/Count ———————————————————————— o.k. ☐

Quality ——————————————————————————— o.k. ☐

Temperature ——————————————————————— o.k. ☐

Prices —————————————————————————— o.k. ☐

Received by ———————————————————————— o.k. ☐

Figure 5-9
A receiving stamp.

what was delivered. Discrepancies are often noted on invoices and then no discrepancy report is made out. Drivers should initial such discrepancy notations verifying them.

Sometimes drivers are given the power to correct discrepancies on the spot. If so, the correction is noted on the invoice and the driver signs to indicate it is correct. This saves time and work for accounting, the seller, and others. Usually two or three copies of the invoice accompany the delivery. In making any notations on the original invoice, carbon papers are used between the original and the others so copies carry the same written record of signatures, changes, or other notations. If only one copy of an invoice comes with the delivery and more are needed, they can be obtained by photocopying. Or the seller can be requested to fax additional copies, a little more complicated and time-consuming task.

Sometimes upon the acceptance of a delivery, all copies will be stamped with a stamp and the date and perhaps time, receiver, driver, invoice number, and other information completed on it. The receiver signs and the driver either signs or initials. Figure 5–9 shows how such stamps might appear.

Discrepancy Report or Slip

When a shipment has some problem, the delivery clerk is often required to complete a **discrepancy report** or **slip**—also called a **credit memo** or **credit slip.** It identifies the shipment by invoice number and perhaps purchase order number, gives date and perhaps time, shipping company, perhaps driver's name, describes the discrepancy, and gives other desired information. If the delivery is returned, the reason for it is given. The receiver signs the report and the driver initials it. It is numbered and the number is put on the shipment invoice. (See later discussion on how this is otherwise handled.) Some discrepancy reports request a credit be given. Figure

5–10a is an example of a discrepancy report. Figure 5–11b shows a discrepancy being found on delivery and the driver signing the discrepancy report.

Often copies of the specifications sent to the seller are used to determine whether discrepancies have occurred. Since the information given in the specifications is kept current and is a written record, they are reliable references.

Date _____ Time _____ Shipper _____

Invoice No. _____ Ordered by PO No. _____ or Phone

(date) _____ or Call Sheet (date) _____ or Other (kind and

date) _____

Discrepancy

_____

_____

_____

_____

Receiver _____ Driver _____

_____

Figure 5–10
An example of a discrepancy stamp used on invoices and other receiving documents to note discrepancies.

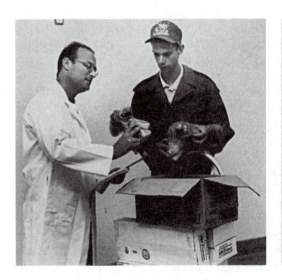 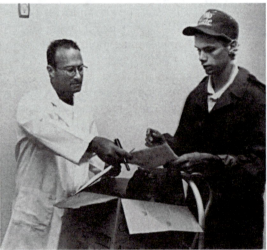

Figure 5–11
An inspection shows a discrepancy and the driver signs the discrepancy report acknowledging it.

Sometimes items are delivered packed in ice, and receivers may be tempted to accept deliveries without removing the ice and then checking weight and quality. This allows for a discrepancy to occur in either weight or quality or both. If a number of the same packages are shipped, ice may be removed from several just to check on the accuracy of quantity, and the others are then accepted. Single shipments should have ice removed, then be checked, and the ice put back (see Figure 5–12).

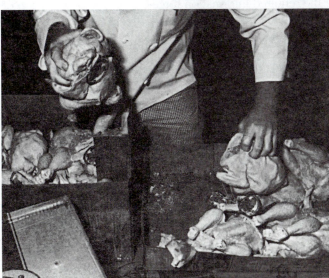

Figure 5–12
To weigh accurately items that have been received packed in ice, the ice must be removed, the actual weight obtained, and the ice replaced.

The Receiving Report

The **receiving report** is a sort of summary of what to expect when a delivery arrives. The time of expected arrival, company shipping, and purchase order number or other order identification are on it. Space is left to record the invoice number accompanying the shipment and to make any remarks required about what was received. Thus, an omission or other discrepancy would be noted. This may not be necessary if a discrepancy report is made out; instead, the discrepancy report number is put on the report.

Some food services do not use a receiving report, believing that all the required information is given on the invoice and discrepancy report, if the latter is used. However, receiving reports do act as a permanent record, recording who shipped, time of arrival, discrepancies, invoice number, whether the goods went to storage or direct, tag number (if used), temperature (if desirable), the quantity, quality, and any other information needed. They can also be a source of information for accounting and for the food and beverage department. These areas often get copies of the report, accountings being accompanied by the invoice, discrepancy report, part of the tag (if used), and other papers relating to shipments needed to prove the delivery, conditions, and price. Accounting uses the receiving report, discrepancy report, and other information to check for credits, billing, and to verify other data. Figures 5–13 and 5–14 are examples of a receiving report and invoice, respectively.

Receiving reports also act as a safeguard against receivers being rushed by drivers who know there is a discrepancy in their order and hope by rushing the receiver to avoid detection of the variation and get acceptance. The requirement to write down the required information forces receivers to do the job of checking and verify that the conditions of the order are met. Once sellers find that they can get by with discrepancies, they may quickly follow up with other discrepancies, adding to their profit and the buyer's cost.

At the close of the day, the receiver completes the receiving report, attaches the invoices, tag parts, POs or other order forms, discrepancy reports, and any other needed information and sends all this to accounting. A copy of the receiving report may be sent to production. One is kept for the purchase files.

Today it is possible to compile receiving reports on computers and then copy receiving information on the computer during receiving. This simplifies record keeping and makes for quick transfer to accounting and other departments. Copies of the specifications, call sheets, POs, or other order data and other needed information used in receiving may also be in the computer, again simplifying the receiving task. Fax machines can also be used to transfer reports and other data to departments and also to sellers.

Variations in Receiving Procedures

Standard receiving procedures may not be used for one reason or another. Thus, some operations use certified or acceptance buying, or use blind receiving, or receive without checking, or have night drop deliveries. In other cases, additional pro-

GENERAL RECEIVING REPORT

MONTH OF _____ 19 __

RECV. BY	DATE	(√) B O	P.O. #	COMPANY	INVOICE #	(√) G R W I	INV. IN	ITEM	$ TOTAL	(√) C R	(√) C O M P	(√) B O	DEPT.	CATEGORY	ACCURUAL $ AMOUNT	INV. ACT.

Figure 5-13
An example of a receiving report.

cedures may be needed, such as writing up back orders or using tags for high-priced items. There are others, but these are the most common.

Certified or Acceptance Buying

Some large firms, government agencies, or local public operations such as school lunch programs, may use **certified** or **acceptance buying.** In such a case, a requirement will be made that the goods be certified as to quality by some outside

SOLD TO:				DATE: _____		
_____						
_____						
_____						
SOLD BY		C.O.D CASH	CHARGE	DRIVER		
LOT	AMT.	UNIT	ITEM	PRICE/UNIT		TOTAL AMOUNT
Received: _____				Received: _____		

Figure 5-14

An example of a receiving invoice.

agent and the receiving firm accepts this as a verification of quality and quantity and does not do its own check. Certification may be by some qualified person or agency, and a certificate is usually issued with the goods. Acceptance buying is a procedure in which federal inspectors are sent copies of a buyer's specifications. A requirement is then made in the purchase agreement that the seller must submit the goods to this inspector for quality and quantity verification. If the goods pass inspection, the inspector sees that all packages are sealed and stamps all approved items, invoices, and accompanying papers with an acceptance stamp. Figure 5–15 is an example of such a stamp. After approval, the goods are then delivered to the buyer by the seller. It is a time-consuming process and buyers would prefer not to do it. The cost of the inspection may be borne by either the seller or the buyer.

Blind Receiving

Sometimes invoices received at delivery have both the quantity delivered and the price written on a black surface so they cannot be read by the receiver. This forces the receiver to check the quantity either by count, weight, or other measure. This is recorded on the invoice and the receiving sheet. Prices are blacked out because the facility does not want receiving to know prices paid for items. The process is called **blind receiving.**

No Inspection on Delivery

Sometimes buyers and sellers agree not to inspect for quality or quantity on delivery. The goods are dropped off, the invoice is signed, accepting it, and the driver

Figure 5-15
A federal acceptance seal indicating the goods meet a buyer's specifications.

leaves. This speeds up the delivery and helps the seller. The buyer also is helped, because the goods can later be inspected at leisure and a better and more accurate inspection made. When such an arrangement is used, the seller agrees to accept the buyer's findings without question. Otherwise, this type of receiving without inspection would fail. In such an arrangement there must be a strong bond of trust between buyer and seller.

Night Drops

If delivery trucks can be on the streets when there is less traffic, more deliveries can be made per hour of time than when the streets are heavy with traffic. Thus, some sellers like to arrange for **night drops** when no receiving clerks or anyone else is there to accept a delivery. In such a case, the delivery person may have a key to enter an area and leave the items. If the area is separate from the other areas of the facility, so the delivery person can only enter there, the system works well. However, if the delivery person can enter the entire premises, there may be some questions as to whether this is a good arrangement. If this is done, there must be a strong bond of trust between the buyer and seller and in drivers used by the seller. Inspection of the goods occurs in the morning when the operation opens. Again, the seller agrees to adjust any discrepancies without question.

In some cases, night drop-offs are made with the goods sealed in large, heavy containers—some of these containers may even be refrigerators or freezers. The delivery truck carries a fork truck so the heavy containers can be lifted up and placed on the receiving dock. Empty containers, left at previous deliveries, are picked up and taken away. Usually the purchase amounts must be large for such a system to work. Some large firms that run their own commissaries use this system to deliver to its operating units with good results. Inspection is often not as thorough, because both receiver and deliverer are from the same firm, but still should be done. Goods cannot always be right in quality and quantity and so must be verified.

Back Orders

When sellers find an item ordered out of stock, they will indicate on the invoice or otherwise that it is back ordered and will be delivered later. Normally, the delivery clerk notes this on the invoice or makes out a discrepancy report, so if a charge is made for the missing item or items, the accounting department and others will be alerted. However, some operations require a **back order** report with a notation that the charge has been deleted from the bill and a copy of the back order report has been given to the driver to take back to the company to make the delivery later and at the same time make a charge for it.

Tags

Receivers often attach **tags** to delivered high-priced merchandise such as poultry, meat, or fish to give better accountability of the product, during storage and use. The tags used usually have two parts—some may even have three—each of which essentially contains the same information taken from the invoice sheet. The item name, supplier, date received, storage location, quality, amount, date of issue, and other information desired may be on parts of the tag (see Figure 5–16). On receipt of the goods, the tag is filled out with the required information, and one part is detached and attached to the invoice sent to accounting, which places the item on inventory. The goods are sent to storage where, upon issue, the second part is detached and sent to accounting to indicate the product has been used. If a third part

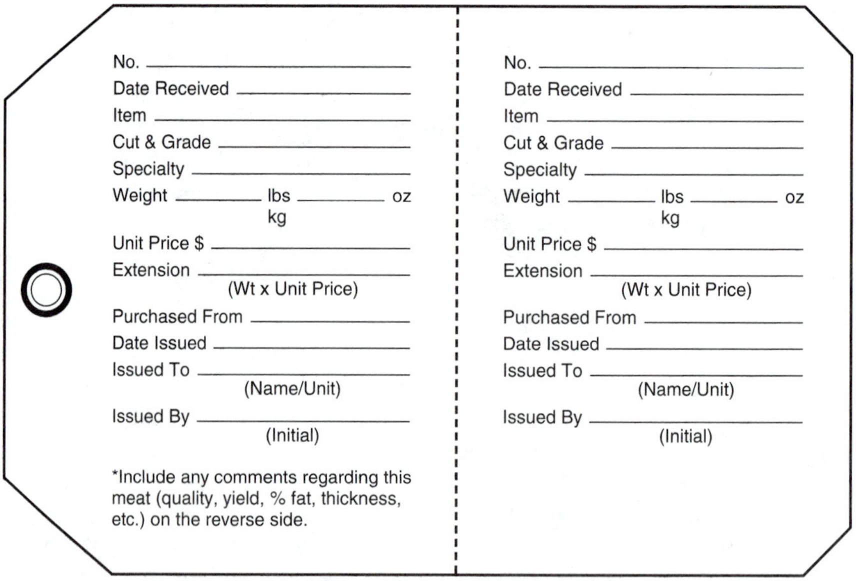

No. ______
Date Received ______
Item ______
Cut & Grade ______
Specialty ______
Weight ______ lbs ______ oz
kg
Unit Price $ ______
Extension ______
(Wt x Unit Price)
Purchased From ______
Date Issued ______
Issued To ______
(Name/Unit)
Issued By ______
(Initial)

*Include any comments regarding this meat (quality, yield, % fat, thickness, etc.) on the reverse side.

No. ______
Date Received ______
Item ______
Cut & Grade ______
Specialty ______
Weight ______ lbs ______ oz
kg
Unit Price $ ______
Extension ______
(Wt x Unit Price)
Purchased From ______
Date Issued ______
Issued To ______
(Name/Unit)
Issued By ______
(Initial)

Figure 5–16

An example of a tag placed on items when delivered. The right completed side is detached and sent in with the receiving report, while the left stays on until issue is made, at which time it too is removed and sent in with the issue report.

is used, this is left on the item and sent with it to the using area, where it is detached and used to fill in the red item report. (This is an inventory of the item in the using area. Issues are added to this inventory, and, as items are used, inventory deductions are made. In this way, use and security of this expensive item may be checked, because sales should equal red item inventory withdrawals. The name "red item" comes from the fact that this type of record is kept on steaks and other expensive red meat items.)

Receiving Wrapup

When the day's receiving is over, cleaning up occurs. The dock may be hosed off and even scrubbed down. Equipment may be washed and stored. The receiving report is completed and all papers accompanying it should be assembled and organized. Direct deliveries and those sent to the storeroom should be differentiated so accounting will know which to charge off as issues and which to put on inventory. It may be desirable to send production a copy of the receiving report so it will know what has been delivered. The storeroom may also get a copy so it will be able to check and see that all items have been properly recorded. As previously noted, the computer may be used to make a permanent record and also to transfer information to others. When all things are done, the receiving report and other papers to be retained by the purchasing department are filed away and receiving for that day is history, but history of a very important kind, for it is here that good security and accountability start. Without good receiving, many things can go wrong. Management should never forget it!

STORAGE

The main goals of storage are to provide security and accountability to products and to maintain their quality. They should not be subject to appropriation by unauthorized persons. The danger of theft is ever present from the time of delivery until the product is served to the patron. Good storage can do much to avoid any pilferage. Good accountability is needed to detect theft and to calculate costs and financial statements, in addition to giving other information of value to purchasing, production, management, or accounting.

Purchasing depends on storage information to know what, how much, and when, plus other information relating to quality retention and shelf life. Production wants to know if the right kind and quantity of goods are on hand or must be purchase requisitioned, plus other information like quality of products. Management wants to know how big inventories are, and if they need to be that big. It is interested in proper security and accountability, in the retention of quality, and in other factors. Accounting needs information on amounts and value on hand, issues, and the like to be able to complete its work. Thus, storage is an important function that serves almost every area of a facility. Additional information on storage can be found in Appendix B.

The Storage Areas

If possible, storage areas should give proper security, light, temperature, air movement, and humidity. Even freedom from vibration may be desirable, as we shall see in the storage of wines. Small operations may not be able to provide all the desirable factors, but, in some cases, like refrigeration and freezer space, specific conditions *must* be met.

In Appendix B a chart and specific information are provided that give much more precise needs for specific products. The following discussion gives some general requirements, but if more exacting requirements are wanted, the chart and information should be consulted.

Common or General Storage

Most operations, even small ones, will have some area set aside for what is called **common** or **general storage.** This is where common items such as flours, canned goods, sugars, shortenings, oils, and many other items are kept. There should be good light, fresh air, a relative humidity not over 60%, and a temperature of from around 60° to 70°F. Temperatures around 100°F reduce storage life to half for some products over that obtained at 60° to 70°F.

Root Vegetable Storage

Some root vegetables can be held at temperatures and a relative humidity of 60% to 70%, but some, like potatoes, should not be held below 50°F, to protect quality. Temperatures above 60°F are not desirable for potatoes and other vegetables. Good air circulation is necessary, but the light can be low or dark. Sacks or containers may be stacked on top of one another on platforms, many up to four or six high.

Fresh Vegetable and Fruit Storage

Do not pack fresh vegetables in storage, even if in containers, too tightly. Even after harvest, these foods are alive and need to have oxygen to respire. Otherwise, they deteriorate, turning dark and sloughy. (Note the air spacer left between rows in Figure 5–17.) A fairly high humidity (75% to 85% relative) is desirable to prevent dehydration. Some operations practice a *wetting process,* that is, bringing in a hose and spraying the storage interior and vegetables with cold water. This raises the humidity and cools the vegetables as the moisture evaporates. It has disadvantages, however, in that it sometimes creates a damp, wet, slippery floor, and some vegetables spoil more quickly when they get an excessive amount of moisture on them; such vegetables do better in an atmosphere of high humidity only. Modern refrigeration equipment, however, is able to provide the proper humidity, so the practice of wetting is dying out as these older areas are being changed. The temperature should be from around 35° to 40°F.

Some fresh vegetables and fruits will hold up under good refrigeration for several or more weeks, but some, like strawberries and other berries, will last only a few days. Such perishable items should be held in the most favorable storage spot for them, and storage personnel should give frequent periodic inspection and alert production to indicate that such items will hold only for a short time.

(a)   (b)

Figure 5-17
(a) Good air spaces between cartons and rows helps hold fresh vegetables longer. It would be even better in this picture if some provision for air spacing were made between the containers on the left and right rows. (b) Frequent inspection of fresh produce should be made to be sure that it is keeping properly. Here even the more stable tomatoes are being inspected to see if they are keeping well. Tomatoes even in good, favorable storage can overripen and become soft or develop white rot.

Meat, Poultry, Fish, Dairy, and Egg Storage

These common animal products do best at a relatively high humidity (90%), and a low temperature, as low as 34°F. It is best to store fish, cut meats, and poultry under moisture-vapor proof wraps, such as plastic. Meat hanging without wraps can dry out and darken faster if held below 34°F, and perhaps this is also about the lowest temperature these items should be held at in a food facility. In commercial storage, however, lower temperatures may be used—just low enough to keep the item from freezing. In some cases, meats, poultry, and fish may be held in rooms in which there are ultraviolet lights, whose rays are supposed to delay the growth of bacteria, molds, and other microorganisms. They do, but the products must be close enough to the lights so the rays reach the products in sufficient numbers and strength to make a kill. Otherwise, the use of such lamps is not effective. (In some cases, meats and some other products like cheese will be held in *ripening* rooms. These storage areas are discussed in the chapters covering the specific products.)

Frozen Storage

In many operations, frozen food spaces are not held at a low enough temperature. This is the fault of designing; not enough heat-extracting equipment or insulation is installed to bring temperatures down to −10°F or lower, as they should be for best frozen storage. Above 0°F, frozen foods can slowly change in texture and also flavor and appearance. Frozen meats develop a grainy texture, and, upon thawing, have a higher drip loss, which results in a product not only of lesser moisture, but also lower flavor and nutrient value. Frozen desserts develop a grainy texture. Humidity should also be fairly high to prevent dehydration. Almost all food placed in frozen storage should be in moisture-vapor proof wraps. Tight wrapping is also needed—the wrap should adhere tightly all over the product (see Figure 5–18). Oth-

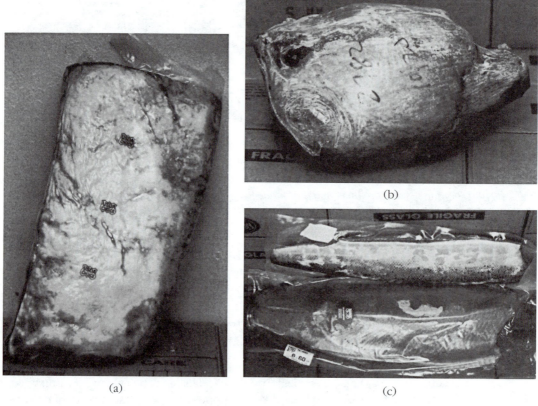

(a)   (b)

(c)

Figure 5–18
These three flesh items show wrapping that fits tightly around the product allowing no air space inside and keeping outside contact out. The wrap around the New York strip loin in (a) is cryovac, which allows the meat inside to ripen but not dry out or develop mold or trimmable waste. We can expect to see much more improved wrapping in the future, some of which will provide a controllable atmosphere around the fresh product keeping it longer.

erwise, there can be a slow withdrawal of moisture from the product depositing between the wrap and product, resulting in what is called *freezer burn*—a dry, gray tough surface develops that is entirely devoid of flavor; when the item is cooked, this dried surface remains in its deteriorated condition.

Storeroom Equipment

In larger operations storeroom clerks must keep records and file these records away. Thus, they will need a work area to do it, and this is often located near the door where issues are made. Equipment there on a table or desk should be a computer, phone, laser gun, typewriter, calculator, and other needed equipment. A file to hold records should be nearby. A work table is also often needed and this too should be located close to the door where issues are made. On it should be scales on which small amounts, even to fractions of an ounce, can be weighed. Another larger scale may be needed and this might be a floor model. Measuring equipment may also be desirable. At times such a work area may be called the **ingredient room.**[1]

Of course, there will also be a need to have perhaps one or two hand-operated trucks that can move platform loads. Knives and tools will be needed to open packages. Depending on the extent of work done, the needs for such equipment will be increased or decreased.

Security

It is recommended that all storage areas be capable of being securely locked and that they be constructed so entry is only through one way. Windows should have bars on them to stop entry. Some locks record opening and closing times. Some storage areas are equipped with fixed cameras that show who is in the area and what is being done. This may be just a permanent record to be reviewed later, but in large operations, security guards in the security office may be able to watch what goes on.

In some operations, cameras also record movement in aisles and other passages. If possible, only storeroom personnel should be allowed in the storage area. Others

---

[1] Just a bit of history: Such a work area is a *must* when food production operates on what is called an ingredient room system. The senior author of this text originally saw this system in use in a New York City Horn & Hardhart central kitchen. It was a method in which the storeroom issues food in exact quantities to prepare specific quantities not in bulk amount. Thus, instead of issuing a sack of cake flour, a sack of granulated sugar, a half case of large eggs, 50 lb of dry milk, and a 50-lb can of cake shortening, the storeroom would issue 10 1/2 lb of cake flour, 12 1/2 lb of granulated sugar, 3 1/2 dozen large eggs, 12 oz dry milk and 4 1/2 lb of cake shortening to make a plain white cake. The requisitions for these quantities came from the production department indicating the delivery point in the kitchen. These ingredients would be delivered there. Thus, workers did not have to leave their work area to go get things. They were thus saving valuable time of highly paid workers. It also gave recipe control to management. Production personnel were required to check all quantities sent to be sure they were correct.

The system was installed in the U.S. Navy Research and Development Facility, where the senior author of this text was director. Katherine Flack, nutrition and food service director for all of New York State's institutions and hospitals, saw the system in operation at the Navy facility, and installed it in the New York system. It was she who named the area where ingredients were weighed out by storeroom personnel the *ingredient room*. From there, the system spread into many kinds of operations.

should be kept outside, perhaps receiving light deliveries over a half or Dutch door. The door can be opened for the delivery of larger, heavier issues.

Keys to storeroom areas should be given good security. Often in off-hours, they are kept by supervisory personnel. They may even be kept in a safe, even in an envelope, which is signed upon opening to indicate who got the key and at what time. When the key or keys are returned, they are put in another sealed envelope. In some instances, when someone in off-hours must go to the storeroom to get things, a log of who went and the time is kept. This record is often kept under the control of management or responsible supervisors. No individual should be permitted to take keys off the premises.

Good security also means that rodents, insects, and other undesirable organisms are kept out of the area. Pest control service may be needed to see that such security occurs. Any deviation from a high standard should immediately be noted, and steps should be taken to see that the situation is corrected. In warm climates, dry fruit and some cereal products may have to be stored in areas that are refrigerated to prevent insect infestation.

Open Versus Closed Storage

Often in smaller operations and sometimes in larger ones, storerooms are opened at the start of the day's work and left open all day with free entry allowed to get items to production personnel. The procedure is often called **open storeroom.** The amount used for a period is often calculated by comparing the result of adding together purchases for the period plus beginning inventory and deducting from the sum the ending inventory. As an example,

Beginning inventory	$10,000
Purchases for period	100,000
Total	$110,000
Less ending inventory	8,500
Amount used (cost of goods sold)	$101,500

In some cases, a requirement may be made that personnel mark what was taken and the amount on a chart, often kept near the entrance to the area. In other cases, only certain personnel may be allowed to have open storeroom privileges.

Storage Costs

Storage costs money. In addition to the cost of the space, refrigeration, freezing, and other costs add to storage cost. Some authorities have estimated that ordinary dry storage room space costs $1.40 to $2.00 per square foot per year.

Storage Procedures

As soon as possible after receipt, goods should be moved into storage, not only for security but to maintain quality. Frozen desserts that melt are usually lost. Eggs standing at room temperature for any length of time lose a lot of quality. Proper surveillance should be given goods in being moved from the receiving area to the storage area. It is generally recommended that no vendor delivery personnel move items to storage, nor should they be permitted any place other than the receiving area unless necessary. It is also not recommended that even those receiving be able to move items to storage. The more the process of receiving to final use can be divided between individuals, usually the better the security. However, in small operations, the same person may receive, store, take from storage, and use. This cannot be avoided even though it is not a favored practice; there is no one else to do it.

As soon as goods are received, they are separated into directs and storeroom items, and the record will show such division. Goods sent to the storeroom are placed on inventory and are considered an asset until used. Upon issue or use, they become a cost. Goods that are directs are charged off as a cost that day. If a shipment is partially stored and partially issued as a direct, the part sent direct is a cost, while that stored goes on inventory.

Storing to Preserve Nutrients

Nutrients in food are lost in storage (1) through extended storage time (the shorter the better); (2) through improper temperature, humidity, or air circulation, through deterioration from dehydration, sunlight (ultraviolet rays), spoilage, chemical or enzymatic change, insect or animal attack, bruising or poor handling; (3) through oxidation and moisture attack; and (4) through other causes that make it necessary to discard the product, such as dirt, soil, and odor absorption. A discussion of these four factors follows.

Extended Time

Time in storage can be especially harmful to vitamin values; minerals are affected much less, and the calorie givers (carbohydrates, proteins, fats, and alcohol) are the least damaged. Few foods or beverages improve in vitamin values with increased age, except perhaps cheese where bacterial or enzymatic change may increase vitamins. Even then there is a time limit to be observed to gain maximum benefit. Slowly, as storage continues, some vitamin values fade away. It is entirely possible late in the season for a fresh item held a long time in storage to be significantly lower in nutrient values over a processed item, frozen versus fresh orange juice, for instance. However, this is also true of canned or frozen foods. Wines and some other items may change in either vitamin or mineral values through chemical changes, precipitation of sediment, or other reasons.

Sanitation and Order

Items kept in storage should be kept in areas that are clean and kept in order not only for appearance, but for ease of finding and allowing for proper accountability. Most governmental regulations today require that items be stored at least 4 inches from floors and walls. Periodic cleaning should occur, and, in some cases, these areas should be sanitized to remove any remaining molds, bacteria, or other microorganisms. Remember, an area can look clean, but it might not be sanitary! Goods kept in clean areas are apt to remain in better shape (see Figure 5–19).

Some managers require that all canned case goods and some other packaging coming in cases be unpacked, priced, dated, and put on shelves. Empty packing cases, if possible, should be broken down, folded, and moved out. If unbroken ones are moved out, it is too easy to move goods out in them. They should go to a designated place where such waste is kept.

Shelving used today should be of the perforated type so as to permit good air circulation and to let soil drop down and through to the floor. It should be strong enough to bear heavy items. Flexible shelving that allows for a change in spacing is desirable. Light items should be placed on the higher shelves and heavier ones on the lower ones. In some cases, bins may be under some shelving. These, with lids, are used to hold bulk goods and are often on rollers. Even shelving that is on rollers is desirable so it can be moved out and cleaning can occur before it is put back.

Only items of the same kind and packaging should be stored in front of one another. Often for better accountability a card, called a **bin card,** is made out, indicating the item and the amount. This is placed in front of where the items are stored and as items are added or removed, the addition or subtraction is noted on the card. Bin cards usually are used for the more costly items. Their use arose from being commonly used on bins where wines were stored. However, they have been found desirable to use for other types of items held in common or other storage.

Figure 5–19
Store items on pallets to keep them off the floor.

Separation of Storage

Special storage areas are usually set aside for cleaning and hazardous materials and for liquor storage.

Cleaning and Hazardous Materials Storage

Many sanitation codes require that cleaning materials and hazardous materials be stored separate from foods. Hazardous materials are those such as poisons, pesticides, strong chemicals, and strong bleaches. If there is only one area for this, it is sometimes advisable to have a space that can be locked for especially dangerous items. If not, at the very least these materials should be stored separately where they can be distinguished easily as being under special care. The shelving on which these items are stored and the floor under should be of a material impervious to attack. Thus, aluminum shelving should be avoided. Stainless steel is best, and hard quarry tile is often used for the floor. A sink with running hot and cold water should be in the area, along with a table for measuring out items.

Liquor Storage

Three kinds of liquor storage are often needed: one for beers and like products held at moderate relative humidity and a temperature of around 34°F, another for wines with common relative humidity or dry and a temperature of about 60°F, and another of common room temperature and humidity for spirits and a few other products. Vibration from passing trains, underground traffic, and common street traffic is undesirable for wines; it disturbs them and harms their quality. Barrel beers should be stored in the coldest area of the beer storage area. They easily sour if allowed to get warm. Beer products should not be allowed to warm up to room temperatures and then be chilled again. It harms quality. Liquor in storage requires good security (see Figure 5–20).

Inventories

Different inventories are used to give security and accountability to foods. One is the periodic physical inventory, another is the perpetual, a third is the in-process inventory, and the fourth is par stock inventory. The par stock and in-process inventory can be one and the same thing, depending on how they are taken and used. Bin cards are a sort of perpetual inventory kept on specific items.

Periodic Physical Inventories

The oldest kind of inventory from the standpoint of use is the periodic **physical inventory.** At one time such an inventory was taken at the end of operating periods when profit and loss, balance sheets, and other accounting information were prepared. They were needed to determine costs and assets. However, some facilities may want information on what is on hand much sooner, not necessarily to complete financial reports but just to inform purchasing, production, management, and others of the status of the supplies on hand and to give accountability. The accountability affords an opportunity to check for shortages: The sum of last inventory and records of amounts received less the sum of amounts issued should equal the physical inventory sum. While the goal is to have no discrepancies, they can and do exist. Some facilities have a rule that any discrepancy over 2% of inventory should be investigated, but it is wiser to try to find the cause of *any* disagreement. Usually they occur because of a failure to record incoming or outgoing stock. Mistakes in physical counts also can cause the error.

Some operations find that a shortened method, called the **ABC inventory** method, works well, avoiding frequent laborious physical inventories. With the ABC method, items are classified by cost value. A items are the most costly, B items second in cost, and C items are the least costly. Management may then require daily physical inventories of A items, weekly for B items, and monthly for C and all other items. The ABC method should not completely supplant the taking of a physical inventory for periodic accounting purposes.

The manner of taking of physical inventories should be prescribed by management. The arrangement of items on the blank inventory sheet and in the storeroom should match. This eliminates search and find. Usually two *reliable* and *capable* individuals, neither of whom comes from either storage or receiving, are often recommended, one to identify and count items and the other to record them. Each page of the physical inventory should be dated and signed by the inventory taker(s).

Today hand recording devices, some compatible with a computer, are available and can eliminate one person and simplify the whole process, even down to mak-

Figure 5-20
Liquors require good storage security.

ing value extensions. Some operations may want such extensions made by the inventory taker, while others may want this done by someone else. Another labor saver is the use of a laser gun to scan labels that record the item identity and quantity and then transfer information into a computer.

Often management itself spot checks the accuracy of inventories to be sure the information is correct. Inventories can be "padded," which means they can contain items that are actually not on hand. This may be done to cover up a dishonest practice. A spot check can sometimes detect this.

Perpetual Inventories

If the quantity and value of specific items are recorded and as quantities are received and issued they are respectively added or deducted from the sum, a **perpetual inventory** is being maintained. In the past, such a record was maintained on cards, which took a lot of time and work, but were requested by management to give up-to-date information on amounts on hand. Some felt the cost was not worth the information given and did not use the system. Today the system can be easily maintained on a computer since much of the basic information for such a system is usually already there as a part of records. In fact, the system can be made almost automatic, just a part of making a record of information on items received, sent to storage or sent as directs, and issues.

In storing items, the principle of FIFO (first in, first out) should be practiced, and the oldest goods moved to the front while the newest are placed back in proper sequence of oldest to newest. Some operations use what is called the DOT system, in which 10 different sets of colored dots are used, with specific dots being assigned to specific days. As goods are stored, the proper colored dot for that day is put on packages, so the storage date is known. If this system is not used, some record the date on the items.

As noted, bin cards are a sort of perpetual inventory, in that they show additions to the amount on hand as goods are received and show deductions from the amount on hand as issues are made. Figure 5–21 is an example of a perpetual inventory card.

Item _____ Code No. _____					
Receipts	Date	Issues	Date	Amount on hand	Date

Figure 5-21
An example of a perpetual inventory card.

Some perpetual systems, besides identifying the item, its code number, receipt or issue, amount on hand, and date, also show a dollar value. Figure 5–21 omits the latter.

In-Process Inventory

At times an operation may want an **in-process inventory.** This is an inventory of items on hand after issue in amount and sometimes also in value. Thus, a kitchen may take an inventory of supplies on hand. In-process inventories are most often used for bar operations and then will be called a **par stock inventory,** because the amount on hand is brought up to a desired (par) level usually at the beginning of an operating period, like every day the bar is opened. When a unit uses such a system, it is common to take an inventory of remaining items at the end of the operating period, say 8 P.M. for a kitchen and 2 A.M. for a bar. The amount needed to bring the stock up once again to a par level is noted and a requisition made out to stores or purchasing to bring the stock up to that level. In a kitchen this might only be for expensive items such as steaks and others that have a fairly high cost. If this is done only for costly items, the system may be called a *red item system.*

Operations that do not use in-process inventories charge issues off as a cost. Otherwise the in-process inventory is an asset until used.

Inventory Costs

Investing in inventory costs money, and a company's finances must be such as to allow for this type of investment. Risk of spoilage or other deterioration or theft, insurance, interest on the inventory, and other costs can be important. Some facilities may find that even a tax put on inventory may be significant. In some states, the average total inventory in liquor stocks is taxed, so facilities try to hold this inventory down for this reason.

A common axiom in buying is "Have as little as possible on hand; get it and use it." Inventories today should be like a fast-revolving checking account, not like a slow-moving savings account, and inflow should about equal outflow and never build a balance. Some manufacturing firms have a policy of "no inventory," arranging to have orders delivered so timed that the goods arrive and immediately go into production. Although a food service may find it dangerous to work this closely, because of the possibility of stockouts (having none on hand), careful planning can save the facility money.

Some facilities set a dollar maximum for inventories. A limit of 4% average inventory to yearly sales is also used. Thus, if sales are $500,000 a year, then an average inventory of $20,000 would be considered satisfactory.

Average Inventory and Inventory Turnover.   Many facilities try to have as fast a turnover as possible. The standard used is often that food inventories should turn over 26 times a year and liquor inventories 8 times a year. The difference is that wine inventories often turn over slowly, so if wine is eliminated, the liquor inventory turnover should be more like that of food.

The way to calculate average inventory and turnover follows:

Step 1. Calculate average inventory. Inventories are taken a number of times during a year. Divide the number of times the inventory is taken by the total sum of these inventories. Thus, if the total of 12 sequential monthly inventories comes to $182,892, divided by 12 months, the result is:

$$\frac{Total\ inventory\ value}{No.\ times\ inventoried} = average\ inventory\ \frac{\$182,892}{12}$$

$$= \$15,241\ average\ inventory$$

Step 2. To get turnover divide average inventory into cost of sales of $400,000:

$$\frac{Cost\ of\ sales}{Average\ inventory} = turnover\quad \frac{\$400,000}{\$15,241} = 26.25\ turnover$$

Inventory's Other Uses

Inventories are not only good for giving amounts on hand and dollar values and accountability, but they also can inform purchasing, management, and others on the speed with which items turn over. Such information is helpful since it may lead to a decision to remove slow-moving items from the menu. Management or others may also be alerted to the fact that such items have remained in stock too long and a way needs to be found to see that they are used up. Inventories also can indicate a need to purchase to bring stocks up to a desirable level. Excessive stock levels can also be detected and a change in purchasing made to correct the situation. The amount on hand may be a guide to future menu planning. Thus, if a facility has on hand a large stock of an item used for producing a specific menu item, the amount on hand may help in planning when that item can be removed from the menu and something else added to take its place. Specific operations may find they are helpful in other ways.

It is desirable to keep inventories at as low a level as possible. Goods on hand are always at risk of deterioration, theft, or other loss. They also cost money not only in space and insurance, but because money is tied up when they are in stock, the interest on the money invested can be a factor. Thus, low inventory levels may have the value of saving money for an operation. For this reason, direct deliveries where goods are received, prepared, and turned into cash help the bottom line more than purchasing goods, storing them, and then later turning them into cash.

ISSUES

An issue is the removal of goods from stores to a department or unit, usually at the request of a requisition. **Issues** remove items from inventory and from the category of being an asset to being a cost. A record is maintained on them for accountability purposes. Accounting uses issues to calculate food cost for the day or period. A direct delivery is considered an issue. An open storeroom system does not give such control and is therefore not favored by many operations.

A form used to record issues is shown in Figure 5–22. Issues are often sequentially numbered so it is easier to identify them and to keep track of them. An issue record may be made in triplicate: one copy for the receiving unit, a second for accounting, and another retained by the stores' unit. It is usual to require that the person receiving the item sign the issue document acknowledging its receipt. At this time, accountability for the item passes from the issuing department to the receiving unit. Sometimes storeroom personnel deliver items to the receiving unit, in which case acknowledgment of receipt is made at the time of delivery and then accountability passes.

In cases where speedy issues are needed, an issue may be made without a requisition, the requisition being forwarded to stores later. Sometimes an issue may be made based on a request by phone, again with the completed requisition being sent later. Stores should keep a record of all issues made without proper requisition so it can follow up later and see that requisitions are forthcoming.

When issues are made, inventory is reduced and an asset is changed into a cost. It is necessary, therefore, to see that an accurate accounting of issues occurs. The total issues for the day plus direct issues are often used as costs for the day. If a perpetual inventory is maintained, the issues will reduce its value, and purchases stored will raise it. It is as important to see that issues are as well protected for security in transportation to using units as in transportation from receiving to storage.

Par Stock Issues

Some operations use a system called **par stock issuing** in which a set amount is always issued. This is common in bar operations. For instance, a cash bar is set up for a reception; it requires a par stock issue. This is supplied. When the event is over, the remaining stock is brought back to issuing, which records amounts used and makes out a charge, crediting the returns.

In par stock issuing, especial in issuing bar stocks, the question may arise on how to inventory returns of partial bottles or how to record issues of partial bottles. Often some fine, almost invisible line is drawn—nail polish is often used—to indicate the quantity level. The amount in the bottle is then estimated and charged out. When a bottle is returned with only a slight withdrawal from the former amount—

Requisition			
Stores _____ Order _____			Date _____
Order _____ Approved by _____		Department _____	
Item	Quantity	Description	Price charge-out
		Total	

Figure 5-22
A requisition for drawing supplies for use. An issue is made on the basis of such requisitions.

say, three-eighths of a bottle was issued with the fine line marker drawn and a quarter bottle is returned—the new amount marks where the new line is drawn and the amount used is charged out. In our example, this would be an eighth of a bottle, and the charge made accordingly.

Par stock issuing may be used elsewhere. For example, a sort of fast-food unit of a resort hotel operating on a beach may need beverages, many fast-food and snack items, and the like to serve the needs of those on the beach. At the close of the day, the entire stock on hand must be sent to storage at the main facility for security and deterioration reasons. It may even be used in some units where it is possible to give security and deterioration protection. Management wants a very strict accounting of what has been used and wants a daily close accounting.

Liquor Issues

Many operations require special procedures for issuing liquor stores. The method used varies with the facility and what it wants. Often, the first concern is security. The package is usually small and can be hidden, so care must be taken that single units rather than cases be taken, although the latter is also possible. In some cases, two individuals are sent to receive issues. This acts as a sort of check on the other person on the team (see Figure 5–23).

Figure 5-23
Liquor issues require special attention to safeguard the items. Here a storeroom clerk is carefully checking requisitions and the issue to be made for good accountability.

It is a common practice in bar issues to require that an empty bottle be returned for a new one to be issued. Bottles are coded with an invisible number to identify that the bottle was one issued by the facility and is not a bottle brought in by an employee who dispenses liquor from his or her own stock and pockets the income. In some cases, it may be required that empty bottles be returned for credit. The bar must save these. Sometimes bars have a chute that allows the bottles to carefully slide to a lower level where they gather and then are later sorted out for return to the various companies who require or want returns.

SUMMARY

Buyers use different ways to order goods on the market. Many are informal such as ordering by phone, via salesperson, or by cost plus, call sheet, blank check, standing orders, computer, or facsimile methods, while others may be more formal such as negotiated purchasing, bid buying, or futures buying. Cooperative buying and the use of purchasing agents may also be used. Ordering large amounts to obtain better prices is justified if there is a savings over the costs of storage. Some of the things a buyer should know about negotiating when ordering are discussed.

Receiving is considered a part of purchasing usually because it is more closely associated with that function than any other and occurs as a step in between ordering and storage, which are parts of purchasing. Normally, in any large organization a receiving report will be made out indicating what goods are expected to be received that day and the conditions for accepting them. At the end of the day this receiving report is completed, indicating what goods were received accompanied by invoices, credit memos, and other papers received in the receiving process. Such information is transferred to both accounting and the receiving office and perhaps to others.

A number of variations may occur in how goods are received. Goods may be accepted on arrival with no inspection or they may be received as night drops, back orders, standing orders, and so forth.

Different kinds of storage are often needed to give security to stores and also to see that they deteriorate as little as possible in storage. These kinds of storage areas include general or common, root vegetable, fresh vegetable and fruit, meat, poultry, fish, dairy, and eggs, and frozen storage. The highest standards of sanitation and order should be maintained in the storage areas. Goods should be protected from damage by handling or improper storage methods. Temperatures should be maintained in the various storage areas suitable to the needs of the items stored there. It is strongly advised that stores that might prove harmful for human consumption or otherwise be a hazard to individuals be kept separate from foods.

Goods should not be left in storage too long. Some operations stamp items stored with a particular color for a particular day so storage personnel will know their age. Practicing what is called first in, first out (FIFO) principles in issuing is a strongly recommended procedure.

An important part of storage maintenance is to see that an accurate record is kept of stocks on hand. The most accurate method, but also the most time consuming, is the taking of a physical inventory, which is an actual count of items on hand and their value. To shorten the process, an ABC method of taking inventory may be used. This is the practice of inventory taking by value of the product, with A items being taken more frequently than Bs, and Bs more frequently than Cs. Inventory turnover is obtained by taking the average value of the inventory and dividing it into cost of sales.

A perpetual inventory may also be maintained. This is an inventory based on amount in stores plus additions to storage minus issues from it. It is adjusted from an actual physical inventory from time to time. Some operations feel that the time taken to maintain such an inventory is not worth the benefit. A bin card is a sort of perpetual inventory for an individual item.

When stores are issued for use, they usually change from an asset to a cost. Issues are usually made at the request of a requisition signed by someone authorized to withdraw supplies. This is called a stores requisition, differing from a purchase requisition that asks for specific items to be purchased. A par stock issue is the issuance of a prearranged set quantity of goods. If a storeroom is left open and personnel are allowed to enter and take items without any record being kept, it is called open storage and the issue step is omitted.

REVIEW QUESTIONS

1. What is a purchase order and how is it used?
2. True or false?: When a buyer buys by bid, the buyer notifies purveyors by phone and then gathers them together where an auctioneer indicates what is wanted and the purveyors then bid on it.
3. True or false?: The savings made in a quantity purchase should be more than the cost of storage.
4. Define *receiving* and state its goals.
5. Should receiving be considered a part of purchasing? Why or why not?
6. Give a profile of the abilities a receiver should have.
7. Indicate what the following are and what purpose they serve in the buying function:
   a. Receiving report
   b. Discrepancy report
   c. Invoice
8. If a receiver feels incapable of judging whether some meat received is choice, who might be called on to do it?
9. What would some of the requirements be for the following kinds of storage?
   a. General
   b. Root vegetable

c. Fresh vegetable and fruit

d. Meat storage

e. Frozen storage

10. If a food service is running a large operation, what kinds of scales should be available at the receiving dock?

11. Name some recommended procedures to follow in taking a physical inventory.

12. What special procedures are often used in issuing liquor?

13. Pair the correct letter designator for a phrase on the right with its counterpart on the left:

____Dot

____ABC inventory

____Par stock

____Open storeroom

____Discrepancy report

____Negotiated purchase

____Call sheet

____Acceptance buying

____FIFO

____Blank check buying

____Ingredient room

____Purchase order

a. Certified buying

b. Complete open buying

c. Informal purchase

d. Credit memo

e. Place where issues are measured or weighed out in exact quantity needed in a recipe

f. First in, first out

g. PO

h. No record is kept of stock taken

i. Stock is stamped a particular color for a particular day to identify when it went into storage

j. Taking inventory based on stock value

k. Quotation list

l. A prearranged, set amount of stock is issued

14. True or false?: A requisition to stores is a specification of the quality of item to purchase.

15. Issues from stores added to direct issues on a particular day equals what?

16. If goods in stores are an asset, what do they become when issued?

KEY WORDS AND CONCEPTS

ABC inventory

back order

bid buying

bin card

blank check (complete open) buying

blind receiving

call sheet (quotation sheet or list)

certified (acceptance) buying

common (general) storage

computer ordering

cooperative purchasing

cost plus buying

directs

discrepancy report (credit memo)

facsimile ordering

fresh vegetable and fruit storage

frozen storage

futures purchasing

house buying

ingredient room

in-process inventory

inventory turnover

invoice

issues

meat, poultry, fish, dairy, and egg storage

negotiated (informal) purchase

night drops

no inspection on delivery

off-the-street buying

open storeroom

par stock inventory

par stock issuing

perpetual inventory

physical inventory

purchase agents

purchase order (PO)

receiving

receiving report

root vegetable storage

standing orders

storage security

tags

CASE STUDY NO. 1

You are a buyer whose expertise is in frozen fruits and vegetables and you work for a large chain of restaurants as its purchasing agent for these products. You must plan for a negotiation conference with a national supplier of frozen potatoes with the intention of granting a year's contract for the supply of frozen potatoes for all units. The supplier has distributors in all major cities and areas where your company has units and so will be able to supply from local sources. What information should you compile to bring to this negotiation conference such as type of potato wanted, cut, packaging, price, minimum order amounts, and past and projected usage? Compile a list of items you expect will need to be discussed in the contract. Bring your list to class and together with the class compile a complete list. Each item listed should be backed by a good explanation of why it is on the list.

CASE STUDY NO. 2

You have been retained as the buyer for a new school district to be formed the next year as a large consolidated unit of smaller school districts. This new district plans to operate a central warehouse that will receive all items needed by the individual school food services. The purchasing department will operate this warehouse and be responsible for delivery of orders for foods and supplies ordered by the schools.

Dairy products, including margarine and butter, and breads and pastry products will not be warehoused or delivered by the purchasing department but will be delivered by the individual companies holding the bid after the central purchasing office has placed the individual schools' orders with the respective bid holders naming the date and time the delivery should be made, the items desired, and amounts to deliver.

A large building has been purchased that will be remodeled as a warehouse unit with storage spaces suitable for canned items, cereal products, frozen foods, fresh fruits and vegetables, nonfood supplies, and so forth. You are directed to assist in the planning of this remodeling with architects and school authorities and also to set up the system to be used for the operation of the purchasing system. This is a massive and challenging task and careful and complete plans must be made for all factors to be covered, such as collecting individual school orders—by phone, fax, e-mail, and so forth. How much lead time must the warehouse have from the individual schools so orders can be assembled and delivered?

The district's menu is planned for a year by the dietary department with individual schools having little freedom to make any changes. This is not only helpful in allowing the individual school to plan ahead and order, it also gives a basis for consolidating a year's need for an item and putting it out for bid. The quantities needed for the year will be calculated by the dietary department but bids will be set up by purchasing. The final selection of companies to be awarded specific bid items will be decided by a committee made up of members from the purchasing department, dietary department, and school authorities.

All meat, poultry, and fish items received from commercial suppliers will be processed so as to be in a state for immediate use such as preformed hamburger patties, chicken cut into individual servings, and meats cut into individual portions. Government-donated items will not be received this way and so a small unit must be set up in the warehouse where these donated whole turkeys, chickens, and hams can be processed into a state where the kitchens can use them for individual portions.

Orders from individual schools will be consolidated into four categories:

a. Those to be delivered by the warehouse

b. Those to be delivered by the bid holders for dairy products

c. Those to be delivered by the bid holder for bread and pastry products

d. Special orders for items needed by the individual schools or central foodservice office.

Individual schools will not play a part in the purchasing task other than sending in their needs to the purchasing department. Occasionally a school's orders might have to be referred to the dietary department to see if they conform to its requirements. Supervision of school kitchens will be the responsibility of the dietary department.

Construct a plan for the proper layout and equipping of just the receiving and issuing areas so you can work constructively with the architects in planning the warehouse's space, location, equipment, and other physical needs. Secondly, set up all forms required, personnel requirements, and so forth, for the operation of receiving so you will have a good workable plan for the operation of the department when you start. The time and effort spent now will eliminate a lot of problems later and save the time and effort that must be expended if things go wrong when the operation starts. When considering the receiving forms, think of how the flow of orders will proceed from individual schools to your office, for transfer to different order sheets, for the actual job of receiving, and for issue and delivery. Also, when shipments are received what receiving sheet will be used by receivers? What must be on such forms so receivers will know if the right amount, right product, and right grade are being delivered? What forms are needed if a delivery is found to be lacking in some essential such as short weight, wrong count, or whatever? Carefully think through all the things that must be done in receiving as you prepare the necessary forms.

CHAPTER 6

The Computer in Purchasing[1]

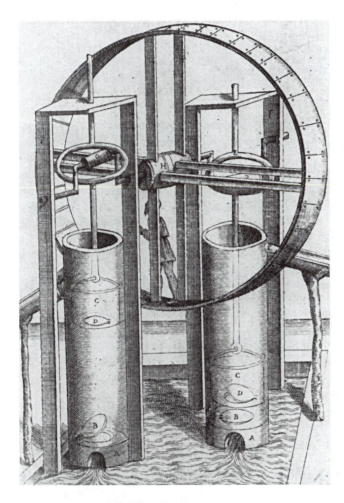

One of the early adding machines that were the ancestors of today's computers. Di Machine, Et Edificii. 1621, Trombe da Rota per Cavar Aqva. From the Louis Szwathmary collection, Culinary Archives and Museum, Johnson and Wales University, used by permission of Dr. Szwathmary and Johnson and Wales University.

Chapter Objectives

1. To indicate the advantages and the role that computers can play in the purchase function.

2. To discuss how one can set up a computer purchase program.

---

[1]This chapter assumes the reader has some basic knowledge of how a computer is operated and what it does. It makes no attempt to tell *how* to set up a computer-run purchasing program, but only to tell what the program might be and how a computer might perform it so buyers and others will know the potential of using a computer.

3.   To point out the latest advances in computer use in purchasing for food ser-
     vices and what might be expected in the future.

INTRODUCTION

About 35 years ago, computers were relatively new machines with limited, specialized uses. They were huge, much slower than today's, had limited capacities, and
even had to be kept in air-conditioned rooms. The invention of the electronic chip
and many technical improvements have brought computers to where they are today.
They are much smaller, faster, less affected by the environment, and relatively inexpensive. Instead of a few, many applications are possible. This has led to their use
in food services, and this use has grown rapidly (see Figure 6–1).

One of the uses to which computers lend themselves in food services is in the
area of purchasing. Practically the whole purchasing function can be computerized,
and the programming to do this is relatively simple. There are what are called
canned or **off-the-shelf programs** that can be purchased. They eliminate the need
to set up a specialized program, but because they do not fit the special needs of a
facility, some may wish to design their own. It is not a difficult job and can then be
tailored to suit exactly the needs of the operation. Figure 6–2 shows where a computerized program can be fitted into the purchasing cycle.

The advantage of using canned programs is that they have been tested. They are
also less expensive than having to set up your own. It is important to purchase from
a reliable company that sells a tested and proven system. Be sure it can be expanded,
if necessary.

Most systems are built around an inventory module and then other modules such
as menu analysis and planning and recipe file modules are interfaced with it. The
system should be compatible with your general ledger and other computer accounting files. If it is not, you should consider purchasing interfacing units to make

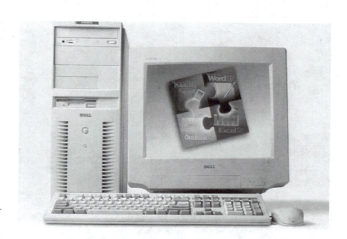

Figure 6–1

*A modern computer that comes with mo-
dem and other features that give users an
inexhaustible amount of information compilation.* (Courtesy Dell Computer.)

this possible. The system should use an up-to-date operating system, such as Windows 95 or Windows NT (or appropriate Macintosh equivalent). Before buying, it is wise to consult current users of a program you are considering to ascertain if they are satisfied with the product. Remember, though, that you should know with certainty your facility's particular needs and establish your computer program based on these needs rather than someone else's.

Although the discussion that follows treats the different files as if they were separate, in today's latest modules they are consolidated into one unit. One of these modules is advertised as doing the following: food and beverage cost control, inventory and inventory analysis, order and purchase history, recipe costing and resizing, menu sales and profit analysis, issues and usage history, comparing average to current use, ROP, last cost or weighted average cost for inventory calculations and other costing, and entire year, or period, or event, or day comparisons. Figure 6–3 shows a list of what one producer claims its program will do.

Training

Before any change to a new computer system is made, employees who will have to use it should be thoroughly trained. Many who have changed with inadequate preparation have found the process to be costly and almost disastrous. In one operation, because of inadequate training in a new **POS (point-of-sale)** system, the problem that resulted increased the amount of from when guests sat down to when

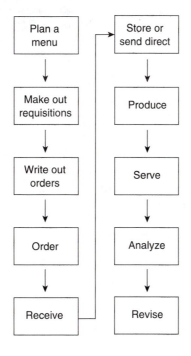

Figure 6–2
One plan of flow in computerizing purchasing.

Work Level 1—If You Just Use Stock On Hand Lists: This is the minimum way to use IPro: Just make inventory check lists and take inventory. All you need to do to make lists is enter item names, prices and quantities. IPro does the stock-on-hand extensions and totals for you so you don't have to do them by hand. This isn't much work but it will save you some time and help you get organized.

Work Level 2—Use "List Processing" for Many Purposes: In addition to making lists for taking stock, you can also use the lists for logging items received, transferred, wasted, sold, etc. and get reports showing the same. However, this is still not "real" control, it's just using IPro as a utility for convenience and saving time.

Work Level 3—Benefits from Item File Setup Work: At this level you only need to enter descriptions of your inventory. You don't normally stop at this work level, but we're making an important point: collecting data gives you the surprisingly great benefits of "discovery" and "setting goals". Chances are excellent that you don't really know what your costs are until you're forced to really look carefully at each item. You will be surprised and shocked by what you don't know. This awareness is the beginning of cost control.

Work Level 4—If You Only Record Purchases: If your time is really precious, just record your purchases or received items only. This gives you the most bang for the buck—there are many very useful reports if you only record your purchases. You can even determine food and liquor cost percentages based on purchases.

Work Level 5—If You Take Inventory and Record Purchases: If you take inventory, record purchases and maybe transfers, you can start to get usage and usage history and averages. You can compare average use to current use, find out if you're understocked or overstocked, and make buy lists based on the last-counted inventory.

Work Level 6—More Benefits If You Enter Recipes: *Inventory* cost control is one thing and *product* cost control is another. You need to know what your recipes cost. Entering your recipes brings benefits of discovery and cost awareness—save thousands of dollars *immediately* when you learn costs are higher than you thought.

Work Level 7—Maximum Results If You Enter Sales Data: If you enter sales data, you'll find the "holy grail" of cost control: *ideal* use, *ideal* cost and stock reduction by sales. This gives you genuine cost control—the ability to compare what *did* happen to what *should* have happened. This is the only way to solve the problems that hurt you the most—theft, waste, overportioning and just plain sloppiness!

Figure 6-3
Some of the benefits one company claims for those using its cost control module. (Courtesy of Advanced Analytical, Inc., 31149 Via Colinas #610, Westlake Village, CA 91362.)

they were served from 34 to 55 minutes. But, after four weeks of using the system, the time dropped to 17 minutes in busy times.[2] Had the situation not improved, it would have been necessary to abandon the computer system and go back to the old system. Too much customer dissatisfaction was occurring to let it go on too long. Problems of increasing time, inaccuracies, and other failures can also occur in the purchasing program, often with disastrous results. When this happens the program is discontinued.

Management must be committed to getting the system going. If employees are left to start up and use the program without guidance and without the interest of

[2]J. E. Herlong, "The Good News About Computers," *Restaurant News* 1996, Vol. 12, No. 9, pp. 15–20.

management, the success of the new program will be in jeopardy. Fortunately, many people today are acquainted with the basic operation of a computer and so they are no longer facing a new "monster" that is going to cause them problems. If management builds on this familiarity and slowly moves into the new program with a thorough training schedule before actually implementing the program, the chance of success is increased. Moving into the program in stages is also helpful, but sometimes not possible.

THE FILES

The purchasing process starts with management setting up a menu designed to please patrons. Thus, in a computer program one might start with a patron profile module that lists menu preferences. A menu file would then follow and then a recipe file that lists a recipe for every item on the menu.

Once the menu is planned, the purchase function can start. A forecast of portions needed might be set up, from which it is possible to calculate amounts needed and to write requisitions for purchase or withdrawal from stores. Purchase requisitions require the buyer to contact suppliers and buy. Information about quality and other factors needed in these purchase items might be derived from a **specification file.** When goods are received the computer will get information on amounts received, vendor, price, invoice number, and so forth. The computer will also be told if the goods go directly to production as a cost or to stores as inventory. An inventory file can be set up to function as a perpetual inventory. Inventory values and total purchases are important in calculating cost of goods sold.

Some operations use a nutrition file to calculate the nutritional value of items served. This information is often printed on the menu, giving patron's healthful information about the items offered. A file that allows menu printing and the production of graphics is becoming a common computer accessory.

The following sections provide a short summary of some of the files mentioned here. It is intended merely to be an overall view, not one that details all factors. You should consult texts written for the express purpose of covering in detail how to set up and operate a program. With the vastly increased capacity of today's computers, many of these files are often consolidated into one, making it possible to reduce amounts stored, increasing efficiency, and simplifying use. They are discussed separately here to simplify and give better organization to the discussion.

Forecast and Menu Analysis File

Forecasting

Some food services compile data on numbers served per meal or day, or even by the hour on days. Events that increase the usual number of patrons, such as a football game or big shopping sale, can give larger patron counts so this might be computerized to aid in future planning purposes. Advance reservations can be transferred to the computer so patron counts can be better estimated. Catering events bring in larger numbers and forthcoming events with guaranteed patron counts can be computerized. Certain days such as Mother's Day bring in large numbers and records of this are valuable for planning amounts needed. Some days are busier than others and the amount of increase or decrease can be recorded for making forecasts.

Menu Analysis

The computer can give a total count of specific items sold and then total them to determine how many items of the group were sold in all. From such information, management can learn about the relative popularity of individual items and perhaps lead patrons to the selection of items management prefers to sell. When the percentage of each item is calculated against the total number of similar items sold, it is called a **popularity index.** Figure 6–4 shows a popularity index taken for five desserts with total sales of 182.

The Recipe File

A file of *all* recipes for *all* menu items should exist, even those for making coffee or tea or hot dogs in buns. All recipes should be standardized to give a known number of known quality and known size portions at a known cost.

Ingredient Listing

All ingredients used should be listed in quantities that relate to how they are purchased, and all other files must be set up the same way so they are all compatible with one another. This may lead to some odd figures, but this is necessary if compatibility of files is retained. Thus, a recipe may call for 3 pints of cream-style corn, which is 48 oz. The corn is purchased in 6/10 cases and each No. 10 can weighs 106 oz net. A case costs $25.44, making the cost per ounce $0.04 (106 oz × 6 cans = 636 oz/case and $25.44/636 oz = $0.04). Thus, while the recipe may call for a measure of 3 pints, the computer will be programmed to make the transfer into (ounces) and then calculate the cost.

You should understand the relationship between volume and avoirdupois (weight) measures. Consider the rule "a pint's a pound the world around"—*sometimes*—ordinary liquids and items like fats and oils comply, but a pint of molasses weighs about 22 oz, not 16, and a pint of flour weighs only 8 oz, not 16. Inaccuracies can raise havoc with getting reliable data. Items also can change when cooked;

Item	No. Sold	Popularity %
Apple Pie	44	24
Chocolate Meringue Pie	38	21
Banana Cake	14	8
Caramel Pecan Sundae	54	30
Fresh Fruit Cup	32	17
Totals	182	100

Figure 6–4
A popularity index for five dessert items.

for instance, rice increases two and a half times while meat loaf may shrink nearly a third. Also today foodservice employees must know metric measures and be able to translate them into our measures or translate our measures into the metric system.[3] Tables of these various measures appear in Appendix G.

Code Numbers, Yields, and Portion Sizes

Code numbers must be assigned to each recipe and also to ingredients in the recipe, and these should also tie in with the code numbers listed in other files. There will be subrecipes and these must be related by codes or otherwise to the recipe to which they relate. Thus, a recipe may call for 3 quarts of Mornay sauce, which is a separate recipe but in this instance a subrecipe. (A Mornay sauce is a basic Bechamel sauce containing cheese.) As with all recipes the Mornay recipe should have its own code number, which the computer reads and prints out the quantity needed to produce 3 qt of Mornay sauce.

The yield of a recipe in portion size must be stated in an amount that is compatible with other files. Thus, while the cook may be instructed to give a portion of "well-rounded serving spoon," the amount of the portion should be 3 oz—which is what this rounded spoon usually equals. The recipe could state "portion: 3 oz (1 well-rounded serving spoon)." All recipes should be costed out so menu planners will know what the item costs and how to price. Figure 6–5 shows a recipe for Lobster Newburg costed out. **Recipe costs** such as this can be grouped together in a file.

Some recipes may have several or more portion sizes, such as a child's portion versus an adult's portion, or an Early Bird portion, which is somewhat smaller than a regular portion. Sometimes the portion may be for three portion sizes, such as a baby bear steak (6 oz) portion, a mama bear steak portion (8 oz), and a daddy bear steak portion (10 oz).

Variations

At times it is not practical to give the computer a measure or a cost of an ingredient, such as a "pinch of saffron," or the cost or measure of fat for greasing a griddle for sauteing veal chops, or a bit of seasoning or flavoring. Instead the total cost of measurable ingredients is taken and 2% of this is added to it for these added but unmeasurable ingredients to give a total recipe cost. Thus, if the total measurable ingredient cost is $149.35, 2% of it or $2.99 would be added to it to give $152.34 as the total recipe cost. Experience shows this works well. Figure 6–5 shows a lobster recipe giving amounts of ingredients to use and the method of making plus cost.

Much other information can be computerized to help in planning menus and in setting up purchase requirements. Figure 6–6 gives one bit of such information on onions. The knowledge of the cost of onions, waste, and other factors presented

---

[3]Sometimes recipes give ingredients by count, such as eggs, and the computer must be programmed to recognize that eggs are purchased by the case of 30 dozen or 360 eggs (30 × 12 = 360). If eggs are $27.00 a case, the price per egg will be $0.075 ($27/360 = $0.075).

```
CODE 7020 LOBSTER NEWBURG

Portions        Size           Yield
   100          6 oz           37+ lbs

 CODE   Ingredients  Weight     Method

 2003    Rice        8 lb.      1. Cook rice; blanch and keep warm
 5785    Flour       1 lb.      2. Make a roux of the fat and flour
 1004    Fat         20 oz.        Add the liquid. Cook to thicken.
 1009    Half        8 Qts.     3. Whisking vigorously add
         & Half                    approximately 2 cups of the sauce with
                                   the egg yolks. Add this to the hot sauce,
                                   stirring vigorously.
 8002    Sherry      1 Qt.      4. Add the lobster meat and heat well.
 1010    Egg yolk    1 Qt.      5. You may add heavy cream but do
 7999    Lobster     12 lb.        not boil.
                                6. Serve 6 ounces of rice covered with
                                   6 ounces of lobster newburg.


COSTING
Total cost for this recipe is as follows:
          Rice       8 lb.     @.20/lb.       1.60
          Flour      1 lb.     @.15/lb.        .15
          Fat        20 oz.    @1.80/lb.      2.20
          Dairy      8 Qts.    @2.00/Qt.     16.00
          Sherry     1 Qt.     @4.50/Qt.      4.50
          Egg Yolk   1 Qt.     @5.50/Qt.      5.50
          Lobster    12 lb.    @10.00/lb.   120.00
                                          $ 149.35
         Plus 2% for Miscellaneous            2.99
         seasonings
         Total recipe cost                 $ 152.34
         $ 152.34/100 portions = $1.52 per portion
```

Figure 6-5

This computer recipe for lobster newburg gives total and portion cost information that is helpful in planning.

here can be of help for those charged with calculating cost and also in setting up quantities to order.

While weights are often preferred in food production, it sometimes is not practical to state a recipe in this measure, but this is rare and occurs usually only on some moving vehicle. One working at sea will understand how unreliable it is to get a weight on a balance scale in a rolling sea. Also, in the kitchen it may be impractical to state that 2½ lb of flour must be used for a cream sauce when the cook has no scale on which to weigh this—the scale is away in the bakeshop—so the measure is 2½ qt and the computer is programmed to make the translation into weight.

Exploding or Sizing Recipes

The computer must be capable of **exploding** or **sizing** recipes, which are terms in computer language meaning being able to increase or decrease the yields of recipes. When computers do this and are programmed properly for it, there is

```
èêêêêêêêêêêêêêêêêêêêêêêêêêêêêêêêêêêêêêêêêêêêêêêêêêêêêêêêêêêêêêêêêêêêêêêêê£
¤                                                                        ¤
úááááááááááááááááááááááááááááááááááááááááááááááááááááááááááááááááááááááááÑ
¤ Number:        2011______                Group:  PRODUCE ________      ¤
¤ Item Desc:     ONIONS, SPANISH ________  Default G/L Code: 2000-001 PRO ¤
¤ Case Desc:     CS= 50 POUNDS ___________ Case Cost:      $      13.000 ¤
¤ Part Desc:     POUND  __________________ Parts Per Case:         50.00 ¤
¤ Unit Desc:      WZ_   Weight Oz.         Units Per Case:        800.00 ¤
¤ Prep Yield %:          100.00            Part Cost:      $       0.260 ¤
¤ Recipe Link: _________                   Unit Cost:      $       0.016 ¤
¤                                                                        ¤
úááááááááááááááááááááááááááááááááááôááááááááááááááááááááááááááááááááááááÑ
¤           Tracking Information     °        Activity Information       ¤
úááááááááááááááááááááááááááááááááááéááááááááááááááááááááááááááááááááááááÑ
¤                                    °                                   ¤
¤ Item Active:          Y            °  Last Cost:        $       13.000 ¤
¤ Daily:                N            °  Last Purchased:      07-28-1992  ¤
¤ Mid Period:           N            °  Total Purchases: $       498.200 ¤
¤ Main Period:          Y            °                                   ¤
¤                                    °  Average Cost:     $        0.018 ¤
¤                                    °  Last Activity:       07-28-1992  ¤
¤                                    °                                   ¤
âêêêêêêêêêêêêêêêêêêêêêêêêêêêêêêêêêêüêêêêêêêêêêêêêêêêêêêêêêêêêêêêêêêêêêêê¥
Prep yield is % of weight left after shrinkage.   ie: meat and produce trimmed.
```

Figure 6–6
Often those responsible for planning in food services need individual cost information, waste information, and other information. This computer printout shows how much information may be computerized and then retrieved. (Courtesy Foodco Corporation, 1002 South State, PO Box 1269, Orem, UT 84059.)

more assurance of obtaining a correct recipe than when an employee tries to do it. Figure 6–7 shows an explosion of an orange cake recipe for 100 portions expanded to 350 portions. However, not all recipes work out by being arithmetically multiplied or divided. Thus, sauces thickened by a starch such as cornstarch or flour do not have the same thickness when exploded this way. As the quantity is increased, the amount of thickener must be increased slightly. Similarly, as the quantity is decreased, the quantity of thickener must be decreased slightly. Also, an attempt to make more than 50 portions of a delicate butter sponge cake might result in disaster because of the delicacy required in handling the product, so no explosion is possible here.

ORANGE CAKE: 112048

Portions   100   Size   2 OZ (2"X 2" Square)   Yield   13+ LB

USE 2 18X26 IN. PANS; FILL EACH 6 1/2 LB

	Ingredients	Weight	Volume	Method
112311	FLOUR, CAKE	3 LB	3 QT	SIFT TOGETHER SALT AND BAKING
141061	MILK, DRY NONFAT	6 OZ	2 C	POWDER; ADD SHORTENING AND
122005	BAKING POWDER	2.5 OZ	4 T	MILK: BLEND AT LOW SPEED 4
122012	SALT	0.5 OZ	2 t	MIN; ADD ORANGE RIND.
126018	SHORTENING	1.35 LB	2 2/3 C	
140611	ORANGE RIND, GRATED	4 OZ	2/3 C	
131003	SUGAR, GRANULATED	3.25 LB	7 C	ADD 1/3 SUGAR: MIX 1 MIN AT
166045	EGGS, WHOLE	2.25 LB	2 PT 1/2 C	LOW SPEED: ADD 1/3 EGGS;
104019	WATER	3 LB	3 PT	MIX AGAIN 1 MIN AT LOW SPEED.
				REPEAT USING ALL SUGAR, EGGS
180113	RED COLORING		2 t	AND WATER: BLEND IN COLORING
180110	YELLOW COLORING		3 t	AND FLAVORING.
180016	ORANGE FLAVORING		2 t	
146063	ORANGE JUICE	2 LB	1 QT	BAKE 350° F ABOUT 30 MIN: WHEN
131003	SUGAR, GRANULATED	1 LB	2 1/4 C	DONE AND CAKE IS HOT SPREAD
				BLENDED SUGAR AND JUICE OVER
				CAKE, LETTING IT SOAK IN.
				CUT EACH PAN 5 X 10; DO NOT
				FROST THIS CAKE.

(a)

ORANGE CAKE: 112048

Portions   350   Size   2 OZ (2"X 2" Square)   Yield   45 1/2 LB

USE 7 18 X 26 IN. PANS; FILL EACH 6 1/2 LB

	Ingredients	Weight	Volume	Method
112311	FLOUR, CAKE	10 1/2 LB	10 1/2 QT	SIFT TOGETHER SALT AND BAKING
141061	MILK, DRY NONFAT	1 LB 9 OZ	7 1/2 C	POWDER; ADD SHORTENING AND
				MILK: BLEND AT LOW SPEED 4
122005	BAKING POWDER	8 OZ	7/8 C	MIN; ADD ORANGE RIND.
122012	SALT	1.5 OZ	7 t	
126018	SHORTENING	4 LB 12 OZ	9 1/3 C	
140611	ORANGE RIND, GRATED		2 1/3 C	ADD 1/3 SUGAR: MIX 1 MIN AT
				LOW SPEED: ADD 1/3 EGGS;
131003	SUGAR, GRANULATED	11 LB 6 OZ	6 QT 1/2 C	MIX AGAIN 1 MIN. REPEAT
166045	EGGS, WHOLE	7 3/4 LB	7 3/4 PT	USING ALL SUGAR, EGGS AND
104019	WATER	10 1/2 LB	10 1/2 PT	WATER; BLEND IN COLORING
				AND FLAVORING. BAKE 350° F
180113	RED COLORING		7 1/2 t	ABOUT 30 MIN: WHEN DONE AND
180110	YELLOW COLORING		10 1/2 t	CAKE IS HOT SPREAD BLENDED
180016	ORANGE FLAVORING		7 1/2 t	SUGAR AND JUICE OVER
				CAKE, LETTING IT SOAK IN.
146063	ORANGE JUICE	7 LB	3 1/2 PT	
131003	SUGAR, GRANULATED	3.5 LB	7 3/4 C	CUT EACH PAN 5 X 10; DO NOT
				FROST THIS CAKE.

(b)

Figure 6-7

(a) An orange cake recipe for 100 portions exploded to give 350 portions (b).

170

Equipment

At times it may be necessary to require that a recipe be made using *only* specific kinds of equipment. Thus, a recipe standardized for the deep, narrower type of steam-jacketed kettle might not turn out the same if made in the more shallow, wider steam-jacketed kettle because of a difference in the evaporative rate between the two kettles. (In the shallow type the surface area exposed to evaporation is much greater.) Thus, if a change in equipment were to occur, the recipe might need to account for a change in the quantity of liquid added to make up for this greater evaporation. (*Note:* Some like recipes to list all the utensils, tools, and equipment used, just to be sure that the preparer gets all things assembled properly and has them on hand when needed.)

Inventory Analyses

Inventory analyses can be of assistance to management and others who need information. The amount to order can be planned with a proper safety and use factor assigned so stock does not run out between time of order and delivery. Inventory analyses can also quickly show usage rates of many items so inventories might be considerably reduced, thus reducing the cost of storage, money invested, and so forth. A computer can help by compiling a **usage file** as shown in Figure 6–8. Cost trends and other market trends can also be compiled and studied. Cost comparisons can also be made quickly between a number of seller prices even though the prices are quoted on different size units, since the basic unit cost such as gallon, pound, ounce, and so on, can be quickly determined. By compiling data for a period and then showing how prices change with the season, good purchasing information can be obtained on when the most favorable prices are apt to exist for items so they can be placed on the menu. **Pricing trends** can also be ascertained by having the computer print out a list of items organized by similar kinds of items with their prices. Figure 6–9 shows such a printout.

Order and Supplier File

Ordering

When the buyer has organized the day's orders from purchase and storeroom requisitions, ordering can proceed. Ordering is simplified with computer use. A salesperson can sit in a buyer's office and take an order, putting it into a laptop computer that is connected via modem to the seller's office, speeding up the process. If an item is out of stock or some other problem exists, the seller's computer informs both the salesperson and the buyer so that adjustments can be made on the spot.

    Direct or *on-line* **ordering** is a method or ordering through a computer when connected by telephone with the vendor's computer. A buyer is able to get information on availability, sizes, grades, price, and delivery date before an order is made. If enough sellers have such a system, it is possible to search the market for the best buy. After placing the order, the seller's computer signals back acceptance, asking for instructions on out-of-stock items or other queries. To be completely usable, both buyers and sellers need to standardize their programs so they are compatible, which,

```
                               One Week Usage Report
                                Reported In Cases

Inventory                Tue        Wed        Thu        Fri        Sat        Sun        Mon     Weekly
Number  Description   01-01-1991 01-02-1991 01-03-1991 01-04-1991 01-05-1991 01-06-1991 01-07-1991 Total
--------------------------------------------------------------------------------------------------------
Food

        01-BAKED GOOD

                                        BAKED GOODS
1086    BREAD BUTTOP WHITE    22.353    52.941     8.235     0.000    21.412    19.588    17.647   142.177
1089    BREAD FRENCH 16"       0.000     0.000     0.000     0.000    25.250    35.417     0.000    60.667
1083    BREAD LT RYE          31.733     0.000     0.000     0.000     0.000     0.000     0.000    31.733
1081    BREAD WHEAT SANDWICH   0.000     0.000    20.417     0.000     0.000     0.000     0.000    20.417
1063    BUN HAMB 4"            7.933     0.000     0.000    17.033     0.000    13.333     0.000    38.300
5019    ENGLISH MUFFIN 2 OZ    0.000     0.000     2.917     0.000     0.000     0.000     0.000     2.917
5038    PIE SHELLS            0.781      0.000     1.302     2.188     0.000     0.521     0.000     4.792
1079    ROLL FRENCH           0.000      0.000     0.000     0.000     7.222     0.000     0.000     7.222
5025    TORTILLA CORN 12"     0.000      0.000     0.000     0.000     2.950     0.000     0.000     2.950
5067    TORTILLA FLOUR 10"    0.000      0.000     0.000     0.625     0.000     0.000     0.000     0.625
5052    WAFFLES              0.000      0.000     0.000     0.000     6.792     0.000     0.000     6.792

        03-MILK & ICE

                                        MILK & ICE
3009    BUTTERMILK           10.938     1.732     0.000     0.000     0.676     5.359     3.464    22.169
3004    CREAM CHEESE          0.000     0.000     0.000     0.000     0.000     0.456     0.000     0.456
3091    HALF & HALF OZ.      14.300     3.472     4.389     0.000     0.000     0.000     3.472    25.633
3080    MILK 2% 5 GAL         2.170     6.222     0.707     2.910     3.177     1.247     4.286    20.718
3057    SOUR CREAM            0.000     0.000     0.000     5.775     0.000     1.010     0.000     6.785
3058    WHIPPED TOPPING       0.808     0.000     0.705     0.000     1.329     1.282     0.000     4.124
3086    WHIPPING CREAM        0.000     0.000     0.000     0.000     2.889     0.000     0.000     2.889
3013    YOGURT                1.885     0.000     0.000     0.586     0.000     0.000     0.000     2.471

        04-GROCERY

                                        GROCERIES
4345    ALMONDS SLICED        0.053     0.000     0.000     0.000     0.077     0.000     0.000     0.130
4272    APPLES SLICED CANNED  0.000     0.000     0.000     0.342     0.000     0.000     0.000     0.342
4342    BAKERS COCOA          0.201     0.080     0.000     0.317     0.000     0.000
4073    BAMBOO SHOOTS         0.000     0.000     0.000     0.000
4028    BEANS GARBANZO        0.000     1.008     0.0
4034    BEANS KIDNEY          0.000     0.64
4036    BEANS LENTIL          0.000
4229    BEANS NAVY DRY        0.000
4204    BREAD C
4113
4263
```

Figure 6-8

A usage report showing inventory by groups and day, giving totals for the week so amounts needed may be estimated by buyers. (Courtesy Foodco Corporation, 1002 South State, PO Box 1269, Orem, UT 84059.)

since there is so much variation in programs used, is a challenging thing to try to do. Perhaps a way will be found through Internet and World Wide Web to make such a system work. The ability to survey sellers' offerings through the Internet makes it possible for buyers to explore many sellers' offerings and then place orders.

Some sellers give buyers a module that contains all their products and product information so the buyer can read it and then order. However, because of price or other changes in the seller's offerings, without frequent updating the system can soon become unusable. It is wise, therefore, to purchase a module that can be updated. Buyers should be careful about tying into systems that might al-

Mon Jan 06, 1992

HISTORICAL PRICING
Pricing Stability Report

Item Number	Item Description	Case Description	Last Paid Price	Bid Date	Bid Cost	Percent Change	Up/ Down	Percent Stability
3018	PICKLE, SLICES	CS=5 GALS (4200 SLICE)	21.00	01-04-1992	21.65	3%	UP	99.29%
				12-02-1991	21.75			
				11-03-1991	22.05			
3019	CORN WHOLE KERNEL FROZEN	CS=1/20 LB	13.65	01-04-1992	16.35	17%	UP	98.58%
				12-02-1991	16.80			
				11-03-1991	16.20			
4000	RELISH SWEET PICKLE	CS=6/1 GALLONS	13.00	01-04-19992	14.50	10%	UP	98.57%
				12-02-1991	14.75			
				11-03-1991	15.10			
4002	TOMATO CATSUP	CS=6/#10 CANS	14.35	01-04-1992	13.00	10%	DOWN	99.66%
				12-02-1991	12.90			
				11-03-1991	13.00			
4003	MAYONNAISE	CS=4 GALLON TUB	19.00	01-04-19992	11.80	61%	DOWN	99.34%
				12-02-1991	11.75			
				11-03-1991	11.60			
4004	GRAIN BARLEY PEARL	CS=20 POUNDS	7.88	01-04-19992	8.00	2%	UP	100.00%
				11-03-1991	8.00			
				11-03-1991	8.00			
4006	FLOUR ALL PURPOSE	CS=1/50 LB	8.25	01-04-1992	5.25	57%	DOWN	98.93%
				12-02-1991	5.20			
				11-03-1991	5.10			
4007	SHORTENING QUICK BLEND	CS=50 LB	28.00	01-04-1992	26.65	5%	DOWN	97.98%
				12-02-1991	26.50			

Figure 6-9

A price stability report showing last price paid and last bid (quoted) price and percent of price change along with price stability price. (Courtesy Foodco Corporation, 1002 South State, PO Box 1269, Orem, UT 84059.)

PURCHASE ORDER

PO NUMBER: 921003   PO DATE: 01-01-1992

V M&M Meats   S   Food Service Solutions
E 3783 South 500 West   E   T 1139 South Orem Blvd.
N Midvale, Utah 83542   N   O Orem, Utah 84058
D   D   (801)225-7907
O 801-269-1861
R

LINE	ITEM NUMBER	ITEM DESCRIPTION	CASE DESCRIPTION	AMOUNT ORDERED	CASE COST	EXT. COST
1	1000	BEEF PATTIES 4-1	CS=10 LB	6.000	17.460	104.760
2	1001	BEEF GROUND 85/15	CS=30 LB	3.000	40.500	121.500
3	1002	BEEF NY STRIP	CS=1 LB	40.000	4.350	174.000
4	1003	BEEF DICED 1/2"	CS=20 LB	2.000	45.250	90.500
5	1007	BARON OF BEEF	CS=1 LB	350.000	1.690	591.500
6	1500	CHICKEN DICED WHT	CS=1/10 LB	2.000	23.520	47.040

TOTAL EXTENSION COST ORDERED = 1129.300

ORDERED BY _____   DATE ____/____/____
AUTHORIZED BY _____   DATE ____/____/____
RECEIVED BY _____   DATE ____/____/____

Figure 6–10

A computer purchase order. Such information when stored can be a source of information on setting up a receiving record, for informing stores of impending orders, and also for informing accounting of orders placed. (Courtesy Foodco Corporation, 1002 South State, PO Box 1269, Orem, UT 84059.)

low sellers access to information in their computers that the buyer would rather be kept confidential.

The computer is often used to print out purchase orders. Figure 6–10 illustrates a PO and Figure 6–11 shows a computer printout of a list of suppliers that can furnish specific kinds of items to a buyer, hence simplifying market searches.

Suppliers

To order by computer, a file of suppliers is a helpful adjunct. This **supplier file** should list suppliers' names, addresses, telephone numbers, and stock information on goods that can be purchased from them. Information as to their service may be included, along with things like billing, receiving, and credit information. The computer can be programmed to come up with suppliers who can furnish special items,

Fri Jan 11

ORDERING INFORMATION

Ordering Data File Report

Item Number	Item Description	Order Frequency	Min. Par Level	Max. Par Level	Vendor Number	Vendor Description	Prep Yield
1000	GROUND BEEF 80/20 MIX	WEEKLY	0.00	0.00	120	MENDELSON WEST	
					131	HINTON FOOD DISTRIBUTORS	
					1	\FOODCO5\COMMSJVS	
1001	ROAST BEEF	WEEKLY	0.00	0.00	131	HINTON FOOD DISTRIBUTORS	
					120	MENDELSON WEST	
					115	UNITED BEEF PACKERS	
					101	ALL AMERICAN FOOD DIST.	
					1	\FOODCO5\COMMSJVS	
1002	BEEF SHOULDER	WEEKLY	0.00	0.00	115	UNITED BEEF PACKERS	
					131	HINTON FOOD DISTRIBUTORS	
					116	ZION FOODS, INC.	
					120	MENDELSON WEST	
1003	STEW MEAT	WEEKLY	0.00	0.00	131	HINTON FOOD DISTRIBUTORS	
					115	UNITED BEEF PACKERS	
					101	ALL AMERICAN FOOD DIST.	
					116	ZION FOODS, INC.	
					120	MENDELSON WEST	
1004	GROUND BEEF, 70/30	WEEKLY	0.00	0.00			
1005	TOP OF RIB	WEEKLY	0.00	0.00	131	HINTON FOOD DISTRIBUTORS	
					101	ALL AMERICAN FOOD DIST.	
					115	UNITED BEEF PACKERS	
					120	MENDELSON WEST	
1006	BRISKETS, UNCOOKED	WEEKLY	0.00	0.00	131	HINTON FOOD DISTRIBUTORS	
					111	SYSCO FOOD SERVICES	
					120	MENDELSON WEST	
					115	UNITED BEEF PACKERS	
					101	ALL AMERICAN FOOD DIST.	
					116	ZION FOODS, INC.	
1007	GROUND VEAL 80/20 MIX	WEEKLY	0.00	0.00	131	HINTON FOOD DISTRIBUTORS	
					115	UNITED BEEF PACKERS	
					120	MENDELSON WEST	
					116	ZION FOODS, INC.	
					1	\FOODCO5\COMMSJVS	
1008	KNOCKWURST, SPECIALS	WEEKLY	0.00	0.00	102	BAY PURVEYORS	
					111	SYSCO FOOD SERVICES	
					131	HINTON FOOD DISTRIBUTORS	
					115	UNITED BEEF PACKERS	
1009	HOT DOGS 8/1	WEEKLY	0.00	0.00	102	BAY PURVEYORS	
					110	HENRY LEE SALES CO.	
					111	SYSCO FOOD SERVICES	
					131	HINTON FOOD DISTRIBUTORS	
					120	MENDELSON WEST	
					115	UNITED BEEF PACKERS	

Figure 6-11

This computer list informs buyers of which vendor sells specific items. (Courtesy Foodco Corporation, 1002 South State, PO Box 1269, Orem, UT 84059.)

thus simplifying the market search. Days when the supplier will deliver are usually noted. Other material may be set up as shown in Figure 6–12. Some operations give suppliers a code number and identify them by that number in the files.

Specification File

Before contacting vendors, a buyer may wish to check and verify grade, brand or quality, packaging, unit of purchase, or get other information on items the facility purchases. Or perhaps the buyer wants to give a vendor this information. Such information will be available in a **specification file.** The facts the buyer wants can be abstracted from the item's specification and placed on the order sheet. If the specification is to be sent to a vendor it can be printed out and then faxed, making transfer easy and quick.

Specifications must be sent out with advertisements for bids so bidders know exactly what is they are to bid on. As noted in the discussion on specifications in another chapter, the two types of specifications are general specifications and product specifications.

Receiving File

When you visit a supermarket, the purchases are run over a glass plate under which a fixed scanner (reader) reads the code on the package, translating it into a number, product name, amount, and price and then printing this information on your sales slip. It also sends the information to the store computer, recording the sale in a **receiving file.** If you are purchasing something in a department store, a portable **scanner** that looks like a little gun is aimed at the Universal Product Code (UPC) and reads the same information.

It is possible today for a food service in receiving to use a portable scanning "gun" to scan the code numbers of sellers and store desired receiving information. The fact that a lot of packages are received from sellers with no UPC code makes this system of little value, but a way to get around this deficiency has been found. Printed sheets (*pick-up* sheets) are available that list code numbers for all items purchased by a facility. The list also contains desired purchase information for each code. This printed sheet can be held in front of a gun scanner to read the printed code and the other purchase information. For instance, a sheet has on it a code number for canned string beans. Four cases of canned string beans are received with no code numbers on them. The receiver picks up the reader, aims it at the proper code number for canned string beans on the printed sheet. Other information printed with the code is also stored: "Blue Lake. Cut. 6/10 $27.85." The receiver then inputs "4" into the reader indicating the number of cases received. Figure 6–13a shows a gun reader about the size of a small hand calculator reading a code; in Figure 6–13b codes are shown as they might appear on the pick-up sheet with desired receiving information. The purchase information on the sheet can be varied to reflect the needs of the receiving facility. When you want to transfer data stored in the scanner to the computer, you connect the scanner to the computer via a docking station and feed the information into the computer for storage. Electronic units are now avail-

Fri Jan 11

Vendor List

Vendor Name & Contact Information

Vendor Number: 101
Vendor Name: ALL AMERICAN FOOD DIST.
Phone Number:
Contact 1:

Address 1: 14735 N.W. 25 TH CRT.
Address 2: MIAMI, FL. 33054
Address 3: (305)949-5350
Contact 2:

Payment Terms

Type: MEA	Discount Days:	0	
Terms: 30 DAYS	Disc. Percent:	0	
Due Days:	30	Status:	

Tax & Historical Information

Last Purch Date: 01-01-1990
Purchases YTD: 0.000
Purch Last Year: 0.000
Discounts YTD: 0.000
Disc. Last Year: 0.000
Distr. Account: <Not Define

Gets 1099?: N
1099 ID#:
1099 Amt. YTD: 0.000
1099 Next Year: 0.000

Vendor Name & Contact Information

Vendor Number: 102
Vendor Name: BAY PURVEYORS
Phone Number:
Contact 1:

Address 1: 2177 N.W. 8TH. AVENUE
Address 2: MIAMI, FL. 33127
Address 3: (305)324-7217
Contact 2:

Payment Terms

Type: GRO	Discount Days:	0	
Terms: 30 DAYS	Disc. Percent:	0	
Due Days:	30	Status:	

Tax & Historical Information

Last Purch Date: 07-30-1992
Purchases YTD: 36363.190
Purch Last Year: 0.000
Discounts YTD: 0.000
Disc. Last Year: 0.000
Dist. Account: <Not Define

Gets 1099?: N
1099 ID#:
1099 Amt. YTD: 0.000
1099 Next Year: 0.000

Figure 6–12
A Printout of the First Two Vendors on a Vendor's List. (Courtesy Foodco Corporation, 1002 South State, PO Box 1269, Orem, UT 84059.)

Figure 6-13

(a) A portable scanner. (b) Fabricated company codes that might appear on a pick-up sheet with other de-sired information. (Courtesy Advanced Analytical, Inc., 31149 Via Colinas, #610, Westlake Village, CA 91362.)

able that pick up data from the scanner and transfer it automatically into the computer without a physical docking station.

The scanner can be used to read vendor invoices, names, and other receiving information desired from the invoice. Scanner information can also be used to add items going into storage and deduct them from inventory when issued. Receiving information can at the same time be sent to accounting, management, production, and others. Figure 6–14 shows the first page of a **receiving report** as a computer might print it out at the end of the day.

Sophisticated scanners are appearing on the market. One completely automatic version can do built-in image processing and has an auto-focus zoom lens with close-up focusing and 24-bit color. Some even have cameras in them to take images in color for transfer into the computer.

Inventory or Ingredient File

Because computers were first introduced in the purchase function to record inventory information, most computer purchase programs are built around the **inventory file.** In fact, with the new computers today that are able to hold such enormous amounts of information, all files may be merged into one module with the inventory file. Whatever the case, all files should be compatible with the inventory file and with each other. The inventory file and other files should be constantly updated so the information is reliable.

An **inventory sheet** should list items purchased by department, such as food, housekeeping, engineering, and office and accounting. Next, within each department, items are listed by group such as linens, soap, toilet paper, wash cloths, face towels, and bath towels in the housekeeping department. Further differentiation into several more subgroups often is necessary, as shown in Figure 6–15.

It is also necessary to store inventory information such as item size and cost of the purchase unit, the issue unit, and the use unit. We need to know the amount of units in an issue unit so use unit price can be calculated for recipes. Thus, if a case

Receiving Report   Date 5/5/97   Page 1 of 4

Item Code	Item Name	Vendor Name	Vendor No.	Invoice No.	PO No.	Invoice Date	Quantity Received	Unit Cost	Total Cost
			Produce						
30022	Lettuce, Iceberg, No 1	O Cty Prod	00954	YC0028V	O11C67	5/3/97	3 cs	17.50	22.50
30029	Onions, Yellow, No. 1	O Cty Prod	00954	YC0028V	O11C67	5/3/97	1 bag	8.45	8.45
30038	Tomatoes, pks, 5X6, No. 1	Wrenz	00941	63792	O11C55	5/5/97	2 lugs	11.45	22.90
30014	Bananas, ripe	Wrenz	00941	63792	O11C55	5/5/97	21 lb	.31	6.51
30006	Avocados, Fuerte, 24's	Wrenz	00941	63792	O11C55	5/5/97	1 lug	15.00	15.00
30014	Cabbage, Domestic, No. 1	Wrenz	00941	63792	O11C55	5/5/97	1 sk	14.50	14.50
30002	Asparagus, Wash. No. 1	Wrenz	00941	63792	O11C55	5/5/97	3 crates	7.20	21.60
30032	Oranges, FL, Navels, No. 1	Wrenz	00941	63792	O11C55	5/5/07	5 ctns	12.00	60.00
Total Produce									171.46
			Meat						
70133	No. 109s Med. Choice	Little	00967	CS0074	O11C72	5/4/97	5 (105 lb)	1.78	186.90
70208	Ground Beef, No. 136	Little	00967	CS0074	O11C72	5/4/97	50 lb	1.39	69.50
70109	Tenderloin, No. 190A, Med Choice	Little	00967	CS0074	O11C72	5/4/97	67 lb	3.87	259.29
70100	Top Sirloin, No. 185D, Med Choice	Little	00967	CS0074	O11C72	5/4/97	59 lb	2.07	122.13
Total Meat									637.82
			Poultry						
60551	Turkey, Tom, Young, No. 1	Shapple	00968	R667	O11C66	5/4/97	66 lb	.90	59.40
60542	Chickens, Broilers, No. 1	Shapple	00968	R667	O11C66	5/4/97	48 lb	.59	28.32
60531	Ducks, Long Island, No. 1	Shapple	00968	R667	O11C66	5/4/97	32 lb	1.55	49.60
Total Poultry									137.32
			Dairy						
4012	Milk, 1/2 pts, 2%	Dennit	00956	TM078	O11C61	5/5/97	4 cs	.32	30.72
4013	Milk, gals, skim	Dennit	00956	TM078	O11C61	5/5/97	10 gal	4.40	44.00
4022	Butter, pats, 100s, 5 lb, AA	Dennit	00956	TM078	O11C61	5/5/97	4 cs	7.25	29.00
4023	Butter, cube, 64 lb, B	Dennit	00956	TM078	O11C61	5/5/97	1 cube	1.30	83.20
4018	Half-Half, pkts, 100s	Dennit	00956	TM078	O11C61	5/5/97	5 boxes	8.00	40.00
Total									226.92

Figure 6–14

The first page of a computer receiving report as it might look at the end of the day. At the start of the day, items like date of invoice, invoice number, quantity delivered, and price would not be on the report but would be filled in at the time of delivery. In this particular report the facility is using its own product code numbers and not UPCs.

of 6/10 canned string beans costs $24.00, and one can is issued, the issue price is $4.00 (24/6 = 4). We can get 20 portions from a can, so the use cost is $0.20 (4/20 = 0.20). Information such as this is needed to calculate recipe or **portion costs.**

The inventory system should be organized to give the storage location of items and their location within this stored area. Inventory sheets should be printed

Item	Kind	Subkind	Unit of Purchase	Inventory Count	Purchase Price	Total Value
Sugar						
	Granulated					
		Regular				
		Breakfast, fine				
		Coarse, sanding				
		Packet				
		Cube				
		Bar				
	Brown					
		Light				
		Medium				
		Dark				
	Powdered					
		XXXXXX				
		10X				

Figure 6-15
Inventory sheet showing sugar subgroups.

to reflect this order, so inventory takers can proceed in inventorying along a straight path and not have to jump around.

Coding of some kind is a requirement. Some operations set up their own codes, but using the UPC system is more desirable because it interfaces with the codes on packages received.

Because not all goods delivered are UPC coded, the use of the scanner described earlier can be duplicated here. Thus, when inventorying, if you see on the shelves five 30-lb cans of frozen strawberries, you can pick up with the reader the printed fabricated code information on the sheet for frozen strawberries and record "5" to complete the inventorying of this product (see Figure 6–13). With such a system, one person with a clipboard in one hand containing the printed UPCs or fabricated codes and other inventory information and a scanner in the other can take an inventory where it usually takes two people, one to count and call out and one to record.

Normally the price given by the computer is the last purchase price, but this can vary with different operations. If the same kind of goods has been purchased at different times at different prices, management may want an average price or the actual price of the item issued. It's simple. No writing, no fuss. Just a quick read, count, and record.

Cost of Goods Sold

In most inventory programs, once the computer gets the price and the number of units at that price, it automatically multiplies these to get the total value. These total unit values can then be added to get total inventory value. Then, the **cost of goods sold** can be calculated using the formula so accounting and management can calculate how well the enterprise has done in the period:

Inventory at beginning of period	$XXXXXX
Add purchases during period	$XXXXXX
Total inventory and purchases	$XXXXXX
Less inventory at end of period	$XXXXXX
Cost of goods sold	$XXXXXX
Dollar sales plus other income	$XXXXXX
Less cost of goods sold	$XXXXXX
Gross profit	$XXXXXX

Then, by deducting other expenses (salaries, wages, rent, light, water, trash removal, etc.) you arrive at *net profit before taxes.*

GRAPHICS

The new computers allow food services to print their own menus, table tents and other advertising, accounting or other forms, and so forth. It is possible to create graphics or to transfer pictures and other graphic art from clip art material into your copy. (*Clip art* is canned graphics for the computer that can be extracted from the clip art file and transferred into your file.) Some desktop programs come with a clipboard gallery from which you can select copy suitable for use in the document being constructed. Color is possible. You can also create your own art and are limited only by the artistic knowledge and skill of the computer operator.

Some facilities like using the computer to do their menus and other small printing jobs. It is faster and gives them greater flexibility. Menus can be changed at will. Printing jobs can be expensive and, once printed, making changes is not easy. Sometimes do-it-yourself menus do not fit into a facility's overall marketing strategy in terms of quality. You must be able to create menus of satisfactory quality to make them look professional and do the necessary job of meeting patron needs and market products for the facility. An article in the May 1997 issue of *Restaurants USA,* "Maximize Menu Merchandising Power," favors the use of a professional menu designer claiming they can usually design a better merchandising menu. This service can, however, be expensive. The article says that the cost of design, copywriting, and printing ranges from $2,000 to $10,000. However, in the very next article, "The Great Menu Contest Winners," the first place grand prize went to a handmade menu costing about "a buck apiece," but most other menu winners were designer originated.

OTHER USES OF THE COMPUTER

Once a module with a foodservice's files are stored in a computer, much analytical and other information is available to management. Portion cost and gross profit of menu items can be calculated. Total food cost and other costs can be compiled. Inventory value is known, and inventory use can be analyzed. If a menu analysis file is set up, the menu can be analyzed to see how well it suited patrons. Much data can be derived for accounting purposes. An analysis is possible of market price trends and usage of supplies. Supplier data is available, and also market information that can be stored to aid in supplier selection and market search. However, most authorities warn against compiling too much data: "Compile only what you need and what you can use" is their advice.

ANALYSIS OF THE PURCHASING TASK

The last step in purchasing is the analysis of how well the entire purchasing program has been performed with a view to reducing costs, errors, waste, and time among other things. Improvement of product quality is another goal. New foods are constantly coming onto the market and these should be scrutinized to see if they might help in solving problems or otherwise lead to improvements. Market developments should be evaluated. The buyer should be constantly searching for new ideas and new ways to improve products or purchase techniques.

The computer gives management much more information with which to make an evaluation. It can also simplify and shorten decision-making efforts. We saw in earlier discussion how menu and inventory analysis can provide information that enables management to improve in that area. Much data in other areas can be gathered to make comparisons and give management and others insight into where beneficial steps might be taken.

If beginning and ending inventories, purchases during period, total sales and other income for period, and other expenses are input into the computer, you can quickly come up with a calculation of net profit before taxes. Next, you can calculate taxes and deduct them from this total to get net profit. The whole procedure is simplified and speeded up over the manual system. (See earlier discussion on calculating cost of goods sold.)

It is also possible to also analyze menus to see how well their items meet nutritional standards. Programs are available that use spreadsheets to show comparative data or to design bar graphs or pie charts or otherwise graphically present information. Such a program may be helpful in day-to-day operations by allowing management to put nutritional values of items on menus or set up advertising material that uses this information.

The **Internet** now makes available a vast amount of information that, if used, can be of help in making improvements. Planners can try out ideas by manipulating data. Playing "what if" can yield much helpful information. Thus, you could take a projected menu and run it through its forecast of portions sold and income, deducting from this the estimated costs, to see if a better profit will result. There are many possibilities.

The use of computer information, plus scrutiny and evaluation, allows you to summarize ideas and make a conclusion as to whether one could have in any way improved the menu and the purchasing procedures. You should not depend on figures alone, but combine their use with observations and constant questioning on whether something could be improved. The Gilbreths, famous industrial engineers, once said, "There's always a better way," and this should be remembered by those who purchase.

SUMMARY

Modern computers have a much greater storage capacity, operate more quickly, and do far more things than early computers did. Before any computer program is installed, you should be sure that it suits your needs and that those who will have to use it are well indoctrinated in its use. The first use of computers in purchasing involved inventory keeping and analysis, and so today most canned programs are built around the inventory file.

The system described in this chapter starts with a menu and menu analysis file from which a menu can be planned. Once this is done, a forecast is made of quantities required and from that amounts to order from stores or to purchase are determined. Then suppliers are contacted and orders placed.

The next step in the program is the receiving. A scanner and printed sheets of code numbers and other desired purchase information are available that can be used in receiving to make the job easier and quicker to do. The results may be more accurate also since only a count of purchase units received need be made by the receiver. This scanner can also pick up the vendor's invoice number and any other invoice information desired, which is then transferred into the computer for permanent storage and for compilation of the receiving report. Received items going into stores can be placed in inventory and directs recorded. The computer can not only store inventory amounts and indicate stock levels and reorder points, but it can keep a perpetual inventory by recording receipts and issues.

The scanner and the printed sheet with codes and desired purchase information can make inventorying simpler, quicker, and easier and can save labor because one person instead of two can do the job. From inventory value, plus other accounting information, you can calculate the cost of goods sold, gross, net, and after-tax profit. From all of the purchasing data gathered, you can derive other helpful information.

The modern computer can also do graphics—if desired, in color—which enables you to make menus, advertising, and other printing jobs. Some authorities, however, feel that professional menu planners can do a better job, making their cost worthwhile.

The last step in purchasing is analysis—after all purchase functions have been completed and the products served to patrons—of how well the purchasing task was done. The computer makes it possible to do a more complete and thorough analysis than can be done by hand. However, you should still use observation and other subjective data with such computer information. After you make an estimate of how well the computer task was done and where it could be improved, the analysis is complete.

REVIEW QUESTIONS

1. What advantages are there to using a canned purchasing program rather than setting up your own?

2. Pair the correct letter designator for a phrase on the right with its counterpart on the left:

_____Reader   a. Off the shelf

_____Modem   b. Set of information on a disk

_____Sizing   c. A universal code

_____Popularity index   d. Changes computer signals so they can be sent over the phone

_____Cost of goods sold

_____Canned   e. Scanner

_____UPC   f. Percent of items sold of the total sold of a group

_____File   g. Computer increasing or decreasing the yield of a recipe

                                     h. Beginning inventory plus total purchases less ending inventory

3. What is a subrecipe?

4. Why might a facility want a supplier file?

5. What information should a recipe file contain?

6. What should an ingredient or inventory file contain?

7. Why should a company installing a new computer system train the staff to use it and then follow up with strong interest afterwards?

8. Describe the use of a scanner, codes, and other pick-up sheet information in receiving and in inventory taking.

9. Why would a recipe have different portion sizes?

10. What must take place before a foodservice buyer can start to purchase items?

KEY WORDS AND CONCEPTS

canned (off-the-shelf) programs

coding

cost of goods sold

direct (on-line) ordering

exploding

forecast file

Internet

inventory analyses

inventory (ingredient) file

inventory sheet

menu analysis file

popularity index

point-of-sale (POS)

portion cost

pricing trends

receiving file

receiving report

recipe cost

recipe file

scanner

sizing

specification file

supplier file

usage file

CHAPTER 7

Meat

Jan. 31, 1852, The Illustrated London News. Ritchie and M'Call's Preserved Meat Establishment, Houndsditch.-The Kitchen. (Australia). March 5, 1870. From the Louis Szwathmary collection, Culinary Archives and Museum, Johnson and Wales University, used by permission of Dr. Szwathmary and Johnson and Wales University.

Chapter Objectives

1. To help buyers understand the importance of meat purchasing to menu performance and to inform them about the physical structure and makeup of meat so they know how meat reacts in cooking.
2. To indicate how meat can be tenderized by various methods.
3. To describe some important features of the meat market, how some meats are processed, and some regulations controlling the marketing of meat.
4. To give some factors on how to calculate the best buys in meat.
5. To discuss the advantages and disadvantages of using frozen meat.
6. To discuss the classification of meat and how it is graded for quality and yield.

7. To detail the use of the Institutional Meat Purchase Specifications (IMPS) and briefly discuss the eight IMPS categories of meats.

8. To review how to identify the various cuts of meat and how to judge grade.

9. To list some criteria needed for the proper purchase of ready-to-serve meats and canned meats and to discuss the use of textured vegetable protein products with meat.

10. To illustrate how meat specifications should be written.

INTRODUCTION

In many operations **meat** comprises more than half the food budget. In addition to being an operation's most costly item, meats are important for patron satisfaction because they are usually the central food of the meal. Menus are often shaped around the main meat item a patron selects in that other foods are chosen to go with the meat, rather than the other way around. Because meat is usually the most important item selected by patrons, its palatability satisfaction decides whether a patron is satisfied with the entire meal. Besides these two important considerations, the meat item selected often determines how much money a patron spends in the operation. For these reasons—cost considerations, patron satisfaction, and check average—buyers should put a lot of effort into the purchase of meats.

Buyers need to know a lot about the cooking of meats. For instance, some meats are suitable only for long cooking by moist heat, while others are best suited for short, dry heat cooking methods. A buyer who purchases a chuck tender—a long, moist heat cooking item—thinking it will make a tender enough steak to broil is going to have to do some dexterous explaining to irate patrons, production staff, and manager. Unless a buyer properly interprets what the menu planner intended in terms of meat items, the menu will fail.

We consume more meat than poultry or fish but this ratio is changing, in part because of a dietary trend toward menu items like fowl or fish, which are usually lower in cholesterol and fat than meats.

Menu Strategy

Planning a menu may be challenged at times by the cost of meat, such costs being more than patrons are willing to pay. Substitutions can be made such as putting on a chicken entree instead of meat. Or, you may use a different cut of meat and prepare it in a proper but client-acceptable way. Or, use lower quality meat that has been tenderized, such as steaks treated with papain, or restructured meat. Using soy meat extenders is also a possibility in some dishes. Or, why not reduce cooking losses by cooking meats at lower temperatures? Be sure to include meat thermometers in such procedures and check oven temperatures to be sure they operate at desired ones. Sometimes, one can serve an item in a slightly different way and thus use a portion of smaller size. For example, putting a steak on a piece of toast can make it appear larger. Others, in planning menus, often try to cut corners on some of the other foods served with the meats and in this way make up for the meat cost.

Perhaps sharpening one's purchasing techniques can do the job. Are good specifications being written? Is there any way in which one can eliminate some factors in what is being purchased but get the same result? Can purchasing in greater quantities help reduce costs? (Be sure in buying larger quantities not to judge only cost per pound AP; there are also storage costs, money tied up in inventory, risk, etc. to consider.) How about submitting meat orders for bid? A complete examination of how the buying is being done might yield some helpful information. We consider these questions in this chapter.

Handling and Cooking of Meats

In Chapter 2 the problem of sanitation and public concern about it was discussed. Meat and poultry were noted to cause illnesses, especially from *Salmonella* and *E. coli* 0157:H7 bacteria. Both bacteria are carried in the intestinal area of healthy animals; both can cause severe cramps, vomiting, and diarrhea. They can be the cause of death or of severe health complications that may last for years. The new HCAAP inspection system discussed in Chapter 2 is now in place, ensuring that meats and poultry are being processed as safely as possible and that contaminated products are being kept from the food chain. Another area now needs to be addressed: Food services need to learn and practice good handling procedures for these products and cook them properly.

Most infections of *E.coli* occur from ground meat that is not thoroughly cooked. Even a hamburger in the pink stage may be a source of infection. Some people are not apt to change their eating of rare steaks or roasts—they will still want even their lamb chops or lamb roast "pink in the middle"—and no food service is going to commit suicide by refusing to serve them the way the public wants them. In their favor it might be said that pieces of meat—not ground—such as chops, steaks, or roasts, if contaminated, will be contaminated on their exteriors not inside and therefore in cooking this contaminated area is subjected to enough heat to make it safe to eat. However, when it comes to serving pink hamburgers or a tartare steak, the line should be drawn. No operation wants to go through what the fast-food operation in the state of Washington went through after serving hamburgers that were contaminated and not thoroughly cooked!

Besides proper cooking, meat and poultry should receive good care in receiving and handling. They should be moved into refrigeration as quickly as possible and not left around at ambient temperatures, which could cause contamination to grow. Items that meat or poultry touch should also receive thorough cleaning and sanitation because the surface of the meat or poultry can contaminate them and then these items can spread contamination to other foods or other items.

PHYSICAL PROPERTIES OF MEATS

Meat Structure

Meat is 45% to 72% moisture with the rest solids such as protein, bone, fat, and some other substances in very minute quantities.

Muscle

Muscle consists of long fibers (long cells) grouped into bundles (*fasciculi*) bound together by connective tissue (*perimysium*). The fibers can be centimeters long and are threadlike cells, slightly tapered at both ends. Figure 7–1 shows a cross-section of a muscle with bundles of fibers grouped to form a muscle. These fibers are filled with moisture, fats, minerals, vitamins, proteins, flavoring substances, and other compounds. Young animals have fine fibers and bundles; these coarsen as the animal ages. Fine bundles, firm, moist flesh with no stickiness, and a good color with a soft sheen indicates good-quality, tender meat.

Connective Tissue

A fibrous membrane called **connective tissue** binds muscle fibers and fastens the muscle to the bone. The basic fiber is called *reticulin,* thought to make **collagen,** a white tissue. As an animal ages, this collagen increases and tends to form cross-links making it into yellow connective tissue called **elastin.** Muscles that get the most exercise—those that move, such as the leg or neck muscles—develop the most connective tissue. Muscles that give support such as the midback muscles develop less.

Tenderness.   Tenderness is correlated with the amount of connective tissue and the feed and treatment the animal gets before and after slaughter. When an animal is slaughtered the muscles are flaccid, but as ***rigor mortis*** sets in the muscles tighten

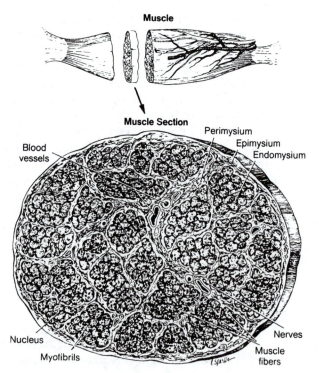

Figure 7-1
Drawing of a muscle in section showing fibers, bundle arrangement, pervading connective tissues, nerves, and blood vessels. (From *Principles of Meat Science* by John C. Forrest et al. Copyright (c) 1975 by W.H. Freeman and Company. Copyright (c) 1988 by Kendall/Hunt Publishing Company. Used with permission.)

up, shrink, and become hard and firm. Meat cooked in this state is tough; we call such meat *green*. Eventually, lactic acid and other substances relax the muscles so they become soft and flabby again, except in some animals the process is not complete. While not completely understood, the condition seems to develop in animals that lack a fat cover. Because young animals usually have little fat cover, they develop this toughness.

If an animal is kept confined and given good feed and care rather than left to live out on the range, the meat is less tough. Kobi beef is a very tender Japanese product. The animal is confined, fed beer mash, and given daily muscle massages, which develops very tender meat. Confining an animal for 180 days to a feed lot and feeding it corn usually develops Prime grade meat, while feeding this way for 150 days develops Choice meat, the second grade.

If a muscle's connective tissue is collagen with little elastin, it can be tenderized by cooking; if the elastin level is high, then cooking is of little help. The reason is that plain collagen breaks down in most heat into water and gelatin; acids such as tomatoes or vinegar speed the reaction. Some meats become tender with little cooking, such as tenderloin, because they contain very little collagen or elastin. However, a shoulder clod usually has too much collagen in it to cook to a tender piece of meat with short, dry heat cooking. Instead, it must be cooked by a longer time via a moist heat process, such as braising, boiling, or stewing. Braising a shoulder clod roast in a specially flavored wine and vinegar marinade makes this piece of meat into a tender pot roast called a sauerbraten.

No method of cooking changes elastin. To tenderize meat high in elastin, we have to break it up by grinding it, pounding it, cubing it, or piercing it with needles. Such meat is thus made into ground meat, cube steaks, pounded before cooking, etc.

Meat can also be tenderized by using enzymes that digest the connective tissue. Thus, meat may be injected with enzymes like **papain** from papaya, *bromelin* from pineapple, or *fictin,* from figs or dipped or dusted with one of these to be tenderized through such digestion. We also inject an animal before death with a papain solution and then slaughter the animal. This way the animal before death distributes the papain throughout the body so it is well and completely distributed. These tenderizers are enzymes that are activated when warmed.

Meat in itself contains enzymes that tenderize the meat. This tenderization from enzymes occurs in ripening meat (discussed later). It can also occur at low-temperature cooking. Meat cooked in a plastic wrap immersed in hot water takes a long time to cook, giving the enzymes a longer chance to work on the meat. The meat, even though cooked a long time, comes out pink and is not overcooked. Roasting at low temperature in an oven that closely controls temperature also gives the enzymes a longer chance to tenderize. Enzymes are destroyed at fairly high heat.

It has also been found that giving carcasses a high voltage electric shock shatters connective tissue, thus making the meat more tender. Freezing can also make meat more tender, by breaking up connective tissue. Meat thawed and refrozen several times may even become slightly mushy because of it.

Restructured meat is tenderized because the meat is frozen and then finely shaved or cut up. This breaks down the connective tissue. It is then thawed, a half percent of salt added, and the meat mixed 8 to 10 minutes, to help draw out the collagen, which acts as a binding agent. It is then shaped into steaks, roasts, or other desired shapes. In this way, tough cuts can be taken and made into tender ones. The product also is quite flavorful because, as we shall see, these tougher cuts have more flavor than the more tender ones.

Meat is usually most tender when raw, less so when rare; it begins to toughen when medium done and can actually be tough when well done. High heat toughens proteins; gentle, low heat is more kind to it. And, finally, on tenderness, we are now beginning to genetically raise animals from strains that develop a more tender meat. Thus, as time goes on we will be able to breed animals that have more and more tender meat. Perhaps someday we won't need teeth anymore to chew it!

Shrink

Heat firms up meat proteins by a process called *coagulation*. Besides becoming firm, the meat fibers denaturate (lose moisture), a process in which the meat fibers shrink and press out juice. We can see this when we put meat on a griddle to fry. Gentle heat induces less shrinkage; high heat causes more. Low shrinkage can mean the meat is more flavorful and we get more portions from it. Some weight loss also occurs in dry heat cooking because of moisture loss. A shrink of 15% to 20% might be considered low.

Bones

Muscles are attached to bones, which give the body solid support and allow the muscles to function in their proper place. Otherwise, with no skeletal structure, animals would be like jellyfish. Bones are largely made of calcium and phosphorus. They first form as a firm cartilage, which is largely protein, but, as the animal ages, this cartilage ossifies (hardens) by being replaced by calcium and phosphorus.

As far as buyers are concerned, bones have no value, adding only to the weight of the meat and therefore its cost. Bones do contribute some flavor from the tissues adhering to them and from their marrow. That is why we crack bones when making stock so the water can get at the marrow. Besides flavor, bones can yield some gelatin. If we add a bit of acid in making a stock from bones, calcium and phosphorus can be dissolved, and, for some people, this can be a good source of calcium in the diet. A bowl of soup made of such stock contributes more calcium than a glass of milk.

Fat

The amount of animal fat consumed is decreasing, while the amount from vegetable sources is increasing. The reason is that animal fat is higher in saturated fat and cholesterol, things people today wish to limit. We can expect this trend toward a lower consumption of animal fat to continue as we raise animals that develop less fat and we trim more fat from meat (see Figure 7–2).

The amount of fat in meat is correlated with age; young animals tend to be leaner than the older ones. Feeding also is a factor; well-fed animals develop more fat. The grade of meat also indicates fat content, the higher grades having more fat. The fat from sheep is the most saturated; beef is next, with pork last.

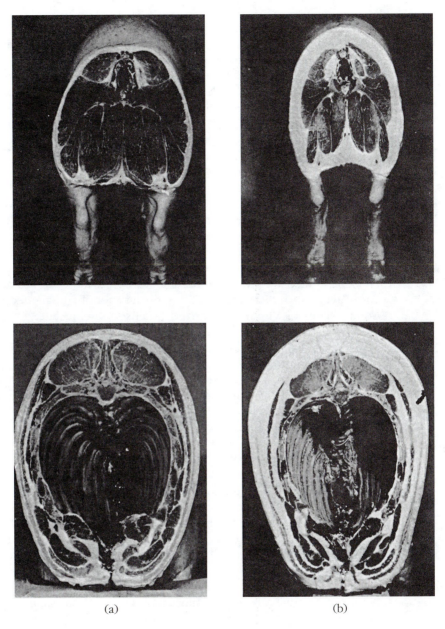

(a)   (b)

Figure 7-2

*Breeding and genetic science is making a change in the amount of fat in meat.
(a) A comparison of the amount of fat found on the carcass of some breeds of hogs.
(b) Thin muscling, shown in the animals in column (a), compared to the heavier
muscled animals, shown in column (b), mean more meat to bone. Note while the
skeletal structures are about the same bone weight, the heavier muscling does not show
a similar equalness in meat yield.* (Courtesy Iowa State University, USDA photos.)

Fat on an animal is found in three general areas. Fat found inside the body is called **body cavity** fat; on the outside it is called **finish;** that distributed within the muscles is called **marbling.** Body cavity fat starts first around the heart and kidneys and then, as the animal fattens, feathers out (shades out) from these thicker areas. Finish begins over the shoulders and rump and then, as the animal fattens, moves downward and forward. Marbling is seen as tiny flecks of fat in the muscles.

Fatty tissues contain from 15% to 50% moisture, which keeps meat moist during dry heat cooking. A roast is baked with the fat side up so as the fat melts it drips down over the meat, basting it and keeping it moist; turkeys are roasted backside up, since the back is where the most fat is. We pull strips of fat through meat in *larding; barding* is laying fatty meat over meat. In both, the fat contributes moisture to the meat in cooking. Low-fat meat is difficult to broil or roast or even sauté without added fat. Lean meats are often better cooked by moist heat for this reason. Under a broiler, lean meat twists up, ending up as a dry, unpalatable product.

Fat is responsible for some of meat's richness and flavor. Fat is an organic substance that absorbs other organic compounds. Thus, the organic flavor esters in an animal's feed are picked up in the body by the fat. Corn-fed pork has a sweet, corn flavor, much different than the sourish flavor of garbage-fed pork. Smithfield County hams of Virginia are prized because they are fattened on peanuts, the peanut flavor carrying over in the flesh. Wild ducks feeding in sea marshes take on a fishy flavor, while those eating wild rice and other grains in the Midwest have a much better flavor.

Thus, in summary, fat adds moistness, richness, and flavor. It nevertheless has some disadvantages in that it adds extra calories and puts more fat and cholesterol into the body.

Color

Myoglobin and **hemoglobin** are two substances that make meat appear red. When heat strikes them they change to **hematin,** a grayish pigment, the color of well-done meat. Oxygen in the air turns myglobin a brighter red, making a substance called **oxymyoglobin.** Thus, ground meat can appear bright red on the outside, while the interior takes on a darker color. Some think the meat is not good, but, if this interior meat is allowed to stand exposed to the air for a time, it too will turn a bright red. **Nitrosomyoglobin** is created when myglobin is exposed to nitrogen as it can be when meat is cured by using nitrites or nitrates. When such meat is cooked, this pigment turns into *nitrosohemochrome,* the pink color of ham, corned beef brisket, and other cured meats. A brownish color in meat comes from *metmyoglobin,* which can be an indication of deterioration and, if accompanied by a wet, slick condition, may indicate the start of spoilage.

When we mix ground ham with veal, beef, and pork to make a ham loaf, the loaf has a pink color inside, caused by the presence of nitrogen in the ham. Sometimes onions dried in nitrogen gas or vegetables raised in high nitrogen soil can furnish enough nitrogen to cause this change. Ice frozen by using ammonia may pick up enough nitrogen from this gas and, if even only 2% of such ice is used in grinding meat to keep the grinder head cooled down, such ice may contribute enough nitrogen to make the meat red when it is cooked.

Meat is still red but about to change to hematin when rare (115° to 140°F or 45° to 55.5°C); it becomes pink at medium (140° to 160°F or 60° to 70.5°C), and gray when well done (160° to 175°F or 70° to 79.2°C). Meat high in acid will show a color change at lower temperatures; thus, ripened meat that develops acid in ripening or meat that is marinated in an acid medium must be watched in cooking, if rare or medium meat is desired. Because meat builds heat in the outer surface when cooking, it is wise to remove meat from the heat before reaching the final interior temperature. The residual heat should bring the meat to the desired stage of doneness. Thus, a 19-lb rib roast can be removed at 110°F (43°C) if it is to be served at around 135°F (57°C). Cooks call such after-roasting cooking *carry-over-cooking*.

Other Physical Properties

Meat flavor, outside of that contributed by fat, is contributed by the nitrogenous and nucleopeptide substances. They also stimulate the gastric cells and develop an appetite. Cooked meat also gets its aroma from these products. As an animal ages, these substances increase in the flesh. Muscles getting the most exercise also contain more of these than the lesser exercised ones. The reason that wild game has a stronger flavor than domesticated animals is that its meat contains more of these flavor substances.

Meat also contains smaller amounts of substances that are still very important nutrients, the most important being proteins that are able to completely support life and reproduction. Fat is usually next in amount and contributes richness, flavor, moistness, and calories. There is very little carbohydrate; most of what there is is called *glycogen*, a body starch. Meat is an important source of the minerals iron and zinc and a number of the B-complex vitamins. Some organ meats are good sources of vitamin A. Thus, meat can be an important food in any diet.

Meat is criticized because it contributes saturated fat and cholesterol. The fat in meat is also *thought* to help support cancers, once they start. The relationship of cholesterol to cancer is not clear. The full story of fat in meat as it relates to health must wait for further research.

Hormones and antibiotics in animal feed or otherwise given to animals to keep them healthy and grow faster have been criticized. The Food and Drug Administration has responsibility in this area and it has set what can be used and the limits to how much can be used. The amount allowed of both of these today are considered within safe health limits.

THE MEAT MARKET

Improved breeds and raising procedures plus the ways in which meat is marketed have changed the market considerably in the last 50 years. More tender animals with higher meat yields in desirable cuts are being produced. A move is also on to reduce the amount of fat animals develop. Animals are being brought to market younger.

Revisions in our grading standards reflect these changes. We no longer feed animals for as long as we used to, so the meat contains less fat. We use a more scientific type of feed to get faster growth, and we use antibiotics and hormones to speed growth and protect animal health (see Figure 7–3). The meat industry has been decentralized. Although Chicago remains the primary market, there is no longer a slaughterhouse there. Instead, animals are now shipped shorter distances to secondary markets such as Kansas City, Omaha, Sioux City, Ogden, and Los Angeles, closer to where animals are grown and where each center can service a more local market.

There are few independent meat companies. Most are now a part of conglomerates such as Greyhound Corporation owning Armour and Company or General Foods owning Oscar Mayer, or Occidental Petroleum owning Iowa Beef Processors. Meat for the market has changed form. Far less carcass, quarter, and wholesale (primal) cuts are shipped; instead, meat is broken down with bone and fat removed, reducing shipping weight and bulk, and shipped as boxed meat. A very significant amount of meat consumed today is boxed meat.

Market Information

Meat pricing and market conditions can fluctuate quickly and buyers need to keep up on trends and market conditions. Much good information is published

Figure 7-3
Typical feeding lots where some animals are rapidly fattened by scientific methods and feed and then sent to slaughter, but many of our even better graded meat animals never go through such a feeding lot. (Courtesy USDA.)

by the government on the amount of animals on ranges and their movement to market, along with prices paid. The USDA will send free daily information on market conditions, amounts slaughtered, going prices, etc. Urner Barry Publications Inc., P.O. Box 399, Toms River, NJ 08754, publishes the Yellow Sheet and can be accessed on the Internet (see Figure 7–4). These two reports are used by almost everyone who purchases a significant amount of meat. The National Livestock and Meat Board in Chicago and the National Association of Meat Purveyors in Tucson, Arizona, are important information gatherers and disseminators of information on meat.

Two USDA publications are also helpful to meat buyers: the *Market News Service Report* and the *Meat Sheet for Boxed Meat Items*. Also a special publication entitled *Meat Price Relationships* is published every other year by Price Analysis Systems, Inc., P.O. Box 9626, Minneapolis, MN 55408. It covers historical prices on 74 meat and poultry items, with their seasonal trend charts. A mathematical model based on this information is used to predict future prices. This can be helpful for buying futures, contracting, budgeting, setting menu prices, selecting and timing promotions, and building or reducing inventories.

AP to EP to AS[1] Costs

One of the problems in purchasing meat is knowing what the portion cost AS is. There is a significant loss of bone and fat as we cut meat down into servable portions. There is also often some trim meat that cannot be used for the portion intended which may have to be utilized as ground meat or stew meat or other. In the appendix of this book, many average EP yields of various cuts of meat from these carcass, quarter, or wholesale cuts are given. However, even if a buyer knows the EP weight, this may not be the final AS weight and thus the final cost. An EP roast can shrink in cooking 35%, a significant loss, and even this is not the end. There is usually about a 5% carving loss. Thus, from a 190-lb forequarter of beef, a 35-lb full rib will be obtained, and from this, a 20-lb roast ready rib. After roasting to a rare stage, one might get a 15-lb cooked rib. From this 12 portions of 8-oz slices of roast without bone and very little fat are obtained. Only by referring to cutting, cooking, and carving loss data such as this can buyers know what the AS yield will be. Records kept on yields AS from AP are helpful as well as published tables on amounts needed (see Appendix F). Also, with such data, it is possible to calculate AS costs and thus know if a proper menu price is obtained, and, in view of the menu price, what is the maximum price the buyer can pay for meat. Unless buyers have such information, they work in the dark, playing a dangerous guessing game. Perhaps we should call it the "Game of Meat Roulette."

---

[1]AP = as purchased often in carcass, quarter or wholesale (primal) cut, EP = edible portion, or in a state of ready to cook (even though some bone and fat may not be edible), and AS = as served, or as we serve it to the patron in a cooked state.

Contract and Acceptance Buying

Meat contracts are usually written for no more than six months; many purveyors want only a month's contract. Some meat buyers cross-hedge (buy futures), making a contract for future delivery to protect an established menu price.

Some buyers use *acceptance buying,* a system in which copies of one's specifications are sent to state or federal meat inspectors, and purveyors first send orders they are to deliver to these inspectors, who check the meat and see that it conforms to the buyer's specifications. If the delivery passes, the inspector stamps the invoice, delivery boxes, or other shipping container and other papers that accompany the order, thus accepting the order. Figure 7–5 shows the stamp used in accepting the goods. The delivery person now can take the goods to the place of delivery, where a quality inspection is no longer needed, since it has already been certified, but quantity and other factors still need checking. Normally, large operations or buyers like the military, school lunch, other federal operations use acceptance buying.

URNER BARRY'S
YELLOW SHEET
URNER BARRY PUBLICATIONS, INC.

Tel. 732-240-5330 • Fax 732-341-0891
Internet: http://www.urnerbarry.com

Boxed Beef Situation

FAT CAT: Boxed beef cutouts trended lower in light trade. Many buyers had already purchased a large percentage of their needs last week and were not active in today's spot market. Retailers and distributors expect next week's demand to be only fair amid end of the month doldrums and the beginning of Lent. Chucks and Rounds traded lower. Loins were mostly steady with the exception of Top Butts, which were in ample supply. Rib values were mixed depending on seller. Slaughter levels end the week 7000 head lower from last week. Cattle weights are running heavier than average. Nearby CME live cattle futures closed down limit.

- Joe Muldowney

U.S.D.A. LIVE COW MARKET QUOTATIONS

($/cwt.)	Sioux Falls, SD	St. Louis, MO	St Joesph, MO	So. St. Paul, MN	San Angelo, TX
Cutter and Boning Utility	37.00-42.00	**	35.00-40.00	37.00-40.00	34.00-41.50
Breaking Utility and Commercial 2-4	**	**	35.00-38.00	38.50-44.00	36.00-43.50
Canner and Low Cutter	32.00-37.00	**	31.00-36.00	33.00-37.00	27.00-34.00
Shelly and Lightweight	**	**	**	27.00-33.00	**

FABRICATED BOXED BEEF ($/cwt.)	Ch.	Ch.	Ch.	Ch.	USDA	USDA
note: ¼" quote=max. avg. fat thickness of ¼"	C/L Spot	LCL Spot	11:20	21:30	Range	Wtd. Avg.
107 Rib	194	194-197	—	—		
109 Rib Roast 22/dn	245	245-250	—	—		
109 Rib Roast 22/up	245	245-250	—	—		
109E B/I Ribeye 15/dn	280	280-290	—	—		
109E B/I Ribeye 15/up	260	260-270	—	—	277-300	287.5
112A Ribeye, Lip On 11/dn	370-375	375-378	—	—	388	388
112A Ribeye, Lip On 11/up	340-345	345-347	—	—	328-359	338.58

(a)

Figure 7–4

(a) An excerpt of a meat price report widely used to indicate market prices. Its color gives it the popular title of the Yellow Sheet. (b) The Yellow Sheet is widely used by meat buyers to get information on amounts, prices, and other marketing information. (Published with the permission and courtesy of Urner Barry Publications, Inc.)

USDA PORK CUTS (OLD REPORT) ($/cwt.)	Range	Wtd.Avg.	USDA PORK CUTS (NEW REPORT) ($/cwt.)	Range	Wtd.Avg.
Reg Hams 17/20........	55	55 E	17-20# TS 1................	57-60	57.67
Reg Hams 20/26.........	46	46	17-20# TS 2................	55	55 E
Reg Hams 26/32........			20-23# TS 1................	49-52	50.35
Reg Hams 32/up.........			20-23# TS 2................	50	50 D
Sel Hams 14/17.........			23-27# TS 1................	48-50	48.4
Sel Hams 17/20...........	53-56	53.89	23-27# TS 2................		
Sel Hams 20/26...........	43-49	45.95	20-27# TS 1................	47-49	48.21
Reg Fz Pic 4/8..........	26	26 B	20-27# TS 2................	46	46
Reg Fz Pic 8/up...........			27#/up TS 2................		
Trimmed Fz Pic 4/8 rs...	UNQ		Picnic, Trim, RS	UNQ	
Trimmed Fz Pic 4/8 ss...	55	55 B	Picnic, Trim, SS	55	55 B
Sq Cut Bellies 10/12......			Belly, Sdls, Fr 10-12#....		
Sq Cut Bellies 12/14.....	39-43	41	Belly, Sdls, Fr 12-14#....	43-47.5	45.25
Sq Cut Bellies 14/16......	39-43	40.29	Belly, Sdls, Fr 14-16#....	43-47.5	44.54
Sq Cut Bellies 16/18......	41	41 A	Belly, Sdls, Fr 16-18#....	44.5	44.5 A
Sq Cut Bellies 18/20......	37	37 C	Belly, Sdls, Fr 18-20#....	39.5	39.5 C
Sq Cut Bellies 20/25......	35	35 A	Belly, Sdls, Fr 20-25#....	38	38 A
Reg Loin 14/18..........	69-77	72.2	Loin 1/4" Trim, 13-19#....	100-102	100.4
Reg Loin 18/22..........	64-70	68.5	1/8" Trm/less, 13-19#....	99-108	101.4
Reg Loin 22/up..........	57	57 B	1/4" Trim, 19-23#.........	90-96	94.5
Trimmed Loin 14/18......	95-97	95.4	combos, 23/Up#...........	57	57 B
Trimmed Loin 18/22......	84-90	88.5	Bnls strap-on, 5-9#.......	148-152	149.8 C
Bnls Cntr Cut Loin..........			Bnls Strap-off, 5-9#......	164	164
Strap On..............	148-152	149.8 C	Tenderloin, 1.25/DN#.......	211-221	217.67 A
Strap Off.................	164	164	Loin Backrib, Fr/Fz, 1.5/dn	350	350
TenderLoin 10's...........			1.75/dn..................		
Tenderloin 125/dn........	211-221	217.67 A	1.75-2.00#.............	255	255 A
Reg Boston Butt 4/8......	42-50	47.24	2.00/up.............		
Reg Boston Butt 8/up.....			Loin Backrib, 1.75/dn	303	303 B
Tr Boston Butt 4/8.........	60-69	65.94	Pic Cshn Meat, 92%, Fr ...	93	93
Sk Shoul 16/dn...........			Pic Cshn Meat, 92%, Fz ..		
Spare Ribs 35/dn Fr......	114	114 A	Boston Butt 4-9#,Fr 1/4" ..	63-72	68
Spare Ribs 35/dn Fz......			1/8"................	72	72 B
Spare Ribs 35/55 Fr......			combo's 9/UP#..............		
Spare Ribs 35/55 Fz......			Sparerib:		
Spare Ribs 35/up Fz.....			Fr,3Bag/3PCVAC,3.8/dn	137	137 A
Loin Back Ribs...........			Fr,2Bag/3PCVAC,3.8-5.8		
150/dn.................	350	350	Combos, 3.8/DN#.......	UNQ	
175/dn.................			Combos, 3.8-5.8#...........		
2/dn........................	255	255 A	Ham Trim, Combo 72% Fr.	34.5	34.5 A
2/up.....................			Ham Trim, Boxed 72% Fr.	UNQ	
42% Trm Fresh..........	22-25	23.67	Ham Trim, Combo 90% Fr.		
Frozen..............			Ham Trim, Boxed 90% Fz.		
72% Trm Fresh.........	31-35	33	Combo 42% Fresh..........	24-26.5	25.5
Frozen..............	41	41	Boxed 42% Frozen..........		
85% Trm Fresh..........			Combo 72% Fresh..........	33-36.5	34.75
Frozen..........			Boxed 72% Frozen..........	41	41
72% Bnls. Pic Fresh......	48	48	Bnls Pic, 72%, Fr.	49.5	49.5
Frozen...........	54	54	Bnls Pic, 72%, Fz.	54	54
Bnls Pic Cush, Fresh...	93	93	Sk. Jowls, Fr.	20-20.5	20.42
Frozen..............			Sk. Jowls, Fz.	24	24
Sk. Jowls, Fresh.........	19	19	Fat, Trace Lean, Fr.	18	18 B
Frozen..............	24	24	Fat, Trace Lean, Fz.		
			Trim,Trace Lean,12-16%,Fr		

Friday, February 20, 1998   No. 36-Vol. 76©
Page 7 - Yellow Sheet - Pork

(b)

Figure 7-4
(continued)

Figure 7-5
The USDA stamp indicates the product meets the buyer's specification. (Published courtesy and permission of USDA.)

Market Pricing

You may wonder when you hear that beef is sold in Texas on the range for $0.60 a pound why you have to pay $2.10 a pound for a No. 109 oven-ready prime rib. The reason is that the beef is in Texas, has to be shipped to a Kansas City feeding lot to be fed corn for five months, slaughtered, cut up, boxed, and sold to a meat dealer who sells it to you. This process involves a lot of cost. And not all of the pounds purchased can be made into salable meat. What about the intestinal area, the skin, the hooves, etc? There is some salvage value in these, but not much. To ship the meat to where it needs to be takes money. Also, think of the labor that has to go into slaughtering, cutting up, boxing, etc.

Or, when you read in the Yellow Sheet that Choice grade No. 109 ribs are $1.87 a pound, remember this is FOB Kansas City in carload (about 36,000 lb) lots. Remember the costs involved in shipping, delivering, storing, etc., and you'll have about $70,000 tied up in ribs after getting them. A place selling eight ribs a night, about 175 orders, would have a 220-day supply on hand. All in all, it is a wonder that the meat industry is able to do the job it does and get the meat to us at the price it does.

Market Regulation

The meat market has been under federal control for 86 years. Sinclair Lewis's *The Jungle,* depicting horrible conditions existing in the meat market, plus President Theodore Roosevelt's release of a panel of inquiry into these conditions, caused so much public concern about sanitation and control, that Congress passed the Meat Act in 1906. It set up operating standards for meat establishments and meat processing and required that meat animals have antemortem and postmortem inspection plus conform to other standards to ensure that the meat was "fit for human consumption." To indicate that meat has met this requirement, federal inspectors stamp meat and meat products containing over 6% meat with an inspected and passed stamp. Figure 7–6 shows the stamps used on meats or on containers containing the required percentage of meat, such as canned goods. Animals that do not meet standards are stamped *condemned, retained* for further inspection, or *suspect.*

The round stamp showing such inspection and approval for use appears on all wholesale cuts of meat. (State stamps often are in the shape of the state.) Inside the stamps is a number called the "official establishment" number, which indicates where the inspection occurred. Thus, if you want to know if what you ordered really are Kansas City steaks, you need only note the number on the package in which the meats are packed, consult the federal government's official establishment list, and find out. If the number is for a Sioux City establishment, you know something is amiss.

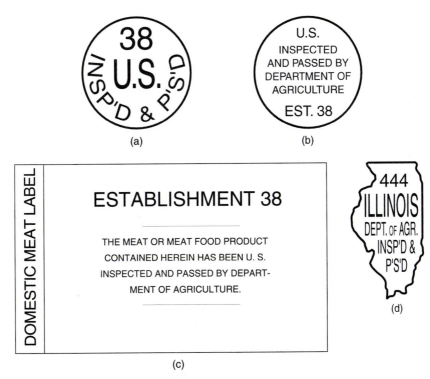

Figure 7-6
Stamps used to indicate meat has been inspected and passed for wholesomeness.
Stamp (a) is used on fresh meat; (b) appears on packaged meats; (c) appears on
boxed meats. States having equal or better than federal inspection standards show
their own approval stamp. (d) The stamp used by Illinois is shown.

Inspection and passed is required of all meats, but grading is voluntary. Meat grades are shown in a continuous shield put on meats by a roller. Initials sometimes appearing under one of the roller stamps are those of the inspector grading the meat (see Figure 7–7). Thus, a buyer can easily find out where the inspection occurred and who graded the meat. Instead of grading, some meat packers may prefer to market meat ungraded or put their own brand on the meat. Ungraded or unbranded meat is called *no roll*. While federally graded meat is supposed to conform to certain standards, brands do not. They are only a claim by the seller of quality. Yield grades are shown also as a single shield, with the yield number of the meat inside (see Figure 7–7b).

In 1996 President Clinton announced new inspection procedures to improve the sanitation of meat products (see Chapter 2). For the most part, the industry changed quickly to meet these new regulations.

Meat grading was established in 1927 under the USDA, the cost being borne by meat packers or by others who request it. The cost is passed on to consumers as an operating expense. There are grades for beef, veal, pork, and lamb. Beef has the most grades since there is more variation in the kinds of animals and their meat cuts

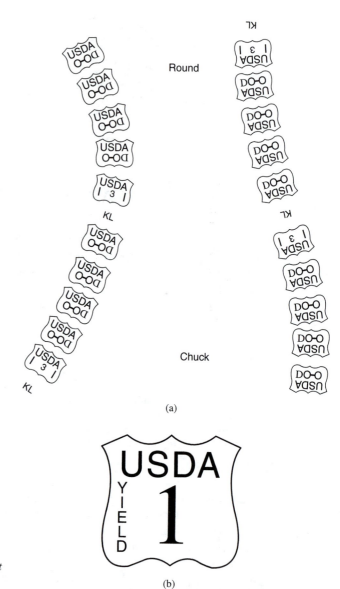

Figure 7-7
(a) The combined grade and yield roller stamp is run from the round to the chuck when no fat is removed from the carcass but is reversed when fat is removed.
(b) The yield stamp used to show the relative yield of the carcass. No. 1 is the highest yield. (Courtesy USDA.)

than among other animals. The lower grades from Commercial on down seldom are marketed, except some of the more tender cuts may be, some of which are also tenderized by enzymes or other means.

In 1967 the Meat Act was amended by the Wholesome Meat Act, tightening standards and establishing state–federal control. If a state has regulations equal to or better than the federal standard, the state is allowed to inspect and stamp its own meats (see Figure 7–6d). If not, the state must comply with the federal standards of 1967. In some cases, if an establishment does not do more than $200,000 per year in busi-

Table 7-1
Large packers and their brands

Packer	Brands of Packer
Armour	Star Deluxe, Star, Quality, Banquet
Cudahy	Puritan, Fancy, Rex, Rival, Thrifty-oh
Hormel	Hormel Best, Hormel Merit, Hormel Value, Hormel
Morrell	Pride, Famous, Special, Allrite
Rath	Black Hawk Deluxe, Black Hawk, Kornland, Crest, Sycamore*
Swift	Premium Proten, Tru Tendr, Premium, Select
Wilson	Certified, Special, Ideal, Leader, Silsco

*The last two brands of this packer are for cows only.

ness and does not ship its meat interstate, it does not have to meet the federal standards, and, if the state has no regulations, it need not meet any standard. However, the courts have so liberally interpreted the "interstate" provision that even such establishments come under the law. Thus, very little meat in this country is not inspected and passed. If a meat carries a state inspection stamp, it cannot be shipped to another state even though it meets or exceeds federal standards.

Packers' Brands

Packers like to sell under their own brands. In this way they can control the quality they want the brand to meet and do not have to conform to federal standards. Some of the largest packers and their brand names are listed in Table 7–1.

MEAT CLASSIFICATION AND GRADING

To purchase meat adequately, a buyer should know (1) how the market is regulated, (2) the classes into which the various kinds of meat animals are segmented, (3) how they are graded, and (4) the manner in which carcasses and their parts are marketed. The terms used to identify each of these factors must be learned, so buyers can communicate properly with marketing agents and obtain exactly what is needed. And, even after knowing all this, buyers must possess the ability to recognize when items conform to what has been specified, so the right item is obtained for the production need. The recognition of the various cuts and their grades is in itself a challenge.

Animal Kinds and Classes

Animal kinds are divided into (a) beef, (b) veal and calf, (c) sheep, and (d) pork. The various classes under these kinds appear in Table 7–2.

Table 7-2
Animal classes

BEEF (BOVINE)	
Bull	Sexually mature male
Bullock	Very young bull
Stag	Castrated after reaching sexual maturity
Cow	Female that has had a calf
Heifer	Female that has not had a calf
Steer	Castrated before sexual maturity
VEAL AND CALF (BOVINE)	
Veal	Young beef, usually under 4 months old
Calf	Beef from 4 to 9 months old
Baby beef*	Very young beef 9 to about 12 months old
SHEEP (OVINE)	
Lamb	Under a year old
Yearling	About 1 year old
Mutton	Over a year old
Ram	Sexually mature mutton
Ewe	Female mutton that has lambed
PORK (SWINE)	
Barrow	Immature male
Gilt	Immature female
Sow	Mature female that has farrowed
Boar	Sexually mature male

Note: These animal classes will be encountered frequently by buyers; students are advised to learn them.
*This class is not recognized in federal classifications, but is sometimes encountered in the market.

The federal government has also established a classification for cured meats, edible by-products, and sausage. In addition to this, buyers should be aware of the many prepreared, canned, and substitute meat products on the market.

Grading

Two grading systems are used for meats; one is for **quality** and the other is for **yield.** Quality grades are found in Table 7–3.

Beef Quality Grading (as of January 1997)

Age or maturity and marbling, considered as one factor, and quality establish the grade for beef. Age is divided: A (under 30 months), B (30 to 42 months), and C, D, and E (over 42 months). Marbling is tiny flecks of fat in meat tissues, and there are seven categories running from practically devoid to slightly abundant (see Figure

Table 7–3
Quality grades for meat animals

Meat Classes	Grades
BEEF*	
Bullocks, steers, and heifers	Prime
Bulls, bullocks, cows, steers, heifers, and stags	Choice
All kinds	Select, Standard
VEAL AND CALF	Prime, Choice, Select, Standard, and Utility
LAMB, YEARLING, AND MUTTON	Prime, Choice, Select, Utility, and Cull
PORK†	Quality of lean must be acceptable to qualify for yield grades
Barrows and gilts	No. 1 through No. 4‡
Sows	

Note: These grading terms will be encountered frequently by buyers; students are advised to learn them.
*Other grades, but seldom used for food service purposes, are Commercial, Utility, Canner, and Cutter.
†Few boars are never marketed as fresh meat but go to the canning market.
‡In 1985 pork grades were revised to recognize the leaner type of hog on the market.

7–8). Quality is a composite evaluation of flesh color, texture, moistness, and firmness and the degree of ossification of bones. Some consideration is given to fat, firmness, amount, and also to other factors.

Age or Maturity and Marbling. Figure 7–9 shows how marbling and maturity are correlated for grading. Only beef under 36 months can make prime; marbling must be slightly abundant or better. Note how these factors change as one goes down the grades in quality. Only a small quantity of beef ever makes prime; it is too fat for the ordinary market. About 94% of the consumer marketed beef *graded* is Choice with the other 6% divided equally between Prime and Select. This makes the Choice grade so wide that the federal government allows the market to divide each grade into bottom and top of the grade, and buyers should indicate whether they want bottom or top when specifying a grade, especially in the Choice grade. Some local markets go one step further and recognize bottom, middle, and top as grade divisions. Most of the beef in this country is not graded. If it were, Select would be about 80%. The half that is graded grades 3% Prime, 94% Choice, and 3% Select.

Bones. Bone condition in grading is judged from size, shape, degree of **ossification,** amount of cartilage, and color of the interior (marrow). The degree of ossification is less and the amount of cartilage is more in younger animals. As animals mature, bones grow harder, larger, and tend to change shape. The interior of bones on young animals is often quite red, while older animals have less redness. Cartilage in the chest cavity, the tail bone, and the "buttons" (round white marks at the juncture of the chine and rib bones) will show more cartilage.

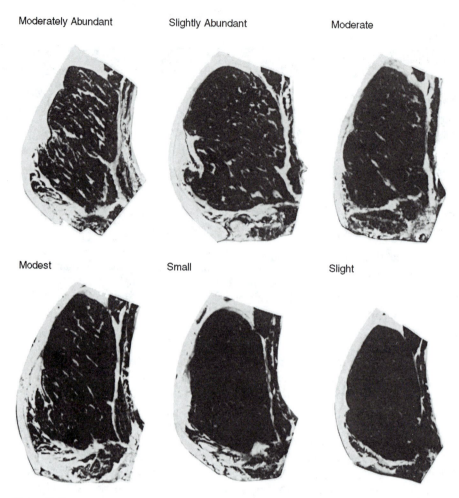

Figure 7–8
Six short-cut rib steaks showing varying degrees of marbling. (Reproduction courtesy of the National Cattlemen's Beef Association.)

Flesh Quality.   Flesh color of young animals is less red but intensifies with age. Bulls may have a color that is a dark purple. Because of a lack of glycogen in the flesh at the time of slaughter, some beef may have an almost black flesh, and this is cause for downgrading; such an animal is referred to as a "dark cutter." Desirable flesh characteristics are a firm, not soft or flabby, feel with a slight moistness, not wet or gummy, and fine fibers that appear silky and possess a soft sheen. Younger animals have a softer feeling flesh. As an animal ages, the fibers become coarser.

Veal and Calf Quality Grading (as of October 1980)
Quality grade standards for veal and calf are somewhat like those for beef, but conformation or fullness of the muscle structure is also a factor. To be of the highest grade, the carcass must be moderately wide and thick in relation to length with full,

Relationship between marbling, maturity, and carcass quality grade*

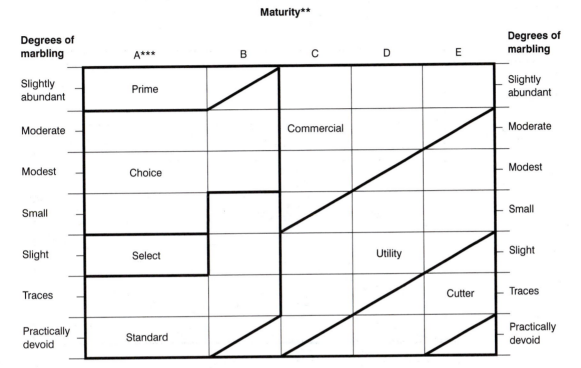

* Assumes that firmness of lean is comparably developed with the degree of marbling and that the carcass is not a "dark cutter."
** Maturity increases from left to right (A through E).
*** The A maturity portion of the figure is the only portion applicable to bullock carcasses.

Figure 7-9
This USDA chart shows how age and marbling limits are established in deciding grade. (Courtesy USDA.)

plump-muscled legs and shoulders and breasts that show a moderate thickness. Thinly fleshed, angular animals are downgraded. Conformation is a part of the quality factor. It is also considered in giving the yield grade.

Conformation is a factor of breeding. Some animals come from heavy beef animals, raised for their meat. Dairy cattle are much less fleshed and more angular in shape, lacking usually full and bulging muscles. Often veal from these animals is slaughtered quite young and may be called **bob veal** on the market (see Figure 7–10.) It will not be of the high quality of specially fed beef offspring that besides having good conformation possess a firmer, white fat and very light, firm flesh. High-quality food services usually take almost all of this—what is called "nature-fed" veal. It is expensive. The New York *Plume de Veau* and the Wisconsin *Provimi* brand veals are considered some of the best on this high-quality veal market.

The amount of fat in the lean is not judged by marbling, but on the amount of feathering (fat inside, intermingled within the lean between the ribs and outside the

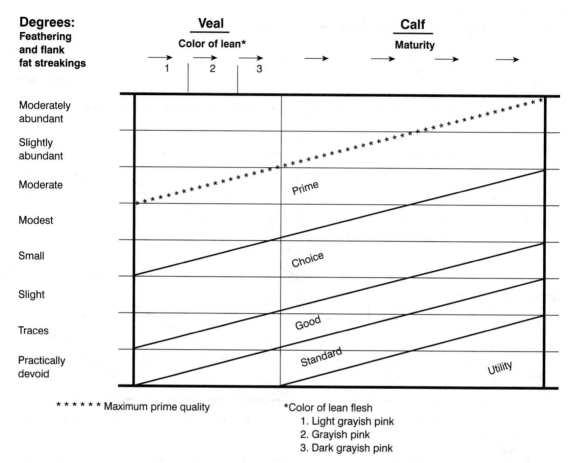

** ** ** ** ** Maximum prime quality   *Color of lean flesh
                                            1. Light grayish pink
                                            2. Grayish pink
                                            3. Dark grayish pink

Figure 7–10
The quality grade equivalent of various degrees of feathering and flank fat streakings in relation to color of lean veal or mature calf. From this figure it can be seen, for example, that degrees of feathering or fat streakings associated with minimum Choice quality for veal increases from minimum traces for carcasses having the lightest color of lean to maximum traces for carcasses with a dark grayish pink color of lean. (Courtesy USDA.)

animal in the amount of fat as it feathers or fades out over the shoulders and loin, reaching down to the lower parts of the body), and the amount of streaks of fat showing within the flank muscles.

The color of veal ranges from a very light pink to a darker one. Dark, grayish-pink to moderately red flesh is characteristic of calf. Veal may be only milk fed or be formula fed, in which case there is a lack of iron in the diet, giving a lighter flesh. The "nature-fed" veal mentioned above has a diet of this kind.

Calf and veal are most plentiful in the summer and fall. As winter continues, the supply decreases and prices go up. At this time, some users turn to the frozen product.

Sheep Quality Grading (as of July 1992)

Age or maturity is the primary factor in establishing grade. It is based on body size, color and character of the flesh, and bone characteristics. Age in the carcass can be

Figure 7-11
A drawing indicating a spool joint found on a yearling or older mutton (left) and the break joint (right) with its eight points found on a young lamb.

indicated by the forelock on the front leg. On lambs, this forelock can be snapped off, showing a ridged break of cartilage. This break is often called a **break joint.** If it is seen in a yearling, it is a sort of blend of the roughness of the break joint and the spool joint. Older animals show a smooth spool joint. Figure 7–11 shows the difference between a spool and break joint. A good amount of fat streaking on the flanks and marbling equal to "slight" or "traces" in fat in beef are sought in the highest grades. A good solid firmness and white creaminess in the fat is also desirable. The color of the lean runs from bright pink in lamb to dark red in mutton. In 1991 the USDA proposed some changes in grading that would encourage the production of leaner lambs. Figure 7–12 shows how the grades of lamb, yearlings, and mutton are established.

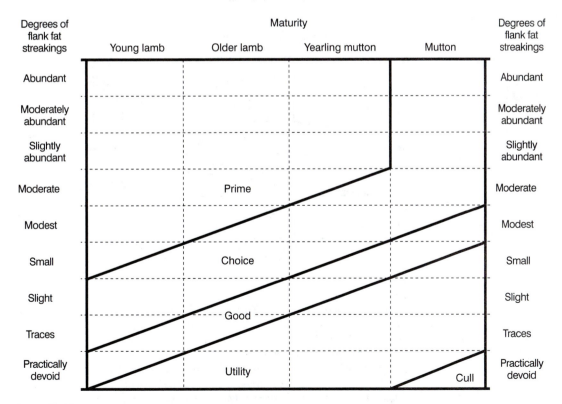

Relationship between flank fat streakings, maturity, and quality

Figure 7-12
Marbling requirements to make a quality grade in sheep. (Courtesy USDA.)

Pork Quality Grading

Names of grades for pork are different than those for beef, calf and veal, or lamb and mutton. Yield is a big factor in deciding grade. Quality of the meat is considered and must be acceptable to qualify for the yield grades of No. 1 through No. 4. The quality of lean at the 10th rib is noted as well as the amount of fat. The color of the lean is also evaluated. Excessive marbling is cause for downgrading. The quality of fat is noted. It must be firm, whitish, and not oily. Bone quality is judged; too much ossification, a lack of a large red marrow, and other factors indicating age are considered. If these factors and others make for an acceptable quality, the animal then is subjected to an inspection and evaluation for yield, and Figure 7–13 shows how this judgment is made. (See a further discussion on yield in the material that follows. Also see Figure 7–14.)

Beef Yield Grading

Beef yield grades are No. 1 through No. 5, with the lowest number indicating the highest yield. These grades are determined by (1) square inches of the ribeye at the ribbing point (between the 12th and 13th ribs), (2) the thickness of fat over the ribeye, (3) the percentage of fat around the kidney, pelvis, and heart areas to total weight, and (4) the hot (right after slaughter) carcass weight. A mathematical formula is used to come up with the yield grade, and this is illustrated in Appendix D.

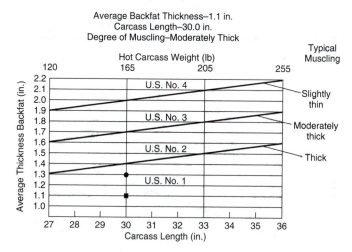

Figure 7-13

Average depth of back fat, carcass length, and degree of muscling indicate the grade of a hot packer-style hog carcass. Thus, a carcass 30 in. long weighing 165 lb with very thick or thick muscles and an average fat depth of 1.1 in. would grade where the square is placed in the chart, but when it trades 2 fat tenths of an inch for 2 degrees of muscling, it moves up to where the dot is shown. A carcass weighing about 150 lb, 29 in. in length, which has an average backfat thickness of 1.5 in. with thick muscling would grade U.S. No. 2. (Courtesy USDA.)

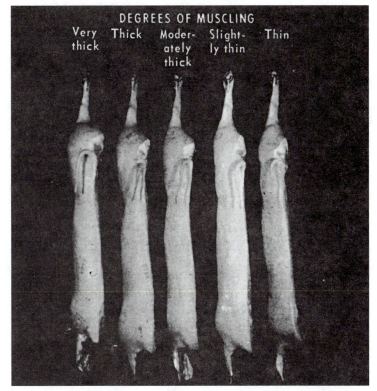

(a)

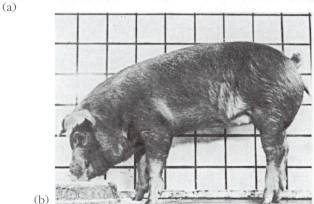

(b)

Figure 7-14

(a) Illustrations of the degrees of muscling used in the grading of pork. A very thick degree of muscling might receive a muscling score of 3.5, the thick a score of 3.0, the moderately thick a score of 2.5, the slightly thin perhaps about a 1.8 score, and the thin a score of about 1.0. (Courtesy USDA.) (b) This young gilt shows desirable conformation characteristics. It has a long body to give a good bacon (belly); thick muscling with the hams longer than the width of the loin; the lower parts of the shoulder and ham are trim and firm; feet are wide apart because of the thick muscling; it is trim in the middle and rear flank; and the jowls are also trim and firm. (Courtesy USDA.)

Table 7-4
Depth of fat over the ribeye or the loin in beef

Yield Grade	500-lb Carcass (in.)	800-lb Carcass (in.)
No. 1	0.3 or less	0.4 or less
No. 2	0.7	0.8
No. 3	1.1	1.2
No. 4	1.5	1.6
No. 5	1.9	2.0

Table 7-5
Yield grades of beef

Quality Grade	Yield Grades*				
	1	2	3	4	5
Prime			X	X	X
Choice		X	X	X	
Select		X	X		
Standard	X	X	X		
Commercial		X	X	X	X

*Because yield grade is based on well-trimmed, low-fat meat cuts, they do not give the desired yield in some of these grades.

Table 7-6
Percent usable beef

USDA Yield Grades				
1	2	3	4	5
74%	71%	68%	64%	61%

Once a beef or any other animal is cut up, a buyer has difficulty in determining what the yield grade might be. Table 7–4 is used by some to make an estimate by measuring the fat over the ribeye on a rib or loin. Often food service buyers are not concerned with yield grades, because by using the IMPS numbers to specify cuts and their weights, plus the amount of fat allowed, one can fairly well establish a desired yield without resorting to the yield grade.

Table 7–5 indicates *normally* how the various quality grades of beef qualify for yield grades. The percentage of usable beef from the various yield grades is given in Table 7–6. (Also see Figure 7–15.)

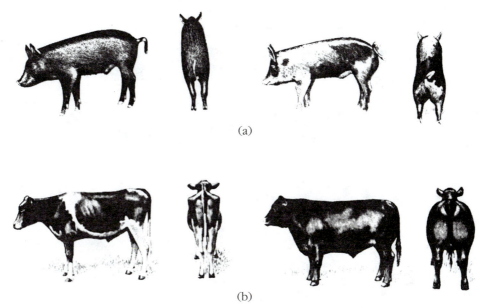

(a)

(b)

Figure 7-15
*Thin muscling, shown in the animals in column (a) compared with the heavier muscled an-
imals on the right (b), mean more meat to bone. Note while the skeletal structures are about
the same size, meaning about equal bone weight, the heavier muscling indicates a greater
meat yield in the (b) animals.* (Courtesy USDA.)

Veal and Calf Yield Grading
Federal yield grades are not used for veal and calf.

Lamb and Mutton Yield Grading
The conformation of a sheep carcass has considerable influence in assigning a yield
grade, especially over the loin, leg, and shoulder. In addition, the amount of external fat and the amount of kidney and pelvic fat to carcass weight are used. One will
find, however, that these yield grades are little used by buyers.

Pork Yield Grading
Pork yield grades are from No. 1 to No. 4. The grade is based on the expected yield
of the ham, loin, shoulder, and belly cuts. Fat is thus graded and excessive fat detracts from the grade. Table 7–7 gives the expected yield, based on chilled carcass
weight, and average **back fat** depth of the various grades of pork. The market usually finds that around 70% of hogs slaughtered grade U.S. No. 1.

A yield test is sometimes made to see exactly what the yield and probable cost
will be from a certain cut. Table 7–8 shows the results of such a test. The prices
used come from purveyor quoted prices on a current market. The value of $7.02
is, of course, only true if the facility can use, besides the No. 109 rib, the diced
beef, the short ribs, the beef bones, and the suet. Usually large operations can

Table 7-7
Expected yields and average back fat of chilled pork carcasses

Grade	Expected Yield (%)	Average Back Fat (in.)
No. 1	60.4 and over	1.5–1.9
No. 2	57.4–60.3	1.9–2.3
No. 3	54.0–57.3	2.3 or more
No. 4	54.0–57.3	Less than 1.5

Table 7-8
Full rib (no. 103) yield test

Full rib (No. 103) 33 1/2 lb @ $1.85/lb =		$61.97
Yield:		
No. 109 (oven ready rib) 20 lb @ $2.35/lb =	$47.00	
No. 135 (diced beef) 5 lb @ $2.00/lb =	10.00	
No. 123 (short ribs) 3 lb @ $1.40/lb =	4.20	
No. 134 (beef bones) 3 lb @ $0.30/lb =	0.90	
Suet 2 lb @ $0.05/lb =	0.10	
Cutting loss 1/2 lb		
Total value of cut-up meat		
	$62.20	
Cutting cost (33 1/2 lb @ 20¢/lb) =	$ 6.70	
Total cost of cut-up rib		$68.90
Amount saved by cutting up a No. 103 rib		$ 7.02

since they often have a varied enough menu to use the by-products. Smaller facilities may not find it worthwhile to butcher out their own meat and use the by-products for employee meals. Another consideration would be whether the facility had someone who can do an adequate job of butchering. Also, it takes special equipment to do such cutting up. Figures 7–16 through 7–19 give some meat yield averages from carcasses compiled by the USDA. Of course, various carcasses and cuts will vary from this, but the information is useful in gaining an estimate. Figure 7–16 compares the muscling as shown on thin and heavy-muscled animals.

Identifying Wholesale and Portion Meat Cuts

Identifying meat cuts is not difficult if one knows the skeletal and muscular set up of an animal. Briefly the skeleton is this: The head and tail are joined by a *spine bone,* which is a group of *vertebrae* joined together. When this spine bone is sawed in two lengthwise, it is called the **chine bone.** Attached to this spine is the **shoulder blade**

BEEF CHART
Wholesale and Retail Cuts

Numerals in circles ◯ refer to wholesale cuts and major subdivisions of such cuts. Letters refer to retail cuts.

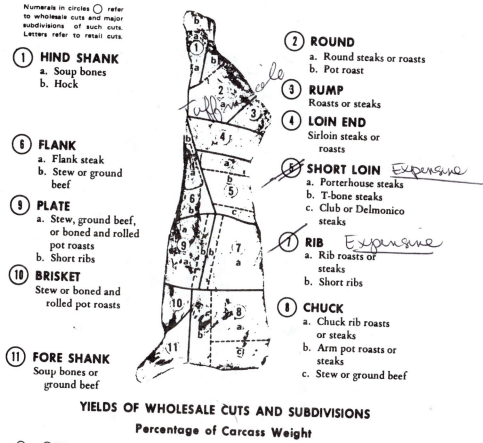

① HIND SHANK
a. Soup bones
b. Hock

⑥ FLANK
a. Flank steak
b. Stew or ground beef

⑨ PLATE
a. Stew, ground beef, or boned and rolled pot roasts
b. Short ribs

⑩ BRISKET
Stew or boned and rolled pot roasts

⑪ FORE SHANK
Soup bones or ground beef

② ROUND
a. Round steaks or roasts
b. Pot roast

③ RUMP
Roasts or steaks

④ LOIN END
Sirloin steaks or roasts

⑤ SHORT LOIN *Expensive*
a. Porterhouse steaks
b. T-bone steaks
c. Club or Delmonico steaks

⑦ RIB *Expensive*
a. Rib roasts or steaks
b. Short ribs

⑧ CHUCK
a. Chuck rib roasts or steaks
b. Arm pot roasts or steaks
c. Stew or ground beef

YIELDS OF WHOLESALE CUTS AND SUBDIVISIONS
Percentage of Carcass Weight

① to ⑥ HINDQUARTER 48.0%	⑦ to ⑪ FOREQUARTER . . 52.0%
① to ③ Round and Rump . 24.0%	⑦ Rib 9.5%
① Hind Shank . 4.0%	⑧ Chuck 24.5
② Buttock . . 15.5	⑨ Plate 8.0
③ Rump . . . 4.5	⑩ Brisket 6.0
④ and ⑤ Full loin inc. suet. 20.5	⑪ Fore shank . . . 4.0
④ Loin end . . 9.0	
⑤ Short loin . 8.0	
Kidney Knob 3.5	
⑥ Flank 3.5	

UNITED STATES DEPARTMENT OF AGRICULTURE
Food Safety and Quality Service

Figure 7-16
Beef Chart: wholesale and retail cuts.

LAMB CHART

Numerals in circles ◯ refer to wholesale cuts. Letters refer to retail cuts.

WHOLESALE CUTS

RETAIL CUTS

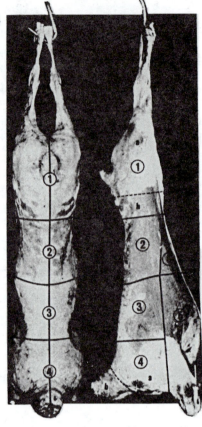

①②and⑥ **HIND SADDLE**

- ① Leg
- ② Loin
- ⑥ Flank

③④and⑤ **FORE SADDLE**

- ③ Hotel Rack
- ④ Chuck
- ⑤ Breast

① **LEG**
a. Roast
b. Chops or roast

② **LOIN**
Loin and kidney chops

⑥ **FLANK**
Stew

③ **RIB**
Rib chops or roast

④ **SHOULDER**
a. Roast or chops
b. Neck slices or stew

⑤ **BREAST**
Stew

YIELDS OF WHOLESALE CUTS
Percentage of Carcass Weight

①②and⑥ Hind saddle 50.0%

① Leg 33.0%

② Loin and ⑥ Flank . . 17.0

③④and⑤ Fore saddle 50.0%

③ Rib 11.0%

④ Shoulder. 25.0

⑤ Breast, inc. shank 14.0

UNITED STATES DEPARTMENT OF AGRICULTURE
Food Safety and Quality Service

Figure 7-17
Lamb Chart.

VEAL CHART

WHOLESALE CUTS

RETAIL CUTS

①LEG
   a. Cutlets
   b. Roast
   c. Stew

①and② HIND SADDLE
   ①Leg
   ②Loin

②LOIN
   a. Loin and
      kidney chops
   b. Stew

③HOTEL RACK
   Rib chops

③and④ FORE SADDLE
   ③Hotel rack
   ④Shoulder

④SHOULDER
   (shank and breast
   not shown)
   a. Roasts
   b. and c. Stew

YIELDS OF WHOLESALE CUTS AND SUBDIVISIONS
Percentage of Carcass Weight

①and②Hind saddle 49.0%
   ①Legs 40.0%
   ②Loin 9.0

③and④Fore saddle 51.0%
   ③Hotel rack . . . 8.0%
   ④Shoulder . . . 43.0

UNITED STATES DEPARTMENT OF AGRICULTURE
CONSUMER AND MARKETING SERVICE
LIVESTOCK DIVISION

Figure 7-18
Veal Chart.

Pork Chart
Wholesale and Retail* Cuts

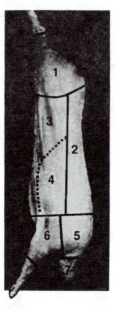

1 Ham
- a. Butt end or half
- b. Shank end or half
- c. Center slices

3 Belly

4 Spareribs

6 Picnic
- a. Picnic roasts
- b. Arm steaks

2 Loin
- a. Loin chops
- b. Rib chops
- c. Loin and rib roasts
- d. Canadian Style bacon

5 Boston Butt
- a. Boston butt roast
- b. Blade steaks

7 Jowl
- a. Jowl bacon square.

*Only some of the more common retail cuts are listed
Numerals refer to wholesale cuts. Letters refer to retail cuts.

EXPECTED YIELDS OF CUTS
Percentage of Carcass Weight (175 lbs.)

Cut	%	Cut	%
1. Ham**	21.0	6. Picnic**	10.3
2. Loin**	20.3	7. Jowl	2.8
3. Belly	13.9	8. Lean Trim**	2.2
4. Spareribs**	3.0	9. Fat	13.6
5. Boston Butt**	7.3	10. Miscellaneous**	5.6

The expected yields shown are an average for the U.S. No. 2 grade. Yields for the cuts identified by
** would be higher for the No. 1 grade, lower for No. 3, and still lower for No. 4.

United States Department of Agriculture
Agricultural Marketing Service
Livestock and Seed Division
Washington, D.C.
1986

Figure 7-19

*Pork Chart: wholesale and retail cuts. Only some of the more common retail cuts are listed.
Numerals refer to wholesale cuts. Letters refer to retail cuts.*

or **scapula** to which are attached the foreleg bone, the **arm bone** or **humerus.** Joining this bone, ending with the hoof, are the **shank bones** (**radius** and **ulna**). Thirteen ribs are next attached to the spine running toward the **hindquarter** area; five are in the shoulder area where we get the arm bone, the cross rib, and other cuts. The lower parts of these ribs make up the **short ribs.** Seven other ribs are found in the rib area which we call the **prime rib** or **rib steak** area, and the thirteenth is in the hindquarter where the **club steak** is taken.

The **pelvis** or **aitch bone** is attached to the rear part of the spine, the forepart of which is called the **sirloin** or **pin** or **wedge bone** area, with the rear part called the **rump** area. The socket to which the round (**femur**) or *hind leg* bone is attached is about midway in the lower middle of the aitch bone. The **tibia** and **fibula** join this round bone, covered at the juncture by the kneecap. The rear hoof joins these two hind leg bones (see Figures 7–20 and 7–21).

The muscles one should know, identified often with their bone structure, are the *longissimus dorsi,* the longest and most expensive muscle in the body (in steaks it is called the **loin eye** or **strip**), runs next to the spine bone from the neck to the rump. In the front shoulder the longissimus dorsi is usually called the *arm muscle.* A small forearm muscle will also be found in cuts made there. The **brisket,** a muscle in the lower neck area in front of cattle, will also be seen on the bottom of these cuts. Cuts from the mid-shoulder area can be identified also by rib bones (called **cross ribs**) and the oval-shaped arm bone (see Figure 7–20a). Farther back in the shoulder is the *blade bone* (*scapula* or *shoulder bone*). Here the longissimus dorsi muscle is called the **chuck.** The **clod** muscle is a meaty muscle that lies over the **rib eye** muscle and will be seen at the top of these cuts. The chine bone is called the *back bone* in these cuts (see Figure 7–20b). The rib eye muscle (longissimus dorsi) is the only muscle seen in the rib area. This is where the prime rib roast and rib steaks come from. Rib steaks in veal, pork, and lamb are called arm steaks (see Figure 7–20c).

The names of cuts from the lower part of the fore area of an animal vary. The lower part of the ribs will be found here (pork in this area differs somewhat from cattle and lamb). In cattle the front meaty part is called the **brisket** and the rear part is called the **plate,** the area from which we get **short ribs.** In veal and lamb these two parts are called the **breast.** In pork, the meaty part is stripped off and used for **bacon** or side pork. Salt pork comes from here. The bones on pork are **spare ribs.** The meat from this area is composed of muscle separated by layers of fat. In pork the fat is more plentiful (see Figure 7–20).

In the hindquarter the **club (Delmonico) steak** contains the eighth or last rib. Right after this under the longissimus dorsi is the **tenderloin (*psoas major*)** muscle. It starts as a small round muscle growing in size as it moves down to the sirloin area. This muscle along with the bigger longissimus muscle (now called the *strip* or *loin eye*) starts at its small end to be **T-bone** steak until it becomes quite large near the sirloin area becoming the lower part of **porterhouse** steak.) In veal, lamb and pork these T-bone and porterhouse cuts are called **chops** (see Figure 8–21). The aitch bone will appear in the sirloin cuts where we get our **round bone sirloin steak,** our wedge bone steak, etc. The muscles are the **top sirloin** (the longissimus dorsi), the tenderloin, and the **knuckle,** a part of the **flank.** The flank is a striated

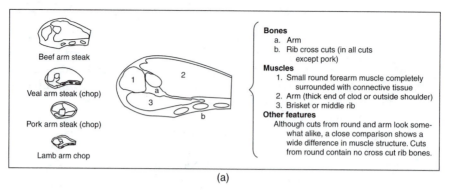

(a)

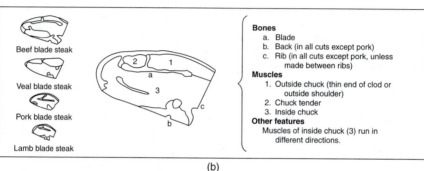

(b)

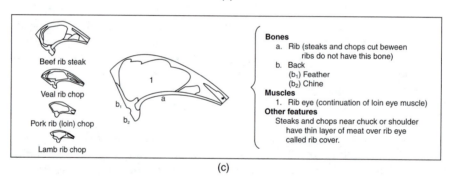

(c)

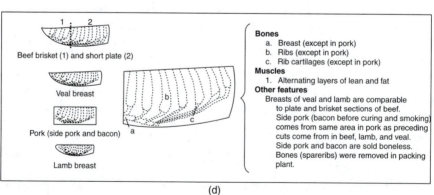

(d)

Figure 7-20

(a, b) Main muscles and bone shapes of the forequarter. (c, d) Main muscles and bone shapes found in the hindquarter. (Reproduction courtesy of the National Cattlemen's Beef Association.)

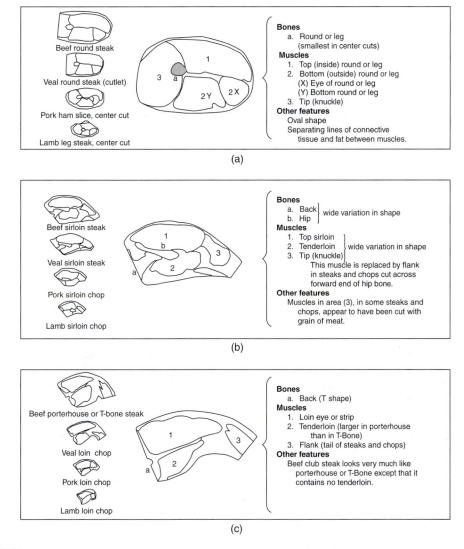

(a)

(b)

(c)

Figure 7-21

(a) The hind leg on beef is called the round; *on veal and calf and lamb, yearlings and mutton, it is called the* leg, *and on pork the* **ham**. *On a beef the round divides into a* top *(inside) and* bottom *(outside), "top" because this is the way the butchers lay the leg on the cutting block for cutting up, "inside" because this is the inside of the animal's leg. The meanings of "bottom" and "outside" should now be obvious. The bottom part of the round is called the* tip *or* knuckle. *(b) Bones and muscles of the* sirloin *on beef, which, when boned out, is often cut into* top *and* bottom *sirloin steaks; if left whole it becomes a sirloin roast. The* flank *or* tip *(knuckle) is often used as a steak and comes from the bottom part of this area. The small part of the* tenderloin *(psoas major) runs along the underneath part of this area. The top part is known as the* strip *(also* loin eye *or* New York *or* Kansas City strip). *It is used as a roast or cut into steaks. In pork and lamb this area is cut into chops, not steaks; it also serves as a roast as a piece. (c) Muscles and bones in the most expensive part of an animal. On a beef it cuts into the* porterhouse *and* T-bone *steaks. If bones out, the top strip is called the* loin eye *(Kansas City or New York strip) and is usually cut into steaks but can be used whole as a roast. The large part of the* tenderloin *(psoas major) is the under strip used for steaks or roasts. When this part of a pork, lamb, or calf is cut into portion cuts, the cut is called a chop and not a steak. A portion of the flank steak is also found in this area. (Reproduction courtesy of the National Cattlemen's Beef Association.)*

221

muscle found as a flap laying off the leg under the belly. The **round** or hind leg on beef is easily identified by the round humerus bone and four muscles surrounding it. The **top (inside) round** is at the top; it is called top because butchers put this part on top in cutting the piece and called inside because it is the inside muscle next to the body. The **bottom (outside) round** is below the top with the eye of the round next to it. The **tip** is the large round muscle at the left of the cut. The top round is the tenderest part of the round. The lower muscle in the tibia and fibula area is called the *heel,* a tough muscle only good for moist cooking (see Figure 7–21).

The **diaphragm,** the muscle separating the lung area from the intestinal area, is also called the **skirt (butcher's) steak,** or **hanging tender.**

MEAT CUTTING

The cutting of meat in food services is becoming a lost art because so few people do it today. Ready-to-use items are now being purchased. Few facilities today have the facilities, the labor, or want the mess and sanitation problems involved in cutting meat. Some few might go halfway and purchase boxed meats and prepare these, but many do not even want this bother. However, because some students might wish to delve further into how meats are cut up and processed into the kind they purchase, Appendix E provides a detailed discussion on meat cutting along with illustrations.

Figure 7–16 shows how a beef side is divided into wholesale (major) cuts and then shows under each the various portion or other cuts derived from these. The percents the forequarter, hindquarter, and wholesale cuts make up of an average carcass are also given. Figures 7–17 and 7–18 give similar information for lamb and veal. Note that instead of forequarters and hindquarters as in beef, the fore and hind parts of these carcasses are called **saddles.** The reason these charts show both sides of the carcass is that sometimes the cut is sold double. Thus, if one orders two legs of lamb, the two legs might come joined. Note also that the hind saddles are cut farther up toward the shoulder than the beef.

Pork as shown in Figure 7–19 is cut differently than beef or lamb or veal. The area over cut No. 4 in this chart is where side pork or bacon is taken, leaving then the spare ribs.

Additional information on the derivation of the various animal cuts is given in Appendix E.

IMPS

The **Institutional Meat Purchase Specifications (IMPS)** were established in the 1940s by the USDA. They established a standardized method for cutting meat and a definition of what meat cuts or products should be. Numbers were assigned to the various cuts or products. Originally there were six different groups of items; today there are eight because of the many new **processed** products on the market. These are the groups with their latest revision date given in parentheses:

Nos. 100 Fresh Beef (1996)	Nos. 500 Cured and Smoked Pork Products (1992)
Nos. 200 Fresh Lamb, Yearlings, and Mutton (1996)	Nos. 600 Cured, Dried, Smoked, and Fully Cooked Beef Products (1993)
Nos. 300 Fresh Veal and Calf (1995)	Nos. 700 Variety and Edible By-Products (1993)
Nos. 400 Fresh Pork Products (1995)	Nos. 800 Sausage Products (1992)

Portion cuts are listed with 1000 numbers. Thus, while an oven-ready rib roast is No. 109, a rib steak from this area is No. 1109. The tables for fresh beef cuts and portion cuts are presented in this chapter (see Tables 7–11 and 7–12). The tables for the other seven groups are given in Appendix E.

The IMPS system was quickly picked up by the National Association of Meat Purveyors (NAMP), which not only listed these standard cuts with their federal definition, but also showed photographs of each meat item, in a booklet entitled ***Meat Buyers Guide.***

Use of the standards quickly spread and today almost all buyers use the IMPS to indicate what they are trying to order. The development of the IMPS made it possible to simplify meat purchasing by using only a number and the name of the cut rather than giving a long explanation of how the cut was to be made along with the name of the cut. Keep in mind, though, that while cutting has been standardized in certain areas, local names are still used, which can cause some confusion when those not used to these local terms encounter them.

[The IMPS are set up so cuts coming from other cuts need not repeat the cutting of previous cuts.] Thus, a beef carcass (No. 100) is divided into sides, a **forequarter** (No. 102) and **hindquarter** (No. 155). If a full rib is cut from the forequarter, it is called No. 103, and from this an oven-ready rib No. 109 will be derived. When one indicates No. 109, all previous cutting and trim are assumed and need not be repeated.

It is not possible in a text of this kind to discuss every IMPS item. Buyers of meat should obtain copies of the IMPS from either the USDA's Meat and Livestock Division or from the NAMP using its *Meat Buyers Guide*. Both contain the same information about exactly how a specific meat cut is prepared for the market. All a buyer has to do is to specify the IMPS number and name of the item, and perhaps the weight range or weight, fat depth allowed, and any other factor desired in the product not covered by the IMPS. Thus, if a buyer wanted to purchase partially boned, cured and smoked, skinless hams, just by stating "No. 504, Ham, Skinless, Partially Boned (Cured and Smoked), 8 to 10 lb each, fresh, approximately 200 lb total" the proper product would probably be obtained. Actually by giving the IMPS number and product name, the buyer has stated that these hams should conform to the following included in the IMPS definition of the product: "The skinless, partially boned ham (cured and smoked) shall conform with the requirements specified for Ham, Short Shank (Cured and Smoked), Item 501, except that the ham shall

Table 7-9
Tolerances permitted in portion-cut weights

Portion Weight Specified (oz)	Tolerance (oz)
Less than 6	¼
6–12	½
12–18	¾
18 up	1

Table 7-10
IMPS weight ranges of various animal carcasses

Range	Lamb	Mutton	Veal	Calf	Pork
A	30–41	55–75	60–90	125–175	120–150
B	41–53	75–95	90–140	175–225	150–180
C	53–65	95–115	140–175	225–275	180–210
D	65–75	115–130	175–225	275–350	

be made completely skinless and the shank shall be removed from the ham through the natural seam separating the shank and the heel (inner shank). All surface fat in excess of 0.25 inch (6 mm) average depth (0.5 in. maximum depth) at any point shall be removed. All trimming, skinning, and defatting may be accomplished either before or after curing, but must be done prior to smoking (exceptions section B part 6). The aitch bone and overlying flesh and shank bones shall be removed without undue scoring or other damage to the ham, leaving the femur bone intact in the ham. The ham shall be encased in an artificial casing, producing a smooth, plump, elongated, oval-shaped, skinless, partially boned, cured and smoked ham." Thus, you can see that using the IMPS number and name of items can save a lot of writing and also end any confusion as to what is actually wanted on both the part of the buyer or seller.

The IMPS also includes many factors that apply to specific items or purchase conditions. Thus, they provide for weight tolerances of portion cuts from their specified weight as listed in Table 7–9. Thus, if 8-oz steaks are specified, individual units can weigh 7 ½ to 8½ oz. Ground patty portions also have a tolerance based on the number per pound. Large cuts have weight tolerances listed in pounds or partial pounds.

The IMPS set up weight tolerances for cuts based on carcass size such that carcasses within certain weights are placed in a specific range. Thus, for beef cuts, carcasses weighing 500–600 lb are in Range A; 600–700 lb, Range B; 700–800 lb, Range C; and over 800 lb, Range D. Thus, a No. 109, Oven-Ready Beef Rib Roast, in Range A would average 14 to 16 lb while in Range D it would range from 22 lb up. Table 7–10 lists the weight ranges for the various animal carcasses.

Another example of these special provisions would be in fat depth allowances; these vary for different cuts and for various animals. Thus, beef steaks can have "not over ½ in. average and not over ¾ in. at any point" and beef roasts "not over a ¾ in. average and not over 1 in. at any one point." Buyers should see that sellers follow these allowances. If a difference allowance is desired, it must be named; otherwise, the IMPS allowance will be followed.

Fresh Beef (Nos. 100s and 1000s)

More beef is marketed than any other classification of meat, but veal, calf, pork, and lamb are gradually increasing at the expense of beef. It is also divided into more types of cuts and portions than any other kind of meat. Tables 7–11 and 7–12 summarize the IMPS listing of the various cuts and portions available in fresh beef. A buyer, by listing the IMPS number, name, and range, can specify with some precision exactly what he wants. Additional material that may have to be added to complete a specification is discussed later in this chapter.

Fresh Lamb, Yearlings, and Mutton (Nos. 200s and 2000s)

Lamb is marketed in far greater quantities than yearling or mutton. Not very much mutton is sold in the U.S. markets, because its flavor is stronger and its texture tougher than American consumers like. Some yearling is sold, but in comparison to lamb, the quantity is small. Buyers can tell lamb from yearling because lamb is a light pinkish red while yearling is beginning to show the deep, dark red of mutton. The size of the bones in the cut or portion can also be an indicator. The IMPS tables for lamb, yearling, and mutton appear in Appendix E.

Fresh Veal and Calf (Nos. 300s and 3000s)

Veal and calf are cut much like lamb, yearling, and mutton. Unlike beef, the legs marketed from these two kinds of animals include what would be the leg, rump, and sirloin of beef. The loin area includes what would be the rib and short loin on beef. While veal and calf are thought of as light meats in contrast to red beef and sheep, the cholesterol content is not low, with many veal and calf cuts being as high as beef. However, the sale of veal and calf has grown because many consumers think differently. Calf can be distinguished from veal by its graduation toward red from the grayish pink of veal and also by bone size. The IMPS tables for veal and calf appear in Appendix E.

Fresh Pork Products (Nos. 400s and 4000s)

Fresh pork has two periods of heavy supply. The piglets born in the January crop come onto the market about six months later and those born in the spring crop come onto the market in the fall. Supplies will be greatest, quality best, and prices most favorable during these two periods.

Table 7-11

Index of IMPS beef products and weight ranges

Purchaser shall specify *IMPS item number, product name, and weight range* to be purchased. The following weight ranges are intended as guidelines. Carcass weights are not necessarily related to the weight of cuts within their respective weight range. Other weights or ranges may be specified.

IMPS Item No.	Product Name	Weight Ranges (pounds)			
		Range A	Range B	Range C	Range D
100	Carcass	500–600	600–700	700–800	800–up
100A	Carcass, Trimmed	475–575	575–675	675–775	775–up
100B	Carcass, Streamlined	335–400	400–470	470–600	600–up
101	Side	250–300	300–350	350–400	400–up
102	Forequarter	131–157	157–183	183–210	210–up
102A	Forequarter, Boneless	104–125	125–146	146–168	168–up
102B	Forequarter, Streamlined	91–110	110–128	128–147	147–up
103	Rib, Primal	24–28	28–33	33–38	38–up
104	Rib, Oven-Prepared, Regular	19–22	22–26	26–30	30–up
107	Rib, Oven-Prepared	17–19	19–23	23–26	26–up
107A	Rib, Oven-Prepared, Blade Bone In	17–19	19–23	23–26	26–up
108	Rib, Oven-Prepared, Boneless, Tied	13–16	16–19	19–22	22–up
109	Rib, Roast-Ready	14–16	16–19	19–22	22–up
109A	Rib, Roast-Ready, Special, Tied	14–16	16–19	19–22	22–up
109B	Rib, Blade Meat	Over 3			
109C	Rib, Roast-Ready, Cover off	13–15	15–18	18–21	21–up
109D	Rib, Roast-Ready, Cover off, Short Cut	12–14	14–17	17–20	20–up
110	Rib, Roast-Ready, Boneless	11–13	13–16	16–19	19–up
111	Rib, Spencer Roll	10–12	12–15	15–18	18–up
112	Rib, Ribeye Roll	5–6	6–8	8–10	10–up
112A	Rib, Ribeye Roll, Lip-On	6–7	7–9	9–11	11–up
113	Chuck, Square-Cut	66–79	79–93	93–106	106–up
113A	Chuck, Square-Cut, Divided	66–79	79–93	93–106	106–up
114	Chuck, Shoulder Clod	13–15	15–18	18–21	21–up
114A	Chuck, Shoulder Clod Roast	Under 15	15–18	18–21	21–up
114B	Chuck, Shoulder Clod Roast, Tied	Under 15	15–18	18–21	21–up
115	Chuck, Square-Cut, Boneless	54–65	65–77	77–88	88–up
115A	Chuck, Blade Portion, Boneless	22–25	25–29	29–34	34–up
115B	Chuck, Arm-Out, Boneless	35–40	40–47	47–55	55–up
116	Chuck, Square-Cut, Clod-Out, Boneless	40–48	48–57	57–65	65–up
116A	Chuck, Chuck Roll, Tied	13–15	15–18	18–21	21–up
116B	Chuck, Chuck Tender	Under–1	1–3	3–up	
116C	Chuck, Chuck Roll, Untrimmed	16–18	18–20	20–22	22–up
117	Foreshank	7–8	8–10	10–12	12–up
118	Brisket	12–14	14–17	17–20	20–up
119	Brisket, Deckle-On, Boneless	9–10	10–12	12–14	14–up
120	Brisket, Deckle-Off, Boneless	6–8	8–10	10–12	12–up
121	Plate, Short Plate	20–27	27–31	31–35	35–up
121A	Plate, Short Plate, Boneless	12–14	14–16	16–18	18–up
121B	Plate, Short Plate, Boneless, Trimmed	8–12	12–14	14–16	16–up
121C	Plate, Skirt Steak (Diaphragm)	1–2	2–3	3–up	
121D	Plate, Skirt Steak (Transversus Abdominis)	1–3	3–4	4–up	
121E	Plate, Skirt Steak (Diaphragm) Skinned	1–2	2–3	3–up	
121F	Plate, Short Plate, Short Ribs Removed	18–25	25–28	28–33	33–up
121G	Plate, Short Plate, Short Ribs Removed, Boneless	10–12	12–14	14–16	16–up
122	Plate, Full	28–37	37–44	44–51	51–up

IMPS Item No.	Product Name	Weight Ranges (pounds)			
		Range A	Range B	Range C	Range D
122A	Plate, Full, Boneless	21–27	27–29	29–32	32–up
123	Short Ribs	2–3	3–4	4–5	5–up
123A	Short Plate Short Ribs, Trimmed	Amount as Specified			
123B	Rib, Short Ribs, Trimmed	Amount as Specified			
123C	Rib, Short Ribs	Amount as Specified			
124	Rib, Back Ribs	Amount as Specified			
125	Chuck, Armbone	77–88	88–103	103–118	188–up
126	Chuck, Armbone, Boneless	59–70	70–82	82–90	90–up
126A	Chuck, Armbone, Clod-Out, Boneless	46–57	57–69	69–77	77–up
127	Chuck, Cross-Cut	86–103	103–120	120–138	138–up
128	Chuck, Cross-Cut, Boneless	68–81	81–95	95–109	109–up
132	Triangle	107–129	129–150	150–172	172–up
133	Triangle, Boneless	83–101	101–117	117–134	134–up
134	Beef Bones	Amount as Specified			
135	Diced Beef	Amount as Specified			
135A	Beef for Stewing	Amount as Specified			
135B	Beef for Kabobs	Amount as Specified			
136	Ground Beef	Amount as Specified			
136A	Ground Beef and Vegetable Protein Product	Amount as Specified			
136B	Beef Patty Mix	Amount as Specified			
137	Ground Beef, Special	Amount as Specified			
137A	Ground Beef and Vegetable Protein Product, Special	Amount as Specified			
155	Hindquarter	119–143	143–167	167–190	190–up
155A	Hindquarter, Boneless	90–108	108–126	126–143	143–up
155B	Hindquarter, Streamlined	96–115	115–134	134–152	152–up
155C	Hindquarter, Trimmed	110–132	132–155	155–178	178–up
158	Round, Primal	59–71	71–83	83–95	95–up
158A	Round, Diamond-Cut	63–76	76–89	89–102	102–up
159	Round, Primal, Boneless	44–53	53–62	62–71	71–up
160	Round, Shank-Off, Partially Boneless	47–57	57–67	67–76	76–up
161	Round, Shank-Off, Boneless	42–51	51–62	62–71	71–up
163	Round, Shank-Off, 3-Way, Boneless	41–50	50–58	58–66	66–up
164	Round, Rump and Shank Off	40–48	48–56	56–64	64–up
165	Round, Rump and Shank Off, Boneless	35–43	43–50	50–57	57–up
165A	Round, Rump and Shank Off, Boneless, Special	38–46	46–54	54–60	60–up
165B	Round, Rump and Shank Off, Boneless, Special, Tied	38–46	46–54	54–60	60–up
166	Round, Rump and Shank Off, Tied, Boneless	35–43	43–50	50–57	57–up
166A	Round, Rump Partially Removed, Shank Off	44–52	52–61	61–70	70–up
166B	Round, Rump and Shank Partially Removed, Handle On	44–52	52–61	61–70	70–up
167	Round, Knuckle	8–9	9–11	11–13	13–up

Table 7–11 *continued*

IMPS Item No.	Product Name	Weight Ranges (pounds)			
		Range A	Range B	Range C	Range D
167A	Round, Knuckle, Peeled	7–8	8–10	10–12	12–up
167B	Round, Knuckle, Full	10–12	12–14	14–16	16–up
168	Round, Top (Inside), Untrimmed	14–17	17–20	20–23	23–up
169	Round, Top (Inside)	14–17	17–20	20–23	23–up
170	Round, Bottom (Gooseneck)	18–23	23–27	27–31	31–up
170A	Round, Bottom (Gooseneck), Heel-Out	17–20	20–24	24–28	28–up
171	Round, Bottom (Gooseneck), Untrimmed	18–21	21–25	25–29	29–up
171A	Round, Bottom (Gooseneck), Untrimmed, Heel-Out	17–20	20–24	24–28	28–up
171B	Round, Outside Round	8–10	10–13	13–16	16–up
171C	Round, Eye of Round	Under–3	3–5	5–up	
172	Loin, Full Loin, Trimmed	30–37	37–45	45–52	52–up
172A	Loin, Full Loin, Diamond Cut	35–42	42–50	50–57	57–up
173	Loin, Short Loin	17–24	24–30	30–35	35–up
174	Loin, Short Loin, Short-Cut	14–20	20–25	25–30	30–up
175	Loin, Strip Loin	11–14	14–18	18–22	22–up
176	Loin, Strip Loin, Boneless	8–10	10–12	12–14	14–up
177	Loin, Strip Loin, Intermediate	10–12	12–14	14–16	16–up
178	Loin, Strip Loin, Intermediate, Boneless	8–9	9–11	11–13	13–up
179	Loin, Strip Loin, Short-Cut	8–10	10–12	12–14	14–up
180	Loin, Strip Loin, Short-Cut, Boneless	7–8	8–10	10–12	12–up
180A	Loin, Strip Loin, Extra Short-Cut, Boneless	6–7	7–9	9–11	11–up
181	Loin, Sirloin	16–19	19–24	24–28	28–up
182	Loin, Sirloin Butt, Boneless	11–14	14–16	16–19	19–up
183	Loin, Sirloin Butt, Boneless, Trimmed	9–10	10–13	13–15	15–up
184	Loin, Top Sirloin Butt, Boneless	8–10	10–12	12–14	14–up
185	Loin, Bottom Sirloin Butt, Boneless	5–6	6–7	7–8	8–up
185A	Loin, Bottom Sirloin Butt Flap, Boneless	1–3	3–up		
185B	Loin, Bottom Sirloin Butt Ball Tip, Boneless	1.5–3	3–up		
185C	Loin, Bottom Sirloin Butt Tri-Tip, Boneless	1.5–3	3–up		
185D	Loin, Bottom Sirloin Butt Tri-Tip, Boneless, Defatted	1.5–3	3–up		
186	Loin, Bottom Sirloin Butt, Trimmed, Boneless	2–3	3–4	4–5	5–up
189	Loin, Tenderloin, Full	4–5	5–6	6–7	7–up
189A	Loin, Tenderloin, Full, Side Muscle On, Defatted	3–4	4–5	5–6	6–up
189B	Loin, Tenderloin, Full, Side Muscle On, Partially Defatted	3–4	4–5	5–6	6–up
190	Loin, Tenderloin, Full, Side Muscle Off	2–3	3–4	4–up	
190A	Loin, Tenderloin, Full, Side Muscle Off, Skinned	2–3	3–4	4–up	
191	Loin, Tenderloin, Butt	1–2	2–3	3–4	4–up
192	Loin, Tenderloin, Short	2–3	3–4	4–up	
193	Flank, Flank Steak	Under–1	1–2	2–up	

Table 7–12

Beef portion cuts

IMPS Item No.	Product	Suggested Portion Weight Range (ounces)
1100	Cube Steak	3–8
1101	Cube Steak, Special	3–8
1102	Braising Steak (Swiss)	4–8
1103	Rib, Rib Steak	8–18
1103A	Rib, Rib Steak, Boneless	4–12
1112	Rib, Ribeye Roll Steak	4–12
1112A	Rib, Ribeye Roll Steak, Lip-On	4–12
1112B	Rib, Ribeye Roll Steak, Lip-On, Short cut	4–12
1121	Plate, Outer Skirt Steak, (Diaphragm)	4–8
1121A	Plate, Inner Skirt Steak, (Transversus Abdominis)	4–8
1136	Ground Beef Patties	Desired ounces or number per pound
1136A	Ground Beef and Vegetable Protein Product Patties	"
1136B	Beef Patties	"
1137	Ground Beef Patties, Special	"
1137A	Ground Beef and Vegetable Protein Product Patties, Special	"
1138	Beef Steaks, Flaked and Formed, Frozen	"
1167	Round, Knuckle Steak	3–10
1167A	Round, Knuckle Steak, Peeled	3–10
1168	Round, Top (Inside) Round Steak	3–12
1100	Cube Steak	3–8
1101	Cube Steak, Special	3–8
1102	Braising Steak (Swiss)	4–8
1103	Rib, Rib Steak	8–18
1103A	Rib, Rib Steak, Boneless	4–12
1112	Rib, Ribeye Roll Steak	4–12
1112A	Rib, Ribeye Roll Steak, Lip-On	4–12
1112B	Rib, Ribeye Roll Steak, Lip-On, Short cut	4–12
1121	Plate, Outer Skirt Steak, (Diaphragm)	4–8
1121A	Plate, Inner Skirt Steak, (Transversus Abdominis)	4–8
1136	Ground Beef Patties	Desired ounces or number per pound
1136A	Ground Beef and Vegetable Protein Product Patties	"
1136B	Beef Patties	"
1137	Ground Beef Patties, Special	"
1137A	Ground Beef and Vegetable Protein Product Patties, Special	"
1138	Beef Steaks, Flaked and Formed, Frozen	"
1167	Round, Knuckle Steak	3–10
1167A	Round, Knuckle Steak, Peeled	3–10
1168	Round, Top (Inside) Round Steak	3–12
1173	Loin, Porterhouse Steak	10–12
1173A	Loin, Porterhouse Steak, Intermediate	10–24
1173B	Loin, Porterhouse Steak, Short-Cut	10–24
1174	Loin, T-Bone Steak	8–24
1174A	Loin, T-Bone Steak, Intermediate	8–24
1174B	Loin, T-Bone Steak, Short-Cut	8–24
1177	Loin, Strip Loin Steak, Intermediate	6–24
1178	Loin, Strip Loin Steak, Intermediate, Boneless	8–24
1179	Loin, Strip Loin Steak, Short-Cut	8–24

Table 7-12 *continued*

IMPS Item No.	Product	Suggested Portion Weight Range (ounces)
1179A	Loin, Strip Loin Steak, Extra Short-Cut	8–24
1179B	Loin, Strip Loin Steak, Special	8–24
1180	Loin, Strip Loin Steak, Short-Cut, Boneless	6–20
1180A	Loin, Strip Loin Steak, Extra Short-Cut, Boneless	4–18
1180B	Loin, Strip Loin Steak, Special, Boneless	6–20
1184	Loin, Top Sirloin Butt Steak, Boneless	4–24
1184A	Loin, Top Sirloin Butt Steak, Semi Center-Cut, Boneless	4–16
1184B	Loin, Top Sirloin Butt Steak, Center-Cut, Boneless	4–16
1185	Loin, Bottom Sirloin Butt Ball Tip Steak	3–10
1185A	Loin, Bottom Sirloin Butt Tri-Tip Steak	3–8
1185B	Loin, Bottom Sirloin Butt Tri-Tip Steak, Defatted	3–8
1189	Loin, Tenderloin Steak	4–14
1189A	Loin, Tenderloin Steak, Side Muscle On, Defatted	3–14
1189B	Loin, Tenderloin Steak, Side Muscle On, Partially Defatted	3–14
1190	Loin, Tenderloin Steak, Side Muscle Off, Defatted	3–14
1190A	Loin, Tenderloin Steak, Side Muscle Off, Skinned	3–14

Proposed changes in the IMPS 400 and 4000, Fresh Pork Products, were published in October 1995. The major changes are an option by the buyer to get added ingredients not presently permitted in these products and an option by the buyer for a maximum fat depth in large cuts in grade No. 1 of ¾ in.; in No. 2, ¼ in.; and in No. 3, ⅛ in. Portion cuts could be specified with a maximum fat depth of ¼ in. or 1/8 in. or practically free of fat, or peeled (denuded) or peeled with membrane removed. Normally, after a year or two of testing, proposed changes are adopted with little change since the Meat Division is careful to get such changes approved by a large majority of meat purveyors before establishing them.

Cured and Smoked Pork Products (Nos. 500s)

A large quantity of the pork marketed is **cured** or **cured and smoked.** Curing is done either by pumping into the meat a heavy salt brine, by soaking in a heavy salt brine, or by adding salt and flavoring ingredients plus preservatives and allowing these products to pull from the meat enough moisture to make a strong salt brine, this latter process being called a **dry cure.** Nitrogen products used in curing meats have been criticized because they can break down in the body into **nitrosamines,** substances suspect of being carcinogenic. Vitamin C reduces the chance of such a breakdown; so if you eat a meal of bacon and eggs but also drink a glass of orange or tomato juice, good sources of vitamin C, the danger of a breakdown into nitrosamines is less.

Some cured items cannot exceed their original or "green" weight after curing. If a product weighs the same or less as before curing, it can be called **cured.** A *dry cure* is one in which 8% to 9% salt and other preservatives are added to meat, which draws out the meat's juices, making a brine, which then soaks into the meat preserving it. A *wet brine cure* is one in which meat is immersed in a seasoned brine of about 55% to 70% salt until it soaks in enough salt to be preserved. It does not lose as much moisture this way. Other meats are cured by pumping them full of a seasoned salt brine using needles to shoot it in, or forcing the brine through the arterial system so it spreads throughout the meat. This adds moisture. When beef is preserved this way, it is called *cured,* as in "cured beef brisket." *Country-cured* meat is given a dry cure with seasoning agents added such as sugar, spices, or honey.

Bacon is a cured meat often purchased. It should appear fresh, the meat should be pink in color and dry, not greasy. It may be purchased in the slab with skin on (No. 536) or off (No. 537) or skin-off sliced bacon (No. 539). The best size skin-on slab to purchase is 8 to 10 lb and about 8 to 10 in. wide. Specify sliced bacon 18 to 24 slices per pound. Preset bacon on sheets is desirable to save labor.

The best size hams (Nos. 503 and 504) run from 12 to 14 lb. A number of excellent imported hams are used in food services. Some of the best are Danish, Westphalian (German), Prosciutto (Italy), Scotch, and Chinese. Capicolli is a cured, boneless, lightly smoked pork butt from Italy. Smithfield hams from Smithfield County, Virginia, where the hogs are fattened on peanuts, have a fine reputation.

Cured, Dried, Smoked, and Fully Cooked Beef Products (Nos. 600s)

Pastrami, dried chipped beef, cornbeef, and a number of other cured, dried, or smoked beef products have long been on the market, but not the wide number of fully cooked beef items that are found today. Our ability to cook-chill products and hold them under refrigeration or to hold them frozen has improved to the point that a huge market has developed in this cooked product line. In many cases, the meat product is combined with other ingredients. Because there is a need for definition of the amount of meat in these products compared to the other ingredients, the government has established guidelines on the minimum quantity of meat an item can contain and still bear that specific name. If the added ingredients are greater in quantity than the meat item, the name of a product must name the added ingredient first such as "vegetables with beef." If the amount of meat is greater, the meat item can come first such as "beef with vegetables." An exception is "pork and beans" and this difference was allowed because the product had been on the market so long before the rule was established that it had become traditional, so beans can predominate in "pork and beans." Tables 7–13 and 7–14 list the minimum amount of meat many fully cooked items can contain. An asterisk indicates raw meat; all others are based on cooked meat.

Variety and Edible By-Products (Nos. 700s)

Liver, kidney, tongue, heart, brains, tripe (first and second stomachs of cattle), oxtails, and sweetbreads are classed as edible by-products by the IMPS. The best liver is thought to be from veal (often called calf's liver), but pork and lamb liver are also considered of good quality. Beef liver is tougher but, if sliced thin and cooked fast for only a short time, can be quite tender. Beef and lamb kidneys are usually the most commonly used. They are often boiled until tender and then used. Beef tongue is most commonly used, but the others may be as well, often as cooked, pickled

Table 7-13

Minimum quantities of meat in some food products

Product	Minimum Quantity	Product	Minimum Quantity
Beans with bacon in sauce	12% bacon*	Beef with barbecue sauce	50% beef
Beans with ham in sauce	12% ham	Gravy with beef	35% beef
Beef with gravy	50% beef	Chili con carne	40% meat*
Beef Stroganoff	30% beef†	Chop suey vegetables with meat	12% meat*
Chili sauce with meat	6% meat*		
Chow mein	12% meat*	Egg foo yung with meat	12% meat*
Deviled ham	No more than 35% fat		
		Egg rolls with meat	10% meat*
Enchiladas with meat	15% meat*	Frozen breakfast	15% meat
Ham and cheese spread	25% ham	Ham chowder	10% ham
Ham spread	50% ham*	Hash	35% meat
Lasagna with meat and sauce	12% meat*	Lima beans with ham or bacon in sauce	12% ham or bacon
Liver, paste, pudding, etc.	30% liver*	Macaroni and cheese with ham	12% ham
Macaroni and beef in tomato sauce	12% beef*		
		Meat casseroles	18% meat, 25%*
Meat salad	35% meat	Meat pies	25% meat*, 18%
Meat turnovers	25% meat*	Meat tacos	15% meat*
Omelet with ham	18% ham	Omelet with bacon	12% bacon
Pork with barbecue sauce	50% pork	Pizza with meat	15% meat*
Sauerkraut with wieners and juice	20% wieners*	Pizza with sausage	12% or 10% dry sausage
Scrapple	40% meat‡	Scallopine	35% meat
Spaghetti with meat balls	12% meat*	Spaghetti with meat and sauce	12% meat*
Spaghetti sauce with meat	6% meat*		
Stews	25% meat*	Spanish rice with beef	20% beef
Sweet and sour pork or beef	25% or 16% meat	Sukiyaki	30% meat*
Tamales with sauce or gravy	20% meat*	Swiss steak with gravy	50% meat
Veal Cordon Bleu	60% veal*, 5% ham* plus cheese	Tamales	25% meat
		Veal birds	60% veal*, 40% dressing
Beans with frankfurters in sauce	20% franks*	Veal fricassee	40% meat*

*Raw basis.
†Plus not less than 10% sour cream.
‡Or meat by-products.

products. Because tongue is somewhat tough, it must be moist-cooked for quite some time and then skinned and used. Beef heart is usually split and moist-cooked to make it tender. It can be stuffed and then slowly braised. The best brains are thought to come from veal; those from other animals are seldom used. Often they are precooked and then prepared in various kinds of dishes. The best tripe is honeycomb tripe, which comes from the second stomach of cattle. Tripe from the first stomach is apt to be more tough and must be moist-cooked a longer time. Oxtails are often braised, but perhaps their most common use is for making oxtail soup. Young cattle and lambs grow a thymus in the throat which is considered a delicacy,

Table 7-14
Miscellaneous specifications and standards for some cooked meals

Item	Purchase Description
Roast beef, frozen	Precooked rounds from choice grade steer or heifer, deli-style, 7–12 lb each. Individually wrapped in moisture- and grease-resistant paper; can be ordered sliced and tied also; boneless.
Roast beef, frozen	Precooked top round from choice grade steer or heifer, 6 ½ lb average, not varying more than ½ lb in individual pieces; boneless.
Roast beef, frozen	Precooked cross-rib, from choice steer or heifer, 12 to 15 lb each, boneless.
Barbecued ground beef, frozen	51½% ground coarse beef, 48½% tomato gravy, cooked basis.
Barbecued meat	The weight of meat when barbecued cannot exceed 70% of the fresh uncooked meat; must have a barbecued (crusted) appearance.
Beef, sliced with gravy, frozen	Meat to be not less than 55% on a cooked basis.
Beef, Burgundy, frozen	45% choice cubed beef, 53% Burgundy wine sauce, 2½% garnish of onions and mushrooms.
Beef casserole, Italian style, frozen	Not more than 50% cooked macaroni; at least 25% cooked beef.
Beef patty, charbroiled, frozen	Cooked, 3% textured vegetable protein may be added; 95% beef, 2% flavoring and spices; 3-oz patties, layer packed.
Beef rolls, frozen	Ground beef in pastry roll with sauce; shall be at least 2 oz ground beef on a cooked basis; 4¾-oz portions.
Beef stew, frozen	25% beef, not more than 20% peas, carrots, green beans, small onions, and celery on a proportionate basis.
Beef and pork fritters	Chop shape 3-oz patties, 53 per case (10 lb), layer packed; 65% lean pork, 30% beef, 3% coating, 2% seasoning
Cabbage rolls, frozen	8-oz portions, 4 oz of filling with remainder cabbage and sauce; filling should be 50% meat.
Cannelloni with meat sauce, frozen	20% meat filling.
Meat balls in sour cream, frozen	55% veal or beef on cooked basis from choice grade meat, 45% sauce; ½ oz meat balls; no extender permitted.
Sirloin tips in mushroom gravy, frozen	From choice top sirloin in ½-oz cubes after cooking, broiled and then added to a gravy. Shall be 41.875% meat on cooked basis, 55% mushroom gravy and 3.125% mushrooms.
Stuffed peppers in sauce, frozen	60% filling and peppers; 40% sauce; filling shall be 50% meat on a cooked basis with corn, rice and seasonings plus moisture 50%.

although those of lambs are quite small. As an animal matures, the thymus glands disappear (see Figure 7–22).

Sausage Products (Nos. 800s)

Sausage may be fresh or cured. Fresh sausage is ground meat that contains seasonings; some nitrite may be added to reduce the danger of bacterial contamination, but this is the only curative agent allowed. It must be refrigerated.

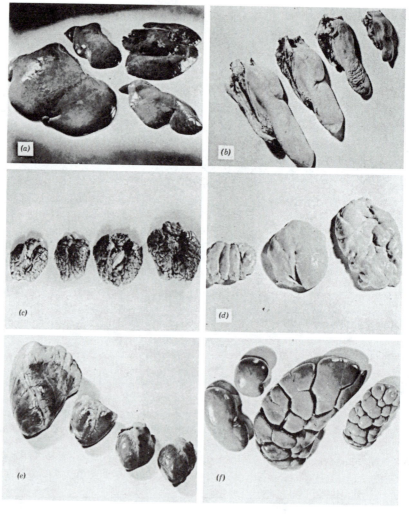

Figure 7–22

Variety meats: (a) beef, pork, veal, and lamb livers; (b) tongues of beef, veal, pork, and lamb; (c) brains of lamb, pork, veal, and beef; (d) sweetbreads of lamb, veal, and beef; (e) hearts of beef, veal, pork, and lamb; and (f) kidneys of lamb, pork, beef and veal. (Courtesy USDA.)

Fresh sausage may not contain more than 3% added moisture; cured can contain up to 10%. Some semidried sausages, such as salami or pepperoni, lose a lot of moisture in curing and do not have to be refrigerated. Smoked cooked sausage such as frankfurters must be refrigerated. Some sausage is so dry, such as pepperoni, that it keeps without refrigeration. If refrigerated, most cured sausage keeps well up to 30 days, fresh sausage for about a week.

Cooking, curing, smoking, fermenting and other processes are used in making sausage. Some even have bacteria added to them to cause desirable reactions. Drying is used as a means of preserving; some salami meat may be predried for a number of days and then after being made are hung to dry out further.

Natural casings are made of intestines, stomachs, colons, or other animal parts; they are edible but shrink in cooking. Collagen casings are edible but they shrink on cooking. Nonedible casings may be made of plastic, fiber, or other materials. They have to be removed before eating. Some sausage such as weiners or frankfurters may be made in plastic casings and then these are removed before marketing.

Specify bacterial count in sausage as not over 100,000 per gram. High-quality, sterilized seasonings should be used. Moisture to protein ratio should not be over 4:1; if the moisture is over this, the product has to be labeled *imitation*. The government allows up to 2% extenders such as cereal to total weight, but all meat sausage can be specified. Type A sausage is chilled; Type B is frozen. Total fat should not be more than 40% for pork sausage (No. 802) and less than this for breakfast pork sausage (No. 810). Specify grinding for these two as first through a 1-in. plate and then through either a $\frac{3}{16}$- or $\frac{1}{4}$-in. plate. Linked sausage should not vary in length over $\frac{1}{2}$ in. Purchase small links 12 to 14 per pound.

Frankfurters or knockwurst (No. 816) should be from 5 to 6 in. in length; normally franks are 7 to 8 and wieners 8 to 10 per pound, but may be specified differently. Lebanon bologna (No. 806) is smoked and uncooked; it is usually made only of coarsely cut beef and stuffed into artificial casings, $3\frac{1}{2}$ to $4\frac{1}{2}$ in. in diameter, weighing 5 to 10 lb. Vienna sausages have a smaller diameter than wieners and are usually skinless and canned.

Liver (Braunshweiger) sausage (No. 803) is cooked and has a slight smoke. The ingredients are largely pork liver and pork. Weights are 5 to 10 lb.

Polish sausage (No. 813) is a smoked, cooked link sausage made of coarsely ground pork with or without finely ground beef. Smoked sausage (No. 811) is cooked and made into links running from 6 to 10 per pound. New England (No. 812) sausage is smoked and cooked and made predominantly from pork chunks, with a small amount of finely ground beef; it comes in casings $3\frac{1}{2}$ to $4\frac{1}{2}$ in. in diameter and weighs from 5 to 10 lb. Specify meat loaves (No. 814) and meat food product loaves (No. 815) as dry heat roasted, steamed, etc., and either chilled or frozen. Finely ground beef, pork, or veal may be used either singly or in combination with any two or all three. The federal government does not allow blood, skin, cracklings, lips, ear, snouts, or such materials to be used. Ingredients such as pickles, olives, cheese, ham, or pasta may be added only in federally governed amounts. A meat loaf that contains an extender over federal limits of 2% must be called "meat food product loaves." Both kinds of loaves usually weigh 4 to 8 lb.

Head cheese (No. 802) is cooked pork head meats or predominantly that with other meats, but ears, livers, spleens, etc., cannot be used. The meat is usually coarsely cut. Caraway may be specified as a seasoning. Specify also whether the product shall be delivered chilled or frozen. Souse is a sausage similar to head cheese.

Salami (No. 804) may be imported from Italy, Germany, Austria, or Scandinavia. Southern Italian sausage is hotter in flavor and contains more garlic than northern Italian types. Genoa and Milan salami are quite dry. Pepperoni has a smaller diameter than salami and is drier and more sharply seasoned. Farmer, Holsteiner, and Cervelat (No. 809) are much like salami. Thuringer is smoked but uncooked. It is made largely from beef and has a distinctive, slightly fermented flavor. Mortadella is made from select, finely ground lean pork with a little beef added, along with small cubes of fat. It is delicately seasoned with cardamon, other spices, and garlic, stuffed into hog bladders, and corded into basket shape. It is cooked and dried, but not smoked.

URMIS

The use of the IMPS for the food service industry was so successful that in 1973 the National Livestock and Meat Board introduced what is today called the **Uniform Retail Meat Identity Standards (URMIS),** and from time to time foodservice buyers might encounter them. Over 300 portion cuts have been identified, described, and given a name based on (1) the kind of animal such as beef, pork, veal, or lamb, with (2) the wholesale (primal) cut from where the cut comes, and (3) the recommended URMIS name. Thus, a beef ribeye steak would be identified as that rather than Spencer steak, Delmonico steak, or just rib steak. This same cut on a veal, pork, or lamb would be identified, respectively, by veal rib chop, pork rib chop, or lamb rib chop. As this system takes over, it will eliminate the confusion often caused by the use of different terms for the same portion of meat throughout this country. Perhaps in the future such names as Kansas City steak, etc., for a beef strip loin may no longer be used and instead just the right name (1) beef, (2) strip loin, (3) steak.

MEAT STYLING FOR THE MARKET

Meat Storage

Meats must be stored often until moved on the market. Fresh meat under proper refrigeration and wrapping will keep for three or more weeks. Meat to be held for long periods of time is wrapped and then frozen.

Fresh meat is best stored under refrigeration at from 34° to 36°F (1.1° to 2.2°C), but if storage is to be for more than a week, the temperature should be dropped to 30° to 32°F (−1° to 0°C). If meat is stored unwrapped it darkens and dries out, causing around a 2% loss per day in weight. Raising the humidity can reduce some of this moisture loss, but the best advice is to wrap meat in moisture-vapor-proof wrapping material. An average $1,500 inventory of fresh meat hanging unwrapped can cause about an $11,000 loss in a year—2% × 365 days × $1,500 = $10,950.

Fast freezing is desirable when freezing meat because small crystals form and this causes less swell within the fibers, thus preserving meat texture. Slow freezing develops larger crystals and more swell, rupturing fibers and causing them to lose moisture, called **drip** or **purge.** Such loss causes the meat to lose flavor, moisture, and nutrients. Varying frozen storage temperatures develop larger crystals and result in greater drip loss. Cook meat from the frozen state, if possible, to avoid this drip loss. (Note, however, that cooking from the frozen state increases cooking time.)

Freezer burn is a surface dehydration that occurs when meat dries out in frozen storage. If moisture-vapor-proof wraps are drawn tightly around the meat, eliminating all space between wrap and meat, such burn can be avoided. Freezer burn appears as a whitish, dry covering that toughens the surface and causes an almost complete flavor and texture loss.

Hold frozen meat in storage at 0°F (−18°C) or less. At a higher frozen temperature, ice crystals will grow larger and cause texture problems in the meat. Also, enzymatic and other changes may be encouraged that may not be desirable. Tables 7–15 and 7–16 give some desirable storage data for meats. Additional storage information is given in Appendix B.

Meat storage can raise the basic cost of meat depending on the type of storage and its length of time. Because temperatures must be kept lower, frozen storage is more expensive than plain refrigeration. The physical cost of building a frozen storage area is also more costly. Frozen costs can run as high as nine cents per pound per month. Meat holds well under good frozen storage for up to 12 months, and under prime conditions somewhat longer. Lamb, yearlings, mutton, veal, and beef hold

Table 7-15

Refrigerator storage timetable—recommended storage time for maximum quality

Meat		Refrigerator (36° to 40°F)
Fresh	Beef cuts	3 to 4 days
	Veal cuts	1 to 2 days
	Pork cuts	2 to 3 days
	Lamb cuts	3 to 5 days
	Ground beef, veal, pork, lamb	1 to 2 days
	Variety meats	1 to 2 days
	Leftover cooked meat	3 to 4 days
Processed	Luncheon meat*	3 to 5 days
	Sausage, fresh pork*	2 to 3 days
	Sausage, smoked	1 week
	Sausage, dry and semi-dry (unsliced)	2 to 3 weeks
	Frankfurters*	3 to 5 days
	Bacon*	1 week
	Smoked ham, whole	1 week
	Ham slices*	3 to 4 days

*If vacuum packaged, check manufacturer's date.

Source: Reproduction courtesy of the National Cattlemen's Beef Association.

Table 7-16
Freezer storage timetable—recommended storage time for maximum quality

Meat in Freezer Wrapping		Freezer (0°F or Colder)
Fresh	Beef cuts	6 to 12 months
	Veal and lamb cuts	6 to 9 months
	Pork cuts	6 months
	Ground beef, veal and lamb	3 to 4 months
	Ground pork	1 to 3 months
	Variety meats	3 to 4 months
	Leftover cooked meat	2 to 3 months
Processed	Luncheon meat	1 to 2 months
	Sausage	1 to 2 months
	Frankfurters	1 to 2 months
	Bacon	1 month
	Smoked ham	1 to 2 months
Frozen Combination Foods,	Meat pies	2 to 3 months
Packaged	Stews	3 to 4 months
	Prepared dinners	2 to 3 months

Source: Reproduction courtesy of the National Cattlemen's Beef Association.

best; pork less well because its fat can get rancid more quickly, especially if air can get at the meat. Ground meats should only be held about three months. Cured and smoked products hold fairly well for about one to three months.

Aging Meat

After meat relaxes after rigor, if meat is allowed to hang in a room at about 36°F (7°C) and 75% to 80% relative humidity, enzymes in the meat act to tenderize it and make it more juicy and flavorful, a process called **dry aging.** The benefits of aging are fairly rapid up to about two weeks, but then the process slows down and, after six weeks, little benefit from it occurs. Because it normally takes 7 to 10 days for meat to get to consumers, all fresh meat gets some aging. To promote it, refrigerated trucks or other means of transport are controlled so this aging occurs during transport. Beef and lamb are aged, but poultry and pork usually are not.

Usually large pieces of meat such as whole carcasses, quarters, or wholesale cuts are aged. Furthermore, meat that is to be dry aged must have a fat cover inside and out sufficient to protect the meat. Once aging starts, a dark blackish-gray mold starts to develop and to penetrate into the fat. This can be delayed by wiping the surface of the meat daily with a cloth dipped into vinegar. The fat must be trimmed from the meat before being used.

Dry aging can be speeded up by raising the room temperature to 60°F (15.4°C), with as much aging occurring in 3 days as in 10 at lower temperatures. However, the danger of spoilage is greater. To control this, vinegar again may be used, or ultraviolet lights are hung close to the meat so its action delays bacterial action. It is also possible to get faster aging by spraying the surface of the meat with spores of the

Figure 7-23
A stamp used to indicate that the meat meets Kosher standards. (From *The Meat We Eat* by John Romans et al. Copyright © 1994 by Interstate Publishers. Used with permission.)

mold that develop, and this process can then occur at the lower temperatures which safeguards against spoilage.

Because money is tied up during the aging process, besides costing money just to do, and because the fat that has grayed must be trimmed off, and because there must be some trim of the blackish, dried surface where flesh is exposed, and because of a moisture loss, dry aged meat is more expensive than regular meat. As much as 10% of the total weight of the meat may be lost in the process.

A less costly method of aging most meat is being used today, and this is the **Cryovac** method. The meat does not need a fat cover as in dry aging and also much smaller pieces can be aged this way. Cryovac is a special tough, plastic film made into bags. The meat to be aged is put into these, the air exhausted, and a heat-shrinking process done which causes the plastic to fit tightly over the meat. This stops a loss of moisture but still allows the desired enzymatic actions to occur at around 36°F. The meat is often shipped in these wraps. When obtained, some liquid will be evident around the surface of the meat inside. This is meat juice that has exuded from the meat. Upon opening the package, a light musty odor may be evident, but this quickly dissipates.

Kosher Meat

Some buyers may find it desirable to purchase meat that is classified for the market as **Kosher** meaning "right and proper" and "correctly prepared." The standards to which these meats must conform come from biblical references and religious practices found in the Mosaic and Talmudic laws largely followed by the Jewish race. The meat must come from animals that have split hooves and chew their cud, which allows cattle, sheep, and some other animals but prohibits pork. A rabbi, trained to slaughter animals as prescribed by these laws must dispatch the animals, and after slaughter the meat must be soaked and salted to remove as much blood as possible. Because it is not possible to remove all the blood on some of the hindquarter cuts of beef, meat from this area cannot be Kosher.

While a Kosher stamp (see Figure 7–23) indicates the meat meets certain religious requirements, it is no guarantee of quality. Such meat must meet federal standards for sanitation and be inspected and passed. Grading for quality must also be done, if there is a need for grade.

Additives in Meat

In processing meat,[2] various ingredients other than meat are added. This reduces the meat or the protein content of the product and buyers may wish to know how much of these additives are in the product. Thus, it is permissible to add water to hams and other items. How much can be added? The federal government regulates the amount of moisture by stating the minimum quantity of **protein on a fat-free basis (PFF)** that a product can contain. Thus the PFF for a ham labeled "cooked ham, no water added" must not be less than 18%, but for a ham labeled "water added," the PFF must not be less than 17%. This method, although a bit more complicated than the old method of just allowing only a certain percentage of water or other ingredient to be added, now more precisely controls the amount of moisture a product can contain. The amount of soy, dry milk, cereal, or other additives that can be added is, however, still controlled by the amounts of the product that can be added.

Nitrates or nitrites are often used to preserve meats such as bacon, ham, sausages, etc. In 1979 cured products without these were allowed on the market, if the label read "not preserved; keep refrigerated below 40°F at all times." Canned hams and other large canned meats are similarly labeled because their size makes it difficult to completely sterilize the entire product. These must often be handled as fresh products, although they are more stable.

Textured Vegetable Protein (TVP)

Many excellent products are being made of soy or other high-protein substances such as rape seed, nuts, or cottonseed. The products may look and taste like ground meats, pieces of chicken, beef, veal, ham, or other meat. Baco-bits, which closely resemble crisp, diced bacon, are made from soy. Soy is used to make milk and other dairy substitutes. Imitation nuts made from soy look and taste like the real thing. Soy protein is used to enrich pastas, flour, or other foods. It supplies a good quality protein without animal fat and so is good for certain diets. It is also a good dietary protein enhancer. Schools are permitted to use the product. A soy–meat ratio of 1:2 is permitted. Using soy as a supplier of protein allows the cost of an adequate diet to be lowered. Undoubtedly in the future we can expect to see more of these protein products in use.

Too much soy added to ground meats that are to be grilled can cause problems. The products stick to the griddle. A better conditioned surface for frying reduces the problem.

Ready-to-Serve Meats

Many prepared meat dishes are marketed, a large share of which have not been brought under federal regulation, except as processed foods that come under the

---

[2]When fresh meat is changed in some manner such as restructuring, smoking, cooking, etc., it is called **processed.** This may be done to help preserve it or give it increased palatability, reduce labor, or give other desirable results.

Pure Food, Drug and Cosmetic Act and other laws. Thus, minimum quantities of meat in them as indicated in Tables 7–13 and 7–14 have not been prescribed by the government and, if buyers desire, they must write in their own minimum quantity allowed. Amounts of added ingredients and other factors affecting quality, appearance, portion size, and so forth must also be included in a specification. Most of these products come frozen or as cook-chill products, ready to reheat and serve. Because the armed forces and other federal and state agencies purchase these products, you may be able to secure copies of their specifications and use these as models for setting up your own.

Canned Meats

If fresh meats are difficult to obtain or refrigeration is lacking, canned meats may have to be used for most meat items. Most food services purchase some.

Some canned meats must be refrigerated because canning does not completely sterilize the interior of the meat. Storage of other canned meats from 40° to 70°F is best. Higher temperatures may encourage undesirable reactions. A number of thick meat products such as hash or stew may be canned by the 18 psi method, in which the food is put into cans at high temperatures in a pressured chamber. This gives a more palatable as well as safer product.

Canned meats should not be kept for more than a year. Freezing can cause a loss of quality, but edibility and nutritional value are not harmed. Freezing, however, may cause the can to swell and break, causing spoilage. Lacquered cans are used to prevent meat from reacting with the metal can linings.

Some of the most commonly used canned meats are as follows: Canned slab bacon in 14-lb rectangular cans with three to four pieces. Canned sliced bacon is also available. Do not keep canned bacon over six months. Canned Canadian bacon may be purchased.

Boned chicken or turkey usually comes in 46-oz or smaller cans. Corned beef comes in cans from 12 oz to 6 lb. Corned beef is packed in No. 2 or No. 10 cans. Canned luncheon meat, pork sausage or pork sausage links, Vienna sausage, frankfurters, chili concarne are also found. This by no means ends the list.

Cooked hams may be oval, round, or pulman shaped. They vary from a few pounds to 16 lb. An 8- to 10-lb ham is best for institutional use. Canned hams over 10% moisture must be labeled "imitation."

Buyers often have to calculate quantities required. Table 7–17 gives the amount of uncooked meat needed to give a small 3-oz portion of cooked meat.

WRITING MEAT SPECIFICATIONS

Meat is one of the most complex and difficult food products to purchase. The wide variety, the different grades, price and value considerations, and market fluctuations make it necessary for buyers to know a lot and be constantly alert in moving in the market. Products must conform to production and customer needs. Well-written

Table 7-17

Servings per pound uncooked meat to yield 3 oz of cooked meat*

Beef		Pork	
Steaks		Chops, Steaks, Cutlets	
Bnls Chuck	3½	Blade (Shoulder)	2½–3½
Chuck, Arm or Blade	2½	Chops, bnls	4
Cubed	4	Loin or Rib Chops	2½
Flank	4	Ham, Cured (center slice)	3½
Porterhouse	2½		
Rib	2	Roasts	
Round	3		
Sirloin	3	Leg (Ham), fresh bi	3
T-Bone	2	Leg (Ham), bnls	4
Tenderloin (Filet Mignon)	3	Smoked Ham, bi	3
Top Loin (Strip), bnls	3	Smoked Ham, bnls	4
Top Round	4	Shoulder (rolled), bnls	3
		Center Loin	3
Roasts		Blade Loin	2
		Top Loin (rolled), bnls	3½
Eye of Round	4	Smoked Center Loin	3
Rib	2	Smoked Shoulder Roll	3
Rump, bnls	2½		
Tip	4	Other Cuts	
Pot Roasts			
Chuck Blade	2½	Back Ribs	1½
Chuck, bnls	2½	Bacon, Regular, Sliced	6
Cross Rib, bi	2½	Country-style Loin Ribs	2
		Cubes	4
Other Cuts		Hocks (Fresh or smoked)	1½
		Pork Sausage	4
Beef for Stew	4	Spareribs	1¼
Brisket	3	Tenderloin	4
Ground Beef	4		
Short Ribs	1½–2½	Variety Meats	
Variety Meats		Brains	5
		Heart	4
Brains	5	Kidney	5
Heart	4	Liver	4
Kidney	4		
Liver	4		
Sweetbreads	5		
Tongue	5		
Veal		Lamb	
Chops, Steaks, Cutlets		Chops and Steaks	
Loin or Rib Chops	2	Leg, center slice	3
Shoulder Steak	2½	Loin or Rib Chop	2½
Round Steak	3½	Shoulder Chop	2
Cutlets, bnls	4	Sirloin Chop	2

Veal		Lamb	
Roasts		Roasts	
Leg, bi	3	Leg, bi	2½
Shoulder, bnls	3	Leg, bnls	4
Rib	2	Shoulder, bi	2
		Shoulder, bnls	3
Other Cuts			
Riblets	1½	Other Cuts	
Cubes	4		
Breast (rolled), bnls	3	Breast	2
Ground	4	Riblets	1¼
		Cubes	4
Variety Meats		Shanks	2
		Ground	4
Brains	5		
Heart	5	Variety Meats	
Kidney	4		
Liver	4	Heart	5
Sweetbreads	5	Kidney	5
Tongue	4½		

* The portions per pound in this table are based on an average serving of 3 oz of cooked, trimmed meat. These portions can vary according to cooking method, fatness of meat, amount of bone, degree of doneness, etc. Thus, they should be used as a guide only. Also, for a larger portion of cooked meat, one will have to adjust the number of servings per pound accordingly.
Note: Bi = bone in and bnls = boneless
Source: Adapted from a table in *Lessons on Meat,* National Live Stock and Meat Board, 1991.

specifications are a must and it requires a knowledgeable and skillful buyer to compile proper ones so the right product is secured at a desirable price.

Specifications need to be written not only to get the right product but also to reduce cost as much as possible. There can often be a wide variation between the price paid AP and the final cost of the product prepared to serve (AS).

It is wise to follow the market and note pricing. The ways to analyze pricing mentioned in a previous chapter now come into play. If meat is purchased in the carcass or primal cut, a buyer must know yields and value of main cuts and by-products. As much as 50% or more of a product may have to be eliminated to get what is desired; some of this 50% may be salvaged as by-products such as bone, suet, meat trim, etc., but the value of these is low and thus the main product must bear most of the AP cost. The buyer should not forget other costs such as labor, equipment cost, and others. Handling costs later in the kitchen need consideration, such as purchasing tray-pack (also called hotel- or shingle-pack) bacon may save a high-priced cook on a busy morning the time it takes to carefully lay out bacon strips from a layer-pack purchase. Good scrutiny by the buyer of these incidental costs may produce significant savings.

The Veterans Administration, U.S. General Services, Armed Forces, state agencies, and other large buying groups have specifications for many meat items. Purveyors can be helpful and work with buyers to set up specifications. Standards of Identity exist for chopped ham and corned beef hash and these can be used to set up specifications for them.

A specification can be made by using a recipe. Thus, if a recipe for chicken à la king calls for 4 lb of cubed, cooked chicken, 1½ lb of mushrooms, 1 lb of green peppers, 1 lb of pimientos, 12 oz of flour, 10 oz of margarine, 2½ qt of chicken stock, 1 qt milk, and 1 pt of evaporated milk, the specification might read "The cooked chicken shall be in natural proportions without skin in approximately ½-in. cubes and be 25% of total weight. Other ingredients shall be of total weight: mushrooms 9%, green pepper 6%, pimiento 6%, flour 4%, margarine 3¾%, chicken stock 30%, milk 12%, and evaporated milk 6%. The medium thick sauce should be of delicate chicken flavor, smooth, not pasty, and other ingredients shall be of natural flavor."

Specifications should require that products meet all sanitary and other requirements of Public Health and the FDA, plus other regulations that support the wholesomeness of products. All products should be free from foreign or objectionable material and insect infestation. Require all meats be inspected and passed by federal or state inspectors—the federal government requires this of all meat products containing over 2% meat. Chilled products should be below 40°F inside and out upon delivery. Frozen products should be solidly frozen.

The following standards are used by one state for cooked meat foods: per gram or cubic centimeter bacterial count should not exceed 100,000, coliform 100, fecal (E. coli) 10, pathogens 0, staphylococcus 100, coagulase positive 0, yeast 100, and mold 100. To check for fat rancidity an iodine, Hanus, or peroxide number can be required; thus, an iodine number of 25 to 100 would be considered satisfactory.

Frozen items should show no evidence of thawing and refreezing, freezer burn, or any off-colors or odors. Items should be delivered in good shape, with good appearance, and without encrusted materials or other substances adhering to them. Roasted, broiled, or fried products should possess a good brown sheen. Tenderness may be specified by requiring a specific Bratzler test number. Type and amount of trim and fat on the surface or a seam fat can be specified. Sliced or cut items can be specified as to thickness, weight, or size. Weight variations allowed should be indicated. Type and amount of breading or other product cover permitted should be specified. Indicate also the kind and quantity of thickening product allowed. In many cases the amount of fat needs specification.

Nutritional content may be important. This may be stated in values per 1000 calories, per meal, or as a percent of the required daily allowance (RDA). Iodine should be present in the same quantity as if iodized salt were used.

Packaging varies for products, but all should be well protected so they reach users in good shape and condition.

Tables 7–13 and 7–14 give helpful information when writing specifications for some processed meats. Table 7–17 lists quantities of raw meat needed to end up with 3-oz portions.

The Specification

Meat specifications appear in many forms, but generally, most will include the following:

1.   Product name with IMPS number and yield grade (where applicable).

2.   Order quantity in pounds, unit, container or other designation. This can be calculated by knowing the number of portions needed and the portion size. Thus, if 40 orders of frenched lamb rib chops are needed with 2 chops per portion, each chop averaging 4 oz, the need would be 40 orders × 2/order × 4 oz or 320 oz ÷ 16 oz = 20 lb EP. If No. 1204a chops are to be ordered, there is no further problem, because these chops come all ready in the form needed, but suppose the establishment wants to process the chops from the primal rack (rib) No. 204 cut? The buyer then needs to know the yield of No. 1204a chops from a No. 204 rack to get the right amount to purchase. It is usually 49% from No. 204 racks, so 20 lb EP ÷ 0.49 = about 41 lb AP, and the buyer will probably specify six 7-lb No. 204 double racks. In doing this calculation, however, the buyer should also make a cost comparison of the cost of purchasing the chops ready to use in No. 1204a form versus cutting them from No. 204 racks. It could be the former is a better buy.

3.   The grade, brand, or other quality factor needed. Usually the buyer gets this information from the food production department. A chef or other person who must prepare the food often knows better what quality is needed to produce the right item and should be consulted. However, buyers also need to know something in this area as a backup verification.

4.   The packaging, size, or other way in which the product is to come. This can take many forms and usually must be suited to the product. Thus, bacon will often come in polyethylene 15-lb boxes preferably tray (hotel)- or shingle-pack, each layer separated by polyethylene paper or other non-grease-absorbing material. Fresh hamburger, 4 oz 3¾ diameter patties might be specified to come in 12-lb lots, packed in strong 200-lb test, fiberboard cartons and sealed in carbon dioxide flushed bags. No. 109 ribs may be specified to come in individually vacuum packed Cryovac wrap in 200-lb test fiberboard cartons, two to the box. Buyers must often consult with purveyors to ascertain the types of packaging available and the best to use. The product needs protection from handling and also to meet sanitary considerations. Frozen meat usually is more stable, but its packaging also needs buyer attention, so unsanitary or damaged products are not received.

5.   The basis on which the price will be named. This is usually based on the pound, but may be by the piece, package, or be some other unit. Sellers need to know this so they quote a price a buyer understands so there is no misunderstanding.

6.   All miscellaneous factors needed to get the right product. These can be varied and considerable. Sometimes it is wise to indicate the intended use; or the point of origin such as Kansas City beef; or the preservation or tenderization method; product form; fresh or frozen and, if frozen, type of freezing; bacterial content; product exterior and interior receiving temperature; type grind or size of dice; ratio of breading or other cover to product; percent fat, fat trim or fat depth allowed at specific

areas; special trim; percent meat mixture; seasonings; processing methods; type of feed; kind, breed, sex, or age of the animal; type of meat aging; range or carcass or primal cut weight; cut thickness or measurement; weight tolerances such as 10-oz steaks ± ½ oz, or number per pound such as "eight wieners to the lb"; boneless or boned, rolled and tied (BRT) give just a few of the factors that might be included.

Specification Examples

The following are examples of specifications for meat giving a number of factors that must be covered to obtain satisfactory products:

A. A university's student union is to serve 500 at a dinner; a 6-oz portion of roast beef is planned and machine slicing will be used. The specification is as follows:
   1. Ribs of beef (No. 110, BRT)
   2. 500 lb (See quantities needed to serve 3 oz. of cooked meat, Appendix F)
   3. U.S. Choice (top)
   4. Boxed ribs, two ribs per box, in 200-lb test polyethylene lined fiberboard boxes Cryovac wrapped, 16 to 17 lb each (Range C).
   5. Quote price per lb.
   6. Cryovac aged minimum 14 days; fresh; fat cover average ½ in., but not more than ¾ in. at any point; seam fat not excessive. Each rib to measure between 15 and 18 in., delivery temperature 36°F exterior and interior of product.

B. A school lunch program wants a three months' bid on 3 ¾ in. by ¾ in. thick, 3-oz frozen hamburger with TVP patties, 20% fat. The quantity required is 8,000 lb. The specification is as follows:
   1. Hamburger patties with 20% TVP (No. 137a)
   2. 8,000 lb
   3. From at least 60% graded standard or better grade fresh beef chucks or rounds and 40% high-quality fresh meat trimmings
   4. Patties shall be round, 3¾-in. diameter, ¾ in. thick, 3 oz each; the meat first put through a 1-in. plate and then a 3⁄16-in. plate; layered in polyethylene lined 200-lb test fiberboard cartons, holding 96 patties in each box, 4-layer pack with paper between patties with entire contents sealed in a carbon dioxide flushed bag.
   5. Quote price per lb.
   6. IQF (individually quick frozen) in a blast tunnel freezer at −20°F (−29°C); bacterial content not to exceed 100,000 per gram and not more than 100 coliform count; deliver to 22 units within a 30-mile diameter area upon individual orders from these units, minimum order 50 lb; delivery time and date to be decided by individual.

C. A good restaurant wants 8-oz boneless strip loin steaks, No. 1178, intermediate (flank or tail not more than 3 in. from loin eye). ROP is 20 lb; order is 80 lb. The specification is as follows:
   1. Beef strip (NY) loin steak, boneless, intermediate No. 1178
   2. 80 lb
   3. U.S. Choice (top)

4. 8-oz steaks± ½ oz; ¾ in. thick; layer-packed, 3 tiers per box, separated by polyethylene; each box to contain 42 steaks or 21 lb.

5. Quote price per pound.

6. Corn-fed 20 days, dry-aged 21 days before cutting; fresh, not frozen; vein or end steaks be rejected; average fat cover ½ in., maximum at any point, ¾ in. (The buyer could add minimum loin eye width 2½ in., maximum 3⅓ in., but this should be met if the other factors are met.)

D. A hospital wants to serve stuffed veal breast roast. The dietary department has ordered 80 lb. The specification is as follows:

1. Veal breast, No. 1313, Range 2

2. 80 lb

3. U.S. Choice

4. Boxed breasts, 40 lb net; each breast to average 6 to 7½ lb and be plastic, vacuum-exhausted wrapped.

5. Quote price per pound.

6. Shall be nature-fed veal; each breast well trimmed with no flank portion, ready for roasting with pocket for stuffing; can be frozen; fresh preferred.

E. A club has french lamb chops on the menu with a forecast of 40 orders, 2 per order to be sold. The specification is as follows:

1. Lamb chops, french, 1204A

2. 20 lb, 80 4-oz chops

3. U.S. Choice

4. Cryovac-wrapped, two 4-oz chops per wrapping, layered in boxes holding approximately 20 lb net.

5. Quote price per pound.

6. Shall come from Range 2 lamb racks (204) averaging 7 lb each (double). Average fat cover depth on each chop ¼ in. No shoulder chops accepted. Must be fresh, not frozen, lamb. (*Note:* IMPS requires these be frenched 1½ in. from the rib end, and so this need not be added. IMPS sets ¼ oz as the maximum plus or minus variation of this weight.)

F. A school dormitory wants ground beef for meat loaf. The specification is as follows:

1. Ground beef, special, No. 137, 20% fat

2. ROP is 50 lb; amount ordered is 120 lb

3. From U.S. Good (bottom)

4. Packed 10 lb in plastic wrap bags, extruded as it comes from the ⅛-in. plate grinder on final grinding; no added moisture; packed 4 bags per box.

5. Quote price per pound.

6. Not over 100,000 plate count and 100 coliform count; product cannot contain any aged meat or aged fat; deliver solid frozen. Use no ice in grinding; use dry ice to cool grinder head.

G. A hotel wants breakfast bacon and sets up the following specification:

1. Bacon, sliced, No. 539, 10–22 slices/lb

2. ROP 10 lb; order 50 lb

3. Acceptable brands: Swift's Premium, Armour's Star, Cudahy's Puritan, or equal

4. Tray or hotel pack, 5 lb each; each box 20 lb net.

     5. Quote price per pound.

     6. Fresh; not frozen; must be delivered not over 7 days from manufacture.

H. A deli sets up a specification for corned briskets of beef; it is as follows:

     1. Brisket, boneless, deckle off, corned, No. 601

     2. ROP 60 lb; order 120 lb

     3. Acceptable brands: Fitzgerald's, Finn's, Breakstone's, Feldman's; shall come from U.S. Top Select briskets.

     4. Briskets shall be between 9 and 12 lb (Range 2), packed individually in plastic bags, drained with no pickling brine.

     5. Quote by the pound.

     6. Deliver chilled, not frozen; shall come from lean briskets, with fat cover not over ½ in. Seam fat shall not be excessive.

I. A cruise ship serves sweetbreads and mushrooms on its luncheon menu. The specification is as follows:

     1. Sweetbreads, veal or calf only, frozen

     2. 30 lb

     3. Packed in 5 lb pails

     4. Quote price per pound.

     5. Shall average 2 to 4 oz each; should not be bloody or heavily veined. Should be firm, solid, good, light reddish cream-colored sweetbreads from the thymus only; only a small quantity of membranous covering. Should come from U.S. Select animals or better.

J. A food service wants cooked Swiss (braised) steaks in gravy in tray-pack pans. The specification is as follows:

     1. Swiss (braised) steaks, cooked, in gravy

     2. 4 cases

     3. Brands "X," "Y," or "Z" acceptable only

     4. Packed in tray-pack pans, flash-18 processed, 2½ lb each net, 24 trays per box.

     5. Price by the case.

     6. High-quality beef must be used so the product is tender and moist. Each steak shall weigh 4 oz on a cooked basis or 7 oz on a raw basis. The remainder of the pack can be gravy (50% maximum), which has a flow of not more than 14 cm in 30 seconds at 20°C in the Bostwick consistometer.

K. A hotel menu offers cornbeef hash as a breakfast dish. Canned cornbeef is desired. The specification is as follows:

     1. Cornbeef hash, canned

     2. 5 cases

     3. Shall be Rath, Hormel, or Oscar Mayer

     4. Packed in 46-oz cans, flash-18 processed, 6 cans per case

     5. Price by the case.

     6. To contain not less than 35% lean cornbeef on a cooked basis, plus fresh, dehydrated or frozen potatoes, or a mixture of these. Optional ingredients are onions, garlic, seasonings, curing agents, beef broth, and beef fat; not over 10% beef broth and 8% added beef broth. Maximum moisture content 72%.

SUMMARY

Buyers must know something about the physical properties of meat and how it performs in cooking so they can purchase meats suitable for the menu need. Meat is from 45% to 72% moisture held mostly in the fat and fibers of the muscles. The finer the fibers, the more tender the meat. Connective tissue binds these fibers, and the amount of connective tissue is also an indication of meat tenderness. The muscles an animal exercises have more connective tissue than those that just give support. As an animal ages this connective tissue also changes becoming something that cannot be tenderized by cooking. It must be broken apart by grinding, cubing, pounding, etc. Tenderizers can be added to meat to help dissolve some of the connective tissue and thus make it become more tender. Aging the meat also tenderizes it. Restructured meat is meat that is finely divided and then reshaped. Such processing gives a tender product.

Fat contains from 15% to 50% moisture and therefore helps to keep meat moist. Fat is responsible for much of the flavor of meat. The fat on an animal is either found as marbling, tiny flecks of fat between meat tissues, or as finish, which is surface fat outside and inside.

The red color of meat is caused by the presence of hemoglobin and myoglobin. Myoglobin turns into oxymyoglobin when air strikes it. If nitrites or nitrates come in contact with these pigments they stay permanently red as they do in cured meats such as ham or corned beef. The pigment is then called nitrosomyoglobin. When meat begins to spoil the red color changes to metmyoglobin, which is a brownish gray. Meat is red up to 140°F; above this it begins to lose color and from 140° to 160°F it is pink; above 160°F it begins to change to the well-done gray color. The pigment now is called hematin. Acid speeds this color change in meat.

The institution of HCAAP came about largely because of outbreaks of *E. coli* poisoning from undercooked hamburgers. Meat under this new inspection program is subjected to much more rigorous testing by plants processing meats. The government by such regulation can control the sanitation of meat up to the point at which it leaves the processing plant, but what happens to it afterward is up to the individuals handling and cooking the products. Thus, food services today should take extra care in handling and cooking of meat to see that good sanitation practices are followed.

Meat is such a costly item and so important to most meals that buyers should see that they have the best market information available for its selection. The USDA meat reports, the Yellow and Green Sheets, and other publications are available to keep buyers informed on market happenings. Buyers should understand how meat is priced on the market. They should also know how to figure the actual cost of meats when served.

The federal government regulates the meat market through various laws largely administered by the Meat and Livestock Division of the USDA. Recently a law was passed requiring state inspection services to meet federal standards. If they do, they can then use their own state inspection stamp of "inspected and passed" but cannot ship such meat out of the state. All meat must be inspected and passed as fit for human consumption; quality and yield grading are voluntary. Much meat is not graded. Most of this ungraded meat or what is called no roll would grade Select.

Kosher meat is meat that is slaughtered by a rabbi using special methods. The meat also receives different treatment than ordinary meat as it moves through the food chain.

Frozen meat is almost as good as fresh meat; there is the problem, however, with the drip or purge that occurs, which is a moisture loss that detracts from the flavor and moistness of the meat. Freezer burn is another problem. If meat has any freezer burn, that portion of the meat is gray and tasteless, regardless of how it is prepared.

Meat should be stored at from 34° to 36°F. It usually loses about 2% moisture a day, which can result in a significant cost in a year's time, if the inventory of meat held is anything substantial. Meats held under refrigeration are best wrapped in moisture-vapor proof wraps to prevent such moisture loss. When meat is held under refrigeration it dry ages, becoming more flavorful and more tender. However, there is a moisture loss and as the meat ages the outer surface fat turns gray, requiring it to be trimmed from the meat. Exposed meat tissue also turns dark and hard requiring its trimming also. Thus, there is a cost in aging. Meat can be aged by a process patented under the name of Cryovac. It prevents such moisture loss and trim.

The federal government divides meat according to age and sex into classes. This in turn influences what grades a carcass can qualify for. Thus, a bull cannot qualify for Prime grade, but quite young bulls, called bullocks, can. Quality is decided by meat color, meat texture, the amount of fat (in beef marbling), and other factors. Meats are graded for yield by noting the amount of fat, the size of the rib eye, and the weight of the carcass when still warm. The quality grade of pork is largely influenced by the yield.

Buyers need to be able to identify the cuts of meat so they can tell if they are getting what they order. How to identify yield from muscle and bone structure is discussed. The use of Institutional Meat Purchase Specifications (IMPS) has become quite standard in meat purchasing. The IMPS system numbers meat cuts and then indicates how such meat should be cut. The size of the cut, fat depth, and other factors are also controlled. The IMPS program was so successful that the National Livestock and Meat Board introduced the Uniform Retail Meat Identity Standards. Buyers may encounter these if they purchase meats through retail outlets.

So many facilities no longer purchase meat in cuts that have to be butchered that meat cutting is becoming a lost art. Only a rudimentary explanation is therefore given of meat cutting, but a much more complete discussion is given in Appendix E for those that wish to study this area.

The writing of meat specifications is discussed. Examples are given.

REVIEW QUESTIONS

1. Why is the purchase of meats usually very important to the successful operation of a food service?

2. What makes meat tough and how is it tenderized?

3. Define the following words, phrases, or statements:

   a. Enzyme   f. Papain

   b. Dry aging   g. Moist cooking

   c. Cryovac   h. Acid on connective tissue

   d. Aging shrink   i. Green meat

   e. *Rigor mortis*   j. Water-bath cooking

4. What good is fat in cooking and for the palatability of meat?

5. Is fat more fattening than alcohol, carbohydrates, or protein?

6. Define these color pigments: myoglobin, oxymyoglobin, nitrosomyoglobin, hematin, metmyoglobin.

7. What is freezer burn?

8. Which of the following statements are true, and which are false?

   a. Dry-cured salami keeps without refrigeration.

   b. Fresh sausage contains 5% added water.

   c. Hams with moisture over 110% of original (green) weight must be labeled imitation ham.

   d. Pumped hams keep less well than dry-cured hams.

   e. Only natural casings shrink in cooking.

9. A full beef loin (No. 172) is purchased for $3.00 a pound. Butchering cost is 20¢ a pound. What is the value of items from a 50-lb loin if the market value per pound of items from this loin and percent yield are as follows?

Items	Value ($)	% Yield from Loin
No. 175, strip loin, boneless reg.	5.60	21
No. 189, tenderloin full, reg.	5.80	13
No. 184, top sirloin, butt, boneless	3.70	18
No. 185, bottom sirloin butt, boneless	4.20	16
Flank end	2.00	4
Trim meat	1.80	3
Bone	.25	17
Fat	.10	7
Cutting loss		1
		100%

What would you purchase, the full loin or parts?

10. Give four good information sources for meat a quantity meat buyer might use to advantage.

11. What does *inspected and passed* mean? How is wholesomeness in meat indicated by stamping? What is an official establishment number?

12. What yield grades does prime beef qualify for? Choice?

13. What is ossification? What are buttons? What role does the condition of bones play in the grading of animals?

14. What is dairy veal? Bob veal?

15. What are the quality grades for beef; calf and veal; lamb, mutton and yearling; pork? What role do the factors of maturity (age), marbling, and quality of flesh play in grading beef? What factors decide the grade of pork?

16. What bones and muscles help identify a beef rib roast? A round steak? A pork chop? A round-arm roast?

17. Match the terms in the left column with those in the right:

_____ *Longissimus dorsi*   a. The main leg bone

_____ *Psoas major*   b. Skirt, butcher's, or hanging tender steak

_____ Knuckle   c. The longest muscle; the ribeye

_____ Chine bone   d. A beef cut over the scapula

_____ Femur   e. The tenderloin muscle

_____ Clod   f. Meat above the kneecap on the round

_____ Diaphragm   g. The spine sawed in two

18. What is a barrow? A gilt? A sow? A boar?

19. What are the IMPS and how do they work?

20. What do the following numbers signify in meat specifications: 100s, 200s, 300s, 400s, 500s, 600s, 700s, and 800s? When an IMPS number is in the thousands, what does it mean?

21. Define the following terms:

a. Range E   f. Sweetbreads

b. Double cut of lamb   g. Boston butt

c. Rack   h. Break joint

d. Aitch bone   i. IMPS

e. Canadian bacon   j. Jowl

22. List the major wholesale cuts for beef, lamb, and pork.

23. If a full loin of beef is divided, what are the three resultant cuts?

24. What are some other names for a top and a bottom round?

25. What are the major differences between pork and breakfast sausage?

26. With what kind of product are the following names associated: Prosciutto, Westphalian, Danish?

27. What limits should one specify in ground meat for bacterial count? For amount of fat?

28. How many ribs does a prime rib roast have if all the ribs in that cut are included? Which ribs (by number) are these?

29. From what animal does a brisket come? What is it?

KEY WORDS AND CONCEPTS

aitch bone (pelvis)

baby beef

back fat

bacon

barrow

beef (bovine)

boar

bob veal

body cavity fat

bottom (outside) round

break joint

breast

brisket

bull

bullock

butcher's steak

calf

chine bone

Choice (grade)

chops

chuck

clod

club (Delmonico) steak

collagen

connective tissue

cow

cross rib

Cryovac

cured

cured and smoked

diaphragm

drip (purge)

dry aging

dry cure

elastin

ewe

femur

fibula

finish fat

flank

forequarter

freezer burn

Green Sheet

gilt

ham

hanging tender

heifer

hematin

hemoglobin

hindquarter

humerus (arm bone)

Institutional Meat Purchase
  Specifications (IMPS)

Kansas City strip

knuckle

Kosher

lamb

leg

loin eye

longissimus dorsi

marbling

meat

Meat Buyers Guide

mutton

myoglobin

nitrosamines

nitrosomyoglobin

ossification

oxymyoglobin

papain

pin bone steak

plate

pork (swine)

porterhouse

Prime (grade)

prime rib

processed

protein fat-free (PFF)

psoas major

quality grading

radius

ram

restructured meat

rib eye

rib steak

rigor mortis

round

rump

saddle

scapula (shoulder blade)

Select (grade)

shank bone

sheep (ovine)

short ribs

sirloin

skirt (butcher's) steak

sow

spare ribs

stag

Standard (grade)

steer

strip

T-bone

tenderloin (*psoas major*)

tibia

tip

top (inside) round

top sirloin

ulna

Uniform Retail Meat
    Industry Identity
    Standards (URMIS)

veal

wedge bone steak

yearling

Yellow Sheet

yield grading

CHAPTER 8

Poultry and Eggs

A girl examining eggs for quality. By Gottfried Schalken (1645–1706) (German). From the Louis Szwathmary collection, Culinary Archives and Museum, Johnson and Wales University, used by permission of Dr. Szwathmary and Johnson and Wales University.

Chapter Objectives

1. To cover the major regulatory measures that control the poultry and egg market and describe the poultry industry and poultry processing for the market.

2. To state the details of kind, class, grades, styles, and type for purchasing poultry and indicate what poultry specifications should contain.

3. To quantify amounts needed to serve 100 portions of various kinds of poultry.

4. To detail factors that determine egg quality and list the egg sizes on the market and weights per case.

5. To discuss factors needed to get adequate quality in processed eggs.

6. To translate processed eggs qualities into equal quantities of fresh or other kinds of eggs and indicate how specifications for eggs should be written.

INTRODUCTION

A big change has occurred in the last 35 years in the production of poultry and eggs. Both are no longer a casual farm crop. Today, huge poultry farms produce most of our poultry, and these are owned largely by major cereal companies such as Ralston and Pillsbury. Today we can produce a heavier chicken in about half the time it once took.

Eggs come out of henneries where thousands of laying chickens may be kept in small cages, just for egg production. Everything is scientifically controlled—breeding, care, feeding, and other production factors now are carefully controlled to give desired results. Our hens are healthier and their environments are more sanitary; a hen today averages over 260 eggs a year and the eggs are more sanitary. The egg market has lost many middlemen because producers now grade, pack, and ship their own eggs or send them to cooperatives or other terminals where this is done. After a drop in consumption—probably because of the high cholesterol content of eggs—consumption has now leveled off.

The consumption of poultry has been steadily rising. In 1989 we were eating 16.6 lb per capita of turkey. In 1996 we ate an average of 19 lb. Similarly in the same period chicken consumption rose from 67.7 lb per capita to over 70 lb. Nearly a third of the meat we eat today is poultry. Our chicken consumption was expected to increase by 6.4% from 1996 to 1997. Besides our own national consumption, we export large quantities of poultry. In 1996 we exported to Russia alone over three-quarters of a million pounds. Duck and rabbit are also finding increased popularity in food services and poultry lends itself well to value-adding, that is, further preparation over the raw, ready-to-cook state. Food services seek value-added items for their menus because they are highly palatable products that get ready customer acceptance and can be made available with little cooking skill needed. Furthermore, the labor saved usually pays for the extra cost.

POULTRY

Regulation

Since 1956 the government has required that all poultry *must* be inspected for wholesomeness before and after slaughter. Postmortem inspection is made on an individual basis, and, until the bird and all its parts, viscera included, are passed, they are not separated. Approved poultry bears the "Inspected and Passed" round circle stamp with a number identifying the establishment where the product was processed. Certificates of inspection are issued on request. Grading is voluntary (see Figure 8–1). The latest standards for poultry were issued in March 1995 and for eggs April 1995.

After poultry is killed, it is bled, then scalded and defeathered. Defeathering is usually done by machine. The bird is then eviscerated and inspected. Unless frozen

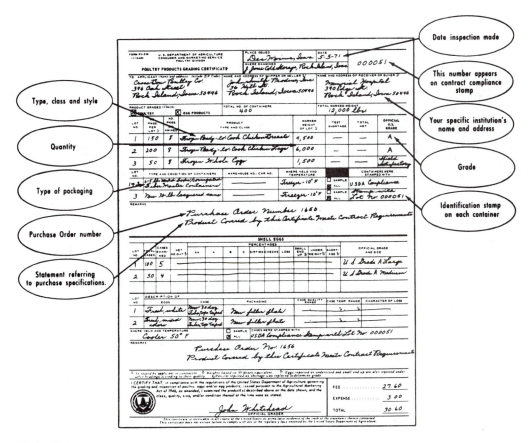

Figure 8-1
USDA's form PY–210 completed by a grader indicating that contract requirements have been met, as outlined in the buyer's specifications. This certificate is attached to the invoice accompanying the shipment. (Courtesy USDA.)

or cooked, it must be chilled immediately to an internal temperature of 40°F, with subsequent storage at 36°F. Chilling and freezing descriptions can be eliminated in specifications by stating "all procedures for chilling or freezing of poultry shall conform to paragraph 381.66 of the *USDA Poultry Products Inspection Regulations.*"

Specifications

A specification for poultry should list (1) kind, (2) class, (3) quality or grade, (4) style, (5) size or weight, (6) type, (7) container or packaging, and (8) temperature required during transport of the shipment and on delivery. Institutions may purchase cooked as well as raw poultry, and additional factors in the specifications may be required for the latter. Some poultry items on the market must meet religious requirements, and specifications may have to list the factors needed to obtain this status.

Table 8–1
Classes of poultry

Chickens

ROCK CORNISH GAME HEN OR CORNISH GAME HEN

A Rock Cornish game hen or Cornish game hen is a young immature chicken (usually 5 to 6 weeks of age) weighing not more than 2 lb ready-to-cook weight, which was prepared from a Cornish chicken or the progeny of a Cornish chicken crossed with another breed of chicken. Rock Cornish fryer, roaster, or hen over 2 lb must conform to the terms used to describe fryer, roaster, or hen chickens.

BROILER OR FRYER

A broiler or fryer is a young chicken (usually under 12 weeks of age), of either sex, that is tender-meated with soft, pliable, smooth-textured skin and flexible breastbone cartilage.

ROASTER-CHICKEN

A roaster is a young chicken (usually 3 to 5 months of age), of either sex, that is tender-meated with soft, pliable, smooth-textured skin and breastbone cartilage that may be somewhat less flexible than that of a broiler or fryer.

CAPON

A capon is a surgically unsexed male chicken (usually under 8 months of age) that is tender-meated with soft, pliable, smooth-textured skin.

HEN, FOWL, OR BAKING OR STEWING CHICKEN

A hen or stewing chicken or fowl is a mature female chicken (usually more than 10 months old) with meat less tender than that of a roaster, and nonflexible breastbone tip.

COCK OR ROOSTER

A cock or rooster is a male chicken with coarse skin, toughened and darkened meat, and hardened breastbone.

Turkeys

FRYER-ROASTER TURKEY

A fryer-roaster turkey is a young immature turkey (usually under 16 weeks of age), of either sex, that is tender-meated with soft, pliable, smooth-textured skin, and flexible breastbone cartilage.

YOUNG TURKEY

A young turkey is a turkey under 8 months that is tender-meated with soft, pliable, smooth-textured skin, and breastbone cartilage that is somewhat less flexible than that in a fryer-roaster turkey. Sex designation is optional.

YEARLING TURKEY

A yearling turkey is a fully matured turkey (usually under 15 months of age) that is reasonably tender-meated and with reasonably smooth-textured skin. Sex designation is optional.

Kind

Poultry kinds are chickens, turkeys, ducks, geese, guineas, and pigeons. Rabbits are classified as a kind. Pea-fowl, swans, quail, wild ducks and geese, pheasants, chukkers, snipes, and others are classified as game bird kinds.

Class

Poultry is differentiated within kind by class, the differentiating factor or factors being either age and/or sex. Table 8–1 lists the kinds and classes of poultry.

MATURE TURKEY OR OLD TURKEY (HEN OR TOM)

A mature or old turkey is an old turkey of either sex (usually in excess of 15 months of age) with coarse skin and toughened flesh. For labeling purposes, the designation of sex within the class name is optional and the three classes of young turkeys may be grouped and designated as "young turkeys."

Ducks

BROILER DUCKLING OR FRYER DUCKLING

A broiler duckling or fryer duckling is a young duck (usually under 8 weeks of age), of either sex, that is tender-meated and has a soft bill and soft windpipe.

ROASTER DUCKLING

A roaster duckling is a young duck (usually under 16 weeks of age), of either sex, that is tender-meated and has a bill that is not completely hardened and an easily dented windpipe.

MATURE DUCK OR OLD DUCK

A mature duck or an old duck is a duck (usually over 6 months of age), of either sex, with toughened flesh, hardened bill, and hardened windpipe.

Geese

YOUNG GOOSE

A young goose may be of either sex, is tender-meated, and has a flexible breastbone.

MATURE GOOSE OR OLD GOOSE

A mature goose or old goose may be of either sex and has toughened flesh and hardened breastbone.

Guineas

YOUNG GUINEA

A young guinea may be of either sex and is tender-meated and has a flexible breastbone cartilage.

MATURE GUINEA OR OLD GUINEA

A mature guinea or an old guinea may be of either sex and has toughened flesh and a hardened breastbone.

Pigeons

SQUAB

A squab is a young, immature pigeon of either sex, and is extra tender-meated.

PIGEON

A pigeon is a mature pigeon of either sex, with coarse skin and toughened flesh.

Source: From USDA, *Regulations Governing the Grading and Inspection of Poultry*, 1995.

Grades

The grades as revised in 1995 for poultry are A, B, C for best to least marketable product, based on (1) conformation, (2) fleshing, (3) fat coverage, (4) freedom from pinfeathers and vestigial feathers (hair and down), (5) exposed flesh, (6) disjointed or broken bones, and missing parts, and (7) discoloration and bruises, and freezing defects. Figure 8–2 shows desirable and undesirable conformation. Official grade stamps are shown in Figure 8–3, while Figure 8–4 shows how birds can differ from grade to grade.

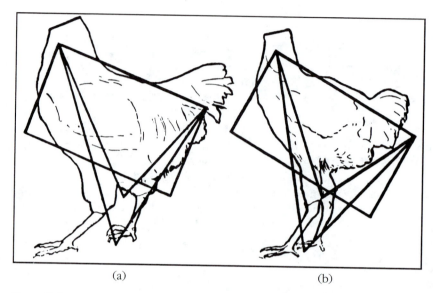

(a)   (b)

Figure 8–2
Bird (a) shows better conformation, promising a higher yield of meat than bird (b). Bird a's body more closely fits into the rectangle and bird b's more closely into the triangle. (Poultry Grading Manual, Agricultural Handbook 31, USDA.)

Style

Poultry may be purchased whole, halved, quartered, or in parts. Whole ready-to-cook (RTC) means the carcass exterior is singed and pinfeathers and vestigial feathers are removed. The head, shanks at the hock joint, crop, windpipe, esophagus, entrails, gall bladder, lungs, and mature sex glands plus the oil gland must be removed. The giblets (heart, liver, and gizzard) must be adequately cleaned, drained, and wrapped in a nonabsorbent paper and may be placed into the body cavity along with neck or may be bulk packed. In 1992, the USDA's definition of chicken parts was changed to make it easier for bird processors to cut a whole chicken into parts. Grades standards and definitions for roast poultry, boneless poultry, skinless carcass and parts, and poultry food products were issued in 1995.

Parts from RTC birds must be proportional to the carcass unless special parts or proportions are specified. Figure 8–5 shows the usual way of dividing a chicken into parts. The following is a summary of the federal government's 1992 definition of what parts named in the specification must be:

Cut-up poultry is any cut up or disjointed poultry or any edible part as described below. It can be specified as in natural portions to whole chicken or with some parts eliminated or added. *Halves* are RTC chickens without necks or giblets, split equally in half along the backbone and breastbone. Specify that breastbones should not be included. **Quarters** are RTC chickens cut into four equal parts, two breasts and two legs, without giblets or necks. *Breast quarters* are breasts halves with or without wing as specified. A portion of the back may be attached, but can

Figure 8-3
Official USDA stamps for ready-to-cook poultry. All poultry bearing federal grades must be inspected for wholesomeness. Grade stamps and inspection stamps may be on the individual bird or on packaging. Federal-state grading means that the program is jointly administered by both. Tags may be on wings, the wrapper, or other location. (Courtesy USDA.)

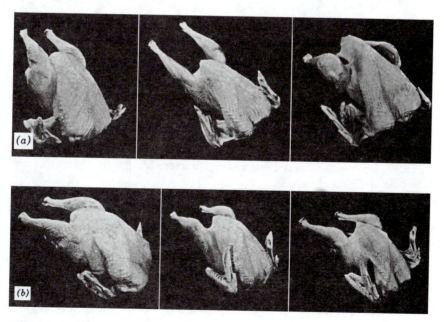

Figure 8-4
(a) Young hen turkey carcasses: (left to right) A quality, B quality, and C quality—the C quality carcass shows better conformation than that of the B quality bird but, because of excessive tears on the leg, is downgraded. (b) Young turkey carcasses: (left to right) A quality, B quality, and C quality. (Courtesy USDA.)

POULTRY PARTS CHART

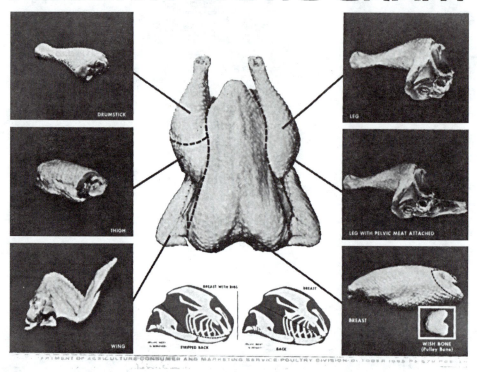

Figure 8-5
The major parts of a chicken are shown here. Note in the bottom center that the dotted line shows the difference between a breast with ribs and a breast without ribs. (Courtesy USDA.)

be specified as removed. **Leg quarters** are thighs and drumsticks with a portion of the back attached.

Breasts shall be separated from the back at the shoulder joint and by a cut running backward and downward from that point along the junction of the vertebral and sternal ribs. Specify in divided breasts that no wishbone or breastbone should be included; neck skin on chickens is not permitted, but on turkey breasts neck skin may (without other specification) be up to the whisker. (1) *Without ribs* means ribs shall be removed; the breasts may be divided in two by removal at the breastbone and wishbones—sometimes breasts are divided into more than two parts; (2) breasts *with ribs* may be whole or divided by cutting along the breastbone. These can be specified as skinless. Breasts may be specified skinless and boneless.

Drumsticks are the lower legs separated at the thigh. **Thighs** are hip portions and may include pelvic meat, but not pelvic bones; back skin is not included. Chicken, turkey, or other legs are joined drumsticks and thighs with no back skin and pelvic bones. Legs with pelvic bone are the poultry legs with skin and pelvic bone.

Wings are the entire wing with all muscle and skin except wingtips may be removed. *Wing drummettes* are the humerus portion of a wing with adhering skin and meat attached. *Wing portions* are poultry wings without drummettes.

Backs include the pelvic bones and all vertebrae behind the shoulder joint. The meat shall not be peeled from pelvic bones. Vertical ribs and/or scapula may be removed or included. Skin shall be substantially intact.

Giblets are equal numbers of hearts, gizzards, and livers.

Size or Weight and Portions Obtained

Proper sizing is important to good portion control. Geese, ducks, and turkeys are specified by individual weight. Chicken, squabs, and some other smaller birds may be specified by individual or group weight such as dozen with an individual allowed weight variation such as for quail "shall weigh 4.5 lb per dozen with no single bird varying more than a ½ oz over 6 oz."

A 2- to 2½-lb. RTC chicken (without neck and giblets) gives four portions of about 8 to 10 oz raw weight with bones and skin. A 1½-lb bird, if halved, gives two good portions. A 3- to 3½-lb RTC duckling after cooking gives four portions: two breast and two leg portions. It is best to serve ducks with bone and skin since slicing takes a lot more bird to show an adequate serving. It takes 12 oz to a pound of RTC goose (raw weight) to make a portion and about 10 to 12 oz of turkey. Turkeys over 18 lb yield more meat per pound than those under 18 lb. The skeleton size of a bird is about the same for a 30-lb bird as an 18-lb one. Normally, a roasted turkey from the RTC to AS state yields around 50% AS meat. In one test, 21½-lb RTC turkey gave about 3½ lb of dark meat slices, 4 lb of white meat slices, plus giblets, wings, and picked meat for a total yield of cooked meat of 12½ lb.

Fowl (hens) of laying breeds over 4½ lb are usually wasteful because of excessive abdominal fat. A 5-lb roasting chicken yields about 30% AS meat, not including giblets or picked neck meat.

Type

Sometimes the market uses specific terms to indicate the time that has elapsed since time of slaughter and whether the bird is fresh, storage, or frozen. **Fresh-killed** means refrigerated at a proper temperature, but not held longer than 3 days; it should be delivered iced with 20 lb of ice used per 80 lb of poultry. *Storage* birds are those held longer than 30 days under refrigeration. *Hard-chilled* means frozen no longer than 60 days, while **frozen storage** means 60 to 100 days of frozen storage. **Fresh-frozen** means birds frozen just recently under rapid freezing methods. **Quick-frozen** means frozen under rapid freezing methods and delivered within a few days of such freezing.

Included in type would be the specification that poultry is to be raw, raw-breaded (maximum breading specified as 30% to total weight), cooked, or cooked-breaded.

Container or Packaging

Packaging for chickens may be 12 to 24 per container. Most turkeys, ducks, and geese are individually wrapped and, depending on size, come packed 2, 4, or 6 to the box. Containers should be plainly marked to show net weight, kind, class, style, grade, and the certificate of inspection number. Buyers close to sources of production may receive fresh-killed poultry, RTC, or parts unwrapped in 25-, 30-, or 50-lb containers. Some shipments arrive in barrels, often iced. If iced, remove the poultry and weigh separately from the ice, checking also for quality. Often fresh-killed poultry shipped some distance is packed in air-exhausted polyethylene wraps.

Frozen poultry is often wrapped in air-exhausted polyethylene wraps to reduce damage from freezer burn, but quick-frozen poultry may be delivered without such wraps because of the time between freezing and delivery.

Shipment Temperature

Specifications should state that frozen poultry is to be shipped in low-temperature refrigerated units that hold the product completely frozen during shipment and that the poultry should be delivered hard frozen. Sometimes a core temperature of not more than 0°F is specified. Often, refrigerated poultry is specified to be shipped in a refrigerated unit held at around 36°F. No poultry should be accepted if above 40°F.

Breed

Yield and flavor can be affected by breed. Most broiler and fryer chickens come from a cross of Rock Cornish cock and a white Plymouth Rock hen. Roasting chickens are young, tender chickens coming from the heavy breeds raised for their meat rather than for the laying of eggs. At times cull hens from egg-laying breeds are on the market because they have lost their laying potential and are marketed at low prices.

Broad breasts, plump short legs, and compact structure are desirable for a high meat yield. Most turkeys are the broad-breasted Beltsville breed. The most common duck on the market is the Peking, a white duck, sometimes called the *Long Island duckling* because so many are produced there. The Toulouse goose is a gray bird weighing from 20 to 26 lb alive at maturity. The white Emden goose, in spite of being a smaller bird, is favored because of bloom of its surface.[1] Homer or Carneaux pigeons are most commonly raised for meat birds. They are usually sold as squabs or very young pigeons.

Bird breed is not normally specified. Most poultry comes from high-yielding broad-breasted stock of the white-feathered variety. Figures 8–6 and 8–7 show two **white breeds** of poultry favored today.

The acceptance service of the federal government can be used by buyers to see that poultry products conform to specifications.

Best Buys

In 1974, the USDA's *Yearbook* listed some value equivalents between whole 2¾-lb broilers and chicken parts; these are given in Table 8–2. These figures are to be used as follows: If the percent given for the part is divided into the whole chicken price per pound, the equivalent price the part should be is derived. Thus, if a buyer wanted to purchase

---

[1] Bloom is the appearance of the surface of the bird. Good bloom is a smooth, rich, soft, fresh-appearing, yellowish-pink on the skin. A white-feathered bird has better bloom on the average than a dark-feathered one. The skin of the latter is apt to be grayish and therefore gives a poorer bloom.

Figure 8-6
Peking ducks are popular on the market; this bird is grown in large numbers on Long Island and for that reason may be called the Long Island duckling. (Courtesy USDA.)

Figure 8-7
A white Chinese gander goose, popular because of its rapid growth to maturity and its white, delicate bloom, giving it good market appearance. (Courtesy USDA.)

chicken breasts with no ribs and the price of whole chickens was 90¢ lb, the price should be $1.23 (90¢ − .733 = $1.228). But, the USDA figures do not include the cost of cutting up whole chickens or other costs when this is done. If a buyer estimates the cutting up cost of chickens is 20¢/lb, the actual cost of the whole chickens is not 90¢ but $1.10/lb. Another point is that if the facility purchases whole chickens, the legs, wings, backs, giblets, necks, etc., will also be obtained. Can these be used to economical advantage? If so, the purchase of whole chickens is warranted.

Sometimes the market might show a price of, say, 49¢/lb for chicken legs, while chickens are selling at nearly $1.00/lb. Why are the legs priced so low? The answer is market demand. The demand for breasts is so great that the normal price can be inflated, while the demand for legs is so low that the equivalent price can be deflated.

At times buyers need to know what percent a part is to the whole chicken. The figures shown in Table 8–3 were calculated from government figures given for 2¾-lb broilers. Thus if a buyer wanted to know about what size the legs of a 2¾ lb (40 oz) broiler would be, the buyer could multiply 40 × 29.66% and see that each leg would be about 12 oz (40 oz × 29.66 = 11.86 oz).

Food services often purchase poultry products processed beyond the RTC or parts stage. To check on the economy of using these products versus producing one's own from scratch, a number of complex calculations have to be made. Buyers should not forget to evaluate the amount of skin or no skin in the processed product and other similar factors. Chapter 11, where convenience foods are discussed, covers some factors that might also have to be considered.

RABBITS

Although rabbits are not poultry, their inspection, grading, and handling are very similar to poultry. Inspection and grading by federal authorities are offered on a voluntary basis.

Fryer rabbits are young domestic rabbits of not less than 1½ to 3½-lb RTC weight and are usually less than 12 weeks old. A roaster is a mature or older domestic rabbit of any weight, usually 4 lb and usually up to 8 months old. Grades are U.S. A, B, and C. Top-grade rabbits have short, thick, well-rounded, and full-fleshed bodies with a broad back, broad hips, and broad, deep-fleshed shoulders. They should be skinned. The muscle texture should be firm and tender. Strips of fat should appear

Table 8-2
Percent equivalence of parts to whole chickens*

Breasts (no ribs)	Breasts (with ribs)	Thighs	Legs (thighs) and drumsticks)	Drumsticks	Wings
73.3	75.5	89.5	93.0	97.5	125

*With natural amount of skin on parts.

Table 8-3
Percent parts are to whole RTC chickens

Breasts (no ribs)	Breasts (with ribs)	Thighs	Drumsticks	Legs	Wings	Backs	Necks and Giblets
24.58	25.85	15.84	13.79	29.66	13.50	22.50	9.17

over the loins, shoulders, and back and there is a fair amount in the interior. Many of the characteristics indicating quality poultry can be used to indicate quality in rabbits.

EGGS

Eggs should be purchased from reliable dealers; there are many chances for error in grading eggs and also in sizing. Eggs should be moved into refrigeration as soon as delivered. Quality can be rapidly lost if eggs stand at room temperature. (Note Figure 8–8.)

Food services purchase eggs as shell eggs, liquid, frozen, or dried. Whole eggs, whites, yolks, and blends are available in the liquid, frozen, or dried form. Buyers should know which to select to obtain the right product for the production need. The weight of an egg is made up of approximately 58% albumen or white, 31% yolk, and 11% shell (see Figure 8–9).

Shell Eggs

Interior factors such as the condition of the yolk and white and the size of the air cell indicate an egg's quality. However, exterior factors such as shell soundness, cleanliness, shape, and texture are considered in grading. Grading is done today using scanners in which eggs move along on a belt with a strong light underneath so the interior condition is visible (Figure 8–10). The grader can note the centering of the **yolk,** the wateriness of the white, size of air cell, any blood spots or other defects. The yolk should be held in the egg center by twisted, ropelike strands of albumen called **chalazae.** The yolk membrane should be firm and strong. Newly laid eggs may show some milkiness of the white, but this is not a defect, as it is lost within a few days. However, eggs sprayed with oil just after being laid and then stored may still show this milkiness, because the oil seals the egg so the carbon dioxide in the egg that causes the milkiness cannot escape. An egg with a sound shell produces a bell-like tone when clicked

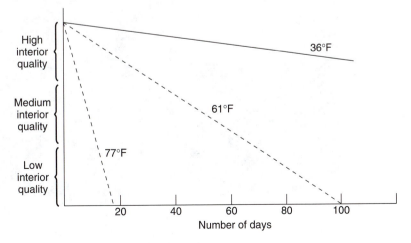

Figure 8-8
Egg quality loss is rapid when eggs are held at high temperatures.

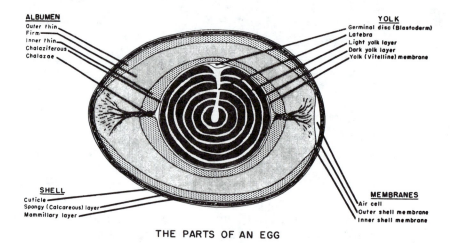

ALBUMEN
Outer thin
Firm
Inner thin
Chalaziferous
Chalazae

YOLK
Germinal disc (Blastoderm)
Latebra
Light yolk layer
Dark yolk layer
Yolk (Vitelline) membrane

SHELL
Cuticle
Spongy (Calcareous) layer
Mammillary layer

MEMBRANES
Air cell
Outer shell membrane
Inner shell membrane

THE PARTS OF AN EGG

Figure 8-9
Parts of an egg. Yolks are anchored in the white by two chalazae cords. As eggs age, the firm white decreases and turns into a thin portion, the air cell grows, the chalazae weaken and allow the yolk to lose its central position. The yolk membrane also weakens, so the yolk may break when the egg is shelled. (Courtesy USDA.)

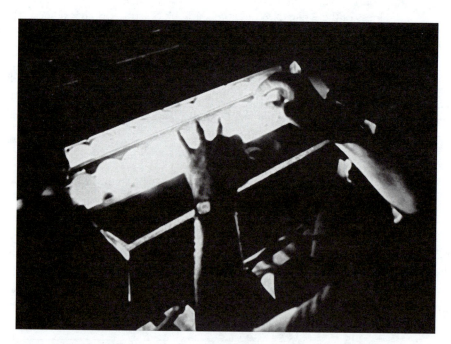

Figure 8-10
Eggs on a moving belt being scanned by a grader. The grader here is picking up sample eggs and twirling them to note interior condition. (Courtesy USDA.)

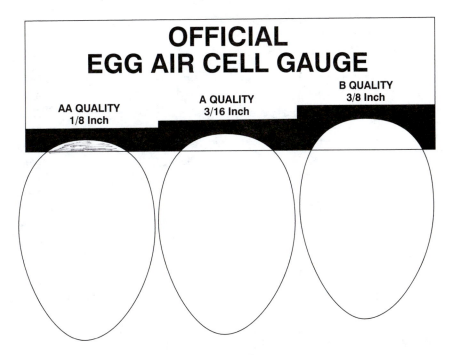

Figure 8–11
An egg grade depends partially on the depth of the air cell in the top interior of the egg. The relative depths to meet grade requirements are shown here. (Courtesy USDA.)

together with another, whereas a slightly cracked one has a flat tone. Cleanliness and shape of shell is a grade factor. From time to time the grader may break an egg and note the white wateriness and measure the height of the yolk with a Haugh meter.

An egg loses carbon dioxide and moisture in aging. As this happens, the **air cell** size increases (see Figure 8–11). The white becomes thin and watery and the yolk flattens out so the egg covers a wide area when broken out. The membrane enclosing the yolk weakens, and the yolk may break when the egg is shelled. A very old egg may begin to show a blackening of the white and develop an offensive ferrous sulfide odor. Such an egg is called "rotten." If eggs are kept properly under refrigeration, they hold quality for several weeks. Even then carbon dioxide and moisture are slowly lost. Most eggs come to market fresh; few storage eggs are marketed.

Egg Standards

Grades
Federal consumer grades dominate the egg market; they are U.S. **Grades AA, A,** and **B;** a U.S. **Grade C** exists but since 1972 these eggs have been required to go into processed eggs because they must be pasteurized to rid them of pathogenic organisms. Eggs called checks (slightly cracked), dirties, leakers, and some others go into the C grade (see Table 8–4).

The grade stamps used are shown in Figure 8–12. Figure 8–13 shows the three top grades of eggs broken out of the shell as raw and cooked. Note as the grade

Table 8-4

Summary of U.S. standards for quality of individual shell eggs (specifications for each quality factor)

Quality Factors	AA Quality	A Quality	B Quality
Shell	Clean	Clean	Clean to slightly stained.*
	Unbroken.	Unbroken.	Unbroken.
	Practically normal.	Practically normal.	Abnormal.
Air Cell	⅛ inch or less in depth.	³⁄₁₆ inch or less in depth.	Over ³⁄₁₆ inch in depth.
	Unlimited movement and free or bubbly.	Unlimited movement and free or bubbly.	Unlimited movement and free or bubbly.
White	Clear.	Clear.	Weak and watery.
	Firm.	Reasonably firm.	Small blood and meat spots present.[†]
Yolk	Outline slightly defined.	Outline fairly well defined.	Outline plainly visible.
	Practically free from defects.	Practically free from defects.	Enlarged and flattened.
			Clearly visible germ development but not blood.
			Other serous defects.

For eggs with dirty or broken shells, the standards of quality provide two additional qualities. They are:

Dirty	Check
Unbroken. Adhering dirt or foreign material, prominent stains, moderate stained areas in excess of B quality.	Broken or cracked shell but membranes intact, not leaking.[‡]

Source: Courtesy USDA, AMS, poultry division.

*Moderately stained areas permitted (½ of surface in localized, or ¹⁄₁₆ if scattered).

[†]If they are small (aggregating not more than ⅛ in. in diameter).

[‡]Leaker has broken or cracked shell membranes, and contents leaking or free to leak.

Figure 8-12

Grade stamps used for eggs. The stamp at the upper left is most frequently seen today. Stamps on the packaging (see Figure 8–14) show the contents have been inspected for quality by a federal inspector. (Courtesy USDA.)

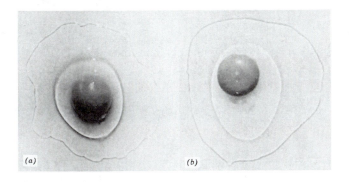

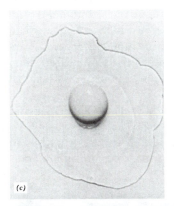

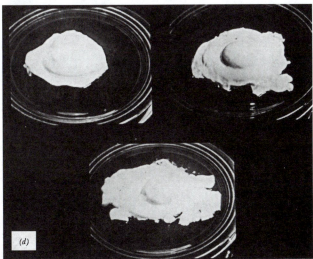

Figure 8-13
*(a) U.S. Grade AA and (b) U.S. Grade A.
(c) U.S. Grade C eggs. Note the difference
in the thicker and thinner portions of the
whites. (d) The three eggs above after
poaching, and (e) a side profile of the U.S.
Grade AA egg after frying.* (Courtesy
USDA.)

lowers how the yolk flattens and the gelatinous white becomes more liquid. The egg size will appear on packages and may occasionally be in the grade shield with the grade. Date of grading and plant number where grading occurred may be shown. Figure 8–14 shows carton stamping.

Size

Shell eggs are marketed into equal size eggs weighing 30 oz (**jumbo**), 27 oz (**extra large**), 24 oz (**large**), 21 oz (**medium**), 18 oz (**small**), and 15 oz (**peewee**) per dozen (see Figure 8–15). Food services usually use large eggs, and recipes are usually standardized for this size, if count is used. The best buy by egg size can be easily obtained by dividing the ounces per dozen into the price per dozen. Thus, if one wanted to know if jumbos at $1 per dozen were a better buy than mediums at $0.84 a dozen, one would get $1/27 oz = 3.70¢ per oz against $0.84/21 oz = 4.00¢ per oz.

Buyers should remember that egg grade and size are not related. Small eggs can be as high a quality as large ones. Shell color also does not influence quality, although in some markets consumers prefer and pay more for brown eggs, while in some other markets brown eggs are not favored against white ones. In cooking performance and nutritive value they are the same.

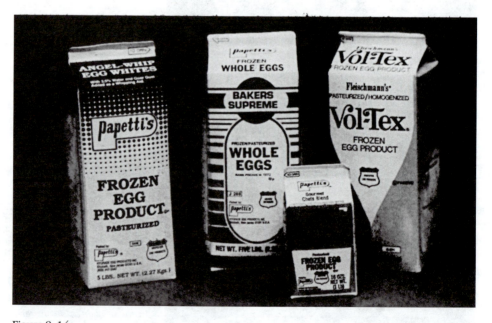

Figure 8–14
An example of an acceptance shield stamp used to indicate that the purchase requirements of a buyer have been met under acceptance buying. (Courtesy USDA.)

Specifications

Specifications for shell eggs should indicate the grade and size plus the following:

- Container and number of dozen per container
- Type of packaging and material
- Shipping temperatures and temperature of eggs on arrival.

Type packaging and material should indicate if the eggs are to come packed in cartons holding a dozen, in cases or ½ cases in cartons holding a dozen eggs, or whether they should come in cases or ½ cases with fillers. The weight of the container plus all other nonegg material should be available to buyers, so when eggs

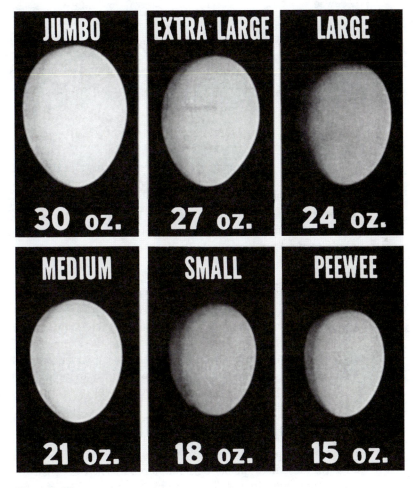

Figure 8–15
The six official egg sizes. Food services usually purchase large eggs and seldom, if ever, use other sizes. The ounces indicate the average weight per dozen for each of these weight classes. (Courtesy USDA.)

Table 8-5

Weight classes for consumer grades of shell eggs

Size or Weight Class	Minimum Net Wt. per Dozen (oz)	Minimum Net Wt. per Case (lb)*	Minimum Wt. for Individual Eggs at Rate per Dozen (oz)
Jumbo[†]	30	56	29
Extra large	27	50½	26
Large	24	45	23
Medium	21	39½	20
Small	18	34	17
Peewee[†]	15	28	

*A case is 30 dozen.

[†]Jumbo and peewee sizes are usually not on the institutional market; food services usually use large eggs.

Note: A lot average tolerance of 3.3% for individual eggs in the next lower weight class is permitted as long as no individual case in the lot exceeds 5%. Shells are 11% of the listed egg weights.

arrive, the total package can be weighed and this tare weight deducted to see if the delivered unit or units meet specifications. Net weights of eggs per dozen, per case, and variation allowed per individual dozen are given in Table 8–5. Large buyers of eggs and dairy products often use the federal government's acceptance service to check grades and sizes (see Figure 8–14). The average weight of fiberboard cartons with fillers and partitions is 11 lb. A *lot* of eggs is two or more cases.

Processed Eggs

Processed eggs may be marketed as cooked, frozen, or dried. All processed eggs must be pasteurized. Some local markets may have liquid eggs in bulk.

It is recommended that operations ascertain if the use of processed eggs for many cooking and baking purposes could save a significant sum of money, not only in egg cost but in labor time in shelling. A comparison of prices between different kinds of eggs may be made using the equivalent information given in Table 8–6.

Frozen Eggs

High-quality whole eggs are frozen for use as omelets, French toast, and scrambled eggs. A lower quality processed egg is used for baking or other purposes. A specification for these high-quality eggs might read: "The eggs shall come from high-quality, clean, edible eggs, free of shells and be reasonably free from blood clots or other defects. There should be no off-flavors or off-odors. No storage, check, dirty, or leaker eggs can be used. They should be in natural proportions of yolks and whites. They should be pasteurized to be free from *Salmonella, E. coli, Staphylococcus,* and *Coliform* of any type." They are packed variously but often come in 30-lb cans.

Table 8-6

Equivalent quantities of processed eggs for 100 portions

Type Egg	Unit of Purchase	Wt per Unit (lb)	Portion AS	Portions per Unit	100 portion Requirement
Frozen, whole	lb	1.00	1 egg = 3 T, 12 eggs = 2¼ c	10 eggs	10 lb or 20 c (1¼ gal)
Frozen, white	Can	30.00	1 egg	300 eggs	10 lb
Frozen, yolks	lb	1.00	1 yolk = 1⅓ T, 12 yolks = 1 c	24 yolks	
Frozen, whites	lb	1.00	1 white = 2 T, 8 whites = 1 c	16 whites	
Dried, whole	lb	1.00	½ oz (2½ T) +2½ T water = 1 egg	32 eggs	
Dried, whole	13 oz	0.81		26 eggs	
Dried, whole	No. 10 can	3.00		96 eggs	
Dried, whole	25-lb pack	25.00		800 eggs	
Dried, yolks	lb	1.00	1 yolk = 2 T + 2 t water	54 yolks	
Dried, yolks	3-lb	3.00	1½ c + ½ c water = 12 yolks	162 yolks	
Dried, whites	lb	1.00	1 white = 2 t + 2 T water		
Dried, whites	lb	3.00	½ c + 1½ c water = 12 whites		

Note: All equivalents are based on large eggs, 24 oz average per dozen. Courtesy USDA.

Frozen eggs for bakery use are available as mixed whole eggs, whites, yolks, salt whole eggs (2% salt or more), fortified whole eggs (which means yolks added), and different blends such as sugar or other ingredients added. Freezing eggs alone gives a toughened product upon thawing, but if some electrolyte is added such as sugar, glycerine, or salt, this toughening does not occur upon freezing. Specify frozen eggs as homogenized.

Dried Eggs

Dried eggs are used largely as whole, whites, or whites prepared for meringues. Specify all dried eggs as inert gas packed and glucose free.

A frozen hard-cooked egg roll, telescoped with the white on the outside and the yolk inside to resemble a hard-cooked egg, is available. One roll is the equal of the slices of about 17 eggs. This egg is marketed under the copyrighted name of Gourm Egg by the Ralston Company. Substitute whole eggs are on the market. They are largely egg whites colored to appear as if yolks were present. One brand on the

Table 8-7

Storage and handling of egg products

Shell Eggs	Specify eggs shall be USDA Inspected and graded and kept in storage and delivered under 45°F. Keep shell eggs under 45°F until withdrawn for use; withdraw only that needed for a *short* period. Refrigerate unused eggs *immediately.* Keep raw eggs away from other foods; thoroughly clean utensils with which raw eggs were used before using for other purposes.
Frozen Eggs	Place products *immediately* upon receiving into refrigeration or frozen storage at 0°F or below. Defrost under refrigeration or under running water in closed containers *not at room temperature.* Keep below 45°F to prevent curdling and off-flavor development. Mix well, since egg solids are not evenly distributed upon thawing. Keep unused amounts under 45°F and use in three days.
Liquid Eggs	Keep 45°F at all times. Use items within 7 days of receipt. Close all used containers in storage and use as quickly as possible.
Dried Eggs	Store in tightly closed containers under 70°F away from strong light. After opening, store in closed containers under 50°F or below. Use only the amount needed; store rest as dry product. Hold products containing dry eggs at from 32° to 50°F.

Note: All egg products should be specified USDA graded.

market is called Egg Beaters. They are eaten for nutritional reasons to avoid the cholesterol found in egg yolks.

The recommended storage and handling procedures for processed egg products are given in Table 8–7.

Eggs and poultry have been cited as contributing to salmonella poisoning. The egg and poultry industries and governmental agencies are working hard to make these products safer through better processing and handling procedures and also in temperature control. Recently the USDA revised its regulations on temperatures for shell eggs during handling in nonheating processing, transportation, and storage, requiring the eggs at no time be allowed to go over 45°F.

Food services should use care in handling these products and see that proper handling and cooking methods are taken to avoid poisoning from occurring. Keep both eggs and poultry products under refrigeration until used. Do not allow them to stand too long. Table 8–7 gives some approved procedures for handling eggs. Also, the bibliography for this chapter gives several excellent references on the care of eggs in quantity cooking. Follow similar low-temperature handling for poultry.

THE POULTRY AND EGG MARKET

The poultry and egg markets have become highly organized. Poultry is raised by larger growers who market their products through large buyers or through their own organization. Eggs may be packed at origin for sale or shipped in huge lots to middlemen who receive them and place them on the market. An industry that was once fairly local and limited to small lot units has now graduated into a massive centralized industry of high capitalization.

Buyers of poultry and egg products must watch the market just as those who purchase meats and marine products must. In fact, they must watch it even more closely because it is much more volatile and can change much more rapidly. This is because poultry and eggs can be produced for the market in a much shorter time than can meat. Marine products are a little different. The market for them can fluctuate wildly at times as catches vary, but even this market is more stable than that of poultry and egg items.

Market reports for poultry and egg products, as for meats and marine products, are published daily, making it possible for buyers to note quantities reaching the market as well as information on prices and possible supply conditions in the future. From this buyers can plan their purchases and recommend to menu planners favorable menu selections. For a food service using a fairly sizable amount of egg or poultry items, such information is of value in creating a more successful business.

Figure 8–16 shows a part of a market report on poultry and eggs. Such information will come to a buyer the day after any market activity, which is normally five days a week. A buyer who watches such reports can note trends and plan purchases. The buyer can also evaluate prices quoted by suppliers to see if they are adjusted correctly according to what the base price is on the market. Market reports are essential if a good buying job is to be done. To paraphrase a popular advertising slogan "No buyer of either eggs or poultry should leave home without them"!

SUMMARY

The Poultry Division of the USDA is authorized under the Agricultural Marketing Act of 1946. The present standards were adopted in March 1995 for poultry and in April 1995 for eggs. Both dictate marketing procedures for these items.

Poultry specifications should usually contain a listing of kind, class, grade, size, type, packaging, and whether the product desired is fresh, cooked, or frozen plus the amount desired and other needed information to obtain the item desired. Kind defines the species, that is, chicken, turkey, duck, goose, guinea, pigeon, or rabbit—the latter being included as a poultry. Class divides kinds into orders, such as Rock Cornish hens, broilers, fryers, roasters, capons, hens or fowl, and roosters; turkeys are divided into fryer-roaster, yearling, or young or mature hens and toms; the rest of poultry kinds is divided into just two orders: young and mature. Grade refers to quality divisions which are A, B, C.

To obtain properly sized portions the specifications should state the size or weight of the bird. Style refers to whether the poultry (whole, halves, quarters or parts) is raw, frozen, cooked, or otherwise processed. RTC means ready-to-cook. The definitions of exactly what the various terms like "halves," "breasts," "legs," "wings," etc., mean are given so when a buyer states just the name of the part desired both the buyer and seller know what is wanted.

Best buys are discussed. The question of whether one should purchase parts when parts are wanted instead of whole birds is analyzed.

COMMODITIES AT A GLANCE

	Previous Day's Close	Weekly Average Year Ago
UB Turkey, Hen, 8-12 lb, East	.54	.5800
UB Turkey,Tom, 16-22 lb, East	.55	.5580
UB Plant Grade 2/UP, NE	.52	.4700
UB Eggs, Large, Table Grade	.73	.8000
USDA Omaha Cattle, CH 2-4, 1,000-1,200 lbs	n/a	68.75
USDA Des Moines Hogs, US 1-3, 210-250 lbs, Country	32.5-34	59.60
Crude Decatur Oil	26.66-27.16	27.16
USDA Des Moines Pork Loins, Reg, Fresh 14-18 lbs	71-77	112.60
USDA Des Moines Skinned Hams SE, Fresh 17-20 lbs.	53-56	69.20
Kansas City Corn, US No. 2, Yellow	2.62-2.63	2.90
Central Illinois Soybean Meal, 44% Truck	172.5-177.5	264.60

WOG CHICKENS		CUT-UP CHICKENS	
Without Giblets		**Eight Piece Cut**	**Nine Piece Cut**
2 1/4-2 1/2 lbs	.6200	.6900	.6900
2 1/2-2 3/4 lbs	.6200	.6900	.6900
2 3/4-3 lbs	.6200	.6900	.6900

CHICKENS

RESALES by First Receivers - All Prices F.O.B. Dealers Dock

PLANT "A"		U.S. GRADE "A"	
2 1/4 lbs. & up	.60-.61	2 1/4 lbs. & up	.60-.61

CHICKEN PARTS		ROASTERS	U.S. Gr. 'A'	ROASTER PARTS	
All prices F.O.B. dealers dock.		Prices paid by first receivers. Resales at varying premiums.		Prices paid by first receivers. Resales at varying premiums.	
Breasts	.90-.91	Iced, 5 lbs. & up	.67	Breasts back in	1.16
Legs	.52-.53	Cryovac, 5 lbs. & up	.81	Legs	.67
Leg Quarters	.39-.40			Wings	.99
Drumsticks	.47-.48				
Thighs	.49-.50				
Wings	.84-.85	**BREASTS**			
Livers 5 lb. tub	.35-.40	Boneless chicken breast, skinless		1.70-1.75	
Hearts	.35-.40	Boneless chicken breast, skin on		1.65-1.70	
Gizzards	.60-.65	**THIGH MEAT**			
Backs & Necks	.19-.20	Boneless & skinless		1.08-1.13	

Figure 8–16

An example of a market report to poultry and egg buyers. (Published with permission and courtesy of Urner Barry Publications, Inc.)

READY TO EAT TURKEY PRODUCTS

SMOKED BREAST		FULLY COOKED TURKEY	
Skin on	$2.15-2.25	Approx. 50% Water	
Skinless	2.25-2.35	Skinless	1.30-1.40
FRIED IN OIL		All White roll	1.00-1.10
Skinless	2.30-2.40	White & Dark rolls	.90-1.00
Skinless, multi p/c	2.35-2.45	Economy White roll	.80-.90
Skinless, netted	2.45-2.55	Economy White & Dark roll	.70-.80
OVEN ROASTED BREAST			
Natural, Handmade, No Sweetners		**SPECIALTY SMOKED ITEMS**	
or Binding Agents + 10% Water		Ham (retail chub)	1.17-1.27
Skin on, 3 p/c	1.95-2.05	Ham (deli)	1.07-1.17
Skin on, (brown top) 3 p/c	2.00-2.10	Pastrami (retail chub)	1.17-1.27
Skinless 3 p/c	2.00-2.10	Pastrami (deli)	1.12-1.22
Skinless, (brown top) 3 p/c	2.05-2.15	Salami (deli)	.97-1.07
Skinless, mini 2 p/c	2.10-2.20	Bologna (retail chub)	.65-.85
No Salt Added		Bologna (deli)	.70-.90
Skin on	2.30-2.40	Hot Dogs (retail)	.75-.95
Skinless	2.35-2.45	Hot Dogs (bulk)	.55-.75
Machine Made, with Sweetner + 20% Water		**READY-TO-COOK**	
With Skin	1.85-1.95	**BONED & TIED RAW ROAST**	
Skinless	1.90-2.00	**Unseasoned***	
Skinless, mini	2.00-2.10	60%-40%	1.50-1.60
OVEN PREPARED BREAST		80%-20%	1.65-1.75
(OVEN COOKED) approx. 30% Water		70%-30%	1.58-1.68
Natural Handmade,		51%-49%	1.42-1.52
Modified Food Starch/Carrageenan/etc		*Seasoned 10-15 cents less	
Skin on 3 p/c	1.85-1.95		
Skinless 3 p/c	1.90-2.00		
Skinless, mini 2 p/c	1.95-2.05		

Figure 8-16 *continued*

Specifications for eggs should include the grade (AA or A), size (jumbo, extra large, large, medium, small, and peewee), and kind (shell eggs, fresh liquid, imitation, frozen liquid, dried, or cooked), plus other information needed to get the right product. In some markets white eggs are preferred, while in others brown ones are. Both have the same nutritional and cooking value.

A lot of eggs is two or more cases of eggs. The average weight of a fiberboard carton with fillers and partitions is about 11 lb. There are on the market some frozen whole eggs that come from such high-quality eggs that they can be used for custards, breakfast eggs such as scrambled or omelets, and other purposes. Bakery-type eggs should not be used for such purposes. They are usually pasteurized to reduce their bacterial content. One may purchase such eggs as whole, whites only, yolks only, and yolks with sugar. Dried eggs may be whole, yolks only, or whites only. Some rather high-quality meringues can be purchased made from a product whose base is dried whites.

Poultry and eggs contain *Salmonella* bacteria, which can cause severe food poisoning. Special care should be taken therefore to see that poultry and eggs do not contaminate other foods nor are used in the kitchen in such a way as to further the growth of this bacteria in the foods in which they are used. For instance, a food such as a Hollandaise sauce can, unless properly handled, be a good source of such poisoning.

A buyer can get considerable information on the market for eggs and poultry. Some of the information has a monetary cost associated with it, while others, like that from the USDA and associations, come without cost.

REVIEW QUESTIONS

1. What are the kinds and classes of poultry? Include age, sex, weight, and other pertinent factors.
2. What factors are considered in grading poultry? What are the grades?
3. What are the differences between the terms ready-to-cook, eviscerated, and parts?
4. Name five factors a specification for poultry should contain.
5. Why are rabbits graded the same as poultry?
6. What are the percentages of the egg of the white, the yolk, and the shell?
7. What do the terms *fresh-killed* and *fresh-frozen* mean?
8. What is the maximum percentage of breading allowed on prebreaded poultry items?
9. What is the maximum temperature that should be allowed in the shipment of poultry?
10. What are the quality indicators of Grades AA, A, and B eggs?
11. Why are substances such as sugar or glycerine added to frozen eggs?
12. What is a chalazae?
13. What are the different size groups for eggs? What is the average weight per dozen? What is the net weight per case of large eggs?
14. What would be the advantage of using Grade A eggs for scrambled eggs for a buffet instead of Grade AA eggs?

15. What quality egg should be purchased for baking? Is it necessary to use fresh eggs for baking?

16. Why is it sometimes cheaper to serve three small eggs than two large eggs for breakfast?

17. How would you compare the cost of different-sized eggs?

SPECIFICATIONS

Chickens, Broilers

1. Chicken, broilers, fresh killed
2. Reorder point (ROP) is two cases; maximum on hand 6 cases; inventory shows 2 cases; order 4 cases.
3. Grade A
4. Dozen per box; birds should be from 3 to 3½ lb each; no weight variation permitted ± this.
5. Price by the pound
6. Shall be RTC without necks and giblets

Turkeys

1. Turkey, frozen, young tom
2. Order 75 to 100 lb per 100 portions needed.
3. Grade A
4. Air-exhausted, polyethylene wrapped, 4 per box
5. Price by the pound
6. Shall be current November pack

Chicken Breasts

1. Chicken breasts, fresh, boneless, skinless halves
2. Five boxes
3. From Grade A birds
4. Layer packed between polyethylene wraps; 20 lb per box; each boneless, skinless breast shall be 5 oz ± ¼ oz.
5. Price by the pound
6. From fresh-killed birds

Eggs, Shell

1. Eggs, fresh, shell, large
2. Three cases

3. Grade A

4. 30 doz/case; foam cases; net weight not under 45 lb

5. Price by the case

Eggs, Frozen

1. Eggs, frozen, whole

2. ROP 10 cans; maximum order 25 cans

3. Order only "X" brand

4. In 30 lb cans

5. Price by the pound

6. Shall not have a total count of over 100,000/g and 10 coli/g

KEY WORDS AND CONCEPTS

air cell	hen
breasts	jumbo eggs
broiler	large eggs
capon	leg quarters
chalazae	mature turkey, goose, guinea, pigeon
chicken	medium eggs
cock	peewee eggs
cut-up poultry	pigeon
drumsticks	quarters
duck	quick-frozen
duckling	Rock Cornish hen
extra large eggs	rooster
fresh-frozen	shell eggs
fresh-killed	small eggs
frozen storage	squab
fryer-roaster	thighs
giblets	tom
goose	white breed
Grade A	wings
Grade AA	yearling turkey, goose, guinea, pigeon
Grade B	
Grade C	yolk
guinea	young turkey
hard-chilled	

CHAPTER 9

Marine Products

Fresco with wine jug and seafood (Langusta, squids, oysters and shells) from an etching, printed in Paris 1763. From the Louis Szwathmary collection, Culinary Archives and Museum, Johnson and Wales University, used by permission of Dr. Szwathmary and Johnson and Wales University.

Chapter Objectives

1. To indicate trends in the fish and shellfish markets and the probable reasons why these items are more popular menu items today.

2. To indicate where and how marine products are marketed, in what forms, when they are usually on the market, and amounts to order.

3. To discuss the regulation of the marine product market.

4. To cover quality factors important in the purchase of marine products.

5. To indicate how certain marine products should be stored, handled, and cooked.

6. To list the different varieties and forms of fresh, frozen, and processed fish and shellfish on the market.

7. To show how to write specifications for marine items.

INTRODUCTION

Marine products covered in this chapter include fish, shellfish, and some other forms of species taken from either freshwater or saltwater. The average yearly consumption of these products reached a peak in 1989 of 16.3 pounds, but has since dropped slightly. This decrease is thought to be because of concerns about the safety of eating marine products. However, they are an excellent food, low in calories and fat compared to meat (see Table 9–1). (See also the discussion of sanitation on page 288). Their protein is of the highest value and they are rich sources of many vitamins and minerals. Except for some shellfish, they are low in cholesterol.

Better management of our marine resources, the use of some fish formerly considered undesirable such as skate and dogfish, better fishing equipment and meth-

Table 9-1
Comparison of nutritive values (100 g or 3½ oz).

	Food Energy (cal)	Protein (g)	Fat (g)	Sodium (mg)
FISH AND SEAFOOD				
Cod (raw)	74	17.4	0.5	90
Breaded fish sticks (raw)	150	15.0	9.0	N/A*
Flounder (raw)	94	16.3	3.2	121
Shrimp (breaded, fried)	190	17.0	9.0	N/A*
Oysters (raw, meat only)	68	8.5	1.8	73
MEAT				
Hamburger (raw)	268	17.9	21.2	65
Sirloin steak (raw, round bone, choice)	313	16.9	26.7	61
Pork loin (raw)	298	17.1	24.9	70

Source: U.S. Department of Agriculture.
*Not available.
Note: Fish fat is high in polyunsaturates, which reduce blood cholesterol, but many shellfish are high in cholesterol. Fish is often a good source of vitamins A and D and the B complex. It is also a good source of certain minerals, especially phosphorus, calcium, potassium, and iodine.

ods, and extension of our territorial boundaries to 200 miles out to sea have increased the amount of marine products we dock each year. A large number of new fish have also been introduced, such as orange roughy, kingslip, highbrow, snapper, painted sweet lips, and leather jacket.

We consume a substantial amount of **farm fish, aquaculture** grown products, and the amount is rising rapidly; our consumption is expected to rise by over 700% by the year 2025. Today only 10% of these products are domestically grown, but this is expected to change upward. Japan, China, Taiwan, Philippines, Mexico, and Central and South America are big exporters to the United States. The quantity of our domestic shrimp catch from our southern waters has decreased substantially only to be more than taken up by aquaculture shrimp. The farming of salmon has increased substantially. Norway, with 375 million pounds in 1996, leads in salmon production; Chile produced 132 million pounds of which the United States consumed 40 million. One of the criticisms food services direct against these products is that they lack the abundant flavor of the naturally (wild) caught item, but otherwise in handling, appearance, and versatility in dishes, the farm product is considered as good or better.

Over 6½ billion pounds of saltwater products are docked each year. On some markets freshwater wild fish are important, but the tonnage is not significant compared to the amount of saltwater items docked. Over 300 different kinds of fish are traded every day in the United States, however, in specific markets the number traded will be much less.

THE MARKET

It is debatable whether the fresh produce or marine products market is the most unstable and variable. Marine products, like fresh produce, are quite perishable and vary considerably in supply during the year. However, with aquaculture and other technological improvements, we are achieving a more stable market, making it possible to predict better availability and price, but buyers must still watch their market closely.

There are five main markets that pretty much decide what is available and the price; they are Boston, New York, Gulf (New Orleans and others), Seattle, and Chicago. Seattle markets Alaskan products, and Chicago is the biggest freshwater market. Each market has its own trading practices, giving rise to confusion in terminology and customs. Identities are not always the same and buyers need to learn what is available on their markets. Most items are sold without label and, because of close similarity, substitutions are possible, some of which are dishonest. Buyers need to learn what substitutions are legitimate. Good, firm specifications provide great assistance in securing the right product.

In recent years, large buyers like chains have been bypassing the national fish markets and dealing directly with the fishing people. These units often set up their own warehouses and distribute the products. A few hotel and restaurant chains can do this but the average food service still purchases from a local dealer who gets the products from a national market.

MARKET REGULATION

Although there is less government control of this market, control is increasing. Grading is being discussed seriously. In 1956, the provisions of the Agricultural Marketing Act were extended to include some processed fish and thus about 20% of our fishery products are inspected and graded. Inspection and grading are largely voluntary. Today the National Marine Fisheries of the Commerce Department grades marine products and sets sanitary standards. Other agencies that enter into control of marine products are the USDA, Department of Health and Public Welfare, and FDA.

Many states also have regulations buyers should know if they buy in them. Some restrict the varieties, size, or sex of marine products that can be caught. Variety names may be regulated. The supplier and user are both held responsible when laws are violated.

In 1995 the FDA set new regulations governing sanitation in marine product processing plants moving in the direction of adopting the HCAAP program. Records must be maintained to show refrigeration, handling, etc. However this covers only processed products. Unprocessed raw marine products are not affected, but there is public pressure to put such products under the same kind of regulation as meat.

Grades

Four grades are used for processed marine products: A, B, C, and Below Standard, with food services using only A and B, the top grades. Grading is based on (1) flavor and odor; (2) imperfections of trim and cutting; (3) blemishes; (4) bones; (5) color; (6) dehydration; (7) skin where it should have been removed; (8) appearance; (9) uniformity of size; (10) texture, including tenderness and moisture; (11) mashed, broken, or otherwise damaged pieces; (12) coating defects, if coated; (13) extraneous material; and (14) packaging and packing.

Some federal and state regulations important to buyers are as follows: Chilled fish must reach an internal temperature of 40°F or lower immediately following processing and be kept at this temperature until delivery. Freezing must occur within 2 hours of processing and reach an internal temperature of 0°F or lower within 72 hours of processing. Potable water must be used for **glazing** (covering products with a thin film of ice); glazing must occur at 0°F or lower. Most fillets in processing may be washed in a sodium chloride solution of no more than 15° salometer for not more than 2 minutes; this time limit and salt limit is set so they do not soak up water and gain weight. Shucked mollusks should not appear bloated or have more than 8% liquid on them on delivery; the time they can be in freshwater is regulated so they do not imbibe water.

Figure 9-1
*The quality grade and wholesome federal
inspection stamps buyers see on some fishery products.* (Courtesy USDA.)

Loose breading is a grade defect. Breading to flesh should be controlled as follows: raw fish portions, 25%; fish sticks, 28%; fried fish portions, 35%; fried fish sticks,
40%; and raw shrimp, 50%; many facilities find this amount of breading excessive.

Figure 9–1 shows the grade and inspection stamp used for marine products.

Certain market or governmental standards require special market sizes or other
factors. Some of these follow and buyers should be aware they exist when purchasing marine products:

Chicken halibut is halibut dressed at 5 to 10 lb; cod from fish dressing 2½ to 10
lb, except fillets, which can come from fish weighing 1½ to 2½ lb; steaks cannot
weigh more than 24 oz. Dressed salmon must weigh over 6 lb and steaks not more
than 24 oz. If they come from the poke (body cavity) area, untrimmed, they shall
have not less than a ½-in.-thick abdominal wall. Sole and flounder fillets should have
the skin removed from both sides, except petrale or English sole,[1] which may have
the skin removed on the blind (ventral) side.

Sanitary Considerations

Some feel that marine life is not as safe to eat as it might be and we need better inspection and safeguards set up to see that it is made more safe to eat. The USDA reports that from 1973 to 1987, the foodborne illness caused by fish and shellfish was
slightly greater than the combined cases from beef and poultry (see Figure 9–2). The
Centers for Disease Control and Prevention recently indicated that of the 3,703 cases
of foodborne illnesses reported, shellfish and fish were reported as causing 14.7%
and 14.7%, respectively. The slightly more than 70% remaining were caused by
meats, poultry, prepared foods, and unknown causes.

Parasitic worms occasionally are found, the round or nematode worms being
most common. A flatworm is next in frequency. Some tapeworms are found. However, few of these parasites, if any, can be hosted by man. Several dangerous bacte-

---

[1]Sole, halibut, flounder, and some other fish belong to the **flatfish** or **bottom fish** family, a variety of
fish that as it matures moves to the bottom of the ocean and lies on its side, the undereye (ventral) moving around to be with the other, looking up. This bottom or flatfish lives largely on the bottom, flapping
along as it moves. The skin on the ventral side is usually clear white, while that on the top side is grayish, brownish, or some other color that blends the fish into its environment.

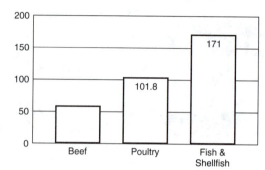

Figure 9–2
*Number of cases of illness per billion pounds
consumed.* (Source: CDC Surveillance Data
& ERS. USDA Consumption Data.)

ria or viruses are sometimes found in fish that live close to the seashore. The most
common illnesses from this source are *ciguartera* and *scrambroid.*

Buyers of bulk raw shellfish should insist that shipments of these products be
accompanied by a Public Health **certificate number** stating that the product came
from certified beds. Such certification is supposed to indicate that the product came
from beds that were inspected and found to contain no contaminants that could be
picked up by the shellfish. Hepatitis, diptheria, and other diseases can come from
shellfish growing in polluted waters. The government requires that a food service
keep the certificate number for at least 90 days. The federal government prohibits
the catching of marine products when the tiny organism called **red tide** is present.
It is a tiny red mite that appears during the warm summer months. Marine products
infected with this mite are poisonous.

SELECTION FACTORS

Economic considerations, use, and other factors dictate what is required to suit menu
needs. Lean fish and most shellfish do not broil or bake well; they are best poached,
boiled, steamed, fried, or deep-fried. Fat fish are best broiled or baked, although they
respond well to some other forms of cooking but usually not any form that adds fat.
(Table 9–2 gives market information and whether fish are fat or lean, and Table 9–3
gives purchase information on shellfish; practically all shellfish are lean. Tables 9–4
and 9–5 give quantities of fish and shellfish to purchase for 100 portions.)

MARKET FORMS

Specifications for fish should state the **market forms** (see Figure 9–3), which are as
follows:

1. **Whole** or **round:** As it comes from the water; perhaps scaled.
2. **Drawn:** Eviscerated and perhaps scaled.

Table 9-2
A buyer's guide for the purchase of fish.

Common Name	Other Common Names	Normal Size in Pounds	Main Production Area	Season	Yield from Round Form	Fat or Lean	Common Market Forms
Barracuda		5–10	California	June	51% to fillet	L	Round, dressed, steaks, fillet
Bluefish		1–7	Mid-Atlantic	All year	52% to fillet	L	Round, drawn, fillet
Bass	Sea, striped, blackfish, black seabass, common, rockfish	2–600 depending on type	Atlantic and Pacific	Depends on type	Around 40% to fillet for all types	L	All forms
Butterfish	Harvestfish	¼–1¼	Mid-Atlantic	June–Oct.	51% to fillet	F	Round, drawn, fillet
Catfish or bullheads		1–10	Rivers, lakes	All year	19% to fillet	L	Round, dressed
Chub		2–5 oz	Great Lakes	All year	33% to fillet	F	Dressed, smoked
Cod, Atlantic		1½–10	New England	All year	31% to fillet	L	All forms
Cod, Pacific		1½–10	Pacific Coast	All year	31% to fillet	L	All forms
Croaker, Atlantic	Hardhead	½–2	South Atlantic	June–Oct.	39% dressed	L	Round, dressed, fillet
Cusk		1½–10	Atlantic	All year	58% to fillet	L	Drawn, dressed
Drum (red)	Channel bass, redfish	2–25	South Atlantic, Gulf	Winter	36% to fillet	L	Round, drawn
Drum (black)	Oyster cracker, oyster drum, sea drum	1–40	Atlantic, Gulf	Winter	38% to fillet	L	Round, drawn
Flounder (sole)	*Atlantic:*		Atlantic				
	Blackback (winter)	¾–2		Late winter	41% to fillet	L	Dressed, fillet
	Fluke (summer)	2–12		Summer	42% to fillet	L	
	Dab (seadab)	¾–2½		April–May	36% to fillet	L	
	Gray	¾–4		April–June	40% to fillet	L	
	Lemon	¾–4		June	41% to fillet	L	
	Southern	2–12		All year	54% to fillet	L	
	Yellowtail or dusty dab	¾–2		Aug.–Jan.	54% to fillet	L	
					44% to fillet	L	
	Pacific:						
	Rex, petrale, sanddab, Dover or English sole	½–2	Pacific	All year	About 40% to fillet form	L	
Grouper		5–12	Gulf	All year	43% to fillet	L	All forms

Table 9-2
continued

Haddock		1½–7	New England	All year	48% to fillet	L	Fillet, sticks
Hake	Boston, squirrel, or white hake; red or mud hake	2 to 5	New England	All year	43% to fillet	L L	Fillet
Halibut		5–75	Pacific or Atlantic	April–Oct.	59% to fillet	F	All forms
Herring, sea		2–4 oz	Atlantic, Pacific	Nov.–Feb.	51% to fillet	F	Round
Herring, lake		⅓–1	Great Lakes	Oct.–Dec.	72% to dressed	F	Round, dressed, smoked
Mackerel, jack		½–2½	Atlantic	April–Oct.	54% to fillet	F	Round, dressed, fillet
Mackerel, Spanish		1–4	South Atlantic, Gulf	Summer		F	Round, dressed
Mackerel, king	Cero, kingfish	5–20	North Atlantic	Jan.–April	53% to fillet	L	All forms
Lingcod		5–20	North Pacific	All year	38% to fillet	L	Dressed, fillet
Mullet		½–3	South Atlantic, Gulf	Sept.–Dec.	53% to fillet	L	Round, dressed, fillet
Perch, white		⅓–¾	Great Lakes	All year	36% to fillet	L	Dressed, fillet
Perch, yellow		½–¾	Great Lakes	All year	38% to fillet	L	Dressed, fillet
Perch, ocean	Rosefish	½–1¼	New England	All year	31% to fillet	L	Fillet
Pickerel		1½–3½	North Lakes	April–Oct.	51% to fillet	L	Dressed, fillet
Pike, blue		½–2	Great Lakes	Sept.–Nov.	44% to fillet	L	Round, fillet
Pike, sauger		½–1½	Great Lakes	April–Oct.		L	Dressed, fillet
Pike, yellow		1–3½	and	April–Oct.	57% to fillet	L	Dressed, fillet
Pike, northern		1–4	Canadian	April–Oct.	39% to fillet	L	Dressed, fillet
Pike, wall-eyed		1–4	Lakes	April–Oct.	41% to fillet	L	Dressed, fillet
Pollock		1½–12	New England	All year	45% to fillet	L	Fillet
Pompano		½–2½	South Atlantic, Gulf	All year	52% to fillet	F	Dressed, round
Sablefish, black cod		1–15	North Pacific	April–Nov.	68% to dressed	F	Dressed, steaks, smoked
Salmon, Atlantic		5–10	Atlantic	June–July	65% to fillet	F	Dressed, steaks
Salmon, chum		5–11	North Pacific	Aug.–Nov.	76% to drawn	F	Drawn, dressed, steaks, fillet
Salmon, king		5–30	North Pacific	April–Aug.	73% to dressed	L	Drawn, dressed, steaks, fillet
Scrod		1½–2½	New England	All year	31% to fillet		All forms

Table 9–3
A buyer's guide for the purchase of shellfish.

Shellfish	Other Names	Main U.S. Producing Area	Peak Production Month	Weight Information, EP Yields, and Miscellaneous Information
Abalone		South Pacific	May	42% meat in shell
Clams, butter		North Pacific	All year	Shell—100 lb/sack; shucked 100–250/gal
Clams, hard*	Quahog, quahaug	North and Mid-Atlantic	All year	Bu—11 lb EP; 80 lb/sack; shucked 100–250/gal
Clams, littleneck		North and Mid-Atlantic or Pacific	All year	60 lb/bu
Clams, razor		North Pacific	Fall	80 lb/box; 16 EP/bu
Clams, soft*		North and Mid-Atlantic	All year	45 lb/bu; 200–700/gal shucked; 16 lb EP/bu
Clams, surf	Skimmer	North Atlantic	June	180–300/gal shucked
Conch				15 lb EP/bu
Crabs				
Blue, hard shell		Mid-Atlantic	All year	10 to 18% meat; 5 lb EP/bu
Rock		New England		10 to 18% meat; 5 lb EP/bu
Blue, soft shell		Mid-Atlantic	May–June	Used whole; 3 lb EP/doz
Dungeness		North Pacific	April–June	22–26% meat
King		Alaska	June	Legs only 14% meat
Lobsters		New England	May–Dec.	25% meat
Lobsters, spiny	Rock or sea crayfish, laguna lobster.	Pacific	Nov.	46% tails only; most of these are imported except the Laguna caught off the coast of California and Mexico
Mussels		New England	May–Dec.	45–55 lb/bu; 10 lb EP/bu; 29% meat
Oysters†				
Eastern		Atlantic	Fall and winter	80 lb/bu; 150–200/gal shucked (Bluepoints)
Pacific	Japanese		Nov.–Jan.	80 lb/sack; 64–240/gal shucked
Olympia	Western		Dec.–Jan.	120 lb/sack; 1600–1700/gal
Scallops				
Bay		Atlantic	Oct.–April	500 per gal shucked; few taken in Pacific
Sea		Atlantic	All year	150 per gal shucked
Sea urchins	Sea eggs			5 lb EP/bu
Shrimp‡				
Gulf		Gulf	All year	12 to 70 per lb
Alaska pink		North Pacific	Dec.–Jan.	150–250 shelled/lb
California		Mid-Pacific	Aug.–Sept.	125–250 shelled/lb

Table 9–3
continued

Shellfish	Other Names	Main U.S. Producing Area	Peak Production Month	Weight Information, EP Yields, and Miscellaneous Information
Squid		North Pacific	June–July	5 to 6 per lb round form
Snails		Atlantic	Winter	Most imported; 20% gross weight is meat
Terrapin	Diamondbacks	Gulf	All year	21% raw muscle
Turtles				
Sea and fresh water			All year	24% raw muscle

*Long shell or surf clams 35% yield; hard-shell clams (round shell) 17% yield drained meat average; hard-shelled clams by areas: New England, 14–20%; Chesapeake, 7–8%; Mid-Atlantic, 10–12%; South Atlantic, 6–8%; Pacific, 24–28%; soft-shell yields: New England, 23–33%, Mid-Atlantic, 27–32%.
†Eastern oyster yield: New England and Mid-Atlantic, 8–11%; Chesapeake, 6–7%; South Atlantic, 4–6%; Gulf, 5–7%; Pacific (Japanese), 10–14%.
‡Yield from frozen headless shrimp in thawing, cooking, shelling, and deveining–43% raw meat.

3. **Dressed (pan-dressed):** Scaled and eviscerated; usually head, tail, and fins are removed. Some, like trout, smelt, and salmon, may not have these removed. Wide differences exist in markets on what is pan-dressed and dressed fish. Trout, because of their fine scales, are not scaled. Pan-dressed usually refers to dressed small fish with head on.

4. **Steaks:** Cross-sections or slices of larger sizes of dressed fish. Portion size and variation from portion size specified should be named.

5. **Fillets (pronounced fil-lets):** The flesh on either side of the backbone and over the fish bones of the thoracic cavity. Some fillets may have tiny bones, such as fillets from mackerel or herring. The skin may or may not be on. For some, breaking up in cooking is lessened when the skin is left on. A fillet cut from one side is called **single** and when double or coming from both sides, it is called a **butterfly** fillet.

6. **Sticks:** Fillets or steaks in lengthwise pieces, usually of uniform size.

7. **Chunks:** Pieces of drawn or dressed fish, sometimes scaled. Figure 9–3 indicates these market forms. Table 9–6 gives some miscellaneous market forms used for fish cuts.

The federal government has also established the following special terms to indicate some forms of marine products:

Type: I—chilled, not previously frozen; II—frozen.

Form: I—unfrozen, whole or round fish; II—frozen and glazed; III (a) single fillets with skin on, or (b) single fillets with skin off—they may also be specified as butterfly (double) or just a or b (fillets must weigh from 3 to 24 oz, except some sole, which can be a minimum of 2 oz; ocean (Pacific) perch fillets as small as 1 oz; yellow perch 1⅓ oz, single whiting 1¼ or butterfly 2⅔ oz, and jewfish, 24 oz minimum;

Table 9-4

A buyer's guide for estimating quantities of shellfish required.

Shellfish	Portion Size or other Preparation Information	Form in Which Purchased AP	Quantity Required for 100 Portions
Abalone	4 oz	Steaks	25 lb
Clams, hard	On the shell: little necks 450–650 per bu or cherry stones 300–325 per bu; 4 per serving	In shell	34 doz
Clams, shucked	Cocktails, approx. 1½ oz	Shucked	1⅛ gal
Clams, chowder	Quahaugs, 150 per bu	In shell	1⅓–1⅔ bu or 2 gal shucked
Crab meat*	Backfin lump from Blue crab or solid meat from Dungeness 1½ oz per cocktail	Solid meat	10 lb
	2 oz for small salads		12 lb
	4 oz for large salads		24 lb
Crab meat*	Lump or flake for creamed, creole or extender dishes, use about 1¼–1½ oz	Solid meat	8–10 lb
Crabs, soft shell	1 each about 4 to 4½" in diameter	Alive	100 crabs
Lobster	¾–1¼ lb chicken lobster or 1½–2 lb and split	Alive Alive	100 lobster 50 lobster
Lobster meat*	See crab meat		
Oysters, blue points	Purchase 300–400 oysters per bu (approx. 75 lb per bu), 4 per serving	In shell	34 doz
Oysters, olympia	For cocktails, 1¼ oz	Shucked	1 gal
Oysters, fried or scalloped	Purchase *counts* ¹²⁵⁄₁₅₀ per gal or *selects* 175–200 per gal	Shucked	2½–3 gal
Oysters, stew	Purchase *standards* 250–300 per gal	Shucked	1½ gal
Scallops, sea	Medium size 175 approx. per gal for deep frying		3½–4 gal
Shrimp, fried	Use Jumbo split or butterflied, about 20 per lb, using 4–5 per portion, or large split or round		20–25 lb
Shrimp	Cocktails 1½ oz, small or Pacific	Shelled	10 lb
Shrimp	Cocktails 5 Jumbo or Large	Green, unshelled†	25–33 lb
Shrimp	Small salad, 2-oz shrimp, ½ c salad	Green, unshelled†	12 lb EP, cooked
Shrimp	Large salad, 4-oz shrimp, 1 c salad	Green, unshelled†	24 lb EP, cooked

*From 10 to 12 cans 14 oz net weight contents of crab or lobster meat are the equivalent of the quantities given here.

†Shrimp are headless AP.

Table 9–5

A buyer's guide for estimating quantities of fish.

Fish	Preparation Information	Estimated Pounds AP Required for 100 Portions			
		Round	Drawn	Dressed	Fillet
Barracuda	5–6 oz steaks			31–38	
Bass, all types	5–6 oz steaks: 4–5 oz fillets		35–50	35	30
Bluefish	Half 1½ lb round fish	75		50	
Bullhead	½ 1-lb fish split			50*	
Butterfish	1 fish to the lb size		50		
Catfish	5-oz fillet	165			30
Chub	1–3 fish depending on size		38		
Cod	4–5 oz fillet	100			30
Cod	5–6 oz steak cut from 8 lb dressed fish			35–50	
Cod, scrod	Split 1¼-lb round scrod into two portions	68		50	
Cod, salt, dry	For fish cakes or creamed cod				10
Croaker	4–5 oz fillet	80			30
Cusk	4–5 oz fillet	64			30
Eels	Smoked 4 oz			25	
Flounder					
Blackback (winter)	†	76		50	30
Fluke (summer)	†	75		50	30
Dab	†	90		50	30
Gray sole	†	80		50	30
Lemon sole	†	80		50	30
Southern	†	58		50	30
Yellowtail	†	70		50	30
Pacific sole	†	82		50	30
California halibut	†	62		50	30
Grouper	5–6 oz steaks cut from 8 lb fish			35	
Haddock	5–6 oz steaks, 4–5 oz fillets	60		50	30
Hake	4–5 oz fillets	74			
Halibut	5–6 oz steaks, 4–5 oz fillets	60		35	30
Herring, sea or lake	Round 1-lb fish per portion	100			
Herring, salted	8 oz split pieces			50	
Herring, smoked	5–6 oz				38
Mackerel	¾-lb split	100	75		
Mackerel, king	4–5 oz fillets				30
Mackerel, Spanish	3 to lb average, split	75	50		

Source: Courtesy USDA.

Fish	Preparation Information	Estimated Pounds AP Required for 100 Portions			
		Round	Drawn	Dressed	Fillet
Ling cod	4–5 oz fillets	62	50		30
Mullet	4–5 oz fillets	60			30
Perch, all types	2 fillets 2–2½ oz each				30
Pickerel	4–5 oz fillets				30
Pike, all types				35–50	30
Pollock	1½–2 lb each or 4–5 oz fillets			35–50	30
Pompano	Use ¾–1½ lb fish split or whole, depending on portion size desired		75	50	30
Sablefish	5–6 oz steaks, smoked 5-oz pieces			35–50 35–50	
Salmon, baking size	Buy 5–12 lb dressed salmon			40	
Salmon	5–6 oz steaks, 4–5 oz fillets			35–50	30
Scup (Porgy)	Purchase dressed 5–8 oz each or split 1-lb dressed fish			35–50	
Shad	Steaks 5–8 oz, fillets 4–5 oz			38	30
Smelt	3–5 fish dressed 12 –16 to lb			35–33	
Snapper, red	5–6 oz steaks cut from 8–9 lb fish			35–50	
Snapper, red	4–5 fillets				30
Shad roe	Purchase *medium* roe averaging 8–10 oz per pair; portion size may vary considerably, depending on type operation				15–30
Swordfish	Steaks 5–6 oz			35	
Tilefish	5–6 oz steaks	82	60	35–50	
Whitefish	Purchase around 4 ib dressed and cut into 5–6 oz portion; filets 4–5 oz			50	30
Whiting	Split 1½-lb rounds or purchase ½-lb dressed fish and use 1 per portion; 4–5 oz fillets	75		50	30
Whiting, king	4–5 oz fillets				30
Wolffish	5–6 oz steaks cut from lb drawn fish; 4–5 oz fillets	90	60		30

*Skinned.

†Small sizes may be split, center bone removed; or selected fillets about 3 to the pound or cut larger fillets into 4- to 5-oz portions.

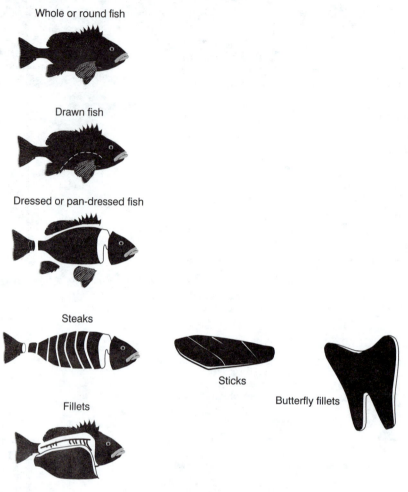

Whole or round fish

Drawn fish

Dressed or pan-dressed fish

Steaks

Sticks

Butterfly fillets

Fillets

Figure 9–3
Market forms of fish. (Courtesy U.S. Department of the Interior.)

IV—steaks ⅝ to 1 in. thick; if frozen, they must be glazed; steaks cannot weigh less than 3 oz and cannot come from napes (necks), including collarbones or longitudinal tail cuts; to make a weight, a steak may be cut in two; V—chunks, glazed, if frozen; VI—pieces of fish flesh, boneless or nearly so.

Style: I—about 25-lb frozen fillet; II—same but not frozen.

Usually an 8- to 12-lb drawn fish bakes best or cuts into steaks best for food service use.

Ground or flaked meat made into reformed products that look and taste like crab, shrimp, lobster, and some others is available. Its trade name is usually **surimi,** an original Japanese product. The ground flaked meat is flavored with the juices of the representative product. It is then mixed to make it cohesive and formed into rep-

Table 9-6
Miscellaneous market forms of fish.

Aberdeen cut	Also called custom, diamond, or French cut. Slanted-rectangle (rhombus) shape, cut from a block, with squared or tapered sides
American cut	Tapered or beveled edges of fillets, pieces, or other fish portions
Bits	Also called bites, nuggets, or cubes; small square, round, or irregular-shaped pieces from frozen blocks; about ½–1 oz each
Cakes	Rounded, preformed, flat cakes of ground, flaked, or minced flesh; can be plain or breaded
Fish n' Cheese	Portion of fish topped with cheese or cheese mixed with ground, flaked, or minced meat and preformed
Portion	A square or rectangular piece cut from frozen blicks, 1½–6 oz each, raw, breaded, or unbreaded; sometimes cooked; grated fish portions are preformed flat pieces made from ground, flaked, or minced flesh; they also may be raw, breaded, or unbreaded; they are sometimes also cooked

resentative shapes. Some products are dyed red on the outside to appear like the real thing. Some breaded surimi shrimp are available. Surimi items have a surprisingly natural flavor and the amounts sold and kinds on the market are increasing rapidly.

Shellfish includes crustaceans (shrimp, lobster, crayfish, spiny lobsters, etc.) and mollusks (oysters, clams, conch, mussels, scallops, etc.). Mollusks are sold in the shell or shucked—shucking is removal from the shell, leaving only clear meat. Scallops are a large mollusk's adductor muscle, which holds the scallop's two shells together. Mussels are usually sold only in the shell. Crustaceans are often sold alive but also cooked in the shell, as fresh solid meat (cooked meat picked from the shell and packed into containers). Most shrimp, crayfish, and spiny lobsters are marketed headless, that is, with the head and thorax removed, leaving only the tail. Lobster tails are the tails of spiny lobsters.

RECEIVING

The condition of marine products is extremely important to menu quality, and special care should be taken upon receiving to see that the product is good before accepting it. Once this is determined, the products should be moved quickly to proper storage since they can quickly deteriorate.

Unfrozen products should be well chilled and not more than 42°F inside; frozen products should be hard frozen. Any suspicion of spoilage should be cause for rejection. Because marine products can lose quality quickly, quality must be checked carefully.

The quality of marine products often depends on their original processing, and season. Some companies produce better items than others. Quick stunning or immobilization, good bleeding, and dressing aids quality. Ships may now be stationed out at sea to speed up the processing of fish. Thus, fish may be caught, frozen, and packaged on board within several hours.[2] Fresh products should be held under adequate refrigeration and moved to market as soon as possible. Freezing should occur by plate, blast, cryogenic, or other speedy methods. Slow freezing destroys cells and contributes to thawing drip; minimum drip occurs if thawing is under 40°F.

When caught, the flesh of fish is soft, but soon stiffens and firms. Fresh fish should be firm and elastic. The flesh should spring back when pressed and not easily pull from the bones. As a fish stales, the flesh softens, becomes flabby and soft, separating from the bone; an indentation of the finger remains in it. The color of the flesh should be bright and clear. White-meated fish should have a white and slightly translucent color, not pink or gray, especially around the backbone. Steaks and fillets should have no traces of brown at the edge. Bright-colored scales with a sheen should adhere tightly to the body. No viscera or blood should be visible. The lining should be intact with no bones protruding. The odor should be fresh and mild. Fish with a strong ammonia or musty, yeasty smell, dull or faded color, scales missing or easily removed, incomplete evisceration, cuts or major bruising, red spots, or yellow or brown discoloration should be rejected. The eyes should be bright and clear, full and bulging, not dull, wrinkled, or sunken. Fish with the inner lining left in tend to keep better. Fat fish can become rancid, often indicated by the appearance of an orange color. Packages of breaded- or batter-covered products should be checked to see if the covering adheres and is in good shape. When thawed, frozen products should meet the standards of fresh.

Much shellfish should be purchased alive, if in the shell. The exception might be shrimp. Some cooked shellfish in the shell may be marketed. Crustaceans turn red when cooked, which distinguishes them from the uncooked or green products. Some cooked crab may have a creamy color outside, flecked with red. Some purveyors, failing to sell their crustaceans alive, may cook them after they perish and market them in a cooked form, so buyers should be aware of this. Fresh shrimp should have a mild odor. The meat should be firm; the texture gets soft and mushy as deterioration sets in. A red-colored shell should show in cooked shrimp with meat that is reddish outside and white inside. Live crustaceans show life by eye, antennae, or leg movement. A lively lobster snaps when picked up; the tail is tightly curled under. As a lobster weakens the tail droops, indicating what is called a *weak*. Dead lobsters hand lifeless, with claws and tail down. Cooked lobsters in the shell should be a bright red, with no disagreeable odor and no smell that is offensive or strongly tainted with ammonia. Cooked lobster can be refrigerated between ice layers for several days only. Live lobsters can also be refrigerated on ice. Some operations have special tanks with circulating water in which they display live lobsters while holding them. Scallops should have a sweet odor and be free of excess liquid.

Live mollusks hold their shell firmly together when pressure is applied to open it; dead ones can often be detected by their open shells, although sometimes, even

---

[2]The federal government in 1980 established what it called its Integrated Quality Assurance Program (IQA), which established desirable handling procedures for marine products. Marine products handled under the standards set by this program may display the IQA label.

though dead, they may still hold their shells firmly together. Sometimes live mollusks left in saltwater can be seen to open and close their shells and clams may extend their necks. Some hold clams in saltwater and put in a bit of cornmeal. The clams eat the cornmeal and disgorge themselves of sand. A slight jar causes the clam to quickly withdraw its neck and close the shell.

Shucked mollusks should be plump, have a clear color and sweet odor, and be free of pieces of shell, silt, and sand. The liquid should be clear. If the mollusks appear bloated or have more than 8% liquid on them, they have probably been water-soaked, increasing their weight. Mollusks should have a pH around 6.0. As they age, they become more acid, a condition that can be detected by tasting the liquor.

Check carefully to see that special specification provisions are adhered to, such as that not more than 2% of the shipment of shell oysters can be dead or that only 1 of 24 live lobsters can be a "weak."

STORAGE

Storage is best for marine products at about 32°F. Handle carefully; bruising encourages bacterial growth. It may be a good idea to rinse whole raw fish and some others in ice water before storing. Whole fish is best packed on clean trays filled with crushed or thin-flaked ice, with plastic cover over the ice. Another plastic cover should be over the fish and another layer of ice over this. Some facilities have trays that pull in and out. See that there is good drainage. Cut pieces of fish should not be stored directly on ice; place in plastic and cover with ice. Fresh fillets are often shipped in 25-lb tins; for best quality remove and place them on layers of ice as described above. Do not have the fish layers too thick. Keep low inventories and rotate on a FIFO basis. Use all items within several days for best quality.

Some food services store mollusks in the shell by spreading them out in thin layers between ice, but see that a plastic wrap separates them from the ice. Properly refrigerated, most live shellfish keep for about a week. Shucked products, properly refrigerated, keep 7 to 10 days. Store them in their containers in a refrigerated area on ice.

Frozen shellfish is stored at 0°F or below—a preferable temperature is –10° to −15°F. (This temperature is also desirable for frozen fish.) Long storage at just below freezing denatures the cells and leaves a drier, pulpy, less flavorful product. Packages should be stacked so good air circulation is possible. Date and follow FIFO. Table 9–7 indicates the freezer storage life of some of the most commonly used shellfish.

Frozen fish can develop what is called **honeycombing,** small indentations in the flesh that look somewhat like honeycomb; it indicates deterioration. *Voids,* hollow places in the flesh, are also undesirable. White cottony spots show freezer burn (dehydration), which destroys texture and flavor. Thaw such products and inspect. Frozen products lose quality and texture if thawed and refrozen, unless one has rapid freezing equipment. Stack frozen packages away from walls and ceiling, and off the floor to allow proper air circulation. Date stock and rotate by FIFO. Do not remove tight-fitting plastic wraps from frozen fish. This helps prevent freezer burn.

Table 9-7
Freezer storage life.*

Species	Storage Life (months)
Clams, shucked	10
Clams, breaded or extruded	12
Blue crab	10
King crab	12
Dungeness crab	10
Northern lobster	12
Spiny lobster	9
Mussels, shucked	9
Oysters, shucked	12
Oysters, breaded	10
Scallops, shucked	14
Scallops, breaded	11
Shrimp, green headless	16
Shrimp, peeled and deveined	14
Shrimp, cooked	12
Shrimp, breaded or extruded	10

*The shelf life assumes adequate glaze, if needed, and a 0°F storage temperature.

Unfrozen, smoked fish should be held at about 32°F, avoiding ice contact. Most products are only lightly processed and can mold or spoil easily. Examine stocks daily. Marinated fish products should be refrigerated unless heat-sterilized in sealed containers. Hard, dried, salted products need not be refrigerated, but protect them from high humidity. See that their wraps also protect them.

SPECIFICATIONS

A specification for any marine product should give the name of the product (use local names, if common), the quantity wanted, the market type, style, form, packaging, etc., any processing such as curing, smoking, freezing, cooking, etc., size, and other pertinent information needed to deliver the right product. If there is no grade, one must purchase by brand or write in the quality wanted. Brand quality has become more reliable as producers learn to produce better products, especially in the frozen line. Since many of the products moving on the market are unbranded or ungraded, buyers must often write lengthy, detailed quality specifications.

Much can be added to protect the buyer concerning packaging and condition of products upon delivery. Glazing should be mentioned, if that kind of product is desired. Prices are usually by the pound, but price by unit, package, number, or other quantity may also be used. Some illustrative specifications for various marine products are presented at the end of this chapter.

PURCHASE INFORMATION

A large number of marine products are marketed in this country, but the amount on any one market is much less, since varieties tend to be local and not widespread. Products are also seasonal and so, even though the amount over the year may be sizable on any one market, the number of items offered at one time may be only a part of what appears over the year. The following is a brief description of the main items that appear. Students should not try to learn all the information given here. It is presented as a source of information for the buyer who wishes to know some facts about a particular marine product (see Figure 9–4).

Fish[3]

Barracuda

Caribbean and Florida waters supply most of the barracuda we use. It is more a game fish than a commercial one, but it is growing in popularity. We often see it served as steaks.

Bass

The most common sea bass on the market are, from the Atlantic, striped, sea, black, and white (common); and from the Pacific, striped, sea, and rockfish. Some freshwater bass is marketed. All are similar. The cooked flavor is a bit stronger than cod but it is a moist, flavorful fish. Supplies are best in early summer and fall from Long Island to northern Maine. The Chesapeake Bay and Pacific areas produce bass throughout the year. Rockfish is often salted and smoked.

Buyers should ascertain the sizes of bass available on their markets. There is much confusion on markets regarding names. Some varieties of drum and grouper are called bass, and different names are given the main bass varieties. For instance, sea bass may be called blackfish, grey bass, or weakfish, and rock bass goggle-eye, red eye, red eye perch, or even sunfish. Bass is a wasty fish and so the yield from AP to EP is low. It is available in all forms.

Blackfish

Blackfish is available all year, whole or filleted; it also goes by the names of bowfin, dogfish, cotton fish, grindle, layer, or spindle cat.

Bluefish

Baby bluefish run ¼ to 1¼ lb; most used sizes are 3 to 8 lb but they can run 20 lb. Pollock, a cod, may be called *Boston bluefish,* but it is not an acceptable substitute for pollock. Other names are blues, snapping mackerel, tailors, and greenfish.

---

[3] A list of illustrations of the most commonly caught fish and shellfish appears in Appendix H.

URNER BARRY'S
seafood
PRICE CURRENT
Tel. 732-240-5330 • Fax 732-341-0891

EASTERN FRESH WHOLEFISH

	Mid-Atlantic		Mid-Atlantic
Blackfish, Tautog........	0.50	American Red Snapper, Gutted	
Bluefish, Jumbo............	-	1-2 lbs..........................	-
lg................................	0.75	2-4 lbs..........................	3.50
Medium.......................	1.25	4-6 lbs..........................	3.00
Small...........................	-	B-Line Snapper	
Butterfish, lg................	1.00+	3/4-1lbs........................	
Medium.......................	0.75	1-2 lbs..........................	
Small........................	0.25-0.30	Sea Bass lg....................	-
Cod, head off, lg..........	2.50	Medium.......................	-
Market........................	2.00+	Small...........................	-
Scrod..........................	1.50-	Striped Bass	
Croaker, lg..................	0.65+	Farm Raised................	-
Medium.......................	-	Skate Wing...................	0.75-
Small...........................	-	Squid, med...................	0.60-0.80+
Cusk............................	-	Swordfish, lg................	5.50-6.00+
Mahi Mahi....................	2.50	Gold Tilefish, lg............	-
Y/T Mixed...................	3.00	Medium.......................	1.60-2.00+
Regular.......................	-	Kitten..........................	1.25-1.40-
Fluke, jumbo...............	3.25+	Weakfish, Sea Trout,	
lg................................	2.50-3.00	lg................................	-
Medium.......................	2.25-2.60-	Medium.......................	-
B/B lg.........................	3.25	Whiting........................	0.75-1.00-
Medium.......................	3.00	King Whiting.................	1.25-
Small...........................	-	Wolffish.......................	-
Dabs, Sea lg................	3.25	Monktail......................	2.50-3.00+
Medium.......................	3.00	Shad Roe, lg................	-
Small...........................	-	Buck............................	-
Sole, Gray lg...............	5.00-	Roe, cut.......................	-
Medium.......................	-	Shark, Mako.................	-
Small...........................	-	Spot	-
Grouper......................	-	Tuna, Bigeye #1...........	-
Hake, White.................	-	Yellowfin #2.................	4.00
Halibut, 10-50		King Mackerel..............	2.50+
Eastern....................	6.00-6.50+	Spanish Mackerel..........	1.75
Western...................	-	**FRESHWATER FISH, Boxed**	
Ling Red Hake............	0.70+	Buffalo Carp.................	-
Mackeral, lg................	-	Jumbo Carp..................	-
Medium.......................	0.75+	Carp, 65 lb...................	0.35-0.40+
Mullet, Lisa.................	0.65	Northern Pike	-
Ocean Perch...............	-	Redfin..........................	-
Pollock.......................	-	Trout dressed...............	-
Pollock, Steak		Yellow Pike, 60 lb..........	-
Head off.................	-	Salmon, Trout, 50 lb.......	-
Pompano, lg................	-	Sheepshead..................	0.30-0.35-
Porgies, Scup lg..........	1.25-1.50	Smelts, 25 lb.................	-
Medium.......................	-	Whitefish, 50 lb.............	1.25-
Small...........................	-	Whitefish, Can., drsd......	-

Figure 9-4
Excerpts of market reports for fresh fish, ocean and farm raised salmon, and frozen shellfish, published to inform buyers of market conditions on various marine products. (Published with the permission and courtesy of Urner Barry Publications, Inc.)

SALMON

Farm Raised - 2000 lb. Average Fresh

WHOLE FISH						FILLETS - Standard Trim/Prem Scale-On PBO			
	FOB Northeast Northeast Atlantic	FOB Miami Chilean Atlantic	FOB Seattle West Coast Atlantic	FOB L.A West Coast Atlantic	FOB Seattle Canadian King		FOB Miami Chilean Atlantic	FOB Miami Chilean Steelhead	FOB N.E. Northeast Atlantic
2-4 lbs.	-	-	-	-	2.00-2.15	1-2 lbs	2.95-3.00	1.90-2.00+	-
4-6 lbs.	1.75-1.85	-	2.05-2.10	2.05-2.10	2.15-2.35	2-3 lbs	3.00-3.10	2.45-2.55+	3.45-3.55+
6-8 lbs.	2.10-2.15	2.00-2.10+	2.25-2.30	2.25-2.35	2.30-2.40	3-4 lbs	3.15-3.25+	-	3.65-3.80+
8-10 lbs.	2.15-2.20	2.10-2.20	2.25-2.30	2.25-2.35	-	4-5 lbs	3.15-3.25+	-	-
10-12 lbs.	2.15-2.25+	2.15-2.25+	2.20-2.30	2.20-2.30	-				
12-14 lbs.	2.15-2.25+	-	2.10-2.20	2.10-2.20	-				
14-16 lbs.	-	-	2.10-2.20	2.10-2.20	-				
16-18 lbs.	-	-	2.10-2.20	2.10-2.20	-				

Wild, Fresh - 2,000 lb. Average, FOB Seattle

GILLNET Head Off	Silver/ Coho	Dark Chum Red Meat	Chum	Sockeye*	Pink		King	Copper River*	
2-4 lbs.	-	-	-	-	-	Under 7 lbs.	-	Under 7 lbs.	-
4-6 lbs.	-	-	-	-	-	7 - 11 lbs.	-	7 - 11 lbs.	-
6-9 lbs.	-	-	-	-	-	11 - 18 lbs.	-	11 - 18 lbs.	-
9 lbs. & up	-	-	-	-	-	18 lbs. & up	-	18 lbs. & up	-

TROLL Head On		Pale Meat					California King	
2 - 4 lbs.	-	-	-	-	-	Under 7 lbs.	-	
4 - 6 lbs.	-	-	-	-	-	7 - 11 lbs.	-	
6 - 9 lbs.	-	-	-	-	-	11 - 18 lbs.	-	
9 lbs. & up	-	-	-	-	-	18 lbs. & up	-	

*Copper River/Ocean Run

H & G Frozen F.O.B. Seattle

GILLNET	Silver/ Coho	Chum Pale Meat	Dark Chum	Semi-Brite Chum	Brite Chum	Red/ Sockeye	Pink	Troll/ Coho	Gillnet King Chinook
2-4 lbs.	-	-	-	-	-	-	0.80-0.85	-	Under 7 lbs.	-
4-6 lbs.*	-	0.50-0.60-	0.80-0.85	-	-	-	0.80-0.85	-	7 - 11 lbs.	-
6-9 lbs.**	-	0.50-0.60-	0.80-0.85	-	-	-	-	-	11 - 18 lbs.	-
9 lbs. & up	-	-	-	-	-	-	-	-	18 lbs. & up	-

*Pink = 3-5 lbs.; **5 lbs. & up

Figure 9–4
continued

Bonito

Bonito cannot be legitimately sold as tuna, although it closely resembles it in flavor and flesh texture.

Buffalofish

The Mississippi River and its tributaries provide our buffalofish; the big catch comes in the Louisiana area from February to August. Other market names are bigmouth, gourdhead, red mouth, channel, razorback, small mouth, suckermouth, bugler, prairie, and rooter. We may see this fish soon being produced in considerable quantities by aquaculture.

Frozen Shellfish

Shrimp 5 lb., Cooked & Peeled	**West Coast**
Oregon, IQF	
250-350 count..	-
350-500 count..	2.90-3.00
Pandalus borealis, Imported	**East Coast**
125-175 count...	-
175-250 count...	-
250-350 count...	3.50-4.00
SLIPPER LOBSTERS - Shell On	**West Coast**
Taiwan, Hong Kong & Thailand	
Under one ounce...	-
1-2 ounce...	6.45-6.65
2-4 ounce...	7.50-7.70
4-6 ounce...	9.15-9.30
6-8 ounce...	-
Meat, Shell Off	
Under 1 ounce..	5.95
1-3 ounce..	7.50-7.75

Figure 9–4
continued

Butterfish

Butterfish is small and is caught from the Chesapeake Bay to Maine during the spring through November. It is rich and buttery and broils well. Other names are harvest fish, dollar fish, shiner, sheepshead, and pumpkin seed.

Carp

Fillets of carp and whole fish are on the market fresh from February through spring. It is a rough fish that grows and prospers under very adverse conditions. It is caught in the Great Lakes and Mississippi area and responds well to aquaculture. Some object to them because they are bony, but the flesh is moist and delicate, and has a sweet, full flavor. Other names are German carp, channel carp, or goldfish.

Catfish or Bullhead

Vast catfish farms exist in the south where they grow well on a minimum of feed, putting on a pound of flesh for every pound of feed. They are good scavengers and eat plants as well as insect and other life. Most are purchased dressed, headless, and skinned and filleted. They are growing in popularity because of their plentiful supply and relatively low price. Other names are blue channel fish, yellow catfish, fiddler, and spotted fish. From round to skinless and boneless the yield is 42%.

Chub
Chub is caught largely in the Great Lakes area and is largely marketed smoked. Only the blackfin variety is marketed fresh. Other names are blackfin, bloater, bluefin, and tullibee.

Cod
Cod is made up of a family of very similar fish such as haddock, pollock or pollack, hake, cusk, whiting, and lingcod. It is marketed fresh for most of the year as round, dressed, steaks and fillets with skin on or off. Most varieties average 10 to 12 lb, but best size is 5 to 8 lb. Scrod is a small 1¼- to 2-lb cod prized for its tenderness and sweet, delicate flavor. Cusk is a fairly fat cod and broils well. Lightly cured and smoked haddock is known as *finnan haddie*. Hake is also sold dry salted, boneless, salted, or smoked.

A lot of cod is sold frozen as sticks, fillets, or fish blocks. Cod is not a legitimate substitute for sole or flounder. Hake is also called whites, muds, Boston, squirrel or black hake, or ling, and pollock Boston bluefish, and Alaskan pollock. Cusk may be called sea whitefish. (The cod called whiting should not be confused with the fish called whiting or silver hake.) Atlantic cod from round to boneless skinless fillets yields 42%; Pacific cod 25% to 35%.

Federal grades for processed cod are A and B. Cod is low in fat. Watch for yellowing and overly soft flesh. In frozen products dehydration gives a rubbery, tough texture. Norway and some other countries are producing large amounts of cod by aquaculture and in the United States it is beginning to be produced this way as well.

Croaker
Virginia waters produce most of the croaker, but it is caught in some quantity north and south of there as well. Most are caught March through October. It is marketed round, or pan-dressed, either fresh or frozen. Other names are hardhead, king belly, and crocus.

Dolphin
Mahi mahi is a dolphin of considerable delicacy, white-fleshed meat. It is not too plentiful and is priced on menus equally with high-cost meat cuts.

Drum
Drum, after cooking, is often mistaken for bass. It is caught from Texas to New England and marketed round, drawn, or filleted. Other names are sea drums, red drum, redfish, red bass, spotted bass, and channel bass.

Flounder or Sole
Sole is a kind of flounder. The Atlantic produces winter sole, lemon sole, yellowtail (Boston sole or dab), grey sole, and sea dab. Fluke and southern are large flounders.

Pacific varieties are rex, petrale, sanddab, and Dover or English sole. The latter resembles the fine English or Dover sole of Europe. Larger sizes of this sole on the market are called *Dover,* while the smaller ones are called *English.*

The best sizes of sole, heads off, are ¾ to 2 lb; fillets from 2 to 6 oz should be purchased. A wide variety of names are given the sole mentioned here and buyers should learn what these are on their local markets. Yield from round to fillets averages 33% to 37%.

True Dover or English sole is imported fresh or frozen. Sizes run 1 to 1¼ lb, 1¼ to 1¾ lb, and 1¾ to 2 lb. Federal grades for frozen sole are A and B.

Grouper
Grouper is an Atlantic-caught fish of high eating quality. It has a high waste loss from round to boneless, skinless fillet. Yield from round to such fillets is from 25% to 45%.

Halibut
The International Pacific Halibut Commission allows the United States to take a share of 65 to 70 million pounds of Pacific halibut from May to October and then closes the grounds to all fishing. Atlantic catches are small. Chicken halibut is from 8 to 10 lb, but good halibut can be obtained from fish weighing up to 20 lb. Federal grades for processed halibut are A and B. Halibut grows well in aquaculture.

Halibut is marketed round, dressed, in steaks, fillets, or chunks. Steaks are sliced halibut pieces, 2 oz or more, packed at random or uniform weight; the latter may be called *portion pack.* Watch for honeycombing in frozen products.

Herring
Both lake (freshwater) and sea herring are marketed. The flesh of herring is fat and somewhat resembles the flavor of mackerel. It is marketed in greatest quantity in the spring and summer. It is also canned, salted, or smoked. Sardines are a family member. Other names for lake herring are cisco and blueback.

Mackerel
Boston or jack mackerel, 1 to 2 lb each, are docked in large numbers from Cape Cod to northern Maine in the spring and summer. Spanish mackerel, 1½ to 3 lb (fillets 6 to 8 oz), is marketed from Boston in considerable quantities. The Pacific mackerel from California is a pilchard and canned as a large sardine. King mackerel can be large enough to cut into steaks. It may also be called cero or kingfish.

Marlin
Marlin, a game fish, is also marketed as a commercial item, though not in great quantities. It is available all year around, fresh or frozen. Black, blue, striped, or white marlin are available.

Mullet
Mullet is a Gulf or south Atlantic fish caught September through December, and marketed fresh or frozen, whole, drawn, dressed, or as fillets. It is also brine-cured, dry-salt cured, or smoked. It is called on different markets common, jumping, silver, striped, or white mullet.

Perch

Rosefish, sea, or ocean perch are docked in Boston. It is small but sautées or deep-fries well. The best freshwater perch comes from what is called pound-net; gill net perch are not as good. Freshwater perch are caught in almost every state in the continental United States. Other names for freshwater perch are red fin, jumbo, English, or lake perch, while sea varieties are also known as brim, deep-sea, or red perch or redfish. Perch respond well to aquaculture.

Pike

Pickerel is a variety of pike and is sold as such under names such as common, grass, jack or lake pike or muskellunge. Other varieties go by the names of perch pike, blue, grass, great northern, yellow, dore, northern, sand or sauger pike or walleyes, jack salmon, salmon jack, lake pickerel or pike perch. Fresh pike is available spring through fall and frozen is available throughout the year.

Pompano

Mexican pompano is actually a permit, an inferior fish, and is not an acceptable substitute for the true pompano that comes from Florida, Bermuda, or Gulf waters. It is a small fish but considered a delicacy. Another name is great pompano.

Porgy

Porgy resembles scup and is sold as such sometimes. It also is known as common porgie, daughy, jolt head, little head, little mouth, saucer eye, and scupping.

Red Snapper

True snapper comes from Gulf or Florida waters; watch for substitutions. "Jap snapper," a grouper, is not an acceptable substitute; however, some varieties caught in the Pacific are. Other names are red or red rock cod, rockfish, or red rockfish.

Sablefish

Sablefish is commonly known as black cod and is frequently smoked. It is a flatfish caught in substantial quantities in the Pacific, but unlike most flatfish is quite fat. Fresh forms are round and dressed.

Salmon

Some Atlantic (Kennebec) salmon are marketed, but Pacific salmon caught from Oregon to Alaska dominate the market. Most Atlantic salmon are sold fresh, much for lox. Ranch (aquaculture) salmon grown in western Canada and the United States are coming onto the market in increasing amounts, making fresh salmon available throughout the year.

Pacific salmon is marketed fresh, frozen, smoked or kippered, and canned. The redder the salmon, the higher the cost. The reddest is Red or Sockeye, 6 to 12 lb, also called blueback or quinault. Silvers (silverside, medium red or Coho), also 6 to 12 lb, and Chinook (king, blackmouth, spring or tyee) salmon, about 10 to 35 lb, have a rich reddish-orange flesh. Pinks or humpbacks are named properly for their flesh color; they run 4 to 8 lb. Chum (keta, fall, silver bright, dog, or white) salmon, 8 to 16 lb, is light colored. Most is river caught in the fall and lacks the quality of the other salmon. The larger the salmon the higher the yield round to dressed; average yield is 65% to 70%.

Scup
Scup, a small fish, is caught from the Carolinas to New England, April through October, and marketed fresh, frozen as round, drawn, filleted, or pan-dressed. It is sometimes called porgy.

Sea Squab
Sea squab puffs up when frightened and so is also called blowfish, puffer, globefish, swellfish, or swell-toad. They are an Atlantic fish, docked December through October, dressed, and marketed either fresh or frozen.

Shad
Shad is famous for its roe, which comes in pairs or strips of two, and is a menu delicacy broiled, baked, batter-fried, or deep-fried. Other fish roe is not equal in quality. It is caught in both the Pacific and Atlantic waters and rivers emptying into them. The females average 4½ lb and males (jack or buck) shad 3 lb. The flesh of the male is considered superior. Skip shad is a small shad.

Sheepshead
Atlantic sheepshead is often not that but butterfish. A true variety is caught in Gulf waters. It is a small fish, closely resembling butterfish. Freshwater varieties are related to perch and are often called white perch. They are caught from the Great Lakes to Louisiana in the Mississippi drainage, the southern caught being best quality. Other names are croaker, freshwater drum, gaspergou, and gray bass.

Skate
Skate is an ugly, odd-shaped flatfish from the Pacific and Atlantic, mostly the latter. On the Boston market it is sold round or drawn, in a form called "saddles", and runs from 1 to 10 lb; in New York, it is available as "wings or saddles," weighing 1 to 10 lb dressed. Other names are Erenacca, Laevis, Raie, rajahfish, stingray, or turbot.

Smelt
The small Pacific smelt may be called Columbia River smelt; they are also called silver, or surf smelt. There are several other sea varieties. Smelt are marketed round, headed, and drawn (dressed), or as boned fillets. The Great Lakes yield a freshwater smelt in the spring.

Spot
Spot is a small fish caught May through November off the coast of the Carolinas to New England; Virginia spot are considered best. They are marketed fresh or frozen as round, drawn, or pan-dressed. They are also called goody, hard head, Lafayette, Norfolk spot, or silver gudgeon.

Sturgeon

Sturgeon is a sea fish often caught in rivers as it comes up to spawn, more prized for its roe than flesh, although it is a good eating fish also. It can grow to huge sizes. Quantities are limited, but is available fresh all year. It may also be called green, lake, sea, or common sturgeon.

Sunfish, Bluegill, or Crappie

Sunfish, bluegill, or crappies are closely related freshwater fish similar to perch. Bluegills are also called blue perch. These may be purchased round, drawn, pan-dressed, or filleted.

Swordfish

Swordfish, a large fish averaging 200 to 300 lb, is much like halibut, but slightly grayer and has less fat, although it broils well. Specify center cuts with no nape (flake) or tail cuts. It is available fresh or frozen. American or Canadian swordfish are higher in quality than the Japanese. Yield: round to dressed 78% to 80% or 55% to 65% loined or filleted.

Tilapia

Tilapia is a high-quality eating fish produced in large quantities in southern farms. This hardy fish grows well in poorer quality waters or conditions. Yield from skin-on, boneless fillets is about 40%.

Trout

A variety of sea trout are marketed. Canada ships some freshwater trout, but most comes from trout farms on the Snake River, Idaho, which average 8 to 10 oz drawn. Danish freshwater trout are good, but Japanese are not. Some Great Lakes trout are found on the Chicago market. Yield: 48% round to skin-on, boneless fillets.

Tuna

Tuna or albacore is also sold on the markets as bluefin, Kawakawa, bonitus, horse mackerel, skipjack, yellowfin, striped albacore, tunny, oriental, big-eye, or southern bluefin. It is mostly known as a canned item, but fresh or frozen is now available year round. Price is conditioned on whether the flesh is white, light, or dark-meated. Yield: 68% to 72% round to loins.

Turbot

Some fish called turbot are caught in our oceans, but the true turbot comes from the coasts of France and the English Channel. It is a flatfish, with somewhat a fine blend of halibut and flounder eating characteristics.

Whitefish

Most whitefish comes from the Great Lakes and Canada and may be called Lake Superior whitefish or shad. It averages about 4 lb in round form and with head on, dressed, is 2 to 3 lb.

Whiting

Whiting is a small fish caught in substantial quantities in the Atlantic. Some Gulf kings (large whiting) are marketed. Other names are kingfish, northern whiting, round head, sea mink, sea mullet, and surf whiting.

Shellfish[4]

Abalone

Abalone is the tenderized sliced pad of a large snail, found mostly in Southern California, but some few as far as Alaska. It cannot be shipped outside California, so most abalone marketed is Mexican, frozen in 5- or 10-lb boxes, each steak 3 to 4 oz. Japan ships frozen and canned abalone.

Clams

Atlantic clams are hardshells found from Cape Cod to Texas and may go by the names of quahaugs or chowder, littleneck and cherrystone, depending on size from largest to smallest. Cherrystones and littlenecks are often served raw. New England soft-shell clams are called trues, steamers, or long-necks. The Atlantic produces a soft-shell crab. Surf or skimmer clams are usually marketed shucked and minced, especially if from the Atlantic. Pacific hard-shell clams, called butter and littleneck, are found in the North Pacific. Pismo clams come from California while the soft-shells or razors come from Washington. Soft-shell clams from either the Atlantic or Pacific may go by the names of sand, nanynose, or maninose clams. The Pacific also produces a cockle clam. The production of aquaculture-grown clams is growing.

Purchase clams in the shell alive. A bushel should weigh 72 lb net. Specify cherrystone count per bushel 320 to 360 little neck 600 to 640, and chowder (quahaug); steamers 400 to 600 (55 lb up per bu). No size is specified for Pacific butter or littleneck clams except they must be mature clams. They are marketed in mixed sizes in 100-lb bags or 80-lb boxes.

Shucked (chilled) clams should come from sound, strictly fresh clams; dead clams (gapers) cannot be used. Potable water must be used in rinsing for not over 5 minutes, and such clams cannot be in water in processing over a total of 30 minutes. They should not have over 8% liquid on them. If frozen, they must reach 0°F in the center within 24 hours. Check shucked clams for foreign matter such as seaweed, or sand; only 4 shell pieces are permitted per quart and no more than 10 cut, torn, or broken clams. Color, odor, and flavor should be good and the texture firm, not soft. The clams should be delivered within 72 hours of shucking and not be over 38°F.

Conch

Conch comes from Caribbean waters. The meat is a creamy white and apt to be somewhat tough but full of rich flavor. It is most often served in a chowder where

---

[4]Shellfish specifications should state that they must come from approved areas under conditions set forth in Parts I and II of the cooperative Program for Certification of Interstate Shellfish Shippers of U.S. Public Health Service Publication No. 33.

it is chopped up and made less chewy. It can be sold live in the shell and as shucked meat.

Crab

Atlantic crabs are (1) blues, a high-quality crab caught in largest quantity around Chesapeake Bay, (2) rocks, a New England crab with brownish flesh, not white as in the blues, and (3) stones, caught around Florida. (When a stone crab is caught only one claw is taken and the crab returned to the water; with one claw the crab is able to survive and grow back a second one!) A soft-shell crab is a blue that has just lost its shell and the new one has not hardened.

Pacific crabs are stone and king, caught in Alaska, and Dungeness caught largely around Puget Sound waters. Only the claws of stone or king crabs are eaten. Minor crab are the California tanner crab and snow crab from Alaska. King crab is a large crab weighing 6 to 20 lb and measuring often 6 feet from one leg tip to the leg on the opposite side. Dungeness crab is sold alive in the shell, cooked in the shell, claw meat only, claw and body meat, and body meat only. Per dozen size is ocean 24 lb and Puget Sound 22 lb.

Blue crab Gulf market sizes are each: hard-shell ⅓ to ⅔ lb and soft-shell ⅛ to ½ lb. The New York market classifies 5½ in. diameter and up bluecrab as jumbo; large prime, 5–5½ in.; prime, 4½–5 in.; hotel prime, 4–4½ in.; large medium, 3½–4 in.; and medium, under 3½ in. Culls are all sizes. Purchase blue crab meat either fresh or pasteurized as lump (top quality), all-body chunk, flake (small pieces of body meat), and claw (lowest quality). The New York market divides lump quality into jumbo and flake or special of the back fin. Mixed must be over 50% lump and the remainder flake. Aquaculture crab is also appearing on the market now. Yields: Alaskan crab, 30% small claws and 50% whole crab; blue crab, 10% to 15%.

Crayfish and Spiny Lobster (Lobster Tails)

Crayfish are small crustaceans without two front claws, caught in inland streams and river inlets or lakes and ponds. They average 6 to 25 per lb. We import some.

Spiny or rock lobster is a large sea crayfish sold without the head and thorax as lobster tails, averaging 6 oz to 1 lb. Some picked, cooked spiny lobster meat is difficult to tell from true lobster meat. New Zealand lobster tails are considered best, but good tails also come from South Africa, Cuba, Florida, and Australia. Some aquaculture tails are appearing. The Laguna or Pacific lobster is a large crayfish sold with head on, weighing 10 oz to 2 lb.

Lobster

The common or true lobster has two large pincher claws near the head. New England produces most of our domestic catch, but we get considerable amounts from Canada. Lobsters are dark bluish green, brownish olive, or blackish brown uncooked, but change to a bright red on cooking. They are purchased alive, frozen, and sometimes cooked. Picked meat is also available.

A lobster with one claw is called a cull; it usually finds its way to picked, cooked meat. Boston grades live lobster jumbo 3 lb and up; large, 1½–2½ lb; quarter, 1¼–1½ lb; and chicken, ¾ to 1¼ lb. A chicken lobster is considered a portion. Lobsters cannot be caught in the breeding season. Immature lobsters are protected by law. Some lobster is also being produced by aquaculture. Yield: 50% from cleaned to picked meat.

Mussels

A mussel is a bivalve resembling an oyster but is razor shaped and about 2½ in. or more long. A bushel in the shell weighs from 45 to 55 lb and contains from 350 to 400 medium-sized mussels. Most come from the North Atlantic, but some fresh-water ones are sold on local markets. Aquaculture-grown mussels are also beginning to appear on markets.

Oysters

Fresh, live oysters are marketed all year. Atlantic oysters come from the Canadian Maritimes to Texas. Chesapeake bluepoints are an excellent white oyster. Long Is-land oysters run about 250 to 300 per bushel. Chincoteagues average 300 to 350 per bushel and Cape Cod oysters, those around Chatham being preferred, run 200 to 250 per bushel. A bushel should weigh about 62 to 67 lb net; light weights are charac-teristic at the season start and heavier ones later in the season.

The Pacific produces the Olympia (western) and Japanese (Pacific) oysters. A gallon of shucked Olympias contains 1,500 to 2,000 oysters. Pacific shucked oysters are graded small 96 to 144 per gal, medium 65 to 95 per gallon, and large 64 or fewer per gallon. Straights are ungraded for size.

Eastern oysters are sold in the shell by the dozen, peck, bushel, or crate or in gallons shucked, fresh, or frozen. Federal standards, per gallon, for shucked eastern oysters are extra large, 160 or fewer; large, 160–210; medium, 210–300; small, 300–500; and very small, over 500.

Shucked oysters should not be in freshwater in processing over 30 minutes and should not have a drainage more than 5%. A gallon should weigh not less than 8 lb net.

Table 9–8 summarizes some market information on oysters. A 3- to 4-oz oyster yields ¼ to ½ oz of meat.

Scallops

Scallops are the adductor muscle or "eye" that opens and closes the shell of a large mollusk. Sea scallops are also called New Bedford scallops and run 100 to 170 per gal. Bay scallops are caught in shallower waters; they are younger and smaller and are considered of better quality. Scallops can be purchased in the shell but usually are sold as clear meat, fresh or frozen. The color of bay scallops is creamy white, light tan, or pinkish white. They run 480 to 600 per gallon. Alaska and other Atlantic waters produce scallops, but the best are thought to come from around New Eng-land. Aquaculture scallops are available on the market.

Shrimp

American waters produce only 200 million pounds of shrimp of the average 860 mil-lion pounds we consume a year; the rest is imported, a considerable amount as aqua-culture grown. Most of our domestic shrimp come from Gulf waters. White and pink varieties are considered better than browns and the deep-water reds. The Pacific coast and north Atlantic produce small shrimp that are used locally and are frequently canned.

Raw or cooked fresh or frozen are available, mostly the latter available in the shell, headless in the shell and as peeled and deveined or not deveined shrimp.

Table 9-8
Market sizes of oysters.

Eastern Oysters				Pacific or Japanese Oysters
Boston Market		**New York Market**		**Seattle Market**
LIVE IN THE SHELL				
Large	500 per bbl	Box	150 per bu	By the sack priced by the pound; 80-lb per sack; average 200 per sack for smaller sizes
Medium	700–750	Medium	200	
Small	900–1050	Half shell	325*	
Extra small	1050–1200	Blue point	400	
SHUCKED PER GALLON				
Count	135–160	Count	160 or fewer	Grades
Select	180–230	Extra select	160–210	A (large) 40–64
Standard	300–350	Select	210–300	B (medium) 65–80
		Standard	300–500	C (medium) 81–96
				D (small) 97–120
				E (small) 121–144
				F (extra small) over 144

*Also called *Long Island,* and may be specified 250 to 300 per bu.

Shelled shrimp are usually glazed; watch for excessive glazing. Raw shrimp are one count smaller after peeling and then another count smaller on cooking.

Sizing of shrimp is per pound and price is related to size.

Table 9–9 gives generally accepted market sizing.

The Gulf markets size shrimp with heads on as large, under 18 per lb, medium, 18–35 per lb; and small, over 35 per lb. The New York and Chicago markets size per pound as shown in Table 9–10.

There are about 5 more large shrimp per pound in the shell than unshelled shrimp. Thus, if the count in the shell were 21 per lb, the count would be 26 per lb of shelled shrimp. Cooking loss in the shell to cooked peeled and deveined is about 50%.

Miscellaneous Marine Products

Sea turtles run from 2 to 100 lb, alive or dressed; freshwater diamondback terrapins are usually sold alive as cows, 1½ to 2 lb, heifers 1 lb, and bulls ½ to 1 lb. Turtle meat is purchased out of the shell raw or cooked. Fresh sea turtles and terrapin are available June through October.

Live frogs run from ½ to 1 lb each, but most operations purchase legs and saddles (lower back with legs) fresh or frozen. Sizes per pound are extra large, 2–3; large, 4–5; medium, 9–12. Florida and Louisiana legs are high quality, and the Japanese generally are as well. On the market, frogs may be called bull, common, or grass.

Eels come live, dressed, and skinned or smoked, and are available fresh or frozen throughout the year; most appear fresh in the fall. Most are imports and aquaculture grown. Round form sizes are large, 2–5 lb; medium, 1–2 lb; and small, under 1 lb. Other names are Anguilla, Capitone, sandboy, sea eel, and shoestring.

Snails are usually sold alive in the shell or canned. Large live snails run about 32 per pound. Cuttlefish (sepia) average ½ to ¾ lb in round form. Squid run 5 to 6

Table 9-9
Usual sizing of shrimp on most markets.

Commercial Name*	Type I, Raw, Chilled or Frozen, Not Peeled	Peeled, Deveined	Type II, Cooked, Chilled or Frozen, Peeled, Deveined
Colossal	15 or fewer	19 or fewer	30 or fewer
Extra jumbo	16–20	20–25	31–40
Jumbo	21–25	26–31	41–60
Extra large	26–30	32–38	61–90
Large	31–35	39–44	91–125
Medium large	36–42	45–53	126 up
Medium	43–50	54–63	
Small	51–60	64–75	
Extra small	61 and over	76 and over	

*These commercial names apply to Type I only and not Type II. The market also classifies shrimp 10 or under per lb as extra colossal and that over 70 per lb as tiny.

Table 9-10
Market sizes of shrimp on the Chicago and New York markets.

Chicago Market		New York Market
Extra jumbo	Fewer than 15	Buyers often purchase by count per pound as under 15, 15–20, 21–25, 26–30, 31–35, 36–40, 41–45, 46–50, 41–60, and over 60; other size terms may be used, small running 41 to over 60/lb and medium 31–40 lb.
Jumbo	16–20	
Large	21–25	
Large–medium	26–30	
Medium	31–42	
Small	43–65	
Very small or bait	More than 66	

per lb in round form. Calimari is a small squid running 2 to 8 oz. Octopus are usually sold in round form; small ones run ¾ lb up.

Canned Products

More canned marine items are consumed than fresh or other type, but consumption is dropping as the popularity of fresh and frozen products increases. Look for neatness of pack, unbroken items, and freedom from bruises, brown blood spots, cracks, blood, entrails, scales, and other defects. Flesh color and liquid should be clear and typical for variety. Unevenly colored flesh or that bearing pink or red streaks is undesirable. A pleasant flavor and odor, free from rancidity, acrid taste, or spoilage should be evident; texture should be firm but not fibrous. Table 9–11 summarizes some information buyers may want to know in purchasing canned products.

Table 9-11

Canned products.

Item	Available as	Remarks
Anchovies	Fillets, rolled with or without filling, or paste	Small Mediterranean fish, 5 to 6 per oz per fillet
Clams	Whole or minced (chopped) in No. 3 cylinders or No. 10 cans	Drained weight should be 45%; liquor should be milky but clear; meat must be tender, flavorful, and free of objectionable flavors
Crab	Regular or vacuum pack and some pastes are packed, all in 3-, 6½-, 7½-, 15-, and 16-oz cans	Should be somewhat free of shell and cartilage, and somewhat firm but not tough or stringy.
Herring (Pilchard)	In tomato sauce, liquid, or mustard sauce	
Lobster	Same can sizes and packs as crab above	
Oysters	Various size cans	Not the equal of the fresh
Roe	Various sizes often in kilo weights when fresh; canned in various sizes	Only true roe of sturgeon can be called caviar; others are labeled with the fish name; imitation from whitefish, shad, salmon, or others; some are dyed black or red (see Figure 9–5).
Salmon	In 4-, 8-, 16-, or 64-oz cans; dietetic packs not more than 60 mg of sodium per 100 gr of drained meat	Best as large body pieces; ½- or 1-lb cans should contain not more than 3 pieces plus a patch, 4-lb, not more than 12 pieces and a patch.
Table 9–11A summarizes buyer information for the purchase of canned salmon.		
Sardines	Norwegian imports (silt or brisling) in 3¼-oz cans; a variety of herring. California pilchard in 15-oz cans.	Most packed in oil; 8 sardines per can. In oil, or mustard or tomato sauce; these sardines are coarser in texture and stronger in flavor than small ones.
	Maine in 3¼-oz cans/100 per case; some 15-oz cans packed. Maine grades its canned sardines.	Small herring, averaging 5 to 6/can; graded fancy, extra standard, and standard.
Shrimp	(See Table 9–11C.)	
Tuna	(See Table 9–11B.) packed in vegetable or olive oil or water; dietetic (low sodium) not more than 50 mg sodium per 100 g; drained weight is 63–64%.	Cannot be bonito; some good Italian *tonno* available. Solid (fancy) must be large pieces; chunk is a mixture of large pieces with 50% passing through a ½-in. screen; flakes are small pieces; grated is granular. The whiter the meat, the higher the quality and price.

خاویار آستر درجه یك

قوطیهای فاقد پلمب و برچسب شرکت سهامی شیلات ایران

از درجه اعتبار ساقط است

Caviar grain Ossetra Premiere qualité
Les boîtes non plombées et sans l'étiqutte spéciale de
la Société Sahami Chilate Iran. ne soet pas valables

Figure 9-5
Some genuine fresh Beluga (Iranian) caviar comes sealed with a metal tag as shown at the top. The label is both Arabic and French.

Table 9-11A
Market types of canned salmon.

Type Salmon	Flesh Color	Flesh Texture
King (chinook)	Light red to almost white	Moderately firm to soft
Red (sockeye or blueback)	Deep red to deep orange	Very firm to soft
Silver (coho)	Red to orange-red or light pink	Moderately firm to soft
Pink	Light pink with orange shading to yellow	Moderately firm to soft
Chum (keta)	Pink to light yellow	Moderately firm to firm

Table 9-11B
Types of canned tuna and can sizes marketed.

Can Size	Type	Net Contents	Drained Weight	Can Size	Type	Net Contents	Drained Weight
211 × 109	Solid	3.50	2.25	401 × 206	Solid	13.00	8.76
	Chunks	3.40	1.98		Chunks	12.50	7.68
	Flakes	3.40	1.98		Flakes	12.50	7.68
	Grated	3.45	2.00		Grated	11.75	7.76
307 × 113	Solid	7.00	4.47	603 × 408	Solid	64.00	43.20
	Chunks	6.50	3.92		Chunks	60.00	37.90
	Flakes	6.25	3.92		Flakes	60.00	37.90
	Grated	6.25	3.96		Grated	59.00	38.30

Table 9-11C
Canned shrimp marketed.

Type Pack	Can Size	Drained Weight (oz)	Number in the can*						Maximum Weight of Defective Shrimp (oz)‡
			1	2	3	4	5	6	
Wet	307 × 201	5½	15	22	31	56	106	†	½
Wet	307 × 208	6¾	19	26	38	68	129	†	⅝
Dry	307 × 208	6¼	19	26	38	68	129	†	⅝
Wet	211 × 400	7	19	27	39	71	133	†	⅝
Dry	211 × 400	6½	19	27	39	71	133	†	⅝
Wet	307 × 400	11¼	32	44	63	115	216	†	1⅛
Dry	307 × 400	10½	32	44	63	115	216	†	1
Wet	307 × 409	13	36	50	71	130	244	†	1¼
Wet	401 × 411	19	52	74	105	191	359	†	1⅞
Wet	502 × 510	38	105	148	210	382	718	†	3 ¾

*Trade sizes are 1, colossal; 2, jumbo; 3, large; 4, medium; 5, small; and 6, tiny or broken.
†There are no maximum or minimum number for tiny or broken.
‡Defective shrimp are those that are broken, improperly deveined, and so on.

Cured Fish

Cod, halibut, trout, whitefish, chub, sablefish, and others are salted and smoked. Mackerel, herring, cod, ling cod, and haddock are salted. Finnan haddie is lightly smoked and salted haddock. It is best to specify "current pack" for cured fish because some products deteriorate with age.

Best Buys

It takes a smart and knowledgeable buyer to know when there is a best buy in the fish or shellfish market. It is a highly dynamic market and can fluctuate rapidly. The buyer needs to keep on top of what is happening and where the market is going.

It is extremely important to know what the yields are for whole, drawn, dressed, fillet, or other products. Wastes can be large and what may seem like a good price becomes an expensive one when scales, skin, head, fins, entrails, and other wastes are calculated, not to mention the labor needed to do this job. Thus, knowing losses in preparation can help a buyer determine quickly which form it is best to purchase.

There are often possibilities for substitution. If the menu includes sole, a buyer has several choices of different kinds of sole, with quality and other considerations being factors as well as cost. Also the possibility of using a frozen product rather than a fresh one may lead to a best buy. With some fish processors using sophisticated methods of catching, processing, and freezing some fishery products, the quality of frozen products has improved to a point that substitution for the fresh product cannot be detected. In a recent test, a panel of top chefs were served cooked samples of a frozen fish and the same fish fresh. They were asked if they could detect which was frozen and which was fresh. Their judgments showed they could not. Also, when they were asked which they preferred, there was no significant difference between the two.

This chapter has presented a number of waste and other factors that can help buyers evaluate the best buys. Using these data in a manner shown in previous chapters for other food categories can help them make their buying decisions. It is dangerous in this market to make quick judgments. Careful analysis of offerings, prices, quality, and other factors is necessary to arrive at a good decision.

SUMMARY

The term *marine products* covers fish, shellfish, and other aquatic life. Our consumption of these is rising although this rise has been slowed because of public concern over the sanitation of some of them. There are five major markets for fish in this country: Boston, New York, Gulf (New Orleans and others), Seattle, and Chicago, the latter selling mostly freshwater fish. Most food services purchase their marine products from local distributors who buy from one or more of these major markets. However, direct marketing is increasing and some large chains that use huge quantities may purchase that way.

Compared with the meat market, the marine market is relatively unregulated. Only processed products are subject to inspection leaving about 80% of the market fairly uncontrolled. The FDA and Commerce Department are the controlling bodies and recently the FDA set up regulations moving processed fish into the HCAAP inspection area. Public Health does regulate the raw shellfish market to some extent by inspecting beds from where such products are taken to see that the waters are uncontaminated. The grades for processed products are A, B, and C.

Upon receipt, fish should be not over 40°F, firm, with tightly adhering scales, bright, full eyes, bones tightly attached to the flesh, a sweet, ocean odor, and a bright sheen to the body with no sliminess. Shellfish preferably should be purchased alive. If so they should show evidence of life. The odor should be sweet and the shells should have a bright, clean sheen. If not purchased alive, the color should be natural, the odor good with no sliminess. Off-color, sliminess, a yeasty, musty, or ammonia odor, excessive bruising, loose scales or protruding bones, a soft, flabby flesh, dull sunken eyes, and other such defects should be cause for rejection. Care should be taken of received products by moving them rapidly to proper storage. Watch for *honeycombing*—small indentations—or *voiding*—hollow spots—on frozen fish. Frozen products when thawed should conform to the standards cited for fresh. The market forms for fish are *whole* or *round, drawn, dressed* or *pan-dressed, steaks, sticks, fillets,* and *butterfly fillets.* Some fish and shellfish are glazed before going into storage; *glazing* is coating the product with a thin coating of ice. This ice layer protects the fish from dehydration and helps to preserve the quality.

Buyers should know the waste in preparing fish and shellfish for service. Some may show a high loss in head, viscera, scaling, skinning, etc. It is not unusual for less than 50% of the purchased product to be edible. Fat fish broil or bake well; lean fish does not and needs moist cooking or cooking in fat.

Marine products should be stored at 32°F. It is best to store fish on layers of ice with a plastic cover over them. Shellfish should similarly be stored layered on ice, but should have a plastic sheet between them and the ice as well as over them. Frozen products should be stored at −10°F or lower.

Specifications for marine products should state the amount, the kind, the market form, the style, packing, processing, etc. A wide variety of high-quality canned and cured fish products are on the market.

Kinds of marine products are discussed so buyers will have some idea of what the various market offerings are. Illustrations of most of the fish products sold in this country appear in Appendix H.

REVIEW QUESTIONS

1. What type regulation does the marine products market get? Do you think this is adequate?
2. What should a buyer look for on receiving fresh fish? Frozen fish? Live fish?
3. How should fresh fish and shellfish be stored? Frozen products?
4. How would you cook a fish high in fat? Low in fat?
5. What are the market forms of fish?
6. Write a specification for a marine product.
7. What is aquaculture and what are your opinions about the quality of products produced by it?
8. From whom does the average food service purchase its marine products?
9. If a buyer is offered a fresh fish or fillets from the same kind of fish by a purveyor, what should the buyer consider before purchasing the fresh fish and getting from them the fillets needed for the menu?
10. Why do we think marine products are more healthful to eat than meats or poultry?
11. Do marine products cause more food poisoning over meats and other food? If so, how much more?

KEY WORDS AND CONCEPTS

aquaculture   butterfly fillet

bottom fish   certificate number

chunks	pan-dressed
drawn	red tide
dressed	round
farm fish	single fillet
fillet	steaks
flatfish	sticks
glazing	*urimis*
honeycombing	voids
market forms	whole

SPECIFICATION EXAMPLES

Shrimp

1. Shrimp, Type II, PDQ
2. 60 lb or 1 case
3. XYZ Brand or equal
4. $\frac{26}{30}$ size, packed in 5-lb lots, 12/case; 6% glazing allowed
5. Priced per pound
6. Shall be Caribbean pinks; evidence of spoilage, freezer burn, or other defects will be cause for rejection of the product.

(*Note:* Type II means frozen, PDQ means peeled, deveined, and quick frozen; since shrimp are not graded, the buyer is purchasing by brand, adding "or equal" to allow other brands to compete; brown shrimp could also be specified instead of pinks; browns are not as desirable because of color but there is no difference in quality, and the yield PDQ is better for browns. Thus, the price is usually a bit, but not a great deal, different.)

Sole

1. Sole, Dover (Pacific), fresh, whole
2. 45 lb
3. Highest quality, fresh-caught, Puget Sound sole
4. Deliver ice packed in standard wooden boxes
5. Priced per pound
6. Shall average 3 to 3½ lb, ± 1 oz.

(*Note:* This is a high-quality sole available in the Seattle market; the 45 lb is an estimate of the steward to yield 50 to 60 6-oz portions of fillet.)

Clams in Shell

1. Clams, littleneck, fresh
2. 2 bu
3. High-quality New England clams
4. Littlenecks shall be 500 to 640 per bu; a bushel shall weigh not less than 75 lb gross (72 lb net)
5. Priced per bushel
6. Clams should be vital and alive on delivery; excessive sand will be cause for rejection.

Trout

1. Trout, brook, fresh, pan-dressed, head on
2. 100 trout
3. Highest-quality, Snake River trout, XYZ brand or equal
4. Each trout should be 12 oz $\pm$ ½ oz, layer-packed individually wrapped in air-exhausted polyethylene wrap.
5. Priced by the pound
6. Must be Snake River fresh brook trout; no other trout will be accepted.

Halibut

1. Halibut, frozen, chicken
2. 50 lb
3. High-quality western halibut from current catch
4. Shall be 10 lb each without glaze—glaze to be not over 6% of total weight; weight tolerance $\pm$ 4 oz.
5. Priced per pound
6. Shall be drawn, headless.

CHAPTER 10

Fresh Produce

Landing Tropical Fruits at Burling Slip, New York. Drawn by A. R. Waud. From Harper's Weekly. (President Grant was in Office cc. 1869–1877.) From the Louis Szwathmary collection, Culinary Archives and Museum, Johnson and Wales University, used by permission of Dr. Szwathmary and Johnson and Wales University.

Chapter Objectives

1. To discuss the nature of the fresh produce market and its regulation, and how fruits and vegetables are prepared for the market.

2. To cover procedures usually followed by food services in specifying, receiving, and storing fruits and vegetables.

3. To cover the quality and purchase factors important in the purchase of the major, and briefly summarize them for minor, fruits and vegetables used by food services.

INTRODUCTION

The produce market is one of our most dynamic and complex, taking a significant share of the dollars many food services spend for food. It is a most important market and it continues to grow in importance as people seek more healthful food. It is one of the most challenging markets in which buyers operate. In 1990 it was estimated that our fresh produce market put more than $4 billion worth of items on our tables.

REGULATION

Considerable regulation of the produce market occurs. States and municipalities and associations have their own regulations, but only federal laws with national application are discussed here.

Agricultural Commodities Act (1938)

The **Agricultural Commodities Act** was passed to provide market stability by requiring fresh produce agents dealing in wholesale or job lots to be licensed and to observe certain fair business practices. Growers may be assigned quotas so an orderly market flow can occur. Low-quality produce can be withheld from the market to prevent it from depressing prices. The act facilitated market confidence and gave a more stable market; quality and marketing procedures were improved.

Agricultural Marketing Act (1953, 1957)

The **Agricultural Marketing Act** orders the Department of Agriculture to create various agencies to establish standards and grades for foods. Thus, the Fresh Fruit and Vegetable Division has been delegated to function in the areas of standards, grading, and other control measures for produce. Today over 160 grading standards have been established for fresh produce alone.

Other Regulations

The Food and Drug Act's provisions for sanitation and plant operation, standards of identity, labeling of packages, and other provisions in this law apply to produce. Under the labeling law of 1990, prepackaged produce must be labeled with nutritional information about the contents. The use of pesticides and other chemicals comes under the GRAS and other regulations. The Public Health's regulation regarding food sanitation must also be met.

THE NATURE OF THE PRODUCE MARKET

The total quantity of fruits and vegetables consumed per capita has been increasing. However, this is not made up by a general overall rise, but a rise in some items, while the consumption of others has fallen. Thus, the fresh potato market has fallen off, but the total amount of potatoes per capita has increased because of the large increase in the consumption of processed potato products. While the consumption of fresh fruits and vegetables has been rising, the consumption of their processed counterparts has been decreasing.

Nutritional Values

Undoubtedly one of the main reasons why fresh produce has increased in popularity is because people are beginning to understand that fresh vegetables and fruits are health-promoting foods. They are high in vitamin content. One serving of some gives a day's need for either vitamin A or C. A number contribute valuable amounts of some of the B vitamins as well as others. Vegetables are also good suppliers of minerals, contributing significant amounts of iron, potassium, calcium, phosphorus, and others. In comparison to some other foods, they are low in calories and fat. Cholesterol is not found in fruits and vegetables, only in foods of animal origin.

Items like legumes, potatoes, squash, and corn contribute significant amounts of complex carbohydrates, which are the form of carbohydrates that are healthiest. Produce also can be a good source of protein. A meal of baked beans and brown bread can provide as much good quality protein as a similar amount of meat. This is also called an "adequate" protein. Produce can also furnish adequate amounts of fiber, the nondigestible substance we need in our diets to promote digestion and elimination. To have good nutrition, it is recommended that persons have at least four good servings a day of some kind of produce.

A Dynamic Market

The produce market can change overnight. A storm in the California lettuce-growing area may destroy a whole crop, and what was a liberal supply suddenly becomes an extremely scarce item with soaring prices. A frost in Florida may do the same. Droughts and other unfavorable conditions can suddenly make drastic changes in both price and supply. In one year a supply can disappear. In 1975 no Texas fresh peas came to market. Canners and frozen food packers had contracted for the entire crop. Likewise, market gluts can appear almost as suddenly. A country producing a large amount of product may view the American market as a favorable place to sell it, and almost overnight the U.S. market is flooded with imports such as strawberries, citrus fruits, melons, peaches, yams, corn, or other fruits and vegetables.

The produce market is also changing rapidly because of technological advances. We can determine now the sugar and starch in fruits and vegetables by shooting laser beams into the item. The flavor and freshness is much improved with better packaging and controlled atmospheric treatment. Not only are we resorting to genetic engineering to develop better appearing, sweeter, and more nutritious produce, but we are also using it to produce items that last longer. Corn, peas, and some other vegetables rapidly change their sugar to starch and lose their fresh flavor. Genetic engineering is changing this, giving these items a longer "fresh" life. Processed fresh produce like chopped lettuce, peeled vegetables, sectioned grapefruit, and others are finding ready markets, changing some aspects of the industry; food services use 70% of what is produced in this new kind of item. The USDA now has established grading standards for cutup produce.

When fruits and vegetables are harvested, they contain what is called "field heat," which, if not quickly removed, can cause a loss of quality. The old way of removing this was refrigeration, which was slow and not too efficient for large masses of product. Then, we introduced **hydrocooling,** cooling with ice or water, but this is expensive and not too efficient, as it requires wetting the items, which was not always good for them (see Figure 10–1). A new dry method, called **vacucooling,** was introduced which was quick and efficient (see Figure 10–2). It works by putting a large lot of produce, such as a truckload or carload, into a tightly sealed chamber

Figure 10-1
Hydrocooling to cool produce with finely chopped ice. (Courtesy USDA.)

and drawing a vacuum, which induces rapid evaporation using heat from the produce. Blast tunnel cooling is also being used to cool some produce. It is a low-cost method and processes larger quantities in a given time.

Better shipping is also changing the produce market. The time it takes produce to get from its place of growth to the market is shortening. Harvest, cleaning, trimming, packaging, and even weighing are being done right in the field. After cooling, produce is loaded on controlled-temperature and controlled-humidity trucks and moved quickly to markets.

Packaging is also causing change. We have improved packaging, using stronger and more protective containers that permit better shipping and handling; film wraps and other kinds of wraps are used to hold freshness, color, and appearance. Film-wrapped cauliflower stays fresh and whiter much longer. Polyethylene wraps delay ripening or deterioration in some products. Air is flushed out of produce in wraps and inert gas like nitrogen or carbon dioxide introduced. This reduces action by the oxygen in air on the produce. Salads packed into 30-lb pouches, sodium sulfite free, now hold the produce in good condition for a week. We are using more flexible packaging, which helps to put more into an equal space. Bacteriastatic wraps are being used to lower bacterial growth. We expect in the near future to see packaging approved that will help reduce bacterial growth in nonsterilized produce. Buyers

Figure 10–2
A vacucooling chamber where produce is placed to lose its field heat rapidly because moisture evaporates and takes heat from produce. (Courtesy USDA.)

may hear the terms "CAP" and "MAP" used to describe packaging. These are abbreviations for **controlled atmosphere packaging** and **modified atmosphere packaging,** respectively. They effectively can bring better produce to market.

The produce market changes rapidly because new kinds or new varieties of produce suddenly appear (see Figure 10–3). Within the last 10 years, the number of fruits, largely tropical or Asian, offered on our markets has grown tremendously. U.S. growers, seeing a good market, also join in and suddenly an item like kiwi fruit that once was scarce and shipped in from New Zealand is heavily produced in Califor-

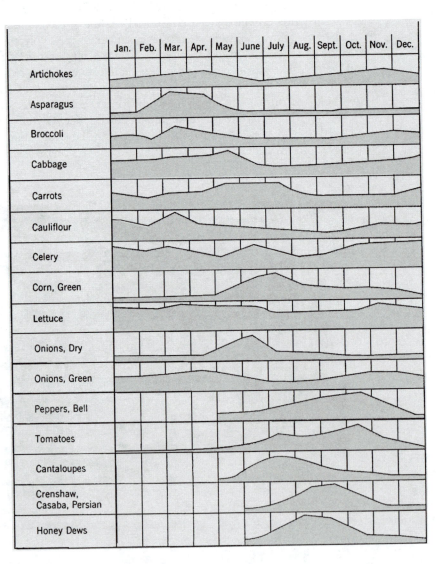

Figure 10–3
Main seasons for some fruits and vegetables.

nia. It is difficult to keep up with the new and changing varieties of apples that each year appear on the market. At one time, the globe onion ruled the market and then, in one year, the grano variety challenged it and now the two share about equally what was once the globe's sole market. In the last few years a large number of baby vegetables have appeared on the market. Besides being a novelty, they are often more tender and more flavorful than their larger counterparts. It is even possible today to get molded fruits and vegetables. This produce is placed into a mold when young and then allowed to develop inside, taking the interior shape of the mold.

Preprepared produce also is causing significant changes. Some operations have almost wiped out their produce preparation sections by purchasing preprepared kinds. The elimination of the waste that had to be handled, besides the reduction in equipment, space, refrigeration, and labor, has made operators see the value in such purchases. It is possible today not only to get potatoes, onions, carrots, and other produce peeled, but also such items as peeled grapefruit and oranges. The kind of prepared salad items on the market today has increased considerably. As labor becomes scarcer and more costly, we can expect to see this trend increase.

Perishability

Fresh produce is a living organism and loses quality rapidly if not handled properly. It respires just as we do. Elevated temperatures speed these respiratory changes; sugar changes to starch, and other enzymatic reactions result in a loss of flavor, appearance, texture, and nutritional values. Each 18-degree Fahrenheit rise doubles respiration and deteriorative change. Cool temperatures and good ventilation are required, the ventilation to remove the spent atmosphere and to bring in new so the organism can "breathe." Fresh produce stored without air to circulate around it "suffocates" and spoils easily. (See Appendix B for desirable storage temperatures for produce.)

Oxygen from the air combines with the carbon in produce, developing heat, carbon dioxide, and moisture. This heat can build up in tightly packed items and cause much more rapid deterioration to occur. Quick removal to cold storage after delivery and loosening tight packs can solve this problem. For example, fresh corn on the cob is often delivered in 50-lb. bags. Opening these bags and spreading the cobs out helps to dispense the heat, preserving the sweetness and texture of the kernels. Some items, such as tomatoes, bell peppers, cucumbers, bananas, avocados, and pineapples, should not receive cold storage.

In ripening, produce emits ethylene, a gas necessary for the ripening process. Some fruits are even placed in special containers that confine the ethylene gas and speed ripening. However, even small amounts of ethylene gas can cause deterioration in leafy vegetables and flowers. A potassium filter (marketed by Shamrock Foods of Denver) has been developed that absorbs ethylene gas, maintaining the quality and prolonging the shelf life of produce.

Some produce gives off odors which can be absorbed by nearby products. Appendix D gives information on these odor-producing items and their proper storage. Separate storage is not always required. Wrapping the odor-producing items is an effective alternative to making new storage arrangements.

Oil-based, flexible plastic wraps are less desirable than resin-based plastics. The latter are rigid containers that can be utilized in the form of mobile plastic carts. Lettuce and other items will keep well and crisp up when stored in carts with tight-fitting covers.

It is important that buyers understand the time that various kinds of produce can hold before deterioration sets in. High waste can occur when buyers overbuy on items and they are left to decay and must be thrown out. It also should be known that ordering certain items at a specified degree of ripeness controls their shelf life. Thus, ordering bananas full ripe gives little or no room for extending use. They must be used within a day of delivery. Ordering them turning ripe gives five to seven days at room temperature before having to use them. Ripened strawberries and other berries should be used as soon as possible—maximum life under refrigeration may be three days. (Tables in Appendix B give the average storage life of much fresh produce.)

Perishable products need proper handling. Some can be easily damaged. Small bruises can grow into decay. After harvest, fruits and vegetables are dependent on the moisture stored in them. Preventing as much moisture loss as possible helps preserve the item. Leave all leafy vegetables connected to the butt so they can absorb moisture. Unless used quickly, loose leaves become a lost item. Do not trim off feeder roots on radishes, carrots, green ions, spinach, etc. These aid in feeding moisture back into the item. Remove yellow, heavily wilted or discolored parts; they only rob the item of moisture. Clean and trim and store as quickly as possible.

It is possible to reintroduce moisture into vegetables by soaking them in tepid (70° to 90°F) water for two to four minutes because warm water opens the pores. Cold water closes them. However, do not soak iceberg lettuce this way. Place it butt down in a tray or sink about 2 in. deep in tepid water. After vegetables have had this treatment, shake or drain off all water and place under refrigeration to crisp. It takes about 24 hours to develop maximum crisping. If plastic bags are used, make sure they allow moisture to drain off. Again, pack loosely so the items can breathe.

Market Variation

Another problem buyers encounter in the produce market is its wide dispersion and the fact that local areas tend to set their own practices. Product terminology can differ; packaging can also. Buyers should know what different market terms mean and what kind of packaging to expect. The same fruit or vegetable may be marketed in boxes or **lugs** on the West coast, in **bushel baskets** in Chicago, and in **bushel hampers** in New York.

The federal government has tried to standardize many of these variations, but has only done so in a major way in grading and, even here, has had to make some allowances. Standards are purposely broad to enable variations in product according to growing area to be included under one standard. Thus, Western peaches, Michigan peaches, and Georgia peaches differ in many ways. Yet, the federal standard is broad enough to include them all. Trying to get one set of grade standards which would include all varieties of apples on the market was also a challenge. However, when it came to citrus fruit, the federal government had to set up separate standards for Florida citrus, for Texas citrus, and for California–Arizona citrus.

With the rapidity with which new kinds of fruits and vegetables or new varieties of old ones appear, the federal government is also pressed to keep up with standards and grades for these products.

Seasons and Place of Origin

The season of the year can make a big difference in what is on the market and its quality. In the winter, imports appear. These are ungraded. They may also vary in sizing and quality from our own products. In the summer, fall, and winter, different apples, pears, and other kinds of items are on the market. Some are only suitable for limited uses, while others may be suitable for a variety of them. Thus, a summer apple like the gravenstein is excellent for pies and for applesauce but poor for baking. It breaks up. A winter delicious is excellent for eating raw or using raw in salads, but it ends up as a withered, dried up product as a baker and hence is a poor product for pies.

A part of this difference in season may be because items come from different areas and vary. California iceberg lettuce is considered the best because of the firm heads and high yield each head gives. The marshall variety of strawberry grown in western Washington near Lake Washington is widely known for its superior color, flavor, and texture. Buyers are willing to pay more for Florida oranges and grapefruit because they know the quality and the higher juice yield are worth it. Colorado melons also command market attention. Climate, soil, and other growing conditions usually account for these differences. However, to do the best job, buyers have to know where to get the most desirable items and it takes a lot of learning and constant updating just to keep up.

To ensure the right item is obtained, buyers may specify the growing region from which produce is to come. Thus, to ensure that heavy, solid heads of lettuce are obtained, the buyer may ask for Salinas Valley, California, lettuce. This avoids receiving the more loosely formed lettuce heads which often come from other growing areas. Specifying the net weight in the package along with the size gives further assurance.

Preference for a particular producing region may change with seasons. A buyer may specify locally grown cucumbers in the summer but change to hothouse-grown in the fall, winter, and spring months. Or, as fall fades into winter, a buyer may change the place of origin for cantaloupes from Colorado to Mexico.

PURCHASING PRODUCE

A lot of information must be available to the purchasing agent to satisfactorily purchase produce. Assuming that the exact product needed is known, the buyer needs to know where it can be obtained and in what packaging, sizing, condition, price, and when it can be delivered. Lead time must be given when placing any order. The following discussion therefore relates to some of the major facets of this phase of the purchasing task.

Purchase Procedures

Because of the perishability of much produce, almost daily ordering must occur. Usually one or two days lead time is required. It is often difficult to purchase a lot of perishable produce by bid, unless some modification of the procedure is made. (See the earlier discussion on bid purchasing.) Call sheet buying is perhaps the most suitable and is most often used. Many times cost-plus is another satisfactory way.

Order amounts should be quantified to the amount needed to adequately meet serving needs, but not be in too much excess, if perishable. This amount may not coincide with the quantity that has to be purchased because purchase units do not break down to that amount. Thus, if 42 pint boxes of strawberries are needed, this is 3½ crates. Purveyors may have a policy of selling only whole purchase units, so four crates must be ordered, a half crate over needs. If the production department is informed, this overage may be planned to be used with some other menu item. Amounts of many items must also be guided by their shelf life. Ordering 10 crates of strawberries with plans to hold the overage for a week for another party would not be good ordering practice. The strawberries might be badly deteriorated by the time they are needed the second time.

Receiving

The perishability of produce means that its receiving must be speeded up and items sent without delay to storage or directly into production. Examine for grade, amount, condition, damage, rot, size, packaging, fill equal to facing, and net weight of contents as specified. Any other factors noted in the specification should be checked. Much fresh produce can easily be infested with rodents, cockroaches, or other pests. Check on receiving for this. During days of high heat or freezing, delivery trucks need either to be temperature controlled. Check temperatures and humidity. Too dry a truck may result in serious wilting. Any items that should be received frozen but are thawed or partially so normally should be refused.

Check for freshness and lack of blemishes or damage. A bright, uniform color typical of the product should be evident. Check for firmness and crispness, degree of ripeness, uniformity of size, etc. Watch for slime or excessive moisture. Precut items such as salad greens, cabbage for cole slaw, and others lose moisture and become slimy as they deteriorate. One look at a bag of such an item gives an indication of the state of freshness of such products. Remember also that storage can change the ripening process and that some products such as bananas, tomatoes, etc., should not be stored under refrigeration. Storage should provide the right temperature, the right humidity, the right amount of light, and separation of items. See the storage charts in Appendix B for more complete information on storage. Date all packages before they go into storage.

Suppliers

For the most part, purveyor selection factors discussed previously should dictate the selection of purveyors of produce. Most produce purchasing is done by phone; a small amount may be done through salespeople, computer, or bid. It is sometimes difficult to get suppliers to use bid buying because of the difficulty of predicting prices in advance. If bid buying is done, some type of escalation clause is often included so prices can be adjusted in case of significant market changes.

Quality or Grades

Wholesale grades for produce are **U.S. Extra Fancy, Fancy, No. 1, No. 2,** and **No. 3. A combination grade** may be seen which is a combination of grades. **Field run** is ungraded produce, just as it was picked.

Normally, the grade most food services use will be U.S. No. 1, top of the grade; but the need sometimes dictates a different grade be obtained. Sometimes a quality above U.S. No. 1 is wanted, but seldom under it. In some cases, a grade for a product needed may not exist and then buyers will have to indicate the quality desired in words such as *highest quality, top market quality, good quality,* etc. Included might be some few words of condition of the product. To be sure the grade is what is wanted, buyers may add in a specification, "The grade of the product upon delivery shall be that named in the specification." Not unusually, a specification might indicate quality by brand such as "Bud" lettuce, "Blue Goose" mushrooms. This is an approved method when the buyer knows the brand.

Names

Unfortunately there is a lack of standardization of names of produce in markets. Different names are often used even in the same market. In as much as possible, all market names used in this text are given for produce in the discussion that follows on individual fruits and vegetables.

Counts, Packaging, and New Weights

Produce is sized and certain sizes are preferred for a standard portion, such as 32 size grapefruit, of which a half makes a good portion. If produce is not packed in the standard package which holds a particular size, the count may be anything the container holds. Thus, tomatoes are sized by the number of rows and columns that can be packed in a standard lug. A lug packed with what is called a **5 × 6 pack** (medium size) will hold five columns of tomatoes with each row holding six tomatoes. (The lug holds two layers so the buyer knows that 60 tomatoes will be obtained.) However, if a purveyor sends an apple box, not a lug, of 5 × 6 tomatoes, there is no established count guarantee. Normally, specifying count or size is not enough; the net weight in the container may be needed to get what one pays for.

Markets tend to standardize their own types of packaging. The trend has been to pack in smaller packages, to reduce handling weight. Some labor unions have also put pressure on package size and weight, refusing to handle anything over 50 pounds. Thus, today lettuce, instead of being packed in the old wirebound crates, which held about 75 pounds, is packed in cartons weighing not less than 40 pounds.

In all specifications for produce, the packaging, size, and count plus *net weight* should be given, where applicable. Just ordering a hamper of spinach is not enough. A loose hamper pack could mean that while package size was delivered, amount was shorted.

Various kinds of packing for produce may be specified. Thus, a layer pack may be specified, as for tomatoes; a cell pack in which the item rests in an individual plastic compartment is becoming much more common because of the protection it gives to products, however, it is a bit more expensive. Loose pack means that the items are packed in a jumble with little or no organization. A bulging pack is used to prevent movement of produce in shipping and handling. The container is packed tightly and full above the top. A stiff but flexible top is put over and tightly fastened down so the produce is now firmly held in place. Saying "struck full" means that the container is only filled to the point at which the contents are just up to the container top, as if filled and then a ruler run over the top to sweep off the extra. "Fill equal to facing" means that top contents and that below the top are the same in size and quality.

AP to EP to AS

Fresh produce is often purchased in the AP (as purchased) state, which usually means that some trim and other treatment is required to bring it to an EP (edible portion) state. Usually, when served raw, EP becomes the AS (as served) state and thus both are the same thing, but if the produce is cooked as carrots might be, the AS served weight will differ from the EP.

It is necessary to know the AP, EP, and AS yields of fresh produce to know how much to order. Fortunately, information has been compiled on how much to order of various produce to make a normal portion. Tables 10–9 and 10–10 at the end of this chapter give the quantity of fresh produce needed for 100 portions. Note Table 10–9 indicates 100 3-oz portions of cooked cabbage requires a half of a 50-lb sack, or 25 lb. But, 100 3-oz portions is only about 19 lb (100 portions × 3-oz portions = 300 oz/16 oz = 18.8 lb). The loss in trimming, etc. of 25 to 19 lb is 6 lb or 24%.

Because the amounts needed in these tables are averages made up of variable yields, buyers and those in production should use these quantities more as guides to amounts needed rather than as an exact quantity needed.

PRODUCE PRODUCT INFORMATION

To purchase produce correctly, one needs to know a lot about the items purchased. Otherwise, the purchase task can lose its effectiveness. In the material that follows, all buying information is given only on the major fruits and vegetables. Because of the large number of less important ones, the information for them is summarized in Tables 10–11 and 10–12 at the end of this chapter.

A date in parentheses after the name of the produce item indicates the date of the federal standard used in the information that follows for that item. Buyers usually should specify **mature** fruit, which means the fruit should be completely ripe.

Fruits

Apples (1996)
While there are over 8,000 varieties of apples, only about 15 are of commercial importance. New varieties are constantly appearing and buyers need to keep up with what is available. Some kinds of apples are on the market all year round.

Apples should be purchased on the basis of (1) intended use, (2) quality, (3) size and packaging, and perhaps (4) place of origin.

Intended Use. Purveyors should be able to give information on best use of new varieties of apples available. Some are very suitable for raw purposes but not for cooking. Some make excellent applesauce but break up too much to be used in cooking. Some apples are better for baking, while others may be best for pies, cobblers, and other similar purposes.

Quality. Two grade standards are used for apples; the Washington State grades are one and used primarily on the market because the state of Washington produces almost 50% of our apples; the second is the federal. Table 10–1 summarizes these grades; note that the U.S. No. 1 federal grade is the equivalent of Washington's grade C. Some changes in apple grading were proposed by the USDA in 1992 to change its grading standards.

Color. Color is one of the most important factors in deciding the grade of apple. This is why the Pacific Northwest's apples are given such high grades. Actually the Washington grade for grade C requires more color than for U.S. No. 1. Since color is not important in apples used pared, Washington grade C and U.S. No. 1 are adequate for that use.

Green apple varieties that take on no red color are not graded by the same color standards.

Very large or very small apples are usually not best quality. Green apples are hard and often tart; overripe ones are soft and mealy. Large apples ripen more rapidly than small ones of the same variety. Proper maturity is indicated by brown seeds, yellowing of the unblushed color, or the development of a blush color on red and blushed varieties and a slight softening of the flesh. Mature apples have a rich, fruity odor, with a crisp texture.

Defects such as decay, internal browning and/or breakdown, scabs, freezing injury, broken skins, bruises, russeting, sunburn, spray burn, limb rubs, hail or drought spots, scars, cracks, insect or mechanical, or other damage all detract from grade.

Size and Packaging. Size affects usefulness. A good portion for eating size is 113's (about three to the pound). Federal sizes for western boxes are from 3¾ in. (56 per box) and 1¼ in. diameter (175 per box). (See Table 10–2 and Figure 10–4.) Western apple boxes hold 41–47 lb, eastern, 50–54 lb. Tray-packed western boxes hold 37–48 lb, and those cell-packed hold 37–44 lb. Specify minimum weight of containers as well as desired size.

Table 10–1

Federal and Washington grades for apples.

Rank in Quality	Grade Name		Grade Characteristics	
	Washington	Federal	Washington	Federal
1st	Extra Fancy	U.S. Extra Fancy	Sound, clean, fully matured smooth, well-formed, free from defects. All good mature fruit; good color, shape, and condition for variety; carefully packed	Mature, not overripe, carefully hand picked, clean, well-formed, free from defects, amount of color specified for variety
2nd	Fancy	U.S. Fancy	Clean, fully matured, and of good color for variety, free from defects, fairly well formed	Mature, not overripe, carefully hand picked, fairly well-formed, free from defects; amount of color specified for variety
3rd	Grade C	U.S. No. 1	Clean, fully matured fruit, fair color and fair shape; condition good, fairly free from defects	Same as U.S. Fancy except color may be lower than U.S. Fancy
4th	None	U.S. No. 1 Early	None	Shall meet all requirements of U.S. No. 1 except for color. This grade is provided for Duchess, Gravenstein, Red June, Twenty Ounce, Wealthy, Williams, Yellow Transparent, and Lodi, or other varieties normally marketed during the summer months
5th	None	U.S. No. 1 Cookers	None	Same as U.S. No. 1 except color; grade provided for apples that are mature but lack sufficient color to meet color standards of U.S. No. 1
6th	None	U.S. Utility	None	Lack color, shape must not be seriously deformed, may have higher waste and labor preparation cost than saved by purchase of this lower grade.

Note: If apples are to be sliced or chopped, a U.S. No. 1 or Combination grade is usually adequate.

Table 10-2
Federal apple sizes.

Count per Western Box	Minimum Diameter Size (in.)*
175	$1\frac{1}{4}$
162	$1\frac{1}{2}$
150	$1\frac{3}{4}$
138	2
125	$2\frac{1}{4}$
113	$2\frac{1}{2}$
100	$2\frac{3}{4}$
88	3
80	$3\frac{1}{4}$
68	$3\frac{1}{2}$
56	$3\frac{3}{4}$

*As measured not around girth but from stem to blossom end transversely.

Note: Federal standards call size 88 or less *very large;* 96 to 125, *large;* 138 to 163, *medium;* 175 to 200, *small;* and 216 to 252, *very small.*

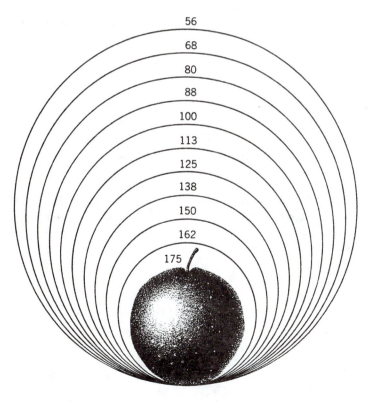

Figure 10-4
Apple sizes and counts per western apple box.

Origin.   Often Pacific Northwest apples are preferred on the market, but that is perhaps because they are so high in quality, are plentiful, and dominate the market. However, New York, Virginia, and apples from other areas of the United States are as good for the purpose intended, except if presented as an eating apple, where color contributes to the Pacific Northwest's apples usually having better appearance.

Storage.   Store apples at 36°–38°F and 85–90% relative humidity. Apples give off odors and gases and so must receive special storage. Consult the storage tables in Appendix B for information on this requirement.

Apples are stored today in commercial warehouses under controlled atmosphere and temperature conditions and keep a long time. Sometimes these apples may have retained quality for over their normal keeping period and, when withdrawn from such storage, move into over-maturity rapidly. Amounts purchased of such apples should be watched. At the end of maturity, apples quickly spoil, showing interior brown rot, decay, or wilt. They yield easily to pressure. Immature apples may never ripen but just shrivel up.

Other Apple Varieties.   Crabapples are about 1½ in. in diameter, used largely for jellies and preserves. A number of fruits with apple names are not apples. The pear-apple (Japanese Pear, Asian Pear, Chalea, Oriental Pear, or Shalea) is not a cross of the apple and pear but a separate fruit. It is rounded and somewhat elongated like a pear with a slight russeting on greenish yellow skin when ripe. Firm and crisp with a light, mealy quality and a combined apple-pear flavor, they are best used raw for salads, desserts, etc. Custard apples (Cherimoya or sherbet fruit) are summarized in a table later. Star apples, a Caribbean fruit, have about 2- to 4-in. diameters with a smooth skin, and a somewhat dull purple or green color. They should be tree ripened. Lady apples, popular in France, have an uneven shape; some have a transparency, making them desirable in fruit displays. Their size is about that of apricots and the flavor somewhat like grapes.

Apricots (1994)

The best apricots are those that are tree-ripened, having a better flavor and sweetness than apricots that are picked and then allowed to ripen. Select mature, clean fruit that is not overripe, soft, or shriveled and is free from decay, cuts, skin breaks, or insect, skinrub, or other damage. Apricots are usually marketed in California lugs, about 24 lb. per lug. Grades are No. 1 and No. 2. Specify fill equal to facing.

Avocados

Florida and California produce almost all avocados for the United States. There are many varieties. California's avocados usually are pear shaped and run 6–12 oz. Florida's avocados are round and run 9–32 oz each. An important factor in selecting avocados is pit size. The California Hass variety has the smallest seed, Fuerte is next; the round Florida fruit has a large pit. However, individual fruit can vary.

Fiberboard or wooden containers are used for shipping. California ships in 12 ½- and 25-lb net lugs, Florida, in 38-lb wood or fiberboard cartons. A ⅕-bu container should contain 36–40 lb. Federal grades exist for Florida fruit; California grades its fruit No. 1 and 2 and Florida No. 1, 2, and 3. California avocados must be over 8% oil.

Good quality fruit is fresh and bright appearing, with a rich, buttery, and soft flesh. Detect ripeness by placing the fruit in the palm and pressing to see if there is a slight yield. The fruit should be heavy for size. Overly soft, mushy, bruised, or decayed fruit, detected by dark sunken spots, should be rejected. Hard avocados can be ripened in two to five days if stored in a warm place (70°–80°F). Store at about 50°F. Production peaks are October to December, with a smaller one occurring from February to April. California ships year-round. AP to EP yield is 60–75%, depending on variety.

Bananas

Bananas come mainly from Central America. The Cavendish variety holds the market. The plaintain is a banana that is usually boiled or baked; it is reddish in color but is not commonly found on the market.

Tree-ripened bananas are insipid in flavor. Ripening in transit or storage is controlled by varying temperature and humidity. Ethylene gas can be used to remove greenness. Fast ripening is done in 3 to 4 days, medium ripening in 5 to 7 days, and slow ripening in 8 to 10 days. Properly ripened fruit has a bright, attractive, yellow color. The fruit should appear fresh, be firm and plump, and have good peel strength. *Full ripe* means no trace of green, with typical ripe-banana color, well flecked with light-brown to dark-brown specks of a size from pinpoints to spots ⅛ in. in diameter. They should be consumed in 24 hours. *Hard ripe* means a bright banana color with no trace of brown, firm texture, and some astringency in flavor; about 3 days are needed for ripening at room temperature. *Turning ripe* means pale banana color with a green tip, little flavor, and sharp astringency. These take 5 to 6 days at room temperature to ripen. Examine for size, fullness of fruit, and degree of maturity. Look for bruised fruit, fruit riper than specified, poorly colored skin, and mold. Chilling discolors the fruit. Store at about 60°F.

Bananas are sold cut from the stem in 10-lb bags or in bunches in 40-lb cartons, about 100–120 per carton. About three medium-sized bananas equal a pound. There are no federal grades. Peeling loss averages 32%. Bananas are on the market in good supply throughout the year.

Berries

The federal government has set standards for blueberries (1995), dewberries and blackberries (1928), cranberries (1971), raspberries (1931), and strawberries (1985). Grades are No. 1 and No. 2. Food services should specify No. 1. The fruit should be well colored for its variety, clean and mature and not soft or overly ripe. Berries should be dry, not wet, free from attached stems or caps, mold, decay, and insect or other damage. Evidence of freezing (softness and lack of bloom and color) should be cause for rejection. Blueberries have no federal sizing, but a buyer can specify per cup (½ pt) Extra Large (less than 90), Large (90–129), Medium (130–169), and Small (190–250). No strawberry should be less than ¾ in. in diameter. Usually berries are marketed in pint or quart baskets, but they may also be purchased in other size units. Specify fill equal to facing.

Cherries, Sweet (1971)

Two types of sweet cherries are on the market, dark or black cherries and those with a cream color, often having a blush of pink or red. Perhaps the best known of the dark varieties is the Bing, and of the cream-colored the Royal Anne. Select mature, fairly well-colored, well-formed, and clean fruit free from decay, insect larvae or holes. Avoid soft, overripe or shriveled, sunscalded or otherwise damaged fruit. The minimum diameter of any fruit should be ¾ in. Specify that fill should be equal to facing. Cherries are usually marketed in California lugs.

Citrus Fruit

Over 3,000 million pounds of citrus fruit are produced in this country per year. California and Arizona are the biggest producers, followed by Florida and Texas in that order. Citrus fruit is one of the most important sources of vitamin C.

Origin Differences. California–Arizona citrus usually has a thick skin, is mildly flavored, with sweet juice and a bright skin color. Florida's fruit has thinner skins, more juice, and a fuller-bodied flavor. Texas citrus falls in between these two producers.

Florida and Texas citrus often have outer skin blemishing or browning called **russeting.** This is caused by a tiny mite that bites into the skin to suck juice, causing the blemish. California–Arizona lacks the humid climate that favors the growth of this mite and so is free of this damage. Besides a quality grade, Florida and Texas citrus have a russeting grade. Thus, Florida grades for least to most russeting are Bright, Golden, Bronze, and Russet; Texas has only Bright and Bronze. Florida's Fancy Bright cannot have more than 1/10 of the surface blemished; its U.S. No. 1 Bright, not more than ⅕; Golden, not more than ⅓; Bronze, more than ⅓; Russet, almost totally covered. Russeting does not affect interior quality, and a facility peeling the fruit may as well purchase the lesser expensive Russet grade since the quality inside is the same as Bright.

Under the Agricultural Commodities Act, the USDA is charged with the responsibility for seeing that, before citrus fruit can be picked for market, it must meet specific standards for ripeness in sugar and acid.

Florida's and to a lesser extent Texas's citrus is subject to what is called **greening,** a green color on the skin that remains although the fruit has fully ripened. If California citrus shows greening, it can be removed by putting the fruit in a chamber with ethylene gas, a process called **sweating.** However, Florida's and Texas's fruit does not respond to this treatment. Sometimes fruit with greening has color rubbed onto the surface. If so, the fruit must be marked "Color Added." It in no way harms the interior quality, and is desirable in some instances. The greener the lime the more highly it is regarded. Lemons showing some greening are supposed to have higher acidity and a better flavor.

Citrus Varieties

The four major kinds of citrus marketed in this country are, in order of amounts produced, oranges, grapefruit, lemons, and limes. Separate federal standards exist for Florida, Texas, and California–Arizona fruit.

Table 10–3

Important characteristics of orange varieties.

Variety	Size	Color	Shape	Rind	Seeds	Flesh	Flavor
SWEET ORANGE VARIETIES							
Hamlin	Medium to small	Yellow orange	Oval to round	Smooth, glossy	Few seeds	Medium juicy	Sweet and mild
Parson Brown	Medium	Rich yellow, orange	Oblongish round	Smooth, ⅛–3/16 in. thick	10–19	Medium fine	Juicy, sweet
Washington navel	Large	Rich reddish orange to orange yellow	Round to tapering at base	Thin, ⅛–¼ in. thick, smooth. Large oil cells	None	Medium coarse	Medium juicy rich, sweet
Pineapple	Medium to large	Deep orange with reddish tinge	Round	Smooth, glossy, ⅛ in. thick	Large, 8–15	Medium fine	Rich and juicy
Homosassa	Medium to large	Deep orange	Round and oval	Smooth and glossy	15	Medium fine	Excellent, rich fragrant
Valencia	Large	Pale orange to yellow orange with tendency to show green	Slightly oval	Smooth or slight pebble; thin, not tough	2–5	Good	Excellent, medium juicy
Ruby red	Medium	Deep orange; red at apex	Roundish thick	Medium smooth, thick	Many seeds		Rich, sweet almost spicy
MANDARIN VARIETIES							
Satsuma	Medium to small	Pale to bright orange	Flat to oblate	Rough, large oil cells	Few	Coarse	Juicy, spicy
Dancy tangerine	Medium	Deep orange	Oblate flat	Thin, glossy		Medium	Rich, juicy aromatic
King	Large	Light to deep orange	Roundish oblate	Very rough	Few	Coarse	Juicy, spicy
Temple	Medium	Deep orange	Oblate	Rough	Few	Moderate	Rich, aromatic, spicy

Oranges.   Two main categories of oranges are marketed: the tight-skinned, and the loose-skinned or kid-glove. The first is far more important in quantity produced. The two main varieties of the tight-skinned are the *Valencia,* a summer orange, and the *navel,* a winter orange, comprising about 80% of the tight-skinned crop. Some other winter varieties are produced such as the *Hamlin, pineapple,* etc., but not in major amounts compared with the two leaders. The major kid-glove varieties are the *mandarin, king, tangerine,* and *Satsuma.* Some crosses with the orange are also seen on the market. One is the tangelo, a cross of the mandarin and pomelo; another is the temple, a cross between the orange and tangerine.

The *kumquat* is a small, oval, tight-skinned orange that is often eaten raw with the rind. It also makes good preserves. The *pomelo* looks like a grapefruit but has a peaked neck, coarse thick skin, and yields much less flesh. Important characteristics of various orange varieties are summarized in Table 10–3.

Grapefruit.   Grapefruit is in good supply in the fall and winter; in the spring, supplies begin to dwindle, and amounts are limited in the summer and early fall months. The Marsh (no seeds) and Duncan are the major varieties. Both are rich in flavor and juicy. The Thompson Pink is an offspring of the Marsh. Other white and pink varieties are seen on the market, but these are the most common (see Table 10–4). Most summer fruit comes from California or Arizona.

The Indian River (FL) and Rio (TX) regions produce high-quality grapefruit. California–Arizona grapefruit have a bright, clear, but thicker skin, slightly less juice, and less body and fullness of flavor (see Figure 10–5).

Lemons.   California and Arizona produce most of our lemons; Florida's are apt to be coarse and large, lacking a good spicy, tart flavor. The main varieties produced are the Eureka (summer) and Lisbon (winter), the latter being produced in greatest amounts, and therefore are less expensive, but because lemons keep well under special refrigerated storage, the advantage is not great. Lemons should have a pleasant citrus odor; if the odor is "fermented," the lemon will have an off flavor.

Limes.   Most limes come from Florida, the Caribbean Islands, and Mexico. The Tahiti variety is the largest and most plentiful. The smaller Key limes of Florida or Mexico, often yellowish green in color and smaller, may be called Dominican or West Indies limes. Peak lime season is summer, but supplies are good all year.

Packaging and Size.   Most packages are fiberboard cartons with some use of bushel baskets, especially Texas, but the market is shifting to mesh or plastic bags or other containers. Washing, packing, and sorting for size, color, and shape is automated. Table 10–5 gives sizes and weights for various area packages. The large 1⅗-bu wirebound box is seldom seen anymore. Note the variation in sizing and package weights between Florida, Texas, and California–Arizona.

Federal sizing for oranges is *large,* 3⅜ in. or more in diameter at right angles to a line from stem to blossom end, 326 g or more; *medium,* 3¼–2¾-in. diameter and 315–325 g each; and *small,* 2½ in. diameter or less and 150–314 g each. Florida's ⅗-bu pack is:

Size	Min. Diameter	Size	Min. Diameter
96s	$3^3/_{16}$ in.	216s	$2^{10}/_{16}$ in.
125s or 126s	$3^3/_{16}$	252s	$2^8/_{16}$
150s	3	288s or 294s	$2^6/_{16}$
175s or 176s	$2^{13}/_{16}$	324s	$2^4/_{16}$*WPC

Table 10-4
Purchase characteristics of some common grapefruit.

Variety	Size (in.)*	Color	Rind Depth (in.)	Flesh	Flavor
Marsh	Medium $3^1/_2$	Light yellow	$^1/_8$ thick	Greenish gray, 11–13 sections, no seeds	Medium acidity and sweetness, faint bitterness
Hall	Large $4^1/_2$	Light yellow	$^3/_{16}$ thick	14 sections, 32 seeds, high juice	Acidity, sweetness, and bitterness strong
Walters	Medium $3^3/_4$	Pale yellow	$^1/_4$ thick	13 sections, 58 seeds	Acidity, sweetness, and bitterness strong
Duncan	Medium to small $3^1/_2$	Light yellow	$^1/_{16}$ thick	Greenish gray, 14 sections, many seeds	Acidity and sweetness medium with noticeable bitterness
Triumph	Small $3^1/_4$	Light yellow	$^1/_8$ thick	11 sections, 37 seeds, very juicy	Mild in acidity, sweetness, and bitterness; delicate flavor

*Inches refer to average diameter of fruit.

Figure 10-5
Note the difference in flesh and rind between the overmature grapefruit on the left and the properly matured grapefruit on the right. Note peaking of the late fruit.
(Courtesy USDA.)

Table 10-5

Sizes and weights of citrus packages.

Fruit	Type Container	Florida Size (bu)	Florida Wt (lb)	Texas Size (bu)	Texas Wt (lb)	CA–AZ Size (bu)	CA–AZ Wt (lb)
Grapefruit	Wirebound box	$1^3/_5$	85	$1^2/_5$	80		
	Wirebound box or fiberboard box	$^4/_5$	$42^1/_2$	$^7/_{10}$	40	$^7/_{10}$*	32 & $33^1/_2$*
	Wirebound box or fiberboard box					$^7/_{10}$	27 or 28
Lemons						$^7/_{10}$	38
Limes	Fiberboard carton	$^4/_5$	40			$^4/_5$	40
	Fiberboard carton	$^2/_5$	20			$^2/_5$	20
	Fiberboard carton	$^1/_5$	10			$^1/_5$	10
Oranges	Wirebound box	$1^3/_5$	90	$1^2/_5$	85	$^7/_{10}$	$37^1/_2$
	Wirebound box or fiberboard box	$^4/_5$	45	$^7/_{10}$	$42^1/_2$	$^7/_{10}$	$37^1/_2$

*This is only for grapefruit grown in the desert areas; Table 10–6 covers other areas of California–Arizona.
Note: All areas also pack in plastic or mesh bags.

The best juice buy is the lowest pound price because, within the same variety, juice yield is by pound weight. However, some buyers feel that the best size juice orange is 56 to 72 oranges, 36 to 48 grapefruit, and 195 to 235 lemons. Size 48 or larger is needed for a half portion of orange; 72s suffice if two halves are served. A half of a 32 per carton size grapefruit is a good serving. Extra large fruit is apt to lack flavor, have a coarse texture and soft flesh; very small citrus usually has an insipid flavor, high acidity, lacking sweetness. Table 10–6 lists the sizes of various citrus fruit. Figures 10–6 and 10–7 give an indication of the relative sizes of oranges and lemons, respectively. Table 10–7 gives average yields of flesh and juice.

Grading.   Food services should use U.S. No. 1, but some Fancy citrus is on the market, better than U.S. No. 1. Florida and Texas have russeting grades also within grades. Since color does not represent internal ripeness, sugar (Brix) and acidity are used to check that. To check quality, cut the fruit and taste. Look for firm, not soft or flabby, well-formed fruit with a fine texture, thin skin, and free from blemishes, hard, dry, or broken rinds, bruises, scab, shriveling, or evidence of decay. Tiny oil sacs in the rind should exist. Citrus is heaviest at the season's start and middle; size is also largest. Rinds get thicker and the tops more pointed as the fruit hangs. Fruit with wrinkled, coarse rinds and pointed sharp necks lack juice and flavor, except a wrinkled, coarse skin in the kid-glove variety of orange does not mean a lack of quality. The federal grades recognize that western citrus has thicker skins. Watch for blue mold, white mold, and mechanical damage. Store oranges at 37–39°F, lemons and limes at 45°–48°F, and grapefruit at 48°–50°F. See the tables in Appendix B for other storage requirements.

Table 10-6
Sizing for citrus fruit.

Size (count)	Diameter (in.) Minimum	Diameter (in.) Maximum
	ORANGES (3/5 BU)	
FLORIDA		
100s	3 6/16	3 12/16
125s	3 3/16	3 9/16
163s	2 15/16	3 4/16
200s	2 11/16	3
252s	2 8/16	2 12/16
324s	2 4/16	2 8/16
OTHER STATES		
100s (48–50)	3 6/16	
125s (64)	3 3/16	
163s (80)	2 15/16	3 3/16
200s (100)	2 11/16	2 15/16
252s (125)	2 8/16	2 11/16
324s (163)	2 4/16	2 8/16
	ORANGES (1 2/5 BU)	
100s	3 7/16	3 13/16
125s	3 3/16	3 9/16
163s	2 15/16	3 5/16
200s	2 11/16	3 1/16
252s	2 7/16	2 12/16
288s	2 4/16	2 9/16
324s	2 3/16	2 8/16
	ORANGES (1/10 BU)	
48s or 50s	3 7/16	3 13/16
64s	3 3/16	3 9/16
80s	2 15/16	3 5/16
100s	2 11/16	3 1/16
125s	2 7/16	2 12/16
144s	2 4/16	2 9/16
162s	2 3/16	2 8/16

Size (count)	Diameter (in.) Minimum	Diameter (in.) Maximum
	TEMPLES AND TANGELOS (4/5 BU)	
54s	3 6/16	
66s	3 2/16	
80s	3	
100s	2 12/16	
120s	2 9/16	
156s	2 5/16	
	TANGERINES	
100	2 15/16	
120	2 11/16	
150	2 8/16	
176	2 6/16	
210	2 4/16	
246	2 2/16	
294	2	
	GRAPEFRUIT (1 3/5 BU)	
36s	5	5 9/16
45s or 46s	4 11/16	5 4/16
54s or 56s	4 6/16	4 15/16
64s	4 3/16	4 12/16
70s or 72s	3 15/16	4 8/16
80s	3 12/16	4 5/16
96s	3 9/16	4 2/16
112s	3 7/16	4
125s or 126s	3 5/16	3 14/16
	GRAPEFRUIT (1 2/5 BU)	
46s	4 5/16	5
54s or 56s	4 2/16	4 12/16
64s	3 15/16	4 8/16
70s or 72s	3 13/16	4 5/16
80s	3 10/16	4 2/16
96s	3 6/16	3 14/16
112s or 113s	3 2/16	3 10/16
125s or 126s	3	3 8/16

Note: Count in container can vary from size term; thus in a 4/5 bu of size 64 grapefruit there will be only 32.
Source: Summarized from federal sizing and count standards, USDA.

Federal standards for citrus fruit are dated as follows: Florida oranges and tangelos (1996), California and Arizona oranges (1957), Texas grapefruit (1969), Florida grapefruit (1996), California and Arizona grapefruit (1950), Texas grapefruit (1969), lemons (1964), limes (1958), tangerines (1948), and Florida tangerines (1996).

Grapes (1996)

Eastern, called slip-skin because the skin slips easily from the meat, and western, called European because they come from European stock, are on the market. There are a number of varieties.

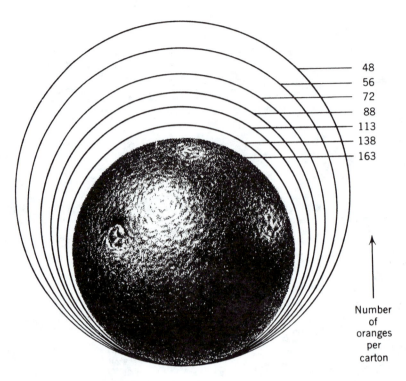

48
56
72
88
113
138
163

Number
of
oranges
per
carton

Figure 10-6
California–Arizona sizes for oranges in standard ⅘-bushel fiberboard cartons.

Grapes at full maturity have best quality. Good quality grapes have green stems, not brown. Stem shriveling indicates age. When a bunch is shaken, few grapes fall. The seeds should be brown and full, not green, and should separate easily from the pulp. Select full, not straggly bunches with full, plump grapes. Sunken areas at the stem indicate age. Grapes with a dead, dull color and a stem that pulls out with meat or brush attached have been frozen. A milky, opaque pulp and flat flavor also indicate freezing (see Figure 10–8). California packs are lugs holding 23- and 28-lb net and flats holding 17–20 lb. If packed in sawdust, the chest should weigh 20–22 to 32–34 lb, depending on size. Eastern crates hold eight 2-qt baskets (18–20-lb net) or 12-qt baskets (26–28-lb net). Purchase Extra Fancy, Table or Fancy Table. Store at 32–40°F.

Kiwis (1997)
Kiwis belong to the gooseberry family. We now get most of this fruit from California. Sizes per California 25-lb lug are 30 or larger, 31 through 38, and 39 or smaller. Grades food services should specify are Fancy and No. 1. Select mature fruit that yields to pressure but is still firm, well formed, clean, and carefully packed.

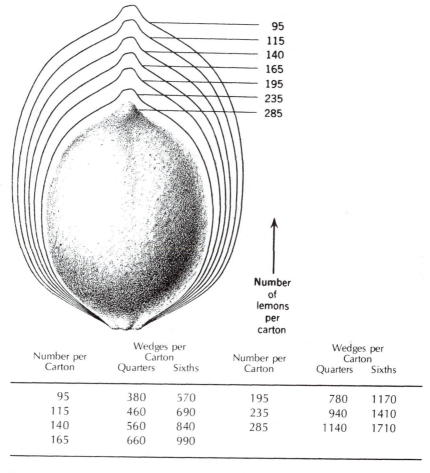

	95
	115
	140
	165
	195
	235
	285

Number
of
lemons
per
carton

Number per Carton	Wedges per Carton		Number per Carton	Wedges per Carton	
	Quarters	Sixths		Quarters	Sixths
95	380	570	195	780	1170
115	460	690	235	940	1410
140	560	840	285	1140	1710
165	660	990			

Figure 10-7

California–Arizona sizes for lemons in standard ⅘-bushel fiberboard cartons.

Table 10-7

Average yields of flesh and juice from citrus fruits, by percent of total weight.

Flesh Type Fruit	(No Membrane) (%)	Juice (%)		
		Arizona	California	Florida
Lemons	64	44	44	
Oranges	65	48	47	54
Grapefruit	47	45	42	46
Limes	57			35

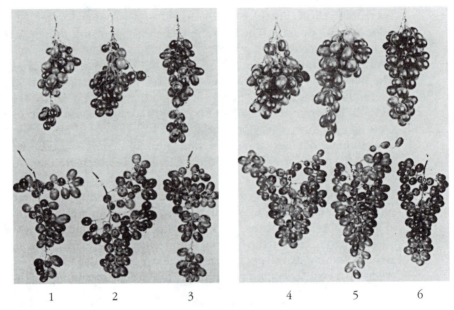

1	2	3	4	5	6

Figure 10-8

The structure of the bunch is considered in grading grapes. Here bunches 1 through 6 are taken hanging. Bunches 1, 2, and 3 are straggly. Bunch 3 is just below the requirement for U.S. No. 1. Bunches 4 and 5 are not straggly but do not meet the standard of "fairly well filled" because of a lack of filling in the upper portions. Bunch 6 meets the minimum standard for "fairly well filled." (Courtesy USDA.)

Melons

Watermelons, cantaloupes, and honeydew melons are the most marketed melons.

Cantaloupe.   Cantaloupes are available throughout the year; domestic supplies peak in the summer and quality is best at that time. California–Arizona ships 70% of the crop, but Colorado produces a significant amount, too. Only cantaloupes with 5-in. diameters or more can be marketed. Packages are half-crates, 38–41 lb, or ⅔-bu crates holding 53–55-lb net. Counts are, respectively, 12–23 and 12–30. Specify Fancy or U.S. No. 1 (see Figure 10–9).

Blossom end softness indicates ripeness; full slip, no trace of stem at the stem scar indicates the melon was ripe when picked; half slip, a bit of the stem showing, indicates a partially ripe fruit on picking but one that will ripen. However the melon may not be of best flavor. Ripeness is also determined by odor, by a raised netting on the skin, and a slight yellowing of the skin. Purchase either by the pound or packages, specifying net weight. Cantaloupes run ¾–4 lb each.

Honeydews.   Honeydews weigh about 6½ lb and are about 6 in. in diameter; they have a slightly oblong shape and a smooth, greenish white rind that, at maturity, is creamy yellow. Purchase full slip melons. Blossom-end softening and a rich, ripe

Figure 10-9
Cantaloupe picked at full-slip stage of maturity shows a stem pulled away from the melon, leaving a clean, cuplike hole.
(Courtesy USDA.)

odor indicate ripeness. The flesh should be thick, greenish, fine-grained, juicy, sweet, and mild in flavor. Decay shows as pink or black dots; a sour smell indicates overripeness and spoilage. Imports make up the deficit in nonproduction months. The honeyball resembles the honeydew but is smaller. Specify U.S. No. 1.

Jumbo crates hold 45–50 lb, standard crates hold 40–43 lb, and cartons 31½ lb. Larger crates may hold 40–45 lb. Crates should come stamped showing crate size, number of melons, and grade.

A number of different melons come onto the market in the fall that are excellent in quality such as the Casaba, Crenshaw, Persian, Spanish, Juan Canary and the Santa Claus (see Figure 10–10), which are late melons. Check ripeness by pressing the **blossom end;** it should give slightly.

Watermelons (1975). Watermelons peak in July and August, but are in fairly good supply from late spring to midfall; imports make them available all year. Shipping is in strong fiberboard boxes, 3–5 melons per box, weighing 55–80 lb.

Ripeness is indicated by a firm, symmetrical shape, a fresh and attractive bloom, giving a somewhat velvety appearance; and a good color varying from a deep, solid green, to gray, depending on variety. The bottom should be yellowish in color. A hollow sound on thumping can indicate ripeness. Immature melons have a hard, greenish, unripe appearance, with a white or pale green underside. Overmaturity is indicated by a slightly dull, lifeless appearance and a soft springy feel when pressure is applied. Taking out a plug is a better judge. The flesh should be of rich color, firm, sweet, and flavorful, and not sour or sloughy. Black seeds indicate ripeness. White heart indicates a poor melon.

Watermelons store well at room temperature for about seven days. A 25- to 28-lb melon divides into portions best. Chill injury harms flavor. Figure 10–11 indicates permitted watermelon shapes within grade.

Nectarines (1997)

Food services should specify Fancy, Extra No. 1, or No. 1. Redness of skin may vary. Most nectarines should have two-thirds of their surface showing blush or red in Fancy grade; in Extra No. 1, three-fourths of the surface should have blush or

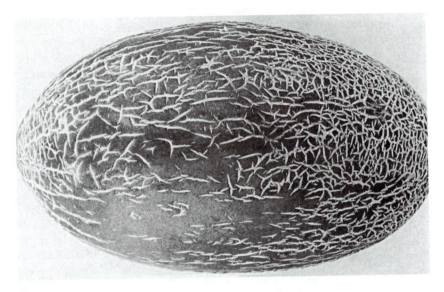

Figure 10-10
The Santa Claus melon. The fruit is oblong, about 12 by 6 in. and weighs around 6 lb. The rind is green and gold, usually with a trace of netting. Flesh is a light green, with a flavor like that of a Casaba. It is a good keeper and may be obtained at times in midwinter. (Courtesy USDA.)

SHAPES OF LONG TYPE MELONS

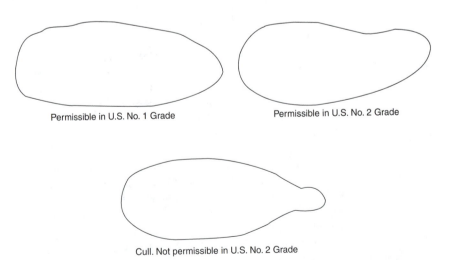

Permissible in U.S. No. 1 Grade

Permissible in U.S. No. 2 Grade

Cull. Not permissible in U.S. No. 2 Grade

Figure 10-11
Shapes of watermelons permitted within grades. (Courtesy USDA.)

redness. The John Rivers variety will not show this amount of redness and still make the grade. Avoid fruit showing green areas on skin since they will not ripen properly. They are marketed in boxes, 25-lb lugs, cartons, or baskets; the container should show the size. Packs shall not be more than three layers deep. Specify fill equal to facing. To test ripeness, smell to get a "peachy" odor.

Peaches (1995)

If not too ripe, peaches hold in refrigeration for about three weeks; however, quality declines about a week after storage. Market peak is July through September (see Table 10–8). Freestone peaches break away from the pits easily; clings do not, and take more labor to prepare because of the extra slicing needed to remove meat from around the pit. Immature fruit is pale yellow, may show greenness, has a poor flavor, high acidity, and a hard, rubbery flesh. Color does not always indicate maturity. Disappearance of green and a creamy yellowing with a full flush of pink, plus softening of the flesh indicate maturity. Packaging is as follows:

Western States	Pounds	All Other States	Pounds
L.A. wooden lug	22–28	4-basket crate	46–52
Sanger lug	10	Bushel basket	50–55
Western peach box	16–22	1⅛-bu basket	35–42
one-layer flat	18–22	1 34-bu or crate	23–28
Wood or fiberboard carton or crate	27		

Table 10–8

Some purchasing characteristics of common peaches.

Variety	Flesh Color	Size and Shape	On Market	General Characteristics
Elberta	Yellow, red blush	Large, oval	August to September	Good shipper and keeper
Hale	Yellow, red blush	Large, round	August to September	Excellent flavor; excellent shipper and keeper
Halehaven	Yellow, high blush	Medium to large, round	August	Excellent flavor
Golden Jubilee	Yellow, slight blush	Large, oval	August	Juicy; good flavor; bruises easily
Hiley	White	Medium large	August	Excellent flavor; juicy
Cumberland*	White, high blush	Large, bell-shaped	July to August	Excellent flavor, high quality
Carman*	White	Medium to large	August	Good quality

*The flesh of semiclingstones separates with difficulty from their pits and may for this reason have limited use in institutions because of extra labor and higher waste.

Georgia or the Carolinas may use six-basket carriers. Three to four peaches to a pound is a common size. Grades are Fancy, Extra No. 1, and No. 1.

Cut and examine for flavor and maturity, and examine for worms and decay. Gum exuding over a tiny mark indicates insect damage. Grades are U.S. Fancy, Extra No. 1, and No. 1.

Pears (1955)

Like apples, pears are purchased on the basis of size, grade, maturity, and use. Full ripeness is indicated by a coloring specific to the variety and softness of flesh. To ripen, open polyethylene wraps and let air enter. Packaging is as follows:

¾ bushel	35–42 lb	L.A. lug or 2-layer carton	22–28 lb
½ bushel	23–28 lb	½ standard box	38–41 lb
Standard apple box or carton	40–54 lb		

The best sizes for food services are usually 110–135 count.

Select clean, bright, and typically colored pears for the variety. Avoid misshapen, soft, or wrinkled fruit. Look for scars or damage or insect or worm injury. Kieffer pears have a gritty texture raw or cooked and so are seldom used. Summer pears do not last long, but winter ones hold a long time in proper storage. Grades are U.S. Extra No. 1 and No. 2 for winter pears and U.S. No. 1 and No. 2 for summer ones; Washington State grades are Extra Fancy and Fancy.

Pineapple (1990)

Pineapple is a year-round crop peaking in April and May. Mexican and Florida fruit appear in February and March and last through June. The best pineapples are said to be those from Hawaii or the Philippines. Ripe fruit has a distinct orange-yellow color with fully developed, waxy, bright eyes or surface squares and a slight whiteness at the base; immature fruit appears small, is purplish green, and has only partially developed, dull eyes. A ripe, rich odor is an indication of ripeness. Select those with dry bottoms, firm eyes, good plumpness, and well-trimmed bases. The fruit should be heavy for size. Base softness, darkening under the skin, mold, or a sour smell show rot. Specifying yellow-ripe indicates firm fruit needing from three to four days to ripen; hard-ripe fruit must be held longer. Half-crates with 9 to 21 pineapples average 35 lb. The best size is 18. Full crates are also marketed. U.S. No. 1 standards require tops to be "not less than 4 in. nor more than twice the length of the fruit." Grades are Fancy and No. 1.

Plums and Prunes (1966)

Food services should specify grades Fancy or No. 1. Packaging is usually in four-basket crates, California peach boxes, or 28-lb lugs. Specify fill equal to facing. Counts should be marked on the packaging.

Table 10–11 at the end of the chapter gives purchase information for a number of fresh fruits not mentioned here.

Vegetables

Artichokes (1968)

The Italian or French globe artichoke is the bud of a thistle. Quality is indicated by compact leaves, plumpness, good symmetry, heaviness for size, and a bright green color. They brown with age or injury. An open bud with a fuzzy center and a dark pink or purple color indicate overmaturity. Bronzed outer leaves indicate frosting, which develops a more tender and flavorful product. Market packages are fiberboard boxes or cartons, 22 lb, and ½ boxes, 20–26 lb. The best portion size usually is 3 to 4 to the pound. Watch for worm holes or base rot. Purchase U.S. No. 1. Baby chokes are sometimes available.

Asparagus (1966)

Asparagus is a spring vegetable but imports make it available year round, although it is somewhat expensive in the off months. Western asparagus is usually marketed in **pyramid crates** that contain wet moss on the bottom. Unless asparagus has about 2 in. of white showing, moisture from this moss will not be picked up by the asparagus. Avoid too much white stem, however. The asparagus should be a bright green, fresh appearing, and have closed, firm, compact tips that snap or break easily at or slightly above the white portion. Specify stalks of "7½ to 8½ in. minimum and none over 10½ in." Wiry, tough asparagus has a dull, dried look, with dark color and open tips. Some varieties have purplish tips when young. Bleached (white) asparagus is available.

A two-compartment pyramid crate holds six 2–2½-in. bunches, weighing net 26–32 lb; sometimes the asparagus is unbunched. Pony crates holding 12 lb net are seen. Washington State's No. 1 equals U.S. No. 1. U.S. No. 1 asparagus should not be less than ½ in. in diameter at the base and at least two-thirds of the stalk should be green.

Broccoli

Broccoli belongs to the cauliflower family and a heading variety may be sold as such. The commonly seen green or slightly purple young broccoli is Italian sprouting broccoli. It is usually marketed in crates. Heaviest supplies are from October to April, but it is a year-round vegetable. Look for fresh, clean, deep green colored, compact buds—open buds or yellowing (flowering) ones indicate age. Wilted, flabby units with yellow leaves should be rejected. Base trim should be even and excess leaves removed. Specify *well* trimmed. Watch for cabbage worms and gray plant lice. Shake to see if buds are firmly attached. Grades are Fancy and No. 1. Cardboard 22-lb boxes hold 14 to 18 bunches. Some broccoli is marketed in florets in plastic mesh bags.

Cabbage (1996)

Different cabbages are in good supply during the year. *Early* is marketed from December to May. It has pointed, conical-shaped, rather loosely packed heads with

Figure 10–12
The lower limit of reasonable solidity for U.S. No. 1 grade heads should be at least fairly firm. (Courtesy USDA.)

smooth leaves. The color is soft green. The next to appear, called *Domestic,* is marketed in early summer and summer. It has a flat top, is moderately green, with a smooth, round head that is fairly firm and tightly formed (see Figure 10–12). The leaves are crisp and brittle. It lasts until fall. Neither domestic nor early cabbage is a good keeper.

Danish is our major cabbage crop, appearing on the market in the fall. It stores and ships well. The heads are smooth, round, very hard, and compact (see Figure 10–13). The color is almost all white except for outer leaves. Cabbage is usually sold in 50-lb netted sacks or in crates or cartons. Some purveyors may sell it by the pound in different containers. Head sizes are:

Large	Early, over 3 lb; domestic and Danish, over 5 lb
Medium	Early, 1½–3 lb; domestic and Danish, 2–5 lb
Small	Early, under 1½ lb; domestic and Danish, under 2 lb

Medium is usually best. Danish must be given a close trim to meet U.S. No. 1 grade, but this is less true for domestic and early. Watch for worms, decay, yellowing leaves, and broken or burst heads. Rub the stem end; if moist, rot is indicated. The color should be typical, the leaves crisp, the head heavy for size, and solid for the variety. Press heads to detect seed stems inside the head; a hard, resisting core is the seed stem and indicates age. Note also broken sections around the stem. Excessive head softness indicates poor quality and high waste. Overly large cores detract from good yield. Specify U.S. No. 1.

Carrots (1968)

Almost all carrots on the market are freshly grown; winter storage carrots are seldom seen since they lack flavor and texture. Carrots are marketed with tops, short-trim tops, and well-trimmed tops; the latter have no more than 1-in. tops and usually are the best buy. Short-trim means not more than 4 in. long, and carrots with tops have tops 12–20 in. long. Carrots should not be less than 3 in. long and be the blunt-end type if peeled in an abrasive peeler. To avoid heavy loss in abrasive peeling, all carrots in the lot should be close to the same diameter, not less than ¾ in. or more than 2 in. at the widest end.

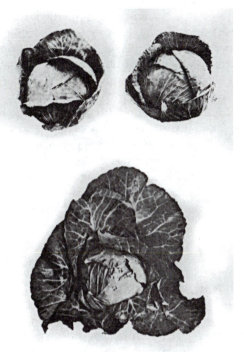

Figure 10-13
Well-trimmed (top) and poorly trimmed heads (bottom) of Danish cabbage.
(Courtesy USDA.)

Topped carrots come in 50-lb mesh bags and wirebound crates; 80-lb crates are seen. Bushel baskets, 50 lb net, are seen on some markets. Baby carrots are often sold in 1-lb bags. Buy U.S. Extra No. 1 or U.S. No. 1. Watch for flabby, wilted, soft, or shriveled carrots; excessively thick masses of leaf stem indicate large cores or hearts and toughness. The carrots should break with a crisp snap when bent. California, Arizona, and Texas carrots are considered sweeter and of better color and flavor.

Cauliflower (1968)
Cauliflower usually comes in 50–60-lb crates. Some heads are film wrapped. Specify well-trimmed heads. Size is unrelated to quality; look for white or creamy white, clean, heavy, firm, compact curds, with a fresh and green jacket of outer leaves, trimmed within 1–2 in. from the curd. Looseness or spread, also called *riciness, fuzzy, barber,* or *old man,* indicates age. Yellow leaves indicate age, but if the head is white, firm, and smooth, quality may still be good. Plant lice show as smudgy, dirty spots. Spotted, speckled, or bruised curds should be rejected. Good fresh, young wrapper leaves may be used for chopped, cooked greens. Large heads usually give best yields. Supplies are most plentiful October through December, but cauliflower is a year-round vegetable. Specify U.S. No. 1, not less than 4 in. in diameter. Cauliflower is also available as florets in 10- to 20-lb plastic bags; some may be vacuum packed.

Celery
The kinds of celery on the market are Pascal (green), white (blanched), and yellow (golden). Pascal dominates the market. It has crisp, juicy stalks with heavy strings or

midribs. Celery is usually shipped well trimmed or clipped with outer branches removed. It is sized, and the number in containers should be specified. The minimum in the standard 16-in. crate is a dozen; 10 dozen or more per crate are called hearts. From 2 to 4½ dozen per crate is usually desired. Standard crates hold 55–65 lb. Specify U.S. Extra No. 1 or U.S. No. 1. Celery supplies peak from November through May, but it is in good supply all year.

Purchase clean, brittle Pascal with 12- to 16-in. stalks, well trimmed with good thickness and solidity; stalks should be straight and not twisted, with good heart formation, solid and not spongy. **Twist** or press to note pithiness. *Green* in a specification means the outer branches should be green or light green. Examine hearts for blackrot, seed stems, insect injury, or insects. **Bowing** is a defect. Detect crispness by bending a stalk until it snaps. Excessive stringiness is undesirable. Wilted or yellow leaves indicate age. Figures 10–14 and 10–15 show celery standards.

Cucumbers (1996)

Cucumber supplies peak April through June and August and September, but they are available in fairly good supply all year. Containers are 1⅓-bushel crates (55 lb), fiberboard cartons (20–22 lb), and ¼-bushel cartons (19 lb). U.S. No. 1 large are suitable, but at low peaks U.S. Fancy may have to be specified. Grade and size are correlated. U.S. Fancy and No. 1 must not be over 2⅜ in. in diameter and must be over 6 in. long. Hothouse cucumbers have no such restrictions. Specify "market type" or "slicing cucumbers" to avoid getting pickling cucumbers. A long, mild, sweet cucumber, called *English* or *European,* is on the market.

Cucumber quality is indicated by a fresh appearance, crispness, good shape, medium size, and a shiny, waxy, dark-green color over at least two-thirds of the

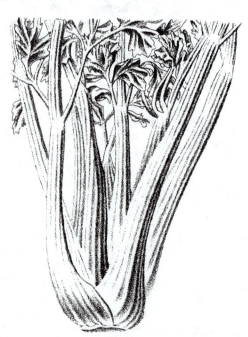

Figure 10-14
Lower allowed limit in compactness in U.S. Extra No. 1 celery. (Courtesy USDA.)

length. Shriveled or withered cucumbers have a tough or rubbery flesh and a bitter flavor. Tender seeds should rest in an almost translucent center that is firm, not jellylike. Overmaturity is indicated by a dull green or yellowish green color, a yellow underside, and a puffy, soft texture. Decay shows as dark, sunken, irregular areas.

Greens, Cooking

Greens for cooking should have fresh, tender, leaves that are bright in color without yellowing, wilting, toughness, coarseness, stringiness, or insect or worm damage. Bruised, broken, or frozen leaves will show wilt. Slime or mold indicate deterioration. Stalks should be fresh, crisp, and snap when bent. Watch for grit, dirt, sand, and extraneous matter. Bushel containers should weigh 19–20 lb net. Specify price per pound and not container.

Dandelion Greens (1955).   These greens peak in March to June but are available all year. Specify U.S. No. 1.

Kale or Borecole (1934).   This vegetable is related to collards or cabbage. Scotch (green, Liberian, or blue) kale has curly or crinkly leaves. Spring kale is a smooth-leaved variety. Specify "washed, bunched, or stripped" kale. Bronzing or browning from cold does not harm flavor but does harm appearance. Specify U.S. No. 1.

Mustard Greens (1953).   Young, tender mustard greens also make good salad greens. Smooth and curly-leaved varieties running from dark to light green are available. Seed stems indicate age and toughness (see Figure 10–16).

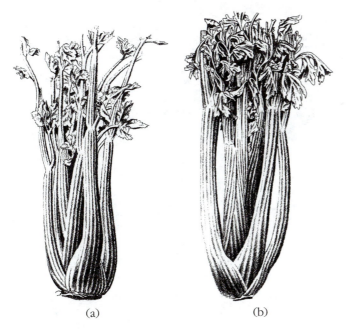

(a)   (b)

Figure 10-15
(a) Well-trimmed celery; maximum extent appearance may be affected by leaf removal or leaf portions on U.S. Extra No. 1 and U.S. No. 1. (b) The lower limit of bowing and twisting. (Courtesy USDA.)

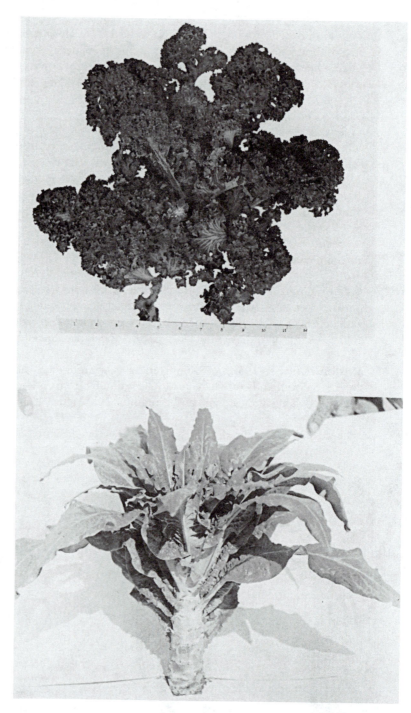

Figure 10-16
Curled kale (top); stem lettuce (bottom); sorrel (opposite). The last can also be used as a salad green. (Courtesy USDA.)

Figure 10-16 *Continued*

Spinach (1987).   Spinach is marketed all year and peaks from March to June. Savoy spinach ships best because its crinkly leaves prevent packing, which smooth-leaved varieties do not. Sprouts, buds, crowns, or coarse leaves and stems indicate poor quality. Spinach also makes good salad greens. Specify U.S. No. 1, but, if scarce, U.S. Extra No. 1.

Belgian Endive.   This green (actually mostly white) is more popular for salads, but makes a delicious boiled or steamed vegetable with lemon butter added. It is a good keeper under refrigeration.

Sorrel.   Sorrel cooks into a slightly bitter, acid green. Garden sorrel has light, dull green narrow and arrow-pointed leaves. Sheep sorrel (oxalis, wood sorrel, sour grass or sour clove) has light, dull-green leaves with light green to reddish stems and round and cloverlike leaves. They are both often found as common weeds.

Greens, Salad
Select clean, fresh-appearing, brightly colored tender greens. Headed greens should have good solidity and firmness of head. Cut-up products should be free of sulfur dioxide or other harmful bleaches or preservatives, be bright, clean, fresh looking, and not bruised.

Chicory, Endive, and Escarole (1964).   Specify U.S. No. 1 chicory, endive, or esca- role; they are all spreading plants with white centers. Chicory is a broad-leaved green with an upright, spreading growth. Endive, sometimes called curly chicory, is flat and spreading with an almost white heart. Outer areas are green. It is 12–13 in. in diam- eter. Supply is best fall to spring. Escarole is about as big as endive with broad, deeper green leaves. It is available all year and peaks in December.

Check these greens for crispness by twisting a leaf or stem. Bushel containers should weigh 25-lb net. Spread to note insects, rot, or other damage. The leaves should be bright and fresh appearing.

Chicory.   French or Belgium chicory or endive (Whitloof chicory) is a slender, solid, small, green-tipped stalk, plentiful in the winter but available all year. It has a slightly bitter flavor, like curly chicory. The leaves are tightly folded around a small core or heart, forming a solid, elongated head. Specify U.S. No. 1. Whitloof endive, curly en- dive, escarole, and chicory can be cooked as greens.

Lettuces.   There are five kinds of lettuce (1975) (see Figure 10–17): (1) *crisphead* (iceberg), (2) *butterhead* (soft and silky), (3) *cos* (romaine), (4) *looseleaf* (bunched or garden), and (5) *stem*. The latter is cooked and served as a vegetable.

Lettuce is packaged variously; the standard carton is most popular, but bushel baskets or hampers, baskets, and a 1⅙-bushel container are also used. Look for rot, decay, tip burn, ragged leaves, excess wrapper leaves, or small heads; color should be bright, fresh, and clean; check for seed stems. Age or long storage is indicated by a distinct reddish tinge or rust on broken surfaces. Stem butts should be small and light in color, either white or a light pink. Deep red indicates age and bitterness. Watch for aphids, freezing, and sunburn. *Well trimmed* for lettuce means there are no more than three wrapper leaves, none of which are exces- sively large or coarse.

Iceberg lettuce has pale green outer leaves and a crisp, white, and tender in- terior. It is available all year, with California, Mexico, and imports making up the supply during low supply periods. Eastern iceberg has a pointed head in contrast to the flat-headed western iceberg. Iceberg ships and keeps well (see Figures 10–17 and 10–18). U.S. No. 1, vacuum-cooled and well trimmed, 2–2½-doz heads per carton, not less than 40 lb net, should be specified. Cartons hold as many as 5-doz heads. Trimmed, washed, cored, and vacuum-packed lettuce is available as well as chopped lettuce in polyethylene bags. No sodium sulfite should be used to keep quality.

Butterhead lettuce (Boston, bibb, or limestone) is a soft-headed lettuce, with fine, soft leaves, oily to the touch, and very tender. All are greener than iceberg, with a yellow-white inner leaf. Boston lettuce is a large-headed variety. Bibb is medium- headed, and limestone has a small head. All are cup shaped, like a tulip. Bibb and limestone are slightly crisper than Boston.

Leaf (garden) lettuce is not headed but comes in bunches of loose leaves, which are curly or smooth with a pale green or green leaf touched with rusted red. It is not

Figure 10-17
The three most common head types of lettuce used on the market: (left) butter (soft-and smooth-leaved); (front center), iceberg (crisp); and (right) cos lettuce or romaine.
(Courtesy USDA.)

as durable as iceberg and cannot be shipped too far. U.S. Fancy may have to be specified in wither.

Cos (romaine) (1960) is a cylindrical, elongated-headed lettuce with a coarse, stiff leaf, and a slightly stronger but sweeter flavor than iceberg. It is green and quite crisp. Purchase U.S. No. 1. *Fairly well headed* means that four or more inner leaves overlap at the top of the plant.

Other Salad Greens. *Watercress* is used as a garnish as well as salad green. It is best in the spring through July, but available all year. Select fresh, bright, green, crisp, and clean cress and watch for worms or insects, yellow leaves, or wilting. It is usually marketed in 10-doz bunches to a 30-lb box. Barrels may hold 25–30-doz bunches. There are no federal standards. *Frisee* is a French white chicory with a green edge; it is slightly bitter. Italian *riccia* and *graziano* are similar. *Radicchio* is a headed red chicory, slightly bitter, with red or white ribs and interior. A head looks much like red cabbage. *Nasturtium* is a common flower with a round, smooth, pale-green leaf with a distinctive spicy, bitter flavor. The seeds may also be used.

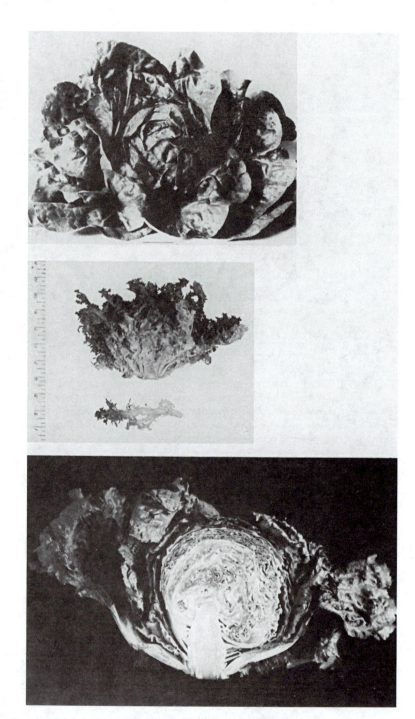

Figure 10-18
Butter or smooth-leaved lettuce (top), curly-leaved endive (center), and a cut head of iceberg (crisp) lettuce showing good head solidity (bottom). (Courtesy USDA.)

A listing of greens, used for garnishes or seasonings, follows—many are related to the families of mint or parsley:

Leafy Plant	Description
Bay leaf	A laurel, grown commonly as a hedge in many areas of the world; it has a spicy, nutty flavor and a hard, shiny, large leaf.
Basil	A roundish, light green, tender leaf that has a soft, delicate flavor somewhat akin to the more pungent flavor of bay leaf.
Burnet	A spicy, full-flavored green leaf that is stronger than sage in flavor; slight acid. It is a member of the rose family.
Chervil	A leafy green like parsley with a spicy parsley-parsnip flavor; it is seen in spring and autumn. A variety of chervil is grown for its root, which is cooked.
Cilantro	Also called Chinese or Mexican parsley; the leaf is very tender and has a rich green color. It is very spicy, with a touch of liquorice flavor. Coriander is the dried fruit of this plant.
Dill	This is a lacy, fernlike-leaved plant with a sweet, delicate but pervasive flavor; it is a flavor associated with dill pickles and other pickled vegetables.
Fennel	A parsley relative, the leaves of which have an agreeable sweet odor and an aromatic taste somewhat resembling anise. The seed is used more than the fresh leaves.
Marjoram	A member of the mint family whose leaves have a distinct, sweet, aromatic flavor with a slightly bitter undertone.
Mint	Green leaves that have a strong, sweet, tangy cool flavor. Peppermint has almost the same flavor but is more bity.
Mustard	The leaves of this plant are sometimes used raw to give a slight mustardy flavor to products that in no way represents the pungency of its seed.
Oregano	A small, tender, light green leaf, that has a flavor like sage-basil-bayleaf but is more pungent and strong. Excellent in salads and Italian sauces.
Parsley	The federal standards have one grade for all varieties; specify U.S. No. 1.
Rosemary	A sweet, fresh, and spicy-flavored leaf that dries into a curved pine-needle shape.
Sage	A velvety, long-leaved plant that has an aromatic, soft pungent flavor that is spicy and somewhat mintlike but slightly more bitter and less pervasive.
Savory	A green leaf with a warm, aromatic, slightly resinous, sagelike flavor; a member of the mint family.
Tarragon	A sweet, nutty flavored, light green small leaf, that has a pervasive, minty flavor.
Thyme	A tiny, round, fully-leaved, curly plant with a strong, sagelike flavor.

Mushrooms (1966)

Our common round, capped mushroom comes in three colors: white, off-white, and tan. All are available all year, usually marketed in 3-, 5-, and 10-lb containers. Precut mushrooms are on the market. Large is over 1⅝ in.; mediums, 1–1⅝ in.; and small, 1 in. or less. Caps should be firm and closed at the stem, with the veil joining the cap unbroken, leaving gills unexposed with few misshapen, dark ones that are bruised, molded, or have other defects. Stems should be closely trimmed, not over 1¼ in. long, clear, and light; dark or black color indicates age. Specify U.S. No. 1, size, and color. Some other mushrooms on the market follow:

- *Chanterelle*—available spring through fall. It has a bright, golden color with a dry texture and peppery, mild flavor.

- *Coral*—a gold, spear-shaped head with a soft, subtle flavor. It is marketed largely in the spring. It has a delicate texture and easily breaks up in cooking.

- *Enoki*—a Japanese, creamy-white mushroom, with a long, fine stem and sweet delicate flavor. Because of its long stem, some call it "a bean sprout with a cap."

- *Morel*—a popular mushroom that is light tan to black. It is a spring product. The dark ones have the best flavor. Insects may be found in the center. Some people find them toxic. The flavor is rich. It can also be obtained dried, which notably increases the rich flavor.

- *Oyster mushroom or pleurotte*—grown in California and France but an Italian mushroom. It has a cap measuring about 8 in. in diameter with a short stem. It is used in sauces or soups or grilled.

- *Portabello*—a large mild, but subtle flavored mushroom that is used to give a delicate flavor to many dishes.

- *Porcini*—an Italian mushroom, now grown all over the world. Stems must be checked for insects. These are good grilled in olive oil with onions. They are also available frozen or dried.

- *Roman or rimini*—a large Italian mushroom. It can have a diameter of 8 in. It is sliced and used in sauces.

- *Shiitake*—a Japanese mushroom, with a wild mushroom flavor and a slight garlic aftertaste, which gives sauces a pronounced flavor.

- *Truffles*—a fungi growing underground and always near a tree. Dogs, pigs, and goats are trained to find them. They are as firm as potatoes and possess a strong odor. French (black) truffles are small, many about the size of ping-pong balls. Italian truffles are white and larger; some can grow to 2 lb. The French season is early December through early March and the Italian one is December to mid-January. A summer truffle grows in France, but it is no match for the others. They are whitish inside and have little odor or taste. Fresh truffles keep refrigerated for about 2 weeks. They should be wrapped in a damp cloth. Freeze-dried or flash-frozen truffles will keep a long time. Truffles are also available canned. They have a musky, fairly strong mushroom flavor, somewhat modified by a faint taste of garlic.

- *Woodears*—a well-known Chinese fungi, also available dried. It has a mild, delicate flavor with rubbery or spongy texture on the inside.

Onions

Three kinds of dry onions are marketed: (1) Late crop or winter (1966), (2) Bermuda-Grano-Granex (1995), and (3) Creole (1943). Onions called long are usually northern grown when days are long, while short ones are often southern grown when days are short.

Dry onions are usually marketed in 50-lb sacks, cartons (48–50-lb net), and bushel baskets or hampers holding 56 lb. Diameter sizes are small, 1–2¼ in.; medium, 2–3¼; and large or jumbo, over 3 in. U.S. No. 1s must be not less than 1½ in. diameter, with red, brown, or yellow kinds having 40% or more of 2 in. and the white kinds having at least 30% 2 in. or more in diameter. U.S. No. 1 boilers may not be less than 1 in. or more than 1⅞ in. in diameter (see Figure 10–19).

Onions are marketed all year, with three peak periods: April and May, June and July, and August to March; the last period dominated by globes, which make up more than 50% of the total dry onion crop (see Figure 10–20). Select bright, clean, hard, well-shaped, dry-skinned, and thin-necked onions. Shaking a bag should give a distinct, dry rustle. Watch for thrips, molds, fungus, or mechanical damage. Store at room or slightly lower temperatures. High humidity encourages rot. Store away from potatoes because dry onions can "steal" potato moisture and rot. Limit stocks to about a two-week supply. Onions give off odors to many foods, so store carefully.

Winter. Winter onions are dominated by globes (red, white, and brown), but other milder, sweeter flavored dry onions such as the sweet Spanish (Valencia) and Walla Walla are included. Winter onions are good keepers but late maturing.

Bermuda. The Bermuda group is sweet and more delicately flavored. At one time the red or white Bermudas held this market, but the Granexs and Granos have now taken over. Many hybrids are also marketed; *Texas sweets* is a term generally applied to all the varieties in this hybrid group.

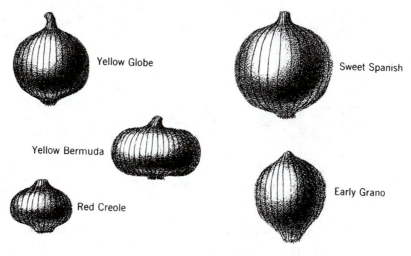

Figure 10–19
Outlines of some of the most commercially important onions on the market. Optimum shape is shown.

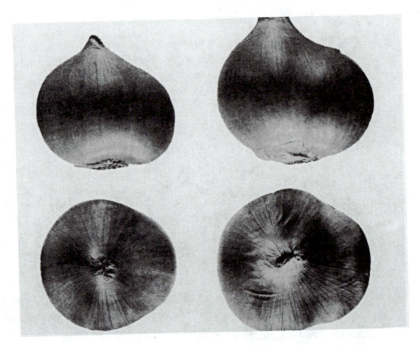

Figure 10-20
The two views of the same onion on the top and bottom left show approximately the lower limit for shape in U.S. No. 1. The two views on the right, top and bottom, show a shape that put the onion into U.S. Commercial grade. (Courtesy USDA.)

Creole.   Creole types are strong and pungent. Some of these are Austrian Brown, Ebenezer, and White Portugal.

The onion market changes rapidly, with new varieties appearing and surging into popularity. Some of the new varieties enjoying present popularity are Abundance, Sweet Spanish (Utah), downing yellow globe, and Southport. Fresh cocktail (pearl) onions are marketed.

Dry shallots look like small onions. They have a very mild onion flavor. They can be obtained in 5-, 10-, or 50-lb bags. Selection factors should be the same as for dry onions. Green onions and shallots are immature plants; green onions (except for the Japanese variety, he-shi-ki) may have bulbs; shallots form none (see Figure 10–21). Market units are cartons holding 4 doz, bushel baskets holding 15–25 lb, and 15¼-in. wooden crates holding 8 doz bunches, 35–40 lb. Large packs of 20–40 bunches, 3 bunches to the pound, are found, tied firmly together. Specify U.S. No. 1, sized small, less than ¼-in. diameters; medium, ¼–1-in. diameters; and large, 1-in. and up diameters. Food services usually use mediums. All should be mild, sweet, and crisp. Green tops should be not less than 8 in. or more than 24 in. Tops should be a bright green and bulbs or lower stems white. Wilted or discolored tops indicate inferior quality; large bulbs indicate age (see Figure 10–22).

Peppers, Sweet (1960)

The Bell (California Wonder) is the usual green pepper marketed. They are available all year, with a peak July through October. Select soft, pliable, good-shaped, thin-fleshed

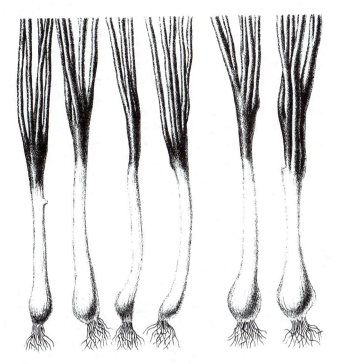

Figure 10-21
*Slight bulb formation (left) is permitted in U.S. No. 1 grade.
Bulb formation called not excessive is permitted in U.S. No. 2
grade (right). Desirable bulb formation is shown in the center.*
(Courtesy USDA.)

Figure 10-22
Leeks, onions, chives, and young shallots are shown from left to right. (Courtesy
USDA.)

peppers with a clear, bright green color and a soft, waxy sheen. Test for crispness and tenderness by puncturing with the thumbnail. Shriveling or excessive softness indicate age or immature harvesting. Watch for deformities or defects. A bleached, discolored area that appears sunken or resembles a water-soaked blister indicates decay (see Figure 10–23). U.S. Fancy sweet green peppers must have a minimum diameter of 3 in. and be 3⅓ in. long; No. 1s must be a minimum of 2½ in. in diameter and 2½ in. in length. Shape affects grade. Red, purple, yellow, and white sweet peppers are on the market.

Hot peppers are available fresh or dried, usually of the chili, pimiento, and cayenne varieties.

Potatoes, Irish (1991)

Our largest single vegetable crop is Irish potatoes; over 12 billion lb are grown per year. It is a year-round crop, with new or immature potatoes coming to market every month. Mature potatoes are harvested in the fall, and stocks last until the next fall. There are 12 leading varieties:

Type	Description	Growing Area	Best Use
ROUND TO OBLONG WHITE			
Katahdin	Large, short, medium thick; shallow eyes	East	*
Chippewa	Large, elliptical to oblong, medium thick; shallow eyes	Mainly New York	†
Kennebec	Large, elliptical to oblong, medium thick; shallow eyes	East	†
Irish cobbler	Medium to large, blunt ends; shallow to deep eyes	Midwest	‡
Norchip	Round to oblong, medium size, shallow eyes, creamy white skin	Midwest	†
ROUND TO OBLONG RED			
Triumph	Medium to large, round, thick; medium deep eyes	Midwest	‡
Red Pontiac	Large, oblong to round, smooth or at times netted; medium deep eyes	East and Midwest	†
Norland	Oblong, smooth red skin, shallow eyes	Midwest	†
Red LaSoda	Semiround to slightly oblong, intense red skin, medium to shallow eyes	Midwest	†
LONG WHITE			
White Rose	Large, oval, flat, many medium deep eyes	West	†
RUSSET			
Russet Burbank	Large, long, oval, heavily netted, numerous shallow eyes	West	*
Norgold	Oblong to long, shallow eyes, netted skin	Midwest	†

*Dry, mealy, and high in starch; good for deep-frying, chips, baking, and mashing.
†Fairly dry and high in starch; good for all purposes.
‡Slightly moist and lowest in starch; good for boiling, hash browns, sautéing, au gratin, or creamed; poor for deep-frying, baking, or mashing.

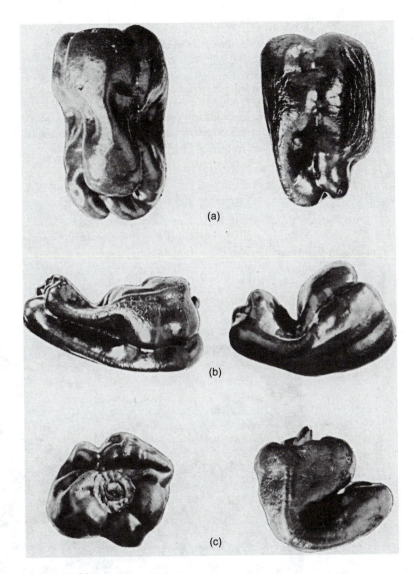

Figure 10-23
(a) Well-shaped, (b) fairly well-shaped, and (c) badly misshapen peppers.
The slight wrinkling noted in some may exist because the pepper is picked
at an immature stage. (Courtesy USDA.)

Bakers are marketed in 50-lb cartons, washed, and sized from 50–140 per carton. Mature potatoes are shipped in burlap, polyethylene, or solid paper sacks, 50-
or 100-lb net, or in 50-lb cartons. Potatoes sized the same have the lowest paring loss
(about 25%); deep-set eyes or thick skin increase this loss.

Grades are U.S. Extra No. 1, No. 1, Commercial, and No. 2 Extra. Extra No. 1s
are cleaner and have fewer defects than No. 1, but both are suitable for foodservice

use. No. 1s must (1) have similar varietal characteristics, (2) be firm, (3) be fairly clean, (4) be fairly well shaped, (5) be free from (a) freezing, (b) blackheart, (c) late blight, southern bacterial wilt, or ring rot, (d) soft rot or wet breakdown, and (6) be free from damage. Size must not be less than 1⅞ in. in diameter, unless otherwise specified. No more than 8% defective potatoes can be found. Specify sizes as:

A	Minimum diameter 1⅞ in. with at least 40% 2½ in. in diameter or more, or 6 oz in weight or more.
B	1½ in.–2¼ in. in diameter.
Small	1¾ in.–2½ in. in diameter.
Medium	2¼ (5 oz)–3¼ (10 oz) in. in diameter.
Large	3 in. (10 oz) to 4¼ in. (16 oz) in diameter.

(See Figures 10–24 through 10–28.)

Some growing areas have found meeting the sizing standards for potatoes difficult, and so these may in the future be changed.

Low-moisture, high-starch, mealy potatoes with a specific gravity of 1.08 or more give a dry, mealy, light, mashed, deep-fried, or baked potato; moist, slightly waxy potatoes, lower in starch and higher in moisture, with a specific gravity of 1.01 to

Figure 10-24
Large, medium, and small potatoes. (Courtesy USDA.)

Figure 10-25
Lower limit, pinched shape for long type in U.S. No. 1. (Courtesy USDA.)

Figure 10-26
The lower limit growth crack and knob, or second growth, for U.S. No. 1. (Courtesy USDA.)

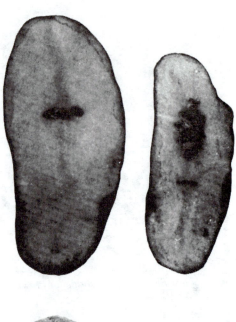

Figure 10–27
Lower limit hollow heart respectively for U.S. Nos. 1 and 2. (Courtesy USDA.)

Figure 10–28
Lower limit air crack and russet scab for U.S. No. 1. (Courtesy USDA.)

1.065, are good for boiling, hash browns, salad, creamed or other form. Maturity, variety, and growing conditions affect the moisture and starch content.

Washington, Idaho, and Oregon russet Burbanks are considered the best baking, mashing, and deep-frying potatoes (see Figure 10–29). North Dakota's Red River valley produces some high-quality russet Burbanks, as well as Wisconsin. Maine's Katahdin potato is fairly good for baking, mashing, or deep-frying. California's Irish rose is a good all-round potato but is usually marketed immature, which restricts use. Immature potatoes (new potatoes) have thin skins, a high moisture content, and are best used as steamed potatoes, boiled potatoes, or for salads because of their heavy and waxy texture and solidness that holds shape.

Potatoes, Sweet and Yams (1963)

The government standards for sweet potatoes and yams are the same. Sweets are lighter in color, drier, and less sweet; yams break up more easily in cooking. Sweet potatoes are preferred for candying or other purposes for which a distinct piece is desired; they are also drier and mealier. Both must be marketed mature. Select clean, firm, potatoes, free from blemishes (see Figure 10–30). They are usually marketed in

Figure 10-29
*(a) Superior, (b) Katahdin, (c) immature cobbler, (d) Kenewick, (e) russet,
(f) mature Irish Cobbler, and (g) Chippewa.* (Courtesy USDA.)

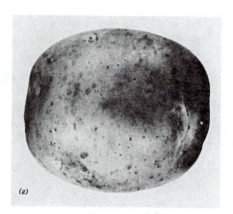

Figure 10-29
(continued)

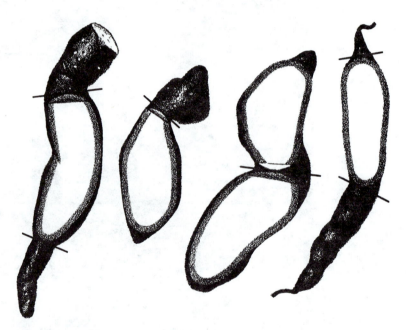

Figure 10-30
Buyers of sweet potatoes should note shapes because too many irregularities can mean a lower yield. These potatoes are termed fairly well-shaped with one or more usable pieces according to USDA standards. (Courtesy USDA.)

24- or 40-lb boxes. Shape affects grade. If the potatoes appear damp, look for rot. Shriveled, soft, and flabby potatoes usually have a poor flavor and are wasteful. Cut to note coarse veining or stringiness. U.S. Extra No. 1 or No. 1 should be purchased. They are marketed all year, but supplies are heaviest in fall and winter. We import some of our needs.

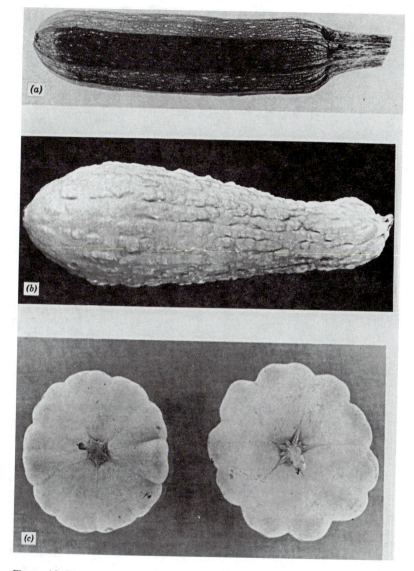

Figure 10-31
Varieties of summer squash: (a) zucchini, (b) straightneck, and (c) cymbling (scallop or pattypan). (Courtesy USDA.)

Squash and Pumpkin

Summer (1984) and winter squash (1983) are marketed. Summer varieties are closely related to the cucumber, and are usually cooked unpared, with seeds, so they must be picked immature with tender seeds in a firm gel (see Figure 10–31). Winter squash is higher in starch, keeps better, and is usually baked or mashed. Some differentiating characteristics of summer squash are:

Kind	Description
Zucchini (Italian)	Long and green cylinder shape
Straightneck	Long, yellowish or whitish; apex is bigger than stem end
Cymbling, scallop, or pattypan	Round and scalloped with a pale, greenish skin; some are slightly warted
Crooknecked	Yellow; larger flower end (apex) than stem; has a bend at the stem end; often has warted skin
Yellow straightneck	Same as crookneck, but relatively straight
Cocozelle	Almost cylindrical, with a very slightly enlarged apex; smooth, widely ribbed skin; dark green or blackish green to pale greenish yellow
Wintermelon	Small variety should be selected when quite young. These are cucumber-shaped with thin, yellow stripes. Popular Chinese vegetable called fahn gwah or marrow squash. Large kind are pale green, frosty-skinned with a greenish white meat. It is often scooped after the top is cut off, the seeds are discarded, and it is gently boiled and filled with a rich soup. The soup is dished with some of the flesh. The rind may be carved with a pictorial design. They may weigh 20 to 30 lb.

Winter squash are hard-shelled. Some may be small, like acorn squash, or larger, like Hubbard (see Figure 10–32). Some are excellent keepers; others do not keep as well, but they are all less perishable than summer squash. The squash should be firm, with a thick, hard, nearly unblemished rind, and be heavy for size. Examine for rot or mold, and press to feel firmness and condition. Buy all squash by the pound. Specify U.S. No. 1 (see Figure 10–33).

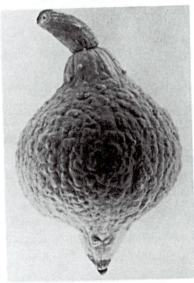

Figure 10-32
The golden hubbard winter squash. (Courtesy USDA.)

Pumpkin is ungraded. It is little used in food services, canned being preferred, usually for use in pies.

Tomatoes

Local tomatoes are available in the summer; then shipments from California, Texas, Florida, Mexico, and other areas take over. These shipped-in tomatoes have a firm, hard meat that really never softens sufficiently in ripening. The flavor is poorer. Sometimes, greenhouse tomatoes are marketed (see Figure 10–34).

Tomatoes come in a variety of containers, some just as a loose jumble pack in apple or other boxes. Packed tomato crates, wirebound or nailed, contain about 60-lb, half-bushel containers that contain 27 lb, and bushel baskets or hampers, 53 lb. Place or cell packs come in two-layer or three-layer flats or cartons, holding, respectively, 18–20 lb and approximately 30 lb. The Los Angeles (L.A.) lug holds 30–34 lb. Climax baskets holding 8, 12, and 16 qt weigh, respectively, 9–11-, 10–20-, and 27-lb net. Hothouse tomatoes are often packed in baskets holding 10 lb.

In 1991 the government changed the sizing of tomatoes. While formerly buyers specified tomatoes by sizing as packed in a layer in rows and columns in a lug such as "6 × 6" (6 in a row in 6 columns), new sizing standards were established using terms such as *small, medium,* etc., with their maximum and minimum diameters. Thus a buyer who used to refer to a 6 × 6 pack now would specify large. Figure 10–35 shows the old sizing and the new.

Buy U.S. No. 1 or a lower grade if market quality is high. Greenhouse tomatoes should be U.S. Fancy or U.S. No. 1. Good shape plus good maturity indicates quality; the tomatoes must be fairly smooth and free from decay, freezing, or damage caused by dirt, bruises, cuts, sunscald, sunburn, puffiness, catfaces, growth cracks, scars, disease, insects, hail, or damage by mechanical or other

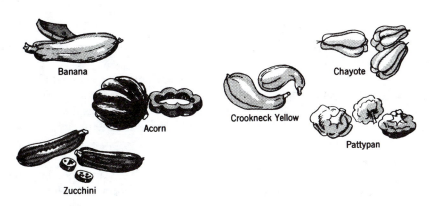

Figure 10-33
Some varieties of squash. Banana and acorn squash keep better than the four summer varieties shown here.

Figure 10-34
Limits of growth cracks and puffiness allowed in U.S. No. 1 grade for tomatoes. The left tomato at the top shows maximum aggregate length of radial growth cracks permitted on 2½-in. tomatoes. The tomato at the right top shows concentric growth cracks affecting appearance to the same extent as maximum aggregate length of radial growth cracks permitted in U.S. No. 1. These limitations apply in all stages of maturity. The lower limit allowed in puffiness is shown in the bottom tomatoes. The proportion of open space permitted depends on wall thickness. Thicker-walled ones may have proportionately greater amounts of open space. Tomatoes with thinner walls must have proportionately lesser amounts. (Courtesy USDA.)

means. Watch for worm damage, decay, mold, and wateriness (see Figures 10–36 and 10–37).

Tomatoes are sold by color. Green means the tomato is completely green, varying from light to dark green. Breakers are green to a tannish yellow, pink, or red on not more than 10% of the surface. Turning means that 10–30% is pink or red. Pink puts the amount at 30–60%, and light red, 60–90%. Red is over 90%. Mixed means any kind in ripeness.

Tomatoes are picked green because they are more firm and ship better. When received, they are placed into ripening rooms and speed ripened by using ethylene or kerosene fumes which changes the color and does little to ripen the interior and thus contribute to better flavor or texture. Best ripening temperature at a food service is about 65°F. They do not ripen under refrigeration. In fact, some authorities say "never refrigerate."

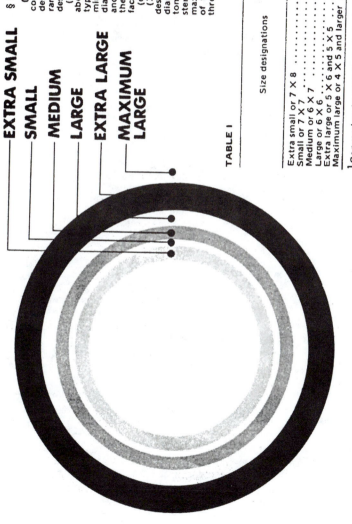

EXTRA SMALL
SMALL
MEDIUM
LARGE
EXTRA LARGE
MAXIMUM LARGE

§ 51.1859   Size.

(a) The size of tomatoes packed in any type container, when specified according to the size designations set forth in Table I, shall be within the size ranges of diameters specified for the respective designations.

(b) In lieu of specifying size according to the above size designations, the size of tomatoes in any type container may be specified in terms of minimum diameter or of minimum and maximum diameters expressed in whole inches, whole inches and not less than thirty-second inch fractions thereof, or millimeters, in accordance with the facts.

(c) For tolerances see § 15.1861.

(1) In determining compliance with the size designations the measurement for minimum diameter shall be the largest diameter of the tomato measured at right angles to a line from the stem end to the blossom end. The measurement for maximum diameter shall be the smallest dimension of the tomato determined by passing the tomato through a round opening in any position.

TABLE I

| Size designations | Inches | | Millimeters[1] | |
	Minimum diameter[2]	Maximum diameter[3]	Minimum diameter[2]	Maximum diameter[3]
Extra small or 7 × 8	1 28/32	2 4/32	48	54
Small or 7 × 7	2 4/32	2 9/32	54	58
Medium or 6 × 7	2 9/32	2 17/32	58	64
Large or 6 × 6	2 17/32	2 28/32	64	73
Extra large or 5 × 6 and 5 × 5 ..	2 28/32	3 15/32	73	88
Maximum large or 4 × 5 and larger .	3 15/32	------------	88	------------

[1] Conversion to metric equivalent made to nearest whole millimeter (mm).
[2] Will not pass through a round opening of the designated diameter when tomato is placed with the greatest transverse diameter across the opening.
[3] Will pass through a round opening of the designated diameter in any position.

Figure 10-35

Tomato sizing. (Courtesy: U.S.D.A.)

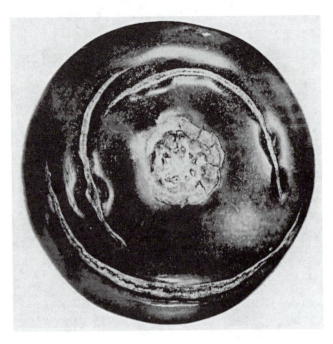

Figure 10-36
Heavy growth cracks or catfaces considerably reduce the grade of the tomato. (Courtesy USDA.)

GRADES

§ 51.1855   U.S. No. 1.

"U.S. No. 1" consists of tomatoes which meet the following requirements:

(a) Basic requirements:

  (1) Similar varietal characteristics;

  (2) Mature;

  (3) Not overripe or soft;

  (4) Clean;

  (5) Well developed;

  (6) Fairly well formed; and,

  (7) Fairly smooth.

(b) Free from:

  (1) Decay;

  (2) Freezing injury; and

  (3) Sunscald.

(c) Not damaged by any other cause.

§ 51.1861   Tolerances.

In order to allow for variations incident to proper grading and handling in each of the foregoing grades, the following tolerances, by count, are provided as specified:

(a) U.S. No. 1.–(1) For defects at shipping point.–Ten percent for tomatoes in any lot which fail to meet the requirements for this grade: Provided, That not more than one-half of this tolerance, or 5 percent, shall be allowed for defects causing very serious damage, including therein not more than 1 percent for tomatoes which are soft or affected by decay; and,

(2) For defects en route or at destination.–Fifteen percent for tomatoes in any lot which fail to meeet the requirements for this grade: Provided, That included in this amount not more than the following percentages shall be allowed for defects listed:

  (i) Five percent for tomatoes which are soft or affected by decay;

  (ii) Ten percent for tomatoes which are damaged by shoulder bruises or by discolored or sunken scars on any parts of the tomatoes; and,

  (iii) Ten percent for tomatoes which are otherwise defective. And provided further, That not more than 5 percent shall be allowed for tomatoes which are very seriously damaged by any cause, exclusive of soft or decayed tomatoes.

Figure 10-37
U.S. grading of tomatoes. (Courtesy USDA.)

Some tomatolike products are tomatillos (ground tomato) and tamarillo (tree tomatoes). The former is a husk-covered fruit growing on vines that look like a tomato plant. They are often cooked in syrup and served as a preserve. These products should be clean and firm with a bright green to yellowish green and have dry husks. Tamarillos are an oval to elongated egg-shaped fruit about 2 in. long with a reddish purple color when ripe. The topepo (Chinese tomato) is a cross between the tomato and the Chinese small green pepper. It is used in salads and should be purchased on the same basis as is used for tomatoes.

BEST BUYS

Because the fresh fruit and vegetable market is so dynamic, buyers should keep it under constant surveillance to take advantage of best buys. A sudden influx of cucumbers on the market might drop prices so that a change in menu would be worthwhile to take advantage of the bargain. Or a sudden rise in price or shortage of an item may make a menu change desirable to avoid a higher price. It is wise to keep in touch with purveyors who often have advance knowledge of possible market changes. One purchasing agent at a large university was alerted by vendors that fresh potato prices would go sky high in the fall because of a heavy freeze in western potato-producing states. He set about purchasing all the processed potatoes available. When the time came and prices jumped, these processed potatoes were used instead of the fresh product. A big saving resulted. Because of the high perishability of many items purchased, buyers need to estimate quantities needed quite closely. Overbuying is to be avoided.

Knowing an item's characteristics and quality factors also helps in deciding which is the best buy. If the menu calls for a peach pie, a buyer should know that a Michigan peach will do as well as a western one and select the most favorably priced one. A McIntosh apple could be substituted for a Delicious for a Waldorf salad if the Delicious were too high priced. Why purchase golden or bright quality grapefruit to peel for a grapefruit and avocado cocktail when russeted grapefruit is lower priced?

Knowing yields is another help in determining the best buy. A case of Florida grapefruit weighing 40 lb yields about 19 lb of sectioned grapefruit (there is about 51% waste), the equivalent of slightly over 2 gal of grapefruit. What price should be paid per gallon for sectioned grapefruit, if the grapefruit costs $18 per case, it takes two hours to do the sectioning, and labor is $4 an hour? Obviously, the sectioned grapefruit costs around $12 and is the equivalent in price. Are the two equal in quality, however? This also must enter into the decision.

Leaf lettuce has a waste of about 26%, romaine of 36%, fairly well-trimmed crisp head of 26%, well-trimmed crisp head of 5%, and soft-headed lettuce of 26%. Is it better to substitute one for the other considering market prices, or is it better to purchase lettuce cut up and ready to use to avoid any labor costs? Besides price and quality, convenience must be evaluated. It may be better to pay just a bit more because of the convenience. Storage may also be a problem, and anything that reduces a storage need is of value. Quality and price are not the only considerations.

If buyers know production needs and work with the production department, some items of lesser quality might be substituted for others. For instance, if a considerable amount of celery is to be chopped and used for soups, salads and other things, No. 2 grade celery might be better because once the product is chopped it cannot be distinguished from the No. 1 product.

Sometimes a buyer finds a bulk pack a better buy. Strawberries usually come in trays of cups but at times they appear just as trays. The yield is higher and the price is often lower per pound of product. The cost of packaging needs to be watched. Packaging, for food services, is something that protects the item and gets it there in good shape. It has little or no merchandising or other utility value. No one sees it except the back of the house. Thus, fancy packaging is a cost that can be dispensed with.

Sizing must also be watched. If tomatoes are to be cut up and yields are considered, you may use a smaller tomato at a lower price than the larger ones used for slicing. Each season and at different times of the season, buyers need to look at the prices of different size oranges which will be juiced. There is only a slight difference in yield, by size; therefore, price can be important.

Evaluations of price on the market AP and eventual cost to the operation should consider hidden factors. Besides labor, what about the cost of energy needed to pare or prepare and cook? Cooking losses need to be considered. Knowledge of yields is a must. Tables 10–9 and 10–10 give the average amount required for 100 portions. Such tables should be used as a constant reference by buyers and those who write menus, not only to know how much is needed for service but for comparing amounts and prices to see which is the best buy.

Table 10–9
Quantities to order of fresh vegetables.

Produce Item	Unit of Purchase	Wt. per EP Yield Unit	%	Portion AS	Portions per Purchase Unit	Units per 100 Portions
Asparagus	lb	1.00	49	4 med spears, or 3	3.83	29¾
Asparagus	crate	28.00	49	cut spears	73.17	1⅓
Beans, lima, green, pod	lb	1.00	40	3 oz	2.13	47
Beans, lima, green, pod	bu	32.00	40	3 oz	68.27	1½
Beans, lima, green, shelled	lb	1.00	102	3 oz	5.44	18½
Beans, snap, green, or wax	lb	1.00	84	3 oz	4.48	22½
Beans, snap, green, or wax	bu	30.00	84	3 oz	134.40	¾
Beet greens, untrimmed	lb	1.00	44	3 oz	2.35	42¾
Beet greens, untrimmed	bu	20.00	44	3 oz	46.93	2¼
Beets, with tops	lb	1.00	43	3 oz	2.29	43¾
Beets, no tops	sack	50.00	76	3 oz	202.67	½
Blackeyed peas, shelled	lb	1.00	93	3 oz	4.96	20¼
Broccoli	lb	1.00	62	3 oz	3.31	30¼
Broccoli	crate	40.00	62	3 oz	132.27	¾
Brussels sprouts	lb	1.00	77	3 oz	4.11	24½
Cabbage, cooked	sack	50.00	79	3 oz	213.33	½
Cabbage, for slaw	sack	50.00	79	2 oz	316.00	⅓

Source: Agricultural Handbook 284, USDA.

Table 10-9 *continued*

Produce Item	Unit of Purchase	Wt. per EP Yield Unit	%	Portion AS	Portions per Purchase Unit	Units per 100 Portions
Carrots, no tops	sack	50.00	75	3 oz	200.00	½
Cauliflower	lb	1.00	45	3 oz	6.56	15¼
Cauliflower	crate	37.00	44	3 oz	86.83	1¼
Cauliflower	crate	50.00	44	3 oz	117.33	⅚
Celery, cooked	lb	1.00	70	3 oz	3.73	27
Celery, raw	lb	1.00	75	2 oz	6.00	16¾
Celery, raw	crate	60.00	75	3 oz	240.00	⁴⁄₁₀
Celery hearts, 24	box	30.00	95	2 oz (raw)	228.00	½
Chard, untrimmed	lb	1.00	56	3 oz	3.00	33
Collards	bu	20.00	81	3 oz	86.40	1¼
Corn, 60 ears	sack	40.00		1 ear	60.00	1⅔
Cucumber, raw	bu	48.00	95	3 oz	243.20	⁴⁄₁₀
Eggplant	bu	33.00	75	4 oz	100.00	1
Endive, escarole, chicory	lb	1.00	75	1 oz	12.00	8⅓
Endive, escarole, chicory	bu	25.00	75	1 oz	300.00	⅓
Kale, untrimmed	bu	18.00	81	3 oz	77.76	1⅓
Lettuce, head	lb	1.00	74	2 oz	6.00	17
Lettuce, head	carton	2 doz	74	⅛ head	144.00	13 heads
Romaine	lb	1.00	64	2 oz	5.12	20
Mushrooms	lb	1.00	67	1 oz	10.72	9½
Mushrooms	basket	9.00	67	3 oz	32.16	3¼
Mustard greens	bu	20.00	59	3 oz	62.93	1¾
Okra	bu	30.00	96	3 oz	153.60	¾
Onions, green, raw	lb	1.00	60	3 oz	3.20	31¼
Onions, mature	sack	50.00	76	3 oz	202.67	½
Parsley	lb	1.00		1 sprig	8 cups	2
Parsley	crate	19.00		1 sprig	9 gal	¹⁄₁₀
Parsnips	bu	50.00	84	3 oz	224.00	½
Peas, shelled	lb	1.00	96	3 oz	5.12	19¾
Peas, in pod	lb	1.00	36	3 oz	1.92	52¼
Peppers, green, raw	lb	1.00	82	1 oz	13.12	7¾
Peppers, green, raw	bu	25.00	82	1 oz	328.00	⅓
Peppers, green	carton	30.00	82	½ pepper	300.00	⅓
Potatoes, pared	sack	100.00	76	4 oz	360.00	.3
Potatoes, stripped and french fried	sack	100.00	54	2 oz	416.00	¼
Potatoes, jacket	sack	100.00	100	1 med	300.00	⅓
Pumpkin, mashed	lb	1.00	63	4 oz	2.52	39¾
Radishes, no tops	lb	1.00	90	1 oz or 4	12.00	8⅓
Rutabagas	bu	56.00	77	4 oz	3.08	32½
Spinach, untrimmed	bu	20.00	67	3 oz	71.47	1½
Squash, summer	bu	35.00	83	3 oz	154.93	¾
Squash, acorn	lb	1.00		½ squash	2.00	50
Squash, hubbard	lb	1.00	58	4 oz	2.30	45
Tomatoes, medium	lb	1.00	91	2 slices	7.50	13½
Tomatoes, medium	lb	1.00	91	wedge	12.00	8⅓
Tomatoes, medium	lug	32.00	91	wedge	384.00	¼+
Tomatoes, medium	bu	53.00	91	3 slices	265.00	⁴⁄₁₀
Turnip greens	bu	20.00	48	3 oz	146.00	¾
Turnips, no tops	bu	50.00	73	3 oz	190.00	½+
Watercress	bunch	1.00	92	½ cup	27.77	4

Table 10-10

Portion size and quantities of fresh fruits required for 100 portions.

Fresh Fruits as Purchased	Unit of Purchase	Weight per Unit (lb)*	Portion as Served	Portions per Purchase Unit (no.)	Approximate Purchase Units for 100 Portions (no.)
Apples	Pound	1.00	1 medium, baked or raw	3.00	33½
	Bushel	40.00	"	120.00	†
	Pound	1.00	2 oz raw, chopped or diced	6.08	16½
	"	1.00	4 oz applesauce	3.48	28¾
	"	1.00	4 oz cooked, sliced or diced	2.52	39¾
	"	1.00	⅙ 9-in. pie (2.12 lb of apples per pie)	2.83	35½
	"	1.00	⅛ 9-in. pie	3.77	26¾
Apricots	"	1.00	2 medium	6.00	16¾
	Lug	24.00	"	144.00	†
Avocados	Pound	1.00	2 oz sliced, diced, or wedges	6.00	16¾
	Lug	12.00	"	72.00	1½
	Box (⅘ bushel)	36.00	"	216.00	†
Bananas	Pound	1.00	1 medium	3.00	33½
	Box	25.00	"	75.00	1½
	Pound	1.00	2 oz sliced for fruit cup	5.44	18½
	"	1.00	3 oz sliced for dessert	3.63	27¾
	"	1.00	4 oz mashed	2.72	37
Blackberries	Quart	1.42	1 oz salad garnish	21.53	4¾
	"	1.42	3 oz	7.18	14
	Crate (24 qt)	34.00	"	172.22	†
	Quart	1.42	⅙ 9-in. pie (0.92 qt per pie)	6.54	15½
	"	1.42	⅛ 9-in. pie	8.70	11½
Blueberries	"	1.97	1 oz salad garnish	28.98	3½
	"	1.97	3 oz	9.66	10½
	Crate (24 qt)	47.25	"	231.84	†
Blueberries	Quart	1.97	⅙ 9-in. pie (0.59 qt per pie)	10.20	10
	"	1.97	⅛ 9-in. pie	13.51	7½
Cantaloupe	Pound	1.00	3 oz sliced or diced	2.67	37½
	1 (No. 36 size)	2.50	½ medium	2.00	50
	Crate (No. 36)	80.00	"	64.00	1¾
Cherries	Pound	1.00	3 oz pitted, raw	4.75	21¼
	Lug	16.00	"	75.95	1½
	Pound	1.00	⅙ 9-in. pie (1.60 lb per pie)	3.75	26¾
	"	1.00	⅛ 9-in. pie	5.00	20

Source: Food Purchasing Guide for Group Feeding, USDA.

Fresh Fruits as Purchased	Unit of Purchase	Weight per Unit (lb)*	Portion as Served	Portions per Purchase Unit (no.)	Approximate Purchase Units for 100 Portions (no.)
Cranberries	"	1.00	1 oz raw, chopped, for relish	15.36	6¾
	"	1.00	2 oz sauce, strained	14.56	7
	"	1.00	2 oz cooked, whole	19.12	5¼
	Box	25.00	"	478.00	†
Figs	Pound	1.00	3 medium	4.00	25
	Box	6.00	"	24.00	4¼
	Box	6.00	"	24.00	4¼
Grapefruit	Pound	1.00	4 fl oz juice	1.61	62¼
	Dozen (No. 64 size)	15.00	"	24.22	4¼
	Pound	1.00	4 oz segments	1.88	53¼
	Dozen	15.00	"	28.20	3¾
	"	15.00	½ medium	24.00	4¼
Grapefruit segments	½-gal jar	4.22	4 oz	10.88	6
Grapes					
With seeds	Pound	1.00	4 oz, seeds removed	3.56	28¼
Seedless	"	1.00	4 oz	3.76	26¾
	Lug	24.00	"	90.24	1¼
Honeydew melon	Pound	1.00	3 oz sliced or diced	3.20	31¼
	1 melon	4.00	Wedge, ⅛ melon	8.00	12½
	"	4.00	3 oz sliced or diced	12.80	8
Lemons	1 lemon (medium)	.23	1 slice	8.00	12½
	"	.23	1 wedge	6.00	16¾
	Pound (about 4 lemons)	1.00	2 oz juice	3.16	31¾
	Carton	36.00	"	113.76	†
Limes	1 lime (medium)	.15	Wedge, ¼ lime	4.00	25
	Pound	1.00	2 fl oz juice	3.52	28½
	Box (⅘ bushel)	40.00	"	140.80	†
Mangoes	Pound	1.00	3 oz sliced or diced	3.57	28¼
	Lug	24.00	"	85.76	1¼
Oranges	Pound	1.00	4 fl oz juice	1.83	54¾
	"	1.00	4 oz sections (no membrane)	2.24	44¾
	"	1.00	4 oz sections (with membrane)	2.80	35¾
California	Carton	38.00	"	106.40	†
Florida	Box	85.00	4 fl oz juice	155.55	†
Medium No.176	Pound	1.00	1 whole	2.00	50
	Dozen	6.00	4 fl oz juice	11.01	9¼
	"	6.00	4 oz sections (no membrane)	13.44	7½

Table 10–10 *continued*

Fresh Fruits as Purchased	Unit of Purchase	Weight per Unit (lb)*	Portion as Served	Portions per Purchase Unit (no.)	Approximate Purchase Units for 100 Portions (no.)
Small No. 250	Pound	1.00	1 whole	3.00	33½
	Dozen	4.00	4 fl oz juice	7.34	13¾
	"	4.00	4 oz sections (no membrane)	8.96	11¼
Orange segments	½-gal jar	4.28	4 oz	17.12	6
Peaches	Pound	1.00	1 medium	4.00	25
	"	1.00	3 oz sliced or diced	4.05	24¾
	Bushel	48.00	"	194.56	†
	Pound	1.00	⅙ 9-in. pie (1.88 lb per pie)	3.19	32½
	"	1.00	⅛ 9-in. pie	4.26	23½
Pears	"	1.00	1 medium	3.00	33½
	"	1.00	3 oz sliced or diced	4.16	24 ¼
	Bushel	46.00	"	191.36	†
Pineapples	Pound	1.00	3 oz cubed	2.77	36¼
	½ crate	35.00	"	97.07	1¼
Pineapple chunks	½-gal jar	4.36	4 oz	17.44	5¾
Plums	Pound	1.00	3 medium	2.67	37½
	"	1.00	3 oz halves pitted	5.01	20
	4-basket crate	28.00	"	140.37	†
Raspberries	Quart	1.47	1 oz salad garnish	22.87	4½
	"	1.47	3 oz	7.62	13¼
	Crate (24 qt)	35.00	"	181.07	†
	Quart	1.46	⅙ 9-in. pie (0.68 qt per pie)	8.85	11½
	"	1.46	⅛ 9-in. pie	11.76	8¾
Rhubarb, trimmed	Pound	1.00	3 oz cooked	5.49	18¼
	"	1.00	⅙ 9-in. pie (1.44 lb per pie)	4.17	24
	"	1.00	⅛ 9-in. pie	5.56	18
Strawberries	Quart	1.48	1 oz salad garnish	20.53	5
	"	1.48	3 oz	6.84	14¾
	Crate (24 qt)	35.00	"	162.40	†
	Quart	1.46	⅙ 9-in. pie (1 qt per pie)	6.00	16¾
	"	1.46	⅛ 9-in. pie	8.00	12½
Tangerines	Pound	1.00	1 medium	4.00	25
	Box	45.00	"	180.00	†
	Pound	1.00	3 oz sections	3.95	25½
Watermelon	"	1.00	3 oz	2.45	41
	1 melon	18 to 30	1⁄16 melon	16.00	6¼

* Legal weights for contents of bushels, lugs, crates, and boxes.
†Number of purchase units needed is less than amount stated.

Table 10-11
Miscellaneous Fresh Fruit Product Purchase Information.

Name	Packaging, Sizing, and Min. Wt of Contents (lb)	Grade to Order	Season	Remarks
Apricots (1928)	4-basket crate, 26 Brentwood lug, 24–25 L.A. lug, 27–30 Common lug, 12–14	U.S. No. 1	June–Aug; some imports	Blenheim, Moorpoark, Royal, and Tilton are most popular varieties
Berries				
Blueberries (1966)	12 pt cup pack, 11 lb	U.S. No. 1	Summer	
Cranberries (1971)	lb bags, 24/case 25 lb carton 100 lb barrel	U.S. No. 1	Peak Sept. Jan.	
Raspberries (1928)	12 pt cup pack 5½–7½	U.S. No. 1	Mid-summer; some imports	
Strawberries (1965)	12 pt or 6 qt cup pack, 9 traypack, 11–15	U.S. No. 1	Early summer, local all year from southern states and imports	
Other berries (1928)	These include blackberries, dewberries, boysenberries (a cross between a loganberry and a blackberry), loganberries, youngberries, bingleberries, elderberries, and sassafrass (June) berry. All except the last two are related to the raspberry.			
Carambola	Various	None	Summer and fall from southern states	Oval, five-angled about size of lemon; bright golden-yellow skin and thick, waxy cuticle; juicy, crisp flesh without fiber. Delicate, tart, flavor; some can be too tart.
Cherimoya or Custard Apple, or Sherbet Fruit				Apple size, light green color, flecked with brown scars; all brown, too old should yield slightly to pressure.
Cherries, black (1971)	Calex lug, 18–20 Campbell lug, 15–16 Wooden lug, 12–14 Market lug, 20 lb	U.S. No. 1	Spring and summer	Examine for worms, soft or overripe, shriveled fruit; should be bright, fresh, full and plump

387

Table 10-11
continued

Name	Packaging, Sizing, and Min. Wt of Contents (lb)	Grade to Order	Season	Remarks
Coconuts	60–100-lb sacks	None	Year-round; fall through winter	Heavy for size; shake to hear if milk present; dry inside may mean moldy; crack, drain, place in oven to warm so meat removes easily; pare peel with vegetable peeler
Dates	Various	None	Largely imports	Plump with smooth skin, and waxy, red or golden color
Feijoa	Various	None		New Zealand oval fruit, about 1½–3 in. long; looks like guava
Figs	5-lb baskets 9 basket crate or flat, 12–15	None	June–Oct.	Sour odor indicates overripe; purchase little; quite perishable
Gingerroot	Various	None	Year-round	Russeted, crooked rhizome; keeps well under refrigeration
Guava	Various	None		Looks like rough apple 1–4 in. in diameter; usually light green when ripe
Kiwi	28–42 count tray pack, about 20 lb/lug 36–49 count carton, 23 lb lug	None		Member of gooseberry family; brown, furry skin, green tart, sweet flesh with ring of tiny black seeds inside
Lichees	Various	None	Late summer and fall imports; Florida produces some	Cherry-size with brown covering; creamy, sweet fruit with pit inside. Keeps well, fresh 2–3 weeks
Loquat	Various	None		Called a cross between pineapple and banana, but not; 1–3 in. long with thin, downy, pale yellow or orange skin
Mango	¼–1 lb, usually tray packed	None	Late spring and summer	Look for plump, fresh, firm fruit, clear in color; press to check ripeness
Mangosteen	Various	None		4–6-oz round fruit; reddish brown outside; whitish pulp; pineapplish aroma and peachlike flavor

Name	Sizes/Pack	Grades	Season	Characteristics
Melons				
Kiwano	12–15 per carton	None	Winter	About 6 in. diameter, 12–14 in. long; yellow-green, sweet flesh
Pipino	9–12 per carton	None	Winter	6–10 lb, 7–10 in. diameter; soft, creamy white, sweet flesh
Santa Claus	Various	None	Fall and winter	
Casaba	Various	None	Late summer to November	
Papaya (Tree Melon)	Hawaiian: 8 oz–2lb; small, 8–13 oz; medium, 13–16 oz; large, 16–32 oz; extra large, over 32 oz; FL, TX, and imports often large melon sized	Hawaiian: No. 1 and No. 2; no federal grades	Most of the year	Spherical to oblong; cavity filled with black seeds; orange, sweet, low-acid flesh
Passion Fruit				
Sweet	Carton, tray pack; 3–6 in. long, orange-brown skin	None		Tough, leathery skin; whitish, translucent flesh
Purple	Egg size, tough, purple skin			Yellow meat, black seeds
Giant (Sometimes called "Watermelon of the West Indies")	10 in. long; tough, yellowish green skin			Purple flesh; sweet and acidic, lacking full flavor of other two
Persimmon, Oriental (Also a southern persimmon of much less market importance)	Lug, tray pack; Flat, 11–13	None	Fall and early winter	Look for well-shaped, plump, smooth, soft fruit with stem attached; slight wrinkling indicates ripeness
Plum	Fiberboard box or carton, 20–24; Standard peach box, 24–28; Sanger lug, 32; L.A. lug, 28–34; 4-basket crate, 28–30	U.S. Fancy or U.S. No. 1	May–Sept.	Different colored varieties and sizes
Plumcot	Same as for apricots	None	Summer	Cross between a plum and apricot
Pomegranate	48–50 lug	None	Fall	Hard, leathery skin, with many, black seeds; mellow, rich reddish meat

Table 10-11 *continued*

Name	Packaging, Sizing, and Min. Wt of Contents (lb)	Grade to Order	Season	Remarks
Prickly Pear (Cactus Pear)	Lugs, tray packed	None		Reddish color when ripe; soft, red, deep red fresh; black seeds are eaten
Prunes (1969)	½-bu box, 28–30 Fiberboard carton, 20 4-basket crate, 28–30 Wooden box, 12–15	U.S. No. 1 or U.S. Fancy	Jul–Oct.	Oregon prune is slightly tart; California or Imperial (French) is sweeter
Quince	Lugs, tray packed	None		
Rhubarb (1966)				
Michigan	5-lb packs	Extra Special, Extra Fancy, Fancy	Hothouse: Jan.–May Local: Apr.–Sept.	Strawberry rhubarb is deep red; break to test for stringiness
Washington	Lug, 20	Extra Fancy, Fancy		
Federal		U.S. Fancy, U.S. No. 1		Federal Fancy must be 1 in. in diameter and not less than 10 in. long
Sapote	Lug, tray pack	None		Called custard apple but not; greenish-yellow apple appearance
Tamarind	Various	None		Seed from a 3–8 in. pod that has a brownish, acid flesh

Table 10-12
Miscellaneous fresh vegetable product purchase information.

Name	Packaging, Sizing, and Min. Weight of Contents (lb)	Grade to Order	Season	Remarks
Baby Vegetables				
Anise	Case or carton	U.S. No. 1	None	Anise is related to the celery family; it has a sweet, licorice-like flavor.
Artichokes	Case, 10			
Red Beets with Tops	Doz bunches			
Gold Beets with Tops	Doz bunches			
Bok Choy	2 doz box,			
Red Brussel Sprouts	Box, 5			
Carrots with Tops	72 count box			
Corn	50 count carton			
Purple Eggplant	Box, 5			
Pattypan green squash	Box, 5			
Gold Pear Tomatoes	12½ pt carton			
Red Pear Tomatoes	12½ pt carton			
Turnips with Tops	Doz bunches			
Green Zucchini	Carton, 5			
Yellow Zucchini	Carton, 5			
Pumpkins	By the piece			
Lettuce and Greens				
Green Oak Leaf	Case			
Red Oak Leaf	Case			
Red Romaine	Case			
Savoy Salad	Crate			
Tango	Case			
Spinach	Case			
Bamboo Shoots		None	Winter, spring, summer	Young, tender rough brown or green tuberlike emerging shoots of emerging bamboo

Table 10-12
continued

Name	Packaging, Sizing, and Min. Weight of Contents (lb)	Grade to Order	Season	Remarks
Bean Sprouts (Mung sprouts are similar but larger)	Various	None	Year	Look for crisp, creamy white full moderately long sprouts—too long indicates age; dark, dull gray indicates bitter and poor flavor
Beans				
Lima (1938) Fordhook or butter Potato or baby	Pods, bu baskets or hampers	U.S. No. 1	Peak: Aug.–Sept.	Fresh, green, tender pods; shelled, plump, tender skins pale green; smell to detect sourness; Italian broad bean eaten as pods is a relative
Fava Broad (Faba, or English or Windsor)	Shelled beans, various			
Beans, String or Snap				Upon opening look for green, immature seeds; look for good maturity and shape, plump with few tails. *Haricort vert* are small, thin green beans; *Chinese (dow kwok)* are pencil size, thin light green beans about 12 in. long
Beets (1955)	Sack, bu basket	U.S. No. 1 & 2		Specify short trim or topped; diameters should not be less than 1½ in.
Beets Greens (1959)	Hampers or bu baskets, etc.	U.S. No. 1		Can come with or without roots (small red beets) but not mixed
Bok Choy (Chinese Chard)	Case or carton	None	All year	Good keeper; purchase for same factors as used for cabbage
Broccoli Greens	bu baskets	None		Greens, not wilted or coarse
Burdock	Hampers or bu baskets			Heart-shaped leaves and purplish flowers; must be quite young to be tender
Cabbage				
Chinese cabbage or celery (Nappa)	Case, carton, hamper or basket	None	All yr.	Long, tapering head with crinkly leaves on a solid core; it is about 4 in. thick and 18–20 in. long;

Name	Packaging	Grade	Season	Description
Red	See cabbage; often sacked, 50	U.S. 1	Best fall	Pointed head, purple-red color
Savoy	See cabbage; often sacked, 50		Best fall	Yellowish-green, crinkly leaves and loosely formed, slightly flattened heads
Cardoon	Carton or basket	None		Member artichoke family; looks like coarse, dark celery; tender inner part usually only used.
Cactus Leaves (Nopales)	Boxed or carton	None	Apr.–May	Long, light green leaves; spines are usually removed.
Celeriac (Celery Root) (1965)	Mostly bu baskets, 45–50	U.S. No. 1	All year	Large knob of turnip-celery, 2½–4 in. in diameter, creamy; usually cooked
Celtuce	Purchase on lettuce standards	None		Celery-lettuce flavor (cel-tuce); Chinese; enlarged stem, no head; leaves eaten only when young; stem peeled and eaten raw or cooked
Chard	Usually in cartons; buy by lb	None		Beet variety; leaves only eaten; reddish green, crinkled leaves; look for fresh, bright leaves with crisp stalks; if wilted or limpd, of doubtful quality; look for insect infestation
Chayote (Vegetable Pear, Mirliton, Mango Squash)	Carton or bu basket	None		Select hard, dark green ones; related to squash-cucumber family, peel and cook
Chestnuts	Purchase by lb	None	Fall	Hard shell must be removed; soak in very hot water to soften brown peel; sweet, light brown meat when cooked
Collards (1953)	Bu baskets or cartons	U.S. No. 1	Summer and fall	Cabbage family member; resembles kale
Corn (1992), yellow or white	5 doz ears per bag, 50 (unhusked: crates, lugs, or boxes)	U.S. No. 1	Peak: July–Sept.; all year	Look for brown tassels and fresh, green, not dry husks and well developed ears inside with full plump, juicy kernels; no clipped husked or unhusked ear shall be less than 5 in.
Eggplant (1953)	Various	U.S. Fancy or No. 1	All year	Well-colored, well-shaped, firm and free from defects

Table 10-12 continued

Name	Packaging, Sizing, and Min. Weight of Contents (lb)	Grade to Order	Season	Remarks
Flowers	By the 50s and 100s; all edible	None	All year	Many kinds available like pansies, nasturtiums, chrysanthemums, etc.
Garlic (1944)	Mesh sacks, 50; fiberboard cartons, 30; often purchased loose by the lb	U.S. No. 1	All year	White variety, Creole, is strong flavor, small cloves; Italian variety same but larger cloves; Tahiti, 3 to 3 in. in diameter large cloves and mildest; Elephant or Giant can weigh 4 oz or more; large cloves, mild flavor
Garnish and Seasoning Herbs				
Arugula	By the oz; usually 8 oz	None		
Basil	By the oz; usually 8 oz	None		Light green leaf with a delicate flavor akin to bay leaf and thyme
Bay leaf	By the oz; usually dried	None		A laurel with a spicy, nutty flavor, and a hard shiny leaf
Burnet	By the oz	None		Spicy, full flavored green, slightly stronger than sage; some acid; member of rose family.
Chervil	By the oz	None	Spring to fall	Parsley appearance; spicy parsnip flavor; a chervil root is also at times available
Chives	By the oz	None		Small onion-like spear with delicate oniony flavor
Cilantro (Chinese or Mexican Parsley)	By the oz	None		Tender, rich green leaf, very spicy with licorice flavor; coriander is the dried fruit of this plant
Dill	By the oz	None		Lacy, fernlike with sweet delicate, pervasive flavor
Fennel	By the oz	None		Parsley relative; leaves agreeable sweet, odor, aromatic taste faintly like anise; seeds used often
Italian parsley	By the oz	None		

Item	Purchase Unit	Grades	Season	Description
Mint	By the oz	None		Strong, sweet, tangy cool flavored green leaf; peppermint more bity
Marjoram	By the oz	None		Mint relative; distinct, sweet aromatic flavor; slight bitter undertone
Mustard	By the oz	None		Slight mustardy flavor, not pungent
Oregano	By the oz	None		Strong flavor like sage-basil-bayleaf
Rosemary	By the oz	None		Sweet, fresh, spicy leaf that dries into a pine needle shape
Sage	By the oz	None		Velvety, long leaf; aromatic, soft, pungent, spicy, mintlike flavor; slightly bitter
Savory	By the oz	None		Green leaf; warm, aromatic, slightly resinous, flavor relative of the mint
Sorrel	By the oz	None		
Tarragon	By the oz	None		Sweet, nutty, pervasive, minty flavored light green small leaf
Thyme	By the oz	None		Tiny, round, fully leaved, curly plant with strong, sagelike flavor; often used dried
Greens, Cooking Fiddleheads	Carton, sack, etc.	None	May–June	Immature ferns as they emerge from the ground and look like a violin head; remove long tails; sweet woody flavor, crunchy texture
Mache (Lamb's Lettuce, or Corn Salad)		None	Winter	Originated in France or Belgium
Horseradish	By the lb	None	Late summer to winter	Pungent root used as seasoning
Jicama	Bag, 10	None	All year	Brownish, round root served raw or cooked; substitute for water chestnut
Kohlrabi (Cabbage Turnip)	lb or bushel	None		2–3 in. diameter bulk that grows above ground; specify crisp and firm bulbs; cut to note stringiness
Melangas		None		Thick rhizome, russet in color; cooked after paring

Table 10–12 *continued*

Name	Packaging, Sizing, and Min. Weight of Contents (lb)	Grade to Order	Season	Remarks
Mushrooms				
Cepe	By the lb	None		Bright, golden color, peppery, mild flavor, dry texture; also dried
Chanterelle	By the lb	None	Spring through fall	
Coral	By the lb	None		Gold, spear-shaped head; soft, subtle flavor; delicate, fragile texture
Cremini	By the lb	None		Creamy white, long, fine stem, and fine delicate flavor; because of its long stem, called "bean sprout with a cap"
Enoki	By the lb	None		
Morel	By the lb	None	Spring	Tan to black; dark ones flavored; drying increases rich flavor; watch for insects in center; some find them toxic
Oyster or Pleurotte	By the lb	None		Large 8-in. diameter cap, short stem
Porcini	By the lb	None		Available fresh, frozen or dried
Portobello	By the lb	None		
Roman or Rimini	By the lb	None		Large 8-in. cap
Shiitake	By the lb	None		Pronounced, wild, garlicy mushroom flavor; pleasant aftertaste
Truffle	By the lb	None	Italian: Dec to mid-Jan; French: Dec.–Apr.*	French: are black and small ping pong ball size; Italian white; some grow to 2 lb; both firm and possess a strong odor and musky, fairly strong mushroom flavor; faint garlic keep well if wrapped in damp cloth and refrigerated; dried, frozen, and canned available
Trumpets	By the lb	None		Trumpet shaped
Woodears	By the lb	None		Chinese fungi usually available dried, but some fresh; mild, delicate flavor with rubbery or spongy texture inside

Item	Container	Grade	Season	Notes
Parsley	Bunched; 1⅔ bu or 1 bu crates; bu containers; boxes, etc.	U.S. No. 1	All year	Fresh, bright green color, free from dirt and yellowed leaves; bunch weighs about 2 oz; a root (Hamburg) parsley is cooked as a vegetable
Parsnips (1945)	Bags or bu baskets, 50	U.S. No. 1	Fall	Select smooth, firm, small to medium with clear, creamy color; reject flabby, crooked roots
Peas (1942)	Bushel, 28 to 30 lb	U.S. No. 1		Use frozen to avoid labor; the Chinese green pea pod is an immature pod of a special variety. One can purchase black-eyed peas in the pod or shelled.
Radishes (1968)	Usually 1 lb polyethylene bags, 24/case	U.S. No. 1	All year	Specify full or clipped top—clipped to no more than ⅜ in; sizes: small less than ¾ in., medium ¾ to 1 in., and large over 1 in. diameters; large apt to be pithy; should be firm, crisp, well shaped, tender, and mild in flavor; Dakon is a large, long white radish of Oriental origin
Salsify (Oyster Plant)	Sacks or boxes	None	Fall	Oyster taste; use parsnip factors for purchase
Shallots	½ by wirebound crates, 8 doz bunches, 40; bu crates, 5 doz bunches, 25	U.S. No. 1	Oct.–May	Fresh bulbs should be ¼–¾ in. in diameter; tops with bulbs should not be over 22 in. long; "clipped top" means clipped back evenly; "trimmed" means some top is clipped away; usually purchased mature, dry
Turnips and Rutabagas (1955)	Often sacked, 50 Turnips with tops in bunches in cartons	U.S. No. 1	Fall	Use beet sizing for beets; reject those over 2½ in. in diameter; rutabagas can be larger; medium size in both best; rutabagas often waxed; specify turnips with tops, clipped tops or no tops
Vendolagas (Purslanem or Fatweed)		None		Small, thick, green leaves with fleshy, tender stems; semi-tropical plant
Waterchestnut		None	All year	Corm (tuber) that grows under water, has brown skin; flavor like chestnut blended with coconut; available frozen or canned, but raw of superior flavor; has crisp texture even after cooking
Yucca (Cassava or Manioc)		None		Root of tropical plant; large, yellow, starchy

*Also a summer white truffle, whitish inside; little odor or taste. Also see Figure 10–38.

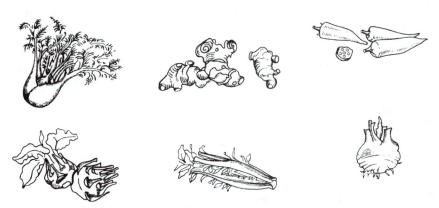

Figure 10-38
Some vegetables not much used in the normal food service except for celery. (right to left, top) Anise is a plant related to celery. It has a licorice flavor plus that of celery. The Jerusalem artichoke is a root rhizome, served raw and cooked; when cooked, it tastes much like the cooked globe artichoke heart. Okra is a vegetable often used in southern dishes. (right to left, bottom) Kohlrabi is a turnip-looking and -tasting bulb that grows above ground. Celery is the commonly used vegetable. Celery root is a plant grown especially for its root and is not part of the regular celery stock.

SUMMARY

The fresh produce market is highly dynamic, and buyers have to keep abreast of developments at all times. A sudden change can mean a loss of considerable sums. Growing and processing procedures are constantly changing. Weather can create a sudden change. Conditions change not only yearly but seasonally and even daily. The product is usually highly perishable; some produce has a shelf life of only a few days. Packaging is changing rapidly with the result that shelf life has been extended for many items. Shipping has also changed with the result that produce now keeps better in shipping and arrives at the markets in better condition. Rapid shipping has made it possible to ship produce from foreign lands, thus extending the seasons in which buyers can obtain items.

Fresh fruits and vegetables are highly nutritious and five portions are recommended in the average daily diet. They furnish valuable minerals and vitamins as well as good fiber. Some are high in carbohydrates. Few are high in fat or sodium.

Upon receiving items, look for clean produce that is free from insects, blemishes, or other defects and damage. Watch for weights. It is best to specify many items by the pound rather than by the container. Some items have a high preparation or high labor cost to prepare and it may be wiser for buyers to purchase the processed item. The market for processed items has grown rapidly.

Because of their high perishability, produce must be quickly stored after receipt and under the proper conditions. Some require a rather high humidity and a temperature just above freezing. However, items like potatoes do not do well under such storage; they develop sugar from their starch, which destroys texture in the cooked product. Some items like tomatoes, bananas, and some other tropical items should not be stored under refrigeration. Some items have to be stored separate from others because they give off odors or absorb them.

Buyers need to know the quality factors that make up the various grades. They also have to know things like size, preparation loss, packaging, areas where the best produce comes from, seasons, etc.

This chapter covers most of the fresh produce available on the market.

REVIEW QUESTIONS

1. What is hydrocooling? Vacucooling? Blast tunnel cooling?
2. What are some of the new technological advances that have helped improve our fresh produce?
3. Why must there be different grading standards for fresh produce according to growing area, such as the three standards for citrus fruit for the Florida, Texas, and California–Arizona areas?
4. What does count mean in fresh produce? Are there several meanings? Do counts always indicate the number in a package?
5. From where in this country do the best lemons come from? Limes?
6. How can one tell when a pineapple is ripe?
7. What kind of oranges would a buyer specify in the summer? The winter?
8. What would be an external specification for the purchase of apples for Waldorf salad for a high-price menu? For a low-price menu?
9. What quality characteristics should you look for in fresh asparagus, broccoli, and cauliflower? What quality characteristics should a buyer look for in all kinds of salad greens and lettuces?
10. What are the best storage conditions for potatoes?
11. What happens when potatoes are held at low refrigerated temperatures? How can one restore quality in them?
12. Washed, sized potatoes are sold in cartons. For what use? What is the net weight of these cartons and what various counts are available at this weight?
13. What packaging is used for various kinds of citrus fruits?
14. What do these terms mean in purchasing tomatoes: *green, breakers, turning, pink, light red, red?*
15. How are tomatoes packed for shipment today? What does the term *5 × 6 pack* mean?
16. How does ethylene gas affect bananas and tomatoes?
17. What are the quality indicators for U.S. No. 1 tomatoes?
18. What should a specification contain to get a good sweet potato for candying?
19. List reasons why fresh produce is more difficult to buy than other products.
20. Define the terms *struck full, loose fill, bulging pack, filled and faced, fill equal to facing.*

21. List and discuss the different requirements of temperature and relative humidity for citrus fruits, potatoes, avocados, lettuce, and apples.

22. List the characteristics indicating quality in all kinds of berries.

23. Indicate the desirable characteristics for all citrus fruit.

24. Discuss the identifying factors among cantaloupes, honeydews, and watermelons.

25. List the kinds of cabbages and select the best one for cole slaw, salad garnish, and cooking.

26. Discuss the various major greens and the reasons for selecting each kind for a salad bar, for a tossed salad, for a Caesar salad, for sandwiches, for garnish.

SPECIFICATIONS

Note: The Culinary Institute of America recommends to its students that specifications for fresh produce be in the following form:

Item	Grade and Availability	How Purchased	Packaging	Weight (lb)
Anise, sweet (fennel)	U.S. No. 1	Firm, feathery, tender stalks, well trimmed and fairly well blanched, minimum diameter of bulb, 2 in., stalk is fresh clean, crisp, and well developed	Carton	60–70
Artichokes (globe or French)	U.S. No. 1 March–May/ Nov.–Dec. (April)*	Trimmed, fairly well formed, plump, fairly compact, but yielding to pressure, tight clinging, fleshy leaf scales of good, uniform, bright dark green color. If separated and open, old	½ carton 40, 44, and 48 count	20
Asparagus	U.S. No. 1 March–June (April–May)*	Fresh, tender and firm, fairly straight with close compact tips; point should be compact; stalks uniform well sized and minimum of ¾ green for entire length; 8–10 in. long; ½ in. or more diameter at base	Carton or case	Pyramids 30 or 18

*Months in parentheses are peak months.

Item	Grade and Availability	How Purchased	Packaging	Weight (lb)
Beans, snap, round green type	U.S. No. 1 May–Sept (June–July)*	Beans of similar varietal character, or fairly uniform size, well formed, bright green or yellow, clean, fresh, young, tender and firm, few stems; long, straight pods; must have definite crisp snap	Bushel	28–30

*Months in parentheses are peak months.

The following are examples of specifications that might be written for some common fresh fruits or vegetables:

Grapefruit

1. Grapefruit segments, fresh, chilled
2. Order 3 gal for every 100 4-oz portions
3. From No. 1 grapefruit
4. Packaged in plastic, sealed gal containers, 4 gal per case
5. Price by case
6. Shall be from Indian River (Florida), Thompson reds

Potatoes, Baking

1. Potatoes, Irish, fresh
2. ROP 5 cartons, maximum stack, 15 cartons
3. No. 1, bakers
4. 50-lb cartons, 100 count
5. Price by the carton
6. Shall be Idaho, Washington, or Oregon mature Burbank russets 1.08 or more specific gravity. Shall be washed. Count size not to vary more than ± 1 oz. Shall not have been refrigerated 14 days before delivery.

Pineapple

1. Pineapple, fresh
2. Order 1 crate for every 100 ⅛ pineapple portions
3. No. 1
4. Crate, 18s, minimum weight per crate 35 lb
5. Price by the crate
6. Shall be yellow-ripe, Hawaiian fruit

Onions, Dry

1. Onions, dry, mature
2. ROP 3 50-lb sacks, maximum 8 sacks
3. No. 1
4. 50-lb sacks
5. Price by the sack
6. Shall be current crop white globes

Lettuce, Iceberg

1. Lettuce, iceberg
2. ROP 5 cartons, maximum 10 cartons
3. No. 1
4. 2 dozen head carton, minimum weight 40 lb/carton
5. Price by the carton
6. Shall be California, Salinas Valley lettuce, vacucooled and well trimmed

Asparagus

1. Asparagus, fresh
2. Order 1⅓ crates for 100 4-spear servings
3. No. 1, state of Washington grade
4. Pyramid crate, minimum weight 38 lb
5. Price by the crate
6. Shall not be less than ½ in. in diameter at base with ⅔ of the spear green.

KEY WORDS AND CONCEPTS

5 × 6 pack (as in tomatoes)

Agricultural Commodities Act

Agricultural Marketing Act

bushel hamper

combination grade

controlled atmosphere packaging (CAP)

field run

greening

hydrocooling

lug

mature

modified atmosphere packaging (MAP)

blossom end on melons

bowing in celery

bushel basket

pyramid crate

russeting

sweating

twisting in celery

U.S. Extra Fancy

U.S. Fancy

U.S. No. 1, No. 2, No. 3

vacucooling

CHAPTER 11

Processed Foods

cc. 1880 American periodical. Extract of happiness. Liebig Extract. From the Louis Szwathmary collection, Culinary Archives and Museum, Johnson and Wales University, used by permission of Dr. Szwathmary and Johnson and Wales University.

Chapter Objectives

1. To briefly summarize the techniques used in food preservation and indicate the basis of quality grading and certification of processed fruits and vegetables.

2. To define standards and terms used on the market for processed foods.[1]

---

[1] A processed food is one that has been changed by some processing method from its natural fresh condition. Thus, for example, a peeled raw potato is a processed food.

3. To detail factors needed to secure the right count, size, or amount of product, including amounts in various packages and also how to obtain drained weight.

4. To indicate the nature, use, and feasibility of using convenience foods.

5. To list amounts required to give a specified number of portions.

6. To present factors needed to obtain specific processed food items.

FOOD PRESERVATION

Since earliest times people have tried to preserve food so that in times of scarcity, there would be something to tide them over. At first humans used nature's own preserved food such as dried berries, nuts, and grains. Then humans found that food could be preserved by drying; later, salting and sweetening were used; honey often was the sweetener. Pickling also was probably known in those early days, a process in which some substances were changed into acid which helped to preserve them, sauerkraut, for instance; salt was used to help this acid preservation process. Smoke was also found to be a preservative and it was combined with salt too to preserve. Chemicals such as sodium **nitrite** or **nitrate (saltpeter)** were also found to be helpful and were widely used to cure meats and some other foods. Alcohol was used in a few ways such as to help preserve wine; alcohol also made it possible to hold some items for a bit longer, but not substantially, as in the case of beer.

Discoveries in Preservation

Food preservation methods in the early 1800s were still quite limited, and often there was hunger, famine, and starvation because food in times of plenty could not be carried through to times of scarcity. Then some scientific discoveries came along that opened up a whole new approach to preservation. **Pasteur** and some others discovered why food spoiled—microorganisms such as yeast, bacteria, and molds—and their control was found to be through heat or freezing.

Appert, a Frenchman, using these scientific discoveries developed a way to preserve food in containers by heating them. For his discovery Napoleon gave him 20,000 francs, a fortune in that time; Napoleon needed preserved food so his troops could travel far distances. The discovery started canning or **appertizing.** Slowly, canning food for the consumer market took off; it was a crude process at first. Thin iron sheets were shaped into cans; tin was used to cover the inside of the can and the food was sealed in the can and heat sterilized. The tin was an inert metal that did not react with many substances and, by preventing contact with the iron of the can, stopped deteriorative chemical reactions.

By the beginning of the twentieth century, canning was a full-fledged business and people were beginning to carry over a wide assortment of rather good foods. Then, we developed freezing and with refrigeration and freezing, a completely new way of food preservation took off with frozen foods beginning to challenge canning as the largest pack.

Rapidly developing technology also made drying and some other processes much more efficient. Freeze-drying, a process in which food is dried while frozen, was developed. Vacu-drying and some other drying techniques were developed, helping in this area. Rapid air transport made it possible to bring foods in from areas having different seasons. Suddenly, people found that the foods available numbered in the thousands rather than just a relatively few. In 1989 the United States produced enough processed fruits and vegetables along with their juices to give every person in this country 10 oz/day.

In the early part of the twentieth century, what was termed "convenience foods" came along, made possible by advancing technology. However, instead of having as the main purpose just the ability to give food a longer shelf life, often these convenience foods were additionally developed to reduce on-premise labor and allow convenience in preparation and the ability to have the food quickly ready for service. Thus today instead of "convenience foods" one hears the term "value-added foods," a better term to describe just what these foods are.

While convenience foods have been looked on as a different food, they are not—they are merely a progression of our use of science and technology in improving our food supply. As we look into the future, we know further advancements in food preservation will occur. Already some foods preserved by radioactive energy are on the market. New advances in packaging are making it possible to preserve fresh produce longer. The caravan moves on.

There is some concern, however, that in making some improvements, we are making our food supply unsafe. To safeguard against this, the government has set up the **GRAS list** (Generally Regarded As Safe list), which lists chemicals and other additives allowed in foods; some may be allowed but only in limited amounts, such as sulfur dioxide, which, if over 200 ppm (parts per million), must be listed on the label as a health hazard. The government also has under its surveillance a number of approved substances that are suspected of being dangerous. Thus, nitrites and nitrates used to preserve meats are under scrutiny because they break down in the body into nitrosoamines, which are suspected of being carcinogenic.

THE MARKET FOR PROCESSED FOODS

The market for **processed foods** is huge and complex. Food is our No. 1 industry and the foodservice industry serves about 25% of it. Thus, even the part of the market that serves this eating out industry is large and complex. This market is well organized and, for its size and complexity, functions with marvelous efficiency. Years of experience and painstaking development have brought this about. Our government functions in it, supplying information, compiling records and statistics, and regulating it. Producers also function well in supplying the materials needed. Often marketing agents and producers of the raw products join together making future plans for production and price. Products move from producers through the hands of many marketing agents, each of which contributes some service.

Processors gather materials and change them in some way to better suit the market. Quantities produced are large and these move out to consumers, gradually being broken down in quantity size until one consumer may purchase only one unit of the millions produced. While few realize it, the efforts of many, many people are required to bring items to the consumer.

REGULATION

Many laws govern the processed food market, but two are of major importance to food service buyers. These and some others were reviewed in a previous chapter.

The **Pure Food, Drug and Cosmetic Act** is highly influential in the field of processed foods, regulating what can or cannot be added to foods, and sets standards for labeling and other things—the GRAS list names additives that are permitted, for instance.

The Agricultural Act allows the USDA to set quality and other standards for processed foods. The **Processed Fruit and Vegetable Division** of the USDA has responsibility for establishing regulatory provisions.

Grading and Brands

Buyers may establish the quality they wish in processed foods either by specifying brand, grade, or describing the quality wanted. Naming the **brand** is sufficient when a buyer knows the brand and its quality. **Grades** establish quality standards that remain fixed for all items covered by the standard. The grades are not specific to a brand, but are a quality level set so buyers and sellers know the quality they are purchasing. It is common to see sellers purchase by grade and then brand the product, selling the product by brand without disclosing the grade quality level.

Usually canners sell their items to brokers and wholesalers without labels, but, if desired, before shipping they can put the buyer's own labels on the goods. While buyers of this kind may purchase by government grade, the label they put on never gives this quality level. Instead, it is the seller's own brand. The purpose is to get food facilities to purchase more by brand than by quality level. When selling by brand, sellers are better able to control products and hold customers.

Often sellers use the same label for all their products, but use different colors to indicate the quality of product inside; thus, Sexton's has its red label representing top quality, its blue label representing its second, and its green label its third.

Buyers need to learn which purveyors sell items at the bottom, midsection, or top of the grade. Some consistently put their brands on items lower in score within the grade, while others put into the package the same grade but a higher scoring product. A brand does not disclose quality and buyers should seek to obtain information on the quality level a brand represents. Three purveyors may offer different brands of a C grade item, with one purveyor's scoring 70, another's scoring 75, and the third's scoring 79. All are grade C, but the third product is most apt to be the better quality.

The listing of quality on the label is voluntary, and buyers will find very few labels give this information. However, some do, and Figure 11–1 shows how this is done. Buyers should be able to get the federal grade by asking the purveyor to give this information. Many buyers specify the score within the grade of many of the processed items they buy.

Until recently the federal government recognized two ways of indicating grades for processed fruits and vegetables. Table 11–1 shows the grading terms used.

In 1990 the government no longer recognized the word terms and used only the letter terms to indicate grades. However, the market does not move quickly, and buyers today still use the word terms.

As indicated, the federal government scores products to establish the grade. The maximum any product can score is 100, and the lowest to get a grade is 70. However,

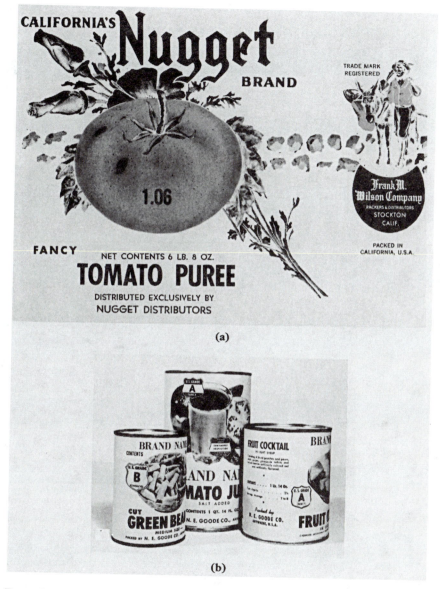

Figure 11-1

(a) An example of a good label giving extra information that is not required by law but tells the buyer much about the product. The "1.06" refers to the specific gravity of the tomato puree. The use of the word fancy indicates that the seller claims the product meets U.S. Fancy quality but makes no claim that it had been federally graded. Under court rulings, this product, if shipped in interstate commerce, may be considered misbranded if it does not meet standards for U.S. Fancy quality. (Courtesy Frank M. Wilson.) *(b) Canned foods that show federal grade stamps.* (Courtesy USDA.)

Table 11–1
Federal grades for processed fruits and vegetables.

	Word terms		Letter terms		Usual grade Score
	Fruits	Vegetables	Fruits	Vegetables	
Top grade	Fancy	Fancy	A	A	90–100
Second grade	Choice	Extra Standard	B	B	80–89
Third grade	Standard	Standard	C	C	70–79

NET CONTENTS
6 LBS. 10 OZS.

	DRAINED	WITH BRINE
NUMBER OF 2 OZ. SERVINGS	36	52
NUMBER OF 3 OZ. SERVINGS	24	35

TENDER YOUNG
SWEET PEAS
MIXED LARGE SIZES
SUGAR AND SALT ADDED
ARTIFICIALLY COLORED

BELOW STANDARD IN QUALITY
ARTIFICIALLY COLORED

ABOVE LEGEND MANDATORY–PEAS ACTUALLY HIGH QUALITY

Figure 11–2
An example of a good descriptive label. Note that the words used have precise mean-ing as to age, quality, and so forth. Because the product is colored with an artificial green coloring, it must be labeled "Below Standard in Quality," but is actually quite high in other factors. (Published through the courtesy of and with the permission of the Green Giant Co.)

any product grading less than 70 is not considered unfit food, but is merely graded as "below standard"; thus, solid water-pack peaches that are considerably broken up and downgraded because of this may be graded below standard but are still excellent for peach pies, where the broken up condition is not important (see Figure 11–2).

The number of grades used for a product is the number needed to move that product on the market. Fruit and vegetable juices usually have only two grades. Fruit spreads like jams, jellies, and others also have two grades. The scores for these are A grade, 85 to 100, and 70 to 84 for either grade B or C.

Figures 11–3, 11–4, and 11–5 show how scores are established for some items. Note a small "1" in front of a score indicates a **limiting rule,** which means that un-

Score Sheet for Canned Fruit Cocktail.

Three standards are indicated: Grades A, B and Sub-standard (SStd).

Size and kind of container _ _ _ _ _ _ _ _ _ _ _ _ _ _ _ _
Container mark or identification _ _ _ _ _ _ _ _ _ _ _ _
Label _
Net weight (ounces) _ _ _ _ _ _ _ _ _ _ _ _ _ _ _ _ _ _
Vacuum (inches) _ _ _ _ _ _ _ _ _ _ _ _ _ _ _ _ _ _ _
Drained weight (ounces):
   ( ) Meets fill of container _ _ _ _ _ _ _ _ _ _ _ _
   ( ) Fails fill of container _ _ _ _ _ _ _ _ _ _ _ _
Brix measurement _ _ _ _ _ _ _ _ _ _ _ _ _ _ _ _ _ _
Sirup designation (extra heavy, heavy, etc.) _ _ _ _ _
Proportions of fruit ingredients:
   Peach: _ _ oz _ _ % ( ) Meets ( ) Fails _ _ _
   Pear: _ _ oz _ _ % ( ) Meets ( ) Fails _ _ _
   Pineapple: _ _ oz _ _ % ( ) Meets ( ) Fails _ _ _
   Grape: _ _ oz _ _ % ( ) Meets ( ) Fails _ _ _
   Cherry: _ _ oz _ _ % ( ) Meets ( ) Fails _ _ _
      Total   _ _ oz 100%
Count:
   Pineapple ( ) Sectors ( ) Diced _ _ _ _ _ _ _ _ _
   Cherry halves _ _ _ _ _ _ _ _ _ _ _ _ _ _ _ _ _ _

Factors		Score Points	
Clearness of liquid media _ _ _	20	(A)	17–20
		(B)	14–16
		(SStd)	[1]0–13
Color _ _ _ _ _ _ _ _ _ _ _ _ _	20	(A)	17–20
		(B)	[2]14–16
		(SStd)	[1]0–13
Uniformity of size _ _ _ _ _ _ _	20	(A)	17–20
		(B)	[2]14–16
		(SStd)	[1]0–13
Absence of defects _ _ _ _ _ _	20	(A)	17–20
		(B)	[1]14–16
		(SStd)	[1]0–13
Character _ _ _ _ _ _ _ _ _ _	20	(A)	17–20
		(B)	[1]14–16
		(SStd)	[1]0–13
Total score _ _ _ _ _ _ _ _	100		

Normal flavor and odor _ _ _ _ _ _ _ _ _ _ _ _ _ _ _ _
Grade _

[1]Indicates limiting rule.
[2]Indicates partial limiting rule.

Score Sheet for Canned Asparagus.

Note three standards are indicated, A, C and Substandard.

Number, size, and kind of container _ _ _ _ _ _ _ _ _
Label _
Container mark or identification _ _ _ _ _ _ _ _ _ _ _
Net weight (ounces) _ _ _ _ _ _ _ _ _ _ _ _ _ _ _ _ _ _
Vacuum (inches) _ _ _ _ _ _ _ _ _ _ _ _ _ _ _ _ _ _ _
Drained weight (ounces) _ _ _ _ _ _ _ _ _ _ _ _ _ _ _
Type _
Style _
Size or sizes (Spears, tips, and points) _ _ _ _ _ _ _ _
Length of cut _
Heads (cut) (percent, by count) _ _ _ _ _ _ _ _ _ _ _ _

Factors		Score points	
Liquor _ _ _ _ _ _ _ _ _ _	10	(A)	9–10
		(C)	7–8
		(SStd)	[1]0–6
Color _ _ _ _ _ _ _ _ _ _	20	(A)	17–20
		(C)	14–16
		(SStd)	[1]0–13
Defects _ _ _ _ _ _ _ _ _	30	(A)	25–30
		(C)	[1]21–24
		(SStd)	[1]0–20
Character _ _ _ _ _ _ _ _	40	(A)	34–40
		(C)	[1]28–33
		(SStd)	[1]0–27
Total score _ _ _ _ _ _ _ _	100		

Flavor (A, C, or SStd) _ _ _ _ _ _ _ _ _ _ _ _ _ _ _ _
Grade _

[1]Indicates limiting rule.

Figure 11–3
Scoring sheets for determining grades. (Courtesy USDA.)

Score Sheet for Frozen Broccoli.

Size and kind of container
Container mark of identification
Label
New weight (ounces)
Style
Count (of stalks)

Factors	Score points		
Color	20	(A)	18–20
		(B)	[1]16–17
		(SStd.)	[1]0–15
Uniformity of size	20	(A)	9–10
		(B)	8
		(SStd.)	[2]0–7
Absence of defects	20	(A)	31–35
		(B)	[1]28–30
		(SStd.)	[1]0–27
Character	40	(A)	32–35
		(B)	[1]28–31
		(SStd.)	[1]0–27
Total score	100		

Flavor and odor
Grade

[1]Indicates limiting rule.
[2]Indicates partial limiting rule.

Score Sheet for Frozen Strawberries.

Number, size, and kind of container
Label: Style or pack: Fruit-sugar ratio (if shown)

Container mark or identification	Containers or sample Cases

Net weight (ounces)
Style
Size or sizes (whole)
Under ⅝″ (percent by count)

Factors	Score points		
Color	40	(A)	36–40
		(B)	[1]32–35
		(C)	[1]28–31
		(SStd)	[1]0–27
Defects	40	(A)	36–40
		(B)	[1]32–35
		(C)	[1]28–31
		(SStd)	[1]0–27
Character	20	(A)	18–20
		(B)	[1]16–17
		(C)	[1]14–15
		(SStd)	[1]0–13
Total score	100		

Flavor and odor
Grade

[1]Indicates limiting rule.

Figure 11–4
Scoring sheets for determining grade. (Courtesy USDA.)

less the item scores at least that much in that factor, it cannot be that grade regardless of the total score. Thus, a sample of fruit cocktail not grading 14 or better for character cannot be graded grade B, even though it scores above 80.

A small "2" in front of a factor score, such as seen in color for fruit cocktail, indicates a **partial limiting rule,** which means that if the color does not score that much or better, it *may* or *may not* be given what its total score indicates according to the discretion of the grader. Thus, fruit cocktail scoring a total of 85 but only 13 for color, might or might not be graded B according to the judgment of the grader. Table 11–2 shows how peas and pears are scored.

Score Sheet for Chilled or Canned Orange Juice.

Size and kind of container

Container mark (packages)

 or

Identification (cases)

Label (including ingredient statement, if any)

Liquid measure (fluid ounces)

Style

Brix (degrees)

Acid (grams/100 ml.: calculated as anhydrous
 citric acid)

Brix-acid ratio (   )

Recoverable oil (% by volume)

Degree of coagulation ( ) None / ( ) Slight / ( ) Serious

Factors		Score points	
Color	40	(A)	36–40
		(B)	[1]32–35
		(SStd)	[1]0–31
Defects	20	(A)	18–20
		(B)	[1]16–17
		(SStd)	[1]0–15
Flavor	40	(A)	36–40
		(B)	[1]32–35
		(SStd)	[1]0–31
Total score	100		

Grade

[1]Indicates limiting rule.

Figure 11-5
Scoring sheet for determining grade.
(Courtesy USDA.)

Figures 11–6 and 11–7 are scoring sheets used respectively for grading raisins and prunes. Figure 11–8 shows an **inspection certificate** for some dried fruits. Federal quality standards exist for dried beans, lentils, and peas. These are U.S. No. 1, 2, and 3.

Labeling

Labels must meet the Pure Food and Drug Division's and other government agency's regulations. A new labeling law now in effect has stiffened these regulations by requiring more meaningful information and much more strict rules on the wording that

Table 11-2

Grading Factors for Peas and Pears.

Factors	Score range from maximum to minimum			
	A	B	C	(Substandard)
PEAS				
Clearness of liquor	9–10	7–8	5–6	0–4
Uniformity of color	14–15	11–13	8–10	0–7
Absence of defects	27–30	23–36	19–22	0–18
Maturity	40–45	34–39	28–33	0–27
Total score range	90–100	75–89	60–74	below 60
PEARS				
Color	18–20	16–17	14–15	0–13
Uniformity of size and symmetry	18–20	16–17	14–15	0–13
Absence of defects	27–30	24–26	21–23	0–20
Character	27–30	24–26	21–23	0–20
Total score range	90–100	80–89	70–79	0–69

can be used. The requirement for nutrient labeling has also been increased with added nutrients.

The required information can be helpful to buyers. If a product falls below the federal standards for quality and fill, the label must state it. The packing medium must be listed along with style pack, variety, and the presence of artificial or imitation flavors or colors, if used. Pictures of the food must be representative of what is inside. The net contents, number of servings, number of pieces in the can, can size, and other information may be required. Many labels use descriptive terms to indicate quality, kind, and so forth; thus, words like *very young, young,* or *mature* are used to indicate age.[2]

Standards of Identity

The **standards of identity** apply to processed foods, and labels must give the proper name of the product and the form it is in the can. Thus, if diced beets are in the can, the label must say "diced beets," and the size of the dice must meet that specified by the government for diced as well as meet other requirements, such as evenness of cuts, broken dice, etc. Buyers should use the names of items as given in the standards of identity so there will be no mistake regarding which product is desired.

Count and Size

Count or size must be specified to get the proper portion size. Buyers should watch sizing—it looks like a larger portion to give two 64-count per No. 10 can pineapple

---

[2]For complete information, consult a copy of the Nutrition Labeling and Education Act of 1990, Public Law 101-535, 101st Congress, H. R. 3562, November 8, 1990.

Work Sheet for Scoring Processed Raisins.

Size and kind of packages and/or cases _
Markings _
Label or brand _
Net weight _
Type _
Size or sizes _
Moisture content _

Flavor	A	B	C
Defects	Maximum		
Pieces of stem:			
Thompson Seedless _ _ _ _ _ _ _ _ _ _ _	1 per 96 oz _ _ _	2 per 96 oz _ _ _	4 per 96 oz _ _ _
Other types _ _ _ _ _ _ _ _ _ _ _ _ _ _	1 per 32 oz _ _ _	2 per 32 oz _ _ _	3 per 32 oz _ _ _
	Maximum (per 16 ounces)		
Capstems:[1]			
Thompson Seedless _ _ _ _ _ _ _ _ _	15	25	35
Muscat _ _ _ _ _ _ _ _ _ _ _ _ _ _ _	10	15	20
Sultana _ _ _ _ _ _ _ _ _ _ _ _ _ _	25	45	65
Seeds in Muscat Seeded only[1] _ _ _ _ _	12	15	20
Loose capstems: Muscat, uncapstemmed _ _ _ _ _	20	20	20
	Maximum (by weight) (percent)		
Undeveloped:			
Thompson Seedless "Small size" _ _ _ _ _ _ _	1	2	2
All other raisins _ _ _ _ _ _ _ _ _ _ _ _	1	2	2
Damaged:			
Thompson Seedless and Sultana _ _ _ _ _ _ _	2	3	5
Muscat _ _ _ _ _ _ _ _ _ _ _ _ _ _ _	3	4	5
Sugared (all raisin types) _ _ _ _ _ _ _ _ _	5	10	15
	Maximum (by count) (percent)		
Moldly (all raisin types) _ _ _ _ _ _ _ _ _ _	2	3	4
Shattered (or loose) individual berries and small clusters of 2 or 3 berries each.	Practically free	Reasonably free	_ _ _ _ _ _ _ _ _ _
Damaged by fermentation (all raisin types). Affecting appearance or edibility.	Not affected _ _	No more than slightly affected.	Not materially affected.
Grit, sand, or silt (all raisin types). Affecting appearance or edibility.	None of any consequence.	None of any consequence.	Not more than a trace.

Color		Maximum by weight (percent)
Thompson Seedless:		
Sulfur bleached and golden:		
Well-bleached (Extra fancy) _	½	
Reasonably well-bleached (Fancy) _ _ _ _ _ _ _ _ _ _ _ _ _ _ _ _	3	Definitely dark berries.
Fairly well-bleached (Extra Choice) _ _ _ _ _ _ _ _ _ _ _ _ _ _	6	
Sulfur bleached: Bleached (Choice) _ _ _ _ _ _ _ _ _ _ _ _ _ _ _	15	
Golden: Bleached (Choice) _ _ _ _ _ _ _ _ _ _ _ _ _ _ _ _ _	20	
	Grade A _ _ 10	Dark reddish brown berries
Muscat: Soda dipped unseeded, and seeded: _ _ _ _ _ _ _ _ _	Grade B _ _ 15	
	Grade C _ _ 20	

Grade _

[1] Not applicable to layer (or cluster) or uncapstemmed muscat raisins.

Figure 11–6
Scoring sheet for raisins. (Courtesy USDA.)

Work Sheet for Scoring Dried Prunes.

Size and kind of container _

Container mark or identification _

Label or brand _

Varietal type _

Size: Count per pound   (Average) _ _ _ _ _ _ _ _ _ _   Uniformity _ _ _ _ _ _ _ _ _

  ( ) Extra large.   ( ) Large.
  ( ) Medium.   ( ) Small.

Moisture content _ _ _ _ _ _ _ _ _ _ _ _ _ _ _ _ _ _ percent; Uniformity _ _ _ _ _ _ _ _ _ _ _ _

Varietal characteristics: ( ) Similar. ( ) Dissimilar.

Defects and summary of allowances[1]	Grade A maximum	Grade B maximum	Grade C maximum	Substandard maximum
Total of all defects, including off-color.	10 percent _ _	15 percent _ _ _	_ _ _ _ _	No limit except as indicated below.
Total of all defects, including off-color and poor texture.	_ _ _ _ _ _ _	_ _ _ _ _ _ _	20 percent _ _	
Poor texture, end cracks, skin or flesh damage, fermentation, scars, heat damage, insect injury, other means, mold, dirt, foreign material, insect infestation, decay.	But no more than 6 percent.	But no more than 8 percent.	_ _ _ _ _ _ _	
End cracks,[2] skin or flesh damage, fermentation, scars, heat damage, insect injury, other means, mold, dirt, foreign material, insect infestation, decay.	_ _ _ _ _ _ _	_ _ _ _ _ _ _	10 percent[2] _ _	
Skin or flesh damage, fermentation, scars, heat damage, insect injury, other means, mold, dirt, foreign material, insect infestation, decay.	_ _ _ _ _ _ _	_ _ _ _ _ _ _	But no more than 8 percent.	
Mold, dirt, foreign material, insect infestation, decay.	3 percent _ _	4 percent _ _	5 percent _ _	5 percent.
Decay _ _ _ _ _ _ _ _ _ _ _ _	But no more than 1 percent.	But no more than 1 percent.	But no more than 1 percent.	But no more than 1 percent.

Total _

U.S. Grade (including all factors) _

[1] Percentages of defects are "by weight."

[2] Except that each 1 percent of end cracks to, and including 8 percent, by weight, shall be considered as ½ percent damaged by end cracks; and any additional end cracks shall be calculated as true percentage, by weight.

Figure 11-7
Scoring sheet for prunes. (Courtesy USDA.)

INSPECTION No.............1267.........

D F A of California

An Association of Dried Fruit and Tree Nut Processors

APPLICATION FOR INSPECTION

Shipper ...FLEETWOOD PACKING CO., INC..... .....SAN JOSE, CALIFORNIA..............

For Steamer ....SEATTLE............ ....JOHNSON.................. Line

.... Car No. .... Route ....

NUMBER OF PACKAGES	STYLE OF PACKAGE	VARIETY AND GRADE	CROP	SHIPPING MARK
450	30 POUND	40/50 SANTA CLARA PRUNES	1992	1267 NORWAY
800	21/1 POUND	FANCY BLENHEIM APRICOTS	1992	
500	30 POUND	SELECT NATURAL THOMPSON SEEDLESS RAISINS	1992	

CONTRACT REQUIREMENTS

(State fully all conditions of sale necessary to enable Inspector to properly pass on shipment.)

FLEETWOOD PACKING CO., INC............. Shipper

OFFICIAL CERTIFICATE OF INSPECTION

THIS IS TO CERTIFY, that on the......1st......day of........March...................., 19..93..., an official inspector of this Association, carefully examined and tested the above described goods prepared for shipment to...................................Norway...................................., and that the same meet applicable DFA standards, are in good condition and of the grade and character described in the above application of shipper.

IN WITNESS WHEREOF, this Association by its............... Secretary duly authorized has this..7th..day of...March., 19..93...., issued this certificate in its corporate name and under it's official seal.

D F A OF CALIFORNIA

By *Frank A. Moseler*

Authorized Officer

F-1

Figure 11–8

A trade inspection certificate for dried fruit. (Published with permission and courtesy of the Dried Fruit Association of California.)

slices than to give one 28-count slice per No. 10 can, but one gets 32 portions from the latter as against the 28 in the other.

The federal government sets the size of containers. Table 11–3 gives the list of approved sizes of cans. Such a list is helpful to buyers who wish to compare amounts of product yielded by different size cans. Suppose a buyer finds that no No. 10 cans of a product are available, but there is a plentiful supply in No. 2½'s. Note in Table 11–3 that a No. 2½ can holds 28.5 oz. A 24-can case would therefore give 24 × 28.5 oz or 684 oz, while a No. 10 case of 6 cans gives 6 cans × 103.7 = 622.2 oz, so a case of 24 No. 2½'s gives 1.1 times as much in net contents as a case of 6/10's (684/622.2 = 1.0993). Thus, if the buyer were to purchase 10 cases of No. 10's of the product, 9 cases of No. 2½'s would give an approximate amount.

Syrup Density

Labels on canned fruit must state type of packing medium. Syrup densities are extra heavy, heavy, medium, or light; sometimes lightly sweetened, water- or juice-packed

Table 11-3
Some common can sizes used for food facilities.

Can Name	Dimensions (in.)		Canner's Designation	Volume (oz)	Approximate Cups	Number per Case
	Diameter	Height				
2Z	2⅛	2¼	202 × 204*			
	2⅛	2⅞	202 × 214	4¾†	½†	12, 24, 48
6Z	2⅛	3½	202 × 308	5¾	⅔	24, 48
8Z tall‡	2 11/16	3¼	211 × 304	8.3	1	24, 36, 48, 72
No. 1 picnic	2 11/16	4	211 × 400	10½	1¼	24, 48
No. 211 cylinder	2 11/16	4⅞	211 × 414	12	1½	24, 36, 48
No. 300	3	4 7/16	300 × 407	13½	1¾	24, 36, 48
No. 1 tall	3 1/16	4 11/16	301 × 411	15	2	24, 48
No. 303	3 3/16	4⅜	303 × 406	15.6	2	12, 24, 36
No. 303 cylinder	3 3/16	5 9/16	303 × 509	19	2⅓	
No. ½ flat	3 7/16	2 1/16	307 × 201			48
No. 2	3 7/16	4 9/16	307 × 409	19.9	2½	12, 24
No. 2 cylinder	3 7/16	5¾	307 × 512	23	3	24
No. 2½	4 1/16	4 11/16	401 × 411	28.5	3½	12, 24
No. 3	4¼	4⅞	404 × 414	33.6	4	12, 24
No. 3 cylinder	4¼	7	404 × 700	46	5¾	12
No. 5	5⅛	5⅝	502 × 510	56	7	12
No. 10	6 3/16	7	603 × 700	103.7	12¾	6
Gallon	6 3/16	8¾	603 × 812	130	16	4, 6

* Diameter is represented by the first number and height by the second; the first digit in each three-digit group indicates inches and the second and third digits, sixteenths of an inch. Thus, 303 by 406 is a can 3 3/16 in. in diameter and 4⅜ in. in height.

†One fluid ounce equals 1/16 pint and 1 cup equals ½ pint. Net weight of contents are not given, because foods vary in density and thus in the net weight contained in cans.

‡Also called No. 55 or the 8-oz can.

items are available. Frequently the higher grades have the heaviest syrups. The heavier the syrup, the less chance fruit has of breaking up.

Different kinds of fruit require different syrup densities. Syrup densities can be tested by using a **Brix** hydrometer or a polarscope. A light syrup on peaches is between 14° and 19° Brix, whereas a light syrup on cherries is 16° to 20° Brix. When fruits are canned, a much heavier syrup is added at the start than what results on standing for a time after canning, since juice from the fruit dilutes the syrup. Apricots *packed* in a 55° Brix syrup will *come out* 25° Brix. Syrup density on packing is called *put in* and the final syrup density after stabilization is called *cut out*. Cut outs are not reliable unless taken 15 days or more from put in. Normally, for every degree Brix, a fruit has 1% sugar, a fact helpful in dietary planning. The amount of non-sucrose sweeteners that can be combined with sucrose in syrups is controlled by the government.

Standards of Fill

Some canned items must be filled to ¾₆ to the container top. Others must be filled to at least 90% of the water capacity. Still others must be filled as "full as practical" without the impairment of quality or breaking or crushing of ingredients. If the **standard of fill** is not met, the label must state prominently "Below Standard in Fill" or "Slack Fill." The federal government in 1968 established a list of suggested net quantities of fill for canned foods. These have been adopted by the National Food Processors Association. Frozen foods must be 100% product stated as net contents. The federal government says no food to which water is added can be labeled "solid" pack. It must be labeled "heavy" pack instead.

Drained Weight

Drained weight is usually not a grade factor, but government standards set a recommended drained weight for a product. Some items like fruit cocktail and canned tomatoes do have a drained weight that influences grade.

Drained weight is the weight left after the liquid has been allowed to drain on a prescribed screen for two minutes. It tells the buyer exactly how much product the package holds. Normally fruits and vegetables are about two-thirds product and one-third liquid. "Net weight of contents" on the label tells the amount of liquid plus product in the can; it does not tell how much product is there, although today some canners also put the yield on the label. Table 11–4 indicates the amounts normally obtained from various products in various size cans.

Density of product can be named instead of drained weight such as for cream-style corn, apple butter, or some thick tomato products. A casual density test is made by stirring a product with a knife and leaving the knife in the center to see if it stands and how long. Another way is to put a small bit of product on a blotter on a smooth, flat surface and measuring after two minutes to see how far the liquid in the product has spread. A more accurate reading can be made by using a consistometer, a device that measures the spread, that is, consistency, of products.

Table 11-4
Sizes and quantities of fruit in some can sizes.

Fruit	Can Size	Amount or Number in Can*	Size Serving or number per Serving	Servings per Can
Apples, heavy	No. 10	7 lb 8 oz		Makes 6 pies
Applesauce	No. 10	6 lb 11 oz	½ c	25
Apricots, halves	No. 10	75–85	3 to 4 halves	23–25
Apricots, halves	No. 2½	$^{20}/_{23}$	3 to 4 halves	6–7
Apricots, whole	No. 10	50	2	25
Apricots, whole	No. 2½	$^{12}/_{16}$	2	6–8
Blackberries	No. 2	1 lb 4 oz	½ c	5
Blackberries	No. 10	6 lb 10 oz	½ c	25
Blackberries, heavy	No. 10	6 lb 7 oz		Makes 4–5 pies
Cherries, RSP	No. 10	6 lb 14 oz		Makes 5 pies
Cherries, sweet	No. 10	$^{240}/_{260}$	½ c (8 to 10)	30
Cherries, sweet	No. 2½	$^{65}/_{70}$	½ c (8 to 10)	7 to 8
Figs, kadota	No. 10	$^{110}/_{120}$	3	30–40
Figs, kadota	No. 2½	$^{28}/_{32}$	3	10
Fruit cocktail	No. 10	6 lb 14 oz	½ c	25
Fruit cocktail	No. 2½	1 lb 14 oz	½ c	7
Fruits, salad	No. 10	6 lb 14 oz	½ c	25
Fruits, salad	No. 2½	1 lb 14 oz	½ c	7
Grapefruit	No. 3 cyl	3 lb 2 oz	½ c	11
Grapefruit, broken	No. 10	6 lb 9 oz	½ c	25
Peaches, halves	No. 10	$^{35}/_{40}$	2	17½–20
Peaches, halves	No. 2½	$^{10}/_{12}$	2	5–6
Peaches, sliced	No. 10	6 lb 14 oz	½ c	25
Peaches, sliced	No. 2½	1 lb 14 oz	½ c	7
Peaches, solid	No. 10	6 lb 10 oz		Makes 4–5 pies
Pear, halves	No. 10	$^{40}/_{50}$	2	20–25
Pear, halves	No. 2½	$^{10}/_{14}$	2	5–7
Pineapple, slice	No. 10	$^{57}/_{64}$	2	29–32
Pineapple, slice	No. 2½	$^{14}/_{16}$	2	7–8
Pineapple, crushed solid pack	No. 10	6 lb 14 oz	½ c	25
Pineapple, crushed	No. 2½	1 lb 13 oz	½ c	7
Pineapple, broken or half slice	No. 10	6 lb 11 oz	½ c	25
Pineapple, broken or half slice	No. 2½	1 lb 13 oz	½ c	7
Pineapple chunks	No. 2	$^{48}/_{55}$ (2½ c)	½ c	5
Pineapple chunks	No. 2½	$^{72}/_{80}$ (3½ c)	½ c	7
Pineapple chunks	No. 10	$^{232}/_{290}$ (12–13 c)	½ c	25
Pineapple tidbits	No. 10	6 lb 11 oz ($^{512}/_{960}$)	½ c	25
Pineapple spears	No. 2	16 spears	3	5
Plums, purple	No. 10	$^{65}/_{90}$	3	22–30
Plums, gage or egg	No. 10	$^{45}/_{55}$	2–3	22
Prunes, dried	No. 10	$^{140}/_{170}$	3–4	50
Prunes, heavy pack, dried	No. 10	$^{210}/_{280}$	3–4	80

*Numbers given here are good averages for institutional use. Data based on experience in use.

PRESERVATION METHODS

Normally food with less than 5% moisture is preserved, although flour is about 13% and some dried fruits are 25%. Foods over 10% salt are usually fairly well preserved, especially if kept chilled. Anything over 55% sugar also tends to remain edible. **Pickling** is a method in which acid in a preserved food becomes about 4 pH and ends about 4 or less. If salt is used, the acid can be reduced. Sauerkraut is pickled shredded cabbage having a lactic acid content of about 1.8% and a 2½% salt content. The creosote in smoke and other products is antagonistic to spoilage agents. Benzoate of soda or benzoic acid up to $\frac{1}{10}$ of 1% is allowed as a food additive to help preserve. Mold in bread is controlled by the use of up to 0.32 parts of sodium or calcium proportionate for each 100 parts of flour. We can also so finely filter liquids that yeasts, molds, and bacteria are removed, leaving a sterile product. This is why we can have a canned draft beer that is not subjected to heat to preserve it in the can.

Refrigeration under 45°F slows micro-agent growth, and below 32°F stops it. Many microorganisms gradually die off in the frozen state.

Slow freezing destroys quality because it encourages coarse crystal growth which can rupture cell membranes and cause the cell to collapse. Rapid freezing develops small crystals which do not swell. In fact, tomatoes, avocados, bananas, and other products can be frozen almost instantly in liquid nitrogen, so with slow thawing these products have a well-preserved cellular structure and a texture like a fresh item. Meat and other flesh products develop a heavy drip loss when frozen slowly or when allowed to remain where freezing temperatures vary, a condition which encourages large crystal growth.

Heat above 140°F destroys most spoilage agents, but, to be sure, foods are treated to higher temperatures to preserve them. Time is a factor in thermicide. A food can be pasteurized at 143°F for about 30 minutes or at 212°F for 1 second. Eggs are held a fairly long time at 138°F to pasteurize them, a temperature below their coagulation point. Cook-chill foods are cooked foods sealed in airtight packages at above pasteurization temperatures and then quickly cooled. If the seal is not broken and the temperature is held below 40°F, many can have a shelf life of 60 some days.

Canning

Canning today is a highly mechanized industry with prepreparation, such as washing, sizing, grading, peeling or shelling, trimming, and loading into cans, and other manipulations all being done mechanically (see Figure 11–9). Canneries are located close to areas of production; in some cases the cannery may be moved out into the field where products are harvested and immediately processed.

Most food is blanched before being placed into cans; this is done to fix color, improve flavor, destroy enzymes or bacteria, soften tissues, or remove gases or dirt. Blanched asparagus is more pliable, going into cans better. Bulky spinach and other greens are compacted so they can be solidly packed into cans. Some fruits have a more uniform color and do not turn brown. After packing the product in the can, a packing liquid is usually added and the cans are closed, exhausted, and sealed. Cooking by steam at high pressure in huge retorts then occurs. After canning, rapid cooling occurs.

Figure 11-9
Sealed cans of food are lowered into a retort, where they are subjected to steam under pressure to sterilize and preserve the food. (Courtesy USDA.)

All cans must be coded with a code that identifies the product, the cannery, and gives other information. The code and the information are filed with the federal government so at any time desirable information about the canned food can be obtained. Cans today are finished inside so they do not react with the foods, replacing the need for spraying inside the can with special lacquers to prevent undesirable reactions between food and the metal.

Flash-18 Method

The **flash-18** method of canning is a novel way of using heat without a long process of high steam temperatures. Instead, a room is sealed tightly with workers inside, and put under a pressure of 18 psi. The room is kept very sterile along with the cans to be used plus other equipment. Workers are required to wear special clothing and gloves so as to reduce chances of contamination. The food then is cooked under this 18-psi pressure which raises the cooking temperature to 253°F, a temperature far above that needed for sterilization. This hot food is then placed into cans and sealed.

When the day's canning is over, workers must remain in the room while the pressure is dropped to normal; otherwise, they would develop the bends, a serious physical condition in which air bubbles form in the blood. After opening the room, the canned food is removed, labeled, and packed into cases. Heavy products such as Spanish rice, cream-style corn, or hash do well under this process, since the process avoids the long cooking in the retort that is necessary to sterilize such thick foods. If cooked by the high-pressure retort method, these foods develop an over-cooked flavor.

Freezing

The shorter the time between harvest and freezing and the faster the **freezing** process, the higher the quality. Preliminary preparation of foods is much the same as for canning, but a blanching in hot water or steam occurs for vegetables to destroy enzymes and frequently to fix color. **Blanching** further wilts foods down or makes them more pliable for packaging. Fruits may be treated with an antioxidant such as ascorbic acid to avoid browning. Vegetables have about 1% salt added, and are usually frozen without liquid. Sugar is added to fruit to preserve flavor, color, and, to a certain extent, texture. A syrup can be used in place of sugar. A "4–1" or a "5–1" on a label indicates the fruit–sugar ratio. There are no recommended drained weights for fruit, but this text gives at times the drained weights obtained from records maintained in one kitchen. Frozen vegetables should be 100% of net weight on the package.

Frozen fruit is usually purchased in 5-, 10-, or 12-oz, and 1-, 6-, 6½-, 25-, or 30-lb units. If the quantity used is large, it can be purchased in larger size units. Vegetables come in 10- or 12-oz, 1-, 2-, 2½-, 3-, or 5-lb packs, but potatoes, peas, corn, and some others may come in larger packs. Some vegetables are sized, but fruits are much less so. Temperatures during shipping and storage should be around –10°F to properly retain quality. As noted previously, fluctuating temperatures are harmful to quality. Thawing and refreezing are also and, if this occurs before the buyer receives the goods, it may not be the quality level specified. For this reason, specifications should state that the "condition upon delivery should be the quality specified."

Drying

Drying is a method of extracting moisture so microorganisms are denied sufficient moisture to grow. Natural drying is allowing items to stand in the air and let the air extract the moisture. Often the sun's energy is used to speed up the process. Much of our dried fruit is dried by this sun-drying process. Another simple method is to introduce heated, dry air to give a speeded-up moisture extraction. Here inert gases may be introduced instead of air to stop oxygen from causing oxidations which develop off flavors. **Vacudrying** is a method of drying by reducing air pressure and then introducing heat. In the rarefied air, the moisture leaves rapidly, giving a quick drying. Continuous vacuum-drying on a belt is used for drying potatoes, onions, and other foods. **Tunnel drying** is a method that uses fast-moving warm air or dry, inert gases going through a tunnel. Eggs or milk can be whipped to a foam and dried that way. A frequently used method is spray drying, in which a slightly concentrated liquid, such as milk, is sprayed into a chamber where moisture is extracted from the fine mist as it drops to the floor. Drum drying uses a heated drum; the drum rotates around in the liquid, picking it up and drying it as it comes out. This dried product is then scraped from the rotating drum. **Freeze drying** freezes the food and, then

Figure 11-10
Trays of peaches spread for drying. (Courtesy USDA.)

under a vacuum, the moisture is pulled from products by the introduction of a small amount of heat. The ancient Aztecs used this method; they would take foods to be dried up into the high mountain peaks and spread it out. It would freeze and then the bright sunlight would furnish the energy to quickly evaporate the moisture. A dehydro-frozen food is a product partially dehydrated and then frozen.

Dried Fruits

Each year we process more than a billion pounds of dried or low-moisture fruits alone (see Figure 11–10). Most fruits should be fully ripe to give maximum sugar and flavor; prunes and figs are allowed to ripen until they fall to the ground. Because of the high level of maturity, there is a chance of damage or defects occurring, and buyers should be sure they purchase well-inspected goods. Damage caused by insects, molds, or decay can easily be hidden after drying, especially if packed in the slab.

Container sizes for dried fruits vary. Food services usually use 25- or 30-lb cases or 4-lb packs, six to the case. If the quantity is small, 1-, 3-, or 5-lb packs should be purchased. Moths, weevils, and other insects attack dried fruits; to avoid this, store in a refrigerated area. Normal storage temperature is 40°–50°F. All dried products can darken and lose flavor if held too long; about a month's supply is the longest holding time recommended.

Look for uniformity of color and a lack of discoloration or off-colors. The best quality fruit has the lightest color, bright and typical for the product. Check for end cracks, lack of ripeness, flesh damage, scars, molds, dirt, extraneous matter, decay, fermentation, and other defects. Insect infestation or damage is common. Reject excessively sugared fruit. Prices vary according to the yield of the season. Sizes and grades of various dried fruits are given in Table 11–5.

Low-moisture fruits are those that contain more moisture than dried. A wide number of different varieties are available in different form. A fruit mix is marketed that can be made into an acceptable fruit cocktail. Even a low-moisture fruit cake mix may be obtained. Dessert mixtures such as apple, cherry, blueberry, raspberry and their blends can be obtained. Low-moisture banana slices are available.

Table 11–5

Sizes for dried fruit, in inches.

Sizes	Figs Adriatic or Kadota	Calimyrna	Mission	Apricots	Peaches	Pears
No. 1 Jumbo	$1\frac{5}{16}$ up	$1\frac{9}{16}$ up	$1\frac{5}{16}$ up	$1\frac{3}{8}$ up	2 up	$1\frac{7}{8}$ up
No. 2 Extra fancy	$1\frac{5}{16}-1\frac{8}{16}$	$1\frac{5}{16}-1\frac{9}{16}$	$1\frac{3}{16}-1\frac{5}{16}$	$1\frac{1}{4}-1\frac{3}{8}$	$1\frac{3}{4}-2$	$2\frac{3}{4}-1\frac{7}{8}$
No. 3 Fancy	$1\frac{3}{16}-1\frac{5}{16}$	$1\frac{3}{16}-1\frac{5}{16}$	$1\frac{1}{16}-1\frac{3}{16}$	$1\frac{1}{8}-1\frac{1}{4}$	$1\frac{1}{2}-1\frac{3}{4}$	$1\frac{1}{2}-1\frac{3}{4}$
No. 4 Extra choice	$1\frac{1}{16}-1\frac{3}{16}$	$1\frac{1}{16}-1\frac{3}{16}$	$\frac{15}{16}-1\frac{1}{16}$	$1-1\frac{1}{8}$	$1\frac{3}{8}-1\frac{1}{2}$	$1\frac{3}{8}-1\frac{1}{2}$
No. 5 Choice	$\frac{15}{16}-1\frac{1}{16}$	$\frac{15}{16}-1\frac{1}{16}$	$1\frac{3}{16}-\frac{15}{16}$	$\frac{13}{16}-1$	$1\frac{1}{4}-1\frac{3}{8}$	$1\frac{1}{4}-1\frac{3}{8}$
No. 6 Standard	under $\frac{15}{16}$	under $\frac{15}{16}$	under $\frac{13}{16}$	under $\frac{13}{16}$	under $1\frac{1}{4}$	under $1\frac{1}{4}$

Note: Figs and pears are measured by width of stem to calyx end, and apricots and peaches are measured by diameters. The size numbers are the same for pears, but the size terms are jumbo, extra large, large, medium, small, and extra small, respectively.

A number of different dried fruit crystals are on the market; these can be used for juice or making beverages. Freeze-dried items are best, but are highest in price. Vitamin C may be added to some.

Dried Vegetables

Dried vegetables available run the gamut from dried legumes to garden vegetables. Most are evaluated for quality on the basis of rehydrating and then, if necessary, cooking. Perhaps the most common dried vegetable used today is potatoes in many forms; onions are next. Low-moisture and freeze-dried vegetables are not marketed in good quantity. Some items, like potatoes, may have vitamin C added to them; dried milk or other items may be added to them also; a dried potato au gratin mix is marketed, for instance.

THE MAJOR PROCESSED FOODS

Canned Fruits and Vegetables

Canned fruits and vegetables require special specification if one is to purchase the best value and the proper item for the need. There are standards of identity that give each item a name, as previously explained, and buyers can rely on these to indicate precisely what is wanted. It is also necessary to state the size can and often the number of these cans per case, such as $\frac{6}{10}$'s (six No. 10 cans per case) or $2\frac{1}{2}$'s (24 No. 2 cans per case).

As noted, the product size can be important, such as a No. 4 pea, or a $\frac{30}{40}$ count pear, or a medium size (2–2½ in.) sliced beet. The federal government has established *recommended* drained weights and this should be given in specifications. Thus, a can of No. 10 $\frac{30}{40}$ half pears should drain out 64.1 oz.

Canned Fruit Spreads

Jams and preserves have fruit suspended in the gel; jam often has mashed or broken fruit, whereas preserves usually have whole fruit. Marmalades are clear jellies in which slices or cut pieces of fruit or peel are suspended. **Jellies** are a clear product made only from fruit juice and sugar. Fruit butters are semisolid pastes of cooked, strained fruit pulp with perhaps added spices. No. 10 cans are purchased if the quantity is used in production, but for table use about 1-oz containers are usually purchased in 12/case packs of 100 each of individual tubs holding about one tablespoon. Large-quantity users may purchase fruit spreads in 30-gal tubs.

Processed Juices

Frozen Juices.   Most sweetened or unsweetened fruit juices are concentrated to a 3:1 water–juice ratio, but some may have a 2:1 to 17:1 ratio. Quality is evaluated after reconstitution on the basis of factors stated above. The flavor should be closer to fresh than canned juices.

Chilled Juices.   Both sweetened or unsweetened chilled juices are marketed; some may be heat treated to obtain a longer shelf life. Juices preserved with chemicals do not qualify as chilled juices.

A specific Brix reading, depending on whether a product is sweetened or unsweetened, is required for each kind of juice, usually varying from 11° to 12.5°, and many may have to meet a certain Brix–acid ratio, often from 11:1 to 17:1 in high-quality juices. Watch for coagulation or material separation. Good flavor and color should be present without noticeable traces of oil from fruit. Color should be good for the product. Dull, dark, murky juice should be rejected. Watch for seed or portions of fruit, rind, cells, pulp, or other extraneous material. Excessive sediment should be cause for rejection.

Canned Juices.   Canned sweetened or unsweetened juices have been subjected to enough heat to be sterile in the can. They should have a bright, sparkling typical color for the product, not dull, dark, or excessively cloudy. The juice should be practically free from sediment or other residue, particles of pulp, seeds, specks, or other extraneous matter. Consistency should be typical for the product. Watch for defects similar to those named for chilled juices.

Some canned concentrated juices are marketed. They should be evaluated after reconstitution on the basis of factors named for canned and chilled juices.

Cook-Chill Foods

Chilled foods have become much more common since improved technology has been able to give them a longer shelf life. **Cook-chill foods** are now commonly used, a product that has merely to be reheated to be servable. The product is cooked in large batches, put into sterile pouches or other moisture-vapor-proof containers while almost at a boiling temperature; they are then sealed, quickly cooled, and then stored in refrigeration. They have a shelf life up to 60 days, but high acid foods may have an even longer one. Often such cook-chill foods are thought of as convenience foods.

Value-Added Foods

Earlier in this chapter a **convenience food** or **value-added food** was defined as a food processed not only to preserve it but also to incorporate other values such as saving labor and convenience. A wide number of such foods are available and the list is growing. Some are of very high quality and compete well with the best of foods made on the premises by experienced, skilled chefs.

Often management or others in an operation are faced with the problem of whether or not it is best to use a value-added food or make food from scratch on the premises. There are many plus and minus factors to consider and each value-added food needs to be considered separately. Most operations find that a mixture of value-added foods and made-on-the-premise foods is best suited for their needs, but some may go 100% to these new foods. The most common usage is a combination of premise-made products and value-added. In one study made by *Restaurants and Institutions* it was shown that operations use value-added items such as salad dressings, desserts, and rolls and breads, while they use premise-made items such as soups and entrees. Value-added foods are most popular with fast food operations while full-service units or hotels and motels tend to use more premise-made items. Smaller restaurants often use more value-added items than larger ones.

Figure 11–11 is a picture of a convenience item that saves a lot of labor. Figure 11–12 shows a laborious process avoided by using a convenience breaded product. Some of the advantages of premise-made items follow. The list is not complete but illustrative of values these items have for a facility. Obviously, an advantage listed here could be considered as a disadvantage of the convenience item.

Advantages of Premise-Made Items

1. The overall cost may be lower.

2. Nutritional values may be higher; it is also easier to calculate nutritional values since ingredients are known. They are not known in the convenience food.

3. Many patrons place a higher value on homemade foods than on convenience products. They feel special pains are taken by competent, skilled chefs to make a differentiated product, special to the operation. They often say, "I can get that convenience stuff at home." The premise-made product conveys better the image the operation is trying to present to the public. The operation cannot advertise "fresh foods," something many patrons desire today.

4. Patrons also do not want foods with additives and they often feel that convenience foods contain too much and that the premise-made product does not. It is a more "natural" food.

5. Vendors may run out of the convenience product, and the operation is left without a supply and is no longer able to produce the item from scratch. Thus, the premise-made product is almost a sure thing; the convenience food is not.

Figure 11–11
The purchase of prepared puff pastry and Danish pastry dough as shown above can save a lot of expensive labor.

Figure 11–12
A breading process like this takes five separate motions, all of which are eliminated in purchasing the prebreaded product. Management must decide, however, if the extra cost of the convenience item is worth the cost of the labor saved and convenience of having items ready at hand in a prebreaded condition.

6. The operation has the labor and the facilities at hand and cannot get rid of them. Management thus feels it has to have the labor and physical facilities there to handle other needs and might as well use it. Otherwise, the cost of the labor and physical facilities are still there while one pays for this also in the convenience item.

7. Competitors cannot serve the identical thing. The product thus can be made unique to the operation.

8. Often package instructions for use of the convenience product are either partial, confusing, or missing, making it difficult for employees to know exactly what to do to serve an adequate product. Also, there is little consistency in the type and quality between different brands and therefore buyers have little freedom in product selection.

9. Employees may feel more secure in making the premise-made item, often fearing that using the convenience product can cause them to lose their job. It is not uncommon for employees to deliberately sabotage the convenience item, because of such feelings.

Convenience foods also have advantages and these contrarily may be disadvantages of the premise-made products. Some of these advantages follow.

Advantages of Value-Added Foods

1. In some cases the convenience product is less expensive considering product cost along with labor, heat, and other costs. Often the cost of the convenience food may seem high but when *all* costs are considered, the convenience product is less expensive. The problem is that often the other costs are not known—they are difficult to obtain—and the operation is driven away by what seems to be a high original cost. In such a situation, these hidden costs must be obtained or accurately estimated so the AP to AS cost of the premise-made product is known and can be compared to the convenience product cost.

   In other cases, it is easy to compare costs. In a product like frozen orange juice compared with freshly squeezed juice, the saving of labor is so evident that one knows the frozen juice is the better from a cost standpoint. The purchase of preportioned meats may save the cost of a butcher and a butcher-shop. Figure 11–13 shows a cost comparison between a convenience product and the same product made on the premises; while not all costs are included, the major ones are.

2. It is easier also to keep track of usage and to control inventories; inventories are also minimized since many separate foods are eliminated and wastes are already taken.

3. Overproduction can be controlled since many of the convenience foods can be quickly prepared to order.

4. Less skilled and less costly labor can be used, since the food has almost all its preparation incorporated in it. Less supervisory time may also be needed.

5. Ordering, inventory size, and work, receiving, storage, cleanup and other times may be lessened and simplified. Record keeping may be reduced, since it is easier to record one purchase than a number and pay one bill for one thing than for a number.

6. Equipment and space needs may be lessened.

7. It is easy to expand menu offerings without increasing labor or physical facilities. Some operations that make most of the offerings to patrons in the dining room may use the convenience item for banquets, thus being able to take care of a large extra load without much extra strain on the facility.

Premise-made

Ingredient	Amount	Cost	Total
Carrots	7 lb	$ 0.49/lb	$ 3.43
Onions	7 lb	0.25/lb	1.75
Celery	7 lb	0.65/lb	4.55
Turnips	7 lb	0.39/lb	2.73
Salad oil	1 pt	5.60/gal	0.70
Stock	5½ gal	1.42/gal	7.81
Total major ingredient cost			20.97
2% major ingredient cost for seasonings			0.42
Energy cost*	20 Kw @ $ 0.10		2.00

Labor:

1½ hr @ $ 4.25/hr		$ 6.37	
½ hr @ $ 10.00/hr		5.00	11.37

Total cost of on-premise 6¼ gal made soup	$ 34.76

Off-premise made

12 2-qt pouches and 1 qt pouch (6¼ gal)	$ 22.10
Energy cost**	1.61
Labor 12½ loads requiring 8 min/load x $4.25/hr	7.08
Total cost of off-premise made soup	$ 30.79

*15-lb aluminum pot (specific heat of aluminum 0.214 Btu/lb) plus 50 lb of soup (specific heat 1.0 Btu/lb) raised 162° F with heating efficiency calculated as 25% and $0.10/kwh.

**5 gal aluminum kettle (0.214 Btu/lb and 2 gal water) specific heat of water 1.0 Btu/lb both raised 162° F plus 50 lb of soup (specific heat 1.0 Btu/lb) raised from 0° F to 212° F with heating efficiency calculated as 25% and $0.10/kwh.

Figure 11-13
Comparative costs of on-premise and off-premise vegetable soups.

8. They are also good to have on hand when there is a runout or when there is a sudden influx of unexpected patrons who must be served.

9. An even supply of a consistent quality product is obtainable. At certain times of the year, product quality of raw materials may not be the best and the products made from them are not of as high quality as desired. Thus, frozen potato strips are processed at the peak of potato quality. Heating them in hot oil in preblanching destroys enzymes that gradually lower quality in the raw product. By freezing the blanched potatoes, this quality is retained. Contrarily, the raw product is stored and by spring the starch–moisture–sugar ratio has changed to a point that now fried potato strips from these stored potatoes are not the best.

10. They are convenient to use, ready at hand. There is no involved preparation, no mess, no fuss or guessing. Management may also have more time to devote to front-of-the-house problems and managing the business.

Make or Buy

The primary responsibility for making a decision to **make or buy** rests with management, but management should have key employees participate in making the decision also.

All factors, pro and con, should be considered and after such deliberation, a decision made whether to make or buy. During the entire decision-making process, vendors of raw materials and also of convenience products should be contacted to get needed information. Such feedback is necessary in making the better decisions. After the product has been purchased and tested, an evaluation should be made to consider whether the decision to use the convenience food was the one that should be made.

WRITING SPECIFICATIONS

The general pattern for specifications given earlier in this text can be followed for processed foods. The names given in this text for the various processed foods are those used by the federal government. Quality can be designated either by brand or grade—if by grade, the total score or even a specific factor score might be given. Packaging will usually be for canned goods by size can and number per case. For frozen goods, the usual purchase size is in 5-lb packs, six per case, but 30-lb cans and other size packaging are also available. Dried vegetables can be by cans—usually %'s—or by box or sack. Dried fruits are usually purchased in 20-lb boxes but are available in other packaging.

The miscellaneous section of a specification will usually be different from that of other foods. It may be necessary to give the type such as with canned snap beans, which are available either as types green or wax. The style also may have to be given such as for snap beans, available styles are whole, whole vertical, sliced lengthwise (French), cut, short cut, and mixed. Sieve size may be required which for snap beans might run from No. 1 through No. 6. In the case of canned fruits, the count and syrup density and even a ratio of mixed items as in fruit cocktail may be needed. Drained weight should be listed. Some items like tomato puree or paste might need a specification of amount of solids. Frozen fruits will require a sugar–fruit ratio.

In some cases specification of nutritional values may be required. Canned fruits in syrup and frozen fruits contain sucrose or other sweetener which may be limited to diabetics and some other individuals. Vegetables will have added salt which is 40% sodium and for those on low-sodium diets, salt-free or low-salt items may be required.

QUANTITIES FOR 100 PORTIONS

The amount required for service is guided by the portion size. Usually a portion of fruits or vegetables is 3 to 4 oz but this can vary from operation to operation. Tables covering the amount of many processed foods needed to serve 100 normal portions appears in Appendix G. These can be helpful in guiding buyers in establishing quantities to order. They are also of assistance to those who must plan for the services of these items.

SUMMARY

Human beings have for many years preserved food to hold it over for times when it was not plentiful, but recently we have also been using preservation methods to add convenience, labor, quality, or other factors. These new foods are called *value-added foods*. A Frenchman by the name of Appert invented canning; he used much of the scientific information that Pasteur and others had found on the nature of bacteria to perfect his canning method.

The federal government, through the Agricultural Marketing Act, the Pure Food and Drug Act, and others, exerts considerable control over the processed food market. The Fruit and Vegetable Division of the Agricultural Marketing Service establishes grades. Sellers, however, prefer to sell their processed products by brands and buyers have to decide whether to use grades or brands when purchasing in this area. The grades for processed foods are usually U.S. Grade A, U.S. Grade B, U.S. Grade C, and Below Standard. Grades are established by scoring a processed food for various quality factors such as color, texture, clarity of juice, evenness of size, etc. However, graders are often guided in their grading by the *limiting rule* or *partial limiting rule*. In the limiting rule, the grader has no choice but to use the rule, but in the partial limiting rule the grader has a choice to use the rule or not. Labeling is regulated and buyers should know what these regulations are. Standards of identity have been established, and counts and sizes, syrup densities, standards of fill, and standards for drained weight have been defined for many processed foods.

The various methods of preserving foods are discussed. Some use the latest knowledge in the technology of preservation. The advantages of using value-added foods are also covered. The writing of specifications is covered and examples given. Quantities needed of processed foods for 100 portions are also discussed.

REVIEW QUESTIONS

1. List six factors that either preserve or help to preserve food.

2. Can you name any "natural" substances that assist in preserving food or extending its shelf life?

3. What are the effects of slow freezing on the cellular structure of fresh fruits and vegetables?

4. What is the flash-18 method of canning? Why is it a good method to use for canning thick substances?

5. Why are foods blanched before processing?

6. How are federal grades for processed foods established? What are the grades for canned and frozen items? For dried fruits? For dried vegetables?

7. What is a limiting rule? A partial limiting rule?

8. If a canned vegetable scores 78 in quality factors, what grade can be assigned to it?

9. If a food grades below standard, does this mean it is not fit to eat?

10. If a label gives the net weight in the package, what does this mean? Drained weight? Brix? Count? Size?

11. If a buyer wants a case of ‰'s, what does he or she mean?

12. List the quality factors for canned, frozen, or chilled fruit juice.

13. What are the physical differences between a jelly, jam, butter, or preserve?

14. What should one look for in inspecting dried fruit for quality?

15. Define what a convenience food is. Why do the authors feel that it should not be considered a new type of food, but only a processed food that is more advanced than some others?

16. If you wanted to purchase enough frozen peas to serve 100 people, how could you find out how much to purchase?

17. As a buyer for a family-type restaurant, how would you set up a specification for 10 cases of ‰'s of canned whole tomatoes, for 30 lbs of frozen sliced peaches, for a 100-lb sack of navy beans, for a 20-lb box of dried pear halves?

SPECIFICATIONS

Apples, Canned

1. Apples, canned, heavy (solid) pack, sliced

2. 1 case ‰'s makes 36 pies

3. Grade A

4. ‰'s, 7 lb 8 oz net weight

5. Price by case

6. Type can be Northern Spy, Greening, Roman Beauty, or York Imperial: minimum drained weight 96 oz/No. 10: shall be unsweetened.

Peaches, Canned

1. Peaches, yellow clings, halves, canned

2. (List quantity wanted for purchase)

3. U.S. Grade 3 (Choice)

4. Packed in ‰'s, count per No. 10, 30 to 35 halves

5. Quote price by dozen cans

6. In heavy syrup, 19° to 24° Brix, minimum drained weight 66 oz per No. 10. Certificate of grade required.

Corn, Creamed

1. Corn, cream style
2. (List quantity wanted for purchase)
3. U.S. Grade B (Extra-Standard) or Green Giant Brand
4. Packed in No. 2 cans, 24/case
5. Quote price by dozen cans
6. Minnesota grown. If not Green Giant, federal certification of grade required.

Asparagus, Frozen

1. Asparagus, frozen
2. (List quantity wanted for purchase)
3. U.S. Grade B (Extra-Standard)
4. Packed in 2½-lb carton; 24 cartons/case
5. Quote price per case
6. Spears (stalks), large, all green; deliver at 10°F interior case temperature or lower.

Strawberries, Frozen

1. Strawberries, frozen, whole
2. (List quantity wanted for purchase)
3. U.S. Grade B (Choice)
4. 30-lb can
5. Quote price per lb
6. Sugar–fruit ratio 1:4; Marshall variety only acceptable.

Tomato Juice

1. Tomato juice, canned
2. (List quantity wanted for purchase)
3. U.S. Grade A (Fancy)
4. 46-oz cans, 12/case
5. Quote price per dozen cans
6. Certificate of quality required.

Jam

1. Jam, apricot and pineapple, Type II
2. (List quantity desired in this order)
3. U.S. Grade A (Fancy)
4. No. 10 can, 6/case; net can contents not less than 8.5 lb
5. Quote per 6/10 case
6. Ratio of apricots to pineapple 3:1; shall be pure fruit.

Raisins, Seedless

1. Raisins, Thompson seedless
2. (List quantity desired in this order)
3. U.S. Grade B (Choice)
4. 25-lb carton, polyethylene lined
5. Quote per lb
6. Soda and oil dipped: Extra Fancy color, size Select.

Prunes

1. Prunes, Italian (tart)
2. (List quantity desired in this order)
3. Trade grade, Extra-large size
4. 25-lb carton, polyethylene wrapped
5. Quote per lb
6. Size $^{30}/_{40}$; moisture content not over 25%.

KEY WORDS AND CONCEPTS

appertizing

blanching

brand

Brix

canning

convenience food

cook-chill foods

drained weight

drying

flash-18

freeze drying

freezing

grades

GRAS List

jam

jelly

inspection certificate

limiting rule

make or buy

nitrite or nitrate

partial limiting rule

Pasteur

pickling

processed food

Processed Fruit and Vegetable
    Division, USDA

Pure Food, Drug and Cosmetic Act

saltpeter

standards of fill

standards of identity

tunnel drying

vacudrying

value-added food

CHAPTER 12

Dairy Products

Vom Butter und Shmaltz butter making. From the Louis Szwathmary collection, Culinary Archives and Museum, Johnson and Wales University, used by permission of Dr. Szwathmary and Johnson and Wales University.

Chapter Objectives

1. To state why consumption patterns are what they are today for dairy products.
2. To indicate how the dairy market is regulated and how it functions.
3. To cover how the price of dairy products is established.
4. To discuss some sanitation standards and who is responsible for enforcing them.
5. To review some standards of identity for dairy products.
6. To identify quality standards for many dairy products.
7. To explain how cheese is made and identify some of the more common cheese products on the market.
8. To discuss the quality standards for butter and margarine.

INTRODUCTION

Dairy products, largely from cow's milk in this country, are popular not only because people like them, but also because they can be important contributors of valuable nutrients. Nutritionists recommend that the average person consume two 8-oz glasses a day of milk or its equivalent in other dairy products. Teenagers who are growing rapidly, pregnant women, and some others should consume more, while smaller children might consume slightly less.

Milk and its products are important sources of protein, and can be of fat as well. The protein is complete, that is, it contains all the essential amino acids needed to support life, growth, and reproduction. Dairy foods are good sources of vitamin A and can be of vitamin D; their contribution of the B-complex vitamins is less but fair, while they contain little vitamin C. The big reason for including dairy products in the diet, however, is because of their contribution of calcium, and to a lesser degree phosphorus. Dairy products contain only small amounts of iron, but what they do have is well absorbed.

The consumption of regular dairy products has been dropping, largely because the milkfat in them is fairly saturated. However, while there has been an overall drop in milk and the higher fat products from it, the consumption of low-fat or nonfat items such as low-fat and skim milk, low-fat cheeses, yogurt, and others has increased. Butter consumption has dropped, because of its fat, while the consumption of ice cream and other frozen dairy products has remained stable. Dairy products should be stored at below 40°F, but serve firm cheese at room temperature for best flavor.

REGULATION

The dairy industry is heavily regulated. Prices for dairy products are largely fixed by state milk boards operating under federal laws. Sanitation standards are very strict. The USDA makes exacting inspections of plants and shipping units handling milk; Public Health watches for contamination. The federal **Milk Ordinance** published by Public Health is a code upon which states model their own dairy codes. Federal law requires that states have as strict, or more strict, a code as this. Government subsidies support the industry and require that certain standards be met for their payment.

There are reasons for such regulation. Milk is produced daily; its production cannot be shut off if no market demand exists. It is highly perishable; it cannot be stored to wait for a better market. Contamination is always a threat, and milk must be handled properly to avoid it. Dairy products can easily be adulterated and the government guards against this. It has established standards of identity to identify what individual dairy products *must* be. Regular milk must be 4% protein, 2% lactose (milk sugar) and 3½% milk fat. Lactase is an enzyme the body must have to digest lactose. Some people purchase lactose-free dairy products because they lack this enzyme.

Pricing

Normal pricing, as decided by normal market conditions, is not prevalent in the dairy market. Under the authority of the Agricultural Marketing Act of 1937, the **Federal Milk Marketing Order Program** functions for 70% of the market; it is so influential that the rest of the market is guided by it. The program sets up a classified pricing plan that establishes prices for three classifications of milk products: Class I, fluid (bottling) milks (milk, skim milk, buttermilk, and so on); Class II, soft milk products (cream, yogurt, cottage cheese, ice cream, etc.); and Class III, hard milk products (cheese, butter, and dry milk). This price fixing between producers and handlers has led to a stable industry—milk supply has been stabilized; market-destroying competition by handlers has been stifled; and a steady flow of dairy products to consumers at reasonable prices has been ensured.

Another factor in pricing is the Class I and manufacturing-grade milk prices paid to Minnesota and Wisconsin producers. These two large milk-producing states dominate the market. Milk Marketing Order Programs in other states are often guided in setting their own prices by the prices in these states.

Sanitation Standards

There are no common sanitation standards for dairy products. Each state or locality sets its own, and these are mandatory. The following are common standards:

Dairy herds must be in good health. Public Health or USDA authorities inspect them to determine their health. Milk must be obtained under highly sanitary conditions. In many codes raw milk cannot qualify for Grade A if its plate count is over 300,000 per milliliter. Shipping to plants must be in modern, refrigerated, sanitized units, and milk is carefully tested on receipt at the plant for conformity with standards for sanitation, taste and odor, and milkfat content. The USDA supervises this testing. Milk not meeting standards can be rejected.

Modern dairy plants are marvels of technology. The milk goes through **pasteurization,** cooling, homogenization, and packaging in a matter of a few minutes, all controlled by computers. Pasteurizing can be done by heating the milk to 145°F for 30 minutes, 161°F for 15 seconds, or 181°F or higher for only several seconds. The latter method is effective and fast, but it gives the product a slightly cooked taste. Some chefs complain that heavy creams pasteurized at this high temperature have a decidedly cooked taste and produce a different reaction when added as a finishing medium to sauces.

Pasteurization temperatures for creams and sweetened or heavy mixes such as ice cream or milk shake mixes are higher than for milk, usually 5°F higher, and often longer. Some use 191°F for 1 second, 204°F for 0.05 second, or 221°F for 0.01 second. These products keep better; some special food services such as cruiselines, for which a long holding period is required, specify products pasteurized at the highest temperatures.

Some fluid dairy products are sterilized at 270° to 280°F for 8 to 10 seconds. A lot of this product is shipped to places where milk is in short supply. The products do not require refrigeration and will not spoil until the carton is opened. Some other areas that need milk, such as Hawaii, make it from dried materials. Butter may be used as the source of milkfat in these products. Although they do not have quite the flavor and odor of fresh milk, they are of sufficiently high quality to meet needs.

HOMOGENIZATION

Homogenization is done by forcing milk under pressures of 2,500 psi or more through tiny orifices to divide fat globules so finely they remain in permanent suspension. Packaging is done by automatic machine in nonreturnable units; the unit is usually made of paraffined or plasticized cardboard. This cardboard stops light, which can destroy riboflavin, an important vitamin in milk.

QUALITY, IDENTITY, AND PURCHASE STANDARDS

No uniform standards for quality or identity of dairy products exist among states; each has its own. There is a federal code, but it is not regulatory. Sometimes the federal code covers products not covered by a state, or vice versa. Some standards are uniform in all states because of federal definition. Thus, milk must be "fresh, clean cow's milk free from objectionable odors and flavors." It should contain "not less than 8.25% nonfat milk solids" and have "a specific gravity at 60°F of 1.028." Standards on other items vary; for example, milkfat varies from 3 to 3.25%, low-fat milk from 0.5 to 2% milk fat, light (coffee) cream from 18 to 20% milkfat, and iced plain milk from 2 to 7% milkfat. The percentage of nonfat milk solids also varies, in nonfat milk from 8.25 to 9% and in milk shake mix from 10 to 25%, for example.

Regulations governing the addition of vitamins A and D (the normal level of vitamin D is 400 units and that of vitamin A is 2000 units USP per quart extra dry milk solids), flavoring substances, and other elements also vary (see Figure 12–1). Buyers who wish to know the local regulations should consult local authorities. The *Federal and State Standards for the Composition of Milk Products, USDA Agricultural Handbook No. 51* (January 1, 1980) summarizes these variations.

Milks

Quality in milk products is based on flavor, odor, and frequently on the quantity of milkfat and milk solids. Bacterial counts may be a part of grade requirements.

Milk is by far the largest dairy product consumed. About 70% of the total milk produced is consumed as that, with only 30% being processed into other dairy products. Food services may purchase some milk products in small containers, such as half-pints of milk.

Milk

Some of the quality requirements of **whole milk** have been stated. Grade A must not have over a 20,000-per-ml plate count or over 10 coliform (some states permit

Figure 12-1
A label for milk giving ingredient and nutrient information. Below is published a
copy of the nutrient information that must be on such packages after May 8, 1994.
(Published with the permission and courtesy of Velda Farms.)

no coli). **Certified milk** is usually raw milk produced under more stringently moni-
tored conditions. It cannot have a plate count of over 10,000 per ml and must have no
coliform. *Soft curd milk* is a special milk treated to make it more digestible. It is mostly
used in infant formulas. *Low-sodium milk* is dialyzed to replace the sodium with potassium, but is otherwise the same as regular milk. For individuals who cannot tolerate
lactose, a milk is on the market which has this removed. Special *cultured milks* often
used for dietary purposes are also available. **Fortified milk** has substances added to
increase the nutritional content, such as vitamins A or C or added milk solids. **Filled
milk** is available. (*Filled* means that a nonmilk fat is added, either as part of or all of
the fat; the product must be labeled "filled.") All of these special milks must conform
to the standards for whole milk except for their special treatment.

   Skim or **nonfat milk** must have 8.25% nonfat milk solids and from 0 to 0.5%
milkfat. **Low-fat milk** is the same but the milkfat maximum is 2%. A 2% milk is also

on the market. *Flavored milk* is regular milk to which a sweetener and/or flavoring such as chocolate is added; if the milkfat or milk solid content is changed from that of regular milk, some codes require it to be labeled as a *milk drink* or with some other term, setting it apart from regular milk.

Eggnog and Milk Shakes

Eggnog is a milk product containing 3.5% to 8% milkfat, 0.5 to 1% egg yolk solids, some sweetener, and flavoring. *Eggnog-flavored milk* is milk containing 3.5% milkfat, 0.5% egg solids, some sweetener, and flavoring. Both of these eggnog products may contain a 0.5% stabilizer.

Milk shake mixes run 2 to 3.25% milkfat, with 10 to 25% total milk solids. *Custard mix* contains 8 to 14% milkfat and 16 to 20% milk solids. Some egg solids may be present. Both may contain about a 0.5% stabilizer.

Soured Milks

Buttermilk traditionally was a fluid left after butter was made, but today it is made from whole, low-fat, or skim milk and soured by bacterial cultures. It has 8 to 8.5% milk solids and a milkfat content consistent with the product from which it is made. Some contain tiny bits of butter. The titratable acidity should be between 0.70 and 0.85%. Souring is done by *Streptococcus lactis, Bacterium bulgarium, Lactobacillus bulgaricus,* or *L. acidophilus.* Some of these bacteria are thought to have a beneficial action in the digestive tract. **Yogurt** is a cultured, spoonable, similarly soured product, 2 to 3.5% milkfat with an 8 to 9% milk solid content. *Low-fat* and *nonfat yogurts* are also on the market. Yogurts may be flavored, or fruits or other products may be added. *Yogurt* is a slightly concentrated milk that is clabbered with a lactic acid bacteria. Many are flavored. They are usually low-fat or no fat.

Concentrated Milks

Evaporated milk is 7.9% milkfat and about 18.0% nonfat milk solids. It may be homogenized and fortified with vitamin D to yield 25 USP units per fluid ounce. It is manufactured by extracting moisture by boiling milk at 130° to 140°F under vacuum. A *nonfat evaporated milk* is available. Purchase may be in cases of 48/6, 6/10-, or 48/14½-oz cans. If water in the amount of 2.2 times the evaporated milk is added, the equivalent of whole milk is obtained. Thus, a 14½-oz can makes a quart of whole milk equivalent. Because lactose (milk sugar) crystallizes easily in such milk, food services often turn cases every six months to retard crystal development. **Condensed whole milk** usually contains not less than 19.5% nonfat milk solids, 8.5% milkfat, and enough sugar to prevent spoilage (usually 45%, which is the equivalent of 19 to 20 lb per 100 lb of fresh milk). A *nonfat condensed milk* is marketed. Condensed milks may be sold in bulk and need not be sterilized in cans as evaporated milk must be.

A *concentrated whole fresh milk* is marketed as either a liquid product or a solid frozen. It has a 10.5% milkfat content. It reconstitutes on the basis of a water-to-concentrate 3:1 ratio. It can be sterilized and given a shelf life of 3 months at room temperature or six months when refrigerated.

Dietary Milks

Dry or *liquid diet foods* made from milk products are marketed. They are usually high in milk solids and are fortified with vitamins, minerals, proteins, and other substances. Some dry or liquid milk products are used for reducing diets and come variously flavored and fortified. Baby formulas are marketed as dry and liquid products. Labels should be checked to ascertain what is in the product.

Dried Milks

Any milk solids with only 2 to 5% moisture in tight seals keeps a long time without deterioration. *Whole dried milk* contains not less than 26% milkfat and a maximum of 4 to 5% moisture. *Nonfat dried milk* usually contains not more than 11% fat and not over 5% moisture. Watch for staleness, a cooked flavor, oxidation, tallowness, caramelization, or other off-flavors. Whole milk can become rancid. Specify that the dried milk must come from pasteurized milk.

Spray-dried milk is usually the highest quality. **Roller-dried milk** processed under vacuum is also of good quality. Milk is spray-dried by first removing a half to three-fourths of the moisture and then spraying this concentrate as a fine spray into a drying chamber; *drum-dried (roller-dried) milk* is obtained by rotating a steam-heated drum or roller in a vat of milk and removing the dried solids as the unit comes out of the milk and dries on the surface. *Instant* is dry milk treated to go into solution rapidly and easily. Regular dry milk is not so treated and has a tendency to lump in mixing. Drum or roller-dried milks are suitable for cooking. Dried buttermilk is on the market.

Malted milk is a dried milk product with about 3.5% moisture, 7.5% milkfat, and the dried solids of a fluid mixture of 40 to 45% nonfat milk and 55 to 60% malt extract. Each pound of malted milk contains the solids of 2.2 lb of fluid whole milk; total milk solids are usually 29%. Double malted milk contains twice as much malt as regular malted milk.

Federal grades for dry whole milk are U.S. Premium, U.S. Extra, and U.S. Standard. Institutions should select either of the first two. Premium grade should have a sweet flavor, with not more than a slight cooked flavor and odor, have a white or light cream natural color, and be free from lumps that fail to break under slight pressure. It should be practically free from brown and black scorched particles. It should not have over a 30,000 bacterial plate count, not more than 90 coliform per gram, and 26% or more milkfat content. Federal grades for nonfat dry milk are U.S. Extra and U.S. Standard. Extra is preferred for foodservice use unless the milk is to be used for manufacturing, bakery production, and so forth. Extra should not have over 50,000 bacterial count per gram and Standard not more than 100,000 per gram. Extra's flavor should be sweet, with no more than a slight cooked, feed or flat, chalky taste and odor, and other factors should be above those for whole dry milk, except for milkfat content.

U.S. Extra is usually specified for dry buttermilk but there is a U.S. Standard. Extra should have a good flavor and odor, and be free from nonbuttermilk flavors. The color should be cream to light brown, it should be free from lumps that do not break under slight pressure, and practically free from black or brown scorched particles.

The acidity should not be less than 0.1% or more than 0.18% expressed as **lactic acid,** moisture not over 4%, and milkfat not more than 4.5%. Bacterial limits are 50,000 per gram.

If the quantity of dried milk used is large, purchase in 50- or 100-lb bags or 200-lb drums. If lesser quantities are used, purchase the milk packed in 6/10 cases, 10-lb bags, and so forth. Purchase by the pound.

Instant milk goes into solution much easier than does regular dry milk and, if the milk is reliquefied rather than used dry, this is a much easier product to use. Specify high-heat-treated milk for milk used for yeast products because regular pasteurized milk has thermophilic bacteria in it that can interfere with yeast development.

Store dry milk in a dry, cool, well-ventilated place. If it becomes higher than 5% in moisture, it will become stale, discolor, lump, and so on. Keep dry milk away from products from which it might absorb objectionable odors. The Dairy Division Laboratory (AMS, USDA, 1819 West Pershing Road, Chicago, 60609) can be helpful in dealing with problems related to dry milk and other dairy products.

Creams

Cream should not have a bacterial count of over 60,000 per ml and not more than 20 coliform per ml. **Half-and-half** is not cream but equal parts of whole 3.25% milkfat milk and 18% cream, which makes it about 10.5% milkfat. *Soured* or *cultured half-and-half* must have, in addition to what has been stated, a 0.2% acidity expressed as lactic acid. *Table (light or coffee) cream* usually runs from 18 to 20% milkfat. **Sour cream** must be similar but have more than a 0.2% acidity expressed as lactic acid. **Whipping cream** comes as **light** (30 to 34% milkfat) or **heavy** (34 to 36% milkfat); it is not homogenized and is usually ripened three days before being marketed. *Whipped cream,* dispensed from aerosols, is 18 to 30% milkfat and contains sugar, flavoring, and stabilizer. A *filled dairy topping* (18% fat) is available that contains milk solids, but the fat is not milkfat. *Sour cream dressings* are 16 to 18% milkfat, with an acidity expressed as lactic acid of 0.2 to 0.5%, and other sour cream and sweet cream products are also marketed.

Frozen Desserts

Frozen desserts should be pasteurized at 155°F for 30 minutes or 175°F for 25 seconds before being frozen. The increase in volume from freezing and whipping, called **overrun,** should be from 80 to 100% for ice cream, around 40% for sherbets, and 25% for ices. **Ice cream,** by weight, should be 8 to 12% nonfat milk solids and 14 to 18% sugar (corn sugar can be 25 to 30% of the total sweetener). A 0.5% of stabilizer such as agar agar, gelatin, or a mixture of monoglyceride and gelatin can be used. The minimum acidity of fruit sherbet and water ice is 0.35%. Some states forbid the sale of artificially flavored frozen desserts. The government standards for frozen desserts in addition to these are given in Table 12–1.

Iced milks have a 2 to 7% milkfat content and 10 to 30% total milk solids.

Table 12-1
Federal ice cream standards.

	Vanilla and Light Flavors	Bulky Flavors	Ice Milk	Fruit Sherbert	Water Ice
Minimum % milk fat	10	8	2	1	0
Minimum % total milk solids	20	16	11	2	0
Minimum lb wt per gal	4.5	4.5	4.5	6	6
Minimum lb total food solids per gal	1.6	1.6	1.3		

Note: Some states may vary in the above percentage requirements.

A 10% milkfat and 20% total milk solid mix is often used for bulky flavors such as chocolate or nut, with about 2% of the flavoring product added. This reduces the final milkfat content to 8% milkfat, which standards allow. Surplus government butter and dry milk can be made into good ice cream and other frozen desserts, but a pasteurizer, homogenizer, freezer, and hardening cabinet must be available. Fluid frozen dessert mixes must have less than 50,000 bacteria per ml and no more than 10 coliform per ml, and dry mixes should have similar counts per gram of product.

Quiescently (unmixed) **frozen dairy products** cannot have an overrun of more than 10%, and cannot be less than 17% by weight total food solids with 0.5% stabilizer. Not more than 0.2% by weight of emulsifier is allowed. Mellorine frozen desserts are made from filled mixes and must be sold under trade names. They cannot be called ice cream.

Philadelphia ice cream is plain milk, cream, sweetener, flavor, and stabilizer. **French ice cream** is Philadelphia ice cream but contains 1.4% by weight of egg solids—1.12% if a bulky flavor. It can be flavored with ground vanilla bean. Low-fat frozen dessert may be from 5 to 10% milkfat. Frozen desserts should be stored at below 0°F and served at 10 to 15°F.

Soft ice cream is a big seller in many operations. A regular ice cream mix can be used or a special one just for making soft ice cream. The mix is frozen in a typical fashion and whipped in a small freezer. When the product is in what is called the "ribbon" stage (the milk folds back and forth, in ribbons, as it comes out of the freezer), it is ready for use. Thus, the only difference in soft ice cream is that it is not hardened. Soft ice cream and shake mixes are usually sold in bulk containers holding three, five, or more gallons. Some operations have refrigerated tanks that are filled by delivery trucks; these refrigerated tanks lead into the machines that freeze the ice cream, thus eliminating handling.

Cheese

Many different **cheeses** are available, and buyers should know their quality factors. Variety depends on the type of milk, bacterial culture, amount of milkfat, processing, aging, and other factors. Quality depends on ingredients, and on how the cheese is made, aged, and stored. U.S. grades are given to some cheeses. A sample of market quotations on different kinds of cheese is given in Figure 12–2.

CHEESE

CHEDDARS
Delivered Dollars Per Pound

Blocks	1.5675–1.7275
Daisies	1.4225–1.9175
Processed 5 lb. loaf	1.6325–1.7600
Processed 5 lb. sliced	1.6525–1.8175
Muenster	1.6100–2.0100

OTHER VARIETIES
DOMESTIC

Blue	1.7650–2.3750
Gorganzola	2.4300–2.4950
Provolone, Fresh	1.4375–1.9450
Romano	2.9625–3.2150
Mozzarella 5 lb. Loaf Part Skim	1.7900–1.9150
Parmesan	3.1750–3.2125

IMPORTED

Argentina, Romano	$2.65–3.29
Reggianito	2.65–3.29
Denmark, Blue	2.64–3.14
France, Roquefort	5.50–6.89
Holland, Edam	2.19–3.09
Gouda	2.39–3.15
Italy, Gorganzola	3.24–5.94
Parmesan	
Pecorino, Romano-Genuine	2.09–2.90
Provolone	3.44–5.50

SWISS CUTS

DOMESTIC	
Grade A	$2.2500–2.5050
IMPORTED	
Austria	$2.2500–2.7500
Denmark	
Finland	2.5900–2.8500
Switzerland	

Figure 12–2
An example of up-to-date market quotations on cheese. (Courtesy Urner Barry Publications.)

Manufacture

Whole, partially defatted, or nonfat cow's milk of approved quality is normally used for cheese, depending on the type. Annatto, a yellow or orangish coloring of carotene derivation, can be included without being noted on the label. The milk must be pasteurized unless the cheese is cured for more than 60 days; such curing destroys harmful bacteria. Federal standards set the moisture and milkfat content. About 100 lb of whole milk makes 10 lb of cheese.

A **clabbered milk curd** is usually the basis of cheese, obtained by coagulating milk with **rennet,** lactic acid-producing bacteria, and other substances. After the milk is pasteurized and cooled to lukewarm temperatures, a starter is added to form lactic acid and sour the milk, which aids in forming a firmer curd. The curd is *cut* into cubes and then is *cooked* by heating. The higher the cooking temperature, the firmer and harder the cheese will be. Cheddar is cooked to below 100°F and Swiss to around 110°F. The curd is then stirred to release whey (freed liquid) so that it can drain off, leaving a solid, rubbery mass called casein on the bottom of the trough in which the cheese is being made. This mass is then piled onto either side of the trough bottom, where it forms a solid substance that can be cut into about 8-in.-wide strips and piled up two to four strips deep—a process called **cheddaring,** which gives cheddar cheese its name although most cheeses are made by this method (see Figure 12–3.) The strips are alternated because the pressure on the bottom strip expresses more whey. Moisture is now close to 50%, and acidity is about 0.45 to 0.60% expressed as lactic acid.

The strips are then *milled* (ground), salted, and piled into hoops—a process called **hooping.** Special molds or bacteria can be added when the milled curd is put into hoops. *Penicillium roqueforti* is a mold that produces blue cheeses; *Propionibacterium shermani* gives the sharp flavor and gas to make the larger eyes in Swiss cheese, and *Penicillium camemberti* makes the richly flavored and soft-textured Camembert. Hoop cloths around the cheese (these have been replaced today, by some cheese manufacturers, with special mold-holders) are then tightened to envelop the curd closely. These rounds, or other shapes, are placed into coolers for several days to dry; they are then moved into *curing rooms*.

Curing, or **aging,** changes the texture from a resilient, rubbery mass to softer, more flexible, and waxy mass. The flavor sharpens, becomes more pungent and biting and smoother. Some cheeses are subjected in curing to temperature, humidity, or salting control. Thus, Swiss may be brine-dipped or salt-rubbed to slow down curing actions. If aging is too rapid, the gas inside can cause the cheese to burst, a phenomenon called a *failure*. The person in charge of curing must have the skill of a brewmaster in a brewery. Figure 12–4 shows some quality factors of good and poor cheese.

Some cheeses ripen from the inside out, such as Swiss and Roquefort. Others ripen from the outside in, such as Camembert, Brie, and Limburger. Inside-out cheeses usually keep well, especially the dry ones such as the hard Granas of Italy. Outside-in cheeses start as firm products but soften during ripening. The cheese then begins to firm and, when it hardens again, it can be an unpalatable product; a powdery, thickly coated brownness on the outside appears. Outside-in cheeses should yield to pressure when they are ready to eat and, when cut, they should be soft and

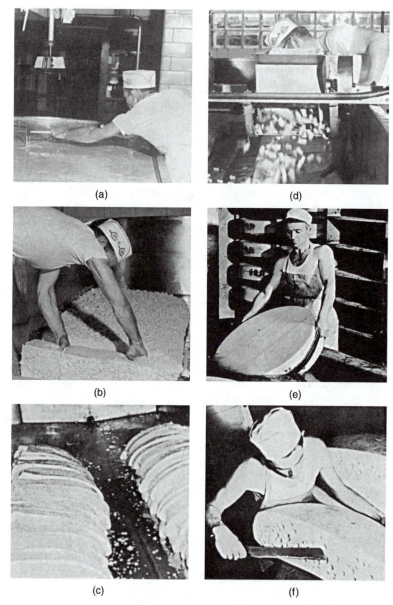

(a)   (d)

(b)   (e)

(c)   (f)

Figure 12–3

(a) After the milk is clabbered by a starter and rennet, it is cut; (b) ditching the cheese, which is cutting it into 8-in.-wide strips and allowing it to drain; (c) piling the strips on one another, a process called cheddaring; (d) milling the cheese to put it into fine pieces, so it can be cultured and packed into hooping; (e) young Swiss cheese is brine-soaked before going to cure to give it flavor and also to help control the curing process; (f) after three months of curing, the Swiss cheese is examined. The large eyes, shiny inside, are an indicator of good quality. Excessive development or dull eyes are marks of poor curing. (Courtesy USDA.)

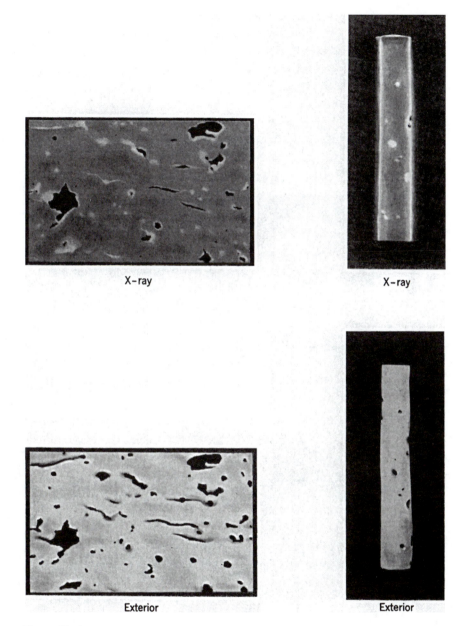

X-ray

X-ray

Exterior

Exterior

Figure 12-4
Pictures on the right show a good grade of cheese with fine holes. On the left, poor cheese is shown with excessive development of holes made by gases during curing. These holes are called **sweet** *or* **Swiss holes.** (Courtesy USDA.)

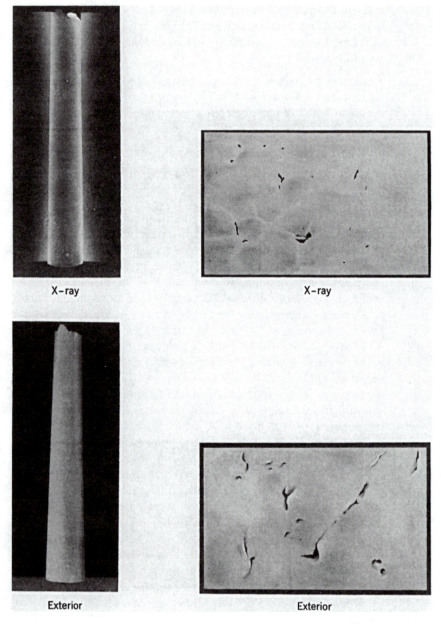

X-ray

X-ray

Exterior

Exterior

Figure 12-4 *Continued*

On the left is cheese that has failed to develop sufficient gas to create holes. Such cheese is called blinds. The top right shows a nizzler while the lower right shows a cheese of adequate cheese hole development.

tacky so that they almost flow. A heavy, rusty crust and a strong ammoniacal odor, plus the loss of the rich subtle flavor, are evidence of overaging. The heavy rind developed in aging of these outside-in cheeses is eaten. Only several weeks' supply should be stocked.

Varieties of Cheese

Cheese is an excellent food of high nutritive value and should be featured on menus. A large number of domestic and foreign cheeses are available. Many of our domestic cheeses are copies of foreign ones, and often good copies, but gourmets may still consider the foreign superior in overall excellence.

Hard Cheeses.   Because the number of hard cheeses is so extensive, only a few of our most commonly ones are described here.

Cheddar or **American cheese** is perhaps most commonly consumed. It is widely produced, and many fine cheddars come from widely dispersed areas such as Oregon, Wisconsin and New York.

Cheddar is a moderately hard cheese, cream to orange in color, with a mild to sharp flavor depending on the time and conditions of its curing. It must not contain more than 39% moisture and have a 50% or more milkfat content on a dry basis. Grades are established on the basis of body, texture, aroma, taste, color, general finish, and appearance. Grades for regular cheddar, curd cheddar, and colby are U.S. AA (Extra), A (Standard), and B (Commercial). Aging is described by *current,* aged up to 60 days; *medium,* aged 60 days to 6 months; and *aged* or *cured,* aged over 6 months.

Swiss or **Emmental (Emmentaler)** (em' ə ler) is a creamy yellowish, smooth, firm, sweet, nutlike tasting cheese with large, round holes. It is cooked to a temperature of 125° to 130°F, which gives it hardness. Special bacteria called propiani produce the rich flavor and large eyes. Curing is difficult. Excess humidity encourages molding and too low a humidity causes rind checks. Federal grades are A, B, and C. The eyes should be well spaced and round or slightly oval, at least $^{11}/_{16}$ to $^{13}/_{16}$ in. in diameter and glossy, not dull or dead. Moisture should not be over 41% and milkfat must be 45% or more. Watch for sticky, dry cheese with a crumbly texture or horizontal cracks that look like fractured glass, called "glassiness," which denotes poor quality. **Nizzlers** have small holes like brick cheese and **blinds** have no eyes at all; both conditions cause downgrading. As Swiss ages, it becomes whiter. Milkfat is 43% and moisture 41% maximum. Length of aging terms are *current,* aged 60–90 days; *medium,* 90 days to 6 months; and *aged* or *cured,* over 6 months.

Monterey Jack is a creamy white, smooth, semifirm, mild-flavored cheese with 50% milkfat or more and 44% moisture. This cheese is aged two to five weeks for normal use. It is a cheddar, and its grades are AA, AS, and B. Small holes should be evident, like apertures between layers of rock, and the surface should be slightly dull, not glazed, with a bright, attractive appearance. It should pull from the mass, tearing rather than crumbling. Poor grades have large, splotchy holes from excessive gas development and a bitter flavor or other off-flavors. *Dry Jack* is coated with a mixture of pepper, oil, and baryta earth (clay) and dried until it is hard and crumbly like Grana cheese.

Colby is a cheddared cheese 10 days old or older. Grades are AA, A, and B. Because it is a young cheese it is somewhat rubbery and mild in flavor.

Soft Cheeses.   A number of soft cheeses, high in moisture, are used by food services. **Cottage** or **farmer cheese** is made by setting a regular milk into a curd and cooking to about 90°F; the curd is then cut and the whey drained; about 1% salt is added. The curd size is regulated by the size of the cutting knife. Moisture should not be over 80%. A salad cottage cheese is sometimes ordered by food services. This should not be above 70% moisture, but not much lower, or the curd becomes hard and dry. Salad cheese is easier to mold. *Pot cheese* is uncreamed popcorn-size curds. Coliform count for these cheeses should be under 50 per gram; combined yeast and mold count should not be over 100; 0.2% calcium chloride can be added to give a firmer curd; gelatin can be added up to 0.5% but not to hold more moisture. *Cook's* cheese is a dry curd as is *Bakers'* cheese. Low-fat cottage cheese should have a 0.5 to 2% milkfat content and an 82.5% maximum moisture content. Regular creamed cottage cheese is 4% milk fat.

Ricotta is a soft cottage cheese of Italian origin. Greek *feta* (fet′ ə) is a soft curd cheese used in many Greek, Balkan, and Arabic dishes; it often comes from goat's milk. It has an acid, sharp, delicate flavor and is somewhat crumbly. *Liptauer* (Liptai) (lip′tô ər) is a Hungarian soft curd, mixed with butter, paprika, mustard, chives, caraway, salt, pepper, capers, or garlic. The curd is often served alone with butter and some seasonings which patrons mix with the curd to suit their taste. Austria has a soft, yellow curd cheese with a smoky flavor that is widely imitated.

Unripened soft curd cheese of high fat content can be ground into a soft paste to make cream cheese. It is at least 33% milkfat. **Neufchâtel** (noo′ chə tel′), originally from Switzerland, is a cream cheese with only a 20% milkfat content but a higher moisture content than cream. Both cream and Neufchâtel can be flavored with pimientos, olives, or other ingredients and used as a spread. *St. Marcelin* (mär′ səl in) is made in Savoy, France; it is a soft, round, cream cheese made from goat's and cow's milk. It has a mild flavor, and a slightly salty undertaste. *Carré Demi-sel* (kär′ ē dəm ē sel′) is a delicious, mild-flavored cream cheese from Normandy that is shaped into a square.

Specifications.   Specifications for hard and soft cheeses usually require the following depending on the type of cheese and what is wanted:

1. *Kind.* This should include the common name of the cheese as given in the standards of identity, if one has been established. Local terms are sometimes used such as "rat" cheese for cheddar. At times, subvarieties under kind may have to be identified.

2. *Grade, brand, or quality.* Only a few cheeses such as cheddar, curd cheddar, colby, Swiss and a few of the other hard cheeses and some soft cheeses are graded and carry the U.S. grade stamp (see Figure 12–5). In other cases, brand must be given or a description of the quality desired.

3. *Aging.* The time and kind may have to be given.

4. *Moisture content.* Standards of identity will establish maximum moisture content for those for which such standards exist. The moisture content of others such as cottage cheese may have to be specified. Often kind of cheese dictates this. The

Figure 12-5
Various grade stamps used to indicate the grade of butter or cheese. (Courtesy USDA.)

description "soft," "moderately hard," "hard," or "very hard" may for some cheeses do the job.

5. *Fat content.* The amount of fat may have to be named such as "low fat" or "4%" for cottage cheese or *"halvet"* (half fat) for the Scandinavian Noekkelost.

6. *Bacterial content.* This may have to be given for some few cheeses.

7. *Origin.* Sometimes this may be important and not only the area of production may have to be given but the exact producer may have to be named.

8. *Kind of milk.* In a few cases this may be required. However, in most cases the kind of cheese named dictates this. Most cheese in this country comes from cow's milk.

9. *Size, shape, or packaging.* Some cheeses come in typical sizes and typical shapes. Others may not. Cheddar cheese today may come in large or small rounds, bricks or in other shapes.

10. *Flavoring.* Usually the kind of cheese named will carry its own special flavor, but in a few cases some within a kind may be flavored with special herbs, wines, or seasonings and may have to be named so as to get the right one. Thus, club cheese is often flavored with various wines and a description may have to be added such as "shall be port flavored."

Butter and Margarine

Butter

Federal standards require that **butter** contain not less than 80% milkfat. It may contain salt and coloring. Unsalted butter is on the market. Butter is usually about 80.3% milkfat, 0.9% milk solids or curd, 2.0% salt, and 16.3% moisture. Cream for butter must be pasteurized at not less than 165°F for 30 minutes or more or 185°F for 15 seconds. About 100 lb of milkfat produces 120 to 125 lb of butter.

After pasteurization, cream can be made more acid (about 0.18% expressed as lactic acid for best flavor) by adding bacteria, or it can be reduced in acidity. Annatto can be used as a coloring, and the label need not state its use. After the cream is churned to produce butter and buttermilk, the buttermilk is drained away. The butter is then washed, salted, and worked. Working is important for a waxy, compact, tenuous body. Overworking gives a loose, sticky, somewhat greasy, body.

Butter is graded Grade AA (93 score), Grade A (92 score), Grade B (90 score), and Grade C (89 score). To score flavor, body, salt, color, and packaging, a grader inserts a trier into a block of butter and brings out a long cylindrical plug to examine. Maximum scores for these factors are 45, 30, 20, 10, and 5 in the trade, but the government uses a different scoring system to arrive at the grades listed here (see Table 12–2). A federally graded **whipped butter** is on the market. It is butter whipped to include air or a gas.

Aroma is a part of flavor, and body consists partly of appearance and partly of texture. The federal standards for butter state that the "U.S. grade of butter is determined on the basis of classifying first the flavor characteristics and then characteristics in body, color and salt. Flavor is the basic quality factor "and is determined organoleptically by taste and smell."

Butter is sold in ¼-lb or 1-lb prints, cubes (64 lb), or sometimes in bulk or other lot sizes. Pats come in 5-lb cartons, usually from 72 to 90 pats per lb. Sometimes these are on paper or plastic chips. Individual portions wrapped in plastic or in plastic cups are available. Figure 12–5 shows some grade stamps used for butter.

Margarine

Federal standards of identity state that **margarine** is a "food, plastic in form, which consists of one or more of the various approved vegetable or animal fats mixed with cream." Optional ingredients are vitamins A and D, butter, salt, flavoring, emulsifiers, artificial color, and preservatives. Labels must state their presence and, for some, the quantities used. In some cases, quantities allowed are controlled. Most margarines contain 15,000 IU of vitamin A per pound. Finely ground soy beans may replace up to 10% of the moisture. The product must be labeled margarine or oleomargarine. Coloring is almost universally permitted today in all states. Some states require that margarine sold in individual pats be triangular in shape and not square and that a sign in the dining area state that margarine is served. The number of pats per pound is the same as for butter. Margarine can be purchased in individually wrapped portions, as chips, in pound or 5-lb boxes, or ¼-lb, 1-lb, or 64-lb cubes. It also is sold in bulk or barrels. Many special margarines are made for food service use such as those for rolled-in doughs or puff pastes. Margarine must not be less than 80% fat.

At one time much margarine was processed from olein (beef) fats, but now soy oil exceeds all other fats used. Cottonseed, corn, and other vegetable fats are also used. Some margarines are blends of animal and vegetable fats. Unsaturated margarines are made from safflower oil or other oils of this type. Hydrogenated corn oil (hardened) or cottonseed oil are saturated, and even though the oil itself is not highly saturated, it is after hydrogenation. Some margarine-like products contain

Table 12-2
Government scoring system for butter.

Example No.	Flavor Classification	Disratings			Total Disratings	Permitted Total Disratings	Disratings in Excess of Total Permitted	U.S. Grade or U.S. Score
		Body	Color	Salt				
1	AA	½	0	0	½	½	0	AA or 93
2	AA	½	½	0	1	½	½	A or 92
3	AA	0	1	0	1	½	½	A or 92
4	AA	½	1	0	1½	½	1	B or 90
5	A	½	0	0	½	½	0	A or 92
6	A	0	½	½	1	½	½	B or 90
7	A	0	1	0	1	½	½	B or 90
8	A	1	½	0	1½	½	1	C or 89
9	B	½	0	0	½	½	0	B or 90
10	B	½	½	0	1	½	½	C or 89
11	B	1	0	0	1	½	½	C or 89
12	C	½	½	0	1	1	0	C or 89
13	C	0	1	0	1	1	0	C or 89

Source: Courtesy Dairy Division, USDA.

considerable moisture and are soft. They cannot be labeled margarine, but may be labeled "spread" instead.

Margarines must be sound, clean, and fit for food. A good specification might read: "Good grade product, sweet, fresh, clean, with firm and uniform body, not sticky or mottled. The color should be a delicate straw yellow, and coloring should not cover inferior merchandise. The products should contain not less than 1% milk solids and 9000 IU of vitamin A per pound. It should contain 80% or more of approved fats and not more than 15% moisture and 4% salt." Packaging should also be stated, and whether it is to come in pats, pats with chips, pound prints, 5-lb prints, 30-lb cubes, barrels, or some other form.

Margarine is evaluated using butter standards. The color should be uniform and the body and texture that of good butter. Flavor should be pleasing, clean, sweet, and free from taint or foreign odor. Off-flavors or odors can be detected if the margarine is warmed slightly. When heated, margarine melts with little foam and browning, but if lecithin is present as an emulsifier, the margarine will foam and brown like butter. The keeping quality of margarine is slightly better than that of butter, and it is less likely to absorb flavors. Store margarine and butter at below 40°F someplace where they will not absorb odors.

The amount of dairy products to purchase for 100 portions is given in Table 12–3.

BEST BUYS

Buyers should investigate the desirability of a food service using processed milks, creams, and other dairy products rather than fresh ones. Dry milk works well in bakery products and also for some cooking purposes. It curdles easily, though, and for this reason may not be acceptable for some items. Evaporated milk is the most stable of all milks and is lower in cost than fresh milk. In many bakery products, margarines work as well as butter. Some of the lower grades of butter often do as well as AA or A and cost less.

Usually the lower the milkfat content of many products, the lower the cost of the item. There is little use in specifying the higher cost items when low-fat ones will do as well. It is seldom that Neufchatel cheese cannot be satisfactorily substituted for cream cheese. Although current or mild cheeses may be less costly, the flavor of aged (cured) cheese is often so much better that less can be used to give a better flavor. The possibility of its use for many cheese dishes should be investigated. Domestic cheeses like the foreign types are frequently suitable, but not always. The real foreign cheese is often of a better flavor and quality.

Higher milkfat frozen desserts and those of lower overrun range are usually superior to the others, but many good low-fat items are on the market, and these should be merchandised to meet the desire for lower fat items.

Because of the nature of dairy products, there is often little chance to search the market or make substitutes to find the best buys. A precise product is needed; changing the quality or using a different item may not result in a suitable product. Buyers are therefore often required to get the product specified and do little manipulation.

Table 12-3

Amount to purchase of dairy products.

Dairy Product as Purchased	Unit of Purchase	Weight per Unit (lb)	Portion	Portions per Purchase Unit	Number Unit per 100 Portions
Cheddar cheese	Lb	1.00	4 oz	4.00	25
Cheddar cheese	Lb	1.00	2 oz	8.00	12½
Cheddar cheese	Lb	1.00	1 oz	16.00	6¼
Cheddar cheese	Longhorn	11–13	2 oz	88–104	1¼
Cheddar cheese	Daisies	20–25	2 oz	160–200	½ to ¾
Cheddar cheese	Flats	32–37	2 oz	256–296	under ½
Cheddar cheese	Cheddars	70–78	2 oz	560–624	under ½
Cheddar cheese	Block	20–40	2 oz	160–320	½ to ¾
Cottage cheese	Lb	1.00	2 or 4 oz	4 or 8	25 or 12½
Cream cheese	Lb	1.00	1 oz	16.00	6¼
Processed	Lb	1.00	1 or 2 oz	8 or 16	6¼–12½
Half-and-half	Pt	1.07	1½ T	21.33	4¾
Half-and-half	Qt	2.14	1½ T	42.67	2½
Light cream	Pt	1.06	1½ T	21.33	4¾
Light cream	Qt	2.13	1½ T	42.67	2½
Sour cream	Pt	1.06	1 T	32.00	3⅛
Sour cream	Qt	2.13	1 T	64.00	1½
Whipping cream	Qt	2.10	1¼ T	51.20	2
Brick ice cream	Qt	1.25	½ c (slice)	8.00	12½
Bulk ice cream	Gal	4.50	No. 12 scoop	22–26	4
			No. 16 scoop	31–35	3
			No. 20 scoop	38–42	2½
			No. 24 scoop	47–51	2
Ice cream cups	3 oz	0.19	1 c	1	100
	5 oz	0.31	1 c	1	100
Sherbet	Gal	6.00	No. 12 scoop	25.00	4
			No. 16 scoop	35.00	3
			No. 20 scoop	42.00	2½
			No. 24 scoop	50.00	2
Fluid milk	Qt	2.15	1 c	4.00	25
	Gal	8.60	1 c	16.00	6¼
	5 Gal	43.00	1 c	80.00	1¼
Condensed milk	14-oz can	0.88			
Evaporated milk	14½-oz can	0.91			
Dry nonfat, instant	Lb*	1.00	1 c fluid	17.06	6
Dry nonfat, regular	Lb†	1.00	1 c fluid	17.06	6
Dry whole, regular	Lb†	1.00	1 c fluid	14.22	7

Source: Adapted from Agriculture Handbook 284, USDA.

* By measure 6½ c.

† By measure 3¼ c.

SUMMARY

Dairy products are important in the diet because they contribute important nutrients, the most important being calcium, phosphorus and vitamin A. The consumption of high milk fat items like butter, cheeses, etc., has been dropping, with lower fat items of the same kind taking their place. The dairy industry is highly regulated. The federal Milk Ordinance sets standards and the Federal Milk Marketing Order Program sets prices, amounts produced, etc.

Milk has a standard of identity that says it must be "fresh, clean cow's milk free from objectionable odors or flavors containing not less than 8.25% non-milkfat solids" with "a specific gravity of 1.028." Other dairy items are similarly defined as to what they ought to be. The kinds of milk, concentrated milks, dry milks, and other dairy products are given standards of identity as to exactly what they must contain.

Milk and some other dairy products are homogenized by forcing the liquid through a frame that has holes tiny enough that the fat globules are divided so finely they do not float to the surface. Most dairy products are pasteurized, but cheese that is aged over 60 days need not be made from pasteurized milk. The curing in that time period destroys any harmful bacteria. Federal grades exist for most liquid milk products, some cheese, and butter.

Frozen desserts are not federally graded but some, like ice creams, have a standard of identity. Thus, ice cream must have at least 10% milkfat, an overrun of not more than 100%, have by weight 8 to 12% nonfat milk solids, and 14 to 18% sugar. Philadelphia ice cream is plain ice cream; French ice cream has eggs in it and may be flavored with ground vanilla.

Most cheese is made by the cheddar process. American (cheddar), Swiss (Emmental), Monterey Jack, and Colby have federal grades. Cheese ripens either from the inside out or the outside in. Those that do the latter gradually grow softer until they begin to become runny. Then they begin to harden, a sign that they are passing their prime. A number of cheeses have special bacteria added to them to produce the item desired. A *nizzler* is a cheese that has developed eyes or holes that are too small (called often Swiss holes or sweet holes); a *blind* has developed no eyes; and a *failure* has burst in curing because it developed too much gas, too fast. Soft cheeses like cottage (farm), ricotta, pot, cream, etc., are made by setting the curd at around 90°F, cutting and then draining off the whey. They are usually lower in fat than the hard cheese and are much higher in moisture content. However, some few low-moisture items are used for baking or other culinary purposes. Salad cottage cheese is about 70% moisture. It is firm enough to hold together for salads.

Butter is made from cow's cream. It must contain not less than 80% milkfat. Grade scores are 93 (AA), 92 (A), and 90 (B). Whipped butter, butter with air or gas beaten into it, is federally graded. Butter is graded largely on its flavor, color, body, and salt content. Margarine is judged on some of the same criteria as are used for butter. It is not federally graded. It usually has vitamin A and vitamin D added to it. It is possible to make some oils into fats by hydrogenation, that is, adding hydrogen to them. This saturates the oil more, so margarines made of highly hydrogenated oils contain almost as much saturated fat as regular butter. Softer margarines are therefore usually less saturated than firmer ones.

REVIEW QUESTIONS

1. Why are prices or marketing procedures for dairy products regulated by the federal government?
2. What is the maximum plate count per milliliter for raw milk to qualify for Grade A milk? For Grade A milk after pasteurization?
3. What are the regular pasteurizing temperatures and times for milk?
4. What is homogenization and how is it done?
5. Why is milk marketed in cardboard containers today, rather than clear glass?
6. What are the times and temperatures of ultrapasteurization?
7. What is the federal standard for whole milk? In your answer, give the percentage of each substance.
8. What is certified milk?
9. What are lactose, lactase, casein, whey, curds?
10. What is the difference between condensed and evaporated milk?
11. What is the milkfat and moisture content of nonfat dried milk? Give maximum percentages.
12. What is overrun and what is the maximum allowed in ice cream?
13. Describe the cheddaring process for making cheese and describe each step in sequence.
14. What does butter contain? Give the percentages of ingredients.
15. What is the minimum fat content for margarine?
16. How is quality judged for ice cream products, fresh milk products, cheese products?
17. What are the major American-made and foreign cheeses used in our food services?
18. What does a large eye that is shiny inside indicate in Swiss cheese? What is a nizzler?
19. What are the percentages of ingredients required in butter?
20. What does 93 score mean? What is its equivalent in letter grades?
21. What is the minimum fat content for margarine? What vitamins are added to margarine?
22. How is quality judged in ice creams, fresh milk products, cheese products?

SPECIFICATIONS

Milk

1. Milk, regular
2. Open order; maintain minimum of 8 cases
3. U.S. Grade A
4. Half-pint (1-cup) cartons, 48 per case
5. Shall be priced per ½-pt carton
6. Shall be 3.25% milkfat or more; minimum nonmilkfat solids 8.25%.

Whipping Cream, Heavy

1. Cream, whipping, heavy
2. 6 qt
3. U.S. Grade A
4. In quart paper cartons
5. Price by the quart
6. Shall be at least 34% milkfat.

Butter

1. Butter
2. Open order; maintain a stock level of 64 lb (1 cube)
3. U.S. Grade AA, 93 score
4. Shall be in pats, 72 per lb, packed 5 lb per box, 6 boxes per case
5. Price by the pound
6. Shall be unsalted, sweet cream butter. Boxes should be layer packed, each layer separated by moisture-proof paper.

Ice Cream

1. Ice cream, pecan brittle
2. 10 gal
3. Shall be —— brand or equal.
4. Shall be in heavy cardboard, interior waxed paper tubular cartons.
5. Price by the gallon
6. Shall be 12% or more milkfat and contain 5% or more of small bits of pecan brittle; maximum overrun shall be 80%.

KEY WORDS AND CONCEPTS

American (cheddar) cheese

blind

butter

buttermilk

certified milk

cheddaring

cheese

clabbered milk curd

Colby

condensed whole milk

cottage (farmer) cheese

cream

cream cheese

curing (aging)

Emmental (Emmentaler)

evaporated milk

Federal Milk Marketing Order Program

filled milk

fortified milk

French ice cream

half-and-half

homogenization

hooping

ice cream

iced milk

lactic acid

low-fat milk

margarine

milk

Milk Ordinance

Monterey Jack

Neufchâtel

nizzler

overrun

pasteurization

Philadelphia ice cream

quiescently frozen dairy products

rennet

ricotta

roller-dried milk

skim (nonfat) milk

soft ice cream

sour cream

spray-dried milk

sweet (Swiss) holes

Swiss cheese

whipped butter

whipping cream (light or heavy)

whole milk

yogurt

CHAPTER 13

Groceries

Print #164. In a general store from a German Childrens Book "on occupations" The Grocer (cca. 1810). From the Louis Szwathmary collection, Culinary Archives and Museum, Johnson and Wales University, used by permission of Dr. Szwathmary and Johnson and Wales University.

Chapter Objectives

1. To cover purchase factors for a group of foods often classified as groceries.

2. To detail product characteristics and important factors required to adequately purchase beverage materials such as coffee, tea, and cocoa.

3. To cover the purchase factors needed to buy cereals, cereal products, and bakery products.

4. To indicate purchase factors needed to buy oils and shortenings.

5. To enumerate product characteristics and other requirements needed to purchase pickled products.

6. To identify and give purchase factors needed to purchase miscellaneous items such as spices, flavorings, sugars and syrups, nuts, vinegars, and leavening agents.

INTRODUCTION

Food services use a large number of items, often classified loosely as **groceries**—items such as beverages, cereals and bakery products, fats and oils, pickled products, flavorings and seasonings, nuts, and others. Although a small quantity of one of these items may be used, the flavor contribution, or the effect it has on a food product, is considerable, so it often pays to purchase a high-quality item—so little is used, the cost per serving is small. Few quality standards exist for these items, so buyers must know the products and the production need to make satisfactory purchases. Brand buying is often advised.

BEVERAGES

Coffee

Coffee, which originated in Arabia, was prized by for many years by Near East cultures. After Venetian traders brought coffee to Europe, it became *the* drink and coffee houses sprang up everywhere. However, some thought it evil stuff, labeling it "Satan's drink." Pope Clement VII was asked to condemn it, but before he did, he thought he ought to try it. He did, liked it, and instead of condemnation, he baptized it, making it Christian, earning the undying love of all coffee drinkers.

Many food services have found that coffee is a highly merchandizable item. Coffee bars exist that only offer an array of flavored coffees and espresso, which can be accompanied by a pastry or snack item. In regular restaurants coffee can be similarly merchandized with meals. The drinking of espresso has become quite popular, as well as other coffee drinks, such as *cafe au lait.*

Coffee is the seed or bean of a cherry-red fruit growing on evergreen shrubs in semitropical or tropical climates. There are four main varieties: **Arabica, Robusta, Liberacia,** and **Stenophylla,** the first two being used most often for coffee. A warm frost-free climate and rocky soil are important to good quality. The best coffee usually grows 2,000 ft or more above sea level; **rio** (river) **coffee** is usually of lesser quality but may still be used in blending to give desired astringency and bitterness. A good growing season—not too wet or dry—contributes to good quality.

The fruit is picked when fully ripe and then the pulp is removed, leaving two greenish white beans. They are then dried, often by sun. Shipment to this country is largely to New York, the primary market for this product. Green coffee has little or no flavor; roasting develops it and ruptures the cells so the flavor can be extracted. Roasting ovens hold over 500 lb each; roasting is at 450° F for 15 to 17 minutes. Three degrees of roast can be given: light (dark chestnut color), medium (brown), and dark (dark brown or almost black). Heavy dark roasts are often used for **cafe espresso.** Roasting increases bean volume about 50%, but about a 15% weight loss occurs. The coffee may be "finished" at the end of roasting, a process in which about a gallon of water for every 100 lb of beans is thrown into the hot coffee, plumping the beans further and giving them a better appearance. Dry finishes also are used. Glazing may be done to improve appearance, protect flavors from oxidation, and assist in clarification, but many believe it only adds weight and improves appearance.

Coffee contains from 0.75 to 2% caffeine, a mild stimulant. Decaffeinated coffee is about 97% caffeine-free. Water-extracted decaffeinated coffee, called natural, Swiss, or European decaffeinated, is considered superior to acid-extracted decaffeinated coffee.

Most coffee is a blend of beans. Our coffees usually contain considerable Brazilian Santos—**Bourbon Santos** are among the best. Colombian coffee is mild and rich, used in best blends. Venezuela has its mild, rich, and flavorful Maracaibo, used little in foodservice blends since it does not hold up well after brewing. Mexican Coatepecs have excellent flavor and good body; its Oaxacas are only fair in quality but have good flavor and life and are used in blends. Jamaica's Blue Mountain coffee is prized by the British, while Puerto Rico's coffee is favored by the Spanish. Java's coffees are much like Santos. Arabia produces the great Mocha, a mild, richly flavored bean with good vitality and holding qualities. Sumatra produces the high-quality, sweet, delicate Ankola and Mandhelling coffees. African Robustas and Liberacias are often used in blends. Hawaiian Kona's are well respected but the amount marketed is small.

Coffee preferences vary by locality. Some areas like a strong, acidic, astringent, and heavy flavor, while others like a mild, rich, full-flavored coffee with limited astringency and acidity. The word *soft* in coffee jargon means fine flavor, readily extracted from the bean, the opposite of *harsh* or *rio*. *Strictly soft cup* indicates top quality. *Character* is made up of aroma and taste, often described by *acid, sweet, neutral,* or *bitter; quality* covers flavor often described as *desirable* or *undesirable*. Some acidity and bitterness are desirable, as is some sweetness, but too much sweetness is undesirable. A neutral coffee is not acid, bitter, or sweet; one called *thin* is neutral and lacks flavor.

Adulterated coffee can contain parched wheat, peas, beans, or chicory, the latter to give color and a more bitter flavor. **Chicory** causes ground coffee to stick together when squeezed. It also sinks quicker and colors cold water brown faster than coffee. Adding iodine to such water shows a blue color. Cut through beans to detect artificially colored coffee.

Grinds vary: Steel cut is a coarse grind with all the coffee passing through a %4-in. screen; medium allows about 50% to go through a 1/16-in. screen, whereas fine passes readily through a 1/24-in. screen. Coarse or medium grinds are used for urns and fine for drip equipment. Turkish coffee or *espresso* is made from very fine grinds.

Coffee is highly volatile and deteriorates rapidly, especially in ground coffee at room or higher temperatures. A coffee kept at room temperature has a flavor rated poor after 8 days of shelf life. Roasted whole beans hold flavor longer than ground. Vacuum or frozen coffee loses flavor slowly. Swelled cans indicate carbon dioxide buildup, but no deterioration. Hard-vacuum bagged polyethylene vacuum-packed coffee holds quality as well as regular vacuum-packed coffee.

Purchase ground coffee in the package size needed for brewing to reduce errors in measurement. Only a two-day supply should be bought, and old stocks used first. The freshest and best coffee comes from beans ground at the brewing site and used immediately.

A good specification would be 20% Bourbon Santos, grading 3s or 4s, high-grown Colombian 40%, high-grown, washed Central American beans 40%. The degree of roast, type grind, packaging, and so forth must be specified.

Pure soluble (instant) coffee is the dry, powdered, water-soluble solids extracted by percolating under vacuum. Some carbohydrate may be added. Freeze-dry processing makes the best instant.

A pound of coffee makes about 2½ gallons of brew, which will yield about twenty 6-oz cups. If an operation is paying $4.80 for a pound of coffee the cost per cup is 24¢ (4.80/20 = 0.24). With the cost of sugar and cream added the cost might be around 28¢ per cup. At a desired food cost percentage of 40%, the menu price would be 70¢, perhaps set at 75¢. That a cup of coffee could rise from 10¢ a cup to this price is incredible, but the figures don't lie.

Tea

Tea is the tiny leaf or bud of a tropical evergreen bush related to the camellia, which grows from 15 to 30 ft high, but is usually pruned to make picking easy. The terminal bud and the next two leaves are the standard *pluck* (see Figure 13–1). Delicacy of flavor starts with the bud; pungency and heavier flavor come with leaf progression. The best tea is usually grown 6,000 ft above sea level. Spring produces the best quality.

Tea has been found by food services to be merchandizable and a number now offer not just ordinary black tea but a number of fine blends from which patrons may make selections. A very nice touch in service is to have the server bring an attrac-

Figure 13-1
Two leaves and a bud, the standard pluck.
(Courtesy of the Tea Council of U.S.A.)

tively arranged caddy filled with these various teas and let the patrons make their selection.

After plucking, tea is **withered** to make the leaves flaccid for **rolling.** Machines roll the leaves, a process which ruptures the cells so they release flavor and enzymes to facilitate fermenting (see Figure 13–2). **Fermenting** is allowing tea to stand so that the tannins oxidize, developing flavor, and causing the color to be black after firing. **Firing** is the introduction of low heat to dry out the leaves.

Hand-rolling and basket-drying by lifting leaves in a basket over a low fire improves quality but raises price. Green tea is not fermented but immediately fired after rolling. Oolong tea is fermented only a short time.

Blends of 5 to 30 different teas are used for tea bags and loose tea to give desirable flavor. Jasmine flowers, orange peel, cloves, or other flavorings may be added. Some specialty teas are not blends but 100% tea of one kind.

Green tea has more tannin than other teas, and thus is slightly more bitter. It has a delicate, greenish yellow, pale liquor and rather fruity flavor. **Oolong tea** is darker, less bitter, still fruity, but possessing a softer flavor. **Black tea** is copper-colored with a soft, mild, subtle flavor lacking in heaviness but slightly acid; some describe the flavor as "brisk."

Figure 13-2
The first stage of manufacture is known as withering. *The leaves are spread evenly and thinly on specially prepared racks and allowed to remain there until they turn into a flaccid condition.* (Courtesy of the Tea Council of U.S.A.)

Table 13-1
Black tea grades.

Trade Size Term	Trade Abbreviation for Grade	Description of Grade
Leaf grades*		
Orange Pekoe	O.P.	Thin, long, wiry leaves that sometimes contain tip leaf; tea liquor is light or pale
Pekoe	P.E.K.	The leaves are shorter and not so wiry and the liquors have more color
Souchong	SOU.	A bold and open leaf; makes a pale liquor
Broken-leaf grades†		
Broken Orange Pekoe	B.O.P.	Best grade generally; much smaller than leaf grades; contains tip; tea liquor has good color and strength
Broken Pekoe	B.P.	Slightly larger than B.O.P., with less color; used as a filler in blends
Broken Pekoe Souchong	B.P.S.	A little larger and bolder than B.P., giving a lighter color; also used as a filler in blends
Fannings	E.N.G.S.	One of the top grades today because of tea bag use; smaller than B.O.P.; gives a good flavored brew with good color; more quickly made because of finer size
Dust	D.	Smallest grade; useful for quick brewing of a good strong cup of tea; used in blends with larger sizes

*About 10% of the crop.
†About 90% of the crop.

Green tea's top grades are Gunpowder, Young Hyson, and Hyson; oolong's are Choice, Finest, and Fine to Finest. Table 13–1 lists the various grades for black tea.

India, Pakistan, Ceylon, Indonesia, Africa, and Russia produce most of our tea. Japan's and China's teas are good, but not of great world market importance.

Tea leaf size heavily influences the grade of tea. Small leaves and buds in brewing lose flavor more rapidly, improving quality. Larger leaves may be broken to reduce size to improve quality. Tea bags are often 100% broken tea. Stems and large leaves in loose tea indicate a lower quality.

CHOCOLATE

The *theobroma cacao* tree that produces the chocolate bean is native to South and Central America but is now found in all tropical and semitropical areas. The pod is 4–7 in. long. Some seeds are aromatic and mild while others are more pungent, acid, bitter, and less fragrant. Blends are common. The beans are shelled and then fermented to reduce bitterness. Then, they are roasted. The dried beans are next broken into small pieces, called *nibs,* and the chaff removed. The nibs are then ground or milled into *chocolate liquor,* which is 45–50% *cacao butter.*

Chocolate contains theobromine and caffeine, both mild stimulants. Bitter chocolate must be 50% or more cacao butter. Hydraulic presses may press out some of the butter and that remaining can then be ground finely to make cocoa. Breakfast cocoa contains not less than 22% cacao butter; some cocoas are much lower than this.

Alkaline treatment breaks down some fiber (cellulose), giving a richer appearance, smoother flavor, and more soluble product in liquids. The Dutchman C. J. Houten discovered this and so the alkaline treatment is often called the **Dutch process.**

Bitter chocolate is straight cacao bean liquor. Sweet or semisweet chocolate contains added sweeteners. Milk chocolate is usually sweetened and contains various quantities of milk. Some bakeshop chocolates may contain lecithin and extra cacao butter. White chocolate is cacao butter with a sweetener, vanilla, and a firming product.

Good chocolate breaks firmly and crisply with clean edges that do not crumble away. It has a full chocolate odor and rounded aroma without being obtrusive. Placed into the mouth, it neither clings stickily to the palate nor feels gritty but melts like butter. Carob is often used as a filler in cheap chocolate.

CEREALS

Most cereals come from the **endosperm** of grains, the inner part of the kernel (see Figure 13–3.) Some few like buckwheat are seeds. By federal regulation, refined cereal products must have added thiamin, riboflavin, niacin, and iron to replace that lost in processing.

Wheat

Flour

Wheat flour is made from what is called **soft** or **winter** and **hard** or **spring wheat.** Hard wheat contains more and stronger gluten and makes a more firm product. It is used for yeast breads and some other bakery items. Soft wheat is used for cakes, cookies, muffins, pie crusts, and other purposes where a tender product is desired. **All-purpose flour** is a blend of soft and hard and is suitable for most purposes, but the quality of products is usually less because the flour is less suitable for the purpose. Hard wheat grows in northern United States and Canada. Hard wheat is sown in the spring and harvested in the fall; soft wheat is sown in the fall and then harvested in the summer. Soft wheat comes from the central states such as Kansas and Nebraska. Soft wheat flour can be identified by touch. Put some in the hand and press. It holds its shape. Hard wheat does not. It crumbles and feels gritty, not soft and smooth like soft wheat flour. Hard wheat is more yellow, because of its higher gluten content. Hard wheats contain 11% or more of gluten; the softest wheat flours contain 7% to 8%.

A gray, dull color indicates poor flour. Good hard wheat absorbs about 65% of its weight in water and still forms a pliable, nonsticky ball. Good soft flour absorbs

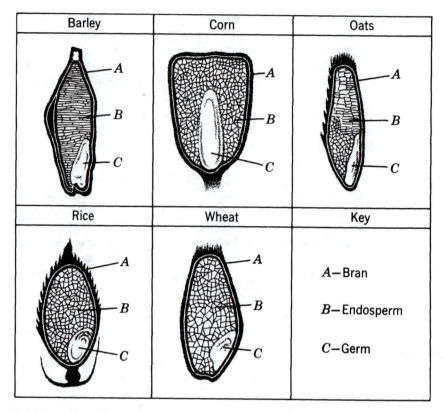

Figure 13-3
The structure of various grains. The interior of the grain contains endosperm from which farina, semolina, hominy, and other products are derived, depending on the grain. (Published with the permission and courtesy of Miller's National Foundation.)

less moisture. A *strong* soft flour can carry high ratios of fat, eggs, and sugar; a *strong* hard wheat flour makes a firm, tenuous product with some chew. Some bakers test flour by making gluten balls and baking them (see Figure 13–4).

Flour is made by properly *blending* clean desired wheat and then running it between rollers, cracking it, and then sifting it. As each *rolling* occurs, the rollers are closer together. Each rolling or sifting is called a **break** or **stream,** and as many as nine may occur. The best flour comes off in the early streams and is called **patent flour,** a product containing the best protein and little ash. The last siftings are called *clears* and make a poor flour, high in ash. The residue left after the last sifting is called *red dog* or *shorts* and is used for cattle or poultry feed.

If all the siftings are used to make a flour, it is called a **straight** or **100% flour.** The best patents are from 40% to 60% of the total flour. Medium (baker's or regular) patents are about 90% of the total flour. Long or family patent is 95%. A filled flour contains more clears than a straight normally would. Whole wheat (graham) flour is straight flour with some of the bran. Unbolted whole wheat flour contains wheat germ in addition to a good deal of bran; it keeps poorly. Figure 13–5 shows how various flours are derived from the wheat kernel.

Figure 13-4

Three gluten balls, before baking, made from equal amounts of (from left to right) bread (hard), pastry (soft), and cake (soft) flour. Note the difference of the amounts of gluten in each, the condition of the gluten indicating strength, and the ability to form a solid, firm structure.

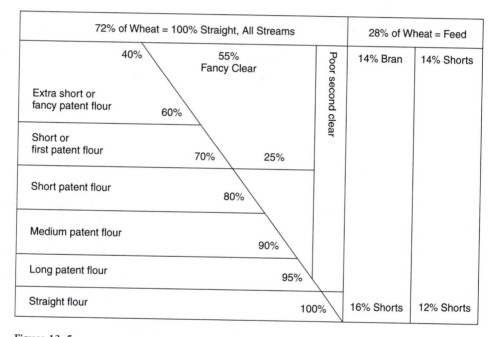

Figure 13-5

Percent of wheat kernel going into different flours. (Published with the permission and courtesy of Millers' National Federation.)

Flour is aged 8 to 10 weeks to condition and bleach it. If chemicals are used for bleaching, the label must state this. Unaged flours perform poorly in products and is often called **green flour.**

Flour is priced at wholesale by the barrel which is 196 lb, or two 98-lb sacks. Food services purchase by the sack or fractions of a sack. Some cake flours are sold in 100-lb bags. Some 50-lb boxed flour is available. Market prices are usually set for the year and so large inventories are not advised. Large users may have their flour delivered in bulk, some in carload lots. Store flour off the floor, with sacks criss-crossed for good ventilation, in a dry, cool area. Flour can absorb odors. Mice, insects, and flooding are dangers to stored flour.

Pastas

Pastas (macaroni products or alimentary pastes) have increased in popularity and they are being served in many ways other than the traditional Italian dishes. They are shaped and dried doughs either of farina, the endosperm of hard wheat, or **semolina,** the endosperm of durum wheat (see Figure 13–6). They are high in protein, semolina making the best pasta because its gluten is stronger. Pastas made from inferior flours are soft and mushy after cooking and do not make for good eating (see Table 13–2).

Government standards permit the addition of ½% to 2% egg white, salt, onions, celery, and bay leaf, in addition to water and flour. If the term *egg* is used, the product must contain 5½% or more egg solids. If the term *milk* is used, not less than 3.8% of milk solids must be present. Protein should be 13% or more. No yellow coloring can be added, nor can pastas be wrapped in yellow paper. If vegetables (e.g., spinach, tomatoes, carrots) are on the label as an added product, their quantity must not be less than 2% nor more than 5%. Whole wheat pasta products are marketed. They do not hold in the steam table as well as regular pastas.

Pasta quality is indicated by a good yellow color and a hard, brittle, or flinty texture, semitranslucent appearance, and a square break making a clean, glassy

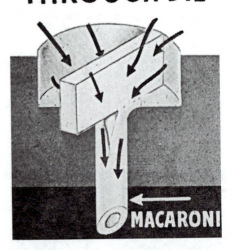

Figure 13-6

How the hole is made in macaroni. The macaroni dough, when pushed against the die, is split by the wings and then pressed together around the lower end of the pin to form a solid tube. As it comes from the bottom of the die, the macaroni is cut into proper lengths.

Table 13-2

Classification of macaroni products.

Type	Name	Size (in.) Trade	Size (in.) Federal Standards
Solid round rods	Vermicelli	$\frac{1}{32}$ diameter	Not more than 0.06 in diameter
	Spaghettini	$\frac{1}{16}$ diameter	
	Spaghetti	$\frac{3}{32}$ diameter	0.06–0.11 in diameter
Hollow tubes, plain	Foratini or maccaroncelli	$\frac{3}{32}$ diameter	
	Forati or perccatelli	$\frac{1}{8}$ diameter	
	Mezzarrelli or mezzani	$\frac{5}{32}$ diameter	
	Macaroni or mezzani	$\frac{1}{4}$ diameter	0.11–0.27 in. diameter
	Zitoni	$\frac{1}{2}$ diameter	
Hollow tubes, corrugated	Mezzani regati	$\frac{1}{4}$ diameter	
	Zitoni rigati	$\frac{1}{2}$ diameter	
Noodles, flat ribbons	Broad	$\frac{1}{4}$ wide, 0.030 thick	
	Medium	$\frac{1}{8}$ wide, 0.033 thick	
	Fine	$\frac{1}{16}$ wide, 0.035 thick	
Sheets, scalloped	Lasagne (the widest)		
	Reginette and margherite		
Elbows, hollow, small, smooth	Tuchetti	$\frac{1}{8}$–$\frac{3}{32}$ diameter	
Elbows, hollow, large, smooth	Ditali lisci	$\frac{1}{4}$–$\frac{7}{16}$ diameter	
Elbows, hollow, corrugated, very large	Rigatoni	$\frac{9}{16}$ diameter	
Elbows, hollow, hexagonal	Bonballati	$\frac{3}{8}$ diameter	
Bunches, curled	Vermicelli rella (morella)		
	Spaghetti rella		
Fancy small pastas	Alfabeto		
	Puntette		
	Stelletta		
	Crowns, and so forth		

fracture. Rod types should be springy and make a good arc before snapping. Poor products break unevenly. Products should be reasonably free from broken, misshapen, or checked pieces. Cook to ascertain texture, taste, odor, and appearance.

Purchase is in 1-lb packages to 300-lb barrels; large users often purchase a lot of pastas in 100-lb bags. Stock only up to a month's supply.

Crackers

Crackers are a flour paste made of salt, shortening, leavening, malt, and a bit of sugar; they are then formed and baked. Many specialty products are now produced, with special shapes and seasonings. Some standards for crackers might be:

Type	Size	Number per lb	Fat (%)*	Moisture (%)†
Regular	¼ in. thick, 2 in. square	120–190	10	5
Small	2 × 1⅛ in.	180–235	10	5
Graham‡	1½–2 in. square	50–95	10	6
Oyster	½–⅝ in. diameter, ⁷⁄₁₆ in. thick	575–700	10	5
Raisin-filled§		30–45	5	11

* Not less than.
† Not more than.
‡ Not less than 30% whole wheat.
§ Not less than 40%, by weight, of seedless raisins. (Salted crackers should have a pound of salt topping per 100 lb of crackers.)

Rice

Pearl rice is a small, round kernel that cooks into a somewhat sticky product, while **long-grain rice** cooks into a separate, whole product. **Brown rice** is only lightly polished with some bran left; it keeps less well than polished rice. *Converted polished rice* is steamed, nutrients are added, and then it is redried. *Instant rice* is precooked and dried; it is often fortified with vitamins and minerals. Purchase in 100-lb bags if use is large. U.S. grades are No. 1, 2, 3, and 4. Trade grades exist.

Corn

Hominy is the endosperm of corn and is made by soaking corn in lye to soften the outer bran for removal and then drying it. **Pearled hominy,** coarser than cornmeal, is used for breakfast cereals. It may be called **samp** and cooked for a cereal product; table or breakfast grits are finer, coming as coarse, medium, and fine. Cream of pearl cornmeal is finer than grits. Hominy flakes are made from thinly pressed paste; they cook rapidly. **Cornmeal** is made from degermed corn endosperm. It can be coarse or fine or white or yellow. *Stone ground* or *old-process* (also called water-ground or old-fashioned) contains the bran and germ. *Corn flour* is finely ground and sifted cornmeal. *Bolted cornmeal* has a high bran content.

Cornstarch is the pure, unmodified, pulverized siftings from corn. Waxy maize starch and modified starches are special cornstarches used for berry pies and for thickening frozen products so they do not break down in freezing. They have greater clarity, softness, and pliability, and make mixtures as thick when hot as cold. Instant starches are precooked and dried. About 14½ oz of cornstarch are required to give the same thickness of 16 oz of waxy maize or converted starch.

Oats

The endosperm of oats, called **groats,** is used largely to make oatmeal. *Scotch* or *regular oatmeal* takes a long time to cook; quick-cooking is made by steaming the groat, cutting it into small pieces, then pressing it flat, and drying it. More cooking and finer division makes quick cooking. Oatmeal should have a bright, uniform, creamy color with the natural flavor of oats, free from rancid, bitter, musty, or other undesirable flavors. Stone-ground oatmeal is called *old-fashioned-stone-,* or **buhr-ground** and often is the long-cooking type. Some oatmeals are called *steel-cut,* which means the kernel is cut into small pieces somewhat like cracked wheat. Whether or not the bran of oats removes cholesterol from the body is controversial.

Barley, Rye, Buckwheat, and Soy

Malt is the main product obtained from barley; *pearled (polished) barley* is used in soups; first grade should have no bran showing. *Brown* (partially polished) *barley* is available. Barley sizes are large, medium, and small.

Rye is used mainly as a flour; because it is low in gluten, some wheat flour of good gluten content is combined with it by bakers. It is available as light, medium, or dark, the amount of bran determining the color. **Pumpernickel** is coarsely ground, whole rye flour.

Buckwheat is not a grain but a seed. Lighter colored buckwheat has most of the bran removed. The darker flours have more bran and a stronger flavor. Wheat flour is used with buckwheat to provide needed gluten.

Soy is a legume, but because it can be made into a meal or flour, it is classed sometimes as a cereal. It is high in protein, but low in gluten, and can be added to foods to increase their protein content. Soy flour gives a yellowish cast to bread; it can be used in pie crusts for flavor enhancement and tenderization. Soy meal is used in some breakfast cereals.

Breakfast Cereals

Breakfast cereals can be classified as ready-to-eat, instant, and cooked. The ready-to-eat breakfast cereal market is highly competitive and companies seek to introduce new brands that will bring more users for its products. Sweeteners, fruit, nuts, fiber, vitamins, protein, minerals, and other ingredients are used to enhance flavor or attract buyers. Often the sale's pitch is one of contributing to better health. Most are made of a paste made largely from finely ground hominy, which is shaped and then baked or toasted. Malt is often a flavoring ingredient. Some items like *puffed wheat* or *puffed rice* are expanded by a process called **gun puffing** in which they are shot suddenly into the air with the pressure inside expanding them as they travel; they are then toasted. A number of puffed oat cereals are also on the market.

Cooked cereals are either the long-cooking or old-fashioned type such as cracked wheat or oatmeal, or quick-cooking such as quick-cooking oats, farina, or cornmeal. *Instant cereals* are those cooked cereals that have been cooked in processing and then finely divided so that they only need to be rehydrated with hot water to be ready to eat. Nutritionists usually prefer that the cooked cereal be the one selected; some look with disfavor at the sweetening of cereals and the addition of so many ingredients that supply calories but little in other food value.

BAKERY PRODUCTS

Many food services purchase their breads, rolls, pies, cakes, and other bakery goods. Few, if any, specifications exist for them.

Breads

Bread and *rolls* should be specified as having crusts of uniform, golden brown color and thickness, even shapes, and gently rounded tops. A slight shred or break may appear on one side. The interior crumb should be clear white or slightly creamy with a soft sheen, and, when a slice is held up to the light, it should be semitranslucent. A grayish crumb denotes inferior flour or poor processing. Grain texture should be soft and velvety, with no large holes and a soft, delicate consistency, not crumbly or doughy. Bread made from either dry or liquid milk should have an 8.2% milk solid content to flour. *Whole wheat bread* should be made from all whole wheat flour and not whole wheat and refined flour, unless that is specified. Breads containing fruits or nuts should have a 5:10 ratio to flour by weight. Calcium or sodium propionate, used to give softness and keeping quality, should not be more than 0.32% to flour in white bread and 0.38% in others. It is best to specify sandwich bread without these propionates, because when they are present the sandwiches tend to soak up moisture from the filling. Cheese bread should have 20% cheese by weight to flour.

Bread should come wrapped in moisture-vapor-proof wraps unless hard-crusted. The number of slices per pound should be specified. Standard loaf slices are ⅜ in. thick, but may vary; 4½ by 4½ in. sandwich bread may have slices ¼ to ½ in. thick. Hard-crusted breads may be called *hearth, Vienna, French,* or *Italian*. **Sourdoughs** are breads having a small portion of overfermented dough added to a normal dough. *Salt-rising bread* is an overfermented bread with a cheesy flavor resulting from adding extra yeast and some cornmeal. *Boston brown bread* is steamed and is a mixture of rye and wheat flour, cornmeal, molasses, milk, salt, and sometimes egg. A large number of specialty breads are now being made to attract buyers and are often finding a ready market.

Cakes

Cakes can be specified as made with water, sugar, flour, whole eggs, butter or vegetable shortening, monoglycerides and diglycerides, corn syrup, nonfat dry or fresh milk, leavening, salt, starch, and flavoring. The size, number of layers, kind of frosting and filling, etc., should also be specified. All colorings, flavorings, spices, nuts, fruits, etc., should meet U.S. certification requirements. The pack should be specified, such as, "one unit per package, 4 per case." Portioning by marking on the top may be desired. Cakes may be specified unfrozen or frozen upon delivery.

Bakery Mixes

No more than a six-month supply of bakery mixes is desirable, because extended storage causes a loss of volume and flavor in products. Specify as being prepared from high-quality, clean, wholesome ingredients. Check competing products for odor, taste, texture, thickness, etc. Mixes prepared by the one-step method are best and should contain dried eggs so fresh eggs are not required. Brand purchase is recommended once quality is ascertained.

Specify cake mixes by type: Type I with dried eggs; Type II requires fresh eggs. Packs are usually 5-lb to 50-lb, often in bags. Frozen waffles often come 20 per sheet, 4 sheets per case or packed 96 to the case, 8½-lb net. For many mixes and ready-to-use products, specify polylined cartons and a 60- or 90-day shelf life. Many prepared yeast and other mixes are now available on the market. All of these save labor and may be quite useful to a facility, providing they give adequate quality and cost.

Bake mixes to judge quality, evaluating taste, odor, thickness, color of crust, texture, color of crumb, grain (should be moist, even, and smooth), and volume. Indicate moisture limits and volume the cooked product must reach (see Table 13–3).

Table 13-3
Moisture percent and volume increase to specify for cake mixes.

Item	Maximum Moisture %	Volume Increase*
Buttercakes	5	2.5 times
Angel cakes	5	3½ in. height†
Cornbreads	9	2.2 times
Plain muffins	6	2.4 times
Biscuits	10	2.4 times
Pancake, waffle, or buckwheat cakes	10	‡
Bread and rolls		3.75 times
Sweet rolls		3.33 times
Cake doughnuts	8½	2.6 times

* Leave baked product in the pan and fill with rapeseed to level full. Measure volume of the seed. Remove the product and fill the empty pan with rapeseed. Measure it. Subtract the volume of the seed when the product was in the pan from the volume when the pan was empty. Divide this by the weight of the product to get specific volume.

† In a 7⅞ × 9⅝-in. tube pan, top and bottom diameter, respectively, add 625 g (1 lb 6 oz) of batter; height after baking should be not less than 3½ in.

‡ After baking the height in the center should be not less than ¼ in. or more than ⅜ in., using 1.6-oz batter and allowing it to flow naturally on a hot griddle.

Pies

Pies often come individually boxed, six per case, and can be either 9 or 10 in. as specified. Freshness is specified by indicating time between baking and delivery. Table 13–4 indicates some specification factors buyers might use.

Cookies

Specifications for crisp cookies should state that they be uniformly baked, and have an even, golden crust color or color suitable to type. The finished cookie should be tender and crisp without any burned or scorched flavor. Broken cookies should not constitute over 5% of the total by weight. Table 13–5 indicates some factors that might be useful in writing specifications.

FATS AND OILS

Dietary recommendations today for best health are that the calories contributed by fats and oils should not be over 30% of total calories, with each gram of fat calculated as contributing 9 calories. Thus, a person with a 2,400-calorie intake should have no more than 800 calories in fat (2,400 × 0.30 = 800) or about 78 grams (800 ÷ 9 = 78) or about 2.7 oz (78 ÷ 28g/oz = 2.7). In addition, these calories should be divided equally between saturated, monounsaturated, and polyunsaturated fats and oils. The aim is to reduce calories and also to select fats and oils that help lower

Table 13–4
Recommended purchase factors for baked or frozen fruit pies.

Pie	Type Fruit	% Fruit in Filling by Weight	% Filling to Total Pie Weight	Other Allowed Ingredients
Apple	Dried or canned Jonathan, Spy, Macintosh	40	67	Water, enriched flour, starch, sugar, vegetable shortening, modified food starch, lemon juice, dextrose, nonfat dry milk, salt, cinnamon, citric acid, leavening, ascorbic acid, and orange oil
Apple/rhubarb	Apples as above and strawberry rhubarb	25 apples 25 rhubarb	67	Water, enriched flour, sugar, starch, vegetable shortening, modified food starch, corn syrup, dextrose, nonfat dry milk, salt, lemon juice, leavening, citric acid, ascorbic acid, U.S. certified food color
Blueberry	U.S. Grade A cultivated genus *Vacinium* blueberries	47	66	Water, enriched flour, vegetable shortening, sugar, modified starch, corn syrup, dextrose, nonfat dry milk, salt, lemon juice, vegetable gum, corn syrup solids, leavening, blueberry and raspberry extracts with other natural flavors, citric acid, cinnamon
Cherry	Montmorency RSP cherries	66*	66	Enriched flour, sugar, vegetable shortening, water, modified food starch, dextrose, nonfat dry milk, salt, lemon juice, citric acid, leavening, cinnamon, U.S. certified food color
Peach	U.S. Grade A firm peaches of the Rio Oso variety	46 sliced and 4 pure peach puree	66	Enriched flour, water, sugar, vegetable shortening, corn syrup, modified food starch, dextrose, nonfat dry milk, salt, lemon juice, dried apricots, citric acid, leavening, ascorbic acid, and U.S. certified food color

*Shall be guaranteed to be substantially above the 25% cherries required by law.

477

Table 13-5

Factors for specifications for cookies.

Type Cookie	Size	Count/lb	Fat (%) (not less than)	Moisture (%) (not more than)
Vanilla wafer	Disk shape ⅜ in. thick, 1½ to 2½ in. diameter	50–120	12	9
Gingersnaps	1³⁄₁₆ to 2⅓ in. diameter	50–70	7½	7
Shortbread		40–65		5
Macaroons*		20–35	12	5
Fig bars†	1½ in. wide, ½ in. thick, 1½ to 4 in. long	14–40	4½	18
Vanilla cake type			17	
Chocolate cake type‡			17	

* Should contain 35 lb of macaroon coconut for every 100-lb soft flour.

† Should contain 50% by weight ground, clean, sound figs.

‡ Should contain 17½ lb of cocoa or 1½-lb chocolate liquor per 100-lb soft flour.

risk of heart attack, stroke, and some other health problems (see Figure 13–7). The public has listened and this has sent the fat and oil market into a tailspin. It has also made a considerable impact on the foodservice industry. Menus now reflect more food choices that meet these dietary recommendations and patrons are responding by selecting these foods.

Today the rush is on to feature less fats and oils in foods and also, when fats are there, to feature the kinds considered health beneficial and to minimize those that are not. A considerable amount of research is being done to develop a product that acts like fat in the product but contributes less calories than fat. Today there are many foods carrying these products but they are foods that are not heated or are heated only slightly because such items break down under heat. And, so the search goes on.

The research to find fat substitutes has gone three ways: substitutes with (1) a carbohydrate base, (2) a protein base, and (3) a nondigestible fat or oil. The first, largely being produced by starch companies like Arco and National Starch, is already marketed, being used in frozen desserts, salad dressings, margarine, and other foods. Modified proteins are also being used, such as the product Simpless. They come from protein substances like milk, whey, or egg whites. Both contribute four calories per gram rather than the nine for fats and oils. Some oils like mineral oil are nondigestible and are not absorbed. They contribute no calories and no saturated or unsaturated fat, yet in many respects act typically as a fat or oil in products. These are being looked at to provide fat-like substances that perform and taste like regular fats but contribute no calories.

Because canola oil has considerble unsaturated and monounsaturated fractions, ranking with sunflower and safflower oils, is plentiful, and is competitively priced, its use has grown rapidly. A margarine made from it has had good sales.

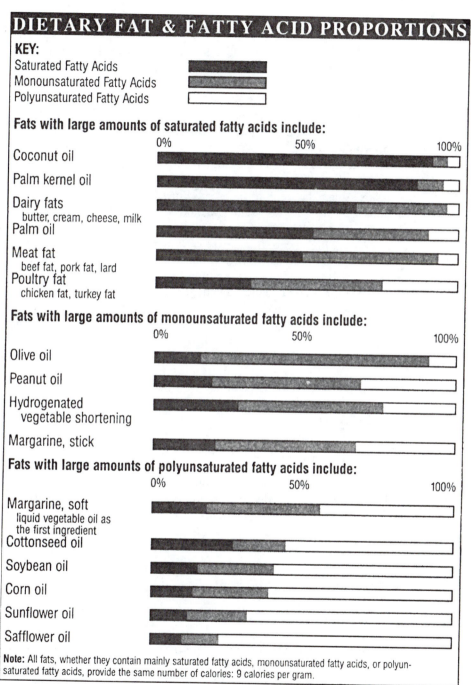

Figure 13-7

Dietary fat and fatty acid proportions. (From *Preparing Foods and Planning Menus,* USDA, Human Nutrition Information Source, Home and Garden Bulletin, No. 232-8.)

What Is a Fat or Oil?

The only difference chemically between a fat and oil is that one is solid and the other liquid. Both are triglycerides, or three fatty acids joined to a glycerol radical. Some of the fatty acids may have all carbon bonds filled in their chain, and these we call **saturated** fatty acids. Others may not have all their carbon bonds filled with carbon, and we call these **unsaturated** fatty acids. If a fat or oil has only one unsaturated carbon, it is called **monounsaturated,** but if it contains two or more, we call it **polyunsaturated.**

Saturated fatty acids tend to make the product solid, while unsaturated ones tend to make the product a liquid. However, as the temperature drops, some oils change into solids. Animal fats tend to be more saturated than vegetable oils, but there are exceptions. Coconut oil is 80% saturated, and only 5% monounsaturated—compare this with canola oil, which is 5% saturated, 55% monounsaturated, and 40% polyunsaturated.

Under high heat, a fat or oil can break down into hydrocarbons, water, acids, and some disagreeably flavored substances. Thus, to obtain a good frying fat buyers must select those that can take high heat in frying. Fats or oils have what is called **shortening power,** which means they give bakery items a desirable shortness or tenderness, a richness, and sometimes a desirable flavor.

An oil can be **hydrogenated** and made into a solid. This is done by adding hydrogen atoms at the unsaturated carbon bond which makes it saturated; this is a process in which oil in a tank, with finely ground nickel, has hydrogen bubbled through it. The nickel acts only as a catalyst, helping to add the hydrogen at the unsaturated bond, but otherwise not becoming a part of the new substance. Thus, cottonseed oil is hydrogenated to make it into a popular solid shortening used for bakery purposes.

Handling Fats and Oils

Fats or oils can discolor or grow rancid by exposure to light, air, or moisture. Air and light should be excluded by airtight, opaque containers. Use dry storage not above 70° F. Thin oil surfaces deteriorate rapidly; an empty oil container can be left to stand and then later be refilled which rapidly develops oil with an off-flavor. Wash all oil containers thoroughly to remove the oil film before using again.

Types of Oils and Shortenings

Lard

Lard is from fresh, clean, sound, fatty tissues of hogs. **Leaf lard,** from fat around the kidneys, is of highest quality. *Moisture* or *kettle-rendered lard* is better than *heat-rendered. Drip-rendered lard* is made by steaming the tissues; if extracted by hot water, the lard is called *neutral*. It is not used much in food preparation. *Dry-rendering* is putting fatty tissues in a steam-jacketed kettle, heating them, and drawing off the liquid lard as it forms. *Natural lard* comes from slowly heated back and leaf fat; it is very white and lacks a definite flavor.

When melted, lard should be a light golden color and not be turbid. When cold, it should be snow white, firm, and moderately resistant to finger pressure with no graininess. Smell and taste when melted; antioxidants are usually added to prevent rancidity. Specify lard with not more than ½% free fatty acids.

Vegetable Shortenings

Cold extraction usually gives a higher quality vegetable oil than heat extraction. Some oils are extracted by solvents and the solvents distilled away. The amount of unsaturation in an oil is often judged by the quantity of iodine the oil can pick up. The value is stated by an iodine number or what is called the Hanus number. A high Hanus number indicates the oil contains considerable unsaturated fatty acids, while a low one indicates a high amount of saturated ones. Thus, lard has a Hanus of 48 to 64, while cottonseed oil has one of 103 to 111. All vegetable shortenings have no cholesterol in them because vegetable products contain no cholesterol. Cholesterol comes from animal products.

Olive Oil

Ripe olives contain 14% to 40% oil. **Extra virgin** or **virgin** or **sublime** means the first pressing and the highest quality. Refined oil comes from later pressing and is not recommended. California and Arizona produce considerable olive oil of good quality. The finest oil is thought to be produced in the Chianti district near Florence and Lucca, Italy. Some oils from Greece and Spain are good. The FDA prohibits adulteration and use of the name *olive oil* if other oils are added.

A good oil should have a light greenish to yellow color with a pleasing flavor and odor, free from strong, green-olive odors and flavors, and free from musty, moldy, butyric, sapateria, rancid, or other off-flavors or odors. Taste before purchasing. Grade A oil cannot have more than 1.4% free fatty acids and the Hanus number should be between 79 and 90.

Cottonseed Oil

The average oil content of cottonseed is 18% to 25%. After hulling and crushing, the oil is hydraulically expelled. Good oil is slightly amber in color, clear, and has a fresh, sweet odor. Dark color indicates low quality and poor refining methods. A high fatty acid content indicates an oil of low quality.

Corn Oil

Corn or maize contains 3% to 6½% oil, and is the by-product of the manufacture of syrup, starch, cornmeal, or hominy from corn. Good oil has a distinctive corn flavor and a light amber, clear color, and a high smoking temperature. Specify **winterized oil,** which has had the heavier fractions (long chain, saturated fats) removed by centrifuging. This prevents it from going cloudy and partially solidifying when refrigerated.

Soybean Oil

Soy oil is heavily used for margarine manufacture. New varieties of seeds now have more than 25% oil. The seeds after oil removal can be ground into flour which can be used to raise the protein content of some foods. Unless the oil is carefully refined and deodorized, a characteristic fishy or bean flavor develops. Its high smoking temperature makes it good for deep-fat frying.

Peanut Oil

From 38% to 50% of the peanut may be oil, which is extracted by crushing and centrifuging. After refining, it has a nutty, pleasing flavor and should be amber in color. Some, a bit darker, can still be of good quality. It has a high smoking temperature and is good for frying.

Unsaturated Oils

The use of highly unsaturated vegetable oils is increasing. While they have as many calories as any other fat or oil, they contribute a higher quantity of mono- and polyunsaturated parts and are thus desirable in diets. Oils from seeds of sesame, rape, sunflower, and safflower are more unsaturated than those from corn, cottonseed, or peanuts. It might be wise to indicate on menus that such oils are used so as to provide more healthy foods for patrons.

PICKLED PRODUCTS

Olives

The **Mission olive,** which came to California with the Franciscan missionaries, is largely used for ripe, black olives. It is firm in texture, rich in oil, and can ripen more and still give a tender, mellow product. Since it is small, large ripe olives must come from olives used for green olives, not as high in quality. Missions are good for **green-ripe olives.** It is green because it is cured immediately after being picked ripe and is not left to turn black as are black olives.

We import large quantities of green olives from Spain and Italy. Sevanillano, Manzanillo, Ascolana, and Mission olives follow in that order in quality of green olives. **Green olives** are also called **queen** or **Spanish.** Pattern- or place-packed olives are called *stick-packed*. Green olives should not have a pH less than 4.0 and a salt content not less than 6%. *Sicilian green olives* are somewhat bitter because they are not lye-soaked before processing. *Salt-cured* oil-coated olives (also called *Greek, Greek-style,* or *oil-cured*) receive a moderate lye soak, are then left to stand to blacken, and then are dipped in oil and packed in salt. The salt withdraws moisture, causing them to shrivel. Uniformity of size and color, flavor, texture, and defects determine the olive grade. The sizes for ripe and green olives are given in Figures 13–8 and 13–9.

Federal grades for green and ripe olives follow:

Green Olives (1967)

- *Grades:* A (90), B (80),[1] C (70).

- *Styles:* Unpitted; pitted without stuffing; pitted stuffed with pimiento, onion, almond, celery; sliced; chopped or minced; broken pitted or salad.

---

[1]Reasonably uniform typical color, which is yellow-green color typical of variety. If olives are stuffed, the stuffing shall possess a good characteristic color for the stuffing used. Packing brine shall be clear and not cloudy. There should be few broken pieces. Workmanship should be reasonably good. Texture should be reasonably uniform, reasonably good with a moderately firm and crisp flesh only slightly tough, which must be characteristic of variety. Reasonably free from slip skins, cutaneous material, pits or pit fragments and other defects.

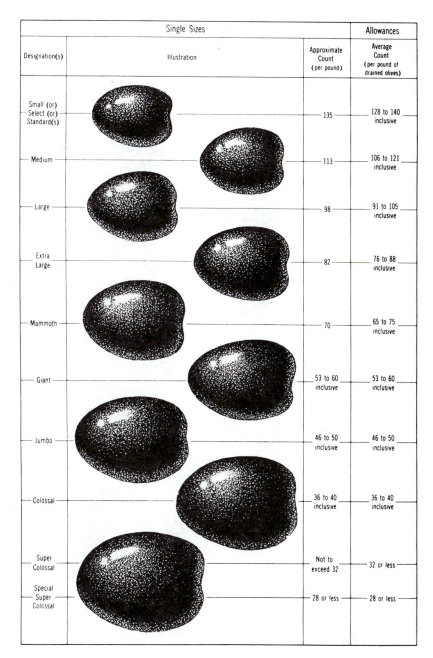

| | Single Sizes | | | Allowances |
Designation(s)	Illustration		Approximate Count (per pound)	Average Count (per pound of drained olives)
Small (or) Select (or) Standard(s)			135	128 to 140 inclusive
Medium			113	106 to 121 inclusive
Large			98	91 to 105 inclusive
Extra Large			82	76 to 88 inclusive
Mammoth			70	65 to 75 inclusive
Giant			53 to 60 inclusive	53 to 60 inclusive
Jumbo			46 to 50 inclusive	46 to 50 inclusive
Colossal			36 to 40 inclusive	36 to 40 inclusive
Super Colossal			Not to exceed 32	32 or less
Special Super Colossal			28 or less	28 or less

Figure 13-8
Ripe olive sizing.

483

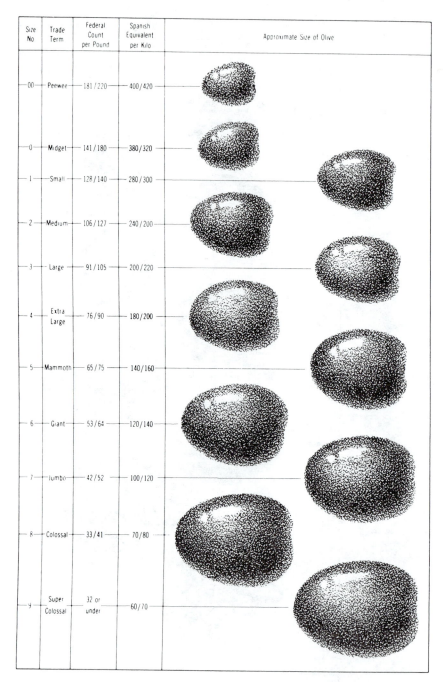

Size No	Trade Term	Federal Count per Pound	Spanish Equivalent per Kilo	Approximate Size of Olive
00	Peewee	181/220	400/420	
0	Midget	141/180	380/320	
1	Small	128/140	280/300	
2	Medium	106/127	240/200	
3	Large	91/105	200/220	
4	Extra Large	76/90	180/200	
5	Mammoth	65/75	140/160	
6	Giant	53/64	120/140	
7	Jumbo	42/52	100/120	
8	Colossal	33/41	70/80	
9	Super Colossal	32 or under	60/70	

Figure 13–9
Green olive sizing.

- *Packs:* Thrown or jumble, place or stick packed.
- *Recommended drained weight:*

Container Size	½ pt	pt	qt	gal
Drained weight	4½ to 5½ oz	9½ to 11 oz	19 to 22 oz	86 to 88 oz

- *Flavorings added:* Plain, spiced with dill, anise, garlic, pepper. (Buyers should ascertain flavoring in olives called Bordelaise, French, Kosher, or Italian. Cuban usually means tomato paste has been added.)

    Note: Sicilian-style green olives have only one grade, No. 1. These are olives of similar varietal characteristics, which are green or straw in color, clean, firm, and fairly well formed; are free from damage caused by discoloration, shriveling, hail, wind, frost, or other means; and possess the normal flavor of Sicilian-style olives.

Ripe Olives (1971)

- *Grades:* A (90), B (80),[2] C (70).
- *Type:* Ripe, green-ripe.
- *Styles:* Whole, whole pitted, halved, sliced, chopped or minced, broken, pitted.
- *Recommended minimum drained weight:* No. 10—Mammoth size or smaller 66 oz, Giant or larger 64 oz, blends of large sizes 64 oz, blends of small sizes 66 oz, halves 50 oz, chopped or minced 10 oz, sliced 50 oz, broken pitted 55 oz.

Pickles

Cucumbers, tomatoes, onions, cauliflower, cabbage, beans, peppers, and other items are pickled. The process may be a natural cure or curing with hot vinegar, salt, sugar, spices, and flavorings.

Natural or *genuine pickles* cure in a 5% salt brine for about four weeks until sufficient lactic acid forms to stop fermentation. Dill, dill emulsion, or vinegar may be added. Adding calcium chloride (alum) gives greater crispness. Tumeric may be added to change the color from a dead one to a light, white-yellow one. Mushy pickles indicate too high a curing pickle. **Floaters** have hollow insides because of too rapid fermentation or undesirable bacterial action. Natural cure pickles keep for about six months if stored in a cold place. Heat treatment increases keeping qualities but lowers overall quality.

---

[2]Color for ripe should be almost black or blackish brown. Color should be uniform or nearly so between olives. Normal color for green-ripe is yellow-green, green-yellow, or other greenish casts and some mottling may be evident. Should be uniform in size. Whole olives should not vary in standard counts more than 3/16 in. in diameter. Cutting on cut styles shall be even with little or no raggedness evident. Fairly free from defects such as blemishes, wrinkles, multilated olives, pits or pit fragments, stems, injuries, or damaged units. Free from harmless extraneous material. The flesh should be reasonably firm.

Many cucumbers for pickles come from **salt-stocks.** Such cucumbers are sent from harvest to salting stations for curing. Here they are fermented in a 7% to 10% salt brine which allows very little fermentation. When made into pickles they lack the flavor and texture of natural cure pickles, but they keep better. Green tomatoes are often given a natural cure like cucumbers. They can also be made from salt stocks. Figure 13–10 shows some federal standards used to judge the shape of cucumber pickles.

Label terms indicate specific flavor and other characteristics for pickles. The following defines some common terms:

Kosher dills	Natural or processed dills with garlic, onions, and peppers.
Polish (Hungarian) dills	Natural dills, usually with onions, garlic, and red peppers.
Sweet dills	Less sweet than sweet pickles flavored with dill.
Sweet	In a sweetened vinegar, spices are sometimes added.
Iceberg dills	Quartered dills; if in smaller pieces they are dill sticks.
Sour pickles	Added vinegar with or without added spices.
Chow-chow	Sour or sweet pickle mixture with prepared mustard; if the term *hot* is used, red peppers are used; cauliflower, peppers, onions, and garlic may be added.
Chutney	A tart, sweet Indian relish of mangoes, green ginger, mustard seed, raisins, East Indian tamarind, chili peppers, black pepper, butter, and spices.
American chutney	Vinegar, green tomatoes, orange marmalade, raisins, lemon peel, dates, lime juice, onion, flour, and spices.
Mixed chutney	May be American chutney or contain pickles, cauliflower, and other ingredients imitating real chutney.
Bread and butter or country-style pickles	Thin cucumber slices cured in strong salt stock and packed heavily in vinegar, spices, sweet syrup, and celery seed.
Capers	Pickled buds from the caper shrub of southern Europe; some may be dried and shipped and then put into a sweetened vinegar solution.

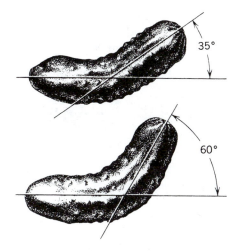

A curved pickle has an angle of 35° to 60° while a nubbin has an angle greater than 60° as shown. The angle is formed by intersecting lines projected from either end approximately parallel to the sides.

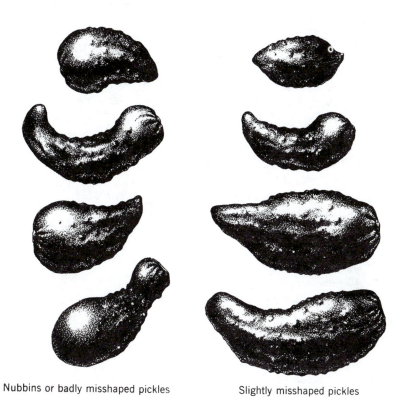

Nubbins or badly misshaped pickles   Slightly misshaped pickles

Figure 13-10
Standards for curved, slightly misshapen, and badly misshapen pickles.
(Courtesy USDA.)

Fresh-pack pickles   Uncured, unfermented cucumbers packed in vinegar and heat-treated to preserve them.

The drained weights some pickles should be are as follows:

Item	Mixture of Cut Pieces	Chopped or Minced Relish
Cucumbers	60–80	60–100
Cauliflower	10–30	10–30*
Onions	5–12	512*
Green tomatoes	10 (max)	10 (max)

*The addition can be optional.

Sweet pickles are cured in a vinegar syrup that helps preserve them along with heat. They should have a firm texture, breaking with a clean snap; no softness or slipperiness, nor hollow, spongy centers should be evident. The interior should be uniform in color and translucent, with no white or opaque flesh or badly shriveled pickles outside tolerance allowances. Taste for quality.

Size affects the sweet pickle grade only when it varies to affect uniformity. Whole sweets are sized: 2¾ in. in length with no variation more than 3 in. and over 4 in. with no greater variation than 1½ in. (see Table 13–6).

Federal grades are U.S. A and B. There are a number of styles. The federal grade for cucumber pickles follow:

Cucumber Pickles (1966)

- *Grades:* A (85)[3], B (70).

- *Recommended minimum drained weight:* Cured, sweet 92%; cured, other than sweet 88%; fresh-pack, sweet 85%; fresh-pack, other than sweet 80%. Fill of cured must be 55% or more and fresh-pack 57% or more of container volume.

Packaging

Pickles usually are purchased in gallon or barrel lots. A case is 4 gal. No. 10 cans or 3¼-qt packs are also common, packed six per case.

Sauerkraut

Finely shredded or cut cabbage fermented in a small amount of water containing 2½ lb of salt per 100 lb of cabbage produces sauerkraut. To retain quality, the kraut

---

[3]The pickles should be free from objectionable flavors, possess the characteristic normal flavor of the pickle type, and should meet standards for acidity, sugar, and salt content. Color should be typical, practically uniform, and practically free from bleached areas. Uniformity in size within reasonable limits is a requirement. Check for damaged units, blemishes, improper processing, soft units, nubbins, curved or misshapen units. Check workmanship on cut styles. There should be no extraneous matter and few stems or other material.

Table 13-6

Sizes and counts per gallon of sweet pickles.

Size Term	Size Number	Approximate Count per Gallon	Length (in.)
Midgets	1 Midget	$^{445}/_{545}$	1½ or less
Midgets	2 Midget	$^{330}/_{444}$	1½–2
Gherkins	1 Gherkin	$^{225}/_{329}$	2–2¼
Gherkins	2 Gherkin	$^{135}/_{224}$	2–2½
Gherkins	3 Gherkin	$^{100}/_{134}$	2½–2¾
Small	1 Small	$^{80}/_{99}$	2¾–3
Small	2 Small	$^{66}/_{79}$	3–3¼
Small	3 Small	$^{52}/_{65}$	3¼–3½
Medium		$^{40}/_{51}$	3½–4
Large	1 Large	$^{26}/_{39}$	4–4¼
Large	2 Large	$^{22}/_{25}$	4¼–4¾
Extra Large		$^{16}/_{21}$	4¾–5¼

Note: A special type of gherkin, called the *Burr gherkin,* is a West Indian fruit, not a true cucumber. It is used for small, sweet cucumber pickles. It is pale green and covered with prickly spines. Some of the smallest midgets and gherkins are made from this product.

is put into enamel-lined cans and heat treated. If no heat is applied, it keeps in a cool place for four to six months.

SPICES

About 0.6% of the food dollar goes for spices. About 60% of a spice's value is aroma; the amount of essential oil or flavoring varies from ½% to 4%. Flavors can be rapidly lost, so purchase only a month's supply. Keep in air-tight containers in a cool place.

Spices are selected on the basis of strength and flavor. Watch for imitations or weak or poorly flavored products. Purchase from reliable spice dealers. Packaging is usually 1 oz, 4 oz, 1 lb, 6 lb, and 10 lb. There are no federal standards for quality, but standards of identity exist. Select fresh spices with a soft, earthy fresh color, pleasant taste, and a fresh pungent aroma. Check for grind quality, wholeness, extraneous material, or broken, shriveled, or damaged units.

FLAVORINGS

Flavorings are esters or essential oils from roots, bark, fruit, sap, leaves, or other plant portions, and are dissolved in solvents such as water, alcohol, or in an emulsion in oil. Some come in dry form. Vanilla beans may be added whole to give flavor and then be removed, or they may be added as a ground product as they are in French ice cream. Artificial flavorings must be labeled "imitation." In the trade, *artificial* indicates flavors similar but not quite like the natural product, whereas *imitation* is a synthetic product. Some flavorings are best natural, but others such as banana, walnut, maple, raspberry, cherry, pineapple, or strawberry are better as synthetics. The flavor is more true and they keep longer.

Some flavorings and spices have what are called "locked-in" flavors. This means the flavor is chemically joined to glucose, giving it more stability; sometimes these are called **plastic flavorings.**

Store flavorings in a cool place, but not under refrigeration because of what is called *cold shock* which harms the flavor, even precipitating some of the essences. Keep flavorings away from sunlight. Purchase only a two months' supply.

Vanilla

A dried, black pod, largely grown in Madagascar and Mexico, contains a bean with about 2% vanilla. The plant belongs to the orchid family. The best Madagascar beans are called Boston. Federal standards for **single-fold vanilla** is the extract from 13.35 oz of beans plus an ounce of vanillin per gallon. Stronger vanillas, such as double-fold, are marketed. **Coumarin** from the Tonka bean has a vanilla flavor, but is not allowed in U.S. vanilla. Vanillin has the same chemical structure as vanilla and comes by distillation of wood from a coniferous tree or from the heavy oil of cloves, the latter being called **eugenol.** To test vanilla extract quality, add a teaspoon to 8 oz of lukewarm milk and taste and smell.

Lemon Extract

Volatile lemon oil in alcohol is lemon extract and must contain not less than 5% oil of lemon and not less than 80% ethyl alcohol. Natural lemon flavor contains 90% terpenes and 4% to 6% each of aldehyde and alcohol esters. Imitation extract is made from oily terpenic aldehyde. It is relatively unstable and must either be made into an emulsion or have added stabilizers.

Other Flavorings

Pure extracts of mint, cloves, cinnamon, tonka, spearmint, peppermint, anise, wintergreen, almond, and orange are usually made with a ratio of natural oil to solvent of 5 to 8 to 100. Some natural fruit flavorings are made. Imitations are usually essences rather than flavors.

CONDIMENTS

A **condiment** is "an agent used to give relish to foods and gratify taste." A blend of spices, flavoring ingredients, vinegar, and tomato is used. Condiments keep well, but inventories should be used soon. Some can show darkening at the end of 3½ months of storage, especially if held at elevated temperatures.

Tomato catsup is strained tomato pulp to which vinegar, sugar, and spices have been added. Chili sauce is the same as catsup, but it is not strained. Their federal grades are discussed in the chapter on processed foods. Often food services purchase these by brand, especially for table use.

Worcestershire sauce is basically soy sauce and vinegar seasoned by items like East India tamarinds, capsicums, cloves, garlic, onions, anchovies, pepper, mushrooms, lemons or limes. It is aged two months before marketing. Chop suey sauce or soy sauce is made from hydrolyzed proteins from soy beans, wheat, corn, yeast, and other products. This, except for table use, is usually purchased 4-gal per case. A well-known pepper sauce is the original New Orleans variety made by steeping vinegar in red pepper or chili pods. Another type is tabasco or hot sauce made by concentrating an extraction from the long-podded tabasco peppers.

SUGARS AND SYRUPS

Sugars

Cane and beet sugar are both pure sucrose. White granulated sugar is sized from coarse to very fine. If finer than coating sugar, it is ground, and **"X"** denotes the fineness; XX is standard, XXXX is confectioner's, commonly used for icing, but 6X may also be. The finest is 10X and makes a mixture with crystals almost as fine as fondant. Some operations purchase an even finer ground sugar called "fondant sugar." Coarse or sanding sugars are used to coat foods. Common granulated sugar is moderately coarse. Berry (fruit or breakfast) sugar is finer and may be used in bakeshops for products needing a sugar that goes rapidly into solution. It is also used for breakfast. Extra fine sugar is used in bars and bakeshops.

Brown sugar's color decides its grade, a color imparted by molasses, not found in granulated sugar. It is about 85% to 92% pure sucrose, 4% moisture, and the remainder invert sugars. Grades run from 1 to 15; 1 indicates the lightest. Trade grades are called *light, medium,* and *dark.* Brown sugar is the same thing as white sugar, except the former still contains some molasses.

Corn sugar is used by some; a standard of identity exists for it. It is sweeter than sucrose and less expensive.

Maple sugar is crystallized from concentrated maple sap. Maple concrete can be purchased for making into syrup or for other purposes.

Syrups

Molasses grades are A, B, C, and substandard with food services using only A or B; A should be not less than 79% solids, 61½% sugar, and not more than 7% ash and medium color. Cloudiness, sediment, or extraneous matter lower grade. Poor molasses is very dark, bitter, and harsh. Taste to judge quality.

Grade AA (Fancy) maple syrup should be light amber; A, medium amber; B, dark amber. The best are clear and brilliant; opaqueness lowers grade. Flavor should be characteristic and clean, free from fermentation or damage caused by scorching or other off flavors. It should be about 65% sugar. Much of the typical flavor comes from ash and impurities. A blend of cane and maple syrups should contain not less than 20% of the latter. Maple syrup and the blend are available in 1-, 2-, and more than 2-oz packages. A gallon weighs 11 lb or more.

Sorghum has a more distinctive flavor than cane syrup and may be slightly bitter and acid; it is not as sweet as cane syrup. It is high in iron, which helps give it its dark color. It is used only in local areas.

Corn syrup is called *glucose, dextrose, confectioner's glucose,* or *unmixed glucose.* It contains 15% moisture, 20% maltose, 30% dextrin, and 35% glucose and is sweeter than cane syrup. Some retail brands are higher in sweeteners.

Maltose is used in bakeshops, largely for yeast breads. It is amber in color and its distinctive flavor limits the amount that can be used. It is about 20% moisture.

Honey should be pleasantly sweet and slightly acid with a color and flavor decided by the flowers from which it came. Fireweed, orange and clover honey are considered the best. Honey should not be over 25% moisture, ½% ash, and 8% sucrose. Clear honey grades are A and B, with A recommended for table use. It should be free of crystallization and comb and be of good flavor, free of smoke, scorching, fermentation or other off flavors. Colors are water white, extra white, white, extra light amber, light amber, and dark amber. Grades for comb honey are U.S. Fancy, No. 1, and No. 2, and comes as section, section frame, wrapped cut-comb honey, or chunk (bulb-comb honey). Individual packs of clear honey of ½ or 1 oz may be purchased or in pint, quart, or gallon sizes. Creamed honey is available for table use.

NUTS

Specify nuts from the current year's crop; buy limited quantities because they easily become rancid or infested. They should be sweet and full-flavored. Broken nuts are purchased if they are to be chopped or broken. Nuts should be clean, free from damage, decay, splits, breaks, oil stain, mold, meat discoloration, or insect damage. Kernels should be well developed (not shriveled), free from rancidity, and well cured. Table 13–7 summarizes buying information on nuts.

VINEGAR

Regular vinegar is a 5% (50 grain) solution of acetic acid and water; it carries the flavor of the item from which made. Flavored vinegars are popular. Vinegar can be made by fermenting wood chips. Wine vinegar is made from wine. Stock only a month's supply. Purchase in gallons, case of four gallons, or in barrels.

Table 13–7
Buying shelled or unshelled nuts.

Kind	U.S. Grade	Remarks
Almonds in the shell	No. 1, No.2	Look for clean, bright, uniform sized nuts, free from extraneous material and damage
Almonds, shelled	Fancy, Extra No. 1	If broken, pieces should not be less than ⅛ in. in diameter
Almond paste	None	Ground almonds, sugar, and egg whites; also called marzipan
Brazil nuts in the shell	No. 1	Also called cream nuts or paranuts
Carob	None	Also called St. John's bread; used as a filler or chocolate substitute
Cashews	None	A lb gives 4 oz unshelled
Chestnuts	None	Most imported from Europe; may be purchased as a flour
Coconut	None	Usually purchased prepared; should be sweet and fresh; available long, medium, or short shred, or very short shred or dipping
Filberts in the shell	No. 1	
Hazelnuts	None	
Macadamias	None	Hawaiian nut, somewhat expensive
Peanuts, Virginia type	Extra large, medium, or small	Specify size by number per lb.
Peanuts, shelled, runner type	No. 1	Specify No. 1 runner-type peanuts for that type
Peanut butter	A or Fancy and B or Choice	Grinds are fine (smooth), medium (slightly grainy), and coarse (chunky); roasts are light or heavy
Pecans in the shell	No. 1 and No. 2	
Pecans, shelled	No. 1 Halves and Pieces, and No. 1 Pieces	Specify halves as 200 to 400 per lb
Pinenuts	None	Also called Indian or pinon nuts; sized from mammoth (250/lb) or midget (750/lb)
Pistachios in the shell	No. 1 and No. 2	
Pistachios, shelled	Fancy and No. 1	
Pistachios	None	
English walnuts in the shell	No. 1 and No. 2	
English walnuts, shelled	No. 1	Colors are extra light, light, light amber, and amber

LEAVENING AGENTS

Yeasts are available in dry, active, active dry, or compressed form; the latter is purchased usually in pound bricks and stored in a refrigerator. Baking powder may be single- or double-acting. Bakers usually indicate their preference by brand. Baking soda is sodium bicarbonate. A pound goes a long way. Baking ammonia is an efficient and good leavener when used in thin-shelled bakery goods. Again, a small amount goes a long way.

SUMMARY

Many dry items, such as coffee, beans, nuts, leavening agents, rice, flour, cereals, vinegar, flavorings, pickled items, fats and oils, etc., are called *groceries*.

Coffee is the bean or seed of an evergreen bush that grows in the tropics or semitropics. The best is produced at elevations above 2,000 feet. Low-grown coffee is called *rio* (river) and is apt to be harsh in flavor. The two varieties of coffee grown the most are the Arabica and the Stenophylla. Coffee must be roasted to develop its flavor. It is blended to obtain desirable flavors. Grind is important and must be suited to the equipment. Coffee can be adulterated, usually with chicory.

The best tea is also high grown and also is a tropical or semitropical product. Two leaves and a bud is a standard pick, after which it is withered, rolled, fermented, and dried. Green tea is not fermented; oolong tea is only partially fermented. Grades of black (fully fermented tea) are Orange Pekoe and Pekoe and grades of green tea are Gunpowder and Young Hyson.

Chocolate is the bean of *theobroma cacao* tree. It too is grown in tropical or semitropical climates and is fermented to remove bitterness. After roasting the beans are broken up into what are called nibs, and then ground. Chocolate must be 50% or more cacao butter. Cocoa is chocolate that has had about 80% of its fat removed and is then ground into a dry powder. Treating cocoa with alkali makes a smoother tasting, better appearing, and more soluble cocoa. It is called *Dutch process cocoa*.

Most cereal products come from the endosperm (inner part) of grains. Bran covers the outside and is usually removed or partially so. Wheat endosperm is ground into flours. The first grindings are called *breaks* or *streams* and make the best flour, called a *patent*. The last grindings are called *clears*, which make a poorer flour high in ash, low in protein, and lacking in typical wheat flour character in baking or cooking. Using all the endosperm except the bran gives a straight or 100% flour. Wheat planted in the spring gives a *hard wheat*, one high in gluten, which makes it suitable for making bread or pasta products. Wheat planted in the late summer and wintered in the field and harvested early in the summer is called *soft wheat* and makes a flour good for pastries and cakes, products that do not need as much gluten. The endosperm of durum wheat, a hard wheat, is called *semolina* which makes a flour suitable for making pastas. Most flours are priced by the barrel, or 198 lb. A half-barrel or 98 lb is usually marketed. Some cake and pastry flours are sold in 100-lb bags.

We use two kinds of rice, long-grain and pearl, mostly the former. Brown rice has some of the bran remaining on it.

Corn is used to make hominy, a product used to make many dry breakfast cereals. It is also eaten as hominy, especially "hominy grits." Cornmeal is ground corn. Corn flour is very finely ground hominy. Cornstarch is the starch of corn. Instant starch is precooked and then dried and reground.

Oats are made from the endosperm of oat grain called *groats*. Many new dry cereal products are today on the market made from oats.

Malt is a sugar that is produced when barley sprouts. It is largely used as a flavoring for dry cereals, in bread making, and for making beer. The endosperm of barley after the bran has been removed is used for soups, as a cooked cereal, etc. Rye flour is used for making rye bread products. Pumperknickel is rye flour with some of the bran left on the endosperm before it is ground into flour. Buckwheat is a seed and is ground to make buckwheat flour, largely used in pancakes. Soy is a legume that is ground into a flour; it is used to enrich bakery goods and other foods. Its high protein content gives foods a higher protein value. Breads and rolls contain propionates which help keep the bread soft and prevent molding. Cakes and pies of many kinds are on the market, especially frozen types.

Fats and oils of many kinds are on the market. Animal fats such as oleo, lard, and so forth, are used to make shortenings. Oils also can be hydrogenated to make them into a fat suitable for use as shortenings. Some oils are hydrogenated to make them solid and are used in margarines. Hydrogenation causes the fat or oil to become more saturated. A saturated fat is a hydrocarbon product with all its free bonds filled with hydrogen. An unsaturated fat is one that does not have all its free bonds filled with hydrogen. A polyunsaturated fat is one that has a number of free hydrogen bonds; a monounsaturated fat is one with only one unsaturated bond. Saturated fat is thought to raise the cholesterol level in the bloodstream but if an unsaturated fat or oil is consumed, these tend to clear cholesterol from the bloodstream.

To reduce the calories in products in which fats and oils are used and also to reduce saturated fat, much research is going on to find fat substitutes. Some have been found that are related to carbohydrates but they cannot be heated, which makes them suitable for use only in salad oils, frozen desserts, and so forth.

Sublime or virgin olive oil comes from the first pressings of ripe olives; it is considered to be the highest quality. Some vegetable oils are *winterized* which is a process in which the oil is centrifuged to force the heavy globules to the outer surface and then separate them from the rest of the oil. It is these globules that solidify when the oil gets cold. Cottonseed, rape seed, sunflower seed, corn, soy, canola, peanuts, and other seeds are also used to make oils.

Pickled products are those allowed to develop acid and their own preservation ingredients. Olives are pickled items. Green or Spanish olives are not fermented. Ripe olives are pickled after ripening and turning black. Green-ripe olives are ripe olives not allowed to blacken before pickling. The Mission variety of olive makes the best ripe olive. A wide assortment of pickles are on the market, but food services use only a limited few such as dills or sweet pickles. Sauerkraut, made from cabbage, is a pickled product.

The purchase of spices is discussed, and also flavorings such as vanilla, lemon, and others. Vanilla is the bean of an orchid. Double-fold vanilla is twice as strong as single-fold. Imitation vanilla is made by distilling the bark of special trees producing a product called *eugenol,* which smells and tastes like vanilla. Coumarin is a product that also has a vanilla odor and taste, but its use is forbidden because it is a poison. Flavorings and spices chemically tied to a glucose have better lasting qualities; they are often called *plastic* flavorings or spices.

Condiments are discussed. Food services use mainly catsup and Worcestershire sauce, although soy sauce and others are used by some facilities.

Our regular granulated sugar is made from sugar beets or sugar cane. Brown sugar and molasses come only from the sugar cane. Corn syrup, maple syrup, honey, and other sugars are covered.

Walnuts, almonds, filberts, and other nuts are covered. A number have federal grades. Vinegar is made often from apples, although there are many other vinegars on the market that have suddenly become popular. Regular vinegar can be made from wood chips. Baking powder, soda, and baking ammonia are the three most commonly used leavening agents.

REVIEW QUESTIONS

1. What does the category *groceries* mean and cover in this text?
2. What is coffee?
3. How and where is coffee grown and how is it processed to become ground coffee in a food service?
4. What is tea and what process causes the development of black, green, and oolong tea?
5. From what does chocolate come?
6. What is the difference between chocolate and cocoa?
7. What is Houten or Dutch process cocoa?
8. How is flour made?
9. Why would a baker want a different flour to make breads and to make cakes, and what kind of flour would be requisitioned to make each?
10. What is a 60% patent flour?
11. To get a good pasta, would you order a semolina or farina product?
12. What is pearl rice, long-grain rice, converted rice, brown rice?
13. What is hominy and what uses do we make of it?
14. What is the endosperm of oats called?

15. What is the most common cereal product used to make dry ready-to-eat breakfast cereals?

16. How can you tell a good loaf of bread?

17. If you want a cake mix with eggs in it, what type would you order?

18. What is a fat and how does an oil differ from a fat?

19. What is another name for sublime olive oil?

20. A liquid oil is hydrogenated. How is this done and what does it do to the oil? Is the oil apt to be more solid? If a margarine contains hydrogenated oil, does the product contain more or less saturated fat than the oil did before hydrogenation?

21. What is winterized corn oil?

22. Why is an unsaturated oil more healthful?

23. What are natural pickles? Kosher dills?

24. What is sauerkraut?

25. What is single-fold vanilla flavoring?

26. Define a condiment.

27. What does an "X" mean when used to designate a sugar?

28. What is the difference between a brown and white sugar?

29. How is maple sugar made?

30. What percent acetic acid does a 50-grain vinegar contain?

KEY WORDS AND CONCEPTS

all-purpose flour	cornstarch
Arabica	coumarin
black tea	Dutch process
Bourbon Santos	endosperm
break	eugenol
brown rice	extra virgin oil
buhr-ground	fermenting of tea
cacao butter	firing a tea
cafe expresso	floater pickle
chicory	green flour
chutney	green olive
condiment	green-ripe olive
cornmeal	green tea

groats

groceries

gun puffing

hard (spring) wheat flour

hominy

hydrogenation

kosher dill pickles

leaf lard

Liberacia

long-grain rice

malt

Mission olive

monounsaturated fat

oolong tea

Orange Pekoe tea

pasta

patent flour

pearl rice

pearled hominy

Pekoe

plastic flavoring

polyunsaturated fat

pumpernickel

queen olive

rio coffee

Robusta

rolling of tea

salt-stock

samp

saturated fat

semolina

shortening power

single-fold vanilla

soft (winter) wheat flour

sourdough

Spanish olive

Stenophylla

straight flour

stream

sublime oil

tea

unsaturated fat

virgin oil

winterized oil

withering a tea

X's (applied to sugars)

CHAPTER 14

Alcoholic Beverages

September 9, 1876 Frank Leslie's illustrated newspaper New York Philadelphia, PA.— The Centennial Exposition—The jury of award on an inspection tour in the wine vaults of agricultural hall. From a sketch by our special artists. From the Louis Szwathmary collection, Culinary Archives and Museum, Johnson and Wales University, used by permission of Dr. Szwathmary and Johnson and Wales University.

Chapter Objectives

1. To cover trends and operational problems that make the marketing of alcoholic beverages to the public more difficult and eventually influence the purchasing program.

2. To cover some of the regulatory provisions used to control the sale of alcoholic beverages.

3. To explain the use of percents or proofs for indicating alcoholic content and how they influence price.

4. To list some of the factors that determine quality in different alcoholic beverages and indicate how buyers can gain good purchase information from labels.

5. To define the different alcoholic beverages purchased and how they are made.

6. To discuss some of the important factors required to purchase alcoholic beverages and how to write a specification for them.

THE CHANGING ALCOHOLIC BEVERAGE MARKET[1]

The drinking of alcoholic beverages is moving toward moderation. Many people now prefer to drink wine, a wine cooler, or even a nonalcoholic beverage at social occasions. This trend has occurred for a number of reasons. Our federal government now requires that all alcoholic beverages carry a warning about the dangers in drinking alcohol.[2] State laws against drunkenness have become much more strict. Organizations such as Mothers Against Drunk Driving (MADD) have pressured legislatures into lowering the blood alcohol level indicating drunkenness. **Dram laws** have been passed that now make those serving alcohol to the public responsible if the individual gets drunk in the operation. These laws carry stiff penalties. Programs to stop the sale of alcohol to minors are rigidly enforced. From a peak in 1976 of 2.76 equivalent gallons of absolute alcohol (200 proof) per capita, the amount has dropped to less than 2 gallons. The double martini lunch is a thing of the past.

By the year 2000, the consumption of alcohol is expected to drop to half its peak level. Although this is an indication that bar and beverage operations will be purchasing fewer alcoholic beverages, it also indicates that the purchase of beverages high in alcohol will drop; instead, purchases will be concentrated more on the lower alcoholic items. Never before has it been so necessary for operations to study their market and purchase wisely.

REGULATION

The alcohol industry is perhaps the most regulated industry in our country. Besides federal laws, there are state laws and the laws of thousands of local communities that control the way the industry operates within their boundaries. Federal regulation and control come largely from the **Federal Alcohol Administration Act (FAAA).** The production and marketing of alcoholic beverages are closely controlled. Standards of identity have been established indicating what alcoholic beverages bearing a specific name must be. Purveyor-customer relations are closely governed. Thus, it is illegal for a supplier to help a retailer get or pay for a license, have a legal or financial interest in the business, rent or purchase space in the seller's operation or furnish free warehousing, extend credit for over 30 days, ship goods on consignment, and a host of others. Those who deal with suppliers should know these regulations and conform to them. Many affect purchasing.[3]

---

[1] *Notice to instructors:* This chapter may repeat information taught in a separate bar and beverage management course and therefore could be omitted from the course of study.

[2] "Government Warning: (1) According to the Surgeon General, women should not drink alcoholic beverages during pregnancy because of the risk of birth defects; (2) the consumption of alcoholic beverages impairs your ability to drive a car or operate machinery, and may cause health problems."

[3] For a complete discussion of these regulations, see the Federal Administration Alcohol Act of 1935, Title 27, U.S. Code.

ALCOHOLIC BEVERAGE MANUFACTURE

Fermentation

The making of alcohol is a simple process of having yeast feed on some carbohydrate. This can be a **mash** of grains, or a **must** (juice) of grapes, or some other substance containing sugar or starch. Yeast turns the carbohydrate into carbon dioxide gas and ethyl alcohol. The carbon dioxide escapes as a gas, leaving the alcohol and some small flavoring and other substances. Thus, two parts of sugar make one part alcohol and one part carbon dioxide. The alcohol is left in the brew or wine, or it can be distilled from it, giving a stronger alcoholic drink, such as brandy.

Special strains of **brewer's yeasts** are added to bring about a correct fermentation. **Fermentation** develops heat that can cause a brew to develop too much acid, undesirable flavors, and other substances. Cooling during fermentation may be necessary.

Yeast can only digest the sugar *glucose*. Thus, sugars like sucrose or fructose or starches cannot be digested by it; fortunately yeast carries an enzyme called **diastase** that changes such sugars or starches into glucose. In some brew, malt is added that is high in diastase. Grapes carry their own yeast. At the time grapes ripen, yeasts gather on the skin, waiting to get at the must when it is pressed from the grapes. Wild yeasts on grapes, utensils, air, or elsewhere can be a problem, and sulfur may be burned to create sulfur dioxide whose fumes are toxic to yeast. Injudicious use of sulfur can give an unpleasant flavor to wine; white wines often capture much sulfur in processing and this, as noted, can be a dangerous substance to some people who have an allergy to it.

Aging

Most wines after fermentation in the fall are aged over the winter months in wood casks to clarify, drop sediment, and improve in flavor. After this **aging,** the wine is bottled. The sediment that drops to the bottom of the cask during this aging can be a source of cream of tartar and other salable substances. The wood of the cask absorbs certain products and encourages other changes. The inside of these barrels may be burned so the charcoal can absorb flavors and also color the beverage—if not enough color is obtained, color is added. Scotch whisky is often aged in used sherry kegs, which give it a distinctive flavor. White wines gradually grow darker; thus, a white wine can be first white, later slightly yellowish, and eventually end up light tan or creamy greenish. Red wines contain anthocyanins and these bright red pigments gradually darken, turning purplish, as does tawny port.

The variety of oak in the keg can influence flavor. Chemical changes occur that may be beneficial or harmful. Spirits lose about 2% a year by evaporation, often called the **angels' share.** After bottling, aging usually stops, except for wines. It is said that "Wines age in the cask, but mature in the bottle." Aging thus must be carefully done for many alcoholic products and the proper time must be carefully watched so the product reaches consumers at top quality.

Top fermented beer beverages are not aged, but lager beer is aged in its making. Budweiser advertises that its top beers are aged in beechwood chips. One of our beer makers now places the date of bottling of its beer so drinkers will know its suitability for drinking.

Proof or Percent Alcohol

The amount of alcohol in a product is indicated either by what is called a **proof** or by the **percent of alcohol.** Wines, beers, and a few other products are listed by percent alcohol. It makes a difference if the percent is by weight or by volume, because alcohol is lighter than water. A pint of water weighs about 16 oz whereas a pint of alcohol weighs about 12.8 oz. The ratio is 1.0 to 0.8. It takes 1¼ pt of alcohol to equal 16 oz. Beers are listed by alcohol weight and wines and spirits by volume. Thus, a 4% beer would be 5% alcohol by volume (4% ÷ 0.8 = 5%) and a 10% wine would be 8% by weight (10% × 0.8 = 8%). A spirit 45% alcohol by volume would be 36% by weight (45% × 0.8 = 36%).

The quantity of alcohol in spirits is indicated by proof. Our proof is twice the percent of alcohol by volume; an 86-proof spirit contains 43% alcohol. Federal rules say whiskey cannot be higher than 110 or lower than 80 proof; proof is indicated by a degree symbol (°).

The British tested proof by dampening gunpowder with the spirit. If the spirit was below 42.8% by weight alcohol, the gunpowder would not burn but at 42.9% it would. This was said to be "proof" that it contained an adequate amount of alcohol, thus originating the term. The British set 42.9% by weight (57% by volume) as their 100 proof, which made pure alcohol 175.25 proof.

Europe uses the metric (also called the **Gay-Lussac** or **continental system**), which lists proof exactly as the percent alcohol by volume. Thus, an 80° American spirit is about 70° in Britain and 40° in Europe. Table 14–1 compares the three systems. Europe uses volume of alcohol for spirits, beer, and wine. This makes its beers often appear to have a higher alcoholic content than ours because we state the content by weight for beers.

Table 14-1
Proof comparisons.

	British	American	European
Pure alcohol	175	200	100
	100	114	57
	88	100*	50
	85	98	49
	80	90	45
	75	86†	43
	70‡	80§	40
	65	74	37
Pure water	0	0	0

*U.S. bonded whiskey.
†The proof of most U.S. blends.
‡The proof of most British whiskeys.
§Lowest proof allowed in U.S. whiskeys.

STANDARDS OF IDENTITY

The Treasury Department has set standards of identity for spirits, beers, and wines. These state what products have to be and what must appear on the labels if they are called specific beverages.

Distilled Spirits

When alcohol is distilled from its brew, it becomes what is called a **spirit.** There are a large number. Some may be quite low in alcohol compared with others, but all qualify for this group if they come from a distilled product. Each has its own distinct taste, aroma, and body; even different brands of the same spirit vary in these. Flavor and body are controlled by the ingredients used to make the fermented brew or by their processing, the spirit's proof, or processing of the spirit after **distillation.** Flavoring compounds are often called **cogeners.**

A spirit is made by first selecting its carbohydrate ingredient; this is often a grain, but can be something like molasses or sugar cane juice for rum or agave cactus juice for tequila. The correct yeast is added and fermentation goes on for about 72 to 96 hours. The higher the distillation temperature, the lower the amount of cogeners that come over with the distillate (see Figure 14–1).

The following terms are often used in describing certain factors relating to spirits:

Term	Definition
Straight	A spirit that comes from the still not over 160 proof; only diluted (rectified) with water to desired proof; if labeled a straight whiskey, it must be aged at least 24 months.
Rectification	Dilution of a spirit to obtain a desired alcoholic content.
Bonded spirits	A bonded spirit must be aged (stored) four years in a government warehouse, must be the product of a single distillery during a single season, and must be 100°. The government's green stamp certifies the spirit is bonded. Bonding is no guarantee of quality, but the better spirits are usually bonded. The IRS of the Treasury Department controls the warehouse, keeping records of spirit entries and withdrawals. No one can enter without being accompanied by a federal official.
Grain neutral spirits	An alcohol distilled from a grain mash that gives a colorless, flavorless, and odorless product at 190°.
Blended spirits	A blended whiskey is 100° straight whiskey blended with other whiskey or neutral spirits not under 80°. The minimum ratio of 100° straight whiskey in such a blend is 20%. Before being marketed, blends are aged a short time, a period called *marrying.* The flavor and body of a blend is much affected by the quality of the straight whiskey, a good blend being made from very good straight whiskey, Scotch, or Canadian whiskey. Many bourbons and other spirits are blends. A blend must carry the reddish pink stamp of the federal government to indicate it is a blend of spirits.

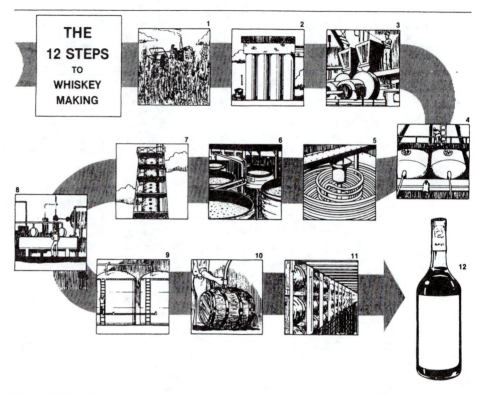

Figure 14-1

The 12 steps to whiskey-making by continuous distillation: (1) The grain is harvested. (2) It is carefully inspected and stored. (3) It is ground into a meal. (4) After the meal is cooked to solubilize the starch, malt is added, changing the starch to sugar. (5) The mash is cooled and pumped into fermenters. (6) Yeast is added to the mash and allowed to ferment, resulting in a mixture of grain residue, water, yeast cells, and alcohol. (7) This mixture is pumped into a continuous still where heat vaporizes the alcohol which is drawn off and the residue allowed to fall to the bottom where it too is drawn off; this is different than the pot still in which the liquid from a fermented brew is placed and the alcohol driven off by heat, the residue is emptied, the pot cleaned, and a new batch put in for distillation; the first is continuous, the second is by batch. (8) The alcohol vapors are caught, cooled, condensed, and drawn off as clean, new whiskey. (9) This new high-proof whiskey is stored in a cistern room. (10) Water is added to lower the proof, a process called rectifying, and the whiskey is drawn into charred oak barrels. (11) The barrels are stored in a rack house for aging. (12) After aging, the barrels of whiskey are drained into the tanks that feed the bottling line; in the case of blends, different whiskeys are put together and grain neutral spirits or other whiskeys are added. (Published with permission and courtesy of the Distilled Spirits Council of the United States, Inc.)

Whiskies

A large number of spirits are called **whiskies.** All come from a mash made of grain.

Bourbon is made from a mash of 51% or more of corn with the balance being any other grain, usually rye or barley malt. **Sourmash whiskey** is made by using part of an old mash to start and assist the fermentation of a new batch, much the same as using a "starter" for sourdough bread. Such spirits have a distinctive sourish flavor. Tennessee whiskey is a sourmash whiskey. Many other bourbons are but the label does not state it. **Corn whiskey** must come from 80% or more of corn. It may lack color because it is stored in noncharred barrels. **Rye whiskey** must be distilled from a mash of 51% or more of rye. Canadian whiskey is made from a mash largely of corn with some rye; bartenders in this country often give a customer asking for rye whiskey, a Canadian whiskey. Most Canadian whiskies are blended either before or after an aging period of at least two years. Most are aged three years.

Imports must conform to our regulations and requirements. Because they contain a large amount of neutral spirits, making them "light" in flavor, they better suit today's American preference in spirits. The taste is now for less flavor, thus the popularity of vodka, which is relatively flavorless.

The federal government requires that our whiskies be distilled at 160°[4] or less and be aged at least two years in charred new oak barrels. Some whiskies are filtered through charcoal before being aged; this process improves flavor by removing harsh components such as fusel oil. It also makes a smoother tasting liquor. If the product is called **light whiskey,** it is controlled to produce a distillate between 160 and 190°. The whiskey can also be stored in used or uncharred oak barrels. Both of these factors give a whiskey with a very light flavor and little body. Also, as noted, a higher grain neutral content gives less flavor.

Scotch whisky (note spelling) is a distinctive product of Scotland, the base of which is a mash of smoked barley for the heavy-bodied types and smoked corn for the lighter bodied ones. Some are distilled by the pot method. Aging is done for at least three years in uncharred oak barrels or used sherry casks. Scotch entering this country must be aged four years unless otherwise labeled. Most Scotch is aged five years or more before it is blended. Low-country Scotch, made in the lowlands, is a light liquor and almost always a blend. It may be blended with what is called high-country barley-based straight liquor and neutral spirits. Some high-country straight Scotch is sold as straight- or single-malt Scotch, is usually of good quality, and commands a higher price.

Irish whisky (again, note spelling) is made from malted and unmalted Irish barley or other grains—it can be a blend of other grain spirits. The grain base may or may not be dried over a coal fire or sometimes peat. Most are pot distilled. It is aged seven to eight years, which produces a smooth and mellow liquor of medium body. It is usually a blend.

---

[4]Note that in this chapter the degree symbol (°) indicates proof unless it is followed by "F" or "C," in which case it indicates degree Fahrenheit or Celsius.

Grain Neutral Spirit Liquors

Gin, vodka, and **aquavit** are made from grain neutral spirits. Gin and aquavit are flavored, but vodka is left pretty much without flavor and odor, with a light body. Many flavored vodkas are marketed.

Vodka is consumed in greater amounts than any other spirit in this country. Vodka is bottled at 80 to 100°; the best brands are carefully filtered through charcoal to remove harsh components. Very little, if any, vodka in this country is made from potatoes.

Gin is flavored neutral spirits usually made by allowing the distillation vapors to pass through flavoring herbs held in a **gin head.** The herbs are usually juniper berries with perhaps cassia bark, coriander seed, orange peel, cardamon, and angelica. Different mixtures of these with juniper berries create different flavors of gins. Gin can be made by steeping neutral grain spirits in these products and then straining them out, giving a product called *bathtub gin.* Compound gin has had juniper and other flavorings added to grain neutral spirits. **London (English) gin** is very dry, lacking sweetness, and is often made by redistilling the grain neutral spirits with the flavoring ingredients added in the still or allowing the vapors to pass through a gin head. **Holland** (Geneva or Schiedam or schnapps) **gin** comes from Holland where it is made from a low-proof, malt spirit base to which juniper and other seasonings have been added. It has a heavy body and carries a flavor from its mash. Its heavy flavor discourages mixing it with other items, such as in a martini. Gin is not aged; golden gin is aged for a short time.

Aquavit is a grain neutral spirit made like gin, but caraway is the main flavoring agent. It is usually served very cold, neat (with nothing else). Beer or food chasers may be used to help remove the threatened strangulation! It is usually at least 100° or more.

Rums

Rum is distilled from fermented molasses or sugar cane. It must be not more than 190° or less than 80°. Rum labels state just "rum" if it is a blend; others indicate they are straight. The place where it is made is also given. New England rum is a full-bodied, straight spirit, distilled at less than 160°. Most of our rum comes from Puerto Rico, which makes a light rum; aging one year yields white or silver rum; amber or gold is aged three years or more. Red label, a heavy, dark rum, is aged six years or more; it has a full flavor with good body. Caramel coloring may be added to make a darker rum. Jamaican rum is a dark mahogany, high in flavor, and full bodied; its base is molasses. It is aged five to seven years and is 80 to 151°. Virgin Island rum is light and unaged. Demeraran rum is made in Guiana; it is lighter in flavor than Jamaican rum but darker in color; proof is 80 to 151°. Barbados and Trinidad rums are medium bodied but full flavored. Haiti and Martinique make a light rum. Liqueur rums are aged like good brandies. The aromatic or Batavia Arak rum comes from Java.

Brandies

Brandy is distilled from fermented fruit or fruit juices and cannot be less than 80°. If labeled brandy, it must come from grapes. If it comes from another product, it must bear the name of the product, such as pear brandy, cherry brandy, or blackberry brandy. Cognac comes from grapes grown in the Charente area in France, where the city of Cognac is located. Usually, the closer the production area is to Cognac, the finer the quality. Armagnac brandy comes from grapes grown in the Department of Gers, southeast of Bordeaux, France. Brandy is usually aged in oak barrels for from 3 to 8 years. Labels need not state age unless it is under 2 years old. Some American brandies are bottled in bond. These must be straight brandy, 4 years or older, and 100°. Specific terms, symbols, or letters on a brandy label indicate age, quality, and so on. The following symbols indicate various claimed qualities: V = very, S = superior, F = fine, P = pale, E = especial or extra, X = extra, and O = old. Buyers should know, however, that each producer of brandies has its own interpretation of what these terms mean. Stars may also mean different things with various brandies. In cognacs, usually three stars mean aging 1½ years; VS means the same thing; VSOP is aged in wood 4½ years or more—usually 7 to 10; extra, vieille réserve, and Napoléon mean aged at least 5½ years. "Fine" champagne means the grapes come from the Grande or Petite Champagne areas, two great cognac areas in the heart of the Cognac district.

American brandy is aged in white-oak barrels for two years or more. It may be straight or a blend. Some can be high in quality. We produce many sweet, flavored brandies. Applejack is distilled from fermented cider, aged in wood at least two years, and sold at 100° or 80°, blended with grain neutral spirits.

Tequila

Tequila (tə kē´lə) is made in Mexico from the sap of the cultivated cactus plant called the maguey or mescal, which we know as the American aloe or century plant. White tequila is unaged; silver is aged up to three years; gold is aged in oak two to four years. If aged a year, it is called *anejo* and if aged longer *muy anejo*. The letters DNG on the label indicate that the liquor meets Mexican standards. Ancient tequila was made from pulque, the juice of the wild mescal.

Cordials (Liqueurs)

The federal government classifies **liqueurs** and **cordials** as the same thing. They are flavored alcoholic drinks, often sweetened. Flavor can be added by percolating with a spirit, and then distilling to get just the essences of the flavoring product. They also can be made by maceration, which is steeping like tea. The spirit with the flavoring is also distilled to get some of the most delicate of the extracted flavors. The third method is to place the flavoring items in a spirit and distill this. For the most part, the flavoring ingredients are fruit—orange, peach, cherry, plum—or seeds from herbs usually, herbs, flowers, peels, or a mixture of these with other items. **Cremes** are very sweet cordials.

Standards of identity require at least 2½% flavoring ingredients in the cordial. Sugar is often more than this. Some cordial formulas are secret, such as Benedictine, Cointreau, and Chartreuse. Some have been made for centuries by monastic orders.

Quality Evaluation of Spirits

Painstaking training and a critical taste are needed to evaluate the quality characteristics of a spirit. Quality is indicated by body, character, clarity, color, and proof. A heavy body is distinguished by a full flavor and aroma, whereas a light one has these characteristics to a lesser degree. Each spirit group has its own individual quality factors. Rums are full-flavored compared with vodkas, which have little or no flavor. Quality differences also exist within similar spirits. A sourmash bourbon has a much different flavor from a regular bourbon. Even vodkas differ in flavor. Aged brandy is distinctly different from the unaged type.

Good flavor is indicated by a smoothness and a lack of strong, raw, harsh, or off-flavors. The aroma should be full, characteristic, and true. A good spirit should have a good taste while in the mouth and for a short time after; there should be no oily, lingering aftertaste. The trend in patrons' taste, in spirits, as noted, is toward a light flavor and body, but this should not limit one's entire offerings. Some patrons want a more full-flavored and heavier bodied spirit. Buyers should know what patrons want and shape their selections accordingly, seeking to give them the qualities they want.

In tasting a spirit, one should be able to identify the true aroma and flavor of the grain, fruit, or other product used in the mash. Molasses gives a heavier-flavored rum than sugar cane. Heavy smoking of the barley gives Scotch a heavy flavor. The distillation process also affects flavor. Fast distillation gives a rougher, but fuller flavor. Character refers to the sensory qualities that distinguish the spirit. Most spirits should be sparkling clear. Spirits vary in color intensity according to how they are made and aged, and how much caramel is added to them. Aging in a noncharred cask gives a lighter colored spirit than aging in a charred one. Barley Scotch is darker than corn Scotch.

Price is not always an indicator of quality; brand can be, but not always. To some extent a buyer of spirits has a simple job because so much of the buying is based on brands and not on quality evaluations. Patrons learn to like brands and request these; bar or well spirits, however, should be selected on the basis of quality and often a taste panel is called together to judge, say, six to seven spirits of the same kind. When the panel makes a decision, the selection often becomes the well stock for a period—three months or six months, for example.

Wine

Wine is the product of partial or complete fermentation of the juice of fruit or berries. Fermented apple juice is called cider and, even though made in a bonded wine cellar, is sold as cider and not wine. Cider is not taxed, nor does it come under federal regulations or permit requirements. To bear only the name *wine,* the product must come from grapes; if made from other fruit, the fruit name must precede the term *wine* (e.g., blackberry wine). Labels must also state the fact that a wine is made from raisins or dried fruits if that is the case.

Wine-Making

Wine quality is affected by the kind of fruit used, the geographical area where it is grown, the climatic conditions of growing, the care the fruit gets during growth and its selection, how the wine is made, and the care it gets after it is made. Aging is also a factor. Most wine is made from grapes.

There are two wine grapes: European *(Vitis vinifera)* and American (chiefly *Vitis lubrusca*), often called the fox grape because of its wild or foxy flavor. Grapes grown for table use, raisins, juice, jellies, or brandy usually make poor wine, although some vintners are beginning to make better wine from table grapes than was previously thought possible.

Most wine grapes grow on American grape roots, since its roots are resistant to phelgra or phlox, a small aphis that once destroyed most of Europe's vineyards. This insect was unknown in Europe, but when some infested American grape plants were imported to England, the phlox quickly spread over Europe. The European grape, being nonresistant to their attack, was almost wiped out. By grafting European vines onto American grape roots, the problem was solved because the American roots could survive phlox attack.

Specific grapes must be used to make specific wines. A Pinot Noir grape must be used for Burgundy, a Semillon for a Graves or Sauternes, a Palomino for sherry, a Johannisberger for a Rhine, and a varying amount of Sangiovese for a Chianti. The blending of juice or wines is common in the United States. In this country, if the name of the grape is used on a label, the wine must be made from 75% or more of that grape. Thus, a buyer selecting an American wine would be more likely to get a wine resembling a French Burgundy if the label read "Pinot Noir" than if it read "Burgundy," which may or may not be like the French wine. And a wine would be more apt to resemble a French claret or red Bordeaux if the label read "Cabernet Sauvignon," the grape used for that wine.

Distinctive American wines are being made from grapes developed here, such as the Zinfandel and Emerald Dry. American vintners claim that blending makes it possible to have a more consistent quality each year and to adjust for variations in sweetness, acid, alcoholic content, flavor, and other factors. If an old wine is blended with a small amount of a young one, a freshness of flavor or fruitiness of flavor results. Some wine merchants in Bordeaux are so skilled at blending clarets that they sometimes produce a wine superior to many estate-bottled ones. The French allow champagne to be blended because it is difficult to get a good wine using the juice of only one type of grape. **Sherry** is a blended wine usually made by the **solera method,** a process in which sun-baked sherries of different ages are blended.

Red grapes produce red wine, the color coming from the skins. Some bitterness or astringency also comes from the skins. A rosé, or pink, wine, called the wine of the night **(vin de nuit),** results when the skins are fermented only a short time, usually overnight. A white wine results from white grapes or red grapes with the skins removed after pressing. Some wines may be colored: port's deep red color comes partially from elderberries added to the wine; sweet white wines may have a deeptan to brownish color, the depth of which is usually an indicator of the degree of sweetness of the wine.

As noted, most wines are kept in the cask during the winter and are bottled in the spring, when a good indication of quality can be gained. Many wine merchants buy in the spring, frequently before the wine is bottled, and may ship in the cask. Some new wines are aged best in cellars or rooms at 55°F, while sherry is cooked or aged best in the sun at temperatures from 100° to 140°F. During aging, wines are run from one cask to another, leaving deposits of lees, tartrates, and so on. Casks are usually kept well filled to prevent undue oxidation. Acetic acid bacteria can oxidize alcohol into acetic acid or vinegar. Most European and other countries clarify wine by decanting, but American wines are frequently filtered to produce a high clarity; this filtering is called **finishing.** Overaging may give an excessively woody flavor.

Age does not necessarily indicate wine quality. Some wines are best consumed young, whereas others are best only after long aging. Normally, white wines last up to six or seven years and should be consumed when three to four years old. Many red wines are good only after they are six or more years old.

Wines, especially white ones, can be a health hazard because of the sulfur they contain. During grape growth sulfur products may be used to control insects or other infestations and this may increase the sulfur content of the grapes. Also, wine casks for white wines are frequently treated with sulfur fumes to kill wild yeasts and this, along with the sulfur already in the grapes, may cause the wine to have a high sulfur content. Because some asthmatic and other individuals are very allergic to sulfur (deaths have even occurred from it), the government requires now that wines containing over 100 parts per million of sulfur must state on the label "contains sulfites."

Wine Storage

Dry wines in bottles should be stored on their side so the corks do not dry out. Sweet and sparkling wines can be stored standing up. Elevated temperatures, light, dampness, and movement (e.g., the shaking of the storeroom area from the passage of subway trains or transporting the wine) may harm wine. Inventories should be carefully controlled and excess stocks avoided. The best storage temperature is about 50° to 55°F. A storage area five ft high and seven ft long holds about 40 cases of wine. Shelves should be 18 to 24 in. deep and divided into bins, so the wines can be located and identified quickly.

Vintages

Labels on wines may show a date that indicates the year (called the **vintage year**) when the grapes were grown. Dates may be important because growing conditions and other factors of that year affect wine quality. California's wines vary less than those of some other areas of the world, because it has a very consistent climate and also blends its wines to get a standard product. Vintage years are therefore less common with these wines, although the use of a vintage year on the label is increasing.

Types of Wines

Wines can be classified by color, place of origin, use, and various other factors.

Wines by color are red, white, and rosé. Red wines are usually full bodied with a hearty, pronounced flavor. They may vary from an orange red, to a bright or deep red, to deep purple. Anthocyanins or red color pigments account for this color; it comes from the grape skins. Rosé is a light rose or pink color. The flavor and body of rosés are closely akin to that of the whites but are often not as dry. (Dry means a lack of sugar, not acid.) White wines have a delicate, fruity flavor with little body. They may vary from an almost clear white to yellow or greenish yellow to a brownish color. White wines and rosés are served chilled; red wines are served at from 60° to 70°F.

Wines may be classified by use as (1) appetizers, (2) dinner or table wines (red, white, or rosé), (3) sweet dessert wines, (4) sparkling wines, and (5) fortified wines. Appetizer wines are aperitifs or aromatic wines, made by steeping flavoring ingredients with the wine, and are usually fairly high in alcoholic content (fortified); they are wines such as vermouths, Campari, Dubonnet, sherry, Marsala, or Madeira. Dinner wines are often served with the meal and are usually dry or fairly so. Sweet dessert wines are either white or red, such as Sauternes, Tokay, or Trockenbeerenauslese. Sometimes these too are fortified, such as port. Sparkling wines have a wide use. They may be used as an aperitif, for social drinking, or as a dessert wine. Champagne, Asti Spumante, sekt, sparkling Burgundy, or sparkling muscat are examples. Fortified wines are often used for social drinking, but can be used as aperitifs or dessert wines. These are 15% or more in alcoholic content.

We often distinguish wines by their place of origin such as French wines, Chilean wines, wines from Burgundy, or *Côtes du Rhone*. Such differentiation helps to indicate the kind of wine. Thus, a California wine is usually much different from one from New York State. It is also common to define the wine by the particular vineyard it comes from, such as Chateau Margaux or Madeira, an island.

Wines may also be classified by the fruit from which they come, or by the shipper (**negociant**) or producer. Brand names help to identify a wine. In France such a proprietary name would be called a **monopole.** A wine may be called generic or varietal. The former refers to a general type of wine, such as a Rhine wine, a Burgundy, or a claret. Varietal wines of this country are those in which a single grape makes up 75% or more of the wine. The use of generic or varietal terms to describe wines is usually limited to American wines. There are other ways to classify wines, and each in some way differentiates a wine so that we know more about it.

Non-U.S. Wines

French Wines.   France is the leading producer of wines and dominates the market, although many wines from Chile, Russia, Australia, and other countries are beginning to cut into this market because they are producing wines that are equal or sometimes superior to the traditionally worshipped French wines. Though France exports much wine, it imports more to meet its needs; this imported wine is of lesser distinction and is called ***vin ordinaire.***

Just because a wine comes from France does not mean it is good or even acceptable. Many poor wines come from there but, of course, many of the world's best do too. It is up to buyers to learn how to select the right ones; knowing a lot about French wines and the year helps.

France has strict controls on its wine industry. Names are tightly controlled by a system called ***appellation contrôlée.*** If a label states *mise du château*, the wine must come from grapes grown *only* on the estate (vineyard) named. Names of vineyards or towns indicate the wine is from grapes grown there; it is not blended. The *Institut National des Appellations d'Origine* and the *Service des Fraudes* are empowered to see that regulations are observed.

All nations belonging to the European Economic Council (Common Market) have agreed to standardize their wine industries according to quality standards established by the Common Market, and this has caused some nations in Europe to set up new controls and standards. Gradually, as the Common Market standards are developed, we will see more and more uniformity in the wines of Europe.

Champagne District. The Champagne district is northwest of Paris and south of Reims, with Epernay in the center. Its wine is a blend usually of Chardonnay (white Pinot) and Pinot Noir grapes. Blanc de blancs are made only from Chardonnay grapes and have a more delicate flavor and a pale, greenish gold color. Only the **cuvé** and the ***première taille*** (first and second pressing respectively,) are used for **champagne;** the third and fourth (*deuxième taille* and *rebèche)* are used for other wines. After fermentation, the wines are stored and then blended in the spring to give proper qualities.

French champagne is made largely by the following ***natural* process:** The bottles have a bit of additional sugar added to renew fermentation. During this second fermentation, the bottles are racked head down and subjected to a process of **riddling,** which shakes the sediment down into the neck (see Figure 14–2). Later this neck is frozen and the sediment is disgorged as a frozen plug with additional sugar added and perhaps brandy if the alcoholic content is not sufficient. This last sugar, called **le dosage** or ***liqueur d'expédition,*** adds more carbon dioxide and may give champagne a sweetness. Labels indicate sweetness as follows:

Brut (br$\bar{u}$) (Nature)*	Very dry	½–1½% sugar
Extra Sec or Dry	Fairly dry	1½–3% sugar
Sec or Dry	Medium sweet	3–5% sugar
Demi Sec	Fairly sweet	5–7% sugar
Doux (d$\overline{oo}$)	Quite sweet	7% or more sugar

Nature on the label should mean that no sugar has been added, but it might not.

Some French champagnes of lesser reputation are made by the **Charmat process.** Instead of bottling after blending, the wine is placed with added sugar into a sealed vat where the second fermentation occurs, but because the vat is sealed, pressure builds from the carbon dioxide gas and fermentation develops. The wine is then bottled under pressure and the bottle corked so the effervescence is sealed in.

American champagnes use these two processes or a third one in which the wine is carbonated to give it effervescence and then bottled.

No vineyard or estate name appears on champagne labels unless it is a small production of one vineyard or producer. Instead, blenders and bottlers such as Möet et Chandon, Mumm, or Mercier are shown.

In some years no champagne may be made because the wine is not good enough. The wines of that year are carried over and blended with the next year's product. There are only a few vintage years. When skins on red grapes are left to ferment a short time, a pink, or rosé, champagne is made.

Burgundy District. The French **Côte d'Or (k$\bar{o}$t d´ôr)** (golden slope), just south of the Champagne district, is made up of the *Côte des Nuits* (kôt d´n$\bar{u}$e´) and *Côte de Beaune* (kôt d´b$\bar{o}$n). The first is famous for its red, rich-bodied wines from the Pinot

Figure 14-2
This worker wears a wire mask when riddling champagne, to protect himself from glass fragments when an occasional bottle explodes. The riddling process consists of slightly turning and shaking each bottle every day for about 6 months.
(Printed with permission through the courtesy of the Wine Institute of America.)

Noir (pē´nō nwar) grape. It is made up of many small vineyards such as the Chambertins or Clos Vougeout (klôs vô q´ō´), the latter so prized that one of Napoleon's generals instructed his soldiers to salute when they marched by it.

Not all red Burgundies are good, and buyers must learn the various vintners and the quality of the product. Some wines may be named after the commune or parish where grown; some may just be labeled *Côte d'Or*. These should be tasted before they are bought because some can be mediocre. A good buyer learns which years produced good wine and buys that.

Chablis (shab´lē) and other wines called white Burgundies come from the north Burgundy districts. They are made from the white Chardonnay or white Pinot Noir grapes, which make a wine with a fine flavor, rich body, and great greenish gold or yellow color. Buyers need to keep up on which shippers or vineyards in any one year have the best offerings because quality can vary.

The area from Chalon to Lyons produces the famous Maconnais (mak´ôn ā) and Beaujolais (bā´jōl ā), dry red wines with less body than Burgundy. They come from the Gamay grape. These wines do not keep as well, but last slightly longer than dry, white wines. Most are blends. *Supérieur* often indicates a wine of better than average quality.

Rhone District. The Côtes du Rhône are just south of the Côtes d'Or and reach down along the Rhone to Marseilles. Avignon, the city where the popes were held prisoners from 1305 to 1377, is in the area. The vineyards of the Chateauneuf-du-Pape (shätonæf dy pap´) (new chateau of the pope) were supposed to have been planted on the order of Clement V. The Cinsant and Syrrah grapes grow well here and, because of the warm climate, the red wines have a deep red color, a heavy body, and a rich flavor just escaping harshness. The reds often throw a heavy sediment, as do the reds from nearby Piedmont in Italy. The Granache grape grows well around the town of Tavel, where the famous pink or rosé wine comes from; they do not hold quality long and should be used within five years.

Bordeaux District. The Bordeaux, or Gironde, area is France's most important wine-growing district, producing the famous red Bordeaux (clarets), the dry, austere Graves, the luscious, golden sweet Sauternes, and their close brethren, the Barsacs. Vintage years are common. Bordeaux reds come from Cabernet Sauvignon grapes, sometimes mixed with others. The sweet and dry whites both come mainly from the Semillon, the Sauvignon Blanc, and the Muscadelle grapes.

In 1855 many wines from the Gironde were ranked by experts, who put the clarets of 61 vineyards into five main classes (or *crus*) and 21 sauternes in two classes. The famous sweet sauternes from the Château D'Yquem (sha tō'dē kem') were put into a class by themselves because they were considered superior. In some years there may be little difference between the wines of the Gironde vineyards, or they may change relative positions, but they still hold their 1855 ranks, to some degree, and buyers can still use this ranking to ascertain the probable quality of the wine. Certainly, clarets from the vineyards of either the first or second class are almost sure to be good any year.

Other French Wine Districts.   Another important wine district of France is the Loire, which produces the famous Anjou rosé and some good white wines. Other good reds, rosés, and whites come from around Anjou, such as Vonvray, Touraine, Pouilly, Sancerres, and Nantais.

Both the Berne and Roussillon areas near the Pyrenees produce some good reds and whites. The Savoy, or Jura, area near Switzerland produces good reds and whites that closely resemble the Italian wines of nearby Lombardy. A Jura white wine called *Château Chalons* (shal'on) is allowed to ferment and age from seven to eight years before it is bottled. It is high in alcohol and lives in the bottle almost as long as the red Bordeaux.

Alsace, near Germany, produces wines much like the German ones and they are put into the tall, slim, light green bottles similar to those of the Moselle area. Many good wines are produced, and the wines of the grape varieties Sylvaner (sil'vanēr), Riesling (rez'liñg), Traminer (tramēn'ər), Gewuerz-Traminer (gəwerz'-tramēn'ər), and Edelzwicker (äd'al swik'ər) are considered very good.

German Wines.   Germany produces many fine wines. German labels must identify the wine by the vintage date, area where the grapes are grown, and name of the shipper. Wines may be estate bottled, come from a general district, or bear the shipper's label as some Bordeaux wines do. The following are some terms used on labels and their meaning:

Auslese (ous lā sə) (late selective picking)

Beerenauslese (ber ən) (select overripe grapes)

Bestes Fass (best′əs fäs) or *Fuder* (füd′ər) (best cask)

Eigengewächs (ī gen gē wekz) (own growth)

Erzeugerabfullung (ĕr zug′ər ab f ōōl ung) or *Aus eigenlesegut* (ous ī gen lā′ sə gōōt) (estate bottled)

Fass or *Fuder Nr.* (cask number)

Fein (fīn) or *Feinste* (fīn stə) (fine or finest)

Gewächs (gē′ weks) (place of origin)

Hochfeine (hok′fīn) (of the best)

Kabinett Wein (kab′ən nit vīn) (special wine—no sugar added)

Kellerabfüllung (kel′ lər ab fool′ung) (cellar filling)

Kellerabzug (kel′ lər ab zug′) (cellar bottling)

Korbrand (kōr brand) (brand of the estate)

Kreszenz (krəz′ enz) (growth of)

Naturwein (nach′ər vīn) (natural wine, unsugared) *Original Abfüllung* (ab fōōl′ ung) (original filling)

Original Abzug (ab zug′) (original bottling)

Qualitätswein (kwol′it ätz vīn aba) (Aba) (wine above ordinary)

Qualitätswein mit Prädikat (mit präd′ i kat) (highest quality)

Schlossabzug (shlôs′ ab zug′) (estate bottling)

Tafel wein (töfl′ vīn) (ordinary wine)

Trockenbeeren (trok ən bē ən) (dry berry)

Ungezuckerter wein (un ge′ zuk ər vīn) (natural wine)

Wachstum (wak′stum) (place where grown)

Wines carrying the terms *qualitätswein mit prädikat* are usually accompanied by one of these quality designators: *kabinett* (special wine, unsugared), *spätlese* (spät′ lā sə) (late picking), *auslese* (selected picking), *beerenauslese* (selected berry picking), or *trockenbeerenauslese* (selected dried-berry picking).

Moselle-Saar-Ruwer District. The Moselle area wines are marketed in tall, slim, green bottles. The wines have a light alcoholic content, about 8% to 9%; they keep well up to six years. They are fragrant, light, crisp, and dry. The best wines come from the middle Moselle, such as Piesporters (pēs′portər), Bernkastel Doktor (bûr̄n kaŝst əl dok tor′), Zeltingers (zel ting′ ərz), and Erdener Treppchen (är den′ ər trep′ chen).

Rheingau District. The Rheingau (rīn′gou) is the northwest area of the Rhine river bend as it moves toward Coblenz, which includes the adjoining west bank of the Main River. Like nearly all German wines, the wines are in tall, slim, brown bottles to protect them from the light. Rheingaus are delicate, with a light body and flavor, a fragrant bouquet, and a brilliant sparkle, but they are apt to be somewhat austere and hard. They are light in alcohol. Quality can vary from year to year. Labels bear the name of the township or the vineyard's name, such as Johannisberger Hölle (jō hän′ is ber gər hōl) or Schloss Johannisberg (shlôs jō hän′ is berg).

Hessian District. Rheinhessen (rīn ′hes sen) (Hessia) on the other side of the Rhine runs from Mainz to Worms. Its wines are somewhat softer and richer than those of the Rheingau and have a slightly higher alcoholic content and a heavier bouquet and flavor. The well-known *liebfraumilch* (lēb frô milk) (milk of the Blessed Mother) comes from this area. Most are blends, and poor ones may be heavily sulfured. When good, it is soft and slightly sweet; the best comes from Nierstein, Nackenheim, or Oppenheim under good shippers' labels. The true liebfraumilch comes from vineyards around the Church of Our Beloved Lady in the City of Worms; it is not labeled *liebfraumilch,* but with the names of the vineyards, Liebfrauen (lēb frô ən), Stiftswein (stiftz' ven), or Kirchenstük (kirk' ən stuk). Niersteiner Domtal (nēr stin ər dum'tel) are blended wines that vary often in quality.

The best Hessian wines come from near the Rhine or alongside it and should be made from the Sylvaner or Riesling (rī sling) grape. Buyers should learn the town and *lagename* (äg ən äm) (vineyard name) from which the best wines come.

Palatinate District (pal at' in āt).   The Rheinpfalz (rīn' pfä lz) (Palatinate) is east of the Rhine, south of Hessia, and next to Alsace-Lorraine. The best wine is produced in the Mittel-Hardt area between Neustadt and Bad Dürkheim, especially around Wachenheim, Forst, Deidesheim, Ruppertsberg, Bad Dürkheim, Kallstadt, Leistadt, and Königsbach. The best wines have a delicate flavor, rich fruitiness, soft bouquet, and great delicacy, but are less crisp and harsh than the Rheingaus. Beerenausleses, the famous sweet wines, are produced here when the grapes become high in sugar and the climate lets them dry on the vines. Because these grapes give little juice, the wine is expensive. The poorest wines *(bodengeschmack)* (bōd ən gē shmak) are coarse, lack flavor, and may taste heavily of the soil.

Other German Wine Districts.   Steinwein (stīn vīn) (stein wine) is a Sylvaner or Riesling white wine produced near Würzburg and marketed in the green, flat, flasklike *bocksbeutel* (boks 'boi təl). Chilean imitations may be marketed in a similar bottle. It should more truly be called a Frankenweine—a light, dry, delicate, and well-balanced wine, with more substantial body than most German wines. Hock comes from the word *hockheimer* (hok' īm ər) which the English shortened. Today it can mean almost any German wine—we also have some American wines called hock. This wine is usually a good, substantial, delicate wine but should not be confused with the Hock vineyard wines in Bodenheim in Hessia. Sparkling Hock and sparkling Moselle are Sekts (sexz) *(schaumweins)* (shaum vīnz); they have good quality usually and they sell at a lower price than champagnes.

Italian Wines.   Italy has never been as fussy as the French and Germans about controlling its wine industry but the Italian government has recently established new regulations and is gradually extending them. The European Economic Council (Common Market) is also an influence in extending control. Buyers should check labels to note whether the symbols **DOC** are there to indicate the wine conforms to the new Italian control standards. The producer, specific wine, shipper, and place of origin or brand are other quality determinants. Even with this, quality varies.

Northern Districts.   All Chiantis (kē an'tā) are not good but usually the best wines are those of the five communes in Tuscany controlled by Chianti Classico, an association that enforces certain standards, which is identified on bottle labels by a black-and-gold seal with a black cock inside. Classico is usually reliable. Chianti bearing the white Della Robbia angel *(putto)* is usually above average. Chiantis from the Brolio vineyard, Rufina, Montalbano, Colli Fiorentini, and Colli Pisani are often reliable. Buyers should select Chiantis carefully because many inferior ones are marketed in the attractive straw-covered flasks (fiascos) (fē'as kō). Common Chiantis are fiery, harsh, and rough, with a rich, full body and somewhat tart flavor. A white Chianti is marketed. Tuscany also produces a light, dry wine of delicate freshness called Vernaccia di San Gimignano (vern a sē ə də san jē mē nan ō). The rich, sweet Vin Santo (vin sant ō) comes from Tuscany.

Piedmont's wines are famous, perhaps the best being Barolo (bar ō lō), a wine of ruby-red color, full body, and a soft, velvety, rich flavor, said to have the taste of roses and the aroma of violets. It casts a lot of lees but lives for a long time; it is marketed in Burgundy-like bottles. The Barbaresco is a light, red wine, resembling clarets, but slightly richer; it is marketed in Bordeaux-type bottles. The Barbera is deep-colored, full-flavored, and full-bodied but somewhat more astringent and harsher than the Barolo; it should be consumed young because it does not hold well. The Freisa (raspberry) is a light red wine with a raspberry bouquet. It is slightly sweet and may possess some spritz. Cortese Bianco or Gavi is a white, pale, light wine with a fresh flavor and delicate bouquet; it also should be consumed when young.

Valtellina, north of Milan, produces some good reds called Valtellina (val tel'ēn ə) or Sassella (sas'el lə), Grumello (grum el' lō), Inferno (in făr nō), Grigioni (gre'ghē-ô ne'), or Fracia (fras' ē'ə), the best vineyards near the town of Sondrio. These are well-developed wines with a reddish black color and usually improve slowly in the bottle. Verona and Venice areas produce the fine, dry, smooth, straw-colored Soave, marketed in light green, slim bottles similar to those used for Alsace wines. The velvety, fruity, delicate, subtle red Valpolicella comes from here. It should be consumed young. The Bologna Lambrusco (lam brōōs kō) is a subtle, red, sparkling wine.

Other northern Italy wines of significance are Est Est Est (It is! It is! It is!), named for the remark of a bishop's valet when he tasted the wine for his master to test its quality. Orvieto (ōr vē ətō) reds and whites are also well thought of, especially the whites.

Southern Districts. Lacrima Christi (lac rimə kristē) (tears of Christ) comes from the Vesuvius area near Naples. It is a soft, slightly sweet, pale gold, aromatic wine; a red, inferior wine with the same name is also made. Most wines south of Naples are rather ordinary, but Sicily has several good ones. The Corvino (kor'vīnō) from the white grapes of the slopes of Mt. Etna is a fine, dry, white wine with a somewhat fiery character. The great Marsala (mar sal'a) is like cream sherry or Madeira (mad' āər).

Austrian Wines. In 1985 Austria set up new regulations governing its wine industry and is expected to grow in importance as a wine-growing country. Four qualities of wine are marketed: *tafelwein, qualitatswein, kabinett,* and *pradikatswein* divided into *spatlese, auslese, eiswein, beerenauslese, ausbruch,* and *trockenbeerenauselese.* If a vineyard, village, or commune is on the label, 100% of the grapes must come from there, but if the vintage or grape variety is on the label, only 85% of the variety is needed. Labels must give unfermented sugar percentages. The approved wines will bear the Austrian Wine Seal which means that the wine has gone through a series of tests and has been approved. The wines of Austria are much like those of the Germans.

Russian Wines.   In 1983 the Soviet Union was the third-largest wine producer in the world, producing over 3½ billion liters per year. Standard regulations are being applied and the grades of wine from best to last are *kollektsioinye*, produced in selected areas with named grape varieties and aged two years in the bottle; *named*, with origin stated and with some aging; and *ordinary*, just as the name implies. Ordinary is the equal of *tafelwein* or *vin ordinaire*.

The main growing areas spread from Moldavia near Romania to the Caspian Sea and much of the Ukraine down into Crimea and neighboring areas. Not much Russian wine reaches the outside world, but with the division of the Soviet Union, we may see some countries begin to market some very fine wines in good quantities.

Spanish Wines.   English mispronunciation of Jerez, where sherry is made, accounts for the name *sherry*. It usually is made from Palomino (pal ō mē′nō) grapes. Three rows of casks are placed one on the other, called the Solera (sōl ārə). The top one contains the youngest wine, the middle the second youngest, and the bottom the oldest. After up to half of the bottom wine is removed for bottling, wine from the middle cask is drawn into the bottom one, filling it, and wine from the top cask is moved to the middle. The top cask is filled with new wine. Setting in the sun in barrels ripens the wine an gives it its special flavor. All sherries are dry, but are made sweet and deeper in color by adding a desirable amount of sweetened grape juice, reduced to a heavy syrup by boiling. Brandy is added to bring the sherry up to an 18 to 20% alcoholic content. The blending of sherries takes great skill. Sherries are classified by their color and sweetness as follows:

Manzanilla (män′zän ē′ə)*	Pale and light bodied	Very dry
Fino (fē′no)	Very pale with more body	Very dry
Amontillado (ä mon tē′äd o)	Golden with some body, nutty	Dry
Amoroso (ä mō rō sō)	Golden to light amber, some body	Medium dry
Oloroso (ōl ō rō sō)†	Deep golden to tan, full body	Sweet
Cream	Deep tan to brown, full body	Very sweet

*Some aged Manzanillas become dark and quite high in alcoholic content.
†This may also be called *cream sherry*.

Spain also produces some excellent dry white wines and some very good dry reds, but buyers should know what they are buying before purchasing them. Most of these come from northern Spain near the Gironde area of Bordeaux and are called *Riojas* (rē ō häs), from the district where they are produced, regardless of whether they are red or white.

Portuguese Wines.   Portugal's most famous wine is **port,** which is a sweet, fortified wine. In certain years a vintage port is produced. Ruby and tawny ports are aged in wood. Tawny port changes color and flavor during aging, becoming less sweet and has a brownish purple color. A crusted port is an aged port of a single year. Most ports are blends. A white port is produced from white grapes.

Only wines produced in the upper Douro River region can be called port. Some other red sweet wines of quality and nature similar to port are called *Lisbon wines.* Portugal is also marketing a fairly large quantity of sparkling rosés, such as Mateus or Lancer's. A delicate, fragrant, slightly tart white wine called *vinho verde,* which should be consumed young, is also well liked.

Hungarian Wines.   Hungary produces the famous sweet wine called Tokay Azu, often called the "King of wines, and the wine of Kings." It is made from sweet grapes that are allowed to ripen on the vines until they develop a slight mold, so the wine has somewhat the flavor of a Sauterne. There are two other dessert Tokays, but they are not as sweet. Hungary produces some excellent dry whites and reds. A dry red wine with a splendid bouquet, rich flavor, and full body is Egri Bikaver (bull's blood). Many Hungarian dry whites resemble those of the Rhine but are slightly richer in flavor and have more body.

Other Non-U.S. Wines.   Switzerland, Chile, Argentina, Australia and New Zealand, Bulgaria, Romania, North and South Africa, South America, Yugoslavia, Czechoslovakia, Greece, the Balkans, Israel, the Middle East countries, Madeira, and others produce some good wines. Buyers who know wines and how to couple them with a good merchandising program can build a profitable offering of such wines and at the same time please customers. For the quality presented, they are usually much lower in cost than some of the better known wines of the world.

American Wines

Many American wines have grown in prestige; each year in competition with other world wines, they do well. Wine today is one of our most popular alcoholic beverages; many people are changing from spirits to wine. It is common at a reception or cocktail party today to see many select a glass of wine or a wine cooler as their drink.

California Wines.   California produces some of the world's finest wines. Napa Valley, north of San Francisco, produces excellent reds, resembling Bordeaux as well as other good light, dry whites, and fuller bodied or lighter bodied reds of high quality. In Sonoma Valley, north and west of San Francisco, some good reds and whites plus dessert wines and champagne are produced. Because of the warmth and sunshine, the best wines of central and southern California are dessert wines, but some acceptable dry whites and reds and some champagnes are produced. California produces some sherries from Palomino grapes using the solera process, but most are heat treated for aging rather than sun-baked, to give them their nutty flavor and deepened color. California also produces some good brandies and some excellent champagnes; some French companies have set up their own vineyards in California and are now producing champagne.

Washington and Oregon Wines.   Some western areas of Washington and Oregon are beginning to produce significant wines. Some of the Washington vineyards have already achieved a good reputation for their products, and this area is expected to continue to grow and develop an excellent line of wines.

Eastern Wines.   The Finger Lakes region, the area along the Hudson River, and the high country in Sullivan County of New York produce excellent wines. New York champagnes from the Finger Lakes region compete in quality with the French product, although they may have a slight foxy flavor from the American grape used. In the United States any sparkling wine can be called champagne, even red, if it is bottle-fermented for sparkle and bears on the label its place of origin (e.g., New York State Champagne).

In Ohio, along Lake Erie from Sandusky to Cleveland, another good wine-producing region exists. The wines from this area are light, well balanced, and pleasant. Both red and white wines are produced, dry and sweet, but perhaps the whites are slightly superior. A few islands in Lake Erie produce a very high quality of wine that is considered some of the best in this country.

Michigan produces a considerable quantity of wine, but only a few of its wines are of sufficient quality to compete with some of the better American or European wines. Missouri, Virginia, Delaware, Tennessee, and the southern Atlantic states also produce some wine; Virginia and Delaware produce some very good semisweet wines. Some good champagnes produced around St. Louis are a blend of American grapes of the region and European grapes from California or wine from California.

The American grape is used for substantially all wines, outside of California, and so the flavor is that of the *lubrusca* (läb rūs′ kə), which has some foxiness. Many people do not object to this, however. It is also true that the middle and eastern wine-growing areas each year import a considerable quantity of California grapes (which are of the European variety) or California wines, and thus reduce some of the foxy flavor in their own wines.

Wine coolers have become popular in operations selling alcoholic beverages. They are popular because of their refreshing quality and because they are low in alcoholic content. Also buyers will find that customers are purchasing more carbonated beverages and beverages such as Gatorade and Power Aid. The fact such drinks as Gatorade are high in electrolytes needed by the body gives them the aurora of being a healthful drink as well as being quite palatable.

Judging a Wine

Louis Forest, a famous Parisian gourmet, said, "The tasting of wine begins, like love, with the eyes." Thus, to judge a wine, pour some into a clear glass holding it before a white napkin in a well-lighted room. The wine should be clear, not murky, and have no sediment in it. The color should be true and typical for the wine. Next, swirl the wine in the glass to note the body. Body is indicated by swirling the wine in the glass and noting how tiny rivulets, called legs, run down the sides of the glass. Body is also indicated by the looseness or adhesiveness with which the liquid moves in the glass. Body can further be evaluated by the feel of the wine in the mouth. The wine should be at the proper serving temperature. In the swirling, some of the aroma should have risen, and this should be smelled. It should have a pleasing smell and no off-odor or excessive fermentation smell. The bouquet (aroma) should be typical for the wine. Swishing a bit into the mouth, the wine should be either sweet or dry, but should not have an excessively tart, bitter, or unpleasant taste. When swallowed, it should leave an agreeable aftertaste.

Some old red and even some young wines may drop sediment called *lees*. Many bottles have a concave bottom to catch and hold them. Such a wine should be decanted before it is judged; this is done by pouring it very carefully into a clean, empty bottle until just a trace of sediment appears in the neck. To better see this trace of sediment, the neck of the bottle can be held near a burning candle. Some wines must be rested after being moved some distance and should not be judged then for several months.

Beers

Beers are beverages containing ½% or more of alcohol, brewed from malt or from any substitute, such as grain, grain products, sugars, or syrups. The federal government classifies beers as beer, ale, porter, and stout. **Saké,** a Japanese beer or wine, is classified as a beer for tax purposes. Beer may be made only in breweries under the control of the federal government.

At least 90% of the beer sold in this country is the lager type. **Lager beer** is produced by a fermentation carried out at low temperatures for a long time. The yeast during fermentation slowly settles to the bottom. For this reason, lager beer may be called **bottom-fermented beer.** This is in contrast with some beers and ales that are **top-fermented** or fermented at a higher temperature, and the yeasts float on top.

Ale is more tart and paler than lager beer and has a more pronounced hop flavor. Porter and stout are ales. Porter is sweeter and less hoppy than ale. It is also brewed from a darker malt. Stout is sweeter than porter. It is also stronger, darker in color, and heavier in flavor than the others in the ale group. The flavor is heavy with malt.

In 1986 the federal government required that all beer labels carry a list of ingredients in the product.

PURCHASING ALCOHOLIC BEVERAGES

The patron decides what kind and brands of alcoholic beverages an operation should purchase, and buyers need to know what patrons want before deciding what to purchase. Patrons usually want certain brands, and they will "call" for them—this gives rise to the term **call liquors,** which are brands specifically asked for by patrons. Well or bar stock, which is served when call brands are not asked for, should suit customer tastes and be priced within their price range. There are trends in drinking, and buyers should know these, as pointed out earlier. Popular, well-advertised brands usually sell well, and when patrons see these labels they have a sense of assurance that the operation is attempting to maintain quality.

Since some states limit which purveyors may carry certain brands, buyers may have little choice from whom they buy. In controlled states, buyers have to purchase from the state or from designated distributors. Prices are also controlled, so there is little use in shopping around for better buys. Some states even dictate ordering, billing, shipping, receiving, and other procedures. Vendors are limited in the kind of advertising and services they can provide. Even in states where there is no control, trade associations and agreements among vendors themselves often restrict free purchasing.

Purchase amounts should be established to maintain a proper stock level. Normally, maximum and minimum stock levels are set, with the minimum level being the reorder point (ROP). Buyers should guard against overstocking. A case of wine costing $72 can easily cost $10 in storage costs before it is sold. Stock should be moved through rapidly. Money does not work if it is tied up in inventory—if it does, it works slowly. Although some alcoholic beverages hold well, others do not. The risk of theft, breakage, and so on should also be considered. Holding down inventory to just meet needs is a good axiom. Management often desires to have an **inventory turnover** from 8 to 20 times annually. Wine turns over most slowly, beers turns over most rapidly, and spirits are between wines and beers.

Beer products preferably should not be held longer than two weeks. Draught beer is perishable and should be sold soon after purchase. It should be held under refrigeration. The dispensing system should be sanitized carefully each day. Beer and ale should be served at 42° to 44°F in clean glasses. A barrel of beer is 31 gal and a half-barrel is 15½ gal. About 460 8-oz glasses are obtained from a barrel considering spillage at 10%. A barrel is about the equivalent of 25 cases of 12-oz bottles.

Spirits should be stored at ordinary room temperature. Dry wines should be stored on their sides so the corks do not dry out. Sparkling and sweet or fortified wines can be stored standing up. Temperatures should be about 60°F or slightly lower for wines.

Purchases are often placed with salespeople. Purchase orders showing order date, purveyor and address, salesperson, delivery date and time, and other necessary information should be on the purchase order (PO). All items should be listed separately by kind, size, brand, and so on, so that complete identification is possible; prices should be given for each item ordered; the name of the person placing the order should be listed.

Prices are set by various factors. Governmental regulations and taxes are a factor (Table 14–2). Case lots should be purchased, whenever possible. However, broken cases should be purchased if the use is small. It is a waste of money to purchase a 12-bottle case of Chartreuse if only one bottle a year is used. Purchase of larger sized containers can reduce cost. Wine to be sold by the glass can be purchased in large jugs or even in 5-gal bulk containers.

Tax today is an important part of the price of alcoholic beverages. A case of 12 750-ml or 25.4-oz bottles of 80 proof spirit carries a $25.70 tax charge or a charge of $2.14 per bottle.[5] Because spirits are diluted with water, a process called *rectification,* a small rectification tax would be applied to this. A 750-ml (25.4 oz) bottle of dinner wine (less than 14% alcohol by volume) would carry a tax charge of $.21[6], while a six-pack of 12-oz cans of beer would carry a tax of about $0.33.[7]

---

[5]12 bottles × 25.4 oz = 304.8 oz/128 oz per gal = 2.38 gal and 2.38 gal × 80 proof/100 proof × $13.50 tax charge per gal (128 oz) = $25.70.

[6]25.4 oz is 0.1984 of a 128-oz gallon and since the tax on a still wine of less than 14% alcoholic content by volume is $1.07, 0.1984 × $1.07 = $0.21.

[7]A barrel (31 gal) of beer carries a tax charge of $18 or $0.5806 per gal and a six-pack contains 72 oz of beer or 0.5625 gal, so $0.5806 × 0.5625 = $0.3266. (The sources of these figures are Tables 14–2 and 14–3.)

Table 14–2
Federal tax schedule.

Distilled Spirits*	$13.50/proof gal
WINE	
Still wines not more than 14% by volume	1.07/gal
Still wines over 14% to 21% by volume	1.57/gal
Still wines over 21% to 24% by volume	3.15/gal
Artificially carbonated wine	3.30/gal
Champagne or sparkling wines	4.30/gal
BEERS	18.00/bbl†
Small brewers producing up to 2 million barrels/yr	
First 60,000 barrels	14.00/bbl
Barrels over 60,000	18.00/bbl

*A gallon or wine gallon is a U.S. gallon of liquid measure equivalent to the volume of 231 cu in. A proof gallon is the alcoholic equivalent of a U.S. gallon at 60°F, containing 50% of ethyl alcohol by volume. A tax gallon for spirits of 100 proof or over is equivalent to the proof gallon. For spirits of less than 100 proof, the tax gallon is equivalent to the wine gallon. As applied to beer, a barrel represents 31 wine gallons. Proof is the ethyl alcohol content of a liquid at 60°F, stated as twice the percent of ethyl alcohol by volume. (A British or Canadian proof gallon is an Imperial gallon of 277.4 cu. in. containing 57.1% of ethyl alcohol by volume.)
†A barrel holds 31 gallons.

Proof or alcoholic content can be a factor in pricing as well as in aging. There is a trend today for patrons to want quality and be willing to pay for it. Some find that offering a very high quality bottled wine or specialty beers at a good price is a way to bring in more profit. Some bars now sell only high-quality wines—they may offer 25 or 100 or more—and mark them up well. Others feature only beers and have a wide assortment of domestic and imported beers. Following trends may be good buying, but buyers should be sure that what they are following is a trend and not just a fad.

The pricing of spirits is highly competitive. Certain brands that command a significant portion of the market can be challenged for a share of the market by competitors who try to lower prices. Nevertheless, popular brands can be somewhat more favorably priced. Volume can be a factor in price; a company may be willing to lower its price if a significant sale can be made. Sometimes discounts are used to lower prices. Buyers may also find special promotions of sellers attractive.

Price comparisons should be made on the basis of equal proof or equal size containers, to ascertain the best buys. If a buyer wants to compare the prices of two spirits at different proofs, the following formulas can be used to get an equivalent price, if proofs are known and bottle sizes are the same:

$$1. \frac{Proof\ of\ (a)}{Proof\ of\ (b)} \times Price\ of\ (b) = Equivalent\ price\ of\ (a).$$

Thus, if one had the same size bottle of two similar spirits, but one (b in this case) was priced $7.55, what should the equivalent price of (a) be if the proof of (a) is 80° and of (b) 86°? $\frac{80°}{86°} \times \$7.55 = \$7.02$, the price that (b) should be to be equal in price because of the proof variation.

Table 14-3
Equivalents of volume in spirit containers.

Bottle	Ounces*	Milliliters
750 ml	25.4	750.00
Fifth (⅕ gal)	25.6	756.50
Quart (U.S.)	32.0	945.60
Imperial quart	38.4	1133.54
Liter	33.9	1000.00
1.75 liter	59.3	1750.00
3.00 liter	101.6	3000.00
Gallon	128.1	3780.00
Imperial gallon	153.7	4534.15

*In these calculations, the metric equivalent of an ounce was taken to be 29.5 ml volume. If this had been weight and not volume, an ounce would be equal to approximately 28.4 g.

To get an equivalent price when bottle sizes vary and the proofs and qualities are equal:

$$2. \frac{\textit{Bottle size of (a)}}{\textit{Bottle size of (b)}} = \textit{Equivalent price of (a).}$$

Thus, if a bottle of 750 ml or 25.4 oz of liquor (b) is $8, what should the equivalent price of a 32-oz (qt) bottle be when proof and quality of both are the same?

$$\frac{32 \; oz}{25.4} \times \$8 = \$10.08 \; \textit{equivalent price of 32 oz.}$$

If proofs vary and bottle sizes vary, one must combine the two formulas. Thus, if a 750-ml bottle of 80° proof liquor costs $6.50, what should the equivalent cost be of an 86° proof liter (1000-ml) bottle? The calculation is 1000/750 × 86/80 × $6.50 = $9.31 the equivalent price of the 1000 ml 86° proof bottle.

Table 14–3 indicates some comparative volumes in ounces and metric measures in various size bottles.

Prices of spirits or other beverages in different sized bottles are never quite equal because it costs more to bottle the same volume in smaller units than in larger ones. Thus, a spirit in a 0.750-L bottle costs more per ounce than the same spirit in a 1.75-L bottle. In using an automatic bar, the large units are thus less expensive.

ISSUING

One of the most important control points in the safeguarding of alcoholic beverages comes in the issuing. Issues should only be made after an authorized withdrawal slip, signed by someone authorized to make such withdrawals, is presented. A complete description of the item and the amount should be on the slip. Items should be marked with some identification indicating that it is an item issued by the operation.

(This is to prevent bartenders and others from bringing in their own products and dispensing them in place of the operation's and pocketing the money—a quick check of bar stock can reveal unmarked bottles in use.) The person receiving the items should sign for them at the time of issue. Only individuals authorized to receive such issues should be permitted to make them. Issues should be safeguarded in transit and should be carefully checked by those stocking them at bars or other places where active stocks are kept.

SUMMARY

Our consumption of alcoholic beverages has changed toward moderation. This is due in part to the actions of antialcohol groups such as MADD. Also federal and state regulations have become more strict and third-party responsibility has caused those engaged in serving alcoholic beverages to take more care to see that patrons do not drink to excess. Our federal government has also warned against the health dangers of excessive drinking. The alcohol industry is our most regulated industry.

Alcohol can be easily made by a process called fermentation. Wine and beers are not distilled but many fermented products called spirits are made by distillation. Wine and spirits usually improve with aging; beers do not. We designate the amount of alcohol in a beverage by stating the weight of the alcohol or its volume. The amount of alcohol in spirits and wine is given in volume or proof and in beers by weight.

The federal government has established standards of identity for most alcoholic beverages. A bourbon must be 51% or more corn whiskey. A true Scotch is produced only in Scotland. To be imported to this country it must be at least 80 proof and aged four years. Irish whisky is like Scotch but the barley is not smoked. Gin, vodka, and aquavit are distilled from a mash grain. Rums are spirits distilled from the fermented products of sugar cane. Brandies are spirits distilled from the fermented mash of fruit. Only a spirit distilled from grapes can be called brandy. If from other fruit, it must carry the name of the fruit such as apricot brandy. Cognac is a brandy made in the vicinity of Cognac, France. Armagnac is a French brandy made in southern France. Tequila is a spirit distilled from the fermented juice of cactus. Cordials or liqueurs are flavored sweetened spirits.

Wine is the product of partial or complete fermentation of the juice of fruit or berries. Only products made from grapes can be called wine. If made from another fruit, it must carry the name of the fruit such as blackberry wine. France has for years dominated the wine market but its supremacy is being challenged by a number of countries. A dry wine is a wine in which most of the sugar from the fruit has been fermented off. A wine over 14% in alcohol has had a spirit added to it to raise the alcohol level. Wines are sometimes classed as appetizers, dry dinner, and sweet (dessert) wines.

The main wine-producing areas in France are Champagne, Burgundy, Bordeaux, Rhône, and some others like Alsace. Germany's main wine-producing areas are Moselle-Saar-Ruwer, Rheingau, Hessian, and Palatinate. Italy has two districts, one north and one south. Its supervising authority over wine is known as the DOC. Austrian wines are much like those of Germany. Hungary, the states of the former Soviet Union, Spain, and Portugal also produce a significant quantity of wine each year. There are many other countries outside of Europe making excellent and considerable wine such as Australia and New Zealand, Chile, and Israel. The main wine-producing districts in the United States are California, Washington and Oregon, and Eastern areas.

The main type of beer consumed in this country is lager, which is made by a slow fermentation and is called bottom-fermented beer. Top-fermented beers include porters, ales, and stouts.

A buyer may have little choice in making some alcoholic beverage purchase decisions. Many guests drink only specific brands so there is no choice there. Some states allow certain sellers to carry specific brands or kinds of alcoholic beverages and so there is no choice in selecting a seller. Prices may also be set and a buyer who tries to get a price concession is breaking the law. Some states require purchases to be made through their own state-controlled warehouses.

Inventories should be kept at a minimum. An inventory turnover of from 8 to 20 times annually is desirable. Purchase orders should be carefully written with complete information. An authorized person must sign the purchase order.

Buyers may have to evaluate purchases on the basis of differences of proof between brands or between bottle sizes. Formulas are given for doing this.

The storage of spirits should be at room temperature; beers should be refrigerated; wine at around 50° to 60°F. Dry wines should be stored on their sides so corks do not dry out.

REVIEW QUESTIONS

1. What should one do about getting employees to report patrons who seem to be becoming inebriated?

2. Who is charged with regulation of the liquor industry?

3. Discuss how alcohol is produced and the conditions that must exist to produce a maximum amount. What part does yeast play in this process? What is the maximum alcoholic content that can be achieved by just yeast brewing?

4. What is a mash? What is a must?

5. At what temperature does alcohol boil? Water? What does this mean in the distillation process?

6. How is sulfur used in making wine?

7. Discuss the aging process used to age different alcoholic beverages.

8. What kinds of containers are used to age Scotch, beer, and wine?

9. What is a Cognac?

10. What is the angels' share?

11. Why is activated charcoal used on distilled spirits?

12. Define proof and percent alcohol. How do different areas of the world calculate proof?

13. What is the proof limit on whiskey in the United States? Minimum?

14. What is the weight of a pint of water? A pint of alcohol? Which beverage would contain the most alcohol, one of 14% alcohol by weight or 14% by volume?

15. Define the following as an alcoholic beverage:

a. spirit	g. Irish whisky	l. aquavit
b. brandy	h. liqueur	m. grain neutral spirits
c. bourbon	i. light rum	n. gin
d. rye	j. dark rum	o. saké
e. Canadian whisky	k. tequila	p. corn whiskey
f. Scotch		

16. What does a gin label mean when it says Holland? London? Compound? Sloe? Bathtub?

17. What is the federal tax per rectified 100 proof gallon?

18. Define wine.

19. What is phelgra or phlox?

20. What is pomace? What common cooking substance do we get from it?

21. Why are rosé wines called *vin de nuit?*

22. List the major classifications of wines.

23. What are the characteristics of German, French, American, and Italian wines that make them different? In what regions in each country are they produced?

24. What is champagne and why is it different from other wines? How is it made? What is riddling?

25. In beer making, what is top fermentation? Bottom fermentation?

26. Why is brand identification so important in the merchandising of alcoholic beverages?

SPECIFICATIONS

The regular form for a specification mentioned in the early chapters of this text can be used for the purchase of alcoholic beverages.

The name should clearly identify what is wanted. If the brand is the vital identifying factor, it might be given here. Thus, one might write: "Bordeaux (claret) wine, Château Latour, 1986." The second factor to list would be the amount required. Third should be the quality determinant, which is often the brand. If it has been mentioned in the name, there is no need to repeat it. Packaging should follow and the size of the unit and number of units to a case or packing should be clearly stated. Thus, one might specify for bourbon used for an automatic bar, "Shall come in 1.75-L bottles, 6 per case." Next, the price per package unit is listed. You must be sure there is no chance for ambiguity here. If the price is to be by case, note it; if the price is to be by bottle, note this. Leave no room for doubt. In competitive pricing the naming of price is omitted. Last, all the miscellaneous factors should be listed. This may be proof for a spirit.

Examples of specifications for some alcoholic beverages follow:

1. Wine, Petite Sirah   (Name)
2. 2 cases   (Amount ordered)
3. Concannon, estate bottled, 1970   (Quality determinant)
4. Case, 12 750-ml bottles   (Packaging)
5. $144 per case   (Price)
6. 12% alcohol, produced and bottled by Concannon vineyards, Livermore, California.   (Miscellaneous)

1. Wine, white table wine
2. 4 cases
3. Piesporter Goldtröpfchen, 1978, Michel Schneider brand, 8% alcohol by volume
4. Case, 12 750-ml bottles
5. $82/case
6. Qualitätswein b.A., Moselle-Saar-Ruwer wine; importer Accent Wine and Spirits

(*Note:* Some German wines can be imported without listing their alcoholic content, if they are listed as a table wine.)

1. Scotch, blended, (100% Scotch whiskies)
2. 1 case
3. Chivas Regal
4. Case, 12 750-ml bottles
5. $180/case
6. aged 12 years, 86 proof

1. Bourbon, Kentucky
2. 5 cases
3. Ezra Brooks, genuine sourmash
4. Case, 12 liter bottles
5. $95/case
6. Aged 7 years, 90 proof

1. Brandy, Cognac
2. 1 case
3. Remy Martin, VSOP, Champagne District

4. Case, 12 750-ml bottles

5. $185/case

6. (nothing needed)

1. Gin, London, dry

2. 2 cases

3. Burnetts

4. Case, 12 liter bottles

5. $88/case

6. 80 proof

1. Beer, Lager

2. 6 kegs

3. Budweiser

4. Kegs or ½ barrels, 15½ gal each

5. Contract price

6. Shall be delivered at a temperature 38° to 42°F.

(*Note:* It is important that beer be kept at a proper temperature because heat can damage it. Also, it is important that the amount of beer be specified in gallons to guard against kegs that have leaked or are not properly filled).

KEY WORDS AND CONCEPTS

aging	cogeners
angels' share	cordials
appellation contrôlée	corn whiskey
aquavit	Côte d'Or
beer	cremes
blended spirits	*cuvé* (first pressing)
bonded spirits	diastase
bottom-fermented beer	distillation
bourbon	DOC
brandy	dram laws
brewer's yeast	Federal Alcohol Administration Act (FAAA)
call liquor	
champagne	fermentation
Charmat process	finishing

gin

gin head

grain neutral spirits (continental)

Gay-Lussac system

Holland gin

inventory turnover

Irish whisky

lager beer

le dosage

light whiskey

liqueur d'expédition

liqueurs

London (English) gin

mash

monopole

must

natural process

negociant

percent alcohol

port

premiére taille (second pressing)

proof

rectification

riddling

riojas

rum

rye whiskey

saké

Scotch whisky

sherry

solera method

sourmash whiskey

spirit

straight spirit

tequila

top-fermented beer

vin de nuit

vin ordinaire

vintage year

Vitis lubrusca

Vitis vinifera

vodka

whiskey (also whisky)

wine

CHAPTER 15

Nonfood Supplies

1815 William Hutton, 30, Paradise Street Birmingham. Manufacturer of Various Articles Plated Upon Steel Viz Dessert Knives & Forks, Fish Knives, Nutcracks, Snuffers, Skewers, Cheese Scopes, Four Pronged Table & Dessert Forks, Table Dessert & Tea Spoons, &c &c and Sundry Other Articles in Imitation of Silver. From the Louis Szwathmary collection, Culinary Archives and Museum, Johnson and Wales University, used by permission of Dr. Szwathmary and Johnson and Wales University.

Chapter Objectives

1. To distinguish between clean and sanitary conditions and the steps and substances needed to achieve both in a food service.

2. To indicate the basic substances needed to satisfactorily perform laundry services.

3. To identify the kind and quality of table flatware, dishes, and glassware needed in food service operations.

4. To discuss the makeup, processing, and use standards required in textiles for foodservice and housing operations.

5. To identify and discuss paper goods and disposable wares.

INTRODUCTION

A food service requires many things other than food if it is to operate adequately, and a substantial amount of money must be spent for these things. Equipment is needed to produce the food; the proper tableware, napery, furniture, and other items must be purchased if the food is to be attractively presented. A facility must ensure those who eat the food that it is not only safe to eat, but clean, and that the facility itself is kept in a clean, sanitary condition. Supplies are needed to do this properly. Workers must also be neat and clean and wear attractive apparel. Flooring and walls, as well as furniture, should be carefully selected and well maintained. Many other items that need to be purchased are included in the non-food category.

It takes knowledge of what is required and how to select the best of such supplies to obtain maximum performance. As in buying foods, there is much to know, and one must be able to search the market and evaluate offerings. This chapter, therefore, presents a broad summary of some of the information needed for a buyer to do an adequate job of purchasing some nonfood items.

CLEANING AND SANITIZING

Clean and **sanitary** are not quite the same. Normally, when we say something is clean we imply it is sanitary, but we may sometimes call something clean when it is not sanitary. An eating utensil, for instance, might appear quite clean and yet harbor harmful, unseen bacteria. A plate might not appear clean because it shows egg left from breakfast after it is washed; but it might be completely sanitary and safe to eat from because, in the final rinse in the dishwasher, the temperature was sufficient to destroy any bacteria. Therefore, in deciding on which cleaning compounds to purchase, a buyer must know the cleaning and sanitary requirements. These may vary for different facilities. A food facility might not need a cleaning compound that sanitizes a floor completely, but a hospital has to have one that not only does a good job of cleaning but sanitizes it as well.

Soil on items is removed not by one but by a number of factors working together. If soil can be moistened, it softens and is more easily removed. Therefore, many cleaning compounds contain substances that help water enter into soil more quickly. Fats and oils resist water so solvents that dissolve them such as naphtha or benzene may be used. Some regulations do not permit the use of carbon tetrachloride in cleaning because it can give off extremely toxic fumes when exposed to fire. Carbon tetrachloride is also suspected of being carcinogenic and of producing liver damage. Special substances may be added to increase the ability of a cleaner to remove soil more easily, such as a special compound in a detergent that removes wax from a floor while cleaning it.

Some solvents work more quickly if they are warm, but a buyer must be sure that the item, when warmed, is not dangerous. Warming benzene or alcohol could result in a dangerous fire. It is best to eliminate such items and use others.

Suds may interfere with cleaning by stopping the soil from absorbing water and stopping the force of the water needed to remove soil. Technically, soil is moistened quickly if the surface tension or the resistance soil has to the penetration of water or other cleaning substances can be broken down. This is often an important factor to look for in a cleaning compound.

Certain chemical reactions can also remove soil. For instance lye or other alkaline substances **saponify** fats and oils; that is, they join with them to make soap. Too much saponification, however, can create so many suds in a dishwasher that effectiveness of sprays and pumps is reduced. Other substances emulsify fats and oils, dividing them into small particles so they remain suspended in water. Other substances, such as egg protein or other proteins, peptize soil; that is, the substance partially digests or changes the chemical structure so the item is much more easily put into solution. Other compounds ionize soil; ionization is a process in which the soil is given an electrical charge that attracts it to other substances so it can be pulled away from the item to be cleaned.

Many cleaning substances contain compounds that keep soil away from an item once soil is removed from it. Thus, we may remove soil from dishes and then have in the cleaning compound a substance that grabs onto the soil and does not let it get back on the dishes. Such compounds are called, respectively, **chelating** or **sequestering compounds.** (A *chela* is the pincer claw of a lobster or crab, and *sequester* means to hide away.)

However, after everything is done to make a cleaning compound as effective as possible, one more factor is required: physical force to remove the soil. Actually, in cleaning dishes in a dishwasher, about 30% of the work is done by the cleaning agent and 70% by the physical force of water forced through sprays. Water and the cleaning agent can help prepare the soil for removal, but mechanical force must remove it.

Water in Cleaning

Although water is an excellent solvent, it must be properly conditioned to be the most effective cleaning agent, and we may have to purchase special compounds to do this. If water is hard, that is, if it contains a large number of alkaline salts, it is not effective as a cleaning agent because many of the mineral salts in the water combine chemically with the cleaning compound, destroying its soil-removing properties. [Water is hard if it contains 10 grains of hard-water salts per gallon; if it contains 17 grains per gallon, it is quite hard. Or, water is hard if it contains 171 parts per million (ppm) of hard-water salts.] Hard water can also leave a film or spots on cleaned items that make the items appear soiled. This is what happens when dishes, glasses, or silverware are spotted after being cleaned.

Hard water can also deposit many of its mineral salts on equipment or in pipes. This reduces the effectiveness of the equipment and eventually plugs up the pipes. Such deposits are called **scale** or **lime**. They are the whitish substance seen inside a dishwasher or on a pan in which hard water was heated. Such scale must be removed.

Extremely soft water is called "metal hungry," which means that it can eat up some metals. It is necessary to treat some water so it will not be too hard or too soft.

We use phosphate, sodium-exchange, resin, or other types of water-softening compounds to make water soft. Or we may have to treat extrasoft water so it does not attack metals. When scale becomes a problem in equipment, we may use descaling compounds that dissolve and remove the liming.

Cleaning Substances

A **soap** is a chemical mixture of a fat and an alkali. Soaps are used much less today than previously because there are many chemical compounds that do a better and more specialized job of cleaning. These compounds are called **detergents,** and they usually contain substances that are either soil removers or water softeners, or both. The most commonly used substances in detergents are the following:

Soil Removers

1. Silicates
   a. Sodium metasilicate
   b. Sodium sesquisilicate
   c. Sodium orthosilicate
2. Carbonates
   a. Sodium carbonate (soda ash or washing soda)
   b. Sodium bicarbonate (baking soda)
3. Phosphates
   a. Trisodium phosphate (TSP)
   b. Chlorinated trisodium phosphate[1]
   c. Pyrophosphate
4. Caustics
   a. Sodium hydroxide (lye or caustic)

Water Conditioners

1. Sodium chloride
2. Sodium hexametaphosphate
3. Sodium tripolyphosphate
4. Tetrasodium pyrophosphate
5. Sodium tetraphosphate
6. Tetrasodium salt of ethylenediaminetetraacetic acid

Most soaps and detergents are alkaline, and frequently are strong enough to give a rather strong alkaline reaction. Some dishwashing detergents may have a **pH**[2] of 11 or more, and these can be dangerous if they get on the body or into the eyes. Be-

---

[1]The chlorine, around 2% of total ingredients, acts as a santizier in the washing process; this, coupled with sanitizing in the rinsing, ensures a better bacterial kill.

[2]A pH of 7 is neutral, neither acid nor alkaline, anything under a pH of 7 is acid, and anything over a pH of 7 is alkaline. A pH of 11 indicates a strong alkaline. A pH of 2 indicates a strong acid.

cause they are highly corrosive to brass, bronze, and aluminum, much milder agents must be used on these metals.

Some cleaning agents are buffered to reduce their corrosive action. An agent used for the hand-washing of pots and pans should not have a pH of over 9 or 10. Dangerous products must be labeled with the amount of active ingredients they contain and worded so that the users will understand they are using a product that might be harmful. Some pot and pan and other detergents have a color reactor that changes when the cleaning properties of the detergents are exhausted.

The cost of dish-washing has been said to be 7% detergent, 8% hot water, 19% breakage, 16% equipment, and 50% labor. Automatic dispensers are advisable for some cleaning equipment to give a steady, even flow of detergent. They may also reduce costs by preventing excessive doses and may improve job efficiency by seeing the right amount is added.

Abrasive powders should contain inert scouring substances that do not scratch a glass plate when rubbed vigorously on it. They should have a pH of 5 (slightly acid) to 11.5 and should rinse easily after use.

Floors require specific types of cleaners. Some asphalt and rubber can be attacked by some types of solvents.[3] Any cleaner used should clean well, dilute easily, mix readily with water, and rinse easily leaving no residue or film. Most should have low-foaming properties, and sanitizing substances may be desirable in some of them. A wax stripper should be easily diluted and applied, possess low-foaming characteristics, rinse well, and leave no residue that interferes with cleaning or re-polishing. Oils or other substances used on dusting or floor mops should not leave a slippery film or other undesirable residue. Floor polishes should have nonslip properties and be self-polishing. A solid floor polish should contain not less than 16% solids, and a liquid type not less than 12%. Polishes should protect floors against abrasion and water spotting; give a high, durable luster that stands up under heavy traffic; and be resistant to heel-marking and soil. They should not powder or pile up under traffic.

Vinyl floors usually do not need waxing; their soft luster is little improved with additional waxing. A mild liquid or other shampoo should be selected for cleaning rugs and furniture. It should clean soil away quickly and easily and not injure the fabric, backing, or colors. It is desirable for a rug cleaner to give antisoiling properties and give a longlasting luster to a fabric. Shampoos used with a rotary electric brush can be labor saving. Some good powder or flake cleaners are efficient in removing inert soil.

Furniture polishes should impart a soft luster and be resistant to the action of water or alcohol. They should not be oily or greasy or attract or hold dust; they should have a pleasant odor and be antistatic and nonflammable, giving a good, long-lasting luster to the surface.

---

[3]The Rubber Manufacturers' Association and the Asphalt and Vinyl Asbestos Tile Institute advise on proper types of detergents to use. The Institutional Research Council (221 West 57 Street, New York, NY 10019) can also be very helpful in giving advice on cleaning agents and in indicating what good specifications for them should contain.

Laundry Cleaners

Some facilities may operate laundries. It has even been found economical to install a small home-type washer and dryer in a food service to wash dishcloths, towels, and other light items. In larger units, a laundry may be operated, and highly specialized substances will be required. Purveyors who sell laundry supplies can be helpful in indicating the most desirable items for solving specialized problems.

Some common stain-removal agents are sodium hydrosulfite or sodium sulfoxalate formaldehyde. Detergents are usually tallow or low-titer (mild) soaps that work well in softened water. They should not be harmful to polyester or other natural or chemical fibers. Fabrics should be soaked in them to test them. Other detergents needed to give a more vigorous cleaning action may contain sodium metasilicate, sodium sesquisilicate, sodium orthosilicate, and TSP, either together or singly. For milder needs, an anionic detergent containing allyarylsulfonates or sulfonated alcohols is used. If the items to be washed are greasy, a carboxylated methyl-cellulose (CMC) is used; when the fabric is not harmed, caustic soda or bentonite clays are used. Most laundries use a sodium hypochlorite bleach or a high-test powdered hypochlorite with about 70% available chlorine. For white cottons, a bleach containing dichlorodimethylhyantoin and trichloroisocyanine acid is good. To remove alkaline substances remaining after rinsing, an acid compound called a **sourer** is used; these are either sodium, ammonium, or zinc fluorosilicate or ammonium fluoride. Some types of fabrics are harmed if any alkaline substance is left in them after washing.

TABLEWARE

The "top of the table" can make an important contribution to the general decor and merchandising. Food that is attractively presented with bright, sparkling, clean glassware, silverware, and dishes of suitable design and color is much more appealing than food not as suitably placed before a consumer. Intense colors such as green, yellow, brown, or orange may decrease appeal, whereas soft colors or white can enhance it.

The quantity of tableware needed depends on a number of factors. A fast turnover operation needs more dishes than a club where leisurely dining occurs. The speed at which items are washed and returned to service may be another factor. If needs are calculated on the number of seats and if the dining area is never fully filled, a higher-than-necessary inventory might be carried. A reserve must be carried, and its size usually depends on how long it takes to get replacements after they are ordered and also whether or not management is willing to tie up the capital required to carry it.

The number and type of menu items served and how frequently they are selected are also influential factors in deciding what and how much is needed. For example, it is not necessary to have an oyster fork for every house seat if only a few orders are sold at a time.

Many operations try to use one type of item for as many purposes as possible. Thus, a bar may eliminate stem cocktail glasses and serve most of its drinks in footless, old-fashion glasses or roly-poly glasses. A common dinner fork can be used for salads and desserts. An 8-oz grapefruit bowl can be used for fruit, dessert, salad, and even small servings of soup; a 6¼-in. plate can be used for salads, bread and butter, and desserts.

Other factors are important. One cafeteria found it could reduce breakage by nearly 25% if it carried enough tableware to get through a whole meal without washing any dishes. Labor and other factors have to be weighed in such a move, however.

PESTICIDES

Food services use pesticides designed largely to eliminate insects such as ants, cockroaches, flies, moths, and weevils. Some are toxic and need care in their storage and in their use. They should not be stored with food; preferably, they should be in a separate storage area that can be locked. Only those who know how to use them should do so, and they should never be used when food is exposed. Some may leave residues that might contaminate food if allowed to remain where food can contact them.

DISHES

Various **ceramics** are used for dishes. Facilities trying to create a certain atmosphere may use earthenware or pottery, but most will use **china (porcelain)**. **Earthenware** (terra cotta, brick, or flowerpot ware) is clay baked to around 1000°F into an unvitrified, soft, porous, and coarse product. It shatters easily and is usually made of low-grade clay. **Pottery** is the same thing, but is baked to a higher temperature. **Stoneware** is baked to around 2200°F, which vitrifies it and makes it into a solid, completely fused product like porcelain. It is usually used for small casseroles, ironstone, storage crocks, mixing bowls, and so on.

China is porcelain, a high-grade refined clay, baked to around 2500°F, so that it is completely fused or vitrified.[4] It must be resilient and withstand sharp shocks and raps. It should be able to be heated to 347°F in a dry oven, removed and plunged into 68°F water immediately and not shatter. The ratio of water to china in this test should be 8:1. No **crazing**,[5] cracks, or other defects should appear. A broken piece of porcelain at least 2½ in. square should not absorb more than 0.03% of its weight in water when boiled in water 5 hours and soaked in cold water for 20 hours or more. Federal standards for taking a blow or rap of a specified intensity in foot-pounds on the body or edge are indicated in Table 15–1.

---

[4]Vitrification is the process of being made into a completely homogenous glasslike product.

[5]When dishware develops cracks in it, it is said to be crazed.

Table 15-1
Federal standards for dishes.

Type Dish	Body Impact (ft-lb)	Edge Impact (ft-lb)
Bowls	0.30	
Fruit dishes	0.24	
Cups to 8 oz	0.06	
Cups over 8 oz	0.10	
Mugs	0.30	
Platters, saucers, plates, plain edges	0.18	0.10
Platters, saucers, plates, rolled edges	0.20	0.15

Ceramic strength depends on the quality of its clay and its processing. Bubbles, impurities, or poor mixing or blending can produce weak spots. A good china clay should be 40% kaolin, 6% ball clay (for plasticity), 18% flint or ground quartz (for strength), 15% feldspar (flint or quartz to give good fusing or vitrifying), and 1% whiting. If aluminum oxide replaces the flint or quartz, strength is increased 1½ times; lightweight china used in institutions is often made of this blend. Although it is strong, it has the defect of adding black marks when it scrapes across other china. Adding ground bone or calcium phosphate gives a more translucent and slightly stronger china called **bone** or **English china.**

Other factors affecting strength are the thickness of the china and "fashioning," such as putting on a rolled edge or an extra rim bead underneath (a scalloped edge is stronger than a plain one). Compactness of shape also strengthens. Putting extra clay in the well or center bottom of the dish helps to strengthen it and reduces star-cracking. If china receives a hard blow in the center bottom, it can show a number of cracks on the upper surface radiating out from the center like the rays from a star. This is called **star-cracking.**

Clay products are made by first forming the clay into the desired shape, called a **bisque.** It is then baked, and it emerges from the kiln as a dull, rough, but hard unit. A glaze, or miffle, is then put on it and it is baked so that the glaze bakes into the dish, producing a hard, bright, durable glaze cover that resists wear and improves appearance. A thin, tough glaze gives good wear. If the glaze is good, a unit should be serviceable for five years.

Decoration is a big factor in cost. Undecorated dishes are usually lowest in cost. Plain-colored or white china with a thin-line band is next in cost, and very simply decorated ware or plain ware with a scalloped edge next. China with a sprayed-on design, print decorated, decal decorated, and hand decorated follow, in that order, in cost. If the unit can be machine printed, the cost is lower. All decorating is done before the glaze is put on except for gold and silver, which must be put on afterward and usually by hand. Thus, gold and silver designs may not wear as well as others because they have no glaze to protect them.

Dishes are usually quoted per place setting, which includes five pieces: cup, saucer, plate, sauce dish, and bread-and-butter plate. A lightweight service costs about 25% more than a heavy one because of the extra loss in breakage during manufacture. Cups, creamers, pitchers, bowls, and other similar items are sold by the number of ounces they hold; plates, platters, saucers, and the like are sold by their actual or overall diameter size or by their trade size, which is the distance between the edge of the well and the opposite outside edge. It is recommended that actual measures be used in specifications, giving the width of the rim desired, if necessary.

Dishes should have good proportion and balance and stack well. Handles and other attachments should be firmly attached and permit easy handling. Deep cups or mugs are not comfortable to drink from because of the distance the head has to move back to empty them; shallow ones cool items too quickly. Heavy ware holds heat longer than lighter ware. Dishes should also be uniform in shape, weight, and thickness and be properly stressed to take shock and wear. A buyer should check the glaze for pitting, depth, and so on. Specifications should give the name of the dish, size, weight, pattern, shape, order number, and perhaps price. Open stock is a pattern held by manufacturers or dealers for immediate delivery—usually within 30 days. Custom-designed china costs more and orders take four to six months, replacements usually two or more months.

The five grades of china from best to poorest are (1) selects, (2) firsts (nearly perfect), (3) seconds (minor defects), (4) thirds (obvious defects but usable), and (5) culls or lumps (badly warped, chipped, or surface-scarred). Run-of-the-kiln is the two best grades plus the best of the seconds. Rejects are those not qualifying for any grade.

Plastic dishware is being used in many operations. It has a soft beauty and does not break; but it stains and abrades, although new methods of surface hardening have lessened these defects. It is also fairly resistant to the action of acids, alkalis, and other substances used in food production. It is light in weight, low in cost, and cleans well. However, it has a tendency to hold water on its surface, so drying is a problem.

Plasticware should be resistant to cracking when heated for eight hours at 170° F. Buyers should use the federal government's commercial standards CS 173-50 for establishing specifications for these items. Melamine and vinyl are the most frequently used plastics, although others are used—some disposable.

Common **glass** is made from silica, soda, lime, and **cullet** (old broken glass). **Crystal** or rock crystal is common glass with lead oxide and potassium silicate added. If boric oxide replaces lime, the product can be used for cooking, as Pyrex is. Corning glass can also be heated, and because it contains metals and other substances to give it strength and durability it is stronger. Pyroceram is a glass originally developed for use in the nose of rockets that had to reenter the atmosphere. It is fused clay, silica, and some rare metals. It makes a highly durable china.

Common glass is the least expensive and increases in cost as other substances are added to it. Decoration can also increase cost. Corning ware is less expensive than decorated china and Pyroceram is about twice as expensive as china. Cut glass is crystal that has been cut so the cut surfaces give it a special brilliance. It is quite expensive.

Glass can be decorated by coloring it or by etching it with fluorine or sandblasting. Or it can be decorated by placing enamel on it by decal or silk screen; the enamel is then fused to the glass by heat. Companies usually require that a gross of an item be ordered before they will put a special decorative design or a logo on glassware.

The least expensive glass is shaped by machine molding or pressing. Glass can also be blown by machine, which reduces its cost over blowing by mouth. A faintly raised line indicates **blown glass** made by machine molding. If a mold is lined with wet clay paste a smoother, brighter surface is obtained, giving what is called line-paste molded glass. Mouth-blown glass is also called custom-made. Some glassware may have the edges hand-beveled or ground down. This increases the cost.

Buyers should check glassware to see that parts fused to it are strong and secure. Glass can be hardened by reheating it so as to reorient the molecular structure on the surface; this is called annealing. Although this gives added durability, if the item is chipped or cracked it is apt to shatter from the heavy force or pull exerted on the item. Corning ware does this. French duraglass does the same thing. A rolled bead, added thickness of glass, a barrel or bell shape, and other things can be done to strengthen glass. Flared and stemmed glassware is weak. Returning the flare to a smaller area strengthens the glass and using a thick, short, fluted stem instead of a long stem reduces breakage. Air bubbles, specks, muddiness, uneven surface, poor balance and proportion, and untrue, rough edges are considered defects. Bottom weight helps reduce top heaviness, and glassware should be tested to see that it does not tip over easily.

FLATWARE (SILVERWARE)

Metal eating utensils such as spoons, forks, and knives are often called **flatware.** It may be made of silver, silverplate, plastic, or stainless steel.

Very few operations use pure silver flatware because of the cost and its softness. Instead silver plate, which is much more durable and less expensive, is used. The interior of plated flatware is a **blank** or metal alloy, frequently nickel and silver. Some blanks today are an alloy of 60 to 67% copper, 17% nickel (to give hardness), and not more than 0.35% iron, 0.5% manganese, 0.05% sulfur, and 0.25% other impurities; the remainder is about 15% zinc. Such blanks are called nickel brass or, erroneously, nickel silver. Sometimes areas of greatest wear may be specified as having 18% nickel to give extra hardness. Britannia, or white metal, used for blanks is a tin alloy containing not less than 80% tin. Blanks containing much iron will rust.

Silver is put onto the blanks by **electrolysis,** a process in which an electrical current picks up silver in a solution and deposits it on the blank. The depth of the silver is based on a standard of the quantity of silver deposited on a gross of standard-size teaspoons, and all other units will have an equal depth. Thus, 8 oz of silver on a gross of teaspoons is called **heavy hotel plate** or quadruple plate; 6 oz is triple; 5 oz is standard or A-1; 4 oz is banquet; and 2½ oz is half-standard. Table 15–2 gives some standards for a rather light blank but good silver coverage frequently used in specifications for **silverplate** flatware.

Table 15-2

Standards for silverplate flatware.

Item	Blank Weight (avoir, oz/doz*)	Silver (troy oz/gross*)
Forks, dessert	18	15
Forks, dinner	24	20
Knives, dessert, hollow handle		15
Knives, dinner, hollow handle		20
Knives, dinner, hollow handle only		10
Knives, dinner, solid handle only		8
Spoons, coffee	13	6
Spoons, dessert	18	15
Spoons, soup	18	15
Spoons, table	24	20
Spoons, tea	11	9

*Blanks are usually stated in avoirdupois ounces and silver in troy ounces.

Sometimes a finished weight is listed in the specification; the following, in ounces per dozen, are frequently used as standards for fairly heavy plateware:

Forks, oyster	10.67	Spoons, dessert	24.33	Knives, dinner*	40.67
Forks, dessert	24.67	Spoons, table	32.00	Knives, dessert*	34.67
Forks, salad	22.67	Spoons, tea	16.33	Knives, tea*	20.00
Forks, dinner	29.33	Spoons, iced tea	16.00	Knives, meat or	
Spoons, coffee	6.40	Spoons, bouillon	16.67	viand*	32.00

*Hollow handle only.

A specification often indicates the standard weight for the blanks by stating the weight of a gross of teaspoons, requiring all the other blanks to conform to this standard. The heaviest blank weight specified for a gross of teaspoons is 11 lb, 10½ lb is next, and the lightest is 9 lb. The weight of the silver plate is also specified in troy ounces or as "extra heavy hotel," "triple," and so on.[6] A tolerance of 15% under the specified weight is permitted on individual units, and 5% of the average of three or more units is permitted in the same shipment.

Wear occurs more at points of use or contact, such as the tips of fork tines, backs of the bowls of spoons, or tips of handles where the object rests on a surface. Specifications may require that such spots be "inlaid" with extra silver, which is brushed, sprayed, or dipped on at these points before silverplating.[7] Usually the specification

---

[6]Instead of this, the actual depth is stated, such as a depth of 20 microns of silver (extra-heavy hotel) or a depth of 0.00125 in. of silver plate (triple), which is about a troy ounce per square foot of surface covered.

[7]Inlays are sometimes put on after silverplating and are burnished to remove evidence of the addition. This works as well as putting it under the silverplate. When this is done, the added silver is called an "overlay."

states that the minimum depth on the middle line of the bearing surface at this inlaid point shall not be less than 0.0018 in. deep after silverplating. An inlaid spoon has about 60% of its silver on the back and 40% on the front.

The quantity of silverplate on flatware is checked by soaking a teaspoon in 19 parts sulfuric acid to 1 of nitric acid, warmed to 180°F, until the silver disappears. A banquet-weight teaspoon should lose about 0.8 grams, a triple plate 1.2 grams, and extra-heavy hotel 1.6 grams. Inlays are checked by allowing the acid to remove the silver only until the inlay is exposed as bright spots or as lines on the bearing point of the blank.

The composition of the blank is not the only factor making silverplate durable. Fashioning is also important. Blanks are stamped out and then receive further shaping, sometimes called grade-rolling, which hardens the blank and also increases thickness where stress occurs and thins the item where less stress occurs. Good grade-rolling also gives the item better balance lines and proportion. A buyer may check strength by doing the following:

1. Placing a fork tine on a hard edge and putting pressure on it to bend it.
2. Bending a spoon where the bowl joins the handle.
3. Checking the junctures of stainless steel blades and handles, noting whether the blade is cemented or soldered in or is solid with the handle (cemented blades loosen easily).
4. Trying to dent a spoon bowl by striking it a hard blow with a hard, sharp object.
5. Checking junctures to see if they are secure, well plated, and well burnished; tacking should not be permitted.

Ware should be checked to see that it has a smooth, even coating of silver and proper placement of inlays or overlays. Knife blades should be good stainless steel and usually **serrated** to give a rough cutting edge. The ware should have good balance in the hand and good grip. Designs should be deep and neatly done. There should be no pitting or other defects. (Silverplate that is heavily decorated or designed shows scratches less easily.) Designs are usually stamped by machine. Figure 15–1 shows how flatware is made.

An institution may use silverplated items called holloware, such as pitchers, platters, creamers and sugars, and the like. Edges should be turned in to give extra strength and reduce chances for denting. Seams should clean easily. Handles should be separated from the unit by insulation if the container is to hold hot items. The insulation should be guaranteed against loosening. Points of juncture should be well soldered with silver or hard solder that has a melting point of 1300° to 1600°F and not the soft solder sometimes used on home ware. The gauge should be heavy enough to take the heavy wear such units are subjected to. Frequently, the blank is copper, but it may be a blend. Points of extra wear may be specified as having an extra inlay of silver. Spouts on pitchers and other units from which liquids are poured should be of the nondrip type. Lids should open to at least 150 to 180° and rest against the handle so the item can be washed and then inverted for good draining.

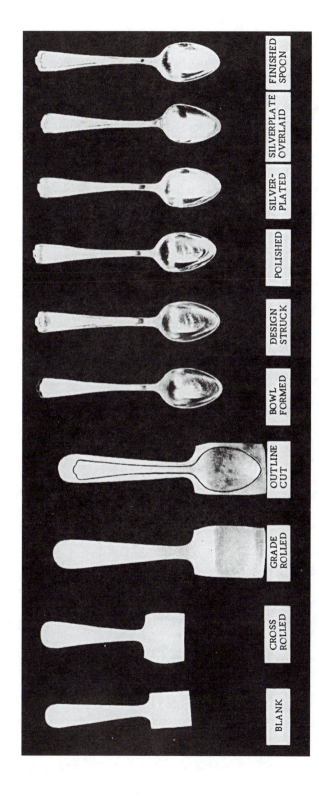

Figure 15–1

Flatware is first made from a blank that is cross- and grade-rolled and then outline cut to give the desired shape. The bowl is then formed by machine and any desired designs are made. It then is polished and silverplated. If specified, an overlay will be put on and final polishing will be done. (Courtesy Edward Don & Co. Reprinted with permission.)

Stainless steel flatware is being used more and more, and very fine quality items that are quite attractive are now available (see Table 15–3). It is a strong, durable metal that is difficult to dent, stain, or scratch. It does not need burnishing, is rust free, and is easy to clean. Unlike silverplate, it does not need replating and resists tarnishing. It requires little care.

Specifications for stainless steel flatware should require either 18-8 or 17-7 chrome-nickel steel (18 or 17% chromium, 8 or 7% nickel and 74 or 76% steel), or a higher chrome alloy called 301, 302, or 410 can be specified. The federal government standard RR-F 450a specifies 410 for knives and 301 or 302 for spoons and forks. A cheaper ware is made using 430-type chrome-steel. Chrome is used to give a soft luster, and nickel and steel are used for hardness and strength. Lower grades of stainless steel show a blue, metallic color that may also be uneven. If too much chrome is present, the alloy corrodes more easily. Stainless steel pits if it comes into contact too much with soft metals such as aluminum or brass. Pitchers, platters, dishes, and other stainless steel ware should be specified as 18-8, 16 gauge, or better. The heaviest gauge used is No. 10, about 9/64 or 0.1345 in. thick. Flatware should be from 0.087 to 0.105 in. (about 12- to 13-gauge) thick.

The best flatware is fashioned by heavy roller pressure (grade-rolled) to vary the thickness and give the item better proportion, lines, and balance; this fashioning also strengthens it. Lower quality ware may be stamped out and have the same thickness throughout. It also shows rough edges where the cutting stamp cuts the piece from the stainless steel sheet. All fork edges should be round and smooth, and the back of handles should be slightly concave. Tines should be smoothly tapered, with their insides ground or coined so that all edges are well rounded. All edges should be rounded and smooth and show no roughness. The items should be free of rough grinding marks, pits, scales, burns, or other imperfections. Usually mirror finish is specified for the inside of spoon bowls and No. 7 finish, called satin, for the other parts.

Knives are best serrated, with serrating at least 1¾ in. from the tip along the blade. The cutting edges of knives should be canneled, and the blade should taper

Table 15–3

Specification sizes for stainless steel flatware.

Item	Approx. Length (in.)	Average Min. Handle Thickness (in.)	Average Min. per Gross
Spoon, tea	6	0.085	8¾
Spoon, dessert (oval)	7⅛	0.095	14
Spoon, bouillon	6	0.085	8½
Spoon, iced tea	7⅝	0.090	9¼
Spoon, table or serving	8¼	0.095	17½
Fork, table (utility)	7⅜	0.090	12
Fork, salad	6⅝	0.065	8
Knife, solid handle	8½		22

uniformly from the tip to a point not more than ¾ in. from the handle. Hollow handles should be securely welded to the blade and not soldered. Solid handles should be integral with the blade.

Since stainless steel is a poor heat conductor, it is seldom used for cooking utensils. If it is, the cooking is done over steam or with steam to obtain a more uniform heat. Frying pans and other cooking units are either double bonded with an iron core inside, which spreads the heat around uniformly, or have a copper bottom to distribute the heat uniformly into the stainless steel. Because stainless steel is durable and does not react with many food alkalis or acids, it is very suitable for use in many pots and pans that are not used for cooking.

Specifications for flatware should indicate the weights, qualities, sizes, material from which it is made, polish or finish, quality of workmanship, and wrapping; it is usually wrapped to ensure against scratching and boxed according to good commercial practices, not more than three dozen per box. A specification may require the submission of samples before the bid is accepted, and payment may be withheld until it is determined that the shipment conforms to the samples.

TEXTILES

A food service uses many different **textiles.** A good seated-service restaurant needs good tablecloths and napkins and workers who appear neat and attractive in their uniforms. Washcloths, towels, and other textile items are needed. Fabrics cover furniture, draperies are made from them, and rugs or carpeting is made of textile fibers. For best service, attractiveness, quality, and lowest cost, a buyer has to know a lot about textiles—how to select and care for them. Gaining applicable knowledge is complicated by constant change. For instance, within a period of a year, almost the entire carpet industry changed from traditional methods of manufacture to a process by which yarns are set into plastic or rubberized backings. And in a short time knits began to be widely used for uniforms. New manufactured fibers may suddenly appear on the market, causing rapid change in fabrics offered on the market and their subsequent care. Wrinkle-proof, waterproof, wash-and-dry, and many other treatments have changed fabric selection considerably.

Because of serious fires that killed many people, many states and communities have enacted strict laws on the kind of textiles institutions can use. These cover the kind of fabric allowed and special treatment that must be given to make them safe to use. Buyers must know what the local regulations are and see that they are met. In addition to safety from fire danger, these laws often include safety measures aimed at preventing accidents. In some areas long, large looped yarns are not allowed in carpeting because women's high heels easily catch in them. Or special construction of textiles may be required to reduce hazards. In certain places, no textiles at all are allowed, to reduce the chances of accident. Buyers should know all of these provisions.

Biohazards

Some concern has been expressed by the public about substances in textiles that can be a danger to health. This often centers around particles that get into the air and cause allergies, asthma, or other problems. The use of asbestos materials is avoided because of the known danger asbestos particles can have to health. Cotton particles are suspected of causing lung problems. Noxious fumes from some substances have also caused complaints. Often these quickly dissipate and cause no problems. Many new textiles do have a "new textile odor," but very little evidence exists to show they are health hazards.

Fibers

Natural Fibers

Natural fibers much used for textiles are cotton, linen, wool, and silk. Others used less often are hemp, ramie, and jute. Cotton, linen, hemp, ramie, and jute are called *cellulose fibers*. They are related to substances such as wood, grass, and other plant tissues. Wool and silk are animal or protein fibers.

   Cotton is one of the least expensive and most used fibers (Figure 15–2). It is attacked by acids but not by moderate alkalis. It is durable, makes nice appearing fabrics because it drapes well, and is comfortable at warm temperatures because it absorbs moisture well. Creasing and wrinkling are problems unless the cotton is made resistant to them. It is stronger wet than dry, which gives it a long laundering life. Cotton seams hold well and show little slippage in uniforms and other fabrics. Cotton launders well and washes rather easily; it shrinks about 5%, but can be made shrink-proof. Good cottons can be woven into very fine yarns, but can also be made into heavy ones for making canvas and the like.

   Linen is a bast fiber, the inner portion of flax. It absorbs moisture well and therefore is excellent for toweling. It does not retain its strength as well as cotton in laun-

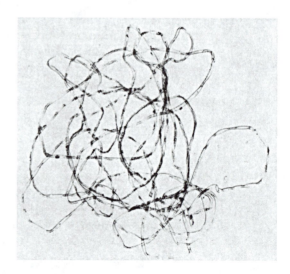

Figure 15-2
Each fiber has special characteristics that make it more or less suitable for uses in textiles. A single cotton fiber looks like this under a microscope. The actual length is 1 ¾ in., nearly 200 times its width. (Courtesy USDA.)

dering and is attacked by alkalis and bleaches more easily. It is expensive but, because it has a soft gloss and a crisp texture, it is especially suitable for table napery. It sheds dirt easily but wrinkles and creases more easily than cotton.

Ramie, also a bast fiber, comes from the stalks of China grass. It is strong, flexible, and makes crisp fabrics that have even better luster than linen. It is therefore used in napery but is more expensive than linen. Jute and hemp are low-cost fibers used for burlap sacks, rope, nets, and so forth.

Wool is the fleece of sheep or other animals, such as camels, llamas, vicunas, guanacos, alpacas, angora rabbits, angora goats (mohair), Kashmir goats (cashmere), and reindeer; even some animal furs are included. Most are expensive. Some, like cashmere, abrade easily and pill—that is, the fibers roll up into tiny balls on the fabric. Mohair has excellent tensile strength and durability and for this reason is used as a furniture covering. Coarse wool is an excellent fiber for making carpeting.

Wool is attacked by alkalis but not by mild acids. It has excellent resiliency and does not wrinkle easily. It springs back into shape after being pressed. It is weaker wet than dry and shrinks badly. It will also felt or pack. It takes dyes fairly well but not as well as some of the competitive man-made fibers such as Acrilan. It will nap well and therefore is a warm fiber because it holds air. Wool has good moisture absorption and feels warm even when damp. To test the strength of the nap of a blanket or other napped item, stick a pin into it and lift up. The pin should not break out; pinching and lifting is about as good a test. When ironed, wool creases well and holds it shape. Because it does not burn easily, it is desirable for blankets and rugs, where cigarettes might be dropped.

Silk comes from the cocoon of a silkworm. Wild silk (*tussah* or *tussore*) comes from undomesticated forest silkworms; it is stronger and coarser. Silk is a poor conductor of heat and is therefore warm. It builds up static electricity. Dyes hold well in it. It is strong but abrades and has less strength when wet. The fabric water-spots easily. It is expensive but is used for some finer draperies, uniforms, and furniture coverings. Silk rug fibers are strong and beautiful. Silk can be weighted, which gives it added weight but can make it lose strength. Acids, especially strong ones, attack silk, as do some caustics.

Man-made Fibers

Many **man-made fibers** are produced today. Rayon and acetate are cellulose-base fibers, and rayon was at one time next to cotton in use. Both are inexpensive.

Rayon lacks resiliency and strength but absorbs moisture well and launders or cleans well. It stretches when damp and shrinks when dry but has good moisture absorbency, especially in toweling. Rayon is highly flammable and should not be used for napped items such as bath mats or for draperies, bedspreads, and the like unless treated to be nonflammable. Modified rayon, such as Fortisan, is good for curtains and draperies because it has low moisture absorption and does not expand or contract. Cross-linked rayons, such as Zantrel, and blends of cotton and rayon are very suitable for uniforms. Rayon can be treated to have wash-and-wear and other minimum-care properties.

Acetates are used largely for draperies or curtains because of their soft, luxurious luster. They hold dyes well but may fade from atmospheric gas attack. They launder and bleach well but must be ironed at low temperatures. Some acetates are easily attacked by alkalis found in mild soaps and detergents, so may not be as suitable for use as some other types of fibers.

There are a number of man-made acrylic fibers. They are light in weight, wash and dry easily, shrink little, and dye well. They are strong and wear well, but some pill easily. They are excellent for carpeting and blankets. Acrilan blankets are much lighter than wool ones and almost as warm. Some, like the modacrylics, are highly resistant to chemicals. Orlon is an excellent acrylic fiber for use on outdoor furniture coverings, awnings, and draperies because it is light resistant and quite durable. It is flammable unless treated. Because of the number of acrylics and the fact that they may not be suitable for some purposes, buyers should check their specific properties before making a purchase. New ones are appearing constantly.

Nylon is one of the strongest fibers made. It has a soft, fine luster that gives it silklike qualities. It is fairly resistant to chemicals and other factors that attack fabrics and has low moisture absorbency, drying quickly. It is static, but can be treated for this, and it yellows in time. Nylon is excellent for carpeting but quite static when so used so it should be treated for static problems. It may be used for uniforms but is hot because it holds heat in. It makes beautiful draperies and upholstering fabrics but tends to slip in the latter use.

Saran is a very durable fiber, excellent for use in outdoor furniture and for carpeting, where stains are a problem. For this reason it is often used for carpeting dining or kitchen areas. However, it is rather harsh and lacks flexibility when used in carpeting.

Olefins are light fibers that equal wool in warmth. They do not wrinkle easily and have good elasticity and washability. They also are fairly resistant to alkalis and acids. Unlike some other woollike man-made fibers, olefins do not pill and have a low static buildup. However, they take dyes poorly and crock easily (**crocking** is a defect in which the dye tends to transfer from the fabric to the body or to other items in contact with it). Mineral and food oils can stain them; they are not strong; and they have poor abrasion qualities. But because of their other qualities they are often used for blankets and similar materials.

Polyester fibers such as Dracon, Fortrel, Kodel, and Vycron are widely used today for drip-dry clothing, curtains, washable rugs, and other items. For tablecloths and napkins, Dacron may be combined 50:50 with cotton. Polyester fibers resist wrinkling and some may pill. They are not easily attacked by mildews, acids or alkalis, or insects.

Glass is mostly used for curtaining materials. It has a beautiful sheen and drapes well, but it can absorb soil, which is difficult to remove. If the fabric is subjected to too much movement, it shatters or abrades. Cleaning is a problem because rough handling can shatter it. Also, it takes dyes poorly.

New man-made fibers are constantly appearing, taking over from those mentioned here, which have been with us for some time. These new products are often far better than the older ones and buyers should check the new against the old to make an evaluation of their suitability for the intended use.

Table 15–4 compares some older and new textile fibers.

Table 15-4
Textile fibers comparison.

Fiber	Good Features	Bad Features
Cotton	Tradition, comfort, low cost	Shrinkage, DP appearance, rot resistance outdoors
Wool	Tradition, comfort, appearance, low flammability	Cost, felting, insect and alkali damage
Silk	Tradition, comfort, appearance	Cost, stain removal, care requirements
Linen	Tradition, comfort, crisp look	Wrinkling, flex abrasion, cost, care
Polyester	Low cost, excellent DP appearance, excellent physical properties	Comfort, oily soiling, stiffness, "image"
Nylon	Elasticity, abrasion resistance, low flammability	Cost, sunlight resistance
Acrylic	Bulky, soft, light, "wooly," outdoor stability	Flammability, elasticity
Modacrylic	Low flammability, shrinkability	Low melting point
Polypropylene	Light weight, excellent mechanical properties, wicking	Low melting point, nondyeable
Aramid	High temperature resistance, light weight with stiffness, flame resistance, extreme toughness	Very expensive, sunlight resistance
Spandex	High stretch and powerful elastic recovery, better than rubber	Expensive
Rayon	Appearance, prints well, comfort	Wrinkles, burns
Acetate	Hand and drape	Poor abrasion resistance and other mechanical properties
Glass	Stiff, strong, cheap, nonflammable	Heavy, abrasion resistance

Source: Courtesy of Robert S. Merkel, Florida International University.

Yarns

Fibers are spun into yarns, that are woven into fabrics. Short fibers make heavy, bulky and weaker yarns and long ones make the finer, stronger yarns used in thinner fabrics. Long wool yarns are called **worsted,** and short ones are called **woolen yarns.** Silk fibers are usually long enough to spin into fine yarns. Staple cotton is long and makes a fine yarn. Combed or carded yarns are short and are made into heavier yarns. Yarn sizes for cotton, wool, and linen are stated in **hanks,** whereas silk and other filament yarns are stated in **denier sizes.**

Weaving

When yarns are interlaced in weaving, a fabric is made. Lengthwise yarns are called **warp** and yarns running across the fabric are called **weft** or **fill** yarns. Warp yarns usually have a higher twist and are of better quality than fill yarns.

Fabric strength is decided by the type of fiber in the yarn, the way the yarn is spun or twisted, its size, and the manner in which the fabric is woven. A loose weave produces a weak fabric called **sleezy** because its yarns move. The number of yarns per inch in the warp and fill has much to do with fabric strength. Thread count is usually stated in number of warp and fill yarns per square inch. Thus, a utility percale used for sheets with a thread count of 90 and 90 (a balanced count) is called Type 180. A fabric with a high count shrinks less, has less tendency to ravel, is stronger, and gives better wear.

The type of weave can be a factor in wear and appearance. Tight weaves that have little or no float (long overlapping) weaves wear the best. Figure 15–3 shows how some of the common weaves are made. Most woven goods have **selvages,** which are the two edges, often woven of stronger warp yarns and much tighter together than the rest of the fabric to give stability and resistance to ravel. Different types of selvages are used, but sheets, towels, and other materials usually have a plain selvage.

Pile weaves are used in toweling, carpeting, or upholstering fabrics. A pile has three dimensions—the warp, the fill, and a loop. **Terry toweling,** the old Axminster carpets, and velvet or velour are examples of this loop (pile or "hairy caterpillar") weave. Chenille is a pile fabric, with an extra fiber across it, which actually gives it four and not three dimensions. This is why a chenille rug is so durable and is often used in institutions where there is much wear but an attractive rug is still desired. A friezé is a pile yarn, tightly twisted, with a stuffer (extra) yarn in it; that makes it popular for furniture fabrics because it has good wearing qualities and the ability to keep a good appearance with hard wear. Mohair yarns made from angora goat wool may be used for friezé or straight-cut pile fabrics to give extra wear, because this fiber is very strong and still resilient.

Pile in a fabric used in an institution should be heavy and dense for durability and, in terry toweling for good moisture absorbency. Dense pile in carpeting and upholstery material prevents shedding pullout and makes the pile stand more erect. It also wears better if of good yarn. A pile that flattens is unattractive in many upholstering or carpet materials. A pile fabric's quality is affected by the number of threads per square inch, the type of fiber and yarn, and the weaving. A pile fabric should be checked by getting hold of the pile or loop and pulling to see if it comes out.

Tufting is a kind of pile weave. Tufting machines use hundreds of needles making an up and down tuft, each needle fixing a loop or tuft of yarn into a base or warp and then brings the yarn up and then down to make the loop fixing the other end of the loop now into the base or warp. Tufting is largely used for carpeting. The warp or base today is usually a plastic. Specify interlock tufting to avoid unraveling (unzipping).

Jacquard weaves may combine basic weaves; they are intricate weaves made by a special weaving machine. Until Jacquard invented the machine, such designs had to be woven by hand, which made them very expensive. Jacquard is used for draperies and furniture coverings. Brocades are produced by a Jacquard loom, but they also are made by hand, which makes them very costly. A damask is woven on a Jacquard loom and is used for linen, cotton, or other tablecloth materials. It has the same design on each side of the fabric.

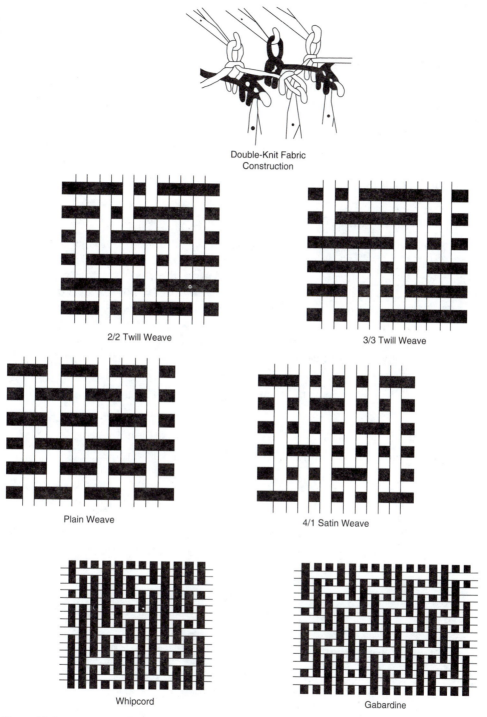

Double-Knit Fabric
Construction

2/2 Twill Weave

3/3 Twill Weave

Plain Weave

4/1 Satin Weave

Whipcord

Gabardine

Figure 15-3
A comparison of some of the common weaves used.

Nonwoven Fabrics

Some nonwoven fabrics are on the market and have limited use, largely as wiping materials in kitchens, bars, dining areas, and others. These are usually made from fibers that have a high moisture absorbency, light weight, and are made in flat sheet form, by pressing or some process that makes a matted sheet composed of loose webbing. They are often purchased as handy wipes or under other brand names. They have limited durability but because of cost are used. They are thrown away after being used. They generally cannot stand up to washing.

Laws and Standards

Specific laws have been passed to protect buyers and give the market better organization. Woolen-fabric labels must state the quantity and type of wool, if the fabric contains more than 5% wool. If the label states the wool is "virgin wool," it must be that; reused wool must be named. Laws also prohibit false or deceptive statements in labels on fabrics. Stuffing in furniture must be identified. The type of fiber or the blends in a fabric must be stated. If a label says a product is shrink-proof, it cannot shrink more than 5%. No label can say a fabric is colorfast because all fabrics fade some. Buyers should learn to read labels. Certain colors on labels indicate the type of washing the fabric can receive:

Purple	Washing at 160°F with bleach
Green	Washing at 160°F without bleach
Blue	Washing at 120°F without bleach
Yellow	Washing at 105°F without bleach
Red	Dry cleaning only

In most hotels, motels, and other institutions open to the public, fabrics must now be treated to be nonflammable.

The textile industry has established a number of self-regulating standards. The American Standards Association developed the *American Standard Performance Requirements for Textile Fabrics* (L-22-1960), and the *Minimum Performance Requirements for Institutional Textiles* (L-24). These establish standards helpful to buyers and have provided a base on which to write specifications. Many of the trade magazines and other publications in the industry also help to maintain standards.

Textile Specifications

A specification for a textile product and the use made of it in the facility must be specifically written for that product. A variety of conditions may underlie requirements; these will dictate what is in the specification. Specifications can be written in considerable detail, naming many of the factors shown in Table 15–5.

Sheets and Pillowcases

Sheets and pillowcases should be specified by type of fabric, which is usually based on a good yarn from staple cotton or a blend of cotton and polyester fiber, if non-

Table 15-5

Textile specification details.

Factor	Explanation
Tensile or breaking strength of the fabric, warp, or fill, either wet or dry	The greatest stretch force a yarn or fabric can take
Resistance against yarn shifting or slippage	About 0.05 or $\frac{1}{20}$ in. (1¼ cm)
Colorfastness under many different factors	No fading after 40 hours under a fadeometer
Maximum shrink	Nonshrink shall not shrink more than 2%
Resistance to abrasion, pilling, moths, mildew, atmospheric or other attack	
Washing or dry cleaning qualities	
Water repellency or ability to resist soil or other factors	
Nonflammability or other treatment, such as wrinkling or crease resistance	

press. A thread count of 70 × 70 is about the heaviest yarn used. This is type 140 yarn and is called **carded cotton muslin.** It should have a minimum tear strength of 70 lb, wet or dry; have 4% maximum sizing and 6% maximum shrink; and weigh 4.6 lb/sq yd. Type 180 (90 × 90 thread count) is called **utility percale** and has a carded or combed cotton thread. Wet or dry tear strength, fill, shrink, and weight-per-square-yard standards should be in tear strength 60 lb, 2% maximum, 5% shrink maximum, and 3.6 lb/sq yd. Luxury or supercale, type 200 (100 × 100), should have 60 lb, 1%, 4%, and 3.6 lb, respectively. Some specifications state that a sheet of torn-length-size of 108 in. should not shrink more than 5 in. in five washings. Sheets and cases should be specified as non-bleach-retentive. If the sheets are colored, the specification should state a colorfastness of 40 hours under a Fadeometer light. Also, these products should be colorfast to high temperatures and bleach. Nonpress sheets and pillowcases have become very popular and buyers should consider strongly their use. Many specify 50% combed cotton and 50% polyester as the fiber ratio. Fitted sheets should also be specified. A fitted sheet is one made to fit around the mattress. The size of the mattress to be fitted should be specified in our and in metric measures. Many add to their specifications stretch corners for easy fitting and also preshrinking, which limits shrink to 1½% or less.

Sheets are specified in torn size, after hemming and washing; a 108-in. torn-size sheet will be about 98 in. This permits a 6- to 7-in. tuck at the head and foot. Some buyers specify sheets at 113 in. torn size, while others find 99 in. long enough. A 6- to 7-in. tuck is usually desired on either side. In some cases, a longer than 6-ft bed is used and sheets must be longer than 108 in. for them.

Buyers should specify pillowcases from tubular rather than flat material because it fits a pillow better. The pillowcases should also be specified to be sized after hemming and to have, after shrinkage, a size 2 in. longer and 4 to 8 in. wider than the pillow. Specify also preshrinking with a shrink in use of 2% or less.

Sheets and pillowcases are usually given a 2- to 3-in. hem. Hems should be stitched with a No. 60/3-ply thread not less than 12 stitches per inch. Hem ends should be backstitched and thread ends tacked to give extra strength and prevent raveling. Bar tacking may be recommended. Selvages should be strong, even, and not more than ⅜ in. wide. The tensile-strength loss of the fabric should not be greater than 10% after 20 washings.

Toweling

Terry toweling should be specified to weigh a minimum of 11.9 oz/sq. yd. and to have double thread, loose twist, and ⅛-in. loops on both sides. The fabric should also have a tight, close weave. Maximum shrink should be 10% for the warp and 4% for the fill or specify nonshrink. Breaking strength of warp should be 50 lb and for the fill, 40 lb. Variations in kind of weave in toweling should be avoided. The various weaves can shrink differently, giving a poor-appearing buckled product.

Honeycomb or huckaback (huck) towels are usually made of carded cotton, rayon, or union (a combination of linen and cotton). Linen has the best moisture absorbency. Specify the minimum weight per square yard as 6.2 oz with maximum sizing 5%, maximum shrink 14% for warp and 5% for fill, and minimum breaking strengths of 58 lb (warp) and 48 lb (fill). Nonshrink can also be specified. (Note that in textile specifications, standards for warp always comes first and those for fill last.) Colors in toweling should be fast to 40 hours under a Fadeometer light. Seams should be from ¼ to ⅜ in. wide with a minimum of 10 stitches per inch. Corners should be backstitched or bar tacked at least ¼ in. back, and raw edges should be turned in for the same distance. Dacron-reinforced selvages wear longer than plain cotton ones. Hemmed towels are not as durable as those with selvage ends. Uniform shrinkage of all materials should be specified.

Dish or glass towels are made from cotton, rayon, linen, or combinations of these. Minimum thread counts should be 54 in. (warp) and 38 in. (fill), and breaking strength for both should be 50 lb; maximum shrink is 14 and 5%. The towels should be fully bleached and line-free. These towels can also be specified as shrinkproof.

Napery

Napery (tablecloths and napkins) may be made from linen, ramie, cotton, rayon, or other fibers. Linen gives a high luster and a crisp, durable fabric that is quite lint-free. Colored napery has some popularity, but white is still the preferred color. Rayon is lower in cost and has good sheen but is weak when wet. Mercerized cotton has good sheen, is not expensive, and wears well. All napery should be able to be washed with bleach at 160°F and be non-chlorine-retentive (chlorine weakens the fabric). A blend of 50:50 cotton and Dacron is often used for nonpress napery. Calendered fabrics have a higher sheen, and singed ones have less lint.

Napery is usually specified as double damask, which is heavy and wears better than single. Good double damask should not have more than 7 float yarns in the fill and not fewer than 195 threads per square inch and a maximum shrink of 8%. It can also be specified as nonshrink. Single damask should not have more than 4 fill floats and not fewer than 140 threads per square inch. Weights should be, respectively, not less than 8 to 10 oz and 5½ oz/sq yd. Single damask with a minimum breaking strength of 75 lb should be specified. Yarn shift should not be more than 0.05 in. on a 2-lb pull.

Indian head, crash, broadcloth, and other tight, solid weaves are used in napery. These are inexpensive compared to damask and give good wear. They should usually weigh from 4 to 5 oz/sq yd. If the following fabrics are used, the following standards are frequently written into specifications: Indian head (suiting), minimum thread count 66 × 76; carded-yarn broadcloths, 116 × 56 thread count and minimum breaking strength of 55 (warp) and 25 lb (fill), and combed-yarn broadcloth, 148 × 74 threads per square inch with a breaking strength of 74 (warp) and 28 lb (fill). Momie cloth (monk's cloth) of mercerized cotton should have a minimum breaking strength for warp and fill of 90 lb, maximum shrinks of 6 and 5%, respectively, and a minimum count of 62 × 56 using yarns sized from 13s to 15s. For low-cost napery, 128-count carded cotton sheeting is used. An 8- to 11-in. hang over the table side is recommended after complete shrinkage has occurred. Seams should be checked for strength and workmanship. Good damask should have a minimum tear-out seam strength of 64 lb. All napery should be able to be washed in 160°F water with bleach.

Blankets

Wool, Acrilan, and Orlon (an olefin) make good, warm blankets. Some new fibers are on the market that might bear investigation. Wool is quite durable and resilient, but Orlon and Acrilan retain nap better. Naps should be strong enough to permit lifting the blanket by the nap. Acrilan is as expensive as wool but lighter. All heavy blankets should have a wet or dry strength of 30 and 25 lb. Warps may be specified as being blended with strong tear combed cotton and made from 2-ply 12½ tpi (twists per inch) yarns. Fillings should have a 7 tpi and a Z-twist for looseness, for warmth and napping. The basic weave should be tight, and holding the blanket to the light should permit the buyer to see a tight weave. Light blankets about 0.12 in. thick should weigh not less than 8 oz/sq yd, and the heaviest 0.24 in. should weigh 15 oz/sq yd.

A twill weave of double fill, and a 1 up and 3 down wale makes the best cotton blanket. Weight should be 1⅓ lb/sq yd with counts of 36 × 30 or more and a breaking strength of not less than 30 and 25 lb. Shrinkage should be a minimum of 11 and 6%. Maximum sizing should be 5%.

Curtains and Drapes

Curtains for glass windows should be quite sheer and permit a large quantity of light to go through them. A good Dacron curtain with a leno weave should have a count of approximately 76 × 64, and quality improves as the count goes up. A ninon weave gives a very sheer curtain and should run 144 threads per square inch. Batiste weaves of combed cotton should be 168 threads per square inch, but if Dacron is the fiber the count can be nearer 150. Twice-stitching on the inner and outer edges of seams should be specified. Draping qualities, washability and ironing should be checked.

Drip-dry curtaining materials are good for institutional use. Curtaining fabrics can deteriorate from sunlight; the least affected to the most are, respectively, Dacron, Orlon, Saran, Fiberglas, Fortisan, nylon, Chromespun, Celasperm, acetates, rayon, Arnel, cotton, and glass. Orlon and Dacron make soft, lustrous curtains that drip-dry and hang well. Fiberglas has great beauty and good draping qualities and will hold its shape well without sag, but it abrades easily unless it is Beta Fiberglas. Rayon is lustrous and low in cost but holds its shape poorly.

Many drapery fabrics are suitable for institutional use. Silk has great beauty and excellent wear but is very expensive. Nylon and some of the other polyesters drape well and have beauty, but some suffer from sunlight attack. Rayon is low in cost and has good appearance but must be treated against flammability and does not retain dimensional length too well in humid climates. Most drapery materials should be specified with a dry-breaking-strength minimum of 35 lb. Momie should be made of heavy yarn and have a 16 × 72 count. Crash or other heavy cotton draperies should have a count of 68 × 76 or more, and Jacquard weaves should be 100 × 30 or over. Seams and hems should be checked, and corners should be mitered.

Upholstery

Appearance, good wear and cleanability are important factors buyers should consider in selecting upholstery materials. Cost must be considered but often a more expensive fabric gives sufficient wear or cleanability or better appearance that it pays to make the investment. Table 15–6 lists some of the most common upholstery fabrics used. Table 15–7 lists some of the popular pile weave fabrics used.

Carpets and Rugs

Today, most carpets and rugs are made by setting yarns into a rubberized or plastic backing. Cut or uncut piles are common, and the Jacquard-type designs or a variation in pile height, called *sculptured,* can be made to give a design in the rug without colors. Tight, short piles of wool, Acrilan, nylon, polypropylene (olefin) or their blends are usually best for institutional use. A square yard of good wool carpeting should weigh around 5¼ lb, acrylics 5 lb, and nylon 4½ lb. Man-made fibers must be

Table 15–6
Upholstery fabrics.

Weave	Count		Flat Weaves oz/54 in. yd	Material
	Warp	Fill		
Brocatelle	85	85	16	Can be cotton, linen, rayon, nylon, silk, or polyester;
Damask	120	50	12	mixtures with nylon or polyesters should not be over 50% of
Matellase	95	75	22	these fibers
Tapestry	72	60	20	
Crash	32	32	15*	100% cotton, vat dyed, 2-ply twisted yarns
Duck	50	40	12*	100% cotton, 2-ply cotton or more, vat dyed. If for outdoors, specify mildew- and water-resistant
Cretonne	60	50	10*	100% cotton, vat dyed, not too durable

Table 15-7
Pile weave upholstery fabrics.

Weave	Count per in.²						oz/54 in. yd		Materials
	Warp				Pile Weaves				
	Pile	Stuffer	Ground	Filling	Loops		Pile	Total	
Plain-rib friezé	36	72	18	29	522		12½	29	Face-warp all mohair; back warp and filling all cotton
Plain friezé	9	72	18	23	103		17	33	50% or more wool or mohair face; backing 100% cotton or rayon or their mixture
Pattern friezé	26			24	312				Pattern may leave bare spots, so 50% or more should be covered with loops; material same as for plain friezé
Mohair velvet, 0.13 in. thick	28	28		48	385		15	25	100% mohair, cut pile
Mohair velvet, 0.14 in. thick	27		54	30	405		12	19	100% mohair, cut pile

*48 in. wide; heavy materials should have a minimum 80-lb dry-breaking strength, and the lightest ones should have a minimum 50-lb dry-breaking strength.

557

spun to 12- to 15-denier thickness to equal thick, heavy, wool yarns. Rayon and cotton are not usually good in institutional carpeting. Acrilan 41, Creslan, Zefran, and Verel are other acrylic fibers used. They usually outwear wool but not nylon.

The yarn in many carpets develops a plus electrical charge, and individuals walking over them develop a minus charge. When the relative humidity is below 40%, 3 kilovolts (kV) or more can build up quickly, which gives a fairly strong shock when someone touches a ground such as a door knob. Carpets can be made to drain off electrical charges by using metallic yarn and grounding the carpet. Where employees get shocks, special nonconductive shoes can be worn; but this is not usually possible for guests. Wool will build up the highest amount of electricity—as high as 12.6 kV; nylon builds up 10 kV, and acrylic or modacrylic builds up 9 kV. With metallic conductors the voltage usually drops down to 2½ kV. Antistatic sprays can be used; these are usually humectants that absorb moisture. Manufacturers are also busily engaged in supporting research to develop antistatic fibers and are succeeding. Specify nonstatic carpeting.

Tight, nubby, twisted piles from strong fiber yarns show footprints less easily and wear better than longer yarns. Long-yarn carpeting, unless made from good, resilient fibers such as wool or Acrilan 41, flatten and are unattractive. They also soil more easily. Nylon shows footprints easily, but a mixture of 50% nylon, 40% acrylics, and 10% rayon or cotton gives good service. Saran resists oil and grease stain, so may be used in dining areas or food service areas.

Carpeting for food service and other operations should be selected for their low-maintenance requirements, nonflammability, resistance against static buildup, and resistance against burns such as those of cigarettes, matches, etc. Durability is an important factor, as well as resistance against soil and stain, and resistance against moisture absorbency such as liquid spills. The fabric material should be aesthetically pleasing and strongly resistant against fading, holding its colors well so the carpeting continues to look fresh and attractive. The carpeting should lay well without wrinkles and kinks, be comfortable underfoot, show a minimum of depression marks from footprints or furniture, and not shrink after installation.

Uniforms

Uniforms must be attractive, fit well, drape well, wear well, and resist soil. They should clean easily and hold a press or be a good quality non-press. Comfort and safety are also factors to consider. Nylon is durable, extremely attractive, and has many other favorable qualities; but it is warm, builds up static, yellows in use if white, and absorbs body stains.

The fiber, yarn, and weave are important in giving wear. Hard, tight fabrics wear best but may develop shine. Some weaves suitable for work uniforms are twills, denim, and plain. Suitings that wear well are whipcord, gabardine, serge, tight twills, and sharkskin. Tweeds and flannels bag and hold a press poorly. They may also be too casual. A number of uniforms are now being made of knit fabrics. These have excellent drape, good appearance, can be treated to hold a press, and drip-dry. Dacron or Orlon in a tight yarn woven into a good fabric gives excellent wear and

Table 15–8

General sizes of cooks' coats.

	Size (in.)				
	Extra Small	**Small**	**Medium**	**Large**	**Extra Large**
Waiter	30	34	38	42	46
Cook	34	38	42	46	52

looks good. Dacron and Orlon are often blended with cotton up to about 50% of the material, which gives a good drip-dry fabric that is cool, wears well, is not too expensive, and washes well.

Uniforms should be specified preshrunk and should not shrink over 1½%. They should have treatment for static qualities, press fastness, antipilling, and nonflammability. Dye fastness, anticrocking features, and ability to resist fading should be specified. Thread counts, tearing strengths, and minimum weight per square yard for the fabric should also be mentioned. The L-24 standards of the American Standards Association (10 East 40th Street, New York City) can be helpful in selecting good uniforms and other textile products. Seams should be well sewn and linings should be specified—rayon makes a good lining. Pockets should be checked for sewing, lining, and strength. Buttonholes need to be noted. Styling is extremely important to employee satisfaction.

The sizes of uniforms can vary between manufacturers, so buyers should check to see that the size specified is proper. It is not unusual to specify chest measurements, sleeve length, armhole circumference, cuff circumference, coat length, hem length, back length, and the like. Table 15–8 lists the general sizes of cooks' coats. Women's uniforms are usually specified as size 10, 12, and so on. Caps come in small, 6⅞ (21¼-in. circumference); medium 7⅛ (22⅜ in.); and large 7½ (23½ in.) sizes. All sizes have a variation, and the tolerance for caps is ± ⅜ in.

Mops

Mops must be durable, hold a large quantity of water, rinse well, and dry adequately. Yarn strengths should be checked. They must be twisted loosely to give good water absorbency, which may weaken them. They should have yarns spun from long staple cotton, possibly blended with some polyester or other fiber. Linen gives good absorbency, durability, and resistance to abrasion, but it increases cost. Specifications can cover the following:

Pounds per dozen	9	12	15	18	20	24
Minimum yards/mop	105	120	135	145	165	190
Width at center (in.)	6	6	6¼	6¼	6¼	6¼
Length (in.)	28	32½	36	40	41	42

PAPER GOODS AND DISPOSABLE WARE

Many operations use **paper goods.** Some operations use them for storage units or other production uses; some use it almost exclusively for service ware. Take-out operations must use it; often such operations will purchase prepackaged items such as a plastic knife, fork, spoon with small salt and pepper packets wrapped in a paper napkin. The ware selected should be attractive and be of good color and design. It is important that they be strongly made and easily handled so accidents are minimized. (Lawsuits because of a lack of attention to such detail can be expensive.) Some localities or states require that all disposables be biodegradable. Others require that such disposable ware be made of unbleached materials. Often the amount of paper goods used is substantial and it is necessary to see that there is adequate storage space for it.

Disposable ware is usually purchased in large lots, a *one-dealer deal* and the purchase is often let out on bid. Often suppliers require a very large order to be placed or an order that requires delivery of a substantial quantity of disposable ware over a long period of time. This is because of the original expense in designing an operation's ware and the cost of making the forms used. An operation makes a considerable original investment in such ware. An operation must also give consideration to the cost of cleaning up grounds and disposing of ware carelessly thrown away by patrons. Some communities are quite strict in their requirements for the proper disposal of these items. An operation also should take whatever measures it can to reduce waste when patrons are allowed to help themselves to the ware.

SUMMARY

To support foodservice operations buyers have to purchase many materials other than foods. Often management makes the purchase decisions on what, where, and how much to buy and the buyer just follows through to complete the negotiation and get the goods.

Clean means that a substance is free of obvious soil, whereas sanitary means that the object is free of any harmful substance. To clean, detergents are used to dissolve the soil; heat is also often an aid to soil removal. Chelating substances in detergents grab hold of soil so it can be removed and sequestering agents hold it away. The kind of water used is important in cleaning. Hard water contains salts that dry on washed objects and leave spots. Lime or scale can plug pipes and interfere with the operation of cleaning equipment. Water softeners are usually used to make hard water soft. Water that is too soft, however, can "eat" metal. Chlorinating substances plus heat are usually used to sanitize. Floors need special treatment to clean and the type of treatment depends on the kind of floor. Laundry detergents should help remove soil but should not harm fabrics. hypocholorite bleaches are used to give desirable whiteness.

Dishware, glassware, and flatware (silverware) needs must be suited to the operation. Usually dishes are made of china or porcelain, a highly refined clay product that is first made into a bisque, then baked, and then glazed and decorated. Porcelain is vitrified by heat, which means that the dishes are heated to a point that the clay fuses into a hard solid substance. Addition of aluminum oxide gives added hardness. Adding ground bone makes china stronger and more translucent.

Glass is made from silica, soda, lime, and cullet (old glass). If lead oxide and potassium silicate are added we get a glass called crystal. Adding boric acid instead of lime to common glass makes it usable as cooking ware. Heating glass to change its molecular structure makes it stronger.

Silverware (flatware) is made by first casting a blank in the shape of the desired unit; such blanks are usually made of brass and nickel, called nickel silver. A silver coating is added to the blank by a process called electrolysis. The amount added is stated by the amount added to a gross of teaspoons. Heavy hotel plate (quadruple plate) has 8 oz. of silver added, triple plate 6 oz., standard 5 oz., and banquet 4 oz. Heavy wear spots have silver added at the wear point; this is called inlaying. Very few operations use pure silverware because of the expense.

Holloware such as pitchers, creamers, and sugar bowls may be made of metalware. It is not unusual to see these made from stainless steel, but some operations use silverplated ware. Holloware may also be made of ceramics.

The stainless steel used for flatware and holloware is usually what is called 18-8 or 17-7 (18% or 17% chromium, 8% or 7% nickel, and 76%, 74%, or 76% steel). Flatware will usually be 12- or 13-gauge and metalware 10-guage stainless steel.

Very little evidence exists to show that particles of textiles are health hazards. The main natural textile fibers are cotton, wool, silk, linen, and ramie, the main man-made fibers are rayon and acetate (both cellulose based and usually made from cotton). Acrylic fibers are nylons, sarans, olefins, and polyesters. Each has special attributes that make them more suitable for specific needs, and buyers should be aware of these attributes.

Textiles are woven fabrics made of interwoven yarns. The lengthwise yarns are called the warp; the crosswise ones are called the weft or fill. Different weaves are produced by varying the manner in which this cross weaving is done. Thus satin is produced by having up to six warps skipped before putting the fill under a warp yarn. Damask is a fabric in which the over and under placing of the yarns are varied to make a design. Jacquard weaves are designs made by machines.

The thread count of a fabric is stated in number of warp and fill yarns in a square inch; thus, a 100×100 (200) thread count means there are 100 warp yarns and 100 fill yarns in a square inch. Pile is a weave that has a loose thread in the fill that makes a tiny loop. This extra thread gives the added moisture absorbency desirable in toweling. Some nonwoven fabrics are on the market.

Laws and standards exist on what fibers and the make-up of textiles must be. Thus, virgin wool must be wool used for the first time. Reused wool, if used, must be indicated. Types of stuffing used in furniture must be identified. If shrink-proof or colorfast features are claimed, the fabric can shrink only a certain percent or can only lose a certain amount of color. All fabrics must contain a label indicating cleaning or washing requirements.

Sheets and pillowcases are usually specified as made of carded muslin 70 ×
70 count (a heavy yarn that gives a rather coarse texture), utility percale 90 × 90
(180) count, or of supercale 200 count. (The latter gives a smooth, pleasant texture
to the fabric.) Wet or dry tear strength, weight per square yard, nonbleach retention, and other desired qualities should be named. A 50% cotton plus 50% polyester gives a nonpress fabric. Pillowcases are best made from tubular rather than
flat fabric sewn together. Sizes for sheets and pillowcases are given in torn size before being made up.

Toweling is usually made of terry towel fabric. Linen fiber gives best absorbency but because it is rather harsh and expensive, cotton is almost always
used. Linen may, however, be used along with other fibers in dish towels.

Napery (tablecloths and napkins) made of linen has a beautiful sheen and
makes a crisp fabric. Damask patterns are usually woven into it. Other plain-
weave fabrics are often used because of the cost of linen. Blankets are usually
made of wool or Acrilan or Orlon. Blankets are napped, which is a process in
which fibers from the yarns are pulled up loosely, giving a furry texture that cap-
tures air and therefore makes the blanket more warm.

Curtains and drapes may be made of silk, but because of silk's expense, other
fabrics such as nylon and glass are usually used. Glass has beauty but abraids if the
fabrics move too much. Rayon is good, but, if used, must be made fireproof because of its high flammability. Upholstery fabrics should be made of strong yarns of
strong fibers so they can stand the wear. They should clean well. Carpets or rugs
are best made of wool but nylon or some other polyesters give good wear and
make good appearing items. Tight, nubby piles are best. Loose piles are dangerous
since heels or other objects can easily get caught in them. Carpeting and rugs
should be nonstatic. Nylon gives good wear and beauty but shows prints easily.

Uniforms must be attractive, fit well, drape well, wear well, resist soil, and
be cool. Nylon makes an excellent uniform, but can be warm; cotton is less expensive, is cool, and gives a good appearance; it can be made into a nonpress
uniform.

Mops are usually made of good quality loosely twisted cotton yarns. Some
polyester in the yarn gives a stronger yarn that wears better.

Some operations use paper goods exclusively for service requirements. Paper
goods should be of solid, good construction so as to give proper and safe service.
Attractive design, color, and convenience in handling should be sought. The purchase of paper goods usually involves a commitment for a large quantity purchase,
usually over a long period, so paper goods suppliers should be carefully selected.

REVIEW QUESTIONS

1. What is napery?
2. What is the difference between cleaning and sanitation?
3. Why might it not be advisable to use carbon tetrachloride for cleaning jobs?

4. What is hard water? What problem arises if using it in dishware washing or for other cleaning jobs? What is the harmful effect of hard-water salts on equipment and in water pipes, boilers, and other units?

5. What is *metal-hungry* water?

6. What is the difference between a detergent and a soap?

7. What is pH? About what pH level are strong soaps and detergents? What is the maximum pH recommended for handwashing soaps?

8. After washing fabrics, a *sourer* may be used. Why?

9. What is porcelain? What are some of the standards established for quality testing of it?

10. What are the advantages of using porcelain dishes over stoneware?

11. What factors contribute to strength in dishes?

12. What is a bisque?

13. What is bone china? English china?

14. How can costs be reduced in purchasing dishware?

15. What are the three top grades of china?

16. What are the advantages of using plastic ware over ceramic ware? The disadvantages?

17. What is common glass?

18. What is pressed or molded glassware? Cut glass? Corning ware?

19. How is stainless steel eating ware made? What quality factors should a buyer look for in purchasing this kind of ware?

20. What are the different grades of silverplated eating ware? How is plated ware made?

21. How can a buyer check the quality of eating ware?

22. What factors should a buyer add to a specification for tableware knives?

23. Define linen, cotton, ramie, wool, silk, polyester, rayon, acetate, nylon, and saran.

24. What is a serious defect in using glass curtaining fabrics for curtains?

25. What factors in the type of material in the yarn, the making of the yarn, and the making of the fabric give fabrics strength?

26. What should a buyer look for in setting up a specification for sheets and pillowcases?

27. What are some special treatments for fabrics that give them special properties?

28. What is a terry towel? A honeycomb or huckaback towel? An acceptable material to be used in dish towels?

29. What are the advantages of using linen for napery versus mercercized cotton? What kind of synthetic material can be added to cotton to produce nonpress materials?

30. Name some of the better upholstery fabrics and their advantages and disadvantages.

31. If one wanted a very durable, but good-appearing carpeting for a dining room, what type of carpeting should be considered? Are there any construction factors that would make the carpeting more preferable than another?

32. If you wanted to purchase uniforms, what would you look for in kind of material, construction, and other aspects?

SPECIFICATIONS

China

1. Plates, dinner, Lotus pattern
2. 10 doz
3. Selects
4. Packed 4 doz per box, foam-layer packed
5. Price by the dozen.
6. Shall be made of highest grade china clay of 40% or more of kaolin, 6% ball clay, 13% flint or ground quartz, 15% feldspar, 5% aluminum oxide, and 1% whiting. Overall size of each plate shall be 10½ in. with a 7-in. well and 3 in. allowed for the rim on either side. Plates shall be fashioned with rolled edge and extra rim bead underneath, with extra clay added in well center to reduce star-cracking. Shall meet federal specifications for absorbency, body, and edge impact standards.

Silverware, Plated

1. Teaspoons, Milford pattern
2. Gross
3. Heavy hotel plate (blanks 11 lb/gross, silver cover 8 oz/gross)
4. Packed 1 doz per box, 1 gross per carton
5. Price by gross
6. Inlaid with 20 microns (0.00125 in.) of silver at the point where the handle and spoon bowl rest; shall not be an overlay. Spoons shall have 60% of their silver on the back and 40% in front.

Textiles

1. Sheets
2. 1 gross
3. Percale, luxury (super) quality, 200 count
4. Packed 1 doz per box

5. Price by the dozen

6. Wet or dry strength 60 lb; fill, 1% maximum; preshrunk (shrink, not over 2%); and weight /sq yd 3.6 lb. Torn size 113 in. torn size permitting 7 in. tuck on regular size double bed mattress.

KEY WORDS AND CONCEPTS

bisque	pH
blown glass	polyester
bone china (English)	porcelain
ceramics	pottery
chelating compound	olefin
china	sanitary
clean	saponify
cotton	saran
crazing	scale (lime)
crocking	selvage
crystal	sequestering compound
cullet	serrated
denier sizes	silk
detergent	silverplate
earthenware	soap
electrolysis	sourer
fireproof fabric	stainless steel flatware
flatware	star-cracking
flatware blank	stoneware
glass	terry toweling
hanks	textiles
heavy hotel plate	tufting utility percale
jacquard weave	vitrification
linen	warp
man-made fibers	weft (fill)
muslin (carded cotton)	wool
napery	woolen yarns
natural fibers	worsted yarns
nylon	yarn
paper goods	

CHAPTER 16

Purchasing Contract Services

Original etching from July 1, 1777 Tenier's Kitchen In The Common Parlour at Houghton. From the Louis Szwathmary collection, Culinary Archives and Museum, Johnson and Wales University, used by permission of Dr. Szwathmary and Johnson and Wales University.

Chapter Objectives

1. To cover some of the basic factors that should be considered in writing contracts for various services.

2. To indicate how a service contract is initiated and how it will be processed.

3. To indicate some of the factors that should be considered in selecting a purveyor of a service.

4. To cover some of the most important services that are usually contracted for and to indicate some of the basic needs in setting up a contract for a particular service.

GENERAL PROVISIONS

The purchasing of contract services varies among different foodservice operations. Some operations need only a few contracts because many are already taken care of, such as waste removal being taken care of by the local government or when most services are provided by the landlord as a part of rental agreement. Some services are one-time services, such as painting the dining area; others may be for a continued period with periodic service visits. Some contract purchases may not involve the purchasing department because they are handled completely by management, such as arranging for insurance or a mortgage loan. In other cases, the purchasing department may not be given any freedom to negotiate; for instance, because a company gives a stipend to a hospital each year, hospital management may feel that the contract for services handled by the company *must* go to the donor.

Some facilities will decide to do their own service, such as having the engineering department take care of refrigeration needs or setting up an in-house laundry to take care of laundry needs. However, this is not always possible. A facility may not have employees with the necessary skills or competence to do the service; some services require licensed personnel to do the work; the facility lacks the necessary equipment; or the work is too dangerous to have ordinary employees do it. A facility might also find that it costs less to give a contract for the service—a contractor that can use nonunion workers may be able to do the work at a much lower cost than a facility that uses higher paid union employees. Or management may feel it has enough to look after without adding other complications and it is worth a little extra cost just to get rid of the problem.

When the decision is made to contract for a service, sometimes it is desirable to have contractors **bid for the work.** This may simplify the negotiation for the purchase department by reducing time and standardizing the negotiation process.

Good **analysis of contracts** before signing them pays off. Although not all items mentioned in the following list apply to all contracts, the list covers in general areas of concern that might need consideration:

- If inspections are to be made, specify the number to be made within a specific period of time and also cover their nature and what the expected outcome of such an inspection should be.

- Labor, parts, and other supplies are specified to meet the needs of the operation and the results required.

- Be sure the contractor has inspected your operation and its equipment and knows all physical and all other conditions required to fulfill the contract.

- If the equipment covered by the contract is under warranty at the time of contract, some charges will be covered under said warranty. When the warranty ceases, a schedule of costs should be specified.

- The contractor should usually be bonded and licensed and should carry adequate insurance.

- Obtain evidence the contractor does completely reasonable work, including any loss caused by the contractor's failure to take appropriate action. The time period within which proper action should be taken should be specified.

- Prepare a complete listing of each piece of equipment to be serviced and its precise location. Do not accept general listings like "all existing refrigeration units."

- Most contracts are for a year, but they may be shorter or longer, depending on the needs. It is advisable to specify a total contract price with payments made periodically. Additional charges that are authorized to be made other than the contract price should be specified.

- If the contract calls for any adjustments after a period of operation, the method and conditions of the adjustment must be clearly stated. Do not accept general wording such as "adjusted at prevailing rates."

- Require notification, preferably in writing, of each inspection or service call made, why it was made, and what was accomplished.

- The contract should specify what is to be accomplished in inspections and servicing and the cost of parts and labor for anything additional should be named. It is often desirable to include a dollar limit on parts and materials that can be used without authorization.

- If emergency calls are made and are not within the contract provisions, indicate what the charges are to be and how many, if any, emergency calls are permitted before such charges start.

- If an extra charge is assessed for work done by supervisory or engineering personnel, be sure the rate is named.

- The language used in specifying when a contract can be cancelled should be studied to make sure there is no possibility of the contract being cancelled without prior notice.

- Before a contract is signed, the experience and qualifications of workers who are to perform the work should be checked.

- Consider the question of security. Contract workers on the premises will have to be trustworthy because it is often impossible to keep a constant watch on them. They may be allowed in places where they could steal items. Often the service company must be bonded and licensed so as to protect those who use the service.

Remember that it is better to have a contract that is too detailed, rather than one that is too brief.

CONTRACT WRITING

The purchasing department may be given the responsibility of writing contracts. Sometimes legal questions are involved and legal counsel must be sought. All details must be spelled out *in writing*. Nothing should be left to chance or spoken instructions.

In setting up contracts, the purchasing department usually does not work alone. Purchasing may do some preliminary work and legal advice may be obtained before the department concerned with the service is contacted to ascertain specific needs and suggestions. Top management may also be brought in at this point if the contract is a big one.

It is important to obtain as many viewpoints as possible to ensure that all necessary provisions are included. Purchasing can then begin to put the contract into written form. This draft should be sent for legal criticism and further refinement, if legal questions are involved. When the contract is returned, it should be ready for final consideration by purchasing, the department using the service, and top management. It is then ready to submit to purveyors of the service. Here additional factors may have to be worked out and the department involved and top management consulted again. Contracts are like specifications in that they spell out what is wanted. Only the price, usually negotiated on the basis of the specification, is added in contracts.

The Purveyor of the Service

Other work done by purveyors of a service should be surveyed carefully before a contract is assigned. The purveyor selected should have a good reputation for reliability, for good service, and for honest and ethical operation. Checking with others who have used the purveyor is a good way to gain information. Better Business Bureaus can help. Interviews with the purveyors can also be revealing, and it may even be advisable to visit their premises to see what kind of equipment and facilities they have.

This complex process of setting up contracts can sometimes be simplified. Purveyors of the service desired may have contracts in ready form. These can be studied and submitted for review by the department concerned, the legal counsel, and top management. Changes or modifications may be suggested and negotiated with the purveyor. Such contracts should receive careful study; they are written to protect and favor the purveyor and not the customer. Provisions may be added by the buyer to give the required protection and service to the customer. The services rendered should be actual, needed, and done in a time and manner suitable to the needs of the facility.

Finalization

Final review and approval by management should be required before a contract is signed. After the contract is signed, a decision has to be made as to who will supervise the performance of the contract. Usually, this is the department for which the service is rendered. The financial or accounting offices may also be given some responsibility because it is their job to see that economy is practiced and value is obtained for resources expended. It is also important that management check from time to time to see that proper performance is obtained from the contractor.

In this chapter on the purchase of contracts, only some of the most important service requirements have been discussed. There are others, such as employment contracts, union contracts, even contracts to outside firms for purchasing, legal, communication, and other services. If a facility does not feel it can adequately handle these contracts, it is advisable to retain a consultant to assist in setting up proper contracts for these services. Often this may be some legal consultant.

ADVERTISING

The food service industry does not have large advertising budgets. Only about 2% of sales is expended for it, but some operations run large advertising budgets. These are often large national chains or businesses that do a lot of business so they can afford such expenditures. Most small operations depend on **word-of-mouth advertising.** However, the trend to use more advertising and to contract it out is increasing.

Some facilities establish general contracts with an advertising agency to handle their public relations and advertising. Such a firm may handle advertising in newspapers, radio, and TV in the local area and also do public relations work such as seeing that stories about the food service appear with as much frequency as possible. The firm may also do mailings and even advertising and publicity in the food service. Such assistance can go even as far as helping in menu presentation. National chains set up big contracts with nationally recognized publicity firms that have highly professional people on their staffs to set up sophisticated and artful programs using TV, magazines, newspapers, and other media to get the company's story across. Small units cannot afford this but can use billboards or newspaper advertising. Publicity promotions such as special dining offers to remember patrons' birthdays or wedding anniversaries may be mailed by a service. The contract may require that copy be submitted before it is used. This requirement should be written clearly, concisely, and briefly—a few words might be enough and should carry precisely the message the advertiser wishes to convey. Chin's restaurant in Las Vegas, voted as serving the best Chinese food in the city, advertised on huge billboards with just the word *FIRST* followed by *Chin's* in smaller letters underneath. It was all that was needed to carry the message. Some advertising contracts made with magazines, TV guides, and newspapers involve taking out a set amount of space for a year or other period. The copy is changed at various times. This same kind of arrangement can be used for billboard advertising.

An agency knowledgeable in the field with a successful history in this area should be selected. If necessary, frequent conferences should be held with management or someone delegated to cover publicity to coordinate efforts with seasonal promotions, business ups and downs, big conventions, and other factors that affect business. It is also desirable for any agency with a contract to publicize a facility to be community-minded and publicize clients through favorable news stories that cost nothing. There are a number of legal cautions to take in advertising. An example would be in selling alcoholic beverages. Thus, it is important for the service doing the advertising to observe the law.

CLEANING

Help shortages or difficulty getting staff to perform cleaning tasks up to the high standards needed may force an operation to contract for **cleaning services.** There may be other reasons, such as lack of proper equipment and the desire to avoid investment in expensive equipment, or the need for specialized skills not available in ordinary workers. Rug shampooing, floor–wall–ceiling care and common cleaning of halls, bathrooms, banquet rooms, public spaces, toilets, and other areas may be covered in such contracts. Night cleaning can also be provided by contract. One of the advantages of a cleaning contract is that the contractor may use nonunion workers and thus be able to do the work for less.

Contracts for cleaning may be made out of necessity. If a food service is on the 26th floor and cleaning of outside windows is not provided in the rental agreement, a contract with a professional service may be necessary to do the job adequately. Health facilities may need special cleaning that requires sanitizing in addition to cleaning. Many facilities cannot cope with their problems of cleaning and sanitation, and the services of an outside agency is the answer. Better management and training could obviate the need for outside help. One authority has said, "If the facility cannot provide proper cleanliness and sanitation, personnel changes should be made."

Contracting for the washing of dishes, pots and pans, and other ware is increasing. The contractee provides the equipment and space while the contractor furnishes the help and often the detergents and other supplies. Again, this is often done to avoid hiring expensive union workers for low-paid jobs.

VENDING

Some operations use **vending services** to dispense foods and beverages, often during times when the regular foodservice units are not operating. However, they may also be used to supplement service during regular hours of operation. Some operations purchase the vending units or lease them and fill and service them themselves, but it is more normal to contract for a vending service in which the vendor supplies the foods, fills the units, maintains the equipment, and in return gives a percentage of the sales to the facility for the privilege of being allowed to operate there. Such an arrangement provides a needed service with little or no trouble to the operation—all that must be furnished is the space and energy to run the units. A vending service may also oversee the operation's personal vending program. Which service to use or whether to contract just the overseeing of a personal vending program must be decided by the operation. The amount of sales is often a critical factor when making the decision.

ENTERTAINMENT

Operations such as night clubs, hotels, cabarets, and even some restaurants may write contracts for **entertainment services.** Usually an agent represents the artists or artist, and the agent will present a written contract form for signature. This should be carefully studied and provisions added to protect the user of the service as well as the agent and artists. Some facilities set up a separate department just to handle entertainment matters. For instance, casinos in Atlantic City and Las Vegas have a special department to handle these contracts, because of their specialized nature. The University of Nevada at Las Vegas even offers a course on entertainment management. If a facility feels it lacks the expertise to handle contracting in this area, it can use a consultant to aid in handling the problem.

EQUIPMENT RENTAL

Caterers, hotels, restaurants, and others may need to rent chairs, tables, dishes, silverware, and other wares on a sporadic and occasional basis. Operations may find this makes financial sense, even though the cost may seem high compared with that of maintaining an inventory so little used. Even refrigerated trucks or other specialized transportation equipment can be contracted for use. There are many advantages in cost and convenience. No storage cost is incurred. The provider of the equipment carries the risk of security and deterioration. Contracts may be written even for setting up and preparing for a meeting, exhibition, show, banquet, or other event. Flower contracts can be made plus contracts for audiovisual equipment, special lighting, and other needs. Even the placement of plants and other decorations can be contracted. Contractors can clean up after the event, leaving everything clean and shipshape for the next event. Management can have peace of mind, providing a proper contract is written.

Facilities may find it desirable to rent coffee-making units, computers, office machines, and other needs on a long-term basis.

In writing the contract for equipment rental, maintenance and repair are often included, and the ramifications of this should be carefully thought out. Just *what* maintenance and repair is covered? How long after a call should service be available? At what hours will service be made? And on what days? Who pays for parts?

FIRE AND SAFETY INSPECTION AND TRAINING[1]

Fire and safety protection are a vital necessity to a facility, for both patrons and employees. It has increased in importance in the last few decades. Local codes for the proper planning of facilities and equipment should be followed. Regulations for safety and protection such as fire codes and **Occupational Safety and Health Administration (OSHA)** regulations should be followed. Consultants may be retained

---

[1]The Occupational Standards and Hazard Act is a federal law requiring businesses and other institutions to establish and follow certain standards and protection in guarding against accidents, fire, and other emergencies.

on contract to train employees and inspect and advise. Assistance may also be retained in setting up fire or emergency procedures. Local fire departments, health departments, and others may do this gratis. Not only should what to do in case of fire, burglary, accidents, bomb threats, earthquakes, and other emergencies be well communicated to patrons and employees, but employees should be trained and drilled so they can act immediately to protect themselves and patrons in an emergency. Some states such as Florida have laws requiring food services to provide training on what to do when a patron chokes on something. Immediate action must occur. Contracts may include such training. Contracts should call for periodic inspection of stairways, halls and aisles, fire alarms, fire escapes, and other factors set up for protection.

Many operations contract for security both within the premises and on the grounds, such as parking lots, or for special protection for guests or others at large gatherings. An important occasion with many guests wearing fine jewelry can be an attraction to burglars. Only one or two incidences of personal hazard to patrons can act to destroy a patronage. Contracts are also written for cash collection, detective services, and so on. Some operations carry insurance that protects them from charges of false arrest.

Contracts for adequate insurance should be made for security, fire protection, accidents, and other possible causes of law suits. Dram shop laws and suits springing from them have raised some insurance rates to almost prohibitive levels. Food poisoning is another common basis of lawsuits. Burglary insurance is advised not only for the operation, but for employees and patrons.

In contracts for security one should require that personnel retained for security be well trained for their jobs and their backgrounds well checked. Some firms have been careless in this and have actually placed former convicted criminals in high security positions where they have victimized the very people they were hired to protect. The firm furnishing the personnel should have a dossier on every employee and be willing to show this to the client on request. Since the contract calls for a special, professional service, these personnel should be clearly capable of performing the service. Their records and backgrounds should show this.

Operations are usually required by law to carry accident insurance; this is generally paid into a state fund set up for this purpose. Health or other programs may also be contracted for.

HEATING, AIR CONDITIONING, AND VENTILATION

Heating contracts should include checks on the efficiency of fuel use and proper periodic adjustment of equipment. Gas flames should have blue cones with white tips. Burners should be properly adjusted for proper air mixing and should be kept clean. Steam boiler flues should be cleaned and flushed periodically; some boilers need descaling treatment. Air ducts should have periodic cleaning and new filters added. In some places air conditioners may be used. These and ionizing units need periodic cleaning and service. Air-conditioning units need balance checks, sometimes as often as every two weeks during hot weather, as do thermostats and other climate control units. A firm contracting for heating, air-conditioning, and ventilation service should give advice on how to achieve more satisfactory results and how to reduce energy and cost of equipment operation. Such **consulting services** often result in substantial savings. The companies that provide fuel or electric energy often have expert personnel that give advice free. Recapture of energy from heat exhaust exchangers or refrigerator compressors can reduce water heating costs. In some areas the use of solar heat units results in savings. Solar units are now easily installed and operated. A company expert in climate control problems can do much to make establishments comfortable. It can reduce drafts, add or reduce static pressure to prevent heat or odor problems, reduce or increase humidity, give even heat, stop noisy equipment, and solve other problems a facility cannot.

LAUNDRY AND DRY CLEANING

Hospitality operations produce a considerable amount of laundry or dry cleaning. Uniforms, table linens, dishrags, towels, carpeting, draperies, furniture, and other items are used, and these should be in first-class, immaculately clean condition. If not, patrons turn away. Contracts for this service are common, because few food services have the facilities to do it, although a small washer and dryer to do dishtowels, rags, and other items may be economical and convenient. Sometimes, management may decide to set up its own laundry and dry cleaning unit, renting the equipment, to maintain desirable standards, even though the cost is higher.

The dry cleaning and laundry industry has been highly organized, and competitive bidding has been often limited with tie-in agreements. Prices, quality of service, and other factors are often similar among purveyors and this may make a facility decide to put in its own unit. In this case, the use of VISA fabrics (treated with a nonwrinkling agent called VISA) is a help. Fabrics containing 50% cotton and 50% drip-dry will also show little or no wrinkling. Table linens, uniforms, and other products made of this material make it easier to do one's own laundry. Disposable materials are also helpful in some cases. Some disposable paper napkins and tablecloths are remarkably like regular linen and can be used for banquets and other occasions.

Contracts may be written for renting clean supplies from a purveyor. The materials may be owned by the facility or by the purveyor furnishing the service; the charge is higher in the latter case. Contracts should clearly cover responsibility for the proper care, maintenance, and responsibility for missing or lost materials. A schedule of performance should be established that provides for the amount of time that can elapse between pickup and return of soiled and clean materials. Inventories on hand have to be based on this schedule, so there is enough at the facility to carry through until the return of the cleaned materials.

MAINTENANCE AND REPAIR

A large number of maintenance and repair contracts can be made covering plumbing, refrigeration, electrical services such as sign service or equipment and electrical maintenance, machinery, utilities, and many other services. Large operations may take care of these services in-house, through an engineering or other department, but smaller units cannot do this because of cost. They may contract or just call in a service provider when the need arises. Each option requires the selection of an experienced service who will render adequate repair or maintenance. Contracts should be written to specify exact requirements. The basis of charges should be stated and what is and what is not covered by the contract. Replacements, spare parts, supplies, and material costs are often based on the purveyor's cost plus a markup. Sometimes a spare part list with prices is included as part of the contract. Often purveyors of the service have printed contracts that contain the provisions they want, but facilities should study these and negotiate any desirable changes or additions. Legal advice is often advisable.

Refrigeration contracts should include cleaning of equipment and areas where dust, lint, and other matter can block good ventilation or air flow. Blocking of cooling units can make compressors run inefficiently. Periodic inspections should include a check on the efficiency of the equipment's operation to see if there is a need for refrigeration fluid or that compressors, expansion chambers, motors, and other mechanical factors are functioning properly. Equipment that meets the standards of the American Refrigeration Institute should be installed, and any replacements, supplies, or other materials used should also meet its standards.

Plumbing contracts often give broad coverage for maintenance and repair. Many operations prefer not to write contracts but call in a plumbing service when there is a need. Minor repairs and maintenance can often be covered by facility personnel, and a plumbing service may be required only for major problems. Contracts should require that all work be done to meet standards of codes in effect in the area. Maintenance should cover repair of leaks, leaky gaskets, elimination of stoppages, rooter cleaning, silencing of noisy pipes, correction of pressure problems, insulation of lines, and other factors needed for good plumbing. Deliming of dishwashers and other equipment, and even the maintenance and repair of water heating units discussed earlier, may be included.

Some facilities may need their own sewage facilities, and sewage disposal or sewage facility management may be included. Treatment of sewage units may have to be done periodically. Health department regulations regarding plumbing and/or sewage operation should be met.

PAYROLL AND ACCOUNTING CONTRACTS

A facility may find that it is more convenient and less expensive to contract for payroll and/or accounting services rather than do its own. Even with a contract, some basic records and accounting must be done to transfer the proper data. The facility should be sure the contract covers all needs and does not over- or underspecify them. The purveyor should be capable of adequately performing the job and have an established reputation for good service.

If trial balances, balance sheets, profit and loss statements, and other accounting summaries are needed, the times for submission of these should be specified, as well as those for IRS accounting. IRS provisions on tip withholding and reporting must be covered. Check writing of paychecks and other wages or salary costs can be done by the service. Complete accounting of individual employee accounts may also be provided. The purveyor of the service should be bonded and in some states licensed.

PEST CONTROL

Some facilities handle their own pest problems such as ants, cockroaches, flies, silverfish, mosquitoes, mice, rats, and other pest invaders, whereas others prefer to retain a professional service. There is a risk if the facility itself does the job and inexperienced personnel handle poisons and pesticides. Any evidence of pests and a failure to eliminate the problem rapidly should be of concern to management because the appearance of only one weevil, mouse, or cockroach often indicates many more. Some serious problems may show almost no evidence of pests, such as termites, which silently work their destruction and are never seen. Only an occasional hatching fly reveals their presence. Once they infest a building, it is no small job even for a professional service to eradicate them.

Contracts should clearly spell out what the service covers, treatment for special problems, and times and frequencies of visits. Responsibility for results should be established and safety to patrons or employees from toxic effects should be stated. Any contamination or failure to eradicate should be the responsibility of the purveyor. Employees of the purveyor should be trained to do a professional job. The purveyor should be bonded to protect the client, should a serious problem occur.

PRINTING

The advent of the computer and other printing and graphic arts equipment that can be used by independent facilities have lessened the printing needs of some operations; many purchase printing only by the individual job to meet sporadic or high-volume needs. Others, lacking such computer equipment, may not write a contract but rather job out work as the need for it occurs. The printing needs may be small. Others find it feasible to contract for the printing of menus, forms, newsletters, and other printing.

REMOVAL SERVICES

In some cases a city or local governmental agency does not provide garbage and trash removal service, and facilities may have to contract their own. The cost of this service may be reduced by providing garbage grinders and incinerators in the facility, but there are always some things that cannot be disposed of in this way and must be carried away.

Contracts for disposal service should specify times and frequency of pickups and include adequate pickup of trash and cleaning around dumpsters. Some contracts even call for cleaning and sanitizing of dumpsters.

Sometimes wastes may have value, such as grease, fats, paper, aluminum cans, or textiles, and the contract should be written for not only disposal but payment for these. Some have a contract for purchase of edible garbage.

Contracts may also be written for leaf or debris removal from parking lots or other areas. Many drive-ins have a special need for debris removal. Some contracts provide special large sweepers and workers to do this type of work, something a facility might find too expensive to do. Such machines often do the job so much quicker and more efficiently. Sometimes this service is included in a contract for ground care in which grass cutting, shrubbery care, and other factors are included.

Contracts should specify the extent and nature of services and fees to be charged for additional services. Thus, a contractor may be given a contract for ground care and for keeping parking places clean, but snow removal, leaf removal, and other needs are paid for at an extra named fee. Snow removal contracts should specify prompt removal after a snow-fall.

TRANSPORTATION SERVICES

Laws may require that elevators, moving sidewalks, escalators, and other similar equipment have periodic servicing and inspection. This can be in addition to governmental inspection and certification. The vital need to make sure people are transported efficiently, safely, and quickly demands that transportation equipment be in good and safe working order whenever the facility is in operation. Outside service may be needed in addition to the more casual and less expert service available from the facility's engineering department or from some other workers. Trying to do the job with in-house personnel is often penny wise and pound foolish. Expensive lawsuits from malfunctioning equipment or unsatisfactory service can play havoc with a facility's profitable operation.

Some operations contract for motor or other transportation of patrons. Airport limousine service is an example for motels and hotels. Institutions may also have to transport their patrons. A retirement home or school may need transportation. Transportation may also be needed for transporting patrons to group parties, New Year's celebrations, and other functions. Operations serving liquor may contract for a service that takes patrons home when they have had too much to drink. A contract may be let for valet service. In some cases, contractors pay a fee to get the service.

Some contracts are written only for lease of the transportation equipment whereas others also include provision of a driver. Some contracts may not set a total contract price but just give a price when the service is needed. Any equipment leased should be maintained by the service in good working order. The responsibility for carrying insurance should be set—does the lessee or the company leasing the equipment carry it?

WATER TREATMENT

Many areas require water treatment, usually to correct water hardness caused by calcium and magnesium salts. Water with below 3.5 grains of hard-water salts is considered fairly soft or soft. Between 3.5 and 9.0 grains it is hard, and above 7.0 it is very hard. Water below 1 grain hardness may be so soft it is "metal hungry" and attacks metals. Treatment is necessary in this case. Water of low hardness is desirable for some cooking purposes; coffee from soft water is insipid compared with that made from moderately hard water. Water departments can advise operations on the average hardness of the water in the area, based usually on the amount of calcium carbonate.

Hardness is usually treated by the resin-ion exchange method. Hard water is run through resin beads that exchange sodium ions for the calcium or magnesium in the hard water. This converts these hard water salts into sodium salts that do not precipitate soaps or detergents or have other undesirable reactions; thus, the water is made soft. The calcium and magnesium are held in the softening unit but must be flushed out from time to time and sodium chloride (common table salt) must be added. Companies contract to add salts and flush the system.

Sometimes water treatment must include iron removal. An oxidizing filter can do this. If manganese or hydrogen sulfide are problems, addition of a chlorine feeder is required in conjunction with filtration through activated charcoal. The chlorine also sanitizes the water. Where sanitizing is needed, chlorine feeders are usually used. Neutralizing filters are sometimes required to reduce sediment, silt, or cloudiness. Where there is a need to remove pesticides, salts, detergents, organic, or even radioactive matter, reverse osmosis units are specified. Sometimes a simpler neutralizing activated carbon filter can do the job. Using a professional service to solve water problems is often the best answer.

SUMMARY

Management is often more concerned with the contracting of services than with the purchase of foodstuffs or supplies. Some services it handles entirely itself such as legal, financial, insurance, capital equipment, and consulting services. When contracts are let, they require careful scrutiny to see that the service desired is obtained. Legal advice should usually be sought. Bidding for the service may be used.

Many operations find that word-of-mouth advertising is their best advertising medium. It is important to see that the message desired is delivered. Some find it advisable to use an advertising agency to achieve desired results. Many cleaning tasks are better done by specialists because the facility employees are not competent to do the work or it takes specialized cleaning equipment. Often a cleaning service can use nonunion employees, which can reduce labor costs for a union facility. This may be true for many other services. Contracts for dishwashing, pot and pan washing, and other cleaning tasks are not unusual.

An operation may desire vending services to supplement its regular service or to provide service when the regular services are closed down. Some facilities purchase their own vending equipment and operate their own vending service. Others may lease equipment and fill these units with their own foods and beverages. Yet others contract with a firm to provide and maintain the equipment and also supply and service the items sold. It is also possible to contract with a firm to supervise the running of your company's vending services.

Entertainment artists usually have agents who contract their services. Personnel that are specialists in this field usually represent the operation and sometimes this is an outside firm. If a lot of entertainment needs to be purchased, a special department separate from the purchasing department may do the contracting.

The rental of equipment is often costly but an operation may find that it pays to rent rather than own certain equipment, especially if the need is casual. However, some operations that consistently need equipment still rent because of convenience, no storage requirements, etc.

Employees should be well trained in fire and safety control. Specialists are often hired to do the required training and also may contract to do inspections. Often local fire, police, and other governmental agencies will give training sessions and do inspections free of charge. Local codes and the regulations of OSHA should be observed. Outside firms are often retained to give security services. It is important to select a security company that has a record of reliability. The backgrounds of all security employees should be carefully investigated before an employee being allowed to hole a security position.

Laws may require operations to contract for various kinds of service. Sometimes the state operates the insurance agency such as workers' compensation. Adequate insurance should be carried to protect the assets of the facility.

The interior climate of an operation is of importance for the comfort of both guests and employees. Heating, ventilation, and air conditioning equipment is run by the operation itself, but an outside firm is often required to see that desirable conditions are obtained. The firm can check and see that equipment is working properly and also assist in getting the desired results at the lowest possible cost. A food service's supplier of fuel or energy can often give valuable advice that costs nothing. The recapture of energy or the use of solar energy can help reduce costs. Some operations operate their own laundry facilities and do all their own cleaning, but sometimes is desirable to hire these services done by an outside firm. Some operations purchase their own laundry needs and then have these serviced an outside laundry. The method used will be decided by the specific conditions and needs the operation.

Some maintenance and repair needs may be contracted, but often such service is accomplished via a specific one-time service call. If refrigeration maintenance is contracted out, it should include cleaning of the units so they function at maximum efficiency. Some operations find contracting for services like payroll and accounting to be efficient because not enough work is required to warrant doing it in-house or the operation lacks the trained personnel to do the work. Pest control contracts are common. The times for performing this service should be spelled out and a check should be made to see that the work is performed as specified.

With the advent of computers many operations find they can do their own printing and achieve professional results. However, many operations still find that having a contract for the printing of menus and other needs is desirable. Specialists in menu construction and printing are often used.

Removal contracts are common for the removal of debris, snow, leaves, etc. Garbage pick-up may be required; if so, the contract should call for specific times and for cleaning of the area; sometimes the washing of containers is specified. It is possible to sell some wastes such as paper, grease, and edible garbage.

Transport equipment such as elevators and escalators are often put on contract for maintenance. Inspection by government authorities is made at periodic times to see that such equipment presents no hazard and is in good working order. Contracts for guest transportation are sometimes made.

Water treatment is sometimes necessary. In some areas the water is hard and must be softened by some process before it is suitable for use. Occasionally problem is encountered with other compounds such as iron salts in the water. Water purification by chlorination and/or filtration may be necessary.

REVIEW QUESTIONS

1. Discuss the reasons for and advantages of contracting for various types of service.

2. List the major details that should be covered in a contract service.

3. List the types of services generally contracted for in hotels and food services.

4. Who should verify the credentials of contracted employees used for security purposes? Why?

5. What are the differences between hiring a consultant and hiring contract services?

6. Who or what should determine the frequency of visits for contract services and the degree of maintenance versus repair?

7. Who carries insurance for the services performed by a contractor?
   Note: A good class exercise would be to divide the class into six groups and have three groups represent a hotel or food service that is negotiating for the following. Group 1—linen service; Group 2—pest control; Group 3—equipment maintenance and repair, such as ice machines or air conditioning. The other three groups can represent purveyors of the three respective services. Evaluate the discussions on how well essential factors were covered, how well they agreed on what services should be rendered, prices, and other factors, and how well the cost of miscellaneous services and other factors were covered.

KEY WORDS AND CONCEPTS

advertising services

bid for work

cleaning services

consulting services

contract analysis

entertainment services

equipment rental

fire protection services

heating, ventilation, and air-conditioning services

laundry and dry cleaning services

Occupational Safety and Health Administration (OSHA)

payroll and accounting services

pest control services

printing services

removal services

safety inspection and training

security services

transportation services

vending services

water treatment services

word-of-mouth advertising

APPENDIX A

The Law of Purchasing

THE PURCHASE OF GOODS

Let's walk toward the "back of the house" for a moment and take a legal look at what goes on in the purchasing and receiving departments.

A lot of goods arrive each day, all worth a great deal. Therefore, we need to pay the same attention to them as we would if it were cash we were receiving and not goods.

What Law Governs?

The law that governs the buying and selling of goods between merchants in all fifty states is Article 2 of the Uniform Commercial Code, known in legal circles as "Sales." Since innkeepers, restaurateurs, bar operators, and others in the hospitality industry are merchants as defined in this article, and since they purchase goods from other merchants, this particular law applies to them. But are innkeepers really merchants as that word is used at law?

U.C.C. 2-104 defines a merchant as "a person who deals in goods of the kind or otherwise by his occupation holds himself out as having knowledge or skill peculiar to the practices or goods involved in the transaction or to whom such knowledge or skill may be attributed by his employment of an agent who . . . holds himself out as having such knowledge or skill." If the innkeeper in fact does

not have the knowledge or skill of a merchant, he should hire a purchasing agent who does.

What Kind of Law Is the U.C.C.?

The Uniform Commercial Code is a rather complicated body of contract law. A product of the past three decades, the U.C.C. must be distinguished from the body of contract law traced to the ancient Egyptians. If we are buying land or a hotel or hiring employees, the ancient laws can be guidelines. If we are buying linens, foodstuff, lamps, chairs and other supplies, we must look to Article 2 for guidance.

Our sales contracts involve the "back of the house" where we receive and store our goods. To facilitate a discussion of purchasing and receiving departments, let's assume we need to purchase 10,000 hand towels for immediate and future use in the hotel.

Easy Enough

To do so, many of us would first look through catalogs of hand towel suppliers. However, examining state statutes to see if the legislature has directed its attention to such matters would be more beneficial. In many states, such statutes exist. To illustrate, Nevada Revised Statutes, 447.090, subsection 3, provides that "sheets shall be at least 98 inches long and of sufficient width to cover the mattress and spring completely." In other states, the size and substance of other items are specified.

Reprinted by permission of John Goodwin, 1987, pp. 141–147.

Any legally oriented innkeeper or merchant who wants to comply with laws which are binding should first examine the statutes. Then you can find what you need at a competitive price in the catalogs and place the order.

Statute of Frauds

Many times we need our supplies in a hurry, so we place the order over the phone, assuming our goods will be shipped faster. However, there is a legal problem to consider since Article 2 has a Statute of Frauds. Such statutes, which have existed since 1677, can cause legal problems when they are least expected.

Article 2-201, U.C.C., states, "A contract for the sale (purchase) of goods for the price of $500 or more is not enforceable by way of action or defense unless there is some writing sufficient to indicate that a contract for the sale has been made between the parties and signed by the party against whom such enforcement is sought or by his authorized . . . agent." While there are three exceptions, the basic law remains. Since our 10,000 linens will certainly cost more than $500, we must use a writing, and the seller should insist that we do. There are two ways we can use a writing.

First, we can place our order by use of a written purchase order signed by an authorized agent. Purchase order forms, prepared by counsel, should have multiple copies for receiving, accounting, and the administrator. Computer forms also may be used.

Still, placing the order over the phone would expedite the process, and there is a proper way to use the oral order.

The order might be placed over the phone by saying, "Please ship 10,000 linen sheets, size 100 inches × 96 inches, catalog item XYZ, at a per-unit price of $6.00 each, FOB our hotel, with delivery by June 1." Then the oral order is simply confirmed in writing and *the agent signs it*. According to U.C.C., 2-201, if the confirmation is sent within a reasonable time, it satisfies the Statute of Frauds unless the seller gives "written notice of objection to its contents" within 10 days after it is received.

Good Policy

All establishments should follow a firm purchasing policy. First, the bulk of orders for goods of $500 or more should be placed in writing. Second, if orders are placed by phone, they must be confirmed in writing and signed by an agent in due course.

Next, a written acknowledgment of the order from the seller might be requested. If there are order changes in the acknowledgment, the U.C.C. places clear responsibility on the buyer.

What Must the Buyer Do?

Once notice is received of a nonconforming shipment, the buyer has two choices: object and tell why the substituted goods cannot be used, or pay the price. A buyer can be held responsible for goods that *were not ordered,* a particular situation which will be examined later.

The buyer must thoroughly review acknowledgments and check them against purchase orders. Not doing so could result in legal problems.

The acknowledgment is a written confirmation of the buyer's order, and he must object to it, if necessary, within 10 days. If the objection is received before the goods are shipped, corrections can be made. If an acknowledgment is not sent, problems can arise when the goods arrive.

The Shipment Arrives

Let's assume that the delivery is different from what was ordered, that is, it is nonconforming. Several things can happen.

We might instruct sales personnel to set the goods aside and not return them. But "acting inconsistently" with someone else's merchandise constitutes acceptance. We then would have to pay for something we did not order. Buyers cannot act inconsistently with goods that belong to someone else.

Another alternative would be to place the goods in stock and use them, if they are an acceptable alternate. If the goods are *cheaper* than what we ordered, there is no problem because by accepting the goods, we have bought them at the lower price. If the nonconforming goods are listed at a *higher* price, legal problems might arise. If we accept them, we do so at the higher price.

How to Handle Nonconforming Goods

Handling nonconforming goods brings into play one of the more interesting parts of Article 2 of the U.C.C. The code makes it clear that if nonconforming goods are received, we must do three things. First, we must inspect the goods; second, we must reject the goods if we do not want them; and third, we must tell the seller why we cannot use the goods. These three requirements are discussed later. If we fail to meet this three-part test, *then we have accepted the goods;* another means of acceptance in a sales-of-goods situation.

The reasoning of this rule is as follows: Since Article 2 applies to merchants, then merchants should have knowledge of what types of goods can be substituted for the ones that have been ordered. If such a substitution is made and the buyer does not object, an acceptance occurs. If the seller sends inadequate substitutions, then he has a right to be told why the substitution is not acceptable. Once the seller is told why the nonconforming goods are unacceptable, then he has the right to "cure" (send conforming goods).

In legal circles, this process is known as the "perfect tender-cure" rule. The buyer is entitled to a perfect tender, or exactly what was ordered. If this is not received, the seller has the right to cure. A seller can only cure if he is told why the goods are not acceptable.

Thus, if we receive nonconforming goods and fail to inspect, reject, and state why, we have accepted those goods and must pay for them. The law applies to both large and small orders of goods. This legality was used against the U.S. Army regarding an order of hams [*Max Bauer Meat Packer, Inc. v. United States,* 458 Fed. 2d 88, 10 U.C.C. Rep. 1056 (U.S. Court of Claims, 1972)]; and Eastern Airlines and 100 nonconforming 727 jet aircraft [*Eastern Airlines, Inc. v. McDonnell Douglas Corp.,* 532 F2d 957, 19 U.C.C. Rep. 353 (5th Cir. 1976)].

How quickly must the buyer follow the perfect tender-cure rule? In the Army case, the hams were rejected in less than five hours. The court held that was too long and the Army had to pay for the order. In the airline case, a few weeks elapsed before Eastern discovered its new fleet of jet aircraft was not what had been ordered. The court held that a few weeks was too long, and Eastern had to accept aircraft which did not meet specifications.

The U.C.C. says rejection must be "seasonable," or in due course. With food that will be prepared immediately, this means a very short period of time.

But What About the Goods?

While we still have the goods in our possession, we hold them under the law of bailment and not under the law of sales. As a bailee, we must use reasonable care to protect and safeguard them until disposition by the owner or the seller. If we use ordinary care and the goods are stolen or destroyed by fire, the loss falls on the seller, making the rejection rule even more important to the buyer.

If the rejected goods are perishable and cannot be safeguarded, then the seller should be notified at once. The seller may instruct us to sell the goods at a loss, or to ship them elsewhere. We are expected, at law, to follow such orders *at the expense of the seller.*

Inspection

To what degree must a buyer inspect the goods? Inspection by sample is all that is required. Examining a box or two from different parts of the shipment meets legal requirements.

Sometimes a shipment is in sealed containers that are not opened until they are used, such as canned goods. If such containers are opened later and the contents are nonconforming, the code also covers the buyer in this situation.

Revoking an Acceptance

If defects are hidden or sealed and are not discovered until later, acceptance can be revoked through a provision in the code. By revoking acceptance, the seller then has the right to cure. If the seller cannot cure, the goods belong to the seller and are held as a bailee by the buyer.

SUMMARY

We have had a general review of the laws that control purchasing at the back of the house. Since merchants are involved, the rules are reasonable, representing a special contract law that covers the sale of goods between merchants. If we as buyers con-duct ourselves as reasonable merchants would be expected to do, we can comply with the rules in most cases.

In our brief discussion, we have not mentioned many topics, such as late delivery, insolvency of a buyer, recapture of goods and others. Article 2 covers all of these problems, and if they arise in buying and receiving, legal advice must be sought.

If we as buyers act in good faith and honesty, monitor our purchasing and receiving departments, and provide a little instruction in the form of house policies, we can get along quite nicely with the contract law called "Sales."

APPENDIX B

General Storage Requirements for Foodstuffs

FRESH FRUITS AND VEGETABLES

"Although it may be necessary to store various fresh fruits and vegetables together, there are some products that should be separated whenever possible. Apples, pears, bananas, peaches, plums, cantaloupes, ripe honey dew melons, avocados, tomatoes, and other ethylene producing fruits or vegetables should not be stored with lettuce (causes russeting), carrots (become bitter), cucumbers, green peppers, acorn or Hubbard squash (loss of green color). Odors from apples and citrus fruits are readily absorbed by meat, eggs, and dairy products. Pears and apples acquire an unpleasant earthy taste and odor when stored with potatoes. Other combinations which should be avoided in storage rooms are apples or pears with celery, cabbage, or onions, celery with onions or carrots, green peppers with pineapples, and citrus fruit with any strongly scented vegetables" such as onions. "Green peppers can taint pineapples if the two are stored together. Onions, nuts, citrus fruit, and potatoes should each be stored separately whenever possible." In many operations, it is not possible to separate products in separate rooms, but storing them as far away as possible in the one storage area is recommended.

The data in this storage section was extracted from the Department of Defense's publication 4145.19-R-1, pp. 5-89–5-124, dated 15, September, 1979. Direct quotes from this material are indicated in quotation marks; summaries of the material are not.

Group 1. The following are high ethylene producers and should be stored separately, if possible:

Apples (see group 3)	Peaches
Apricots	Pears
Berries (except cranberries)	Persimmons
Cherries	Plums and prunes
Figs (not with apples, odor transfer)	
Grapes	Pomegranates
	Quinces

Store group 1 at: 32°–34°F (1°–3°C)
Relative humidity of 90–95%

Group 2. Store the following together:

Avocados	Olives, fresh
Bananas	Papayas
Casaba melons	Persian melons
Crenshaw melons	Pineapples (not with avocados)
Eggplant (see group 5)	
Grapefruit	Tomatoes, green
Guava	Tomatoes, pink (see group 4)
Honeydew melons	
Limes	Watermelons
Muskmelons but not cantaloupes	

Store group 2 at: 55°–65°F (13°–18°C)
Relative humidity 85–95%

Group 3. Store the following together:

Apples (Grimes Golden, Jonathan, Yellow Newton, and McIntosh)	Lychees (see group 4)
Cantaloupes	Oranges
Cranberries	Tangerines
Lemons (50–55 F if stored for over a month)	

Store group 3 at: 36°–41°F (2°–5°C)
Relative humidity 90–95%

Group 4. Store the following together:

Beans, snap (not with fresh peppers)	Squash, summer
Lychees (see group 3)	Tomatoes, pink (see group 2)
Okra	Watermelons (see groups 2 and 5)
Oranges	
Peppers, red and green	

Store group 4 at: 50°–55°F (10°–13°C)
Relative humidity about 95%

Group 5. Store the following together:

Cucumbers	Pumpkins and winter squashes
Eggplant (see group 2)	
Ginger (not with eggplant; see group 7)	Watermelon (see groups 2 and 4)
Potatoes (mature)	

Group 6a. Store the following together:

Artichokes	Mushrooms
Asparagus	Parsley
Beets, red	Parsnips
Carrots	Peas
Endive and escarole	Rhubarb
Figs (see group 1)	Salsify
Grapes	Spinach
Greens	Sweet corn
Leeks (Not with figs or grapes)	Watercress
Lettuce	

Note 1: Grapes fumigated with sulfur dioxide (SO_2) or containing chemicals with sulfur dioxide should not be stored with other fruits or vegetables.

Note 2: Group 6a is compatible with group 6b, except for figs, grapes, and mushrooms.

Group 6b. Store the following together:

Broccoli	Horseradish
Brussels sprouts	Kohlrabi
Cabbage	Onions, green
Cauliflower	Radishes
Celeriac	Rutabagas
Celery	Turnips

Store groups 6a and 6b at: 32°–34°F (0°–10°C)
Relative humidity 95–100%

Note 1: Do not store green onions with rhubarb, figs, or grapes, and probably not with mushrooms or sweet corn.

Group 7. Store the following together:

Ginger (see group 5)	Sweet potatoes
Potatoes, immature	

Store group 7 at: 55°–65°F (13°–18°C)
Relative humidity at 85–90%

Group 8. Store the following together:

Garlic	Onions, dry

Store group 8 at: 32°–34°F (0°–1°C)
Relative humidity 65–70%

A number of products stored at too low a temperature can suffer chill damage. Thus, apples will develop internal browning, brown core, soggy breakdown, and soft scald; eggplant surface scald and rot; melons pitting, surface decay, and failure to ripen; ripe tomatoes, water soaking and softening and decay along with a loss of fresh flavor.

FROZEN PERISHABLE SUBSTANCES

"Storage temperature for all frozen subsistence items shall not exceed 0°F. For ice cream, the recommended temperature is −10°F and in no case should the temperature exceed 0°F."

Months of storage life of frozen foods at 0°F or below

Apples	18	Meals, precooked	6
Apple juice, concentrated	30	Milk, homogenized	1
Asparagus	12	Milk, concentrated whole	1
Bacon, sliced	12	Okra	18
Beans, green, lima and wax	12–14	Onion rings, fried or raw	14
Beef	12	Orange juice, concentrated	24
Beef, corned	6	Oysters	8
Beef, ground, diced, etc.	9	Pastas dishes, cooked	6
Beef, liver, tongue, etc.	4	Pastrami	6
Berries	18	Peaches	18
Broccoli	14	Peas, blackeye	12
Brussels sprouts	12	Peas, green	14
Butter, well wrapped	18	Peas and carrots	14
Cakes	12	Peppers	6
Carrots	24	Pies, cream	6
Cauliflower	14	Pies, fruit	12
Cherries, RTP, pitted	24	Pineapple	12
Cheeses	12	Pineapple juice, concentrated	24
Chicken, parts	8	Pizza or pizza shells	6
Chicken, whole, RTC	10	Pork, barbecued	6
Clams, shucked	6	Pork, carcass or cut up	8
Corn	8	Pork, cured and smoked	6
Corn on the cob	9	Potatoes, all kinds	12
Crabs	8	Rhubarb	18
Dates	12	Sausage, cured, dried	6–8
Duck	10	Sausage, beef	6
Eggs	12	Sausage, liver	3–4
Fish, fillets, steaks	6	Sausage, breakfast	2
Fish sticks, portions	2–3	Scallops	8
Frankfurters (weiners)	6	Soups	12
Grapefruit juice, concentrated	24	Spinach	10
Grapefruit sections	24	Squash, cooked	24
Greens, leafy	14	Succotash	12
Hams	6	Sweet yeast goods	2
Ice cream and frozen desserts	9	Tamales	6
Lamb	12	Topping, dessert	24
Lard, shortening, etc.	12	Turkey, boneless, cooked	7
Lemon juice, concentrated	12	Turkey, boneless, raw	7
Lime juice, concentrated	12	Turkey, whole	–
Lobster tails	8	Veal	12
Lobster, whole	8	Vegetables, mixed	12
Margarine	12	Waffles or hot cakes	2

Approximate chill storage days of perishable foods

Item	Storage °F	Approx. Storage Life
Artichokes	32	14
Apricots	32	7–21
Asparagus, fresh	36	10
Avocados, rough skinned	40–45	14–28
Avocados, smooth skinned	55	14
Bacon, sliced, skinless	32–35	42
Bananas, green	56–58	7–10
Bananas, ripe	56–58	2–4
Beans, green or wax	45–50	7–10
Beans, lima, shelled, unshelled	32	7
Beef, carcass or cut up	35	10–14
Beef, ground	35	4
Beef, cured	35	35–42
Beets, topped	32	120–180
Beets, bunched	32	14
Berries	32	2–3
Blueberries	32	14
Broccoli	32	10–14
Brussels sprouts	32	21–35
Butter, well wrapped	32	30
Cabbage, red and summer	32	21–42
Cabbage, winter	32	90–120
Cabbage, Chinese	32	7–10
Cantaloupe	32	5–14
Carrots, mature, topped	32	120–170
Carrots, immature	32	28–42
Casaba melon	45–50	28–42
Cauliflower	32	14–28
Celeriac	32	90–120
Celery	32	30–42
Cherries, sweet	30–31	14–21
Chicory	32–34	10–30
Cheese, blue veined	32–35	180
Cheese, Swiss, American, etc	32–35	360–540
Cheese, cottage	32–35	14
Cheese, cream	32–35	30
Cheese, mozzarella	35	30
Cheese, parmesan and other dry	32–35	180–360
Clams, shucked	32–35	4
Cookie dough	32	90
Corn on the cob	32	4–8
Cranberries, fresh	36–40	60–120
Cranberry sauce	50	180
Cream	32–35	7–10
Cream, sour	32–35	14
Cream, ultra pasteurized	32–35	84
Crenshaw melon	45–50	14
Cucumbers	50–55	10–14
Dates, pitted, cured	32	180
Eggnog	32	14
Eggnog, ultra pasteurized	32	84
Eggs, shell	29–31	150–180
Eggplant	45–50	7–10

Item	Storage °F	Approx. Storage Life
Fennel	32	60–120
Figs, fresh	32	7–10
Frankfurters (weiners)	32–35	21
French dressing	50	80–90
Fruitcake	40	300
Fruits, dried	32–40	180–360
Garlic, dry	32	180–210
Ginger, rhizomes	55	180
Gooseberries	31–32	14–28
Grapefruit	58–60	28
Grapefruit sections	35–45	540
Grapes, American types	32	21–56
Grapes, European types	30	60–180
Greens, escarole, endive, etc.	32	14–21
Greens, collards, kale, etc.	32	10–14
Ham, cured, canned	32–35	270
Smoked	32–35	28
Honeyball melon	45–90	21–28
Honeydew melon	45–90	21–28
Horseradish, prepared	32	90
Horseradish root	30–32	300–360
Huckleberries	32	7–10
Jams, jellies, etc	50	180
Kohlrabi	32	14–28
Kumquats	33–35	60–120
Lamb	32–35	7–10
Lard	45	120–240
Leeks	32	30–90
Lettuces	32–34	14–21
Lettuces, chopped	32–34	5–7
Lobster, live in water	33–50	7
Lemons	55	30–90
Lemon juice	50	120
Limes	48–50	42–56
Luncheon loaf	32–35	14–21
Mangoes	55	60–90
Margarine	32–35	7 years
Milks, regular	32–35	7–10
Milks, ultrapasteurized	32–35	84
Mushrooms	32–34	3–4
Mustard, prepared	50	90–270
Nectarines	31–32	14–28
Okra	45–50	7–10
Olives	45–50	28–42
Onions, dry	32	180–240
Oranges	40–44	28–56
Orange juice	32	21
Oysters, shucked, in ice	32–35	4
Papaya	50	120
Parsley	32	30–60
Parsnips	32	60–180
Peaches	32	14–28
Peanut butter	50	180

Item	Storage °F	Approx. Storage Life
Pears	31	30
Peas, unshelled	32	7–14
Peppers, sweet	45–50	14–21
Peppers, dry, chili	32–50	180
Pepperoni, dry	32	28
Persian melons	45–50	14
Persimmons	30	90–120
Pies, fruit, fresh	35	3
Pineapple, ripe	45	147
Plums	32	21–28
Pomegranates	32	14–28
Pork, wholesale cuts	32–35	5
Poultry, all forms	30	5
Potatoes, sweet	55–60	120–210
Potatoes, white, new	40–50	60–120
Potatoes, white, mature	40	150–240
Potatoes, peeled	35	5–9
Potatoes, irradiated	40–45	360
Prunes, Italian	32	14–21
Pumpkins	50–55	60–90
Quinces	31–32	60–90
Radishes	32	10–12
Rhubarb	32	14–28
Rolls, brown and serve	32	21
Rutabagas	32	120–180
Salad dressings	50	90
Salmon steaks	32–35	4
Salami, dry	32–35	60
Salsify	32	60–120
Sausage, various	32	10–14
Scallops	32–35	4
Shallots, cured	32	21–28
Shortening, sealed	32	1800
Shrimp, unpeeled, in ice	32	14
Syrups	50	365
Spinach	32	10–14
Squash, summer	32–40	4–5
Squash, fall and winter	50	60
Swiss chard	32	10–14
Tangerines	32	14–28
Tomatoes, mature green	55	7–21
Tomatoes, pink	55	4–7
Tomatoes, firm ripe	55	3–5
Tomatoes, full ripe	32–35	21
Turnips	32	120–150
Veal, wholesale cuts	32	6
Watercress	32	7
Watermelon	40–50	14–21
Yeast, active, dry	30–39	180–360
Yeast, compressed cake	30–32	30–90
Yogurt	30–35	30

Dry storage, semiperishable foods

Item	Keeping Time in Months (Approximately)		
	40°F	70°F	90°F
Apricots, canned	48	24	12
Apricots, dried	24	3	1
Apricots, freeze dehydrated	24	12	5
Apricot nectar, canned	48	24	12
Asparagus, canned	36	18	9
Baby foods	24	12	6
Baby formula, canned	24	12	6
Bacon, sliced, canned	48	24	12
Bakery mixes, commercial	12	6	3
Baking powder, canned	24	12	6
Baking soda, boxed	indef.	indef.	indef.
Barley pearl, bagged	60	48	24
Beans, dry	24	12	9
Beans, green, canned	36	18	9
Beans, dried, cooked, canned	72	36	18
Beef, cooked, canned	72	36	18
Beef, dehydrated, canned	60	24	12
Berries, canned	36	18	9
Beverage bases: cocoa powder	72	36	24
Beverage base, powders	48	24	12
Biscuit mix	36	18	3
Bouillon, etc.	48	24	12
Bread crumbs, boxed	8	4	2
Cakes, fresh	2–4 days		
Candy, boxed, caramels	12	9	4
Candy, hard	72	36	18
Candy, starch jelly, box	24	12	6
Carrots, canned	60	30	15
Catsup, bottle or can	36–48	18–24	12–9
Cereals, ready-to-eat	24	12	6
Cheese cake mix	12	6	3
Cherries, maraschino	36	18	9
Cherries, canned	36	18	9
Chicken, canned	60	36	18
Chili con carne, canned	48	30	15
Chili sauce, bottled	48	24	12
Chocolate, cooking, bitter	48	24	12
Chocolate, sweetened types	48	24	12
Chocolate syrup	72	36	18
Chutney	48	24	12
Clams, canned	72	36	18
Cocoa, canned	36	18	9
Coconut sweetened, canned	36	18	6
Coffee, instant	36	18	9
Coffee, ground, bagged	9	2	1
Cookies, carton	6	4	1
Cornbread mix, canned	24	12	3
Corn, all kinds, canned	72	36	18
Corn chips, packaged	1	½	¼

Item	Keeping Time in Months (Approximately)		
	40°F	70°F	90°F
Corn flake crumbs, boxed	24	12	6
Cornmeal, packaged	24	12	6
Crackers, graham, packaged	4	2	1
Crackers, others	12	6	3
Cranberry sauce, canned	36	18	9
Cream substitutes	12	6	1
Currants, packaged	24	12	6
Dessert powder, gelatine	72	36	18
Dessert powder, dessert	48	24	12
Eggnog, canned	12	6	1
Eggs, dehydrated, canned	60	36	18
Figs, canned	48	24	12
Flavorings, bottled	indef.	indef.	indef.
Flours, bagged	24	12	6
Fruit cakes, boxed	12	6	1
Fruits, candied, canned	12	6	3
Fruit cocktail, canned	48	24	12
Fry mix breading, bagged	36	18	9
Gelatin	72	36	18
Grape juice, canned	24	12	6
Grapefruit, canned	48	24	12
Grapefruit juice, canned	48	24	12
Hash, corned beef or roast beef, canned	72	36	18
Hominy grits, package	24	12	6
Hominy, canned	72	36	18
Honey, extracted	48	24	12
Jams and jellies	36	16	9
Lard, carton	12	6	3
Lemon juice, dehydrated, canned	72	36	18
Luncheon meat, canned	60	36	18
Macaroni, carton	72	36	18
Mayonnaise, jar	12	6	3
Meringue powder	48	24	1
Milk, dry, nonfat	32	16	8
Milk, evaporated, canned	24	12	6
Milk, whole, dry, canned	6	3	1
Mincemeat, canned	48	24	12
Molasses, canned or jar	48	24	12
Mustard, prepared	36	18	9
Mushrooms, canned	48	24	12
Noodles, chow mein, packaged	8	4	2
Noodles, egg	72	36	18
Nuts, shelled, packaged	60	24	12
Nuts, unshelled, packaged	24	12	6
Okra, canned	48	24	12
Olives, green, jar	48	24	12
Olives, ripe, canned	48	24	12
Olive oil, canned	18	6	4
Onions, dehydrated	36	24	12
Orange juice, canned	48	24	12
Peaches, canned in syrup	48	24	12

Item	Keeping Time in Months (Approximately)		
	40°F	70°F	90°F
Peanut butter, jar	36	18	9
Pears, canned in syrup	36	18	9
Peas, canned	72	36	18
Peas and carrots, canned	60	30	15
Pickles, various	24	12	6
Pie crust mix, canned	36	18	6
Pie fillings, various, canned	24	12	6
Pie crust, graham cracker, container	8	4	2
Pimientos, canned	48	24	12
Pineapple juice	48	24	12
Pineapple, regular pack	48	24	12
Plums, canned, red types	36	18	9
Plums, canned, other	48	24	12
Popcorn, unpopped, canned	72	36	18
Popcorn, unpopped, carton	2	¼	⅛
Potato chips, packaged	1	½	¼
Potato chips, canned	12	6	3
Potato granules, canned	60	36	18
Potato slices, canned	36	18	9
Prunes, dry, carton	18	9	5
Pumpkin, canned	36	18	9
Raisins, dried, carton	18	9	5
Rice, instant, carton	36	18	9
Rice, milled, bagged	48	24	12
Rice, parboiled, bagged	30	20	10
Rolls, bagels, bagged	1 day		
Rolls, common, bagged	2 days		
Rolls, English muffins, bagged	1 wk		
Salad dressing, jar, spoonable	8	5	2
Salad dressing, jar, pourable	7	5	2
Salad oil, canned	24	12	6
Salmon, canned	72	36	18
Sauces, meat, condiment type	60	30	15
Sauerkraut, canned	36	18	9
Sardines, canned	72	36	18
Sardines in tomato sauce, canned		15	8
Shortening, baking or deep frying types, canned	48	24	12
Shrimp, canned	72	36	18
Syrups	72	36	18
Soups, canned	60	30	15
Soups, dehydrated, packaged	24	12	6
Soup and gravy bases, canned	60	30	15
Spaghetti, packaged	72	36	18
Spices	48	24	12
Spinach, canned	60	23	12
Starch, packaged	96	48	24
Sugars, bagged	36	18	6
Tamales, canned	24	24	12
Tapioca, packaged	96	48	12
Taco shells, corn, packaged	12	6	3

Dry storage, semiperishable foods (continued)

Item	Keeping Time in Months (Approximately)		
	40°F	70°F	90°F
Tea, carton	35	18	9
Tomato juice, canned	36	18	9
Tomatoes, canned and puree	48	24	12
Tomato paste, canned	36	18	9
Tomatoes and okra, canned	48	24	12
Topping, dry, canned	36	24	6
Tuna, canned	72	36	18
Turkey, canned	72	36	18
Vinegar, liquid, bottled	60	30	15
Yeast, bakers, active dry, canned	6	1	½
Yeast food, bag	48	24	12

Notes:

1. Relative humidity over 50–55% can lead to rusting of cans and over 60% can cause molding in most boxed or bagged foods.

2. Salt in a relative humidity over 90% cakes; it is still usable.

3. Turn canned milks every 30 to 60 days; separated or grainy milks can be used for cooking.

4. Cream-style liquids break down on freezing but can be reformed by vigorous beating with a whip. Frozen baked products may be somewhat altered in grain, but will usually return to normal on reheating.

5. Packaged or otherwise exposed chocolate can absorb flavors.

6. Store flours, sugars, and other bagged goods on platforms that raise it off the floor. It is also best to cover with tarpaulins.

APPENDIX C

Economic Order Quantity

Economic order quantity (EOQ) is a composite calculation that considers order cost, usage, and storage costs when determining quantities to purchase. It also can be used to calculate the most economical dollar amount to order at or the most economical amount to order.

EOQ is suitable for use by large buyers, and some small buyers may even find it useful for items they purchase in large quantities. Fast-moving or perishable items do not lend themselves to EOQ. Thus, coffee should be ordered to last only a few days. Coffee delivery, therefore, should be steady and frequent, not sporadic.

Small variations between dollar amounts and amounts to order do not make a big difference; thus, making a small adjustment to save storage space or limited funds can be done without too much difference. An explanation of the most favorable amounts to order in dollars and in units follows.

AMOUNT TO ORDER IN UNITS

The calculation to ascertain the number of units to order is

$$EOQ = \sqrt{\frac{2(a \times b)}{c \times d}}$$

Thus, if one wanted to know how many No. 10 cases of C grade chopped canned tomatoes to order, the calculation might be

a = average order cost	$10
b = usage during period	240 cases
c = percent of item value in storage cost	15%
d = unit value	$14 per case

$$\sqrt{\frac{2(\$10 \times 240)}{0.15 \times \$14}} = \sqrt{\frac{\$4800}{\$2.10}} = 47.8 \text{ cases}$$

EOQ is 48 cases

AMOUNT TO ORDER IN DOLLARS

$$EOQ = \sqrt{\frac{2(a \times b)}{c}}$$

where

a = order cost average	$10
b = usage during period times unit cost	$3360
c = percent of item value in storage costs	15%

$$\sqrt{\frac{2(\$10 \times \$3360)}{0.15}} = \sqrt{\frac{\$67,200}{0.15}} = \sqrt{\$448,000}$$
$$= \$669.33$$

APPENDIX D

Formulas for Calculating Yield Grades of Meat

BEEF

Beef yield grades are determined on the basis of the following formula: Yield grade = (2.50 + 2.50 × adjusted fat thickness in in.) + (0.20 × % kidney, pelvic, and heart fat) + (0.0038 × hot carcass weight in lb) − (0.32 × ribeye area in.^{2}). Thus, if a 750-lb carcass, hot weight, had an adjusted fat thickness of 0.5, an inside fat of 2% of total carcass weight, and 16.5 in.^{2} of ribeye surface, the calculation would be as follows:

Basic value	*2.50*
2.50 × 0.5 in.	*1.25*
0.20 × 2.5 in.	*0.50*
0.0038 × 750 lb	*2.85*
	7.10
0.32 × 16.5 sq in.	*5.28*
Yield grade	*1.82 (Yield grade is No. 1.)*[1]

---

[1]Yield grades fall between the whole numbers; they are not rounded up or down. Thus, a yield grade of 1.0 to 1.99 is No. 1.

LAMB AND MUTTON

Lamb and mutton yield grades are determined on the basis of the following formula: Yield grade = 1.66 + (0.25 × % of pelvic and kidney fat) + (6.66 × adjusted fat thickness over ribeye) − (0.05 × leg conformation grade). Thus, a lamb carcass with a 1.5% pelvic and kidney fat value, a 0.1-in. fat thickness over the ribeye, and a 14 leg conformation code would have a yield grade of 1: [1.66 + (0.25 × 1.5%) + (6.66 × 0.1) − (0.05 × 14) = 1.6298].

PORK

Pork yield grades are determined on the basis of the following formula: Yield grade = (4.0 × backfat thickness over last rib in in.) − (1.0 × muscling score). Muscle scores are 1 = thin, 2 = average, and 3 = thick muscling. Thus, a barrow or gilt that had a 1.1-in. backfat thickness and a 1.8 muscling score would have a yield grade of U.S. No. 2: (4.0 × 1.1 in.) − (1.0 × 1.8) = 2.6.

IMPS Tables Other Than Fresh Beef and the Division of Beef into Wholesale Cuts

Tables E–1 through E–9 give the IMPS numbers of meat cuts other than beef. The figures at the end of this appendix show how the forequarters and hindquarters of beef are divided into the wholesale cuts from which individual cuts purchased by food services are taken. Figure E-1 shows the skeletal structure of beef, and Figures E–2, E–3, and E–4 show the lines of division of beef and how to cut it.

Table E-1

Index of products and weight range for lamb and mutton (in pounds)

Item No.	Product	Range A		Range B		Range C		Range D	
		Lamb	Mutton	Lamb	Mutton	Lamb	Mutton	Lamb	Mutton
200	Carcass	30–41	55–75	41–53	75–95	53–65	95–115	65–75	115–130
202	Foresaddle	15–21	28–38	21–27	38–48	27–33	48–58	33–38	58–65
203	Bracelet (Double)	5–6	8–11	6–8	11–14	8–10	14–17	10–12	17–19
204	Rib Rack (Double)	3–5	6–8	5–6	8–10	6–7	10–13	7–8	13–14
205	Chucks and Plates (Double)	12–16	22–30	16–21	30–38	21–26	38–46	26–30	46–52
206	Chucks (Double)	11–14	19–26	14–19	26–33	19–23	33–40	23–27	40–46
207	Square Cut Shoulders (Double)	8–10	14–19	10–13	19–24	13–16	24–29	16–19	29–33
208	Square Cut Shoulder, Boneless	3–4	6–8	4–6	8–10	6–7	10–12	7–8	12–16
209	Breast, Flank On	4–6	8–11	6–7	11–13	7–9	13–16	9–11	16–18
209A	Breast, Flank Off	3–5	7–10	5–6	10–12	6–8	12–16	8–10	16–18
210	Foreshank	1–1.5	2–3	1.5–2	3–4	2–2.5	4–5	2.5–3	5–6
230	Hindsaddle	15–21	23–38	21–27	38–48	27–33	48–58	33–38	58–65
23	Loin (Double)	5–6	8–11	6–18	11–14	8–10	14–17	10–12	17–20
232	Loin, Trimmed (Double)	3–4	6–8	4–5	8–10	5–7	10–12	7–8	12–15
233	Leg (Double)	11–14	19–26	14–19	26–33	19–23	33–40	23–27	40–46
233A	Leg, Lower Shank Off (Single)	5–7	9–12	7–9	12–15	9–12	15–19	12 up	19 up

Table E–1

Index of products and weight range for lamb and mutton (in pounds) (continued)

Item No.	Product	Range A Lamb	Range A Mutton	Range B Lamb	Range B Mutton	Range C Lamb	Range C Mutton	Range D Lamb	Range D Mutton
233B	Leg, Lower Shank Off, Boneless	4–6	8–11	6–8	11–13	8–11	13–17	11 up	17 up
233C	Leg, Shank Off (Single)	5–7	8–10	7–9	10–12	9–12	12–15	12 up	15 up
233D	Leg, Shank Off, Boneless	4–6	7–9	6–8	9–11	8–11	11–14	11 up	14 up
233E	Hindshank, Heel Attached	Under 1	1–1.5	1–2	1.5–3	2 up	3 up		
234 234A	Leg, Oven-Prepared Leg, Oven-Prepared, Boneless, & Tied	4–6	8–10	6–8	10–13	8–9	13–16	9–11	16–18
235	Back	9–12	17–23	12–16	23–29	16–20	29–35	20–23	35–39
236	Back, Trimmed	6–8	11–15	8–11	15–19	11–13	19–23	13–15	23–26
237	Hindsaddle, Long Cut	20–27	36–49	27–34	49–62	34–42	62–75	42–49	75–85
238	Hindsaddle, Long Cut, Trimmed	17–23	33–41	23–29	41–52	29–36	52–63	36–41	63–72

Note: When single chucks, backs, and so on are specified, their respective weights must be half that prescribed for double cuts in the table. The weight range of cuts shown in this table do not necessarily reflect any relation to the carcass weight ranges. Studies have shown that not all carcasses within a given weight range produce cuts that are uniform in weight. Therefore, in ordering cuts, purchasing officials should specify the weight range(s) desired without regard to the carcass weights shown in the various ranges.

Table E–2

Index of portion-cut products and weight range table

Item No.	Product	1 oz	2 oz	3 oz	5 oz	6 oz	8 oz	10 oz
1300	Cubed Steaks	X	X	X	X	X	X	
1301	Cubed Steaks Special	X	X	X	X	X	X	
1306	Rib Chops	X	X	X	X	X	X	X
1309	Shoulder Chops	X	X	X	X	X	X	X
1332	Loin Chops	X	X	X	X	X	X	X
1336	Cutlets	X	X	X	X	X		
1395	Veal for Stewing*	Amount as specified						
1396	Ground Veal*	Amount as specified						
1396A	Ground Veal Patties*	Amount as specified						

Note: Because it is impractical to list all portion weights, those identified by the letter X are suggested only; other portion weights may be specified, if desired.

*May also be prepared from calf in which case the name *calf* shall apply.

Table E–3

Index of products and weight range table for veal and calf (in pounds)

Item No.	Product	Range A		Range B		Range C		Range D	
		Veal	Calf	Veal	Calf	Veal	Calf	Veal	Calf
300	Carcass	60–90	125–175	90–140	175–225	140–175	225–275	175–225	275–350
303	Side	30–45	63–88	45–70	88–113	70–88	113–138	88–113	138–175
303A	Side, 2 Rib Hindquarter	30–45	63–88	45–70	88–113	70–88	113–138	88–113	138–175
303B	Side, 1 Rib Hindquarter	30–45	63–88	45–70	88–113	70–88	113–138	88–113	138–175
303C	Side, Boneless	23–38	48–77	38–54	77–86	54–67	86–106	67–86	106–135
304	Foresaddle, 11 Ribs	29–44	61–86	44–69	86–112	69–86	112–137	86–111	137–175
304A	Foresaddle, 12 Ribs	31–46	64–89	46–71	89–115	71–88	115–140	88–113	140–178
305	Bracelet, 7 Ribs (Double)	6–11	13–18	11–15	18–23	15–19	23–28	19–24	28–35
305A	Bracelet, 7 Ribs (Double)	6–11	13–18	11–15	18–23	15–19	23–28	19–24	28–35
306	Hotel Rack, 7 Ribs (Double)	5–9	9–14	9–12	14–18	12–14	18–22	14–18	22–28
306A	Hotel Rack, 7 Ribs (Double)	5–9	9–14	9–12	14–18	12–14	18–22	14–18	22–28
308	Chucks, 4 Ribs (Double)	22–40	50–71	40–56	71–90	56–70	90–110	70–90	110–141
308A	Chucks, 5 Ribs (Double)	23–41	52–73	41–57	73–93	57–72	93–114	72–92	114–145
309	Square Cut, Chucks, 4 Ribs, (Double)	11–20	25–36	20–28	36–45	28–36	45–55	36–47	55–72
309A	Square Cut Chucks, 5 Ribs, (Double)	12–21	27–40	21–29	40–51	29–37	51–63	37–48	63–80
309B	Square Cut Chuck 4 Ribs, Boneless	10–19	23–33	19–26	33–41	26–33	41–51	33–43	51–65
309C	Square Cut Chuck, 5 Ribs, Boneless	11–20	25–35	20–27	35–43	27–34	43–53	34–45	53–67
309D	Square Cut Chuck, Neck Off, 4 Ribs, Boneless & Tied	9–18	22–32	18–25	32–39	25–32	39–49	32–42	49–63
309E	Square Cut Chuck, Neck Off, 5 Ribs, Boneless & Tied	10–19	24–34	19–26	34–42	26–33	42–52	33–44	52–66
310	Shoulder Clod	2–4	5–7	4–5	7–8	5–7	8–10	7–9	10–12
310A	Shoulder Clod, Special	2–4	5–7	4–5	7–8	5–7	8–10	7–9	10–11
310B	Shoulder Clod Roast	2–4	5–7	4–5	7–8	5–7	8–10	7–9	10–11
311	Square Cut Chuck, 4 Ribs, Clod Out, Boneless	9–18	22–32	18–25	32–39	25–32	39–49	32–32	49–63

Table E–3
Index of products and weight range table for veal and calf (in pounds)

Item No.	Product	Range A Veal	Range A Calf	Range B Veal	Range B Calf	Range C Veal	Range C Calf	Range D Veal	Range D Calf
311A	Square Cut Chuck, 5 Ribs, Clod Out, Boneless	10–19	24–34	19–26	34–42	26–33	42–52	33–44	52–66
311B	Square Cut Chuck, 4 Ribs, Clod Out, Boneless & Tied	9–18	23–32	18–25	32–39	25–32	39–49	32–42	49–63
311C	Square Cut Chuck, 5 Ribs, Clod Out, Boneless & Tied	10–19	24–34	19–26	34–42	26–33	42–52	33–44	52–66
312	Foreshank	1–2	2–3	2–3	3–4	3–4	4–5	4–5	5–7
313	Breast	3–6	7–9	6–8	9–12	8–10	12–15	10–12	15–19
330	Hindsaddle, 2 Ribs	30–50	63–88	50–70	88–112	70–88	112–138	88–114	138–175
330A	Hindsaddle, 1 Rib	29–49	61–86	49–69	86–110	69–86	110–135	86–112	135–172
331	Loin, 2 Ribs (Double)	6–10	13–18	10–14	18–21	14–18	21–28	18–23	28–42
331A	Loin, 1 Rib (Double)	5–9	11–16	9–13	16–19	13–17	19–25	17–22	25–39
332	Loin, 2 Ribs, Trimmed (Double)	5–8	11–15	8–11	15–19	11–14	19–22	14–17	22–28
332A	Loin, 1 Rib, Trimmed (Double)	4–7	9–12	7–10	12–16	10–13	16–19	13–16	19–25
333	Full Loin, Trimmed	6–9	11–15	9–12	15–19	12–15	19–24	15–18	24–29
334	Legs (Double)	24–40	50–70	40–56	70–90	56–70	90–110	70–90	110–140
335	Leg, Oven-Prepared, Boneless	9–15	18–26	15–21	26–33	21–26	33–40	26–33	40–51
336	Leg, Shank Off, Oven-Prepared, Boneless	7–11	13–19	11–15	19–24	15–19	24–29	19–23	29–33
337	Hindshank	1–2	2–3	2–3	3–4	3–4	4–5	4–5	5–7
339	Leg, Short Cut	9–16	20–28	16–23	28–36	23–38	36–44	38–47	44–52
340	Back, 9 Ribs	11–19	22–30	19–26	30–42	26–31	42–51	31–40	51–65
340A	Back, 8 Ribs	9–17	20–28	17–24	28–40	24–29	40–49	29–38	49–63
341	Back, 9 Ribs, Trimmed	9–15	18–25	15–20	25–33	20–25	33–40	25–32	40–51
341A	Back, 8 ribs, Trimmed	7–13	16–23	13–18	23–31	18–23	31–38	23–30	38–49
342	Hindsaddle, 9 Ribs, Long Cut	35–58	73–102	58–81	102–131	81–100	131–160	100–130	160–204
342A	Hindsaddle, 8 Ribs, Long Cut	33–56	71–100	56–79	100–129	79–98	129–158	98–128	158–198
343	Hindsaddle, 9 Ribs, Long Cut, Trimmed	33–55	69–96	55–77	96–124	77–96	124–151	96–123	151–192
343A	Hindsaddle, 8 Ribs, Long Cut, Trimmed	31–53	67–94	53–75	94–122	75–94	122–149	94–121	149–188

Notes:

1. When single hotel racks, square cut chucks, loins, legs, etc., are specified, their respective weight shall be one-half of that prescribed for double cuts in the table.

2. The weight ranges of cuts as shown in this table do not necessarily reflect any relation to the carcass weight ranges. Studies have shown that all carcasses within a given weight range will not produce cuts that are uniform in weight. Therefore, in ordering cuts, purchasing officials should specify the weight range(s) desired without regard to the carcass weight shown in the various ranges.

Table E-4
Index of IMPS pork products and weight ranges (in pounds)

Item No.	Product	Weight Ranges			
		Range A	Range B	Range C	Range D
400	Carcass	120–150	150–180	180–210	210–up
401	Fresh Ham	14–17	17–20	20–26	26–up
401A	Fresh Ham, Short Shank	14–17	17–20	20–26	26–up
402	Fresh Ham, Skinned	14–17	17–20	20–26	26–up
402A	Fresh Ham, Skinned, Short Shank	14–17	17–20	20–26	26–up
402B	Fresh Ham, Boneless, Tied	6–8	8–10	10–12	12–up
402C	Fresh Ham, Boneless, Trimmed, Tied	6–8	8–10	10–12	12–up
402D	Fresh Ham, Outside, Tied	4–8	8–10	8–12	12–up
402E	Fresh Ham, Outside, Trimmed, Tied	4–6	6–10	10–up	
403	Shoulder	8–12	12–16	16–20	20–up
404	Shoulder, Skinned	8–12	12–16	16–20	20–up
405	Shoulder, Picnic	4–6	6–8	8–12	12–up
405A	Shoulder, Picnic, Boneless	2–4	4–6	8–12	8–up
405B	Shoulder Picnic, Cushion, Boneless	(amount as specified)			
406	Shoulder, Boston Butt	2–4	4–8	8–up	
406A	Shoulder, Boston Butt, Boneless	2–4	4–8	8–up	
407	Shoulder Butt, Cellar Trimmed, Boneless	1½–3	3–4	4–7	7–up
408	Belly	10–12	12–14	14–18	18–up
409	Belly, Skinless	7–9	9–11	11–13	13–up
410	Loin	10–14	14–18	18–22	22–up
411	Loin, Bladeless	10–14	14–18	18–22	22–up
412	Loin, Center Cut, 8 Ribs	4–6	6–8	8–10	10–up
412A	Loin, Center Cut, 8 Ribs, Chine Bone Off	4–5	5–7	7–9	9–up
412B	Loin, Center Cut, 8 Ribs, Boneless	2–4	4–5	4–6	6–up
412C	Loin, Center Cut, 11 Ribs	5–7	7–9	9–11	11–up
412D	Loin, Center Cut, 11 Ribs, Chine Bone Off	4–6	6–8	8–10	10–up
412E	Loin, Center Cut, 11 Ribs, Boneless	3–5	5–6	6–7	7–up
413	Loin, Boneless	6–8	8–10	10–12	12–up
413A	Loin, Boneless, Tied	6–8	8–10	10–12	12–up
413B	Loin, Boneless, Tied, Special	6–8	8–10	10–12	12–up
414	Loin, Canadian Back	3–4	4–5	5–6	6–up
415	Tenderloin	½–1	1–1½	1½–up	
415A	Tenderloin, Side Muscle Off	½–1	1–1½	1½–up	
416	Spareribs	2½–dn	2½–3½	3½–5½	5½–up
416A	Spareribs, St. Louis Style	1½–2	2–3	3–up	
416B	Spareribs, Breast Bones	¼–⅓	⅓–½	½–¾	¾–up
416C	Spareribs, Breast Off	2½–dn	2½–3½	3½–5½	5½–up
417	Shoulder Hocks	¼–¾	¾–1½	1½–up	
417A	Ham Hocks	(not applicable)			
418	Trimmings	(not applicable)			
420	Pig's Feet, Front	(not applicable)			
420A	Pig's Feet, Hind	(not applicable)			
421	Neck Bones	(as specified)			
422	Loin, Back Ribs	1½–dn	1½–1¾	1¾–2¼	2¼–up
423	Loin, Country-Style Ribs	2–3	3–up		
435	Diced Pork	(as specified)			
496	Ground Pork	(as specified)			
496A	Ground Pork and Vegetable Protein Product Patties	(as specified)			
496B	Pork Patty Mix	(as specified)			

Note: Purchaser shall specify *IMPS item number, product name, and weight range* to be purchased. The following weight ranges are intended as guidelines. Carcass weights are not necessarily related to the weight of cuts within their respective weight range. Other weights or ranges may be specified.

Table E-5

Portion-cut pork items

Item No.	Product	Suggested Portion Weight Range (oz)
1400	Fillets	3–8
1406	Boston Butt Steaks	4–8
1407	Shoulder Butt Steaks, Boneless	3–8
1410	Loin Chops	3–8
1410A	Loin Rib Chops, With Pockets	5–8
1411	Loin Chops, Bladeless	3–8
1412	Loin Chops, Center Cut	3–8
1412A	Loin Chops, Center Cut, Chine Bone Off	3–8
1412B	Loin Chops, Center Cut, Boneless	3–8
1413	Loin Chops, Boneless	3–8
1413B	Loin Chops, Boneless, Special	3–8
1438	Pork Steaks, Flaked and Formed, Frozen	Amount as specified
1495	Pork For Chop Suey	Amount as specified
1496	Ground Pork Patties	Amount as specified
1496A	Ground Pork and Vegetable Protein Product Patties	Amount as specified
1496B	Pork Patties	Amount as specified

Abbreviation of the product name is recommended. Abbreviations, when used, shall be as follows:

Boneless—Bnls
Center Cut—Cntr Cut
Blade—Bld
Bladeless—Bldls
Ground—Grnd
Short Shank—Sht Shnk

Shoulder—Shld
Skinned—Sknd
Special—Sp
Tenderloin—Tender
Trimmed—Trmd

The above products names and abbreviations have been reviewed and approved by USDA, FSIS, Meat and Poultry Technical Services, Standards and Labeling Division, Washington, DC.

Table E-6

Index of cured, cured and smoked, and fully cooked pork items (in pounds)

Item No.	Product	Range A	Range B	Range C
500	Ham, Short Shank (Cured)	10–14	14–17	17–20
501	Ham, Short Shank (Cured and Smoked)	10–14	14–17	17–20
502	Ham, Short Shank, Skinned (Cured)	10–14	14–17	17–20
503	Ham, Short Shank, Skinned (Cured and Smoked), Fully Cooked	10–14	14–17	17–20
504	Ham, Skinless, Partially Boned (Cured and Smoked)	8–10	10–12	12–14
505	Ham, Boneless (Cured and Smoked), Fully Cooked	8–10	10–12	12–14
505A	Ham, Bonless, Tied (Cured and Smoked), Fully Cooked	8–10	10–12	12–14
508	Ham, Boiled, Boneless (Cured), Fully Cooked	8–10	10–12	12–14
509	Ham, Boneless (Cured and Smoked), Fully Cooked, Special	5–11	11–16	
510	Ham, Honey Cured (Smoked), Partially Boned, Spiral Cut	8–10	10–12	12–14
511	Ham, Chunked and Formed (Cured), Fully Cooked	8–10	10–12	12–14
511A	Ham, Chunked and Formed (Cured and Smoked), Fully Cooked	8–10	10–12	12–14
512	Ham, Diced (Cured)			

Table E–6

Index of cured, cured and smoked, and fully cooked pork items (in pounds) (continued)

Item No.	Product	Range A	Range B	Range C
512A	Ham, Diced (Cured and Smoked)	As specified by purchaser		
514	Pork, Diced (Cured)			
515	Pork Shoulder (Cured)	8–12	12–16	16–20
516	Pork Shoulder (Cured and Smoked)	8–12	12–16	16–20
517	Pork Shoulder, Skinned (Cured)	8–12	12–16	16–20
518	Pork Shoulder, Skinned (Cured and Smoked)	8–12	12–16	16–20
525	Pork Shoulder Picnic (Cured)	4–6	6–8	8–12
526	Pork Shoulder Picnic (Cured and Smoked)	4–6	6–8	8–12
527	Pork Shoulder Picnic (Cured and Smoked), Boneless, Tied	6–8	8–10	10–12
530	Pork Shoulder Butt, Cellar Trimmed, Boneless (Cured and Smoked)	1.5–3	3–5	5–8
531	Pork Shoulder Butt, Boneless (Cured and Smoked), Special	2–4	4–6	6–8
535*	Belly, Skin-On (Cured)	10–12	12–14	14–16
536*	Bacon, Slab (Cured and Smoked), Skin-On, Formed	10–12	12–14	14–16
537*	Belly, Slab (Cured and Smoked), Skinless, Formed	10–12	12–14	14–16
538*	Bacon, Slab, Center-Cut (Cured and Smoked), Skinless, Formed	8–10	10–12	12–14
538A*	Bacon, Sliced, Center-Cut (Cured and Smoked)	Number of slices per lb 12–14;		
539*	Bacon, Sliced (Cured and Smoked), Skinless	14–18; 18–22; 22–26; 26–30; 28–32; or as specified		
541*	Bacon, Sliced (Cured and Smoked), Ends and Pieces	5 and 10 lb containers or as specified		
545	Pork Loin (Cured and Smoked)	10–14	14–17	17–20
546	Pork Loin, Bladeless (Cured and Smoked)	10–14	14–17	17–20
547	Pork Center Loin, 11 Ribs (Cured and Smoked)	5–7	7–10	10–12
547A	Pork Center Loin, Boneless (Cured and Smoked)	3–5	5–7	7–10
548	Pork Center-Cut Loin, 8 Ribs (Cured and Smoked)	4–6	6–8	8–11
548A	Pork Loin, Center-Cut, Boneless (Cured and Smoked)	2–4	4–6	6–10
550	Canadian Style Bacon (Cured and Smoked), Unsliced	3–4	4–6	5–6
550A	Canadian Style Bacon (Cured and Smoked), Sliced	5 and 10 lb containers as specified		
555*	Jowl Butts, Cellar Trim (Cured)	1–2.5	2.5–4	
556*	Jowl Squares, (Cured and Smoked)	0.8–2	2–3	
558*	Spareribs, Fully Cooked	1.5–3	3–5	5–up
559*	Spareribs, (Cured and Smoked)	1.5–3	3–5	5–up
559A*	Pork Spareribs, Fully Cooked, St. Louis Style	1.5–2	2–3	3–up
559B*	Pork Spareribs (Cured and Smoked), St. Louis Style	1.5–2	2–3	3–up
560*	Hocks, Ham (Cured and Smoked)	0.5–1	1–1.5	1.5–2.5
561*	Hocks, Shoulder (Cured and Smoked)	0.5–1	1–1.5	1.5–2.5
562*	Clear Fatback (Cured)	6–8	8–10	10–12
563*	Feet, Front (Cured)	0.8–1.5		
	PRECOOKED PORTION ITEMS			
1513	Ham Patties (Cured), Fully Cooked	3–5 oz.	As specified by the purchaser	
1531	Ham Steaks (Cured and Smoked), Boneless	5–12 oz.	As specified by the purchaser	
1545	Pork Loin Chops (Cured and Smoked)	3–8 oz.	As specified by the purchaser	
1548	Pork Loin Chops, Boneless, Center Cut (Cured and Smoked)	3–8 oz.	As specified by the purchaser	
1596*	Pork Patty, Precooked	3–8 oz.	As specified by the purchaser	

*Style option not applicable to this item.

Table E-6
Index of cured, cured and smoked, and fully cooked pork items (in pounds) (continued)

Item No.	Product	Range A	Range B	Range C
Abbreviation of the product name is recommended. Abbreviations, when used, shall be as follows:				

Blade—Bld   Trimmed—Trmd
Boneless—Bnls   Short Shank—Sht Shnk
Bladeless—Bldls   Shoulder—Shld
Ground—Grnd   Center Cut—Cntr Cut
Tenderloin—Tender   Skinned—Sknd
Smoked—Smk   Special—Sp

The above products names and abbreviations have been reviewed and approved by USDA, FSIS, Regulatory Programs, Standards and Labeling Division, Washington, DC.

Table E-6
Miscellaneous specifications and standards for some frozen meats

Item	Purchase description
Roast beef, frozen	Precooked rounds from choice grade steer or heifer, deli-style, 7–12 lb each. Individually wrapped in moisture- and grease-resistant paper; can be ordered sliced and tied also; boneless.
Roast beef, frozen	Precooked top round from choice grade steer or heifer, 6½ lb average, not varying more than ½ lb in individual pieces; boneless.
Roast beef, frozen	Precooked cross-rib, from choice steer or heifer, 12 to 15 lb each, boneless.
Barbecued ground beef, frozen	51½% ground coarse beef, 48½% tomato gravy, cooked basis.
Barbecued meat, frozen	The weight of meat when barbecued cannot exceed 70% of the fresh uncooked meat; must have a barbecued (crusted) appearance.
Beef, sliced with gravy, frozen	Meat to be not less than 55% on a cooked basis.
Beef, Burgundy, frozen	45% choice cubed beef, 53% Burgundy wine sauce, 2½% garnish of onions and mushrooms.
Beef casserole, Italian style, frozen	Not more than 50% cooked macaroni; at least 25% cooked beef.
Beef patty, char-broiled, frozen	Cooked, 3% textured vegetable protein may be added; 95% beef, 2% flavoring and spices; 3-oz patties, layer packed.
Beef rolls, frozen	Ground beef in pastry roll with sauce; shall be at least 2 oz ground beef on a cooked basis; 4¾-oz portions.
Beef stew, frozen	25% beef, not more than 20% peas, carrots, green beans, small onions, and celery on a proportionate basis.
Beef and pork fritters, frozen	Chop shape 3-oz patties, 53 per case (10 lb), layer packed; 65% lean pork, 30% beef, 3% coating, 2% seasoning.
Cabbage rolls, frozen	8-oz portions, 4 oz of filling with remainder cabbage and sauce; filling should be 50% meat.

Table E-6

Miscellaneous specifications and standards for some frozen meats (continued)

Item	Purchase description
Cannelloni with meat sauce, frozen	20% meat filling.
Meat balls in sour cream, frozen	55% veal or beef on cooked basis from choice grade meat, 45% sauce; ½ oz meat balls; no extender permitted.
Sirloin tips in mushroom gravy, frozen	From choice top sirloin in ½-oz cubes after cooking, broiled and then added to a gravy. Shall be 41.875% meat on cooked basis, 55% mushroom gravy and 3.125% mushrooms.
Stuffed peppers in sauce, frozen	60% filling and peppers; 40% sauce; filling shall be 50% meat on a cooked basis with corn, rice and seasonings plus moisture 50%.
Liver, Beef, frozen	Raw, 4/lb, Style A, Selection 1, skinned, sliced, IMPS 702SL.
Veal Cutlets, frozen	Shall come from the large muscle of the shoulder or leg. Should be clear slices and not knitted or cubed. Each cutlet to be 4 oz not over or under ¼ oz. Maximum breading 20%, 80% meat.
Veal Drumsticks, frozen	Finely ground meal containing not over 1% salt, 2% cereal, 3½% dry milk (nonfat). Added moisture shall not exceed 7½%. Breading shall be first by dipping into wheat (white) flour and then a mixture of 50% eggs and 50% milk and then into fine crumbs or prepared breading mix. Breading shall not be more than 25% of total weight. Shall be 2 or 4 oz each, as specified. Shall be layer-packed separated by moisture- and grease-resistant paper.
Pork, Breakfast Patties, Cooked, frozen	Fresh pork sausage. Rounds should not be less than 2 in. in diameter and ³⁄₁₆ inch thick.

Table E-7

Index of cured beef products (in pounds)

Item No.	Product	Weight Range 1	Weight Range 2	Weight Range 3
600	Spencer Roll, Corned	Under 15	15–22	22 up
601	Brisket, Boneless, Deckle Off, Corned	Under 9	9–12	12 up
602	Knuckle, Corned	Under 8	8–15	15 up
603	Knuckle, Dried	Under 5	5–8	8 up
604	Top (Inside) Round, Corned	Under 16	16–27	27 up
605	Top (Inside) Round, Dried	Under 10	10–15	15 up
606	Bottom (Gooseneck) Round, Corned	Under 11	11–18	18 up
607	Bottom (Gooseneck) Round, Dried	Under 8	8–14	14 up
609	Rump Butt, Corned	Under 8	8–12	12 up
613	Tongue, Cured	3–5		
614	Tongue, Smoked	3–5		
617	Process, Dried Beef	Under 8	8–14	14 up
618	Sliced Process Dried Beef			
619	Sliced Dried Beef	¼ pound, ½ pound, 1-pound individual		
620	Sliced Dried Beef, Ends and Pieces	packages, or bulk or layer packed		

Note: Because it is impractical to list all weight ranges for these products that purchasers may desire, those included in this table are suggested only. Other weight ranges may be ordered if desired.

Table E-8
Index of products and weight range for edible by-products (in pounds)

Item No.	Product	Range 1	Range 2
701	Beef Liver	Under 13	13–16
702	Beef Liver, Sliced (Frozen)	Under 13	13–16
703	Beef Liver, Portion-Cut (Frozen)	4-to-the-pound	4-to-the-pound
704	Calf Liver	Under 6½	6½–8½
705	Calf Liver, Sliced (Frozen)	Under 6½	6½–8½
707	Veal Liver	Under 3	3–5
708	Veal Liver, Sliced (Frozen)	Under 3	3–5
710	Pork Liver	Under 5	
713	Lamb Liver	Under 1½	
716	Beef Tongue	3–5	
720	Beef Heart	3–5	

Note: Because it is impractical to list all weight ranges for edible by-products that purchasers may desire, those included in this table are suggested only. Other weight ranges may be ordered if desired.

Table E-9
Index for IMPS sausage products—series 800

Item No.	Product	Suggested Weight Range
800	Frankfurters	4, 6, 8, 10, 12 links per pound
801	Bologna	1 to 12 pound units 16, 18, 20, 25 slices per pound
802	Pork Sausage	1, 2, 3, 4, 5, 6 pound rolls 6, 8, 10, 12, 14, 16 links per pound 2, 3, 5, or 7 pound bags 5, 6, 7, 8, 9, 10, 11, 12 pound units
802A	Pork Sausage, Patties	2.5 or 3 oz. patty
802B	Pork Sausage, Cooked	1.5 or 2 oz. patty 2, 3, 5, or 7 pound bags
802C	Whole Hog Pork Sausage	6, 8, 10, 12, 14, 16 links per pound 1, 2, 3, pound rolls 2, 3, 5, or 7 pound bags 5, 6, 8, 10 pound units 1.5 or 2 oz. patty 2.5 or 3 oz. patty
803	Liver Sausage	5 to 8 pounds
804	Cooked Salami	7 to 12 pounds 16, 18, 20, 25 slices per pound
805	Minced Luncheon Meat	5 to 10 pounds 16, 18, 20, 25 slices per pound
806	Lebanon Bologna	5 to 10 pounds 16, 18, 20, 25 slices per pound
807	Thuringer	4 to 8 pounds 18, 20, 25, 30 slices per pound
808	Dry Salami	2 to 5 pounds 20, 25, 30 slices per pound
809	Cervelat	2 to 5 pounds 20, 25, 30 slices per pound
810	Breakfast Sausage	1, 2, or 3 pound rolls 8, 10, 12, 16 or 19–21 links per pound 5, 6, 8, or 10 pound units

Table E-9

Index for IMPS sausage products—series 800 (continued)

Item No.	Product	Suggested Weight Range
811	Smoked Sausage	6, 8, 10, 19–21, 48–51 links per pound
812	New England Brand Sausage	5 to 10 pounds 16, 18, 20, 25 slices per pound
813	Polish Sausage	3–5, 11–13 inches in length
814	Meat Loaves	4 to 8 pound loaves 16, 18, 20, 25 slices per pound
815	Meat Food Product Loaves	4 to 8 pound loaves 16, 18, 20, 25 slices per pound
816	Knockwurst	5, 6, 7, 8 links per pound
817	Breakfast Sausage, Cooked	19 to 21 links per pound
818	Italian Sausage	4, 6, 7, 8 links per pound 1, 5, 6, 8, 10 pound units 2, 2.5 or 3 oz. patty
819	Ham Links	14 to 15 links per pound
820	Head Cheese	4 to 8 pounds 16, 18, 20, 25 slices per pound
821	Pepperoni	1 to 2 pound sticks 10 to 15 slices per ounce
822	Bratwurst	4, 6, 7, 8 links per pound
822A	Bratwurst Patty	2.5 or 3 oz. patty
824	Pork Rib Shape Patty	3.0, 4.0 or 5.0 oz. patty
825	Canned Luncheon Meat	30 ounce or 6 pound cans
826	Scrapple	1, 5, 10 pound units

Note: Purchaser shall specify *IMPS item number, product name, formula, and weight range.* The following weight ranges are intended *only* as guidelines. The purchaser may specify any other weight range, link, or slice count desired.

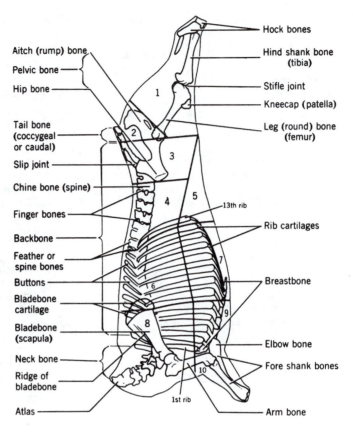

Figure E-1
The skeletal structure of beef. (Courtesy USDA.)

Aitch (rump) bone
Pelvic bone
Hip bone
Tail bone (coccygeal or caudal)
Slip joint
Chine bone (spine)
Finger bones
Backbone
Feather or spine bones
Buttons
Bladebone cartilage
Bladebone (scapula)
Neck bone
Ridge of bladebone
Atlas

Hock bones
Hind shank bone (tibia)
Stifle joint
Kneecap (patella)
Leg (round) bone (femur)
13th rib
Rib cartilages
Breastbone
Elbow bone
Fore shank bones
1st rib
Arm bone

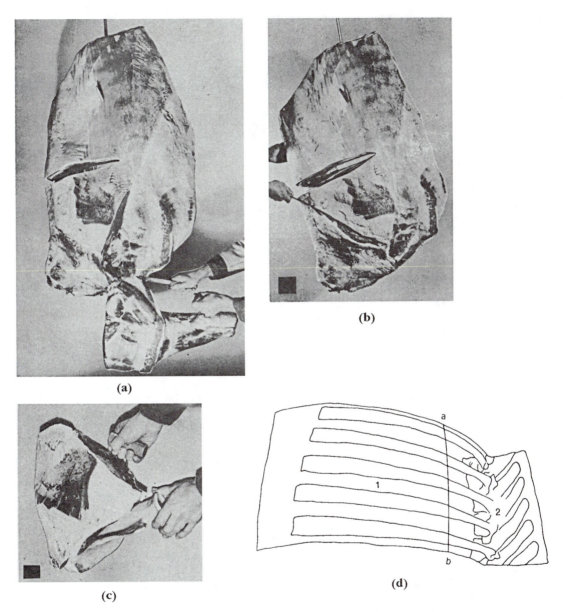

(a)

(b)

(c)

(d)

Figure E-2

(a) The first cut usually made in a forequarter is the cut that separates the shank. (b) The triangular cut shown here removes the clod, the muscle that sets over the shoulder blade or scapula. Note that the wing has been partially separated from the cross-cut or New York chuck by cutting between the fifth and sixth ribs. (c) The clod lifts off easily from the scapula blade. (d) This shows the bones of the 5-rib wing taken from the forequarter with the rib and plate divided along line ab. (Photos taken at a demonstration of meat cutting by Vern Olmstead.)

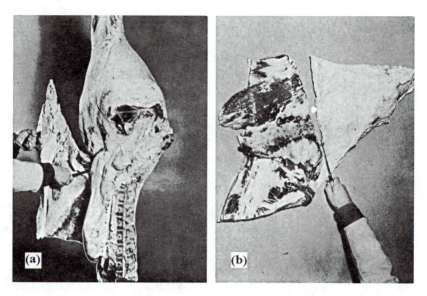

Figure E-3
A hindquarter of beef is best cut up from the hook. Illustration (a) shows the first cut the removal of the flank from the round and loin and (b) the flank being stripped of its fatty tissue. (Photos taken at a meat cutting by Vern Olmstead.)

Figure E-4
The round and loin are frequently cut as shown. The short loin ends at line ab, the loin end or sirloin is found between lines ab and dec. The rump forms the triangle made by lines fec. The tenderloin is indicated by the dotted line and the rear part behind line ab, marked as "1" is the butt tenderloin. A full loin is all parts under line dec. The short loin can yield cuts such as a T-bone (Nos. 1173 and 1174), bone-in-strip loin (Nos. 1177, 1178, and 1179), boneless strip loin (No. 1180), and tenderloin (Nos. 1189 and 1190). The top and bottom butt sirloin steaks (Nos. 1184 and 1185) come from the sirloin.

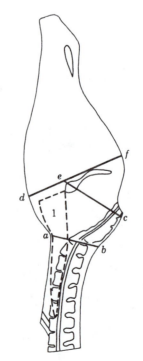

Servings per Pound of Uncooked Meat

*Servings per pound uncooked meat to yield 3-oz cooked meat**

Beef		Pork	
STEAKS		**CHOPS, STEAKS, CUTLETS**	
Bnls Chuck	3½	Blade (Shoulder)	2½–3½
Chuck, Arm or Blade	2½	Chops, bnls	4
Cubed	4	Loin or Rib Chops	2½
Flank	4	Ham, Cured (Center Slice)	3½
Porterhouse	2½	**ROASTS**	
Rib	2	Leg (Ham), fresh bi	3
Round	3	Leg (Ham), bnls	4
Sirloin	3	Smoked Ham, bi	3
T-Bone	2	Smoked Ham, bnls	4
Tenderloin (Filet Mignon)	3	Shoulder (Rolled), bnls	3
Top Loin (Strip), bnls	3	Center Loin	3
Top Round	4	Blade Loin	2
ROASTS		Top Loin (Rolled), bnls	3½
Eye of Round	4	Smoked Center Loin	3
Rib	2	Smoked Shoulder Roll	3
Rump, bnls	2½	**OTHER CUTS**	
Tip	4	Back Ribs	1½
POT ROASTS		Bacon, Regular, Sliced	6
Chuck Blade	2½	Country-style Loin Ribs	2
Chuck, bnls	2½	Cubes	4
Cross Rib, bi	2½	Hocks (Fresh or Smoked)	1½
OTHER CUTS		Pork Sausage	4
Beef for Stew	4	Spareribs	1¼
Brisket	3	Tenderloin	4
Ground Beef	4	**VARIETY MEATS**	
Short Ribs	1½–2½	Brains	5
VARIETY MEATS		Heart	4
Brains	5	Kidney	5
Heart	4	Liver	4
Kidney	4		
Sweetbreads	5		
Tongue	5		

Servings per pound uncooked meat to yield 3-oz cooked meat (continued)*

Veal		Lamb	
CHOPS, STEAKS, CUTLETS		CHOPS AND STEAKS	
Loin or Rib Chops	2	Leg, center slice	3
Shoulder Steak	2½	Loin or Rib Chop	2½
Round Steak	3½	Shoulder chop	2
Cutlets, bnls	4	Sirloin chop	2
ROASTS		ROASTS	
Leg, bi	3	Leg, bi	2½
Shoulder, bnls	3	Leg, bnls	4
Rib	2	Shoulder, bi	2
OTHER CUTS		Shoulder, bnls	3
Riblets	1½	OTHER CUTS	
Cubes	4	Breast	2
Breast (Rolled), bnls	3	Riblets	1¼
Ground	4	Cubes	4
VARIETY MEATS		Shanks	2
Brains	5	Ground	4
Heart	5	VARIETY MEATS	
Kidney	4	Heart	5
Liver	4	Kidney	5
Sweetbreads	5		
Tongue	4½		

Note: bi = bone in; bnls = boneless.

* The portions per pound in this table are based on an average serving of 3 oz of cooked, trimmed meat. These portions can vary according to cooking method, fatness of the meat, amount of bone, degree of doneness etc. Thus they should be used as a guide only. Also, for a larger portion of cooked meat, the number of servings per pound will have to be adjusted accordingly. Adapted from a table in *Lessons on Meat,* National Livestock and Meat Board, 1991.

APPENDIX G

Amounts to Order of Processed Food

Table G-1

Canned vegetables—portion size and quantity required for 100 portions

Canned Vegetables as Purchased	Unit of Purchase	Portion as Served	Portions per Purchase Unit (No.)	Approximate Purchase Units for 100 Portions (No.)
Asparagus				
Cuts and tips	No. 300 can	3 oz	2.86	35
	No. 10 can	"	20.19	5
Spears	No. 300 can	6 medium	2.57	39
	No. 10 can	"	18.53	5½
Bean sprouts	"	3 oz	18.37	5½
Beans, dry—kidney,	No. 303 can	6 oz	2.13	47
lima, or navy	No. 10 can	"	14.40	6¾
Beans, lima, green	No. 303 can	3 oz	3.68	27¼
	No. 10 can	"	24.14	4¼
Beans, snap, green or	No. 303 can	"	3.05	33
wax	No. 2½ can	"	5.51	18¼
	No. 10 can	"	20.87	5
Beets	No. 303 can	"	3.52	28½
Diced	No. 10 can	"	23.92	4¼
Sliced	No. 303 can	"	3.25	31
	No. 10 can	"	22.53	4½
Whole baby beets	No. 303 can	"	3.31	30¼
	No. 10 can	"	22.88	4½
Carrots				
Diced	No. 303 can	"	3.31	30¼
	No. 10 can	"	23.92	4¼
Sliced	No. 303 can	"	3.31	30¼
	No. 10 can	"	22.88	4½
Chop suey vegetables	"	"	34.00	3
Collards	No. 303 can	4 oz	2.71	37
	No. 2½ can	"	4.73	21¼
	No. 10 can	"	14.93	6¾

SOURCE: Food Purchasing Guide for Group Feeding, USDA.

Table G–1

Canned vegetables—portion size and quantity required for 100 portions (continued)

Canned Vegetables as Purchased	Unit of Purchase	Portion as Served	Portions per Purchase Unit (No.)	Approximate Purchase Units for 100 Portions (No.)
Corn				
Cream style	No. 303 can	"	4.00	25
	No. 10 can	"	26.48	4
Whole kernel	No. 303 can	3 oz	3.52	28½
	No.10 can	"	23.30	4½
Kale	No. 303 can	4 oz	2.71	37
	No. 2½ can	"	4.73	21¼
	No. 10 can	"	14.93	6¾
Mushrooms	No. 8 Z	3 oz	2.66	37¾
	No. 10 can	"	22.67	4½
Mustard greens	No. 303 can	4 oz	2.71	37
	No. 2½ can	"	4.73	21¼
	No. 10 can	"	14.93	6¾
Okra	No. 303 can	3 oz	3.51	28½
	No. 10 can	"	20.14	5
Okra and tomatoes	No. 303 can	"	5.01	20
	No. 10 can	"	33.65	3
Olives, large				
Ripe				
Pitted	No. 1 tall	2 olives	21.33	4¾
Whole	"	"	25.60	4
	No. 10	"	187.69	*
Green, whole	Gallon	"	250.25	*
Onions, small, whole	No. 303 can	3 oz	2.99	33½
	No. 10 can	"	19.86	5¼
Peas, green	No. 303 can	"	3.41	29½
	No. 10 can	"	22.39	4½
Peas and carrots	No. 303 can	"	3.68	27¼
	No. 10 can	"	24.14	4¼
Pickles				
Dill or sour				
Sliced or cut	Quart jar	1 oz	22.00	4¾
	No. 10 jar	"	72.00	1½
	Gallon jar	"	90.00	1¼
Whole	No. 2½ jar	"	19.00	5½
	Quart jar	"	21.00	5
Sweet				
Sliced or cut	"	"	24.00	4¼
	No. 10 jar	"	78.00	1½
	Gallon jar	"	95.00	1¼
Whole	No. 2½	"	20.50	5
	Quart jar	"	22.00	4¾
Pickle relish				
Sour	Quart	"	25.75	4
	No. 10 jar	"	91.75	1¼
	Gallon jar	"	114.50	*
Sweet	Quart	"	28.00	3¾
	No. 10 jar	"	100.00	1
	Gallon jar	"	125.00	*

Canned Vegetables as Purchased	Unit of Purchase	Portion as Served	Portions per Purchase Unit (No.)	Approximate Purchase Units for 100 Portions (No.)
Pimientos, chopped	No. 2½ can	½ cup	4.80	†
	No. 10 can	"	17.39	†
Potatoes, small whole	No. 2 can	2–3	4.00	25
	No. 10 can	2–3	25.00	4
Pumpkin, mashed	No. 300 can	4 oz	3.64	27½
	No. 2½ can	"	7.24	14
	No. 10 can	"	26.50	4
Sauerkraut	No. 303 can	3 oz	4.37	23
	No. 2½ can	"	7.66	13¼
	No. 10 can	"	26.74	3¾
Soups				
Condensed	No. 1 picnic	1 cup diluted	2.50	40
	No. 3 cylinder	"	11.50	8¾
Ready-to-serve	12-fl-oz can	1 cup	1.50	66¾
	25-fl-oz can (No. 2½)	"	3.12	32¼
Spinach	No. 303 can	4 oz	2.71	37
	No. 2½	"	4.73	21¼
	No. 10 can	"	14.93	6¾
Squash, summer	No. 303 can	"	2.75	36½
	No. 10 can	"	17.50	5¾
Squash, winter	No. 300 can	"	3.64	27½
	No. 2½ can	"	7.24	14
	No. 10 can	"	26.48	4
Succotash	No. 303 can	3 oz	3.47	29
	No. 10 can	"	23.40	4¼
Sweet potatoes	No. 3 vacuum or squat	4 oz	3.74	26¾
	No. 2½ can, with syrup	"	4.78	21
	No. 10 can, with syrup	"	18.00	5¾
Tomatoes	No. 303 can	"	4.00	25
	No. 2½ can	"	7.00	14½
	No. 10 can	"	25.52	4
Tomato products				
Catsup	14-oz bottle	1 oz	14.00	7¼
	No. 10 can	"	111.00	1
Chili sauce	12-oz jar	1 tbsp	20.27	5
	No. 10 can	"	177.30	*
Juice, concentrate‡	6-fl-oz can	4 fl-oz	6.00	16¾
Turnip greens	No. 303 can	4 oz	2.71	37
	No. 2½ can	"	4.73	21¼
	No. 10 can	"	14.93	6¾
Vegetable juices	23-fl-oz can	4 fl-oz	5.75	17½
	46-fl-oz can	"	11.50	8¾
	96-fl-oz can	"	24.00	4¼
Vegetables, mixed	No. 303 can	3 oz	3.63	27¾
	No. 10 can	"	23.57	4¼

*Number of purchase units needed is less than 1. †Number of purchase units needed is determined by use.
‡See vegetable juices for canned tomato juice.

Table G–2

Frozen vegetables—portion size and quantity required for 100 portions

Frozen Vegetables as Purchased	Unit of Purchase	Portion as Served	Portions per Purchase Unit (No.)	Approximate Purchase Units for 100 Portions (No.)
Asparagus				
Spears	Pound	4 medium, cooked	3.38	29¾
	Package	″	8.44	12
Cuts and tips	Pound	3 oz cooked	4.27	23½
	Package	″	10.67	9½
Beans, butter (lima)	Pound	″	5.33	19
	Package	″	13.33	7½
	″	″	16.00	6¼
Beans, lima, green	Pound	″	5.33	19
	Package	″	13.33	7½
Beans, snap, green or wax	Pound	″	4.85	20¾
	Package	″	12.13	8¼
Blackeye peas	Pound	″	5.92	17
	Package	″	14.80	7
	″	″	17.76	5¾
Broccoli				
Spears	Pound	2 medium	4.57	22
	Package	″	11.43	8¾
Cut or chopped	. Pound	3 oz cooked	4.53	22¼
	Package	″	11.33	9
Brussel sprouts	Pound	″	5.12	19¾
Carrots, sliced or diced	Pound	″	5.12	19¾
	Package	″	12.80	8
Cauliflower	Pound	″	4.80	21
	Package	″	12.00	8½
Collards	Pound	″	4.75	21¼
	Package	″	11.87	8½
Corn				
On cob	Pound (about three 5-in. ears)	1 ear, cooked	3.00	33½
Whole kernel	Pound	3 oz cooked	5.17	19½
	Package	″	12.93	7¾
Kale	Pound	″	4.11	24½
	Package	″	10.27	9¾
	″	″	12.32	8¼
Mustard greens, leaf or chopped	Pound	″	4.27	23½
	Package	″	10.67	9½
	″	″	12.80	8

SOURCE: Food Purchasing Guide for Group Feeding, USDA.

Frozen Vegetables as Purchased	Unit of Purchase	Portion as Served	Portions per Purchase Unit (No.)	Approximate Purchase Units for 100 Portions (No.)
Okra, whole	Pound	″	4.37	23
	Package	″	10.93	9¼
	″	″	13.12	7¾
Peas, green	Pound	″	5.12	19¾
	Package	″	12.80	8
	″	″	15.36	6¾
Peas and carrots	Pound	″	5.23	19¼
	Package	″	13.07	7¾
Peppers, green Whole	″	½ pepper, cooked	12.00	8½
	″	″	30.00	3½
Diced or sliced	Pound	1 oz cooked	15.52	6½
	Package	″	38.80	2¾
Potatoes French fried	″	10 pieces	8.00	12½
	″	″	40.00	2½
Small whole	Container	3 cooked	16.67	6
Spinach	Pound	3 oz cooked	4.27	23½
	Package	″	10.67	9½
	″	″	12.80	8
Squash, summer, sliced	Pound	″	4.64	21¾
	Package	″	11.60	8¾
	″	″	13.92	7¼
Squash, winter, mashed	Pound	4 oz cooked	3.68	27¼
	Package	″	9.20	11
Sweet potatoes Whole	Pound	1 whole, cooked	2.63	38¼
	″	4 oz cooked	3.92	25¾
Sliced	Package	″	9.80	10¼
	″	″	11.76	8¾
Succotash	Pound	3 oz cooked	5.65	17¾
	Package	″	14.13	7¼
Turnip greens, leaf or chopped	Pound	″	4.27	23½
	Package	″	10.67	9½
	″	″	12.80	8
Turnip greens with turnips	Pound	″	4.75	21¼
	Package	″	14.24	7¼
Vegetables, mixed	Pound	″	5.07	19¾
	Package	″	12.67	8

Table G-3

Canned fruits—portion size and quantities required for 100 portions

Canned Fruits as Purchased	Unit of Purchase	Portion as Served	Portions per Purchase Unit (No.)	Approximate Purchase Units for 100 Portions (No.)
Apples, solid pack	No. 2 can	4 oz	4.48	22½
	No. 2½ can	"	6.48	15½
	No. 10 can	4 oz	24.00	4¼
		⅙ 9-in. pie	24.00	4¼
Apple juice	23-fl-oz can	4 fl oz	5.75	17½
	46-fl-oz can	"	11.50	8¾
	96-fl-oz can	"	24.00	4¼
Applesauce	No. 303 can	4 oz	4.00	25
	No. 2½ can	"	7.24	14
	No. 10 can	"	27.00	3¾
Apricots, halves	No. 303 can	3–5 medium	4.00	25
	No. 2½ can	"	7.00	14½
	No. 10 can	"	25.00	4
Blackberries	No. 303 can	4 oz	4.00	25
	No. 10 can	"	26.48	4
Blueberries	No. 300 can	"	3.64	27½
	No. 10 can	"	26.24	4
Boysenberries	No. 303 can	"	3.76	26¾
	No. 10 can	"	26.48	4
Cherries				
Red, sour, pitted	No. 303 can	"	4.00	25
	No. 10 can	4 oz	26.24	4
		⅙ 9-inch pie	24.00	4¼
Sweet	No. 303 can	4 oz	4.00	25
	No. 2½ can	"	7.24	14
	No. 10 can	"	27.00	3¾
Cranberries, strained or whole	No. 300 can	2 oz	8.00	12½
	No. 10 can	"	58.50	1¾
Cranberry juice	1 pt	4 fl oz	4.00	25
	1 qt	"	8.00	12½
	1 gal	"	32.00	3¼
Figs	No. 303 can	3–4 figs	4.00	25
	No. 2½ can	"	7.00	14¼
	No. 10 can	"	25.00	4
Fruit cocktail or salad	No. 303 can	4 oz	4.24	23¾
	No. 2½ can	"	7.52	13½
	No. 10 can	"	27.00	3¾

SOURCE: Food Purchasing Guide for Group Feeding, USDA.

Canned Fruits as Purchased	Unit of Purchase	Portion as Served	Portions per Purchase Unit (No.)	Approximate Purchase Units for 100 Portions (No.)
Grapefruit juice	18-fl-oz can	4 fl oz	4.50	22¼
	46-fl-oz can	"	11.50	8¾
	96-fl-oz can	"	24.00	4¼
Grapefruit sections	No. 303 can	4 oz	4.00	25
	No. 3 cylinder	"	12.48	8¼
Lemon juice	32-fl-oz can	2 fl oz	16.00	6¼
Lime juice	"	"	16.00	6¼
Orange juice	18-fl-oz can	4 fl oz	4.50	22¼
	46-fl-oz can	"	11.50	8¾
	96-fl-oz can	"	24.00	4¼
Oranges, mandarin	No. 10 can	4 oz	25.50	4
Peaches				
Halves or slices	No. 303 can	2 medium	3.00	33½
	No. 2½ can	"	7.00	14½
	No. 10 can	2 medium	25.00	4
		⅙ 9-in. pie	24.00	4¼
Whole, spiced	"	1 each	25.00	4
Pears, halves	No. 303 can	2 medium	3.00	33½
	No. 2½ can	"	7.00	14½
	No. 10 can	"	25.00	4
Pineapple				
Chunks and cubes	No. 2½ can	4 oz	7.52	13½
	No. 10 can	"	27.00	3¾
Crushed	No. 2½ can	"	7.52	13½
	No. 10 can	"	27.24	3¾
Sliced	No. 2½ can	1 large	8.00	12½
	No. 10 can	1 large or 2 small	25.00	4
Pineapple juice	18-fl-oz can	4 fl oz	4.50	22¼
	46-fl-oz can	"	11.50	8¾
	96-fl-oz can	"	24.00	4¼
Plums	No. 2½ can	2–3 plums	7.00	14½
	No. 10 can	"	25.00	4
Prunes	No. 2½ can	4 oz	7.52	13½
	No. 10 can	"	27.52	3¾
Raspberries	No. 303 can	"	4.00	25
	No. 10 can	"	27.00	3¾
Strawberries	No. 303 can	"	4.00	25
	No. 10 can	"	27.00	3¾

Table G–4
Frozen fruits—portion size and quantities required for 100 portions

Frozen Fruits as Purchased	Unit of Purchase	Portion as Served	Portions per Purchase Unit (No.)	Approximate Purchase Units for 100 Portions (No.)
Apples, sliced	Pound	4 oz ⅛ 9-in. pie (1.50 lb per pie)	4.24 4.00	23¾ 25
	Package	4 oz	10.60	9½
	"	"	21.20	4¾
	Can	"	127.20	*
Apricots	Pound	"	3.80	26½
	Can	"	95.00	1¼
	"	"	114.00	*
Blackberries	Pound	"	4.12	24½
	Can	"	123.60	*
Blueberries	Pound	"	4.32	23¼
	Package	"	10.80	9½
	Can	"	108.00	1
	"	"	129.60	*
Cherries, red, sour, pitted	Pound	4 oz ⅛ 9-in. pie (1.5 lb per pie)	4.00 4.00	25 25
	Can	4 oz	120.00	*
Grapefruit sections	Pound	"	4.00	25
	Package	"	12.00	8½
Grapefruit juice, concentrate	6-fl-oz can	4 fl oz	6.00	16¾
	32-fl-oz can	"	32.00	3¼
Grape juice, concentrate	6-fl-oz can	"	6.00	16¾
	32-fl-oz can	"	32.00	3¼
Lemon juice, concentrate	4-fl-oz can	2 fl oz	10.00	10
	6-fl-oz can	"	15.00	6¾
Lemonade, concentrate	6-fl-oz can	"	21.00	5
	18-fl-oz can	"	63.00	1¾
Melon scoops	Pound	3 oz	5.33	19
	Package	"	34.67	3

SOURCE: Food Purchasing Guide for Group Feeding, USDA.

Frozen Fruits as Purchased	Unit of Purchase	Portion as Served	Portions per Purchase Unit (No.)	Approximate Purchase Units for 100 Portions (No.)
Orange juice, concentrate	6-fl-oz can	4 fl oz	6.00	16¾
	12-fl-oz can	"	12.00	8½
	32-fl-oz can	"	32.00	3¼
Peaches, sliced		4 oz	3.80	26½
	Pound	⅛ 9-in. pie (1.33 lb per pie)	4.50	22¼
	Can	4 oz	24.70	4¼
	"	"	38.00	2¾
	"	"	114.00	*
Pineapple Chunks	Pound	"	4.00	25
	Can	"	40.00	2½
	"	"	120.00	*
Crushed Pineapple juice, concentrate	6-fl-oz can	4 fl oz	6.00	16¾
	32-fl-oz can	"	32.00	3¼
Raspberries	Pound	4 oz	4.00	25
	Can	"	26.00	4
	"	"	40.00	2½
	"	"	120.00	*
Rhubarb		4 oz	4.24	23¾
	Pound	⅛ 9-in. pie (1.50 lb per pie)	4.00	25
	Package	4 oz	10.60	9½
	Can	"	42.40	2½
	"	"	106.00	1
	"	"	127.20	*
Strawberries	Pound	"	4.00	25
	Can	"	26.00	4
	"	"	40.00	2½
	"	"	120.00	*
Tangerine juice, concentrate	6-fl-oz can	4 fl oz	6.00	16¾
	32-fl-oz can	"	32.00	3¼

*Number of purchase units needed is less than 1.

Table G–5
Dried vegetables—portion size and quantities required for 100 portions

Vegetables, Dried, Regular, and Low-Moisture, as Purchased	Unit of Purchase	Portion as Served	Portions per Purchase Unit (No.)	Approximate Purchase Units for 100 Portions (No.)
Regular				
Beans (includes white beans, lima beans, kidney beans, blackeye beans, and peas)	Pound	3 oz cooked	12.37	8¼
Peas (includes any type, whole peas, split pea, and lentils)	"	"	11.89	8½
	Bushel	"	713.60	*
Low-Moisture				
Onions, sliced	Pound	"	22.24	4½
Potatoes, white				
Flakes	"	4 oz cooked	20.84	5
	Package	"	52.10	2
Granules	Pound	"	20.24	5
	Package	"	50.60	2
Sweet potatoes, flakes	Pound	"	11.76	8¾

SOURCE: Food Purchasing Guide for Group Feeding, USDA.
*Number of purchase units needed is less than 1.

Table G–6

Equivalent fresh products to one pound of dehydrated product

Fruits	Equivalent Weight (lb)	Vegetables	Equivalent Weight (lb)
Apples	11.00	Asparagus, diced	30
Apricots	7.10	Beans, green, 1/2 in. cut	12½
Cherries (pie)	7.00	Beets, powdered	12
Dates	1.75*	Cabbage, diced	21
Figs	1.35*	Carrots, diced	12
Peaches	7.10	Celery, diced	30
Pears	11.00	Garlic, sliced	4
Prunes	1.71*	Greens, flaked	15¼
Strawberries	11.00†	Horseradish, powdered	5½
		Leeks, powdered	11
		Okra, powdered	11
		Onions, dry, flaked	9
		Onions, green, flaked	14
		Parsley, flaked	7
		Peas, green, whole	5
		Peppers, green, diced	20
		Pimiento, powdered	28
		Potatoes, diced	8
		Potatoes, granules and flake	12
		Pumpkin, powdered	12
		Tomato, flaked	20
		Turnips	16
		Sweet potatoes, flaked	7

SOURCE: Data abstracted from U.S. Department of Agriculture tables.
*Commercially dried fruit.
†Freeze-dried.

APPENDIX H

Fish and Shellfish Docked from American Waters

Following are illustrations of the most commonly caught fish and shellfish. Beneath the names of each are locations where they are found.

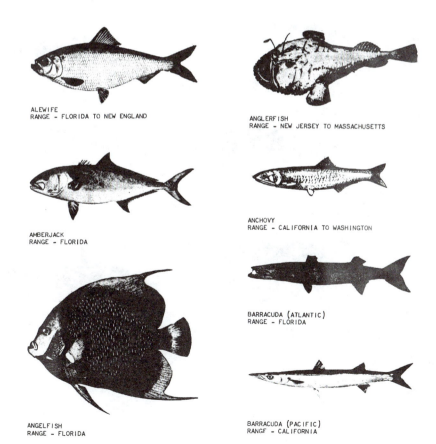

ALEWIFE
RANGE - FLORIDA TO NEW ENGLAND

ANGLERFISH
RANGE - NEW JERSEY TO MASSACHUSETTS

AMBERJACK
RANGE - FLORIDA

ANCHOVY
RANGE - CALIFORNIA TO WASHINGTON

BARRACUDA (ATLANTIC)
RANGE - FLORIDA

ANGELFISH
RANGE - FLORIDA

BARRACUDA (PACIFIC)
RANGE - CALIFORNIA

BLUEFISH
RANGE - GULF OF MEXICO TO NEW ENGLAND

BURBOT
RANGE - GREAT LAKES

BLUE RUNNER OR HARDTAIL
RANGE - GULF OF MEXICO

BUTTERFISH
RANGE - FLORIDA TO NEW ENGLAND

BONITO (ATLANTIC)
RANGE - NORTH CAROLINA TO MASSACHUSETTS

CABIO
RANGE - FLORIDA TO VIRGINIA

BOWFIN
RANGE - FRESH-WATER

CARP
RANGE - FRESH-WATER

BUFFALOFISH
RANGE - FRESH-WATER

CATFISH
RANGE - FRESH-WATER

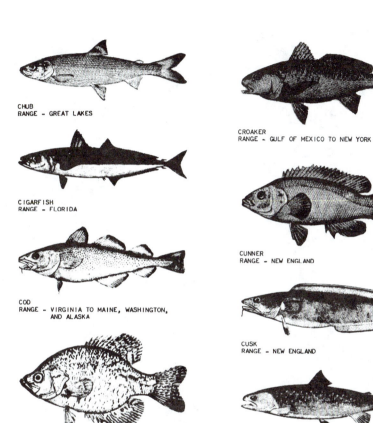

CHUB
RANGE - GREAT LAKES

CROAKER
RANGE - GULF OF MEXICO TO NEW YORK

CIGARFISH
RANGE - FLORIDA

CUNNER
RANGE - NEW ENGLAND

COD
RANGE - VIRGINIA TO MAINE, WASHINGTON,
        AND ALASKA

CUSK
RANGE - NEW ENGLAND

CRAPPIE
RANGE - FRESH-WATER LAKES

DOLLY VARDEN TROUT
RANGE - PACIFIC

CREVALLE
RANGE - SOUTH ATLANTIC AND GULF STATES

DOLPHIN
RANGE - FLORIDA TO NORTH CAROLINA

DRUM, BLACK
RANGE - TEXAS TO NORTH CAROLINA

LEMON SOLE
RANGE - NEW YORK TO MAINE

DRUM, RED
RANGE - TEXAS - MARYLAND

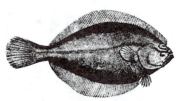

DAB
RANGE - MASSACHUSETTS TO NOVA SCOTIA

EEL, COMMON
RANGE - FLORIDA TO NEW ENGLAND AND IN
        MISSISSIPPI RIVER, LAKE ONTARIO

BLACKBACK OR WINTER FLOUNDER
RANGE - NORTH CAROLINA TO MAINE

EEL, CONGER
RANGE - FLORIDA TO NEW ENGLAND

FLUKE
RANGE - TEXAS TO MASSACHUSETTS

GRAY SOLE
RANGE - MASSACHUSETTS TO MAINE

FLYING FISH
RANGE - PACIFIC AND ATLANTIC OCEANS

FRIGATE MACKEREL
RANGE - MIDDLE ATLANTIC

GARFISH
RANGE - FRESH-WATER

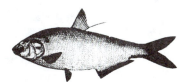

GIZZARD SHAD
RANGE - NORTH CAROLINA TO MARYLAND,
        GREAT LAKES

GOLDFISH
RANGE - LAKES AND RIVERS

GRAYFISH
RANGE - PACIFIC

GROUPER
RANGE - TEXAS TO SOUTH CAROLINA

GRUNT
RANGE - FLORIDA

HADDOCK
RANGE - NEW ENGLAND STATES

HAKE, RED
RANGE - CHESAPEAKE BAY TO NEW ENGLAND

HAKE, WHITE
RANGE - CHESAPEAKE BAY TO NEW ENGLAND

HAKE (PACIFIC)
RANGE - PACIFIC

HALIBUT
RANGE - PACIFIC COAST - NEW ENGLAND

633

HARDHEAD
RANGE - CALIFORNIA

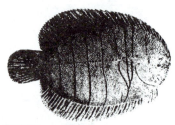

HOGCHOKER
RANGE - CHESAPEAKE BAY

HARVESTFISH OR "STARFISH"
RANGE - NORTH CAROLINA TO CHESAPEAKE BAY

HOGFISH
RANGE - FLORIDA

HERRING, LAKE
RANGE - GREAT LAKES

JEWFISH
RANGE - FLORIDA

HERRING, SEA
RANGE - NEW JERSEY TO NEW ENGLAND, PACIFIC
        COAST STATES AND ALASKA

HICKORY SHAD
RANGE - FLORIDA TO RHODE ISLAND

JOHN DORY
RANGE - MIDDLE ATLANTIC STATES

KING MACKEREL
RANGE - TEXAS TO NEW YORK

MACKEREL, ATLANTIC
RANGE - CHESAPEAKE BAY TO MAINE

KING WHITING
RANGE - TEXAS TO MASSACHUSETTS

MACKEREL, JACK
RANGE - CALIFORNIA

LAKE TROUT
RANGE - GREAT LAKES

MACKEREL, PACIFIC
RANGE - CALIFORNIA

LAMPREY
RANGE - FRESH-WATER

MENHADEN
RANGE - GULF OF MEXICO TO NEW ENGLAND

LAUNCE
RANGE - NEW ENGLAND

MOONEYE
RANGE - GREAT LAKES

LINGCOD
RANGE - CALIFORNIA TO ALASKA

MOONFISH
RANGE - FLORIDA

MULLET
RANGE - TEXAS TO NEW JERSEY

SARDINE, PACIFIC (PILCHARD)
RANGE - CALIFORNIA TO WASHINGTON

OCEAN POUT
RANGE - NEW ENGLAND

PINFISH
RANGE - FLORIDA TO NORTH CAROLINA

OCEAN PERCH (ROSEFISH)
RANGE - NEW ENGLAND

POLLOCK
RANGE - MIDDLE ATLANTIC AND NEW ENGLAND STATES

PADDLEFISH
RANGE - GULF OF MEXICO, MISSISSIPPI RIVER

POMPANO
RANGE - TEXAS TO NORTH CAROLINA

PIGFISH
RANGE - FLORIDA

PIKE OR PICKEREL
RANGE - FRESH-WATER

QUILLBACK
RANGE - FRESH-WATER

636

RATFISH
RANGE - WASHINGTON TO ALASKA

SALMON, CHINOOK OR KING
RANGE - CALIFORNIA TO ALASKA

ROCK BASS
RANGE - GREAT LAKES

SALMON, CHUM OR KETA
RANGE - OREGON TO ALASKA

ROCKFISH
RANGE - CALIFORNIA TO ALASKA

SALMON, PINK
RANGE - WASHINGTON TO ALASKA

RUDDERFISH
RANGE - CALIFORNIA

SALMON, RED OR SOCKEYE
RANGE - OREGON TO ALASKA

SABLEFISH
RANGE - PACIFIC COAST STATES AND ALASKA

SALMON, SILVER OR COHO
RANGE - CALIFORNIA TO ALASKA

SAUGER
RANGE - GREAT LAKES

637

SCULPIN
RANGE - PACIFIC COAST STATES AND ALASKA

SEA TROUT OR WEAKFISH, GRAY
RANGE - FLORIDA TO MASSACHUSETTS

SCUP OR PORGY
RANGE - FLORIDA TO NEW ENGLAND

SEA TROUT OR WEAKFISH, SPOTTED
RANGE - MARYLAND TO TEXAS

SEA BASS
RANGE - FLORIDA TO NEW ENGLAND

SEA TROUT OR WEAKFISH, WHITE
RANGE - GULF OF MEXICO

SEA CATFISH
RANGE - TEXAS TO CHESAPEAKE BAY

SHAD
RANGE - FLORIDA TO NEW ENGLAND

SEA ROBIN
RANGE - CHESAPEAKE BAY TO NEW ENGLAND

SHARK
RANGE - ATLANTIC COAST, GULF, PACIFIC COAST STATES

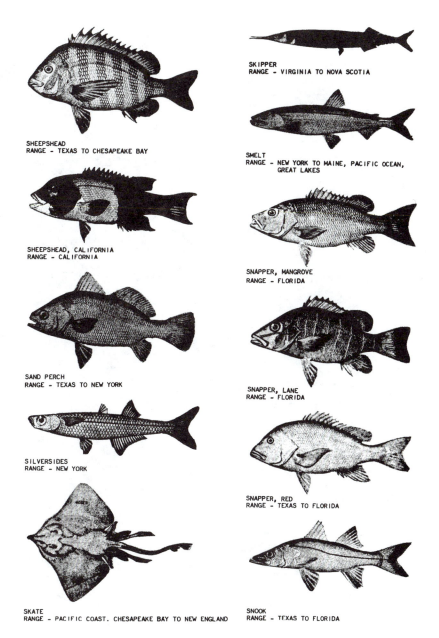

SHEEPSHEAD
RANGE - TEXAS TO CHESAPEAKE BAY

SHEEPSHEAD, CALIFORNIA
RANGE - CALIFORNIA

SAND PERCH
RANGE - TEXAS TO NEW YORK

SILVERSIDES
RANGE - NEW YORK

SKATE
RANGE - PACIFIC COAST. CHESAPEAKE BAY TO NEW ENGLAND

SKIPPER
RANGE - VIRGINIA TO NOVA SCOTIA

SMELT
RANGE - NEW YORK TO MAINE, PACIFIC OCEAN,
        GREAT LAKES

SNAPPER, MANGROVE
RANGE - FLORIDA

SNAPPER, LANE
RANGE - FLORIDA

SNAPPER, RED
RANGE - TEXAS TO FLORIDA

SNOOK
RANGE - TEXAS TO FLORIDA

639

SPADEFISH
RANGE - FLORIDA

SPANISH MACKEREL
RANGE - TEXAS TO VIRGINIA

SPOT
RANGE - GULF OF MEXICO TO MIDDLE ATLANTIC STATES

SQUAWFISH
RANGE - CALIFORNIA

STEELHEAD TROUT
RANGE - OREGON TO ALASKA

STRIPED BASS
RANGE - NORTH CAROLINA TO NEW ENGLAND, CALIFORNIA
        TO OREGON

STURGEON
RANGE - COASTAL AND RIVER AREAS

STURGEON, SHOVELNOSE
RANGE - FRESH-WATER

SUCKER
RANGE - FRESH-WATER

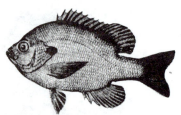

SUNFISH
RANGE - FRESH-WATER

SWELLFISH
RANGE - CHESAPEAKE BAY TO MIDDLE ATLANTIC

SWORDFISH
RANGE - NEW ENGLAND AND CALIFORNIA

TRIGGERFISH
RANGE - FLORIDA

TAUTOG
RANGE - CHESAPEAKE BAY TO NEW ENGLAND

TRIPLETAIL
RANGE - FLORIDA

TENPOUNDER
RANGE - FLORIDA

TUNA, ALBACORE
RANGE - PACIFIC COAST

THIMBLE-EYED MACKEREL
RANGE - CHESAPEAKE BAY TO NEW ENGLAND

TUNA, BLUEFIN
RANGE - CALIFORNIA, NEW JERSEY TO MAINE

TILEFISH
RANGE - MIDDLE ATLANTIC AND NEW ENGLAND STATES

TUNA, LITTLE
RANGE - MASSACHUSETTS TO TEXAS

TOMCOD
RANGE - PACIFIC COAST, MIDDLE ATLANTIC AND
        NEW ENGLAND STATES

TUNA, SKIPJACK
RANGE - CALIFORNIA

WHITE PERCH
RANGE - NORTH CAROLINA TO MAINE

TUNA, YELLOWFIN
RANGE - PACIFIC

WHITING
RANGE - VIRGINIA TO MAINE

WHITE BASS
RANGE - GREAT LAKES

WOLFFISH
RANGE - MASSACHUSETTS AND MAINE

WHITEFISH, COMMON
RANGE - GREAT LAKES

YELLOW PERCH
RANGE - GREAT LAKES, OTHER LAKES

WHITEFISH, MENOMINEE
RANGE - ALASKA, GREAT LAKES

YELLOW PIKE
RANGE - GREAT LAKES

BLUE CRAB
RANGE - TEXAS TO RHODE ISLAND

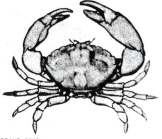

STONE CRAB
RANGE - FLORIDA

DUNGENESS CRAB
RANGE - PACIFIC COAST STATES AND ALASKA

HORSESHOE CRAB ›
RANGE - MARYLAND TO NEW YORK

KING CRAB
RANGE - ALASKA

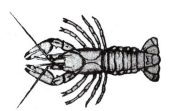

FRESH-WATER CRAWFISH
RANGE - RIVERS AND LAKES

ROCK CRAB
RANGE - NEW ENGLAND

SPINY LOBSTER
RANGE - CALIFORNIA AND FLORIDA

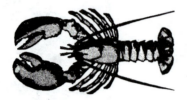

LOBSTER, NORTHERN
RANGE - VIRGINIA TO MAINE

HARD CLAM
RANGE - FLORIDA TO MAINE

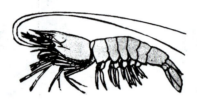

SHRIMP
RANGE - TEXAS TO NORTH CAROLINA, MAINE,
        CALIFORNIA, WASHINGTON, AND ALASKA

RAZOR CLAM, PACIFIC
RANGE - OREGON, WASHINGTON AND ALASKA

BUTTER CLAM
RANGE - PACIFIC COAST

SOFT CLAM
RANGE - MIDDLE ATLANTIC TO NEW ENGLAND,
        PACIFIC COAST STATES

LITTLE NECK CLAM
RANGE - PACIFIC COAST

CONCH
RANGE - FLORIDA TO MAINE

LIMPET
RANGE - NEW YORK AND NEW ENGLAND

FRESH-WATER MUSSEL
RANGE - FRESH-WATER STREAMS

SEA MUSSEL
RANGE - NORTH CAROLINA TO MAINE

OYSTER
RANGE - TEXAS TO MASSACHUSETTS, PACIFIC COAST

BAY SCALLOP
RANGE - FLORIDA TO MASSACHUSETTS, WASHINGTON

SEA SCALLOP
RANGE - NEW JERSEY TO MAINE

STARFISH
RANGE - ATLANTIC AND PACIFIC COAST

TERRAPIN
RANGE - TEXAS TO NEW JERSEY

GREEN TURTLE
RANGE - FLORIDA

LOGGERHEAD TURTLE
RANGE - FLORIDA TO NEW JERSEY

FROG
RANGE - FRESH-WATER, MARSHES, POND

HAWKSBILL TURTLE
RANGE - GULF OF MEXICO, AND ATLANTIC COAST
TO NEW YORK

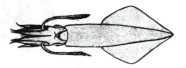

SQUID
RANGE - VIRGINIA TO MAINE, CALIFORNIA AND
WASHINGTON

SOFT-SHELL TURTLE
RANGE - LAKES AND RIVERS

SPONGE
RANGE - FLORIDA

IRISH MOSS
RANGE - NEW ENGLAND

Bibliography

CHAPTER 1

U.S. Dept. Of Labor, Bureau of Labor Statistics, *Occupational Handbook,* Bulletin 2470. Washington, DC, 1996–1997.

U.S. Dept. Of Labor, Employment and Training Administration, *Dictionary of Occupational Titles,* Vol. 1, Washington, DC, 1991.

CHAPTER 2

Allen, Robin Lee. "Meat Inspection Is Only the Beginning." *Restaurant News* (July 1996).

Bertranoli, Lisa. "After the Outbreak." *Meat Processing* (October 1996).

Chapman, Nancy. "Two Roads to Nutrition Labeling on Menus." *Restaurant Digest* (November 1996).

Clapp, Steve. "Mega-Reg Raises Temperatures." *Meat and Poultry* (December 1996).

Erdman, David. "Irradiation: A Valuable Ally in the War on Pathogens." *Meat and Processing* (July 1996).

Glickman, Dan. "HACCP Act Means Safer Future." *Michigan Chronicle* (August 27, 1997).

Hunter, Beatrice. "Making Foods Safer." *Consumers Research* (July 1996).

Lewis, Neil A. "Meat Safety Rule No Longer 'Catch as Catch' " *New York Times* (July 7, 1996).

Marriot, Richard E. "FDA Fresh Labeling Regulations Go 'Light' on Menus." *Restaurant News* (May 1996).

Mitchell, Jackie. "Monitoring Your Health and Safety Policy." *Food Service Management* (September 1996).

Moran, Michael. "Improving Your Menus' Market Potential." *Food Service and Hospitality* (Fall/Winter 1996).

NRA Editorial Board, "Japan's *E. coli* Crisis Underscores Need for US Operators' Vigilance." *National Restaurant News* (September 1996).

Parker, Davis. "Creating Awareness." *Restaurant Hospitality* (September 1996).

Puzo, Donald F. "The Federal Government Is Spending More on Food Safety But Doing Less Than in 1989." *Los Angeles Times* (June 13, 1996).

Treto, Paul Anthony. "Operations Management: Two Roads to Nutrition Labeling on Menus." *Restaurant Digest* (November 1996).

CHAPTER 3

Allen, Robin Lee. "FDA Ordered to Include Menus in Food-Labeling Law." *National Restaurant News* (July 1996).

Eames, Donald, and Gregory Norkus. "Developing Your Procurement Strategy." *The Cornell Hotel and Restaurant Administration Quarterly* (May 1988).

Evans-Correla, Kate. "Tools of the Trade." *Purchasing* (October 1991).

Fraceschini, D. Robert. "Here's How to Get the Most Value Out of Your Packaging Buys." *Purchasing* (January 16, 1986).

Gardner, Karen. "Predicting Food Prices." *Nations Restaurant News* (April 1997).

Kessler, David. "Concerned About NELA Impact on Small Business." *Prepared Foods* (May 1992).

Kushner, Gary Jay. "Food Regulatory & Legislative Outlook." *Food Processing* (January 1992).

McMullek, Shannon. "Purchasing Companies Thrive as Industry Surges." *Hotel Business* (June 1996).

Rooney, Brian. "Innovative Purchasing Provides Bulk Sales to Smaller Companies." *San Francisco Business Times* (May 1988).

Thienpont, Charles. "Forecast." *Restaurant Business* (September 1996).

"Tracking the Markets." *Nations Provisioner*. Toms River, NJ: Urner Barry Publication (January 1997).

Van Wagner, Lisa R. "FDA Reviewing Deluge of NLEA Comments." *Food Processing* (April 1992).

CHAPTER 4

Coltman, Michael M. *Hospitality Industry Purchasing,* New York: Van Nostrand Reinhold, 1989.

Porter, Anne. "Supplier Evaluation Revisited." *Purchasing* (July 1991).

Steffanelli, John M. *Purchasing,* 3rd ed. New York: John Wiley & Sons, 1992.

Virts, William B. *Purchasing for Hospitality Operations,* East Lansing, MI: Educational Foundation, American Hotel-Motel Association, 1987.

CHAPTER 5

Campbell, Liz. "Taking Care of Business." *Food Service and Hospitality* (April 1996).

Demetrakakes, P. "Data Beyond the Door." *Food Processing* (September 1996).

Falola, Norm. "Insure Safe Purchasing and Receiving." *Restaurant Hospitality* (April 1996).

Greymour, David. "Strategy for Buying Food." *Food Service Management* (September 1996).

Hayes, David, and Herman Zaccarelli. "Made to Order Purchase Orders." *Cooking for Profit* (June 1996).

Liberson, Judy. "Shared Responsibility." *Lodging Magazine* (September 1996).

Patterson, Pat. "Checks and Balances Prevent Disputes Over Orders." *Nations Restaurant News* (October 1996).

Patterson, Pat. "Differentiating Between Standards and Specifications." *Nations Restaurant News* (May 1996).

Patterson, Pat. "Finding Bargains and Knowing How to Police Them." *Nations Restaurant News* (February 1996).

Patterson, Pat. "Keeping Inventories 'Up to Par'." *Nations Restaurant News* (November 1996).

Patterson, Pat. "Product Consistency Is the Key to Maintaining Quality." *Nations Restaurant News* (April 1996).

Patterson, Pat. "Sharp Negotiations Help All Parties Reach Goals." *Nations Restaurant News* (August 1996).

CHAPTER 6

Durocher, Joseph. "Back in the Front." *Restaurant Business* (February 1996).

FAB, Inc. "Computer Program Pools City Buying Power." *Institutional Distribution* (March 1996).

Farsad, Behshid, and Stephen Lebruto. "A Measured Approach to Food-Inventory Management." *Cornell Hotel & Restaurant Administration Quarterly* (June 1993).

Kapner, Suzanne. "NRA to Launch First International Foodservice Technology Expo." *Nations Restaurant News* (March 1996).

Kasavana, Michael. "Back Office Soft-ware." *Restaurant Business* (October 1989).

Lockwood, Russ. "Money in the Bank." *Restaurant Business* (January 1992).

"New Technology." *Restaurant Business* (January 1990).

"Online Purchasing." *Restaurant Business* (July 1991).

Patterson, Pat. "The Professional Buyer—Computer Assisted Inventory Management." *Institutional Distribution* (June 1990).

Patterson, Pat. "Small Operations Can Take Advantage of Big Services." *Nations Restaurant News* (May 1993).

Tanyeri, Dana. "Are You Ready for the Revolution?" *Institutional Distribution* (March 1991).

"The Future." *Food Management* (November 1990).

Weinstein, Jeff. "13 Things You Need to Know Before Buying a POS System." *Restaurant and Institutions* (February 1993).

CHAPTER 7

Boykin, Calvin C., Henry C. Gillam, and Ronald A. Gustafson. *Structural Characteristics of Beef,* AER No. 450. Washington, DC: USDA 1980.

Edwards, Joseph. "Trends in Beef Cattle Production in the US." *World Animal Revue,* No. 5, 11–15.

Murkoski, S. A., and M. I. Schurer. *Meat and Fish Management.* North Scituate, MA: Breton, 1981.

National Association of Meat Purveyors, *Meat Buyers Guide to Portion Control Meat Cuts* and *Meat Buyers Guide to Standard Meat Cuts*. Tucson, AZ, 1996.

National Livestock and Meat Board, *Meat Evaluation Handbook*. Chicago, IL, 1968.

National Provisioner, Toms River, NJ: Urner Barry Publication, 1997.

The Hotel, Restaurant, Institutional Meat Price Report. Toms River, NJ: Urner Barry Publication, 1997.

USDA, *Standards and Grades for Beef*. Meat and Livestock Division, Washington, DC, 1997.

USDA, *Standards and Grades for Lamb, Yearlings, and Mutton*. Meat and Livestock Division, Washington, DC, 1992.

USDA, *Standards and Grades for Veal and Calf*. Meat and Livestock Division, Washington, DC, 1980.

USDA, *Standards and Grades for Pork and Pork Products*. Meat and Livestock Division, Washington, DC, 1995.

Warwick, Everett J., and James E. Legates. *Breeding and Improvement of Farm Animals,* 7th ed. New York: McGraw-Hill, 1989.

CHAPTER 8

American Egg Board. *The Incredible Edible Egg*. Park Ridge, IL, 1989.

American Egg Board. *The Egg Handling and Care Guide*. Park Ridge, IL, 1990.

"Background on *Salmonella Enteritidis* and Eggs." Washington, DC: Egg Nutrition Center, 1990.

"Facts About *Salmonella Enteritidis* and Eggs." Washington, DC: Egg Nutrition Center, 1990.

"Formed Turkey Products Right for the Times." *Meat Processing* (September 1996).

Handy, Elizabeth. "Eggs, Nature's Prepackaged Masterpiece of Nutrition." *Agricultural Handbook,* Washington, DC: USDA, 1869, pp. 139–145.

"Making Turkey Ever More Consumer Friendly." *Meat Processing* (July 1996).

McNamara, Don, M. Ph.D. "Effects of Fat-Modified Diets on Cholesterol." *Annual Nutrition Reviews,* 273–290, 1987.

"*Salmonella* and Eggs: Myths and Facts." Washington, DC: Egg Nutrition Center, 1991.

USDA. *Acceptance Service for Meat and Meat Products,* Marketing Bulletin No. 47. Washington, DC, 1970.

USDA. "Egg Grading Manual," *Agricultural Handbook 75*. Washington, DC, 1990.

USDA. *Institutional Meat Purchase Specifications*. Washington, DC, 1992.

USDA. "Meat Products." Meat and Poultry Inspection Program, Washington, DC, 1992.

USDA. *Official U.S. Standards for Grades of Carcass Beef*. Washington, DC, 1992.

USDA. "Purchasing Dried Egg Mixtures." Washington, DC, 1991.

USDA. "Purchasing Frozen Whole Eggs." Washington, DC, 1990.

USDA. "Standards for Meat and Meat Products." Meat and Poultry Inspection Program, Washington, DC, 1977.

USDA. *USDA Grades for Pork Carcasses,* Marketing Bulletin No. 52. Consumer and Marketing Service, Washington, DC, 1992.

CHAPTER 9

Berne, Steve. "Cyrogenic Freezing Gives Oysters New Shelf Life." *Prepared Foods* (September 1996).

"Fish Farms Proliferate and So Does Concern." *Regional News* (Olympia, WA) (April 24, 1994).

"Fish Farms Told to Wear Diapers." *Regional News* (Olympia, WA) (January 15, 1994).

Halsey, Eugenia. "New Rules Aim to Make Seafood Safer." Washington, DC: Food and Drug Administration, (October 1996).

Hedden, Jenny. "The Row Over Fish." *Restaurants USA,* (December 1995).

Huet, Spencer, and Marcel Dean. *Textbook of Fish Culture,* 2nd ed. New York: Grolier Electronic Publishing, 1995.

Redmayne, Peter. "A Fisherman's Guide to Seafood Distribution." Anchorage, AK: Salmon Market Information Service, 1995.

Toufexis, Anastasia. "Dining with Invisible Danger." *Time* (March 27, 1989), 28–38.

Trum Hunter, Beatrice. "Fish Poisoning." *Consumers' Research* (April 1989), 8–9.

Trum Hunter, Beatrice. "Improving the Fish Inspection Program." *Consumers' Research* (August 1989), 13–15.

U.S. Code of the Federal Registry. "Regulations Governing U.S. Standards for Grades for Fishery Products." USDC (October 1988).

U.S. Federal Supply Service. *Federal Standard Stock Catalog.* "Fishery Products," Washington, DC: U.S. Printing Office, various dates.

"U.S. Sleeping Giant of Aquaculture Begins to Stir." *Quick Frozen Food International* (January 1990), 94–95.

U.S. Subchapter G, Part 260. "Processed Fishery Products." Inspection and Certification Division, USDC (October 1, 1988).

"What's That Wiggling in My Sushi?" *Science News* (May 13, 1988), 300.

Young, Frank E. "Is Fish Safe to Eat?" *Consumers' Research* (August 1989), 10–12.

CHAPTER 10

Canan, Kerri. "Apples." *Restaurant Business* (August 1996).

Patterson, Pat. "A Hard Sell: Buying Produce Is No Easy Day in the Park." *Restaurant News* (November 1995).

Petusevsky, Steven. "Healthful Dining Options." *Restaurant Hospitality* (September 1996).

Scaeli, Leopold K. "Wild Mushrooms." *Cooking for Profit* (May 1996).

CHAPTER 11

Berne, Steve. "Fresh Soups Achieve 120-Day Shelf Life." *Prepared Foods* (August 1996).

Hollingsworth, Pierce. "Can Comeback." *Food Technology* (September 1996).

CHAPTER 12

Kosikawski, Frank V. *Cheese and Fermented Milk Foods*. Ann Arbor, MI: Edwards Brothers, 1966.

Milk Industry Foundation. *Milk Facts*. Washington, DC, 1985.

Pszczola, Donald E. "Low-Fat Dairy Products Getting a New Lease on Life." *Food Technology* (September 1996).

Sapeka Corporation. "Cheese 60, 54—54, France." Paris, 1985.

USDA. "Federal and State Milk Market Orders." Washington, DC, 1990.

USDA. "Federal and State Standards for the Composition of Milk Products." *Agricultural Handbook 51*. Washington, DC, 1980.

CHAPTER 13

Bailey, Clyde H. *The Chemistry of Wheat Flour*. New York: Chemical Catalog Co., 1989.

Brockenbrough, J. Gill, Jr., and Peter Coe. *Coffee*. Greenborough, NC: Pot Pourri Press, P. O. Box 18312, 1989.

Eckey, E. W. *Vegetable Fats and Oils*. New York: Van Nostrand, Reinhold, 1954.

Encyclopedia Americana, Vol. 27, p. 899. "Vanilla." Danbury, CT: Grolier, 1988.

Hallmich, Nancy. "Consumers Sink Teeth into Olestra Chips." *USA Today* (September 1996).

Katz, Fran. "Vegetable Oils Follow Healthy Directions." *Food Processing* (February 1996).

Segal, Marian. *Fat Substitutes, a Taste of the Future?* Rockville, MD: U.S. Public Health, FDA, 1991.

Solomon, Goody. "Some Vanilla Sold in Mexico." *Miami Herald* (March 29, 1984).

Spices: What They Are and Where They Come From. New York: American Spice Trade Association, 1956.

Weiss, Theodore. J. *Food Oils and Their Uses*. New York: Van Nostrand Reinhold, 1970.

"Whole Bean Coffee Sales Are Growing 20% Per Year." *Beverages* (June 1994).

Wieland, Henry. *Cocoa and Chocolate Processing*. Park Ridge, NJ: Noyes Data Corp., 1972.

CHAPTER 14

Bell, Donald A. *Wine and Beverage Standards*. New York: Van Nostrand Reinhold, 1990.

Bellucci, Elio C. "Protect Patrons from Third Party Assaults." *Southern Beverage Journal* (January 1989).

Dee, Dorothy. "Riding the Crest with Bottled Waters." *Restaurants USA* (February 1990), 19–20.

Ford, Gene. *The Benefits of Moderate Drinking*. San Francisco, CA: Alcohol, Health and Social Wine Appreciation Guild, 1988.

Grossman, Harold. *Grossman's Guide to Wines, Beers and Spirits,* revised by Harold Lembeck. New York: Charles Scribner's Sons, 1977.

"How to Implement an Alcohol Awareness Program." *Restaurants USA* (February 1990), 13.

Julyan, Brian K. "How to Store Table Wines." *Restaurants USA* (October 1990), 30–31.

Johnson, Hugh. *Modern Encyclopedia of Wine,* 2nd ed. New York: Simon and Schuster, 1987.

Kotschevar, Lendal H., and Mary L. Tanke. *Managing Bar and Beverage Operations.* East Lansing, MI: Educational Institute of the American Hotel and Motel Association, 1991.

Kotsiggris, Costas, and Mary Porter. *The Bar and Beverage Book.* New York: John Wiley & Sons, 1985.

Mariani, John F. "Short and Simple Restaurants Trim Liquor Inventories." *Market Watch,* No. 7 (1990), 80–87.

Oz, Clarke. *The Essential Wine Book.* New York: Simon & Schuster, 1985.

Prugh, Thomas. "Point of Purchase Health Warning Notices." *Alcohol, Health and Research World,* No. 4 (1990), 10.

Schoonmaker, Frank. *Encyclopedia of Wines.* New York: Hasting House, 1964.

Simon, Andre L. *Guide to Food and Wine.* London: Cohens, 1960.

"U.S. Consumption of Distilled Spirits Hits a 27 Year Low." *Wall Street Journal,* No. 79, 1990, p. A6.

Wiegand, Ronn, R. "Profit from the Growing Wine Market." *Night Club and Bar,* No. 8 (1989), 14–16.

Winkle, A. J. *General Viticulture.* Berkeley, CA: University of California Press, 1962.

CHAPTER 15

Barrett, Don. *Technical and Environmental Service Module.* Capre Tech Services International, May 1991.

Barrett, Kathy. *IAQ Historical Perspective 1988–1992.* Capre Tech Services International, May 1992.

Bertagnoli, Lisa. "Material Matters." *Hospital Management* (September 1996).

Grimshaw, Rex W. *The Chemistry of Clays and Allied Materials,* 4th ed. New York: John Wiley & Sons, 1971.

Hollin, Norman, and Jane Saddler. *Textiles.* New York: McGraw Hill, 1970.

Institute Research Co. *Cleaning Agent Standards.* New York, n.d.

Kotschevar, L., and Margaret Terrel. *Food Service Planning.* New York: Macmillan, 1984.

Liberman, Judy. "Setting the Table." *Lodging* (June 1996).

Mark, H. F., F. S. M. Atlas, and E. Cernia, *Man-Made Fabrics.* New York: John Wiley & Sons, 1967.

Morgan, H. *Metalwork and Enameling,* 5th ed. Mineola, NY: Dover Publishing, 1971.

Norton, F. *Fine Ceramics.* New York: Holt, Rinehart and Winston, 1960.

Index